THE MONTEVERDI VESPERS OF 1610

THE MONTEVERDI VESPERS OF 1610

MUSIC, CONTEXT, PERFORMANCE

JEFFREY KURTZMAN

OXFORD

UNIVERSITY PRESS

*This book has been printed digitally and produced in a standard specification
in order to ensure its continuing availability*

OXFORD
UNIVERSITY PRESS

Great Clarendon Street, Oxford OX2 6DP

Oxford University Press is a department of the University of Oxford.
It furthers the University's objective of excellence in research, scholarship,
and education by publishing worldwide in

Oxford New York

Auckland Bangkok Buenos Aires Cape Town Chennai
Dar es Salaam Delhi Hong Kong Istanbul Karachi Kolkata
Kuala Lumpur Madrid Melbourne Mexico City Mumbai Nairobi
São Paulo Shanghai Taipei Tokyo Toronto

Oxford is a registered trade mark of Oxford University Press
in the UK and in certain other countries

Published in the United States
by Oxford University Press Inc., New York

© jeffery Kurtzman 1999

The moral rights of the author have been asserted
Database right Oxford University Press (maker)

Reprinted 2003

ISBN 0-19-816409-2

To Kathi, with love and gratitude

Preface

MONTEVERDI'S sacred music, largely ignored by many Monteverdi scholars engrossed in studies of the madrigals and the operas, has long fascinated me. The composer's surviving sacred repertoire, the majority of it collected in three very large publications representing a remarkable variety of stylistic treatments of the mass, vesper psalms, Magnificats, hymns, motets, the Litany of Loreto, and spiritual madrigals, probably reflects only a fraction of the sacred music he actually composed. In fact, sacred music occupied Monteverdi throughout his entire life. At the age of only 15 he first presented himself to the musical world as a composer of three-voice motets in the *Sacrae cantiunculae* of 1582, followed in the next year by a collection of *Madrigali spirituali* for four voices, only the bass part of which now survives. There is evidence in the first extant letter from Monteverdi's hand that he composed sacred music for the Gonzaga court well before he published the *Missa in illo tempore* and *Vespro della Beata Vergine* in 1610, and Denis Stevens, also on the basis of remarks in Monteverdi's letters, has suggested that Monteverdi composed twenty-nine masses for Christmas Eve, one for each year of his employment at St Mark's in Venice (see Chapter 1). If this is true, then the single masses published in the *Selva morale et spirituali* of 1641 and the posthumous *Messa a quattro voci et salmi* of 1650 comprise only small gleanings from a vast field of activity, forever lost to us. By extension, it is probable that the psalms, hymns, and motets published in these two large collections also represent only a portion of a much larger *œuvre* emanating from Monteverdi's long career at St Mark's. Though we may lament such losses, the body of music that remains to us is vast enough to occupy Monteverdi scholars for the foreseeable future.

My own preoccupation with Monteverdi began with a graduate seminar taught by Charles Hamm at the University of Illinois at Urbana-Champaign, in which we attempted to understand Monteverdi's mensuration signs and their proportional relationships—a topic still unresolved in the Monteverdi literature and the subject of Chapter 20 of the present volume. Witnessing how little research had been devoted to Monteverdi's sacred music, I subsequently resolved to write my dissertation in this area, eventually resulting in a thesis on the Vespers of 1610 and a published collection of essays on the Mass and

Vespers.[1] The current book is an extension of both that collection of essays and the preparation of my critical edition of the Vespers for Oxford University Press. I had wanted to provide for the edition an introduction to performance practice issues as they related to the Vespers, but as I delved ever deeper into performance practice of the late Renaissance and early *Seicento*, the material grew well beyond the scope of an introduction. Since I had been assembling for many years material on the history of Italian Vesper music in the Renaissance and *Seicento* and had also been enlarging my analytical studies of Monteverdi's sacred and secular music, Bruce Phillips, Music Book Editor of Oxford University Press, suggested a separate book on the 1610 Vespers, as companion to my critical edition, that would explore the Vespers in their historical and modern context, attempt to provide analytical insight into the music, and examine the performance practice issues pertinent to the Vespers. The result of his suggestion is the present volume, which, despite the amount of effort that it represents, still seems incomplete and inadequate to the author, since Monteverdi's Vespers seem to raise virtually every controversial, ambiguous, and ultimately unresolvable issue in early seventeenth-century sacred music. The reader may well find that after viewing so many facets of the Vespers as through a prism, all of the questions with which he or she began remain, in the final analysis, without definitive answers. I console myself with recognition that such an outcome is in the nature of the subject-matter and that unresolvable questions are often the most interesting for scholarship. Examining such questions increases our understanding, even if it may not provide us with definitive solutions.

This volume is divided into three principal parts: (I) the context of Monteverdi's Vespers in terms of the liturgy for vespers, vesper publications of the sixteenth and early seventeenth centuries, and the stylistic context of the first two decades of the *Seicento*; also included is a survey of modern controversies over the Vespers, illustrating how scholars and performers have variously interpreted its historical context, its liturgical use, and performance practice; (II) an analytical study of the music of the Vespers, including a detailed examination of the fascinating *Nigra sum*, and (III) an enquiry into seventeenth-century performance practice issues raised by the Vespers and suggestions for their solution. Several appendices provide detailed supplementary material.

Chapter 1 will present the sources of Amadino's 1610 print and examine the history of controversy over this publication, including a discussion of principal modern editions and recordings as well as the many hypotheses that have been

---

[1] Jeffrey G. Kurtzman, 'The Monteverdi Vespers of 1610 and their Relationship with Italian Sacred Music of the Early Seventeenth Century' (Ph.D. dissertation, University of Illinois at Urbana-Champaign, 1972); id., *Essays on the Monteverdi Mass and Vespers of 1610* (Houston: Rice University Studies, 1978).

put forward regarding the print's origins and purposes. Chapter 2 will discuss the liturgical background of Monteverdi's collection and treat the question of the relationship between plainchant antiphons and polyphonic psalm settings. In Chapter 3, the sixteenth-century polyphonic repertoire for vespers, especially the published repertoire of the second half of the century, is surveyed. The next chapter, Chapter 4, will extend the survey of the published vesper repertoire into the first two decades of the seventeenth century, where the historical and stylistic context of Monteverdi's print will be examined in an effort to discover influences on his compositional methods and style as well as highlight the unique features of his Vespers.

Understanding the unique aspects of Monteverdi's music allows us to estimate his influence on other composers in the decade following the publication of his Vespers. Yet musical context is a subject of enormous scope, and the complete musical context of Monteverdi's Vespers cannot be studied in a book focusing on the Vespers itself. Indeed, the musical context of the *Seicento* is only gradually unfolding as more and more scholars in recent years have devoted their efforts to individual composers and repertoires of this period.[2] At the present time, the only general survey of Italian sacred music in the Monteverdi period is Jerome Roche's invaluable *North Italian Church Music in the Age of Monteverdi* (1984). The study of the musical context of Monteverdi's Vespers in Chapter 4, therefore, will be limited to those composers and compositions that can be directly related in some way to Monteverdi's style and technique in the Vespers.

At this point the discussion will turn to the music itself. Chapters 5–10 are divided into two segments, the first comprising prefatory remarks on various methods of analysis that have been developed in recent times for addressing Monteverdi's music and a study of compositions based on a cantus firmus, the second examining the four motets without cantus firmus. The first segment is divided for convenience into four chapters; Chapter 5 is on analytical methods, Chapter 6 on the response and psalms, Chapter 7 on the Magnificats, and Chapter 8 on the hymn and *Sonata*. The second segment includes a detailed study of *Nigra sum* in Chapter 9 and a less detailed examination of the remaining three motets in Chapter 10. The analyses in these chapters attempt to reveal Monteverdi's treatment of the cantus firmus, his structural techniques, his stylistic variety, his variation procedures, his treatment of texture, his harmonic

---

[2] For a bibliography of this context, already requiring substantial supplementation, see section II of K. Gary Adams and Dyke Kiel, *Claudio Monteverdi: A Guide to Research* (New York: Garland Publishing, Inc., 1989). At the time of this writing, Anne Schnoebelen, Elizabeth Roche, and I are in the midst of preparing for Garland Publishing a twenty-five-volume series of 17th-century Italian music for the mass and the office as well as representative examples of the motet repertoire of the first half of the century.

language, modal and tonal aspects of his music, and his methods of interpreting his texts. The relationship between the Vespers and Monteverdi's concept of the *seconda prattica* is likewise explored.

The final section of the book (Chapters 11–22) deals with the many performance practice issues raised by the Vespers, treating them one at a time. Performance practice questions are often quite complicated, and the arguments subtle. In an effort to make these chapters sufficiently readable, the principal theoretical and historical sources as well as my suggestions and conclusions are contained in the main body of the text, while the footnotes for each chapter examine the secondary literature and the many debates over these issues. Thus the footnotes form a kind of musicological gloss on the more general discussion in the chapters themselves.

Six appendices serve to supplement the main body of the text. Appendix A lists the psalm *cursus* for first and second vespers for feasts throughout the liturgical year. Appendix B quotes Latin rubrics for vespers and for the use of the four seasonal Marian antiphons from a 1583 Roman breviary. Appendix C contains the text, in both Latin and English, as well as a structural outline, of each of the ten cantus firmus compositions of the Vespers in order to give the reader a rapid overview of each of these pieces. This appendix thus serves as a supplement to the analytical discussion in Chapters 6–8.

Appendix D comprises a discography of the Vespers. Annotations in the discography do not constitute 'record reviews', but rather indicate the different approaches various directors and ensembles have taken to performance practice and liturgical issues in the Vespers. Appendix E is a list of sixteenth- and seventeenth-century sources cited in the text, arranged alphabetically by composer, while Appendix F lists theoretical sources of the sixteenth and seventeenth centuries cited in the text, as well as facsimile editions and English translations of these treatises. The Bibliography comprises secondary literature and modern editions of music, the latter grouped in a separate category. While the Bibliography lists John Whenham's recent book, *Monteverdi: Vespers (1610)* (Cambridge: Cambridge University Press, 1997), it unfortunately became available too late to be included in my discussion of the literature on the Vespers in Chapter 1 and elsewhere.

This volume is conceived as a handbook on the Vespers, organized to follow a logical thread from cover to cover, but also usable in segments or individual chapters depending on the reader's interests. Those concerned with the historical aspects and background of the Vespers may wish to refer to Chapters 1–4 only, while scholars interested in the analysis of Monteverdi and early seventeenth-century music in general may find the analytical chapters useful. Performers, whether singers, instrumentalists, or choir directors, may find the performance practice section or individual chapters on specific performance practice topics helpful. The materials in the appendices allow for a variety of quick references to various subjects and sources discussed in the text.

Throughout this book, specific pitches are given in italics and lower-case letters according to the standard nomenclature of octaves (i.e. *c′* = middle C). References to a note or chord designating a pitch-class, but not a specific octave, are given in capital letters in roman type. Bar numbers refer to those in my edition of the Monteverdi Vespers published by Oxford University Press.

Since this book is published in England, I have adopted British nomenclature for note values. Because this terminology may be unfamiliar to some American readers, it may prove useful to set forth here both the Renaissance forms, which appear from time to time in the text, and the American equivalents, which do not:

Renaissance term	British term	American term
breve	breve	double whole note
semibreve	semibreve	whole note
minim	minim	half note
semiminim	crotchet	quarter note
fusa, croma	quaver	eighth note
semifusa, semicroma	semiquaver	sixteenth note
biscroma	demisemiquaver	thirty-second note

The meaning of the terms 'cadence' and *clausula* can also generate cross-cultural confusion apart from their evolving usages between the Renaissance and the present. By *clausula*, I refer to the two-part Renaissance and early Baroque cadence whereby a sixth expands to an octave or a third contracts to a unison. Rules of *musica ficta* require the sixth to be major and the third to be minor. I use the word 'cadence' to refer either to a *mediant* or final closure in a chant melody, or to a closure or half-closure involving three or more parts. Even though a *clausula* constitutes one type of cadence, it is useful to distinguish between the two terms since Renaissance three- and four-part polyphony typically constructs cadences out of a two-part *clausula* harmonized by the other two parts, often with a leap of a fourth or fifth in the bass.

Three- and four-part cadences are of four principal types: (1) 'complete', 'perfect', 'authentic', or 'full', meaning a V–I closure; (2) 'plagal', meaning a IV–I closure; (3) 'incomplete', 'interrupted', or 'half', meaning suspension of the cadence progression on V; and (4) 'evaded' or 'deceptive', meaning an unexpected resolution, most often entailing a V–VI progression.

Some chapters of this book constitute revisions or expansions of my earlier publications. Chapter 3 was originally presented as a shorter paper at the Musicological Institute of the University of Frankfurt in 1982 at the kind invitation of Helmut Hucke, as well as at the first Durham Conference on Baroque Music, 1984. It was subsequently revised and enlarged for publication in *De musica et cantu: Studien zur Geschichte der Kirchenmusik und der Oper. Helmut Hucke zum 60. Geburtstag* (1993), 419–55. The editors of this volume, Peter Cahn and Ann-Katrin Heimer, have kindly given their permission to reprint it here in a further revised version. While much of the discussion in this chapter is related to the Monteverdi Vespers only in so far as it establishes the general Renaissance background from which the vesper repertoire of the early seventeenth century developed, I have considered it useful to include this chapter to make the material more readily accessible to readers in Great Britain and North America, especially since so little information is available in the musicological literature on vesper music of this period.

Chapter 4 updates and expands significantly my article 'Some Historical Perspectives on the Monteverdi Vespers', originally published in *Analecta musicologica* (1974) and in revised form in my *Essays on the Monteverdi Mass and Vespers of 1610* (Rice University Studies, 1978). I am grateful to the editors of both publications for permission to incorporate the earlier versions into the present revision. Some of the material in Chapters 6–10, devoted to analysis of the music, also appeared in my *Essays on the Monteverdi Mass and Vespers* and is likewise used here with the kind permission of the editor of Rice University Studies.

In the course of my studies of the Monteverdi Mass and Vespers, I have accumulated numerous debts to librarians and fellow scholars. Among librarians, I owe particular thanks to the late Sergio Paganelli and to Giorgio Piombini of the Civico Museo Bibliografico Musicale of Bologna, Italy, for numerous kindnesses and extraordinary assistance as well as permission to publish my edition of the Vespers based principally on the Civico Museo's copy of the original 1610 print. Thanks are also due to many librarians and libraries that have provided me with microfilms and otherwise assisted my research in sixteenth- and seventeenth-century music. These include especially the staff of the Civico Museo of Bologna, Don Emilio Maggini of the Biblioteca del Seminario in Lucca, Antonio Brasini of the Biblioteca Comunale in Cesena, Siro Cisilino and subsequently David Bryant of the Cini Foundation in Venice, Santo Baratti of the Church of San Giuseppe in Brescia, Aniela Kolbuszewska of the University Library in Wrocław, Agnieszka Mietielska-Ciepierska of the Jagellonian Library in Cracow, and many other librarians, who must go unnamed, at the British Library, the Biblioteca Comunale in Assisi, the Biblioteca Capitolare in Verona, the Conservatorio Giuseppe Verdi and the Fabbrica del Duomo in Milan, the Archivio Dorio Pamphilj and the Biblioteca Casanatense in Rome, and the University Library in Uppsala, Sweden. Numerous other European and American libraries have opened their doors to my research and supplied me with microfilms of their holdings. The list is unfortunately too vast to mention individually here.

Many scholars have unselfishly shared their ideas and information with me and have assisted me by reading and criticizing various chapters of the text. Stanley Boorman, Robert Kendrick, Kevin Mason, Joshua Rifkin, Sally Sanford, Alexander Silbiger, and Carl Smith have all read and offered very useful suggestions on portions of the text. Jerome F. Weber provided valuable assistance, including the loan of recordings, in compiling Appendix D. Stephen Bonta and Tim Carter have read the entire book in earlier drafts, while Eva Linfield has been especially helpful in critiquing the analytical portion of the book in two different drafts. The present form of these chapters and a number of ideas and concepts contained in them reflect her cogent and penetrating criticisms. Jeffery Kite-Powell and Stewart Carter were most generous in sharing with me, in advance of publication, chapters from *A Performer's Guide to Renaissance Music* and *A Performer's Guide to Seventeenth-Century Music*, respectively. Paola Besutti verified liturgical texts from the rite of Santa Barbara for me in the Archivio Diocesano Mantovano, while her husband, Roberto Giuliani, has provided information for Appendix D. Kan Leung, my assistant, has been immensely helpful with computer inputting, proof-reading, and editing. I have received assistance with matters of Latin grammar from Professors William Harris of Middlebury College, Kristine Wallace of Rice University, and James Patout Burns of Washington University. Professor Wallace supplied the translation of Monteverdi's dedication in the Introduction, note 2. Special thanks go to Nathan Eakin of the Gaylord Music Library at Washington University for his always courteous and ready responses to my countless reference queries.

The Institute of Mediaeval Music and W. W. Norton & Co. kindly gave me permission to publish diagrams from *Girolamo Diruta, 'The Transylvanian'*, ed. Murray C. Bradshaw and Edward J. Soehnlen, and from Howard M. Brown and Stanley Sadie, eds., *Performance Practice: Music after 1600* in Chapters 8 and 22 respectively, and Harold Copeman likewise gave his kind permission for me to publish tables from his book *Singing in Latin* in Chapter 23. Permission to publish Examples 4.2.2b and 4.3 was graciously granted by Garland Publishing, Inc. Finally, I am greatly indebted to Fiona Little for her detailed and fastidious copy-editing of what must at times have seemed an inordinately complicated manuscript.

All of my readers have offered valuable suggestions and criticisms for which I am very grateful and without which this book would be much the poorer. Most of their recommendations are reflected in my final text; nevertheless there are a few issues where I have stubbornly adhered to my original position or preferred my own way of saying things. Despite all their efforts and my own to correct errors, avoid omissions, and escape traps of poor logic or unclear exposition, I am certain to have fallen short and must assume responsibility myself both for the mistakes and vagaries that have escaped me and for the views and analyses that may ultimately prove in error. After years of labour and thought, one can only sigh and say, *Ohimé, avrei potuto fare meglio.*

My work has been aided by many granting agencies over the years. I wish to acknowledge the support of the Martha Baird Rockefeller Fund for Music, the National Endowment for the Humanities, the John Simon Guggenheim Foundation, the American Council of Learned Societies, the Deutscher Akademischer Austauschdienst, Middlebury College, Rice University, and Washington University for fellowships and grants that have contributed to this book. Without their aid, I would not have been able to make the many excursions to European libraries to collect the materials that form the substance of Chapters 3 and 4. Sabbaticals from Middlebury College, Rice University, and Washington University have given me the time to concentrate my efforts on research and writing unencumbered by other duties.

Equally important have been the years of fruitful discussion and interaction regarding seventeenth-century Italian music with my colleagues and friends Stephen Bonta, David Bryant, Tim Carter, Graham Dixon, Beth Miller, Massimo Ossi, Jerome and Elizabeth Roche, Anne Schnoebelen, and John Suess. From them I have learned at least as much as from my own research. The loss of Jerome Roche to an untimely death has been a severe blow, both to me personally and to seventeenth-century Italian studies.

No amount of thanks can express the gratitude I owe my wife and dedicatee, Kathi, for her infinite patience, encouragement, and moral support on the many occasions when my travels and my work disrupted family life or inconvenienced her and our children. She has made a much larger contribution to this book than she realizes.

Contents

᪣✿᪣

List of Music Examples

⟨❦⟩

[1] Repr. from Jeffrey Kurtzman, ed., *Vesper and Compline Music* (Seventeenth-Century Italian Sacred Music, xi; New York: Garland Publishing, Inc., 1995). I am grateful to Garland Publishing for permission.

[2] Ibid.

Introduction

MONTEVERDI'S *Vespro della Beata Vergine*, published together with his *Missa in illo tempore*, has been a familiar item in music histories and the subject of intense interest among early music performers and enthusiasts for many years.[1] And well it should be, given the grand dimensions, vocal and instrumental virtuosity, musical colour, and extraordinary variety characterizing the collection of fourteen compositions subsumed under the title *Vespro della Beata Vergine* in the composer's Bassus Generalis part-book. The importance of this publication to Monteverdi himself is underscored by its dedication to Pope Paul V.[2] Interest in the Vespers has led to several modern editions and innumerable performances and recordings, some of very high quality, employing historical instruments and up-to-date knowledge of early seventeenth-century performance practices.[3] By now, the Vespers of 1610 are truly in the public domain, familiar to large numbers of musicians and music-lovers.

---

[1] For bibliography concerning the Vespers, see Denis Arnold and Nigel Fortune, eds., *The Monteverdi Companion* (London: Faber and Faber, 1968), 310–22; and eid., *The New Monteverdi Companion* (London: Faber and Faber, 1985), 340–51. For an extensive bibliography of all aspects of Monteverdi's life and work, see K. Gary Adams and Dyke Kiel, *Claudio Monteverdi: A Guide to Research* (New York: Garland Publishing, Inc., 1989).

[2] The dedication illustrates the weight Monteverdi gave to this, his first major sacred publication. The wording of the dedication is filled with the formulas of praise found in so many others of the period except for two personal references. One of his purposes in publishing this music, he says, is that 'the mouths of those speaking unfair things against Claudio may be closed.' This remark may have been aimed at Giovanni Battista Artusi's censure of his contrapuntal skill, about which Monteverdi may still have chafed in 1610. The other personal remark refers to this music as the result of his 'nocturnal labours'. I am grateful to Prof. Kristine Wallace for the following translation: 'When I wished to send forth into the light certain ecclesiastical pieces in musical modes to be sung in chorus, I had decided to dedicate [them] to your Majesty, Pontiff of Pontiffs, than which truly none in the world of mortals approaches nearer to God, but because I recognized that to the greatest and highest, things very mean and small were not politely dedicated, plainly I would have changed my plan if it had not finally come into my mind that material concerning divine matters by a certain right of its own demands that the title-page of the work be inscribed, or rather imprinted, with the name of him who has the keys to heaven in his hands and holds the helm of empire on earth. Therefore that the sacred harmonies, illuminated by your extraordinary and almost divine glory, may be resplendent and that by [your] supreme blessing being given, the humble hill of my talent may daily grow more and more green, and that the mouths of those speaking unfair things against Claudio may be closed, having thrown myself at your most holy feet, I offer and present these my nocturnal labours, of whatever sort they are. Wherefore, again and again I beg that you may deign with kindly countenance and cheerful mind to accept what I humbly offer, for thus it will happen that with more lively mind after this and with greater labour than before I shall be able to serve both God and the Blessed Virgin and you; farewell and live long, happy.'

[3] See App. D.

This attention has also given rise to controversy, especially over what actually constitutes Monteverdi's Vespers. Vesper services for feasts of the Virgin, whether first or second vespers, comprise certain principal musical items, based on the structure of the vesper liturgy (see Chapter 2 for a more detailed discussion of the vesper liturgy in the sixteenth century and early seventeenth century). These items are the versicle and response *Deus in adjutorium . . . Domine ad adjuvandum*; the five psalms *Dixit Dominus*, *Laudate pueri*, *Laetatus sum*, *Nisi Dominus*, and *Lauda Jerusalem*, each preceded and followed by its own antiphon from either the Common of Feasts of the Virgin or from the Proper of the Time; the hymn *Ave maris stella*; and the Magnificat, also preceded and followed by its own antiphon from the Common or the Proper. Other versicles, prayers, and the chapter are also chanted to simple lection tones in a vesper service.

Monteverdi's publication of 1610 contains polyphonic settings of all of the principal musical items for vespers on feasts of the Virgin except the liturgical antiphons, which varied according to the feast. In addition, his publication also includes a second setting of the Magnificat and five non-liturgical pieces, singled out on the title-page: *cum Nonnullis Sacris Concentibus* (with some sacred concertos). One of these *sacri concentus* follows after each of the psalms within the body of the print: *Nigra sum*, *Pulchra es*, *Duo Seraphim*, *Audi coelum*, and the *Sonata sopra Santa* [*sic*] *Maria ora pro nobis*. The texts of these five compositions differ from the antiphons prescribed in the Roman Breviary or any other known seventeenth-century breviary for any feast of the Virgin, and although two of them, *Nigra sum* and *Pulchra es*, are related to antiphon texts for the Virgin in the Roman use, Monteverdi's texts are longer than the liturgical versions and their settings appear in different positions (after the first and second psalms) from the position of the official antiphons (third and fourth antiphons for the Common of the BVM and fifth antiphon for the Feast of the Assumption, respectively).[4]

The most heated controversies generated by Monteverdi's collection have been over whether or not these five *sacri concentus* constitute part of the Vespers or are separate items, unrelated to the Vespers, as might be inferred from the title-page. The wording and grammar of the title-page have themselves given rise to varying interpretations and disputes on this issue. Even those who include the five *sacri concentus* as part of the Vespers do not always agree as to where they are to be placed. Other controversies and disagreements have arisen over various aspects of performance practice, especially the transposition of the pieces notated in *chiavette*, the size and constitution of the choir, the role of doubling instruments, and the choice of continuo instruments. Every

---

[4] *The Liber Usualis with Introduction and Rubrics in English* (New York: Desclée Company, 1980), 1259, 1606. In the 16th and 17th centuries *Nigra sum* belonged to the set of antiphons for the Feast of Holy Mary of the Snow, which was subsequently taken over for the Common of the BVM.

performance, recorded or live, involves significant levels of interpretation, even when based on a thorough knowledge of early seventeenth-century performance practices.

Surveying the fourteen compositions in the *Vespro della Beata Vergine*, it seems as if Monteverdi were intent on displaying his skill in virtually all contemporary styles of composition, utilizing every modern structural technique. Stylistically, he ranges from chordal *falsobordone* to virtuoso vocal displays, from recitative to complex polyphonic textures, from simple presentations of the psalm tone with organ accompaniment to lush vocal sonorities and colourful instrumental obbligatos. Structurally, Monteverdi explores a different organizational method in each of the pieces. Only the two Magnificats share a common organizational outline, and even here there are some significant structural differences between the two versions. Monteverdi's objective was clearly to carry to new heights the Renaissance aesthetic concept of *varietas* and to provide as many forms of musical splendour as he could muster. In this respect his collection of vesper music goes far beyond any other sacred music publication of his day, though it is clear from descriptions and pay records that vespers was celebrated in many locations with great pomp and large musical forces on important feast-days. Monteverdi's, however, is by far the most elaborate version to have been printed in the early seventeenth century.

Despite the almost bewildering variety of music, there is a definite order to this splendid conglomeration of diverse structures, styles, and techniques. All of the liturgical texts are composed around a cantus firmus, which comprises the reciting note in *Domine ad adjuvandum*, the psalm tones in the psalms, the plainchant hymn in *Ave maris stella*, and the Magnificat tone in the Magnificats. Of the *sacri concentus*, only the *Sonata sopra Sancta Maria* employs a cantus firmus: the Litany of the Saints with the name of Mary inserted as the specific saint addressed. Within the limitations imposed by the cantus firmi, most of which are quite similar to one another, Monteverdi varies his adornments of the borrowed chants with seemingly inexhaustible imagination. In the opening response, the reciting note is sung with chordal *falsobordone* by the choir, but with instruments weaving an elaborate tapestry of sound around the singers, based on the fanfare toccata from the opera *L'Orfeo*.

The psalm *Dixit Dominus* also employs *falsibordoni*, but these are interspersed with passages for the full six-voice choir, with solo duets, and with elaborate polyphonic melismas echoed by instrumental ritornellos. The whole forms a coherent, fundamentally symmetrical structure. Virtuoso soloists emerge from a choir of eight solo voices in *Laudate pueri*, and the cantus firmus, though not continuously present, is transposed on several occasions to permit greater variety of harmony and tonality. *Laetatus sum*, in which the psalm tone is used only sporadically, is structured over four separate repeated bass patterns, two of which are themselves varied in their repetitions. These bass patterns support the solo psalm tone, complex polyphonic textures, virtuoso duets, and even *falsobordone*. The remaining two psalms, *Nisi Dominus* and *Lauda Jerusalem*, each illustrate different forms of the polychoral style. *Nisi* divides the ten-voice choir into two different ensembles, one echoing the other, with an ever-present long-note cantus firmus in the two tenor voices. *Lauda Jerusalem* is for seven voices, with the tenor continuously carrying the cantus firmus, sometimes transposed, until the doxology, where it shifts to the soprano. The other six parts are divided into two three-voice choirs of soprano, alto, and bass, which respond to one another in close imitation.

The Magnificat tone is closely related to the psalm tones, but the use of its *initium* in every verse of the Magnificats provides more opportunity for harmonic variety. Both Magnificats consist of discrete settings of each of the twelve verses, each verse based on the Magnificat tone and each a distinct piece with its own style, texture, and performing forces. Ten of the twelve verses of the first Magnificat *a 7* are related in one way or another to verses from the second Magnificat *a 6*, although there are a few changes in the order of succession to create a more symmetrical arrangement in the Magnificat *a 7*. Each Magnificat comprises a giant set of variations on the Magnificat tone.

The hymn is also based on the appropriate plainchant, but in this rather conservative piece the melodious cantus firmus appears in the top voice throughout. Monteverdi deals with the challenge of seven verses all sung to the same melody with yet another form of variation. Each successive verse is scored differently, ranging from eight-voice choir, to each of the two four-voice choirs, to different soloists from each of the choirs. The final verse then repeats the music of the first verse, once again illustrating Monteverdi's propensity for symmetry in his large-scale structures. Adding further variety is an instrumental ritornello following the second to fifth verses. The instruments for the ritornello are not designated, so further variety may be introduced by altering the instrumentation from one statement to another.

The five *sacri concentus* stand to some degree apart from the other compositions in consisting of four few-voiced motets and an instrumental sonata with litany. As already mentioned, only the *Sonata* employs a cantus firmus. *Nigra sum*, for solo voice, is in the newly invented rhetorical style of contemporary monody, as is the first part of *Audi coelum*. *Pulchra es*, on the other hand, is a virtuoso duet, including a triple-metre section in the melodious aria style. This piece celebrates the luscious sonority of voices paired in thirds. Even more virtuosic is *Duo Seraphim*, with the most elaborate ornamentation notated in any surviving motet of the early seventeenth century. *Audi coelum* is an echo piece, combining recitative with virtuoso melismas in its first part, but bursting into six-voice polyphony in its second half in response to the text *omnes hanc ergo sequamur* (let us all, therefore, follow her).

The *Sonata sopra Sancta Maria* is an unusual piece, an enlarged version of a genre of instrumental compositions with vocal ostinatos of which only a few examples survive. The style of the work is derived to some degree from the canzonas of Andrea and Giovanni Gabrieli. But after the purely instrumental opening section (beginning like a pavane-and-galliard pair with the same music presented first in duple metre and then in triple), the instruments are joined by the soprano cantus firmus intoning eleven times the Litany of the Saints addressed to Mary. Meanwhile, the instruments continue uninterruptedly, in a virtuoso style analogous to that of the singers in some of the other *sacri concentus*, the psalms, and the Magnificats.

The five *sacri concentus* seem to be arranged according to a specific plan. The number of principal voice parts increases from one in *Nigra sum* to two in *Pulchra es* and three in *Duo Seraphim*, and then reduces again to two in *Audi coelum* and one in the *Sonata sopra Sancta Maria*. In terms of total forces, however, there is a steady augmentation from the first to the last, for *Audi coelum* concludes with a six-part choir, while the *Sonata* has eight instrumental parts plus basso continuo in addition to the single vocal part. The increasing number of forces has been used to argue that the *sacri concentus* were not printed in a succession designating their order of performance, but rather that Amadino simply followed the typical practice among sixteenth- and seventeenth-century printers of presenting compositions in an order determined by the number of parts.[5] However, this explanation does not account for Amadino's placement of the *sacri concentus* between the psalms. In virtually all other surviving prints of vesper music also containing motets (the only exception is a 1619 print by Paolo Agostini described in Chapter 4), the motets or concertos are placed in a separate group, usually at or near the end of the print. In those cases where the number of voices differs, the motets or concertos are indeed normally arranged according to the increasing number of parts.

Modern performances of the Vespers may be without regard to historical performance practices or may attempt to utilize the information we have to adhere more or less closely to a seventeenth-century style of performance. 'Historically informed performance' has become much more popular in the last few decades, especially in Great Britain, but has also gained significant ground in North America. The topic is complicated and difficult because so many

---

[5] David Blazey, 'A Liturgical Role for Monteverdi's *Sonata sopra Sancta Maria*', *Early Music*, 17 (1989), 181.

aspects of performance in the early seventeenth century were left up to the performers themselves, not just as matters of aesthetic choice, as in continuo realization and vocal and instrumental ornamentation, but also in terms of practical necessities. Choirs differed in size and in the capabilities of their soloists. Instruments may or may not have been available. Liturgical needs may have differed from one occasion to another. Tuning systems may have varied, and Latin pronunciation certainly varied from one locale to another. Different churches or other performing spaces had varying acoustical properties. The operating principal in seventeenth-century music was clearly to make performance decisions according to the practical needs and exigencies of the occasion, in addition to giving wide latitude to improvisation by vocal and instrumental soloists and continuo players.

In Monteverdi's Vespers we see the efforts of a composer to control more and more aspects of performance through detailed notation of ornamentation, specification of instrumentation, and even detailed organ registration rubrics. Monteverdi does not attempt to notate all of these things all of the time, but we can see in the part-books for the Vespers his personal interest in taking some control out of the hands of performers and placing it in his own. This does not mean, however, that Monteverdi did not still expect performers to make many of the same kinds of practical and aesthetic decisions that they did in other composers' music. Indeed, whatever restrictions he hoped to impose on performers' liberties, he must have known that anyone performing his music apart from those under his immediate direction would follow their usual habits, substituting instruments other than those designated, adding ornamentation where Monteverdi writes none, selecting different organ registration, and in general following their own whims and the practical necessities of their own particular performances.

Thus we have two kinds of 'historically informed performance' to try to understand.[6] One is an 'ideal' performance based as closely as possible on Monteverdi's notation and rubrics and what we know of the singers, instrumentalists, and other performing conditions under which he worked. Such a performance attempts to recreate what we think Monteverdi himself would have wanted. Unfortunately, while we have his notation and rubrics, we have very little knowledge of Monteverdi's performance conditions. There is not even any documented performance of music from the Vespers in Mantua. Only a performance in St Mark's in 1613 seems reasonably certain (see Chapter 1), and in this case we do have some information as to the size of the regular vocal and instrumental ensemble at St Mark's as well as the number of extra singers and instrumentalists employed for the occasion.

---

[6] I am grateful to Joshua Rifkin for this suggestion.

The second kind of 'historically informed performance' is based on a broader understanding of the norms and range of early seventeenth-century performance practices. This second type recognizes that Monteverdi's Vespers would not always have been performed by Monteverdi himself in the circumstances and under the conditions that he envisaged. Other seventeenth-century musicians would have applied their own practical and aesthetic criteria to performing this music, so that an 'historically informed performance' can also take its point of departure from what we can learn of seventeenth-century approaches to performance in general. The chapters on performance practice issues in this book attempt to deal with both types of 'historically informed performance', beginning with Monteverdi's own notation and rubrics and what is known of performance practice in Mantua (very little) and Venice (more), and expanding to the broader basis of the entire Italian peninsula. Theoretical treatises are the principal source of information in establishing performance practices, but letters and descriptions of performances are also sometimes helpful. As always with historical performance practices, there are rarely definitive answers, and all the scholar can do is attempt to circumscribe the range of possibilities as we discover them.

Modern performers have yet a broader range of possibilities in contemplating performances of the Monteverdi Vespers. They can ignore historical performance practice questions altogether and interpret the music in the same style as a large work for soloists, chorus, and orchestra by Verdi or Brahms, or, at the other extreme, they can specialize in early music and attempt to apply all of the seventeenth-century criteria that scholars have uncovered to their performance of this music. The former approach has become less and less acceptable in recent years, while the latter is reserved to only a few ensembles. Most performances will fall on a scale somewhere in between. Even early music groups usually consist of both male and female singers, already radically compomrising the sonority that Monteverdi and his contemporaries would have expected. The chapters on performance practice in Part III of this book are intended to provide musicians with the information currently available to help them decide where on that scale they wish to situate themselves, from as 'pure' a replica of seventeenth-century performance practices as possible to the opposite extreme. Moreover, the position on the scale may well vary with the performance practice issue. A mixed ensemble, for example, might perform improvised ornamentation and use period instruments, but also sing with a continuous, perceptible vibrato, play in tempered tuning, and ignore historical Latin pronunciation. Indeed, virtually all modern performances by early music ensembles represent some compromises in what is known of early seventeenth-century performance practices. But, as Lewis Lockwood indicates in the passage quoted in Chapter 11, the most important matter is for performers to make the music come alive, whatever their position. My hope is that the various sections of this book will help make Monteverdi's Vespers 'come alive' in its many dimensions: its historical context, its remarkably sophisticated construction, and seventeenth-century criteria for its performance.

I. CONTEXT

I

Sources, Controversies, and Speculations:
The Early and Modern History of
Monteverdi's Vespers

THE two seventeenth-century sources for Monteverdi's Vespers are discussed and compared in the critical notes to my Oxford University Press edition of the Vespers.[1] The primary source, the only one containing all of the music, is the original 1610 print by Ricciardo Amadino, complete and partial copies of which are located in a number of European libraries.[2] The full text of the title-page reads:

SANCTISSIMAE/ VIRGINI/ MISSA SENIS VOCIBVS,/ AC VESPERAE PLVRIBVS/ DECANTANDAE,/ CVM NONNVLLIS SACRIS CONCENTIBVS,/ ad Sacella sive Principum Cubicula accommodata./ OPERA/ *A CLAVDIO MONTEVERDE/* nuper effecta/ AC BEATISS. PAVLO V. PONT. MAX. CONSECRATA./ [coat of arms of Paul V]/ Venetijs, Apud Ricciardum Amadinum./ M D C X.

The initial five lines of the title appear in a slightly amplified and different form on the frontispiece of the Bassus Generalis part-book:

SANCTISSIMAE/ VIRGINI/ MISSA SENIS VOCIBVS,/ AD ECCLESIARVM CHOROS/ Ac Vesperae pluribus decantandae/ . . .

The first two compositions in the Vespers portion of the print, *Domine ad adiuvandum* and *Dixit Dominus*, were reprinted in

RELIQVIAE/SACRORVM/CONCENTVVM/GIOVAN GABRIELIS,/ IOHANLEONIS HASLERI,/ utriusq; praestantissimi Musici:/ Et aliquot aliorum praecellentium aetatis nostrae artificum/ Motectae, VI. VII. VIII. IX. X. XII. XIII. XIV. XVI. XVIII./ XIX. vocum, noviter expromtae/ *à* GEORGIO GRUBERO NORIMB./ [printer's mark]/ NORIMBERGAE,/ Typis & sumptibus Pauli Kauffmanni./ M.DC.XV.[3]

Controversies over Monteverdi's print begin with Amadino's title-page itself. Denis Stevens, in interpreting the Bassus Generalis version, placed special

---

[1] The sources for the *Missa in illo tempore*, which, with the exception of Amadino's print, differ from those of the Vespers, are discussed and compared in my edition of the *Missa in illo tempore* (Stuttgart: Carus-Verlag, 1994).

[2] A complete list is given in RISM, *Einzeldrucke vor 1800* and in the critical notes to my edition.

[3] RISM, *Recueils imprimés XVIᵉ–XVIIᵉ siècles*, 1615².

emphasis on the size of type of each line of the title.[4] Since the type size of *MISSA SENIS VOCIBUS* is larger than that of any of the other musical items, Stevens claimed that 'Monteverdi wanted his six-part Mass to occupy the most important position on the title page'.[5] Noting the very small type size of the phrase *Ac Vespere pluribus decantandae* in relation to the phrase *cum nonnullis . . . nuper effecta*, he translated the latter as meaning 'with some sacred pieces, works recently composed by Claudio Monteverdi and intended for princely chapels and apartments'.[6] On the basis of the differential in type size, Stevens considered the *sacri concentus* to be 'obviously equal if not superior in importance to the phrase about Vespers' and 'quite apart from the Mass and Vespers'.[7] Consequently, his edition omitted the *sacri concentus* as well as the Magnificat *a 6*. While the phrase *cum nonnullis sacris concentibus* certainly requires interpretation, there is nothing to be learned from type sizes on the frontispiece. Except for the names of dedicatees, type size figures primarily in the graphic design of title-pages in sixteenth- and seventeenth-century Italian music prints, not in the relative importance of compositions in the publication. There are countless publications in which the largest and most significant musical items are not reflected by the largest type.

In fact, the meaning of the phrase *ad Sacella sive Principum Cubicula accommodata* and the items to which it applies is not unequivocally clear. In Latin grammar, *accommodata*, a neuter plural, could not modify *cum nonnullis sacris concentibus* alone, but must modify more than one item in a series, perhaps all three of the items listed in the title (*Missa, Vesperae, sacri concentus*). To modify the phrase *cum nonnullis . . .* alone, the ending would have had to have been *accommodatis*. If the music had originally been intended for the ducal chapel of Santa Barbara, it would have been fully appropriate to use the final phrase *cum nonnullis . . .* to refer to the *Missa in illo tempore* as well as the *Vesperae* and the *sacri concentus*.[8] On the other hand, Monteverdi specifies the intended ensemble for the Mass on the Bassus Generalis title-page: *ad ecclesiarum choros* (for church choirs). This added phrase, referring to the Mass alone, may have been intended to distinguish the Mass, as a work for church, from the Vespers and *sacri concentus*, which were suited to chapels or princely chambers, thereby limiting *cum nonnullis . . . accommodata* to the second and third items of the series.

In the fourth line of the title, *pluribus* refers back to *vocibus*, that is, *pluribus* is an adjective modifying the dative form of *voces* (Vespers to be sung by 'several

[4] 'Where are the Vespers of Yesteryear?', *Musical Quarterly*, 47 (1961), 316–17; and the preface to *Claudio Monteverdi: Vespers*, ed. Stevens (London: Novello, 1961), p. iv.

[5] 'Where are the Vespers', 316.

[6] Ibid. 316–17.

[7] Ibid. 317.

[8] Denis Arnold noted already in the first edition of his biography of Monteverdi that 'in accordance with normal Latin usage *accommodata* goes with both *Missa* and *Vespere*.' See Arnold, *Monteverdi* (London: J. M. Dent and Sons, Ltd., 1963), 137 n. 1.

voices' or 'many voices' in contrast to the six voices [*senis vocibus*] of the Mass, *not* 'several Vespers'). The insertion of *ad ecclesiarum choros* on the Bassus Generalis title-page does not alter the relationship between *vocibus* and *pluribus*. *Decantandae* could refer either to the *Vesperae* alone or to the *Missa ac Vesperae*.[9] A reasonable literal translation of the principal title-page, therefore, reads: 'For the Most Holy Virgin, a Mass for Six Voices and Vespers to be sung by several voices, with several sacred songs, [the whole, or at least the Vespers and the sacred songs] suited for chapels or the chambers of princes. Works by Claudio Monteverdi, made [composed] not long ago and dedicated to His Holiness Pope Paul V.'[10] Roger Bowers proposes a slightly different interpretation of the title-page from mine and offers a more literary translation: 'To be sung to the most holy Virgin: a Mass for sixfold voices and Vespers for more, with some sacred symphonies—works suited to the chapels or chambers of princes, lately wrought by Claudio Monteverdi and dedicated to the most blessed Paul V. Pontifex Maximus.'[11] The previously published translation that most accurately represents Monteverdi's meaning is that by Denis Arnold in 1963 (omitting the dedications): 'Mass for six voices suitable for church choirs, and vespers to be performed by larger forces (together with some motets) suitable for chapels or the apartments of princes.'[12]

While the separation of the *sacri concentus* from the *Vesperae* on the title-page fuelled Stevens's argument that the *sacri concentus* were 'quite apart from the Mass and the Vespers', the matter is further complicated by the heading that appears

[9] Gottfried Wolters's German translation of the title-page correctly notes that if *accommodata* were to modify *cum nonnullis sacris concentibus*, its ending would have to be *accommodatis* (Wolters incorrectly spells *accommodata* with a single *m*). However, he also suggests that *accommodata* may modify *cubicula*, which is grammatically impossible. See *Claudio Monteverdi: Vesperae beatae Mariae Virginis*, ed. Wolters (Wolfenbüttel: Möseler Verlag, 1966), 204–5. Wolfgang Osthoff's Italian translation incorrectly attached *accommodata* only to the *sacri concentus*. See Osthoff, 'Unità liturgica e artistica nei *Vespri* del 1610', *Rivista italiana di musicologia*, 2 (1967), 315.

[10] I am grateful to Profs. William Harris, Kristine Wallace, and James Patout Burns for assistance with the Latin grammar of the title.

[11] Bowers sees *decantandae* as referring to *Sanctissimae Virgini*, while I have interpreted it as referring to *Vesperae*. Either interpretation is grammatically correct, but it does not make sense for *decantandae* to refer to *Sanctissimae Virgini* for several reasons: (1) mass and Vespers are sung to God, not to the Virgin, even if they are dedicated to the Virgin; (2) the position of *decantandae* would exclude the *sacri concentus* from those works 'sung to the Virgin'; (3) the *sacri concentus* include the only works in the print whose texts are actually addressed to the Virgin: the *Sonata sopra Sancta Maria* and *Pulchra es*. Bowers's translation also interprets *Principum* as a genitive referring to *Sacella* as well as *Cubicula*, whereas the presence of *sive* before *Principum* and the placement of *Principum* before rather than after *Cubicula* tend to separate this word from *Sacella* (but this does not mean that Monteverdi might not have had princely chapels in mind). Bowers considers the full stop after *accommodata* a printing error. The full stop makes no difference in the interpretation, however. Bowers acceptably sees *accommodata* on the principal title-page as referring to all three sets of musical items, and the purpose of inserting *ad ecclesiarum choros* on the Bassus Generalis title-page as distinguishing between church choirs as the suitable medium for the Mass and the other items as suited to the types of musicians found in 'ducal and princely households'. See Bowers, 'Some Reflection upon Notation and Proportions in Monteverdi's Mass and Vespers of 1610', *Music & Letters*, 73 (1992), 396.

[12] *Monteverdi*, 137 n. 1.

at the beginning of *Domine ad adjuvandum* in the Bassus Generalis part-book: *Vespro della B. Vergine da concerto, composto sopra canti fermi* (Vespers of the Blessed Virgin in the concerted style, composed over cantus firmi). This rubric would seem to apply to everything that follows, including the *sacri concentus*, though the latter, apart from the *Sonata sopra Sancta Maria*, are not based on cantus firmi. Aside from questions about the role of the *sacri concentus*, the purpose of the second Magnificat is not immediately clear. These matters will be considered further in the course of the discussion below.

The first two words of Monteverdi's title have until now escaped discussion because of their obvious relationship to the contents of the print, but the naming of the Blessed Virgin may have had particular significance for Monteverdi and the Gonzagas. The city of Mantua, like Venice, considered itself to have a special relationship with the Virgin. The seventeenth-century Mantuan historian Ippolito Donesmondi, under the heading 'Special Prerogatives of Mantua', declared that 'the Blessed Virgin promised to S. Anselm that she would eternally be its [Mantua's] protector'.[13] Therefore Monteverdi's leading dedication of his music to the Virgin represented not only recognition of the print's liturgical contents, but very likely an acknowledgment of the special role of the Virgin in the life of Mantua and its ruling family.[14] Donesmondi also claimed a close relationship between Pope Paul V and the Gonzagas. At the request of Duke Vincenzo, the Pope came to Mantua in 1607, granting a large number of perpetual indulgences upon the occasion of his visit to the Church of St Andrea and out of reverence for its relic of the Most Precious Blood of Christ.[15] Thus the two dedicatees of Monteverdi's print, the Virgin and the Pope, were evidently chosen for multiple reasons, including their associations with the Gonzagas and Mantua.

The first republication of music from the 1610 print after Monteverdi's time was by the Bolognese scholar, composer, and prelate Giambattista Martini. Martini, whose private collection of prints and manuscripts now forms the Civico Museo Bibliografico Musicale in Bologna, published the first Agnus Dei (transposed down a fourth) from the *Missa in illo tempore* in his monumental

---

[13] *Cronologia d'alcune cose più notabili di Mantova* (Mantua: Aurelio and Lodovico Osanna fratelli, 1615), 26.

[14] Helmut Hucke has seen the print as principally votive in character. See Hucke, 'Die fälschlich so genannte "Marien"-Vesper von Claudio Monteverdi', *Bericht über den internationalen musikwissenschaftlichen Kongress Bayreuth 1981* (Kassel: Bärenreiter, 1984), 295–305.

[15] 'Favorì nell'entrare del presente anno M.DC.VII. il Pontefice Paolo, la Chiesa di Sant'Andrea in Mantova, per rispetto del pretiosissimo Sangue di Christo, d'indulgenze molto ragguardevoli durante in perpetuo, ad istanza del Serenissimo; e fra l'altre, ne'giorni di Sant'Andrea, dell'Ascensione, di Nostro Signore, e per la notte del venerdi santo, è plenaria; . . .'. See Ippolito Donesmondi, *Dell'istoria ecclesiastica di Mantova . . . parte seconda* (Mantua: Aurelio and Lodovico Osanna fratelli, 1616), 409. Donesmondi also claims that the Pope had determined to make the duke's second son Ferdinando, when still quite young, a cardinal because of his devotion to the Church, and that the Holy See had a special affection for the merits of the House of Gonzaga (ibid. 414).

counterpoint treatise of 1774–5. For Martini, the Agnus Dei served as an example not only of excellent counterpoint, but also of ecclesiastical music designed 'to arouse in the soul of listeners affects of devotion, obsequiousness, and veneration toward the majesty of God' in contrast to Monteverdi's madrigals with their emphasis on expression of the words and free use of dissonance.[16]

Music from the Vespers portion of the print was first published by Carl von Winterfeld in his study of the music of Giovanni Gabrieli and his contemporaries in 1834.[17] Winterfeld included in his volume of examples transcriptions of the first part of *Dixit Dominus*, up to the end of the first ritornello, and the first half-verse of the *Deposuit* from the Magnificat *a 7*.[18] Winterfeld also devoted several pages of discussion to the Mass and Vespers, noting the contrast between old and new style, briefly surveying the varied styles found in the collection, and describing in more detail *Dixit Dominus*, the Magnificat *a 7*, the *Sonata sopra Sancta Maria*, and the hymn *Ave maris stella*.[19] Winterfeld was struck by what he considered the symmetry of the entire Vespers, and was the first to sense a large ground-plan behind the succession of pieces. Nevertheless, he found the motets trifling and shallow and Monteverdi's music throughout the Vespers lacking in the 'fullness of an inner, pious life'.[20]

Around the turn of the twentieth century, the Italian scholar Luigi Torchi published the *Sonata sopra Sancta Maria* in his series *L'arte musicale in Italia*.[21] This was the first complete composition from the 1610 Vespers to be published in a modern edition. Torchi's diplomatic transcription, without continuo realization or any editorial markings, constituted the best edition of music from the Vespers for two generations. Torchi placed the *Sonata* in public view for the first time, leading to transcriptions of the piece for modern ensembles, such as a 1907 version for tenor, string quartet, and piano or harmonium, and a 1919 orchestral setting for soprano choir, brass, harp, harpsichord, organ, and five-part orchestral strings.[22]

Nearly one hundred years after Winterfeld had first introduced Monteverdi's sacred music to the public, the first complete edition of the composer's 1610

---

[16] *Esemplare osia Saggio fondamentale pratico di contrappunto sopra il canto fermo*, 2 vols. (Bologna: Lelio della Volpe, 1774–5), ii. 242–50: 'il fine principale della Musica Ecclesiastica essendo di eccitare nell'animo degli Ascoltanti affetti di divozione, di ossequio, e di venerazione verso l'infinita Maestà di Dio . . .' (p. 242). Martini's commentary on the Agnus Dei is reprinted in full in Paolo Fabbri, *Monteverdi* (Turin: E.D.T. Edizioni, 1985), 158–60. For the significance of the transposition down a fourth, see Ch. 17 below.

[17] *Johannes Gabrieli und sein Zeitalter*, 3 vols. (Berlin, 1834; fac. edn. Hildesheim: Georg Olms, 1965).

[18] Ibid. iii. 112–15.

[19] Ibid. ii. 52–8.

[20] Ibid. 58.

[21] 8 vols. (Milan: G. Ricordi, 1897–1908?), iv, 51–72. This volume also contains editions of the madrigals *Cruda Amarilli* and *O Mirtillo*.

[22] The piano quintet version is in MS in the Sibley Music Library, Rochester, NY. The transcription is by Luigi Torri, though the parts are inscribed 'Pisa 24. Febbraio 1907. Alfredo Luchi'. The orchestral version is edited by Bernardino Molinari (Milan: G. Ricordi & Co., 1919).

print was finally issued in 1932 by Gian Francesco Malipiero in volume xiv of his complete edition of Monteverdi.[23] Malipiero's was not a scholarly edition in the modern sense. There are few critical notes and many errors in both text and music. Its editorial additions are limited for the most part to accidentals and an uncomplicated and not always appropriate realization of the Bassus Generalis. Nevertheless, Malipiero's edition was of considerable value, since it made the complete music of the 1610 collection available to musicians for the first time. Moreover, his method was to provide a more or less diplomatic transcription of the original, thereby avoiding the editorial excesses and confusions of several later editions, not to speak of other volumes in his own series.

Hans F. Redlich was involved in correcting the proofs for Malipiero's edition, and, in his own words, 'decided there and then to prepare a practical arrangement. Such an arrangement was necessary because of the peculiar state of incompleteness in which all music of the early baroque period (based on the musical shorthand principle of the *basso continuo*) has been left to posterity by its creators.'[24] According to Redlich, 'the modern edition has not only to reconstruct a complete orchestral score, but must add expression-marks galore, alter the time-signatures, revalue cumbersome rhythms and write out complete parts for the organ and the harpsichord'.[25] Despite being based on the Malipiero edition, Redlich's version was vastly different from it. He omitted the psalms *Nisi Dominus* and *Lauda Jerusalem* (two pieces of rather shallow choral grandeur, according to Redlich) as well as the Magnificat *a 6* and rearranged the other compositions in the order *Domine ad adjuvandum*, *Dixit Dominus*, *Laetatus sum*, *Laudate pueri*, *Duo Seraphim*, *Nigra sum*, *Pulchra es*, *Audi coelum*, *Ave maris stella*, *Sonata sopra Sancta Maria*, and Magnificat *a 7*. To these compositions Redlich added tempo, articulation, and dynamic markings, divided the vocal forces into *soli* and *tutti*, realized the continuo in a very elaborate, contrapuntally complicated, and highly ornamented manner, provided large-scale orchestration for the ritornellos, and added obbligato instruments.

Redlich's edition, originally in manuscript, was executed in 1934 and first performed in Zurich on 24 February 1935 by the Häusermann Choir under the direction of Hermann Dubs.[26] The Schola Cantorum in New York, directed by Hugh Ross, performed selections from this edition in 1937; Dubs revived the

[23] *Tutte le opere di Claudio Monteverdi* (Vienna: Universal Edition, 1932), xiv/1–2. For a list of modern editions up to 1986, see K. Gary Adams and Dyke Kiel, *Claudio Monteverdi: A Guide to Research* (New York: Garland Publishing, Inc., 1989), 38–9.

[24] 'Monteverdi's "Vespers" ', *Listener*, 943 (6 Feb. 1947), 260.

[25] Ibid.

[26] Ibid. Subsequent performances were given in Winterthur and Lausanne. Dubs and the Häusermann Choir performed *L'Orfeo* on 10 Nov. 1936. The performance information in this paragraph is derived from Redlich's article in the *Listener*, from Redlich, 'Monteverdi's Religious Music', *Music & Letters*, 27 (1946), 209 and the preface to *Claudio Monteverdi: Magnificat Sechsstimmig*, ed. Karl Matthaei (Kassel and Basle: Bärenreiter-Verlag, 1941). Matthaei was familiar with the performances based on Redlich's MS edition, and agreed with Redlich's claims that the continuo tolerated a 'richer, motivic-elastic decoration'. Matthaei's own realization of the Magnificat *a 6*, however, is much more

Vespers in the Großmünster in Zurich on 12 October 1941; and in 1943 the Swiss Radio Beromünster broadcast Redlich's version of the Vespers, under the direction of Hermann Scherchen. Additional Swiss broadcasts followed, and the edition was first performed in England by the Morley College Music Society (whose director was Michael Tippett) under the leadership of Walter Goehr on 14 May 1946. The Morley College Music Society then repeated its performances in July 1946 and January 1947. Paul Collaer also directed a performance in Brussels in 1946. Finally, Redlich's edition of the Vespers was broadcast on the BBC's Third Programme on Thursday, 13 February 1947.

Redlich's edition finally reached print in 1949,[27] was reissued in a slightly revised version in 1952, and served as the basis of a gramophone recording in 1953.[28] The recording drew scornful criticism, much of it condemning Redlich's edition.[29] The response of Leo Schrade, who had prepared his own edition of the Vespers for a separate recording, is a classic of musical invective:

Recently there have been a good many performances of Monteverdi's works, especially numerous in the case of the Vespers, in concerts and over the radio, and all of them so remarkably remote in spirit and letter from Monteverdi's original that the time seems to have come for frank criticism. For arbitrary, inartistic performances will, in time, seriously affect understanding for Monteverdi's work. . . .

The recording of Monteverdi's Vespers here reviewed, shows all the deplorable features we have mentioned: a version over-romantic, with little musical taste and understanding of style, but with serious changes in the original text. The deviations from the original are indeed so serious that they can no longer be regarded as legitimate 'interpretations' but must be qualified as arrangements, violating both scholarship and musicianship. . . .

A first question that the recording brings up concerns the selection of the compositions from the Vespers. For the recording does not present the complete Vespers. . . .

A second question that must be raised concerns the order in which the compositions appear. Monteverdi planned his Vespers as a perfect unity, both liturgical and artistic; and the unity is such that is should not be tampered with. Liturgically, the psalms, the hymn, and the Magnificat occupy the center of importance, and they follow each other as the rite of the Vespers prescribes. While Monteverdi resorted to certain liberties in the choice of antiphons linked to the psalms and Magnificat (not of course to the hymn), he at least was careful to choose related, Marian texts and to keep in mind the proper position of solo compositions as antiphons prefatory to the psalms. . . . It has been stated that the original does not have sufficient indications of either the media or the manner of performance, and this alleged lack of indication was, therefore, the

---

modest than Redlich's of the Magnificat *a 7*. Matthaei also retains Monteverdi's organ registration rubrics, which Redlich had discarded.

[27] *Monteverdi: Vespro della Beata Vergine* (Vienna: Universal Edition, 1949; rev. 1952). Redlich discussed his edition in 'Claudio Monteverdi—zum Problem der praktischen Ausgabe seiner Werke (Vesper 1610)', *Schweizerische Musikzeitung*, 74 (1934), 609–17, 641–6, as well as in 'Claudio Monteverdi: Some Problems of Textual Interpretation', *Musical Quarterly*, 41 (1955), 68.

[28] Vox PL 7902. The Swabian Choral Singers and the Stuttgart Bach Orchestra were conducted by Hans Grischkat. See App. D, item 2.

[29] See Hans Nathan, 'Two Interpretations of Monteverdi's *Vespro della Beata Vergine*', *Music Review*, 15 (1954), 155–6, and Leo Schrade, 'Monteverdi: *Vespro della Beata Vergine*', *Musical Quarterly*, 40 (1954), 138–45.

pretext for all kinds of additions and arrangements. Only somebody who never saw the original can make such an assumption. . . . Since the recording follows Redlich's score, the performance exhibits all the errors and shortcomings of that edition. In fact, the deplorable deficiencies of the performance are to a large extent due to the editorial arrangement used by the musicians. . . .

As regards the arbitrary addition of parts, it is vexing enough when a Respighi nonchalantly adds his music to a score of Monteverdi; we have a harder time when the score is enriched by a musicologist. But whether composer or musicologist, he has no right to subject us to a kind of study in a course of 'free composition.'[30]

Schrade then continues with detailed criticism of various aspects of both the edition and the performance.

Redlich defended his conception of the Vespers, describing the 1610 print as a pot-pourri of unrelated pieces: 'a loose collection of diverse liturgical compositions rather than . . . a single artistic unit'.[31] Redlich stressed the difference between the printed music of the early seventeenth century and the many treatises and descriptions of performances that discuss ornamentation, doubling instruments, and multiple continuo instruments. He defended his ornamentation of continuo lines on the basis of comments by Heinrich Schütz and Michael Praetorius.[32] Aside from disagreement over liturgical and artistic unity in the Vespers, the dispute between Redlich and Schrade was principally over performance practice. Schrade, as will be discussed below, had the more sophisticated view of the liturgical aspects of the Vespers, but he saw Monteverdi's rubrics, detailed ornamentation, and reproduction of the upper parts of some pieces in the Bassus Generalis part-book as indications of the completeness of Monteverdi's score, not to be tampered with. While Redlich misunderstood the liturgical nature of Monteverdi's print, he correctly saw it as incomplete in terms of seventeenth-century performance practice, requiring 'filling out' on the part of performers. Aside from the liturgical impropriety of Redlich's edition, the question at stake is the character of his arrangement and its proximity to or distance from seventeenth-century practices. From Part III of this book, it will be apparent that Redlich understood far more of early seventeenth-century performance practice than Schrade.

Schrade, in his 1950 study of Monteverdi, had already recognized that the response, psalms, hymn, and Magnificats were the standard liturgical items for

---

[30] See Schrade, 139–41. For background on the recording of Schrade's edition and the Schrade–Redlich controversy, see Jim Davidson, *Lyrebird Rising* (Portland, Oreg.: Amadeus Press, 1994), 402–3.

[31] 'Claudio Monteverdi: Some Problems of Textual Interpretation'. Redlich had already described the succession of pieces under the heading Vespers in the 1610 print as an 'accidental-additive collation'. See Redlich, *Claudio Monteverdi: Leben und Werk* (Olten: Verlag Otto Walter, 1949), 145. In the enlarged English translation of this book, the entire passage is rendered: 'The addition of the "nonnulli sacri concentus" clearly betokens the elastic character of the whole arrangement, whose fortuitous grouping together as a unit implies no further mutual obligation with regard to performance' (Redlich, *Claudio Monteverdi: Life and Works*, trans. Kathleen Dale (London: Oxford University Press, 1952), 128).

[32] 'Claudio Monteverdi: Some Problems of Textual Interpretation', 69–70.

Vespers on feasts of the Virgin.[33] He also drew associations between the motets *Nigra sum* and *Pulchra es* and the two liturgical antiphons with these same text incipits. He assumed that the five *sacri concentus* were 'to function in the place of the proper antiphons . . . for the liturgy of the day is observed in the rest of the collection'.[34] Schrade's own edition (in manuscript and never published) was recorded at virtually the same time as Redlich's,[35] and was reviewed more favourably than Redlich's by Hans Nathan, but Nathan still complained of 'several arbitrary *a cappella* passages (in *Lauda Jerusalem* and occasionally in *Laudate Pueri*) as well as a few disturbing *tempi* which are apparently not the conductor's doing'.[36] Nathan also emphasized that the recording and Schrade's edition presented the Vespers in their entirety and their original order (omitting the Magnificat *a 6*).

Schrade's reaction to the Redlich edition and recording not only may have reflected a scholar's indignation at what he considered unscholarly and unmusical work, but may also have been prompted by Redlich's earlier critical reviews of Schrade's own book.[37] Redlich, in response, turned some of Schrade's own arguments against him and accused Schrade in his manuscript edition of 'taking from it [Redlich's edition] not only the title and features of general presentation, but also a number of editorial characteristics'.[38] Redlich also cited discrepancies between Schrade's edition and the recording based on it and repeatedly criticized Schrade's disinterest in performance practice questions. Thus began the cycle of debate and controversy over interpretations of the Vespers, centred on two principal issues: liturgy and performance practice.

Contemporaneous editions of music from the Vespers included a partial and faulty edition by Georgio Ghedini in 1952, with the motet *O quam pulchra es* from Leonardo Simonetti's anthology of 1625 inserted, and Gottfried Wolters's partial edition of 1954, containing the response, the five psalms, *Audi coelum*, the *Sonata sopra Sancta Maria*, the hymn, and the doxology of one of the Magnificats. This edition was without continuo realization and was derived

---

[33] *Monteverdi, Creator of Modern Music* (New York: W. W. Norton & Company, Inc., 1950), 251–4.

[34] Ibid. 253. This is also the viewpoint expressed in Schrade's review of Redlich's recording.

[35] L'Oiseau-Lyre OL 50021–2 (1953). See App. D, item 3. Live broadcasts by the same performers took place on the BBC's Third Programme on 19 and 21 Feb. 1954. See Redlich, 'Editions of Monteverdi's Vespers of 1610', *Gramophone*, 31 (1954), 503.

[36] 'Two Interpretations', 155. Redlich defended his own and Schrade's a cappella omission of the basso continuo on the basis of its being a *basso seguente*, and therefore optional. See Redlich, 'Two Interpretations of Monteverdi's *Vespers*', Correspondence, *Music Review*, 15 (1954), 255–6. Redlich later criticized the tempos in the recording based on the Schrade edition as 'excessively fast'. See Redlich, 'Claudio Monteverdi: Some Problems of Textual Interpretation', 68.

[37] Redlich, 'Aufgaben und Ziele der Monteverdi-Forschung: Zu Leo Schrades Monteverdi-Buch', *Die Musikforschung*, 4 (1951), 318–32; and review of Schrade, *Monteverdi, Creator of Modern Music*, *Music Review*, 13 (1952), 316–18.

[38] 'Editions of Monteverdi's Vespers of 1610'.

from Malipiero's own faulty version.[39] A year later Redlich published another revised version of his own edition, this time based on the original print rather than Malipiero, and evidently responding to the criticism of his earlier omissions, since he now included thirteen of Monteverdi's compositions, excluding only the Magnificat *a 6*.[40] Redlich's revised edition and Schrade's manuscript version were the first since Malipiero to go back to the original source.

By the late 1950s, new editions of the Vespers were appearing frequently, for Walter Goehr, who a decade before had conducted the first performance of Redlich's initial edition in England, issued his own version in 1957.[41] Goehr followed Schrade, rather than Redlich, in his interpretation of the liturgical order of the print, except that Goehr considered the *Sonata sopra Sancta Maria* as the antiphon to the Magnificat because of the proximity of its text to the Magnificat antiphon *Sancta Maria succurre miseris*.[42] The other motets he treated as antiphons, noting, however, that *Duo Seraphim* and *Audi coelum* do not belong to the liturgy of Marian feasts. Goehr, like Redlich and Schrade, based his edition on the 1610 print, but he was a noted performer, not a scholar, and his effort to render the music in a modern form proved extremely clumsy. Reductions in note values, frequent changes in metre, extensive added orchestration, missing parts, exchanges of parts, poor continuo realization, and multiple other editorial sins made this effort highly problematic for practical use.[43]

Despite Schrade's and Goehr's view that the Vespers represented a liturgical and artistic unity, others were still troubled by the fact that none of the five *sacri concentus* texts is strictly in agreement with any liturgical antiphon for a vespers of the Virgin. Denis Stevens, for example, in the preface of his 1961 edition of the Vespers, proclaimed 'Let us state then, quite categorically, that the following texts are not antiphons, nor have they any connection with Vespers of the Blessed Virgin: *Nigra sum*; *Pulchra es*; *Duo Seraphim*; *Audi coelum*; *Sonata sopra Sancta Maria*.'[44] According to Stevens, Monteverdi 'certainly never envisaged

---

[39] *Claudio Monteverdi, Vesperae Beatae Mariae Virginis (Marien-Vesper) 1610* (Wolfenbüttel: Möseler Verlag, 1954). The five psalms and the hymn were also published as separate editions. See the review by Redlich, 'Monteverdi and Schütz in New Editions', *Music Review*, 19 (1958), 73–4.

[40] *Claudio Monteverdi, Vespro della beata vergine/Marienvesper* (Vienna: Universal Edition, 1955). According to Wolters, *Claudio Monteverdi: Vesperae beatae Mariae virginis* (Wolfenbüttel: Möseler Verlag, 1966), 205, Redlich's edition was published in Kassel and Basle by Bärenreiter.

[41] *Claudio Monteverdi: Vespro della Beata Vergine (1610) da concerto, composta* [sic] *sopra canti fermi* (Vienna: Universal Edition, 1957).

[42] Ibid., p. iii. Jürgen Jürgens and Andrew Parrott both place the *Sonata sopra Sancta Maria* in this position in their recordings of the Vespers. See the discussion below of the article by David Blazey, who argues a similar case.

[43] See the reviews by Redlich, 'Monteverdi and Schütz in New Editions', 72–3, and Wolfgang Osthoff, 'Claudio Monteverdi: Verspro della Beata Vergine (1610)', *Die Musikforschung*, 11 (1958), 380–1; and Denis Stevens's review of a BBC performance from this edition, 'Monteverdi's Vespers', *Musical Times*, 99 (1958), 673.

[44] *Monteverdi Vespers*, p. v. Stevens excluded these compositions as well as the Magnificat *a 6* from his edition. See also Stevens, 'Where are the Vespers of Yesteryear?', 316–25; and Giuseppe Biella, 'La "Messa" il "Vespro" e i "Sacri Concenti" di Claudio Monteverdi', *Musica sacra*, 2nd ser., 9 (1964), 105–15.

the kind of performance that has become customary in recent years, with psalms and motets reeled off one after the other just as Amadino had printed them'.[45] Consequently, Stevens omitted these five compositions and supplied for each psalm a plainchant antiphon. In a plainchant service, the tones of the psalms are selected according to the modes of the liturgically appropriate antiphons for that service, but with polyphonic settings of psalms, each psalm represents a single tone and the choirmaster can no longer choose a psalm in the tone that matches the liturgically correct antiphon (see the discussion of this issue in Chapter 2). Stevens, therefore, did the opposite: he chose antiphons in the same modes as the tones of each of the psalms and the Magnificat, indicating that the antiphon was to be repeated after each psalm (but omitting the rubric after the Magnificat). The result, though, is a series of antiphons that do not represent any single liturgical service. Stevens explained the presence of two Magnificats in the print (the Magnificat *a 6* was omitted from his edition) as serving first vespers (on the vigil of a feast) and second vespers (towards the end of the feast-day itself). With regard to Monteverdi's instrumentation, he recommended the substitution of oboes and possibly even clarinets for Monteverdi's cornettos, and the addition of bassoons to the basso continuo.[46] Critical notes are somewhat sparse; nevertheless, Stevens's edition is accurate and the basso continuo realization is in seventeenth-century style, making his version a significant improvement over earlier editions, if still not wholly satisfactory. Stevens issued a recording based on his edition in 1967.[47]

In contrast to Stevens, Gottfried Wolters published a new edition in 1966 in which all of Monteverdi's compositions following the rubric *Vespro della Beata Vergine* (except the Magnificat *a 6*) were published in the order of the 1610 print.[48] This edition was a considerable advance over Wolters's earlier edition as well as all other versions. It was based on Monteverdi's print (editors had finally given up using Malipiero as their source) and was the first to provide a detailed critical report. Numerous suggestions for instrumental doubling, for

---

[45] *Monteverdi Vespers*, p. vi. Stevens was even more insistent on this point in a contemporaneous article: 'The lengthy cantata-like texts of . . . [the four motets] could never be used as antiphons, and it is unforgivable to pretend that they are.' See ' "Monteverdi's Vespers" Verified', *Musical Times*, 102 (1961), 422. The appearance of Stevens's edition and article sparked another acrimonious debate, this time between Redlich and Stevens. See *Musical Times*, 102 (1961), 422, 564–5, 643, and 713. Stevens later accepted the inclusion of the *sacri concentus* in a vesper service on artistic grounds in the liner notes of the 1966 recording by Michel Corboz (New York: Musical Heritage Society, n.d.; see App. D, item 4): 'When we listen to the "Vespers" in the order of the printed editions, we cannot help being struck by the grandiose architectural design, so carefully thought out, which is responsible for this sequence of masterpieces. The judicious alternation of smaller and larger works, the progression of each category independently of the other, the variety in tonality (for we may speak of tonality in the modern sense, rather than of modes); all this goes to show that the "Vespers" are not simply a collection of magnificent pieces, but a great and unified conception—a monument comparable in importance and grandeur with Bach's B minor Mass.'

[46] *Monteverdi Vespers*, pp. vi–vii. Stevens notes the unavailability of cornettos at that time and considers trumpets an unsatisfactory substitute.

[47] Vanguard VCS-10001/2. See App. D, item 8.

[48] *Claudio Monteverdi: Vesperae beatae Mariae virginis.*

instrumental ritornellos, and for use of soloists and choir in the psalms, Magnificat, and hymn are given in an appendix rather than encumbering the score itself as in Redlich's and Goehr's editions. Wolters's basso continuo realization is mostly simple in style, according to the precepts of early seventeenth-century continuo practice, except in the few-voiced motets, where it is more elaborate, perhaps overly so. The chief difficulty with Wolters's edition is its reduction of note values in triple metre and the substitution of numerals for mensuration signs that are not only confusing and inconsistent, but sometimes make triple time look duple. Nevertheless, this edition was the best available at the time and has been widely used by performers.

Wolters considered Monteverdi's publication a liturgical work, and the *sacri concentus* as replacements for the plainchant antiphons that would normally follow each psalm. In an appendix to the edition, Walther Lipphardt gave suggested plainchant antiphons to precede each psalm. Since, like Stevens, Lipphardt could not find antiphons from any liturgical service to fit the succession of tones of Monteverdi's psalms and Magnificat, he selected a series of antiphons, mostly derived from the Song of Songs and traditionally associated with Marian feasts or the Common of Virgins. Four of these came from a modern antiphonal, but one was derived from a twelfth-century manuscript antiphoner. As far as he could, Lipphardt matched the modes of these antiphons with the tones of Monteverdi's psalms, but had to concede defeat in two cases where he could find no antiphons with Song of Songs texts in the matching modes.[49]

With the notion of the 1610 Vespers as a complete liturgical unit becoming more widely accepted, Jürgen Jürgens prepared in 1966, the same year as Wolters's edition, the first complete recording of the series of compositions in Monteverdi's print as a liturgical service, omitting only the Magnificat *a 6* as superfluous.[50] In the notes to this recording, Wolfgang Osthoff hedged on the role of the *sacri concentus*: 'It is not even said [in the print] whether these are to replace the antiphons or to represent "concertante" insertions independent of them. . . . *Duo Seraphim* presents a special problem from this point of view.'[51] Jürgens's recording inserts plainchant antiphons both before and after the psalms, the *sacri concentus* then following after the repeated antiphons. The *Sonata sopra Sancta Maria*, however, as a litany, is displaced until after the hymn and versicle, anticipating the Magnificat antiphon *Sancta Maria succurre miseris*.[52]

---

[49] According to Wolters, the first performance of the Vespers with Gregorian antiphons took place on 5 Aug. 1954 as part of the Festliche Tage Junge Musik in St Michael's church in Passau (ibid. 204 n. 3).

[50] Telefunken SAWT 9501/02-A. See App. D, item 5.

[51] Ibid., liner notes.

[52] Walter Goehr, as noted above, had already recognized the relationship between the *Sonata* and the Magnificat antiphon. See also n. 42 above.

Osthoff also notes the impossibility of finding liturgically appropriate plain-chant antiphons whose modes match the tones of Monteverdi's psalms; there-fore the selection was made from antiphons derived from the Song of Songs which do match the tones of the psalms, but not that of the Magnificat.[53] After the antiphon to *Lauda Jerusalem*, the plainchant chapter is sung immediately before the hymn, and the versicle is performed after the hymn. Similarly, the plainchant *Benedicamus Domino/Deo gratias* follows the repetition of the Magnificat antiphon and closes the service. Osthoff admits that the series of antiphons 'cannot . . . be ascribed to any particular festival of the Virgin Mary', but paradoxically concludes that 'this self-contained series of antiphons also seems to us to have first made truly clear and understandable the liturgical order and the structure of Monteverdi's Vespers of the Blessed Virgin'.[54]

Until the time of Wolters's second edition and Jürgens's recording, the litur-gical issues raised by the Vespers had been examined rather superficially through modern liturgical books. In 1967, the 300th anniversary of Monteverdi's birth, Stephen Bonta published the first thorough account of the vesper liturgy in relation to seventeenth-century vesper publications and explored the liturgical question posed by Monteverdi's five *sacri concentus* on the basis of seventeenth-century sources. His study supported the notion that these pieces were intended as substitutes for the official antiphon texts, which a celebrant could have intoned *sotto voce* while the motets and *Sonata* were being performed.[55] The crux of Bonta's argument was that once a composer had set a series of vesper psalms in particular tones in *canto figurato*, it became virtually impossible to find antiphons to match these tones, and even if one could, they were liturgically incorrect. According to Bonta, the solution to this problem was to abandon 'both tonal unity and liturgical propriety'.[56] The missing antiphon at the Magnificat, Bonta suggested, should be supplied by an instrumental composi-tion, according to the suggestion of the contemporary theorist Banchieri.[57] Banchieri also recommended playing the organ after the *Sicut erat* of a psalm, indicating that repetition of a plainchant antiphon would not have intervened.

---

[53] Despite the derivation of antiphons for both the Wolters edition and the Jürgens recording from the Song of Songs, they have only one antiphon in common.

[54] Telefunken SAWT 9501/02-A, liner notes. see App. D, item 5.

[55] Stephen Bonta, 'Liturgical Problems in Monteverdi's Marian Vespers', *Journal of the American Musicological Society*, 20 (1967), 87–106. Many of Monteverdi's biographers did not concern themselves with the issue of liturgical or artistic unity in the Vespers until after Bonta's article. Denis Arnold, for example, skirted the question in the first edition of *Monteverdi* (1963), only saying of the print: 'Its size and contents suggest that it was a presentation volume, not meant for ordinary practical use' (p. 138). The second edition of 1975 repeated the same sentence, but in response to Bonta's article added at a later point, 'When the motets, psalms, hymn, Sonata and Magnificat are given, as they usually are today, as an entity (and for this there is a strong case to be made out), the total concept appears to inhabit a world of its own' (p. 147).

[56] 'Liturgical Problems', 96.

[57] Ibid. 98–101. See the quotation from Banchieri in n. 110 below.

Even the *Caeremoniale Episcoporum*, the official book of rules for liturgical celebrations, sanctioned the practice of the organ substituting for the antiphon, as long as the antiphon was recited by one of those officiating.[58] This point contradicts Jürgens's repetition of the antiphon after each psalm in his recording as well as Stevens's instructions to repeat the antiphon in his edition.

Complaints and admonitions of church officials against the practice of substituting texts offer evidence of the reality of such practices (see further discussion of this issue below and in Chapters 2 and 4). Indeed, Bonta interpreted the large seventeenth-century repertoire of motets and instrumental music as solving the problem of Proper texts in the mass and office by making available music in *canto figurato* for substitution where plainchant no longer fit modally or aesthetically and where *canto figurato* settings of Proper texts would have been too cumbersome and infrequently used to warrant composition. The anomalous Trinitarian text of *Duo Seraphim* did not enter into Bonta's discussion; in fact, he considered the texts of all the *sacri concentus* as appropriate for Marian feasts. With regard to the two Magnificats, Bonta accepted Stevens's suggestion that they were to serve for both first and second vespers.[59]

In the same year Wolfgang Osthoff argued that the 1610 print constituted a complete service, principally on aesthetic grounds.[60] Osthoff also offered further evidence, in the form of an eyewitness account, of the practice of performing motets and instrumental music between psalms in vesper services. Corroborating evidence was subsequently provided by Thomas D. Culley in his studies of music at the German College in Rome and in Jesuit colleges in other countries.[61] Anthony M. Cummings also uncovered a widespread practice of

---

[58] 'Liturgical Problems', 99–100.

[59] Ibid. 92, 97, 104–5. If the use of substitute texts had become a common practice, justifying viewing Monteverdi's *sacri concentus* as replacements for plainchant antiphons, then it would also seem possible to borrow Gregorian antiphons from other Marian feasts, as both Wolters and Stevens did, whether to provide texts that are Marian in orientation or to match the tones of Monteverdi's psalms and Magnificats.

[60] 'Unità liturgica e artistica', 319. Osthoff quotes a letter by the German musician Paul Hainlein, who heard vespers on the Feast of the Immaculate Conception, 8 Dec. 1647, in the church of St Francis in Venice: 'Die psalmen seindt gewest: Dixit Dominus, Laudate pueri, Letatus sum, Nisi Dominus, Lauda Jerusalem, auch ein Himnus vor dem Magnificat, hernach Alma redemptoris mater. Aber zwischen jedweter psalm ein Motetten oder Sonata gemacht, darunter ein Bassist und Discantist, welche von der Roma eine gesungen, von der Madona, seindt auch wort auß dem 46 psalm genomen worden dieses inhalts, daß sie deß Türcken macht zerstöhren, bögen und schildt zerbrechen, schiff und Galleen verbrennen und seine gantze macht in den abgrundt des Meers stürtzen wolle.' However, Osthoff argued the unity of the Vespers principally on aesthetic grounds and considered the addition of plainchant antiphons as extraneous intrusions. Guido Pannain, in the same year, also claimed artistic unity for the Vespers. See Guglielmo Barblan, Claudio Gallico, and Guido Pannain, *Claudio Monteverdi* (Turin: Edizioni RAI Radiotelevisione Italiana, 1967), 343–4.

[61] *Jesuits and Music, i: A Study of the Musicians Connected with the German College in Rome during the 17th Century and of their Activities in Northern Europe* (St Louis: St Louis University, 1970), 78 and 85; and id., 'Musical Activity in some Sixteenth Century Jesuit Colleges with Special Reference to the Venerable English College in Rome from 1579 to 1589', *Analecta musicologica*, 19 (1979), 7.

substitutions for liturgical texts in the mass in Italy in the sixteenth century,[62] and James H. Moore cited documentary evidence of the performance of motets between the psalms at vespers in Venice.[63] James Armstrong's study of Giovanni Francesco Anerio's *Antiphonae* of 1613 demonstrated not only that antiphon texts could be rather freely rearranged, substituted, or altered, but also that the modal relationship between antiphon and psalm was considerably loosened, perhaps even eventually dissolved through the *canto figurato* settings of both psalms and antiphons or antiphon substitutes.[64] Various church decrees attempting to eliminate the interpolation of unauthorized texts and compositions in both the mass and the Divine Office also testify to the frequency of such practices.[65]

The score Jürgen Jürgens had originally prepared for his 1966 recording was eventually published by Universal Edition more than a decade later.[66] In the preface to this edition Jürgens had evidently changed his mind about the need for plainchant antiphons and the position of the *Sonata sopra Sancta Maria*. Taking his point of departure from the Bassus Generalis rubric *Vespro della B. Vergine da concerto, composto sopra canti fermi*, he stated unequivocally,

> The sequence of the vesper movements in the printed edition follows strictly the liturgical order of a vesper [*sic*], so that we find here additional confirmation of the compositional unity of the 'Vespers'; all alterations in the order must therefore be seen as arbitrary interference with the unity of the work as it was conceived. . . . The concert character of the work is underlined by the fact that in place of the Gregorian antiphony required by the liturgy, groups of soloists are used; their texts are in part antiphonies and in part free invention.[67]

Jürgens's reasoning for this shift of orientation is rooted in the conclusion that the Vespers do not constitute a liturgical service. According to Jürgens,

[62] 'Toward an Interpretation of the Sixteenth-Century Motet', *Journal of the American Musicological Society*, 34 (1981), 43–59.

[63] *Vespers at St Mark's: Music of Alessandro Grandi, Giovanni Rovetta and Francesco Cavalli* (Ann Arbor: UMI Research Press, 1981), 151–2.

[64] 'The *Antiphonae, seu sacrae cantiones* (1613) of Giovanni Francesco Anerio: A Liturgical Study', *Analecta musicologica*, 14 (1974), 89–150.

[65] Bonta quotes a few such decrees in 'Liturgical Problems', 96. Two decrees from 1628 and 1639 warning against substitutions for the correct antiphons are given in English translation in Graham Dixon, 'Agostino Agazzari (1578–after 1640): The Theoretical Writings', *Royal Musical Association Research Chronicle*, 20 (1986–7), 48. On motets as liturgical substitutions see also Culley, *Jesuits and Music*; Gino Stefani, *Musica e religione nell'Italia barocca* (Palermo: S. F. Flaccovio, Editore, 1975); Moore, *Vespers at St Mark's*; Anthony M. Cummings, 'Toward an Interpretation'; and Jerome Roche, *North Italian Church Music in the Age of Monteverdi* (Oxford: Clarendon Press, 1984), 40–7. For an unusual approach to the polyphonic setting of all five antiphon texts as a single motet, see the discussion of Pietro Maria Marsolo's *Motecta quinque tantum vocibus . . . liber secundus* of 1614 in Chapter 2.

[66] *Claudio Monteverdi: Vespro della Beata Vergine* (Vienna, 1977). The Universal Edition catalogue number is 16646. See the review of this edition (which also surveys previous editions) by Denis Arnold in *Early Music*, 6 (1978), 463–4; and my review in *Music Library Association Notes*, 37 (1980), 981–3. Universal Edition also published a miniature score version of this edition with abbreviated preface as Philharmonia No. 470.

[67] *Claudio Monteverdi: Vespro della Beata Vergure*, pp. viii–ix. Jürgens's preface is published in both German and English.

Ever since Monteverdi's 'Vespers' was rediscovered, musicologists and musicians have been trying to establish the liturgical reference of the work, and a series of reconstruction attempts have been published. None of these has arrived at a satisfactory solution; they all come to the conclusion that the 'Vespers' comprise a single sacred work without reference to a fixed liturgy.

For if a liturgical version were in fact the basis for the work, it would be necessary to place a tonally appropriate antiphony before and after each Psalm and before and after the Magnificat, and to omit the solo concerti which in Monteverdi's concept replace the antiphonies.

All such attempts were bound to fail for this reason alone: Monteverdi had chosen a Gregorian canto fermo which had no corresponding liturgical antiphony which would fit in tonally with Monteverdi's psalm tone. It is thus impossible here to adhere to the liturgical rule whereby antiphonies and psalm-tones should correspond—except by using non-liturgical, i.e. transposed, antiphonies—and this much-discussed theory can finally be eliminated.[68]

Jürgens's view of the unity of the series of compositions, therefore, was based on opposite criteria from Bonta's. Whereas Bonta (and Wolters before him) saw the *sacri concentus* as replacements for plainchant antiphons, Jürgens at this time saw the entire collection as extra-liturgical—a churchly concert in which antiphons no longer played a role and the problem of matching the modes of antiphons to the tones of Monteverdi's psalms and Magnificats simply did not exist. His 1977 edition, therefore, presents all of Monteverdi's music except for the Magnificat *a 6* in the order of Amadino's print, without interpolation of plainchant antiphons (or other vesper chants). Jürgens's edition also provides performance practice suggestions and critical notes, but both are deficient in detail, and the score does not distinguish between Monteverdi's original and Jürgens's frequent editorial interventions in terms of rubrics, *colla parte* doubling, *musica ficta*, varying continuo instruments, and shifts between soloists and tutti. Only Jürgens's ornamentation is notated unambiguously as editorial.

Just when it seemed that the liturgical and/or artistic unity of the *Vespro della Beata Vergine* had been broadly accepted, further questions and suggestions for alternative interpretations began to surface. In the liner notes to his 1984 recording of the Monteverdi Vespers, Andrew Parrott, together with Hugh Keyte, argued that the five *sacri concentus* were indeed 'intended to substitute for liturgical movements', but that their order in Amadino's print was confused.[69] Parrott recorded the motets *Nigra sum*, *Pulchra es*, and *Audi coelum* in the positions they occupy in the print after the psalms *Dixit Dominus*, *Laudate pueri*, and *Nisi Dominus*. However, he displaced the *Sonata sopra Sancta Maria* after the Magnificat as an antiphon substitute for the canticle (Monteverdi did not provide any composition at this point in the print); and *Duo Seraphim*, which,

---

[68] *Claudio Monteverdi:Vespro della Beata Vergure*, p. ix. Jürgens issued a second recording of the Vespers, Ambitus AMB 383826, based on this thesis in 1989. The performance presents the first thirteen compositions in their order in the print (omitting the Magnificat *a 6*), and eschews all plainchant additions. See App. D, item 29 and the discussion of this recording below. For a related view of the Vespers as non-liturgical, see the discussion of the article by Helmut Hucke below.

[69] EMI Angel DSB-3963, 1984. See App. D, item 21.

according to Parrott and Keyte, 'cannot be an Antiphon substitute at a Marian vespers, since it is Trinitarian in reference', was moved to near the end of the service as a substitute for the *Deo gratias*. Parrott then placed a *Sonata a 2* by Giovanni Paolo Cima after *Laetatus sum* in the original position of *Duo Seraphim* and a *Sonata a 3* by Cima after *Lauda Jerusalem* in the original position of the *Sonata sopra Sancta Maria*. Parrott also added Monteverdi's 1624 setting of the *Salve Regina* to the end of the service, since liturgical practice required a performance of one of the seasonal Marian antiphons after vespers if compline were not to follow.[70] In addition to the polyphonic items, Parrott provided plainchant antiphons from the Feast of the Assumption before each psalm and the Magnificat, as well as all of the other liturgical chants that complete a vesper service on this feast-day (the chapter, prayers, versicle, and responses).[71] Parrott, therefore, accepted the notion that all of the compositions in Monteverdi's print, other than the *Missa in illo tempore*, furnished music for a single vesper service, but a complete liturgical service required a different order from the print itself as well as additional music. Noting the *chiavette* notation of *Lauda Jerusalem* and the Magnificat, Parrott transposed these works down a fourth.[72]

Also in 1984, Helmut Hucke published a paper, originally read in 1981, in which he argued that there is no such thing as a 'Marian vespers' in the liturgy, and that Monteverdi's collection was never intended as a liturgical service, but rather as 'non-liturgical, princely devotional music in a quasi-liturgical form'.[73] Particularly bothersome to Hucke were the non-liturgical texts of the five *sacri concentus* and the absence of a relationship between *Duo Seraphim* and the Marian liturgy. However, I fail to see the difference between a 'Marian vespers' (an invalid concept for Hucke) and Monteverdi's own rubric *Vespro della Beata Vergine* or the rubrics *De Beata Vergine* or *Vespro della Madonna* found in other prints (see Chapters 3 and 4). I also see no incompatibility in Monteverdi's print serving for both a liturgical service and a source of devotional music. Much more interesting in Hucke's article was an interpretation of the texts of many of the compositions from the collection in terms of Renaissance biblical exegesis.

In 1986, Bernhard Meier contributed to the argument in favour of a 'unified' Vespers on the basis of his analysis of the modes of the four motets (excluding the *Sonata sopra Sancta Maria*). According to Meier, the discovery of the modal basis of the motets places them on the same tonal basis as the psalms, hymns, and

---

[70] For the text of the relevant rubric from a contemporary breviary, see Ch. 2 n. 3.

[71] James Moore has documented the practice at St Mark's of still performing the plainchant antiphon before the psalm when organ music substituted for the antiphon after the psalm. See *Vespers at St Mark's*, 176.

[72] See the discussion of *chiavette* and their role in signalling transposition in Ch. 17. Parrott defended his transcriptions in 'Transposition in Monteverdi's Vespers of 1610: An Aberration Defended', *Early Music*, 12 (1984), 490–516.

[73] 'Die fälschlich so genannte "Marien"-Vesper', 298.

Magnificats with their Gregorian cantus fermi.[74] Meier's case is weak, however, since all of Monteverdi's music of this period, including the secular music, is rooted to some degree in the modal system he inherited.

In the next year, Jürgen Jürgens, who had recorded the first version of the Vespers as a reconstructed liturgy in 1966, complete with antiphons and displaced *Sonata sopra Sancta Maria* (see the discussion above), recorded another performance from an exactly opposite point of view.[75] This time Jürgens performed only the items in Monteverdi's print, in their original order, with no chant other than the versicle *Deus in adjutorium*. In his liner notes Jürgens railed with the zeal of a convert against any interpolations or alterations in the succession of pieces in Monteverdi's print, without, however, mentioning his earlier recording and its vastly different perspective.[76]

A new and very interesting proposal regarding the origin of the Vespers was made by Graham Dixon in 1987, suggesting that most of the music of Monteverdi's 1610 print was not initially intended for a feast of the BVM at all, but rather for the feast of Santa Barbara, celebrated in the Gonzaga ducal church of Santa Barbara.[77] The ducal church (also known as a basilica) has its own rite, compiled in the late sixteenth century and sanctioned by the Pope, which differs in many details from the Roman rite.[78] One of these differences lies in the cycle of psalms for various feasts. The psalms for the Common of Virgins, which in the Roman rite are the same as for all Marian feasts, are in the rite of Santa Barbara *Dixit Dominus*, *Confitebor tibi*, *Beatus vir*, *Laudate pueri*, and *Lauda anima*.[79] Each of the Marian feasts from the Proper of the Time, however, either

---

[74] 'Zur Tonart der Concertato-Motetten in Monteverdis Marienvesper', Ludwig Finscher, ed., *Claudio Monteverdi. Festschrift Reinhold Hammerstein zum 70. Geburtstag* (Laaber: Laaber Verlag, 1986), 366.

[75] See n. 68 above.

[76] See Jürgens's arguments against liturgical unity in the preface to his 1977 edition of the Vespers, quoted above. Jürgens's preface and liner notes are polemical in tone, based on rather garbled scholarship and *non sequiturs*. Nevertheless, some of his conclusions are probably correct. See my own discussion of the order of compositions in Monteverdi's print below.

[77] 'Monteverdi's Vespers of 1610: "della Beata Vergine"?', *Early Music*, 15 (1987), 386–9.

[78] For a brief account of Guglielmo Gonzaga's persistent efforts to establish his own liturgy see Pierre M. Tagmann, 'The Palace Church of Santa Barbara in Mantua, and Monteverdi's Relationship to its Liturgy', in Burton L. Karson, ed., *Festival Essays for Pauline Alderman* (Provo, Ut.: Brigham Young University Press, 1976), 54–5. More detailed is the account in Iain Fenlon, *Music and Patronage in Sixteenth-Century Mantua*, 2 vols. (Cambridge: Cambridge University Press, 1980), i. 79–117. Differences between the rite of Santa Barbara and the Roman rite have been studied by Paola Besutti in 'Ceremoniale e repertorio liturgico della basilica palatina di Santa Barbara in Mantova' (thesis, University of Parma, 1984–5); ead., 'Catalogo tematico delle monodie liturgiche della Basilica Palatina di S. Barbara in Mantova', *Le fonti musicali in Italia*, 2 (1988), 53–66; ead., 'Un tardivo repertorio di canto piano', *Tradizione manoscritta e pratica musicale: I codici di Puglia* (Florence: Leo S. Olschki, 1990), 87–97; ead., 'Testi e melodie per la liturgia della Cappella di Santa Barbara in Mantova', *Atti del XIV congresso della Società internazionale di musicologia* (Turin: E.D.T. Edizioni, 1990), 68–77; ead., 'Giovanni Pierluigi da Palestrina e la liturgia mantovana', *Atti del II Convegno internazionale di studi palestriniani* (Palestrina: Fondazione G. Pierluigi da Palestrina, 1991), 157–64.

[79] Santa Barbara Breviary, Prima Pars, fo. 221ᵛ, Pars Secunda, fo. 139ᵛ.

requires the same psalms as the Roman rite for both first and second vespers, or has a separate set for first vespers: *Dixit Dominus, Confitebor tibi, Beatus vir, Laudate pueri*, and *Laudate Dominum*.[80] This latter set corresponds to the *cursus* common to many vespers of male saints in the Roman rite (but also employed for first vespers on the feasts of St Agnes and St Agatha—see the psalm *cursus* in Appendix A). For the feast of Santa Barbara herself, annually celebrated in the ducal church with considerable ceremony, the psalms for first vespers are this latter *cursus*, while those for second vespers are the same as those for Marian feasts and the Common of Virgins in the Roman rite—the same *cursus* found in Monteverdi's 1610 Vespers.[81] The other major feast of the ducal chapel's patron saint, the Feast of the Translation of Santa Barbara on 22 April, requires the same psalms for first and second vespers as the feast of Santa Barbara itself.[82]

Therefore, as Dixon argues, the psalm *cursus* of Monteverdi's Vespers need not originally have been planned for a Feast of the BVM, but rather could have originated in connection with second vespers on either of the two feasts of Santa Barbara, 22 April or 4 December. As he suggests, such an elaborate ceremony on the 4 December feast might have been performed in 1607 or 1609.[83] December of 1608 seems out of the question, since Monteverdi was at his parents' home in Cremona seeking release from the ducal service (see below).[84] 1609 is the more likely possibility, since Monteverdi was completely preoccupied during the autumn of 1607 and the spring of 1608 with preparations for the opera *Arianna* and *Il ballo delle ingrate* in connection with the marriage of Margherita of Savoy and Prince Francesco, which, after many delays, took place on 24 May 1608 (see below).[85] It seems unlikely that he would have had time to complete an elaborate vesper service in the same period, and Monteverdi's and

---

[80] The Marian feasts in the Santa Barbara Breviary are the Conception of the BVM on 8 Dec., the Purification of the BVM on 2 Feb., the Annunciation of the BVM on 25 Mar., the Visitation of the BVM on 2 July, Holy Mary of the Snow on 5 Aug., the Assumption of the BVM on 15 Aug., and the Nativity of the BVM on 8 Sept. Of these, the Purification, the Annunciation, the Assumption, and the Nativity are all listed as *duplex maior*. Feasts with the *Dixit–Laudate Dominum cursus* for first vespers are the Visitation, the Assumption, and the Nativity. I am grateful to Paola Besutti for checking my own notes against the Santa Barbara Breviary. Tagmann, in 'The Palace Church of Santa Barbara', 57, is confused in his list of psalms for Marian feasts. Knud Jeppeson, in 'Monteverdi, Kapellmeister am S.ta Barbara?', in Raffaello Monterosso, ed., *Claudio Monteverdi e il suo tempo* (Verona: Stamperia Valdonega, 1969), 312–13, takes the first vespers *cursus* of the Visitation as his basis of comparison with the Monteverdi Vespers, thereby obscuring the identity between the Santa Barbara breviary and the Roman rite in the *cursus* for second vespers and first vespers on most Marian feasts.

[81] Breviary of Santa Barbara, Pars Prima, fos. 223–5.

[82] Ibid., fo. 264ᵛ.

[83] 'Monteverdi's Vespers of 1610', 387.

[84] See Domenico De'Paoli, *Claudio Monteverdi: Lettere, dediche e prefazioni* (Rome: Edizioni de Santis, 1973), 33–7, and Eva Lax, *Claudio Monteverdi: Lettere* (Florence: Leo S. Olschki Editore, 1994), 20–4. Eng. trans. in Denis Stevens, *The Letters of Claudio Monteverdi* (Cambridge: Cambridge University Press, 1980), 57–61.

[85] The complex circumstances surrounding this wedding are described in Stuart Reiner, 'La vag' Angioletta (and Others)', *Analecta musicologica*, 14 (1974), 26–88.

his father's letters to Duke Vincenzo and the duchess describing his pressures and unhappiness during this time mention nothing about the added pressure of a large liturgical work.[86]

A key factor in Dixon's argument is the presumed unsuitability of *Duo Seraphim* for vespers of the Virgin. However, a Trinitarian motet was perfectly appropriate for Santa Barbara, who was martyred for her espousal of the Trinity; indeed, the fourth and fifth psalm antiphons for this feast make reference to her devotion to the Trinity.[87]

Further strengthening the association of at least part of the 1610 Vespers with the ducal church is Paola Besutti's demonstration that the form of the *Ave maris stella* chant used by Monteverdi in his setting of the hymn is closer to the version from the rite of Santa Barbara and to that used by the former *maestro di cappella* of Santa Barbara, Giaches de Wert, than it is to contemporaneous Roman rite versions.[88] While there are differences between Monteverdi's cantus firmus and its text underlay on the one hand and those of the Santa Barbara chant and Wert's cantus firmus on the other, Wert's is also not identical to the Santa Barbara chant, and two important structural identities differentiate all three versions from contemporaneous Roman chants. Taking Dixon's thesis as her point of departure, Besutti speculates that Monteverdi may have originally intended his Vesper music as a means of applying to Vincenzo Gonzaga for the post of *maestro di cappella* in Santa Barbara, which became vacant at the end of 1608 or the beginning of 1609 with the death of Giovanni Gastoldi.[89] Gastoldi had been ill for quite some time and his demise was anticipated. In fact, Monteverdi's father's letter to the duke of 9 November 1608, lamenting Claudio's exhaustion, ill health, and poverty (Claudio was at home in Cremona at the time), asked for his son's release from ducal service, or at least, for service limited 'to the church' [Santa Barbara].[90] However, Antonio Tarone temporarily occupied the

---

[86] Monteverdi's father's letters are published in Fabbri, *Monteverdi*, 148–50; Eng. edn., 100–2.

[87] Breviary of Santa Barbara, Pars Prima, fo. 223^r. For the texts of these antiphons, see Dixon, 'Monteverdi's Vespers of 1610', 387. A brief account of the legend of Santa Barbara and the multiple reasons why Guglielmo may have chosen this saint are given in Fenlon, *Music and Patronage*, i, 100–1.

[88] 'Ricorrenze motiviche, canti dati e "cantus firmus" nella produzione sacra di Claudio Monteverdi', paper delivered at Convegno, Claudio Monteverdi: Studi e prospettive, Mantua, 21–4 Oct. 1993, published as '"Ave Maris Stella": la tradizione mantovane nuovamente posta in musica da Monteverdi' in Paola Besutti, Teresa M. Gialdroni, and Rodolfo Baroncini eds., *Claudio Monteverdi: Studi e prospettive, Atti del Convegno (Mantova, 21–24 ottobre 1993)* (Florence: Olschki, 1998), 57–78. The basis of Besutti's argument is not only the melodic similarity between Monteverdi's and the Santa Barbara version, but also the peculiar similarities of text underlay. Jeppeson had argued the opposite, but was mistaken in a portion of his comparison between the Santa Barbara chant and Monteverdi's cantus firmus. See 'Monteverdi, Kapellmeister an S.ta Barbara?', 315.

[89] Liner notes to a 1987 recording, Harmonia Mundi France 901247.48; see App. D, item 24. According to Pierre Tagmann, 'La cappella dei maestri cantori della basilica palatina di Santa Barbara a Mantova (1565–1630): Nuovo materiale scoperto negli archivi mantovani', *Civiltà mantovana*, 4 (1969–70), 380, Gastoldi was last mentioned in the archives as *maestro di cappella* on 3 Jan. 1609.

[90] Baldassare Monteverdi's letter is reproduced in Fabbri, *Monteverdi* (1985), 149–50.

position until April 1609, when Stefano Nascimbeni was appointed *maestro di cappella*.[91]

Circumstantial evidence also suggests an association of at least some of the music in the 1610 print with the ducal church. Dixon connects the adherence to plainchant cantus firmi in Monteverdi's psalms and Magnificats with the conservative character of the liturgical practices fostered by Gugliemo Gonzaga in establishing the rite of Santa Barbara. Gastoldi, *maestro di cappella* at Santa Barbara from 1592 to early in 1609, occasionally used a cantus firmus in his Vesper psalm settings and often composed in a very conservative, largely homophonic, style.[92] As Dixon remarks, 'The style which Monteverdi adopts in the Vespers psalms is a compromise between the new compositional tendencies (seen in *Orfeo*) and the traditional chant practice. Such a fusion of idioms would have allowed him to use his most up-to-date techniques in composing for the basilica, while not endangering the traditional ethos of the liturgy there.'[93]

Dixon similarly sees Monteverdi's use of the toccata from *L'Orfeo* in the Vespers response *Domine ad adjuvandum* as also connecting the 1610 print with the ducal church:

> The scoring of the toccata in *Orfeo* for 'Un Clarino con tre trombe sordine' strongly suggests that this piece must have had a particular ceremonial role in the context of the Mantuan court. The designations 'clarino' and 'trombe' are only exceptionally found in art music of this period, and the use of mutes suggests that these are outdoor instruments being allowed inside for a particular purpose. Monteverdi is unlikely to have taken a piece with a particular political connotation for the Gonzaga, and used it in a seemingly haphazard way outside court.'[94]

Additionally, the litany *Sancta Maria ora pro nobis* appears in other polyphonic contexts, in one case a motet with the name *Sancte Marce* and in another with *Sancta N.*, the abbreviation standing for *nome*, indicating that the name of any saint may be inserted.[95] Thus, the original form of the text of this piece could have been *Sancta Barbara ora pro nobis*, as Dixon surmises, perhaps requiring slight alterations in the rhythm of the published setting.[96]

The two texts *Nigra sum* and *Pulchra es*, while long associated with the BVM, might also have been applicable to other female saints. Only *Audi coelum* specifically refers to and names Mary on several occasions; her name is integral to the construction of the text and not subject to substitution.[97] *Audi coelum*, therefore, must have been composed either for a Marian feast or as devotional music for

---

[91] Tagmann, 'La cappella dei maestri', 381.

[92] See Ch. 4. for brief discussions of some of Gastoldi's psalms and Magnificats. Fenlon also comments on the conservative nature of the music for the ducal chapel; see *Music and Patronage*, i. 117.

[93] 'Monteverdi's Vespers of 1610', 388.

[94] Ibid. See the discussion of trumpet mutes and their effect on pitch in Ch. 6 below.

[95] See the discussion of these pieces in Ch. 4

[96] 'Monteverdi's Vespers of 1610', 387.

[97] See the discussion of *Audi coelum* in Ch. 10.

the court. Similarly, the hymn *Ave maris stella* is 'proper' to feasts of the BVM; the vesper hymn for the two feasts of Santa Barbara is *Exultet celebres virginis inclytae*.[98] Nevertheless, as mentioned above, the version of the *Ave maris stella* chant used by Monteverdi seemingly derives from the rite of Santa Barbara, so that the hymn was probably composed for a Marian vespers of some kind for the ducal chapel. In fact, the church of Santa Barbara had a separate altar to the Virgin, so it is likely that there would have been numerous solemn celebrations of Marian feasts in the ducal church.[99]

That instruments were used in the ducal church on the feast of Santa Barbara is demonstrated by the dedication of the *Apparato musicale* of 1613 (RISM F1813) by Amante Franzoni, *maestro di cappella* in the ducal church from some time in 1612. In this dedication Franzoni refers to his mass, which contains instrumental music, as 'solemnly sung on that day' [the feast of Santa Barbara in 1612].[100] The *Apparato musicale* also contains a setting of *Duo Seraphim* and a version of the litany *Sancta Maria ora pro nobis*, the latter entitled Concerto and set for soprano solo accompanied by four trombones.[101] The appearance of these two compositions in a print expressly connected with the church of Santa Barbara suggests that Monteverdi's settings of the same texts may similarly have been associated with the ducal chapel, though not necessarily with the Feast of Santa Barbara itself.[102]

Dixon's hypothesis is plausible, for it would not have been necessary for most of the music of the 1610 print to have originated in connection with a Marian feast. Moreover, music originally for separate services could have been assembled by Monteverdi into the 1610 publication under the rubric *Vespro della Beata Vergine*. Dixon's assumptions at least provide an explanation for the inclusion of the motet *Duo Seraphim* in the 1610 print, without, however, resolving the question of the relationship of its Trinitarian text to Marian Vespers.

A recording based on Dixon's proposal, performed by 'The Sixteen' under the direction of Harry Christophers, was issued in 1988.[103] This reconstruction of second vespers on the feast of Santa Barbara inserts the appropriate plain-

---

[98]   Santa Barbara Breviary, Pars Prima, fo. 223ʳ.

[99]   Besutti, 'Ceremoniale e repertorio liturgico', 16. Until the construction of the church of Santa Barbara, the Gonzaga family chapel in the cathedral was located in the chapel of Santa Maria dei Voti. See Fenlon, *Music and Patronage*, i. 23.

[100]   'la Messa solenemente in detto giorno cantata'.

[101]   See the discussion of these pieces in Ch. 4.

[102]   While Franzoni is explicit in the dedication about the mass being performed on the feast of Santa Barbara, in reference to the motets of the collection he merely says that they were added to the mass: *pregato ancor da particolari amici, di darla* [the mass] *alle stampe accompagnata da quei Concerti*. Whether or not the *concerti* originated in connection with the 1612 feast of Santa Barbara, they likely were associated with the ducal church simply by virtue of Franzoni's position as *maestro di cappella* there. See also Graham Dixon, ' "Behold our Affliction": Celebration and Supplication in the Gonzaga Household', *Early Music*, 24 (1996), 250–61.

[103]   *Monteverdi: Second Vespers for the Feast of Santa Barbara*, Hyperion CDA 66311/2. See App. D, item 26.

chant antiphons from the Santa Barbara Breviary before each of Monteverdi's psalms as well as the Magnificat, but reorders Monteverdi's five *sacri concentus*. *Pulchra es* is shifted from its position after *Laudate pueri* in Monteverdi's print to follow *Dixit Dominus* in the recording. Similarly, *Nigra sum* is placed after *Laetatus sum*, the position originally occupied by *Duo Seraphim*. The apparent rationale for this is the role of *Nigra sum* as the third antiphon (for the psalm *Laetatus sum*) in the Common of the BVM.[104] *Duo Seraphim* is shifted from its original position after *Laetatus sum* to follow the final psalm, *Lauda Jerusalem*, and *Audi coelum*, originally positioned after *Nisi Dominus*, is displaced to near the end of the service, substituting for the Advent Marian antiphon that would have been sung if vespers concluded the day's services. The *Sonata sopra Sancta Maria [Barbara]* appears at the very end, after the final prayer, presumably as the litany that was often sung at the end of vesper services (see below). In lieu of the displaced *sacri concentus*, instrumental sonatas from a manuscript compiled by Giovanni Amigoni, a Mantuan musician, are inserted after *Laudate pueri* and *Nisi Dominus*. A motet to Santa Barbara, *Gaude Barbara* by Palestrina, is also added after the post-Magnificat prayers, in accordance with the common sixteenth- and seventeenth-century practice of performing a motet after the Magnificat.[105] The hymn for the Feast of Santa Barbara is presented in plainchant, and other chants completing the service are also included, such as the chapter, blessing, prayers, versicles, and responses. Since *Ave maris stella* has no part in a vespers of Santa Barbara, the hymn is added at the end of the recording in order to present 'the complete 1610 Vespers music'.[106]

David A. Blazey, whose dissertation studies the Litany in Italy in the seventeenth century,[107] accepts the idea that Monteverdi's four motets are to serve as antiphon substitutes in the Vespers, but sees a different role for the *Sonata sopra Sancta Maria*.[108] He demonstrates the close relationship between the litany text *Sancta Maria ora pro nobis* and the Litany of Loreto on the one hand and the Magnificat antiphon for feasts of the BVM, *Sancta Maria succurre miseris*, on the other.[109] Blazey also cites Banchieri's suggestion that an organist should play a

---

[104] The antiphons for the Common of the BVM in modern liturgical books are derived from the 16th- and 17th-century feast of Holy Mary of the Snow. *Nigra sum* appears as the third antiphon for this feast in the Santa Barbara Breviary (Pars Secunda, fo. 180ᵛ.).

[105] See e.g. 'Culley, Jesuits and Music', 81–2.

[106] Hyperion CDA66311/2 liner notes. The 1610 print is not complete, however, for the Magnificat *a 6* is not included. Dixon's hypothesis can lead to a number of different reconstructions, all of which are in some sense arbitrary; only one of these could be chosen for the recording. See my review of this recording in *Early Music*, 17 (1989), 429–35. The music is listed in order in App. D, item 26.

[107] 'The Litany in Seventeenth-Century Italy', 2 vols. (Ph.D. dissertation, University of Durham, 1990).

[108] Blazey, 'The Litany', i. 241–9; id., 'A Liturgical Role for Monteverdi's *Sonata sopra Sancta Maria*', *Early Music*, 18 (1989), 175–82.

[109] This is the Magnificat antiphon for second vespers on the feast of Holy Mary of the Snow in the Santa Barbara Breviary (Pars Secunda, fo. 180ʳ), as well as in the Roman breviary. The liturgy of this feast became the liturgy of the Common of the BVM as early as the 17th century. Monteverdi

'*Franzesa Musicale*, or something else if he likes' after the Magnificat.[110] Similarly, Giovanni Battista Fasolo in 1645 gave instructions for short organ pieces called *fughe sopra l'obligo* as substitutes for the Magnificat antiphon.[111] Blazey notes that Monteverdi's and other similar sonatas are principally instrumental in character, while their employment of 'the melodic formula of the litany as used in the ostinatos is closely associated with the text of the Magnificat antiphon "Sancta Maria succurre miseris"'.[112] Blazey also calls attention to the relationship in character between the *Sonata* with its obbligato instruments and the Magnificat *a 7*, which relies heavily on obbligato instruments.[113] He therefore concludes that the *Sonata sopra Sancta Maria* was intended as an antiphon substitute for the repeat of the antiphon after the Magnificat rather than for the psalm *Lauda Jerusalem*. This hypothesis also places the *Sonata* at the end of the service, not only in the position where instrumental music was often performed, but also in the position where litanies were sometimes sung in the seventeenth century. To account for the fact that his interpretation renders the position of the *Sonata* in the Amadino print out of liturgical order, Blazey suggests that Amadino merely interspersed the *sacri concentus* between the psalms in ascending order of number of parts, thereby giving them an arbitrary ordering from the standpoint of their position in a liturgical service.[114]

Blazey's hypothesis is also plausible, though his assumption about the ordering of the *sacri concentus* is troubling. As with the reordering of the *sacri concentus* in the reconstructions of Parrott and Dixon, Blazey's hypothesis requires us to assume that Amadino made some kind of liturgical error in his highly unusual placement of the motets and the *Sonata* after each of the psalms (see below for further discussion of Amadino's placement of the *sacri concentus*). Yet the one piece of hard evidence we have of Monteverdi's intentions is just this ordering. It may be in error, but there is no evidence that the ordering is incorrect or arbitrary, and each of these hypotheses requires us to assume so. Indeed, the difficulties scholars have had in explaining the role of the Trinitarian text of *Duo*

himself published a setting of this Magnificat antiphon in 1627. On the relationship between the antiphon and the Litany of Loreto, see Blazey, 'The Litany', i. 238–44.

[110] Quoted in Blazey, 'A Liturgical Role', 178: 'Doppo il Magnificat suonasi una Franzesa Musicale, ò altro se piace'. Banchieri also provided four capriccios to play after the Magnificat in the 1605 edition of *L'organo suonarino*.

[111] Blazey, 'A Liturgical Role', 178. Fasolo's *Annuale* was previously mentioned in Bonta, 'Liturgical Problems', 99–100.

[112] 'A Liturgical Role', 178–9.

[113] Ibid. 179–80. In drawing this relationship, Blazey does not take into consideration the Magnificat *a 6*, which is without obbligato instruments.

[114] 'The Litany', i. 21, 55–7, 61–8, 72, 78, 102–6, 108; id., 'A Liturgical Role', 180–1. See also Jerome Roche, 'Musica diversa di Compietà: Compline and its Music in Seventeenth-Century Italy', *Proceedings of the Royal Musical Association*, 109 (1982–3), 63; and Colleen Reardon, *Agostino Agazzari and Music at Siena Cathedral, 1597–1641* (Oxford: Clarendon Press, 1993), 43 n. 38, 69–70. The most common roles for the litany were in processions, on Saturdays, and after Compline. See Blazey, 'The Litany', ch. 2.

Seraphim or the unusual character of the *Sonata sopra Sancta Maria* with regard to the other motets have prompted some scholars to seek hypothetical solutions other than the possibility that Amadino actually printed the *sacri concentus* in their intended relationship to the psalms. While the solutions proposed by Parrott, Dixon, and Blazey are plausible and must be given serious consideration, it is also possible that they are solutions to a non-existent problem. It may be that we simply do not understand how freely non-liturgical texts may have been interpolated into liturgical services, or there may have been other reasons unknown to us for Monteverdi including a setting of *Duo Seraphim* in a vespers of the BVM and the *Sonata sopra Sancta Maria* as an antiphon substitute for *Lauda Jerusalem*. I am more reluctant than Parrott, Dixon, and Blazey to ignore the available hard evidence—the succession of pieces in Amadino's print—in favour of solutions to what may be problems of our understanding rather than of Monteverdi's liturgical intentions. For seventeenth-century musicians, the order of pieces in his Vespers may have posed no problem at all.

A few other publications from the first third of the seventeenth century are organized in ways tending to support the assumption that Monteverdi's *sacri concentus* were meant to serve as antiphon substitutes. Three such prints are discussed in some detail in Chapter 4. The earliest is Giovanni Battista Fergusio's *Motetti e dialogi per concertar a una sino à nove voci* of 1612, in which there are four sets of six motets, each set followed by a Magnificat. This unique grouping, not seen in any other print of the period, suggests six antiphon substitutes for the psalms and Magnificat of a vesper service, followed by the Magnificat itself. A slightly later print, Paolo Agostini's *Salmi della Madonna* of 1619, contains multiple settings of each of the five psalms of the Marian *cursus*, each psalm setting followed by a motet.[115] One of the motets in each group associated with a single psalm text is labelled *antifona prima*, *antifona seconda*, and so on. These *antifone* are polyphonic settings of the liturgically correct antiphon texts from the feast of Holy Mary of the Snow, in other words, the Common of the BVM, while the texts of most of the other motets, apparently serving the same function in relation to the psalms as the *antifone*, are not liturgical antiphons at all. A third publication, Leandro Gallerano's *Messa e Salmi concertati* of 1629, has a short motet preceding one setting of *Dixit Dominus* and another preceding one setting of the Magnificat. Each of these motets is described in the table of contents as an *Introducione*. These motets may well have been intended as substitutes for the plainchant antiphons; they each appear *before* the liturgical item rather than afterwards, as seems normally to have been the case.[116] Stephen Bonta had

---

[115] See a list of the contents of this print in Ch. 4.

[116] For a discussion of the practice in Venice, see Moore, *Vespers at St Mark's*, 175–7. Some of the contemporary references speak of a motet or instrumental piece between the psalms, thereby failing to connect the interpolated composition specifically to the psalm before or the one after.

already pointed out that Giovanni Battista Fasolo's *Annuale* of 1645 provides instrumental pieces *loco antiphonae post Magnificat* (in place of the antiphon after the Magnificat).[117] Indeed, many prints of vesper music in the seventeenth century include one or more instrumental pieces at the end. Other evidence of motets substituting for antiphons in vespers is described in Chapters 2 and 4.

After the publication of Jürgens's edition of the Vespers in 1977, no further editions appeared until the mid-1980s. The first of these was by Clifford Bartlett in 1986, originally prepared for the recording by Andrew Parrott (see above) and based on Malipiero and Wolters.[118] This version included downward transposition by a fourth of *Lauda Jerusalem* and the Magnificat *a 7*, but omitted the Magnificat *a 6*. Bartlett subsequently issued another edition in 1990, produced from a computer, also omitting the Magnificat *a 6* but presenting the remaining pieces in the same order as the 1610 print.[119] The edition contains critical notes, but does not provide a realization of the Bassus Generalis; basso continuo figures are supplied instead. *Lauda Jerusalem* and the Magnificat *a 7* are transposed down a fourth, but the advantage of an edition produced on the computer is that transposition to any pitch level can be readily accomplished upon request for any of the compositions.[120] Bartlett has made the Magnificat *a 6* separately available in a computer-produced score, thereby providing, for the first time since Malipiero, the complete vesper music of the 1610 print.

Bartlett has also made available a liturgical guide, called a 'work in progress', as a companion to the edition. The guide usefully reproduces the rubrics, together with English translations, for all of the office hours except compline from the 1604 edition of the *Directorium chori* of Giovanni Guidetto.[121] The liturgical guide additionally contains antiphons for the principal Marian feasts throughout the year (including Holy Mary of the Snow) for those who wish to perform the antiphons before each psalm and the Magnificat. Bartlett's approach to the antiphons, however, is different from that of Wolters and Stevens, both of whom sought Marian texts in modes matching as closely as possible the tones of Monteverdi's psalms and Magnificat, but in doing so violated the liturgical appropriateness of the antiphons. Bartlett, by contrast, presents the liturgically correct antiphons for each feast, but many of them are transposed to match their psalms. What 'match' means, however, is problematic, for the ver-

---

[117] 'Liturgical Problems', 99–100.

[118] *Monteverdi, Vespro della Beata Vergine* (Huntingdon, Cambs.: King's Music, 1986).

[119] *Monteverdi, Vespro della Beata Vergine* (Huntingdon, Cambs.: King's Music, 1990). See the brief comments in the review by Paul McCreesh, 'Monteverdi Vespers: Three New Editions', *Early Music*, 23 (1995), 326.

[120] See Ch. 17.

[121] *Monteverdi Vespers (1610): Guide to Liturgical Context* (Huntingdon, Cambs.: King's Music, 1989). Bartlett refers to the *Guide* as 'work in progress, not a finished document'. The source for Bartlett's rubrics is Ioanne Giudetto, *Directorium chori ad usum omnium ecclesiarum cathedralium, & collegiatarium* (Rome: Stephanum Paulinum, 1604).

sions of antiphons given in some cases conclude with the opening note of the psalm tone cantus firmus, in other cases terminate with the same note as the final of the psalm or Magnificat, in yet others end a fifth above the final of the psalm or Magnificat, in still others end with the final of the transposed Magnificat (down a fourth), and in several cases do not match at all.[122]

The Monteverdi year of 1993 (the 350th anniversary of his death) stimulated multiple efforts at producing new editions of the Vespers. A facsimile of the 1610 print based on the Bologna copy was issued in 1992 with a very brief introduction by Grreta Haenen.[123] A study score by Jerome Roche was published in 1994[124] and a revised version of Denis Stevens's 1961 edition also appeared in the same year.[125] Roche's score is the first since Malipiero to include all fourteen compositions within a single edition. In addition to a preface briefly addressing the principal issues surrounding the Vespers, Roche provides critical notes, texts, and translations in a separate appendix, and a liturgical appendix with the vesper liturgies, including untransposed plainchant antiphons for the Common of the BVM and the feast of the Assumption of the BVM. Stevens, in his revised edition, adds the motets he had omitted in 1961, but retains many of the errors of the earlier edition, retains its modern instrumentation, divides *Nigra sum* into a dialogue for two voices, adds two editorial parts to the *Sonata sopra Sancta Maria*, and ignores much of the research on the Vespers accomplished since 1961.[126]

My own edition published by Oxford University Press serves as companion to the present volume and provides the complete music, with complete critical notes, plainchant antiphons, and original texts with English translations. *Lauda Jerusalem* and the two Magnificats are given both in their original, untransposed notation as well as transposed down a fourth. The complete Bassus Generalis is also included in its original open score format.

Since 1987, a number of new recordings of the Monteverdi Vespers have appeared aside from the *Second Vespers for the feast of Santa Barbara* by Harry Christophers discussed above. It is impossible in this space to discuss them in detail and the reader is referred to the discography, Appendix D, for a list and descriptions of these recordings. I will note here only a few salient characteristics.

Except for the Christophers recording, these recent efforts have tended to present the compositions in the order of Monteverdi's print with the exception

---

[122] See Ch. 2 for my discussion of the various ways in which plainchant antiphons may have been accommodated to psalms and Magnificats.

[123] *Claudio Monteverdi: Sanctissimae Virgini Missa senis vocibus ac Vesperae* (Peer, Belgium: Alamire, 1992).

[124] *Claudio Monteverdi, Vespro della Beata Vergine* (London: Eulenburg Ltd., 1994). See McCreesh, 'Monteverdi Vespers'.

[125] *Claudio Monteverdi, Vespers 1610*, ed. Denis Stevens (London: Novello, 1994).

[126] See McCreesh, 'Monteverdi Vespers', 326–7.

of three that displace the *Sonata sopra Sancta Maria* (Wikman, Bernius, and Jacobs, items 25, 27, and 39 in Appendix D) and one that substitutes a Frescobaldi ricercare for the *Sonata* (item 33 in Appendix D). Several add plainchant antiphons and other chants from various feasts (Harnoncourt (item 23), Bernius (item 27), Savall (item 28), Pickett (item 30), Jacobs (item 39), Pearlman (item 42)). The antiphons in the recording by Jordi Savall are taken from the feast of Santa Barbara, making his version another 'quasi' vespers of Santa Barbara (Savall does not omit *Audi coelum*, does not alter the text of the *Sonata*, and does not replace *Ave maris stella* with the hymn for Santa Barbara). All of these recordings except Wikman's employ period instruments. Savall transposes *Lauda Jerusalem* down an augmented fourth, Van Asch (item 36) and Junghänel (item 37) transpose it down a whole tone, and Pickett and Renz (item 34) transpose both *Lauda Jerusalem* and the Magnificat *a 7* down a fourth. Only the new recording by John Eliot Gardiner (item 31) includes the Magnificat *a 6* in addition to the Magnificat with instruments, while the recording by Hermann Max (item 33), which eschews obbligato instruments, presents the Magnificat *a 6* only.

John Eliot Gardiner's recording was made in connection with performances in St Mark's Basilica, Venice, on 10–11 May 1989, and a video version was also produced (the Magnificat *a 6* did not figure in these performances and was only added later to the CD version). This video is visually and sonically magnificent, though scarcely the 're-creation' that Gardiner contends. Especially problematic is Gardiner's introduction, which associates the Vespers too closely with Venice and unaccountably describes the motets as 'secular' and their texts as not tolerable in Rome (where Palestrina had given a major impetus to Song of Songs settings with his motet collection of 1583–4 based exclusively on texts from the Song of Songs!). The performance itself, with soloists, choirs, and instrumentalists moving frequently among the two pulpits, various balconies, and various parts of the chancel, is designed more for dramatic effect in a concert atmosphere than to represent the character of a liturgical performance from Monteverdi's time. Indeed, there is no evidence to suggest that singers and instrumentalists in St Mark's performed from any more than a very restricted number of locations, depending on the liturgical function.[127] Gardiner's children's choir (with both male and female voices) and the gestures, such as a tenor kneeling in front of an altar while intoning a doxology or raising his hands towards heaven while singing the Gloria of the Magnificat, make for effective religious theatre but have no historical basis. Gardiner does follow the order of contents of Monteverdi's print, though he does not include any of the plainchants that would be required for an actual 're-creation'.[128]

---

[127] What is known of performance practice in St Mark's is documented in Moore, *Vespers at St Mark's*.

[128] For a critique of Gardiner's recording, see Graham Dixon, 'Fine if Unauthentic Interpretations', *Classic CD* (Feb. 1991), 97.

My own perspective on the contents of Monteverdi's 1610 print was first outlined in my dissertation on the Vespers in 1972.[129] I agreed with Bonta's position on the use of the *sacri concentus* as antiphon substitutes and provided additional evidence from the prints of Fergusio and Agostini.[130] I also concurred with Osthoff's contention that the Vespers constitute an artistic unity. Bonta, especially, was quite explicit about this liturgical and artistic unity: 'the weight of both external and internal evidence suggests that it should be published and performed in its original form, with nothing omitted, and with a canzona or two added near the end of the service. Any other type of edition or performance is a violation of Monteverdi's artistic intentions, and runs counter to what we know of the musico-liturgical practice of his time.'[131]

My own view, however, as presented in both my dissertation and an article published in 1974,[132] is more flexible; I do not believe that a complete liturgical service is the only option Monteverdi had in mind. While the Amadino print may be used in the published order to provide music for a large-scale polyphonic vesper service, Monteverdi probably also intended other possibilities. The very phrase *ad Sacella sive Principum Cubicula accommodata* on the title-page suggests a variety of locations for performance. The two Magnificats, one with and one without instruments, suggest two different performance circumstances: if appropriate instruments were available, the Magnificat *a 7* could be presented; if not, the Magnificat *a 6* with organ accompaniment only (as in item 33 in Appendix D). Similarly, Monteverdi indicates that the instrumental ritornellos in *Dixit Dominus* are optional. The same may be true for the ritornellos in *Ave maris stella*, which have no rubric. The hymn certainly could be performed without these ritornellos, or with a reduced version of the ritornellos played by the organ. Even the opening response could conceivably be sung as a simple *falsobordone* without the instrumental accompaniment and interludes, or the organ could play the instrumental interludes. Indeed, the tenor part-book has the rubric *Sex vocib. & sex Instrumentis, si placet* ('For six voices, and six instruments, if one wishes'). It is possible, therefore, to use most of the music from Monteverdi's print for a vesper service without instruments participating other than the organ—only the *Sonata sopra Sancta Maria* would have to be omitted from the service; the response, too, if not included, could be sung in plainchant.[133] The omission of instruments would have made Monteverdi's

---

[129] 'The Monteverdi Vespers of 1610 and their Relationship with Italian Sacred Music of the Early Seventeenth Century' (Ph.D. dissertation, University of Illinois at Urbana-Champaign, 1972), 55–69.

[130] See the discussion of additional evidence from contemporaneous prints in Ch. 4. See Ch. 2 for a discussion of the tonal problems and performance options entailed in using plainchant antiphons, whether by themselves or in conjunction with Monteverdi's *sacri concentus*.

[131] 'Liturgical Problems', 106.

[132] 'Some Historical Perspectives on the Monteverdi Vespers', *Analecta musicologica*, 15 (1974), 29–86.

[133] Clifford Bartlett makes the same observation about a vespers without instruments in his edition *Monteverdi, Vespro della Beata Vergine* (1990). For a recording that follows this procedure to some degree, omitting the instrumental accompaniment and substituting the continuo ensemble for the

collection more widely usable, although in the early seventeenth century an increasing number of churches had instrumentalists in their permanent employ and many recruited instrumentalists and extra singers for special feasts to be celebrated with unusual pomp, such as the feast of a church's patron saint (see Chapter 4).

Additionally, there is no reason why individual items could not have been extracted from Monteverdi's print without having to utilize others. The four few-voiced motets could each have served as devotional music or been inserted into the office or the mass on any occasion where their texts seemed appropriate. A vesper service, depending on the importance of the feast, might comprise a polyphonic setting of the first psalm, or even two or three psalms, plus the Magnificat, but not the other psalms or antiphons.[134] A vesper service for another virgin saint might utilize Monteverdi's psalms and one of the Magnificats, but would require a different hymn and quite possibly different motets as antiphon substitutes, if motets were used at all. All of these functions could have been served by Monteverdi's 1610 collection, and it seems likely that he envisaged just such flexibility, ranging from the extraction of a single composition to a complete liturgical service in the order presented.[135]

Part of our difficulty in understanding Monteverdi's intentions in the Vespers stems from our very limited knowledge about the circumstances leading to the composition of the music in the 1610 print and the motivation for publishing it in the form in which it appeared. The most direct evidence we have is from a letter written by Monteverdi's *vice maestro di cappella*, Don Bassano Casola, to Cardinal Ferdinando Gonzaga in Rome, dated 16 July 1610:[136]

Monteverdi is having printed an a cappella Mass for six voices, of much study and labour, since he was obliged to manipulate continually, in every note through all the parts, always further reinforcing, the eight motifs that are in the motet *In illo tempore* of Gombert. And he is also having printed together [with it] some vesper psalms of the Virgin with various and diverse manners of invention and harmony, and everything over a cantus firmus, with the intention of coming to Rome this autumn to dedicate them to His Holiness. He is also in the midst of preparing a group

instrumental interludes in the response, omitting the ritornellos in *Dixit Dominus*, and performing the ritornellos in the hymn with the continuo ensemble, see App. D, item 33.

[134] See the discussion of this practice in Rome in Thomas Noel O'Regan, 'Sacred Polychoral Music in Rome 1575–1621' (D. Phil. dissertation, University of Oxford, 1988), i. 85–7.

[135] Edward Lippman, in a review of the L'Oiseau-Lyre recording of the Vespers (App. D, item 3), noted the flexibility explicit in Monteverdi's title and suggested that 'if one of the Magnificat settings is omitted (as it is in the present recording), the music can be used intact . . . [and] it is equally permissible to look upon the work as a collection of music that could be used only in part' ('Monteverdi: *Vespers of 1610*', *Musical Quarterly*, 41 (1955), 406).

[136] Some confusion exists on the precise dating of this letter. Davari and De' Paoli give 16 July, while Vogel dates it 26 July. See Stefano Davari, *Notizie biografiche del distinto Maestro di Musica Claudio Monteverdi* (Mantua: G. Mondovi, 1885), 23; Domenico De' Paoli, *Claudio Monteverdi* (Milan: Editore Ulrico Hoepli, 1945), 159; and Emil Vogel, 'Claudio Monteverdi', *Vierteljahrsschrift für Musikwissenschaft*, 3 (1887), 430. De' Paoli's more recent biography, *Monteverdi* (Milan: Rusconi, 1979), 250, gives 10 July.

of madrigals for five voices, which will consist of three laments: that of Arianna, still with its usual soprano, the lament of Leandro and Hero by Marini, the third, given him by His Highness, about a shepherd whose nymph has died. The words [are] by the son of Count Lepido Agnelli on the death of the little Roman [the singer Caterina Martinelli].[137]

Casola's description of the Mass and Vespers is neither complete nor accurate in every detail. The eight motifs (*otto fughe*) from the Gombert motet are actually ten in number. In mentioning the *Salmi del Vespero . . . tutte sopra il canto fermo*, Casola has in mind the five vesper psalms and very probably the two Magnificats, but he omits any reference to the response, motets, hymn, and *Sonata sopra Sancta Maria*. Whatever inaccuracies and omissions there may be in Casola's remarks, it is nevertheless evident that Monteverdi's compositional work on the collection seems to have been largely if not entirely finished by this date, a circumstance that would certainly have been necessary for the publication to have been dedicated 1 September and available for Monteverdi to take to Rome in the autumn.[138]

The next reference to the Mass and Vespers appears in a letter written on 14 September 1610 by the Gonzaga prince, Francesco, to his brother the cardinal. Francesco remarks that Monteverdi is coming to Rome to have some religious compositions published and to present them to the Pope.[139] The discrepancy between Francesco's letter and the evidence of Amadino's print, dedicated in Venice on 1 September, is probably the result of a misunderstanding on the prince's part. His letter was posted from Pontestura, west of Casale Monferrato, where Francesco was on holiday, and his knowledge of Monteverdi's intentions and of the publication of the Mass and Vespers by Amadino may have been incomplete and imprecise.[140]

The purpose of Monteverdi's trip was twofold, for he was also seeking entrance for one of his sons into the Roman seminary.[141] When Monteverdi

---

[137] 'Il Monteverdi fa stampare una Messa da Cappella a sei voci di studio et fatica grande, essendosi obligato maneggiar sempre in ogni nota per tutte le vie, sempre più rinforzando le otto fughe che sono nel motetto, *in illo tempore* del *Gomberti* e fà stampare unitamente ancora di Salmi del Vespero della Madonna, con varie et diverse maniere d'inventioni et armonia, et tutte sopra il canto fermo, con pensiero di venirsene a Roma questo Autumno, per dedicarli a Sua Santità. Và ancho preparando una muta di Madrigali a cinque voci, che sarà di tre pianti quello dell'Arianna con il solito canto sempre, il pianto di Leandro et Hereo del Marini, il terzo, datoglielo, da S.A.Sma. di Pastore che sia morta la sua Ninfa. Parole del figlio del Sigr. Conte Lepido Agnelli in morte della Signora Romanina.' Text from Vogel, 'Claudio Monteverdi', 430.

[138] That he did take a copy to Rome for presentation to the Pope is demonstrated by the presence of an Altus part-book with the coat of arms of Pope Paul V on the cover in the Biblioteca Doria Pamphilj in Rome.

[139] See De' Paoli, *Lettere*, 50; and De' Paoli, *Claudio Monteverdi*, 160.

[140] Casola's letter distinguishes clearly between Monteverdi's intention to have the Mass and Vespers published and his plan to go to Rome to dedicate them to the Pope. It is only Francesco who connects the publication of the collection with the journey to Rome.

[141] A letter of Monteverdi's, dated 28 Dec. 1610 and very probably addressed to Cardinal Ferdinando Gonzaga in Rome, describes the composer's hopes for admission and a benefice for his 9-year old son, Francesco. See De' Paoli, *Lettere*, 50–3, and Lax, *Lettere*, 31–3. Eng. trans. in Stevens, *The Letters*, 76–8.

actually departed for the Holy City is unknown, though it must have been after 14 September, since Francesco's letter requests Ferdinando's aid in obtaining a papal audience.[142] When Monteverdi first arrived in Rome, his behaviour was puzzling, as is indicated by a letter discovered by Susan Parisi. In this letter of 7 October 1610 from the Mantuan official Rainero Bissolati to Cardinal Ferdinando Gonzaga, who was away on holiday, Bissolati says 'this morning by chance I ran into Signor Claudio Monteverdi who says he has been in Rome for three days and has been staying in an inn [*Camera locanda*]. He hasn't even let himself be seen or heard of by us so I insisted that this evening he come to your Illustrious Lordship's palace where I will give him hospitality as we did Captain Balciani.'[143]

Since Mantuan court musicians normally stayed in the cardinal's palace or the residences of other nobles or cardinals on visits to Rome,[144] Monteverdi's incognito lodging at a public inn suggests that he wished to conduct some kind of private business away from prying eyes before letting the Gonzagas know he had arrived (the letters from Casola and Francesco quoted above demonstrate that he would have been expected at some point at the cardinal's palace). What this business might have been is unknown, but as will be suggested below, it is probable that Monteverdi was at this time searching for employment outside the Gonzaga court and away from the problems he had suffered there. It is quite probable that Monteverdi was making discreet inquiries at the beginning of his sojourn in Rome.[145] Monteverdi did eventually lodge in Ferdinando's palace, as is indicated in a letter of 30 October from Giulio Gualtieri to the cardinal announcing the arrival of Don Bassano Casola, who would 'lodge with Monteverdi and the master of the house'.[146]

The only evidence that Monteverdi may have had an audience with Pope Paul is the surviving Altus part-book with the Pope's coat of arms in the

---

[142] De' Paoli, *Lettere*, 50.

[143] 'q.ta mattina a caso ho ritrovato il S.r Claudio Monteverdi, che dice esser tre giorni in Roma, loggiato a Camera locanda, senza mai lasciarsi vedere, ne sentire da noi cosi ho fatto tanto, et con mio gran sforzo, che venghi in q.ta sera nel palazzo di V.S.Ill.ma dove lo trattaro conforme al S.r Cap.o Balciani, credendomi d'incontrare l'intentione sua d'haver fatto bene.' See Susan Parisi, 'Once Fired, Twice Almost Rehired: An Assessment of Monteverdi's Relations with the Gonzagas', paper delivered at Convegno, Claudio Monteverdi: Studi e prospettive, Mantua, 21–4 Oct. 1993 published as 'New Documents concerning Monteverdi's relations with the Gonzagas' in Besutti, Gialdroni, and Baroncini, eds., *Claudio Monteverdi: Studi e prospettive*, 477–511. I am grateful to Prof. Parisi for a copy of this paper, from which the original text and her translation are taken.

[144] Ibid.

[145] Noel O'Regan's studies of sacred music in Rome in this period give some idea of the number of churches and oratorios, aside from the Cappella Sistina and the Cappella Giulia, where Monteverdi might have sought employment. See O'Regan, 'Sacred Polychoral Music'.

[146] Parisi, 'Once Fired': 'Hieri sera arrivo D. Ottavio con D. Bassano chi mi dica haver perso V.S.Ill.ma a Poggibonzi con dir che il S.r Chieppio sara qui stasera che lo metterò nelle stanze dove stava il S.r Claudio et proviserò di servirlo in modo che riceva ogni satisfattione et D. Bassano fara vita con il Monteverde et il M'ro di casa.'

Biblioteca Doria Pamphilj.[147] However, it is certain the composer made a favourable impression on the Cardinals Montalto and Borghese (the latter the Pope's nephew), for they wrote to Duke Vincenzo in Mantua on 23 November and 4 December respectively, describing Monteverdi in glowing terms.[148] If Monteverdi was not still in Rome at the time of these letters, he must have returned to Mantua only shortly before. His next extant letter is the one from 28 December mentioned above, posted from Mantua.

Despite his efforts, Monteverdi was unsuccessful in obtaining a benefice and admission for his son into the seminary, and there seem to have been few concrete results from his journey. The evidence of his visit left behind comprises the set of part-books, of which only the Altus, cited above, survives, and a manuscript copy, restored twice, of the *Missa in illo tempore* in the Vatican library (Cappella Sistina MS 107). This version is prefaced by the same dedication to Pope Paul V as Amadino's print, with only slight differences in orthography. Since the Sistine Chapel did not use accompanying instruments of any kind, the Bassus Generalis of Amadino's print is absent from the Vatican manuscript.

Of note in the letter from Don Bassano Casola quoted above is the list of laments in preparation, two of which were published four years later in the Sixth Book of Madrigals.[149] There was often a substantial time-lag between the completion of Monteverdi's compositions and their eventual publication. Some of the madrigals from Book IV (1603) and Book V (1605) were already in circulation by 1600, as proved by the discussion and quotation of excerpts in *L'Artusi, ovvero, Delle imperfezioni della moderna musica*, printed in that year.[150] *L'Orfeo* was premièred in the spring of 1607 but not published in its first edition until 1609. Casola's letter reveals a four-year delay in the appearance of the laments.

These apparently normal time-lags suggest that parts or perhaps even all of the Mass and Vespers may have been completed well before the late summer of 1610. The close connections between portions of the Vespers and *L'Orfeo* also imply an earlier date for some of the pieces, especially *Domine ad adjuvandum*. It is, in fact, quite possible that the compositions in Amadino's very large print of 1610 represent a gradual accumulation of material over the span of several, or even many years. Preparations for the Gonzaga wedding celebration of 1608,

---

[147] See Claudio Annibaldi, 'L'archivio musicale Doria Pamphilj: Saggio sulla cultura aristocratica a Roma fra 16° e 19° secolo (II)', *Studi musicali*, II (1982), 287, 291. This part-book has handwritten emendations where other copies of the Altus have printed paste-over corrections, indicating that the Pope's copy came from very early in the print run, perhaps as an advance copy specially bound.

[148] Vogel, 'Claudio Monteverdi', 356.

[149] These are the cycles *Lamento d'Arianna* and *Lagrime d'amante al sepolcro dell'amata*.

[150] Excerpts in Eng. trans. in Oliver Strunk, *Source Readings in Music History* (New York: W. W. Norton & Company, Inc., 1950), 393–404. The polemics between Artusi and Monteverdi, lasting until 1608, are discussed in Claude V. Palisca, 'The Artusi–Monteverdi Controversy', in Denis Arnold and Nigel Fortune, eds., *The Monteverdi Companion* (London: Faber and Faber, 1968), 133–66 and reprinted with very slight changes in their *The New Monteverdi Companion* (London: Faber and Faber, 1985), 127–58.

about which Monteverdi complained bitterly in a letter long after the festivities were over, occupied all his time in the autumn of 1607 and the spring of 1608, leaving him exhausted at the beginning of the summer.[151] But work on the Mass and Vespers may have progressed during the summer of 1607 and the summer and autumn of 1608, and throughout much of 1609. It should be recalled that Pope Paul V visited Mantua in 1607, and it is possible that some of the music of the print eventually dedicated to him might have been performed for him during his stay.[152] Some of the pieces in the print, particularly the more conservative psalms *Nisi Dominus* and *Lauda Jerusalem*, could conceivably date from much earlier than 1607. Indeed, both of these compositions have unusually few errors in Amadino's print, suggesting that Monteverdi delivered to the publisher very accurate manuscripts, perhaps resulting from multiple performances and the opportunity to correct errors. On the other hand, the piece that lies between these two in the print, *Audi coelum*, is replete with errors, implying a hastily prepared manuscript that may have resulted from very recent composition and perhaps even no opportunity for performance.

Denis Stevens has suggested that the composition of some of the music for the Vespers reaches much further into the past than the few years before its publication.[153] According to him, *Dixit Dominus*, in an early version without ritornellos, as well as the Magnificat *a 6*, may stem from Duke Vincenzo's expedition to Hungary in 1595, an expedition on which Monteverdi and other musicians accompanied him and performed a vesper service on the eve of the battle of Vysegrad. A contemporary account indicates that the music for this service might have been composed by Monteverdi (*forse il compositore dello stesso Vespro*).[154] Stevens also suggests that *Laetatus sum*, reflecting gypsy fiddle music in the Lombard rhythms of the passage at *Propter fratres*, may have been written shortly after Monteverdi's return from this expedition. The motets *Nigra sum*, *Pulchra es*, and *Duo Seraphim* could have been written, according to Stevens, in the first few years of the new century. Because of their larger textures, he places *Nisi Dominus*, *Lauda Jerusalem*, and *Audi coelum* at about 1603–5, the time of publication of the Fourth and Fifth Books of Madrigals. The response and the *Sonata sopra Sancta Maria* he associates with *L'Orfeo* of 1607, and he dates these pieces 'during the aftermath of this work'.[155] The Magnificat *a 7* he considers to

---

[151] Monteverdi's letter is dated 2 Dec. 1608. See De' Paoli, *Lettere*, 33–9, and Lax, *Lettere*, 20–4. Eng. trans. in Stevens, *The Letters*, 55–7 as well as in Arnold and Fortune, eds., *The Monteverdi Companion*, 26–9. Monteverdi's father, Baldassare, also wrote two letters to the Duke and Duchess of Mantua in autumn 1608 seeking his son's release from ducal service. See De' Paoli, *Lettere*, 30, 33. The texts of these letters are in Fabbri, *Monteverdi*, 148–50; Eng. edn., 100–2. The political circumstances surrounding the wedding are documented in Reiner, 'La vag' Angioletta (and Others)'.

[152] See n. 15 above.

[153] 'Monteverdiana', *Early Music*, 21 (1993), 565–74.

[154] Ibid. 566. This passage was quoted in Fenlon, *Music and Patronage*, i. 194, doc. 63.

[155] Stevens, 'Monteverdiana', 569.

have been completed before 1605. There remains from the 1610 print only the *Missa in illo tempore*, which, on the basis of Casola's letter, Stevens thinks Monteverdi finished in 1609.[156]

All of this is highly speculative. Even Casola's letter states no more than that Monteverdi 'is having printed' the works Casola names. Only the madrigals later published in 1614 are mentioned as in progress: 'He is also in the midst of preparing a group of madrigals.' The letter does not preclude the possibility that the *Missa in illo tempore* is several years old.

It is difficult to evaluate such speculations, since there is so little evidence to substantiate most of them. Monteverdi himself spoke vaguely of masses and motets in his first extant letter of 1601,[157] and we have no way of knowing how much sacred music he may have composed in Mantua that was never published and later lost. The most likely of Stevens's suggestions is the composition of the response and the *Sonata* at about the time of *L'Orfeo*. But the very modern vocal style and the virtuoso demands of *Nigra sum*, *Pulchra es*, *Duo Seraphim*, *Audi Coelum*, and the two Magnificats also bear a relationship to *L'Orfeo*, not only in their common requirement for virtuoso singers, especially tenors, but in the instrumental requirements for the Magnificat.

It is just as easy to speculate on other occasions in Mantua that might have given rise to some of the pieces in the 1610 print. For example, on 29 December 1605 the beatification of Luigi Gonzaga was celebrated with a procession from the cathedral of San Pietro to the Jesuit church of the Holy Trinity.[158] Moreover, in the same period, three canvases by the court painter Peter Paul Rubens, including one of Gugliemo Gonzaga and his son Duke Vincenzo I adoring the Trinity, were mounted above the altar of this church.[159] Such occasions could easily have featured the Trinitarian motet *Duo Seraphim*.

Peter Holman has also suggested a diverse origin for at least some of the music of the Vespers, citing 'no consistency in the way particular instruments are allocated to particular partbooks. . . . This suggests that the manuscript material used as printer's copy consisted of a number of separate sets of parts, not a single co-ordinated set of material for the whole "work", as is produced for modern performances—which is another reason for thinking that the individual items had a diverse origin and existence.'[160]

---

[156] Ibid.

[157] De' Paoli, *Lettere*, 17, and Lax, *Lettere*, 13. Eng. trans. in Stevens, *The Letters*, 37. This letter requests an appointment to the position of *maestro di cappella* (at court, not in the ducal church of Santa Barbara) recently vacated by the death of Benedetto Pallavicino.

[158] See Susan Parisi, 'Ducal Patronage of Music in Mantua, 1587–1627: An Archival Study' (Ph.D. dissertation, University of Illinois at Urbana-Champaign, 1989), 162.

[159] Ibid. 209 n. 158. These three paintings were Rubens's only major commission from the Gonzagas. See Fenlon, *Music and Patronage*, i. 122–3 and the photograph of the canvas with Guglielmo and Vincenzo on p. 120.

[160] '"Col nobilissimo esercitio della vivuola": Monteverdi's String Writing', *Early Music*, 21 (1993), 585.

I concur that the music of Monteverdi's 1610 print was probably composed at various times for various occasions, perhaps in groups of pieces. There is considerable affinity, for example, among the first three psalms, *Dixit Dominus*, *Laudate pueri*, and *Laetatus sum* (see Chapter 6). The other two psalms, *Nisi Dominus* and *Lauda Jerusalem*, also have much in common with one another and are the most accurately notated compositions in the print. The four motets, *Nigra sum*, *Pulchra es*, *Duo Seraphim*, and *Audi coelum*, are likewise quite similar in conception but are wholly unrelated to the *Sonata sopra Sancta Maria*. The latter shares instruments with the Magnificat *a* 7, while the two canticles share a virtuoso vocal style with the last three motets. The hymn stands stylistically alone except for its instrumental ritornellos. It is certainly conceivable that Monteverdi composed groups of these works on different occasions and assembled them into a liturgical whole for purposes of his 1610 publication.

Uncertainties about the origin of the contents of Monteverdi's collection are matched by uncertainties regarding possible liturgical performances of this music in Mantua. While there is no firm evidence of portions of Monteverdi's Vespers being performed in Mantua, it seems likely that many, if not all, of the compositions comprising this print would have served for one or more liturgical celebrations in the city in the few years preceding their publication in 1610. The close relationship between the toccata to *L'Orfeo* and *Domine ad adjuvandum* argues for use of the latter in Mantua some time around or after February of 1607, when *L'Orfeo* was first performed. Likewise, the vocal and instrumental forces required for the Vespers are similar, though not identical, to those assembled for *L'Orfeo*. The close relationship between the chant used in *Ave maris stella* and the unique version of the rite of Santa Barbara suggests that the hymn had been performed in the basilica. The parallel between Monteverdi's *Sonata sopra Sancta Maria* and the Franzoni concerto with the same text mentioned above suggests that this litany with instrumental accompaniment might have been traditional in the ducal church. While *Duo Seraphim*, with or without its second section, was a popular text in the late sixteenth and early seventeenth centuries, its recurrence in the Franzoni collection with exactly the same version of the text used by Monteverdi suggests once again a relationship between Monteverdi's setting of this Trinitarian text and the basilica of Santa Barbara. Coupled with the visit to Mantua of Pope Paul V in 1607, these associations imply the possibility of a singular, festive liturgical event during that visit connecting the Pope, the Gonzagas, Mantua, the Virgin Mary, and St Barbara as patrons and protectors of the duchy and the city. However, because there is no direct evidence whatsoever connecting this music to any such liturgical celebration in Mantua, room has been left open for much other speculation among scholars. The proposal of Graham Dixon has already been discussed above; other suggestions will be evaluated here.

Pierre Tagmann has speculated that composition of the Vespers was stimulated by the birth of Duke Vincenzo's granddaughter, Maria, on 29 July 1609,
and that portions of the Vespers may have been performed on 15 August 1609,
the Feast of the Assumption, or 8 September 1609, the Feast of the Nativity of
the Virgin.[161] What we know of Monteverdi's whereabouts in this period derives from two letters to Alessandro Striggio, written in Cremona and dated 24
August 1609 and 10 September 1609.[162] In the first Monteverdi acknowledges
receipt the day before of a letter from Striggio containing a text from the duke
that he wanted Monteverdi to set to music. Monteverdi also makes reference to
a conversation with some cornetto and trombone players that seems to have
taken place some time in the recent past, in Cremona rather than Mantua, as is
clear from the letter of 10 September where he reports a further conversation
with these musicians.[163] It is not impossible that Monteverdi was in Mantua for
Assumption Day, but in the interval between 29 July and 15 August he could
at most have rehearsed a performance, certainly not composed a large body of
music. No record of such a performance survives. From the subsequent letter of
10 September, it is clear that Monteverdi had remained in Mantua between 24
August and 10 September. Thus the dates and the contents of these letters
render Tagmann's suggestion impossible.

Iain Fenlon has argued that 'given the system of patronage under which composers worked, it is almost certain that a work of this kind was originally
written for a specific occasion, even with particular forces in mind'.[164] Assuming
that the Vespers were composed between early 1607 (the period of *L'Orfeo*) and
early 1610, Fenlon suggested that the Vespers were first performed on Sunday,
25 May 1608 at 'a special ceremony in Sant'Andrea inaugurating a new order of
knighthood in honour of Christ the Redeemer'.[165] This ceremony marked the
beginning of the 1608 wedding festival, and featured the installation by Duke
Vincenzo of the bridegroom Francesco

as the first member of the new order, investing him and the other new knights with robes and
decorations. The knights then kissed the Duke's hand, bowed to Prince Francesco, and took their
places for the liturgical part of the ceremony. Now the *Te Deum* was chanted and then, after an

---

[161] 'The Palace Church of Santa Barbara', 53–60.

[162] De'Paoli, *Lettere*, 40–6, and Lax, *Lettere*, 25–30; Stevens, *The Letters*, 64–5, 68–70. See also Arnold
and Fortune, eds., *The Monteverdi Companion*, 30–4; eid., eds., *The New Monteverdi Companion*, 23–5 (10
Sept. letter only).

[163] Details regarding these musicians may be found in Elia Santoro, *La famiglia e la formazione di
Claudio Monteverdi: Note biografiche con documenti inediti* (Cremona: Athenaeum Cremonese, 1967), 80.

[164] 'The Monteverdi Vespers: Suggested Answers to some Fundamental Questions', *Early Music*, 5
(1977), 381.

[165] Ibid. 383. Fenlon's information comes from the court chronicler, Federico Follino, *Compendio
delle sontuose feste fatte l'anno M.DC.VIII. nella città di Mantova, per le reali nozze del Serenissimo Prencipe D.
Francesco Gonzaga, con la Serenissima Infante Margherita di Savoia* (Mantua: Aurelio et Lodovico Osanna,
1608), 19–26. The Mantuan ecclesiastical historian Ippolito Donesmondi also describes the ceremony
in *Dell'istoria ecclesiastica di Mantova . . . parte seconda*, 419–26.

oration by the Bishop of Mantua, solemn (polyphonic) Vespers were celebrated by the Bishop dressed pontifically. At the end of this service the treasured relic of the Precious Blood was displayed on the high altar and the Duke together with his son, the other new knights, and the members of the nobility who had witnessed the ceremony returned to court.[166]

25 May 1608 was Pentecost Sunday, and the singular difficulty with Fenlon's hypothesis is that the vespers in question would not have been a vespers of the Virgin.[167] The feast of Pentecost required the psalms *Dixit Dominus*, *Confitebor tibi*, *Beatus vir*, *Laudate pueri*, and *Laudate Dominum* at first vespers and the same *cursus* with the substitution of *In exitu Israel* as the fifth psalm for second vespers. Therefore, Monteverdi's response, *Dixit Dominus*, *Laudate pueri*, and either of the two Magnificats from the 1610 print could have been used on this occasion, but not the entire Marian service.

Jordi Savall, on the other hand, has suggested that the Vespers were first performed on 25 March 1610, the feast of the Annunciation, in the basilica of Santa Barbara in honour of the daughters of Francesco Gonzaga (note Paola Besutti's association of Monteverdi's version of the *Ave maris stella* chant with the rite of Santa Barbara, discussed above).[168] This hypothesis is plausible, though Savall offers no evidence to support it.

Although speculation regarding the origins and use of the Vespers has ranged widely, the fact is that we actually know no more about the origins of the music of the 1610 print than we did at the time Vogel first published Casola's letter in 1887. On the other hand, there has been much more consensus regarding Monteverdi's motivation in assembling and publishing the *Missa in illo tempore* and the *Vespro della Beata Vergine* in a single large collection. This motivation likely stems from Monteverdi's frequently expressed dissatisfaction with his employment in Mantua. We see this already intimated in his first extant letter of 28 November 1601.[169] Pressures on the composer also came from the attacks of the Bolognese theoretician Giovanni Maria Artusi in a public debate that dragged on from 1600 at least until 1608.[170] From 1604 to 1608 Monteverdi's letters are filled with complaints about difficulties in drawing his salary, poverty, overwork, physical exhaustion, and ill health brought on by the Mantuan climate.

---

[166] Quoted from Fenlon, 'The Monteverdi Vespers', 383.

[167] Donesmondi confirms that the founding of the order occurred on Pentecost. See *Dell'istoria ecclesiastica di Mantova*, 419–26.

[168] Liner notes to item 28 in App. D.

[169] De' Paoli, *Lettere*, 17–18, and Lax, *Lettere*, 13–14; Eng. trans. in Stevens, *The Letters*, 37–8; and Arnold and Fortune, eds., *The Monteverdi Companion*, 22–3.

[170] See Palisca, 'The Artusi–Monteverdi Controversy', *The Monteverdi Companion*, 133–66 and *The New Monteverdi Companion*, 127–58. See also additional comments on the controversy in Tim Carter, 'Artusi, Monteverdi, and the Poetics of Modern Music', in Nancy Kovaleff Baker and Barbara Russano Hanning, eds., *Musical Humanism and its Legacy: Essays in Honor of Claude V. Palisca* (Stuyvesant, NY: Pendragon Press, 1992), 171–94.

The low point in Monteverdi's life at Mantua came paradoxically at the high point of his professional career there. On 10 September 1607, some seven months after the première of *L'Orfeo*, his wife Claudia Cataneo, a singer, died, leaving him with two motherless sons. But he hardly had any time for grieving. In the autumn of 1607 and spring of 1608 he was wholly occupied with hasty preparations for the wedding celebrations of the coming spring.[171] In the midst of these preparations, on 7 March 1608, the 19-year-old singer Caterina Martinelli, who was scheduled to play the leading role in the imminent production of Monteverdi's new opera *Arianna*, died of smallpox.[172] Caterina had been Monteverdi's pupil and lodger ever since she was first brought to Mantua in 1603.[173] The role had to be assigned to someone else, an actress, and rehearsals became frantic. In addition to composing and rehearsing *Arianna*, Monteverdi composed and rehearsed *Il ballo delle ingrate* for the wedding festivities, which finally took place in late May and early June. Having suffered the death of his wife and his pupil within the space of a few months, the latter in the midst of pressure-filled preparations for the wedding celebrations, Monteverdi was exhausted and sick by the middle of the year. He returned to his father's house in Cremona in early July and remained there for several months. In November his father petitioned first the duke and then the duchess for his son's release from ducal service, but the duke wrote back at the end of the month ordering Monteverdi to return to court.[174] On 2 December Monteverdi wrote to the duke's councillor Annibale Chieppio claiming:

> unless I take a rest from toiling away at music for the theatre, my life will indeed be a short one, for as a result of my labours (so recent and of such magnitude) I have had a frightful pain in my head and so terrible and violent an itching around my waist, that neither by cauteries which I have had applied to myself, nor by purges taken orally, nor by blood-letting and other potent remedies has it so far been possible to get even partly better. My father [a physician] attributes the cause of the headache to mental strain, and the itching to Mantua's air (which does not agree with me), and he fears that the air alone could be the death of me before long. Just think then, Your Lordship, what the addition of brainwork would do if I were to come and receive graces and favours from His Highness's kindness and clemency, as he commands.[175]

Monteverdi then went on with a long list of complaints, concluding with a request that Chieppio assist him in obtaining an honourable dismissal from the

---

[171] The political circumstances surrounding this wedding are documented in Reiner, 'La vag' Angioletta (and Others)'.

[172] Edmond Strainchamps, 'The Life and Death of Caterina Martinelli: New Light on Monteverdi's "Arianna" ', *Early Music History*, 5 (1985), 155–86. Caterina's tomb was inscribed by Duke Vincenzo: 'she died in the eighteenth year of her youth, the ninth of March, 1608.'

[173] Stevens says she moved to another house on 7 Nov. 1606. See *The Letters*, 53.

[174] Ibid. 56; for Monteverdi's father's letters see n. 86 above. The father's letter to the duke of 9 Nov. 1608 indicated that his son would be willing to serve in the church alone (Giovanni Giacomo Gastoldi, *maestro di cappella* of Santa Barbara, was mortally ill). This request was not fulfilled, however.

[175] Stevens, *The Letters*, 58. For the original Italian, see De' Paoli, *Lettere*, 33–4, and Lax, *Lettere*, 21.

duke's service. These efforts failed, however, and Monteverdi was back at court by mid-January, where Duke Vincenzo attempted to assuage the composer's feelings by raising his salary and establishing an annual pension.[176] The pension became a further sore point, however, for Monteverdi had difficulty in collecting it from the Mantuan treasury, a matter he doggedly pursued for the remainder of his life.

Thus, by 1610 Monteverdi had long been dissatisfied with his employment. But the intrigues and vagaries of Gonzaga court life could hardly have been different in character from those of other Italian courts; therefore, if he were to seek stable employment elsewhere, it would have to be in a major ecclesiastical position. However, Monteverdi was unpublished and unknown outside Mantua as a composer of church music, and his first step would have had to be to publish a major collection with a prominent dedication, demonstrating his capabilities, in the hope of attracting widespread attention. This is precisely what he accomplished in publishing a conservative mass, a contrapuntal *tour de force*, together with a modernistic vespers in the most varied combination of sacred styles yet printed in Italy. If Monteverdi was indeed seeking a new position in Rome, as Redlich, De' Paoli, and Arnold have previously suggested, the Mass would have been an appropriate introduction to the Cappella Sistina, while the Vespers would have been of interest perhaps to the Cappella Giulia (the choir of St Peter's Basilica) and certainly to the many churches, confraternities, and colleges that produced elaborate music involving virtuoso singers and instruments for the feasts of their patron saints and on other important feast-days.[177] Similarly, the combination of elements in this print would have been well suited to Venice and other major centres of the Veneto, such as Verona, Brescia, and Bergamo. In Milan, the *Missa in illo tempore* may have appealed, but the Vespers were very different from typical Milanese sacred music of the time.[178]

On Christmas Day in 1611 some psalms of Monteverdi were performed in the cathedral in Modena, but were reportedly received very poorly.[179] The only psalms in common between the feast of Christmas and Marian feasts are *Dixit Dominus* (at both first and second vespers) and *Laudate pueri* (at first vespers). The Magnificat, which was often referred to as a 'psalm' in the sixteenth and

---

[176] Stevens, *The Letters*, 57; Fabbri, *Monteverdi*, 151; Eng. edn., 104.

[177] See Redlich, 'Monteverdi's Religious Music', 210; De' Paoli, *Lettere*, 50; and Arnold, *Monteverdi* (1975), 24. The variety and character of elaborate sacred music performances in Rome are described in O'Regan, 'Sacred Polychoral Music'. See also the other articles on music in Roman churches by Dixon and O'Regan listed in the Bibliography. The appropriateness of the *Missa in illo tempore* for the Sistine Chapel is underscored by the fact that it is the Mass alone that survives among the Vatican manuscripts, while the surviving Altus part-book with the entire Mass and Vespers in the Biblioteca Doria Pamphilj belonged to the private collection of the Pope.

[178] My thanks to Robert Kendrick for his observations on sacred music in Milan in this period.

[179] The account is quoted in Fabbri, *Monteverdi*, 174: 'Geminiano Capilupi, over Lovetto mastro di capella, a fatto cantare certi salmi del Monteverdo mastro di capella del duca di Mantova, che sono stati a nausea di tutti.' See also Eng. edn., 120.

seventeenth centuries, is, of course, also common to all vespers. Given the reported reaction of the listeners and the liturgical demands of Christmas, it is possible that the psalms performed at Modena were entirely different from those published in 1610. Since the performance was conducted by someone other than Monteverdi and the congregation's reaction was unfavourable, it is unlikely that Monteverdi was using this occasion to audition for a position in Modena.

None of these efforts had a positive outcome, and in the summer of 1612 Monteverdi suffered the indignity of being abruptly dismissed from the duke's service in Mantua.[180] Monteverdi's original patron, Duke Vincenzo I, had died in February of that year, and his son Francesco acceded to the throne encumbered by huge debts piled up by the extravagances of his late father. Francesco determined to cut expenses and reduce the size of his retinue, and after his coronation in June, some of the court's high officials and a quarter of the musicians were released. Francesco's austerities had evidently engendered considerable worry and unhappiness among the musicians, for one had run away to Florence, another was seeking employment in Rome, and the famous singer Adriana Basile complained bitterly of neglect, while a plot to steal her had been rumoured. These events and rumours were embarrassing to Francesco, who also became personally unhappy with the Monteverdi brothers. On 6 July 1612, he wrote to his brother Ferdinando, the cardinal, in Rome:

> Your Illustrious Lordship knows how much obligation Monteverdi and his brother have to serve me on account of the honorable stay that they have had in this house for so many years, and because of the great esteem that I have always shown toward both of them; now it appears to me that either to ruin me or for some other reason they have rebelled, and they treat me with every term of disrespect, claiming that other shelter is not lacking to them; and because I would like to take revenge for my reputation I had the idea to dismiss both of them immediately from my service when they least expect it; . . . Your Illustrious Lordship should not be surprised that, since Monteverdi is the subject he is, I should condescend to part with him; for if you knew with what hope of advantage and from what ulterior motives he and his brother are dealing with me you would side with me completely.[181]

On 29 July 1612, Francesco fulfilled his intention and abruptly dismissed both Claudio and Giulio Cesare Monteverdi. In a letter of 6 November 1615, Monteverdi described his departure from the Gonzaga court thus: '[I] left that Most Serene Court so disgracefully—by God—after being there for twenty-one years I took away no more than twenty-five scudi.'[182] Despite several attempts by the Gonzaga dukes to lure him back to Mantua in subsequent years,

---

[180] See Susan Parisi, ' "Licenza alla Mantovana": Frescobaldi and the Recruitment of Musicians for Mantua, 1612–1615', in Alexander Silbiger, ed., *Frescobaldi Studies* (Durham, NC: Duke University Press, 1987), 59–62. The following account of Monteverdi's dismissal is taken from this article.
[181] Ibid. 60–1.
[182] Quoted from Parisi, 'Licenza alla Mantovana', 64. See De' Paoli, *Lettere*, 77; Lax, *Lettere*, 42–3; Stevens, *The Letters*, 104.

Monteverdi steadfastly refused, citing over and over again the penury, misery, and indignity he had suffered at the court of the Gonzagas.[183]

Early in the autumn of 1612 Monteverdi travelled to Milan, where Aquilino Coppino had published three books of spiritual contrafacta of his madrigals in 1607 (reprinted in 1611), 1608, and 1609.[184] Rumours circulated that Monteverdi was seeking the post of *maestro di cappella* of the cathedral in Milan and had failed miserably at the audition, but the position was not, in fact, vacant, and letters to the Duke of Mantua from a Mantuan singer, Francesco Campagnolo, and Mantua's ambassador in Milan, Alessandro Striggio, squelched these rumours. Striggio indicated instead that 'he [Monteverdi] was most honored by gentlemen [*cavalieri*] and welcomed and cherished as much as possible by the musicians [*dai virtuosi*], and his works were sung here with great praise in the most notable places'.[185] According to Striggio, Monteverdi had not sought the position of *maestro di cappella* at the Duomo, then occupied by Vincenzo Pellegrini; nevertheless, his visit to Milan as an unemployed musician of considerable reputation must have been to seek opportunities of some kind, whether in secular surroundings or in another major church of the city. But like his visit to Rome, this sojourn in Milan produced no tangible results.

Finally, in the following year, Monteverdi found the stable church position he sought, the most visible and prestigious post in northern Italy, as *maestro di cappella* at St Mark's in Venice. The last documentary reference to what might be music from the Mass and Vespers of 1610 comes in connection with Monteverdi's audition (*prova*) for this position in the summer of 1613. The post had become vacant on 10 July of that year through the death of its incumbent, Giulio Cesare Martinengo.[186] In August, Monteverdi underwent a trial performance of his music prior to his appointment as the new *maestro*. A document of 19 August 1613 reads:

The most illustrious Procurators, wanting to elect a *maestro di cappella* of the church of St Mark in place of the Reverend Maestro Giulio Cesare Martinengo, and having written by order of the Procurators [*SS. SS. Ill.*^{ma}] to the most illustrious ambassador in Rome, to all of the most illustrious rectors of the *terra firma*, and to the residents of the *Serenissima Signoria* in Milan and Mantua to obtain information about individuals qualified in this profession for the aforementioned service;

---

[183] See Parisi, 'Once Fired, Twice Almost Rehired'.

[184] See RISM 1607[20] and 1611[15] and François Lesure and Claudio Sartori, eds., *Bibliografia della musica italiana vocale profana publicata dal 1500 al 1700* (Pomezia: Staderini spa, 1977), ii, items 1944, 1945, 1946, 1947. The only copy of the 1608 publication was destroyed in World War II, while only three part-books of the 1609 publication survive. See Claudio Sartori, 'Monteverdiana', *Musical Quarterly*, 38 (1952), 403–6. Sartori recounts the history of Monteverdi's relations with Milan and Milanese musicians from 1589 to 1625. See also Margaret Ann Rorke, 'Sacred Contrafacta of Monteverdi Madrigals and Cardinal Borromeo's Milan', *Music & Letters*, 65 (1984), 168–75.

[185] '. . . è stato onoratissimo da' cavalieri, e dai virtuosi benveduto et accarezzato al possibile, e le sue opere si cantano qui con gran lode nei più notabili ridotti.' Quoted in Fabbri, *Monteverdi*, 176. For a slightly different translation, see Tim Carter's English edition, 123.

[186] Procuratori di San Marco di Supra, Reg. 140, 1607–1614, a di 1 agosto [1613].

from the responses having learned that the person of the most worthy [*D.*^{*mo*}] Claudio Monteverdi, formerly *maestro di cappella* of Duke Vincenzo and Duke Francesco of Mantua, has been recommended as the foremost candidate; of the quality and worth of whom the Procurators [*SS. SS. Ill.*^{*mi*}] are greatly confirmed in this opinion, both from his published works and those which in these days the Procurators [*SS. SS. Ill.*^{*mi*}] have sought to hear, to their complete satisfaction in the church of St Mark with its musicians. Therefore, by unanimous ballot they have determined that the aforementioned most worthy [*D.*^{*mo*}] Claudio Monteverdi should be elected as *maestro di cappella* of the church of St Mark at a salary of three hundred ducats per year and with the usual and customary gifts . . .[187]

Monteverdi also received a house in the canonry and 'gift' of fifty ducats (*per donativo*) from the Procurators, to cover his travelling expenses and sojourn in Venice.[188]

Account records of the Procurators from 22 August refer to payments for ten extra singers (*cantori extraordinarij*) for performances in St Mark's on the anniversary of the accession of the doge (24 July) and for the entire office for the Ascension of Our Lady (the feast of the Assumption, 15 August).[189] On that day another payment was ordered for carrying two organs back and forth to San Giorgio Maggiore on the island of St George for Monteverdi's rehearsal (*prova*). Earlier entries also refer to these celebrations. One on 24 July had recorded payment to the fifteen regular instrumentalists (*sonatori ordinarij*) for having played on the anniversary of the doge, and one on 19 August had recorded payment to fourteen *sonatori ordinarij* for having played at mass on the feast of the Assumption.[190] This entry may refer to the *Missa in illo tempore*, with fourteen instruments doubling its thick texture, although another mass in more modern style, no longer extant, was also possibly meant. According to the document of 22 August, the payment was to be made by order of the *maestro di cappella*, whereas the one dated 19 August was by order of the *vice maestro di cappella*. Evidently, Monteverdi had not yet been officially named the *maestro* when the payment of 19 August was inscribed, but was already considered the *maestro di cappella* by the scribe on 22 August (after having been officially elected on 19 August, four days after the Procurators had heard the Ascension Day services). The printed music mentioned in the election document of 19 August must have been the Mass and Vespers of 1610, Monteverdi's only printed sacred music since his youthful *Sacrae cantiunculae tribus vocibus* of 1582. The music by Monteverdi heard by the Procurators on the feast of the Assumption very likely comprised either extracts or a complete service from the *Vespro della Beata*

[187] Procuratori di San Marco di Supra, Reg. 140, 1607–1614, a di 19 agosto. See Fabbri, *Monteverdi*, 177–8; Eng. edn., 124. The document was first published by Guido Sommi Picenardi in 'Alcuni documenti concernenti Claudio Monteverde', *Archivio storico lombardo*, 22 (1895), 135–6.

[188] Ibid.

[189] Procuratori di San Marco di Supra, Reg. 7, Cassier Chiesa, 1610–1614.

[190] Ibid. The extra payment may have been required because performing on the doge's anniversary was probably not listed as one of the regular duties for the musicians.

Vergine, although the election document mentions works other than the ones already published (possibly a different mass). Whether Monteverdi's music was performed on 24 July for the anniversary of the doge is unclear.

Pay records from 10 September refer to what was evidently a separate rehearsal in San Giorgio Maggiore and to another performance.[191] The first record indicates payment for twenty instrumentalists (*XX. sonatori ordinarij*) for having participated in the rehearsal of a mass by Monteverdi (*del nº. maestro di capella*) as well as playing in St Mark's on the same day as the rehearsal. The second record indicates that six additional musicians were to be paid for having sung in St Mark's on the Feast of the Nativity of the Madonna (8 September). Further confirmation of the performance of a mass on that day is found in another record of 9 September, indicating payment by order of the *maestro di cappella* to fifteen instrumentalists (*15 sonatori ordinarij*) for having played in St Mark's at mass on the Day of the Madonna.[192] The mass for the feast of the Nativity was probably a different work from the mass for the feast of the Assumption, since it is quite unlikely that Monteverdi would have repeated the same work after so short a time. Since most payments seem to have been recorded very shortly after the services for which the musicians were employed, and the pay record of 10 September specifically mentions the feast of the Nativity, it seems that Monteverdi was fully occupied in Venice in late August and early September (and perhaps even from late July) with more than one major celebration. After leaving Venice to return to Mantua, Monteverdi officially took up his duties at St Mark's in early October.[193] We hear not another word in the seventeenth century of Monteverdi's Mass and Vespers of 1610.

Without further documentary evidence, we may never come to definitive solutions to the many questions raised by Amadino's print of 1610. But another reason why we have experienced such controversy over the Monteverdi Vespers is that we have tended to view this collection in historical isolation. We have been attracted to the Vespers by its obvious aesthetic worth and its dazzling display of modern styles and techniques, but our understanding of the work as historians has been vague at best. Not only do we have no earlier liturgical music by Monteverdi,[194] but until recently we have known nothing about vesper music

---

[191] Procuratori di San Marco di Supra, Reg. 7, Cassier Chiesa, 1610–1614.

[192] Ibid. I am unable to account for the discrepancy between *XX sonatori ordinarij* in the document of 10 Sept. and *15 sonatori ordinarij* in that of 9 Sept.

[193] Monteverdi wrote to Mantua from Venice on 12 Oct. describing his recent journey, during which he was robbed by highway bandits. From the letter, it appears that he arrived in Venice at midnight on Saturday, 5 Oct. See De' Paoli, *Lettere*, 62–5; Lax, *Lettere*, 37–40; Stevens, *The Letters*, 90–3; Arnold and Fortune, eds., *The Monteverdi Companion*, 36–8; eid., *The New Monteverdi Companion*, 30–2.

[194] Monteverdi's very first publication, at the age of 15, was the set of three-voice Latin motets: *Sacrae Cantiunculae tribus vocibus . . . Liber Primus nuper editus Venetijs Apud Angelum Gardanum, 1582*. The composition of masses and motets is mentioned in his first extant letter of 28 Nov. 1601, and the *Dichiaratione* written by Giulio Cesare Monteverdi and published as the preface to the *Scherzi musicali* of

and motets of his immediate predecessors and contemporaries. Yet information about the liturgical and musical context of Monteverdi's Vespers might not only offer us new perspectives on controversies and performance issues surrounding Monteverdi's music, but also give us a better idea of how this remarkable collection relates to the vesper and other sacred music of his contemporaries. Among the key questions are: How does Monteverdi's publication relate to the publication practices in this repertoire? What aspects of his music reflect contemporary currents in sacred music? Were there other composers whose music influenced Monteverdi? What aspects of his 1610 print are original with Monteverdi and represent unique contributions to the repertoire? What influence might Monteverdi have had on his contemporaries? These are among the questions that the next three chapters will attempt to address.

1607 mentions Claudio's 'responsibility for both church and chamber music' (*il carico de la musica tanto da chiesa quanto da camera che tiene*). The *Dichiaratione* is published in De' Paoli, *Lettere*, 394–404. Eng. trans. in Strunk, *Source Readings in Music History*, 405–12. The 1601 letter is in De' Paoli, *Lettere*, 17–18; Lax, *Lettere*, 13–14; Stevens, *The Letters*, 37–8; Arnold and Fortune, eds., *The Monteverdi Companion*, 22–3.

2

The Liturgy of Vespers and the
'Antiphon Problem'

⟨❧⟩

THE Roman liturgy of vespers in effect at the time when Monteverdi's *Vespro della Beata Vergine* was published by Ricciardo Amadino in 1610 had been established by the *Breviarium Romanum* of Pope Pius V in 1568. The Pius V breviary was the sequel to the deliberations of the Council of Trent (1545–63) and replaced the reform breviary of Cardinal Quiñones, which had served the Roman liturgy from 1535 to 1568. The new breviary was conservative, restoring much of the pre-sixteenth-century office, and it remained in force until the reform breviary of Pius X in 1911. A more radical reform resulted from the Second Vatican Council in 1971.[1]

Following the Council of Trent, churches with special papal dispensation or having divergent liturgical traditions more than two centuries old were allowed to retain their liturgies. Both the ducal church of Santa Barbara in Mantua and St Mark's Basilica in Venice had their own liturgies, the former by virtue of papal dispensation, the latter by reason of antiquity. Monteverdi's publication of 1610, however, fulfils the needs of the Roman rite, rather than reflecting the specific liturgies of either Santa Barbara or St Mark's (see Chapter 1 for a discussion of the thesis that at least some of the contents of the *Vespro della Beata Vergine* may have originally been composed for the feast of Santa Barbara). Indeed, Monteverdi's dedication of his print to Pope Paul V in Rome would have been inappropriate had its contents been aimed uniquely at either of these special rites.

The principal elements of the Roman vesper service are as follows:[2]

---

[1] Brief histories of the office may be found in Cheslyn Jones, Geoffrey Wainwright, and Edward Yarnold, SJ, eds., *The Study of Liturgy* (Oxford: Oxford University Press, 1978) and Robert Taft, SJ, *The Liturgy of the Hours in East and West* (Collegeville, Minn.: The Liturgical Press, 1986).

[2] The table is based on Taft, *The Liturgy of the Hours*, 313, which is derived in turn from Gabriele Winkler, 'Über die Kathedralvesper in den verschiedenen Riten des Ostens und Westens', *Archiv für Liturgiewissenschaft*, 16 (1974), 100. General rubrics for vespers from a 1583 Venetian printing of the Pius V breviary read as follows: 'At vespers: Pater noster: Ave Maria: Deus in adiutorium, &c. Then five psalms are said, with five antiphons, as indicated in the Proper, or the Common. On Sundays or on ferial days: antiphons and psalms are always said as in the psalter (when Paschal Time, the psalms are said under one antiphon) unless [there are] other Proper antiphons, as [for example] assigned to Sundays in Advent. After the psalms and antiphons, the chapter, hymn, verse, antiphon at the Magnificat with the

Invitatory: Psalm 69 (℣ Deus in adjutorium meum intende. ℟ Domine ad adjuvandum me festina.)

Current psalmody: five psalms (The *cursus*, or cycle, of psalms varies with the type of feast (e.g. feasts of male saints, feasts of the Virgin or other female saints, Sunday vespers) or specific feasts of the Temporale (e.g. Christmas, Corpus Christi, etc.)). Each psalm is preceded and followed by its antiphon. The antiphons are all proper to the particular feast being celebrated, except for the Common of the Saints and during Paschal Time (between Low and Trinity Sundays). In Paschal Time all five psalm antiphons are simply *Alleluia*.

Lesson (designated 'Chapter' in the *Liber usualis*). The lesson, like the psalms, varies with the type of feast or specific feast).

Hymn (the hymn, like the psalms, is proper to the type of feast or specific feast).

Versicle: Psalm 140:2 (℣ Dirigatur Domine orati mea. ℟ Sicut incensum in conspectu tuo.), except on Saturdays.

Magnificat (preceded and followed by the Magnificat antiphon, which is proper to the specific feast or to a particular Common of the Saints. Magnificat antiphons at Sunday Vespers during Paschal Time are proper, but in the Common of the Saints are sometimes replaced by *Alleluia*.).

The combinations of ordinary texts, proper texts, and texts which serve for various categories of feasts are complicated, vary considerably, and cannot be subsumed under any general rule. The conductor wishing to perform a complete vesper service should consult the *Liber usualis* for the appropriate details as well as for prayers both before and after the office and possible commemorations after the Magnificat antiphon. Those wishing to perform a vesper service more nearly in accord with the 1568 breviary should consult a breviary published prior to the reform of Pius X in 1911. The principal musical differences between the breviary of Pius V and the reformed breviary of 1911 are the suppression in the latter of a short responsory preceding the hymn and occasional differences in the selection of the hymn. Other details differ as well, but do not affect the principal musical elements.

   From 1568 until the breviary of 1911, general rubrics suggested that one of the four seasonal Marian antiphons should be sung at the conclusion of vespers

canticle, and the [office] prayer are said, all according to the time or the saint for that particular office. When prayers are said, they are said before the [office] prayer; the commemorations, if any, of the Cross, Saint Mary, the Apostles, and the peace are sung afterwards, as said above in their particular rubrics.' Regarding antiphons, the rubrics say: '. . . . on doubles at vespers, matins, and lauds only, the antiphons are said complete before the psalms and are repeated complete after the psalms; and in the other hours, and in offices that are not doubles, the antiphon is only begun at the beginning of the psalm, then it is said complete at the end. And when the antiphon begins like the psalm, after the beginning of the antiphon there is said what follows in the psalm without repetition of the beginning [of the psalm], from that place where the antiphon left off . . .' See App. B for original text.

if this were the last office hour of the day (i.e. if compline were not sung).[3] These antiphons, with their seasonal rubrics as given in the Pius V breviary, are *Alma Redemptoris Mater* (from the first Sunday in Advent to the [feast of the] Purification); *Ave Regina Caelorum* (from the [Feast of the] Purification to the fifth day in Holy Week); *Regina Caeli laetare* (Paschal Time); and *Salve Regina* (from the octave of Pentecost until Advent). The Litany of Loreto may also have concluded a vesper service on many occasions.[4]

The psalm and Magnificat antiphons of the vesper service pose certain complications in performance. When a vesper service was performed entirely in plainchant, the tone of the psalm or Magnificat was expected to match the mode of the antiphon which preceded and followed it. Since psalm and Magnificat chants consisted of standard formulas while every antiphon chant was different, it had been an easy matter to provide each psalm and the Magnificat with a plainchant in each of the eight tones plus the mixed *tonus peregrinus* for the psalm *In exitu Israel*. The choir was then expected to select the psalm or Magnificat tone to match the mode of the antiphon.

Not only did the antiphon mode and psalm or Magnificat tone match, the absolute pitch level at which they were sung was also adaptable to the comfort of the choir. Numerous treatises from the sixteenth and seventeenth centuries testify to the need for organists to be able to transpose when accompanying a choir in order to set a pitch standard that was comfortable for the choir.[5] As a

---

[3] From the 1583 breviary quoted in n. 2: 'The antiphons of the Blessed Mary placed at the end of the psalter are said singly after compline according to the various seasons, as noted there, except on the three major days of Holy Week before Easter. They are said outside the Choir, however, only at the end of compline and at the end of matins, or after lauds if this is how the [morning?] office ends; otherwise, if another hour follows, at the end of the final hour. Whenever another hour is finished, they are always to be sung in the Choir and the exit is made from Choir . . . it is . . . not said when the mass follows after another hour.' See App. B for original text. The passage pertaining to where the antiphon is sung is problematic in its reading and interpretation. The translation given here suggests that the seasonal Marian antiphon was sung somewhere in the church (perhaps in front of a statue of the Virgin), rather than in the Choir, after compline and after matins, lauds, or even another hour—whichever one concluded the [morning?] office. After all other hours (such as vespers), however, the antiphon was sung from the Choir, after which the monks exited. If compline were sung after vespers, then the Marian antiphon would only be used at compline, since the latter would be the final hour. The fact that many publications of polyphonic vesper music in the sixteenth and seventeenth centuries include the four seasonal Marian antiphons confirms the interpretation that one of the antiphons could be sung at the conclusion of vespers if compline did not follow. I am grateful to Prof. J. Patout Burns for his assistance with the translation and its interpretation.

[4] See David A. Blazey, 'The Litany in Seventeenth-Century Italy', 2 vols. (Ph.D. diss., University of Durham, 1990), i. 21, 55–7, 61–8, 72, 78, 102–6, 108. See also Colleen Reardon, *Agostino Agazzari and Music at Siena Cathedral, 1597–1641* (Oxford: Clarendon Press, 1993), 43 n. 38, 69–70.

[5] Zarlino had already devoted a chapter to this subject in *Le istitutioni harmoniche* (Venice, 1558; fac. New York: Broude Brothers, 1965), 319–20. According to Zarlino, transposition to all notes of the keyboard are possible, and he gives two examples, one with a two-flat signature, the other with a two-sharp signature. Zarlino warns that 'When . . . the mode of a composition is transposed, musicians should be warned above all to arrange it in such a manner and place that, in both ascent and descent, all notes are present which are necessary for the constitution of the mode, that is, which yield the whole tones and semitones necessary for the mode's essential character.' Eng. trans. in. Vered Cohen, *On the Modes: Part Four of 'Le istitutioni harmoniche', 1558, Gioseffo Zarlino* (New Haven: Yale University Press, 1983), 52. Juan

consequence, no matter what the notation of the mode and tone, all modes and tones were sung in the same limited range, in some instances, perhaps, with the same reciting note.[6] Such 'transpositions', in modern terms, of the mode and tone would not have been perceived as transpositions by the choir, but merely as selecting a suitable reciting pitch, since the notation of the mode and tone had no bearing on absolute pitch. For the organist, however, who would have had to adapt the position of his fingers on a keyboard with fixed pitch, the choice of reciting pitch did indeed involve transposition in the modern sense.

A similar procedure prevailed even when psalms began to be sung polyphonically in chordal *falsobordone*, where the psalm tone, often in the top part, was harmonized in four voices with simple root-position chords (at first improvised, then later notated).[7] By the late sixteenth century, *falsibordoni* were no longer so closely tied to the reciting note of the psalm tone; rather, the cantus firmus was 'treated freely or not even used'.[8] Nevertheless, the bipartite structure of the psalm tone, consisting of recitation followed by mediant and final cadences, governed the structure of all *falsibordoni*. *Falsibordoni* were untexted and were nearly always published in multiple tones, usually all eight, sometimes including the *tonus peregrinus* as well. Even in this form of polyphony, the *maestro di cappella* could select the tone of the psalm to match the mode of the antiphon. Moreover, the choice of a comfortable pitch standard was still not problematic, since the composite range of all the voices of a typical *falsobordone* was still relatively narrow and could be moved substantially upwards or downwards.

Bermudo gave the same admonition to organists. See Bernadette Nelson, 'Alternatim Practice in 17th-Century Spain', *Early Music*, 22 (1994), 250. Since organs were normally tuned in mean-tone tuning, split keys were required for a number of transpositions, the number of available transpositions depending on the number of split keys. See Ch. 22 below regarding organ tunings. Adriano Banchieri provided specific transpositions for the organist in *L'organo suonarino opera terzadecima* (Venice: Amadino, 1605), fac. ed. Giulio Cattin (Amsterdam: Frits Knuf, 1969), 40–3, and in *Cartella musicale* (Venice: Vincenti, 1615), 71. Girolamo Diruta talks extensively about transposition with numerous examples in *Seconda parte del Transilvano* (Venice: Alessandro Vincenti, 1622), bk. iii. 4–11; bk. iv. 7–16. See App. F below for complete citations of these treatises and English translations. For French sources on this subject, see Robert Frederick Bates, 'From Mode to Key: A Study of Seventeenth-Century French Liturgical Organ Music and Music Theory' (Ph.D. diss., Stanford University, 1986).

[6] For discussions of this subject see Almonte C. Howell, Jr., 'French Baroque Organ Music and the Eight Church Tones', *Journal of the American Musicological Society*, 11 (1958), 106–18; Vincent J. Panetta, Jr., *Treatise on Harpsichord Tuning by Jean Denis* (Cambridge: Cambridge University Press, 1987), 44–50, 75–7, 84–7; Nelson, 'Alternatim Practice'; and Jeffrey G. Kurtzman, 'Tones, Modes, Clefs and Pitch in Roman Cyclic Magnificats of the 16th Century', *Early Music*, 22 (1994), 641–64.

[7] The origins and development of the *falsobordone* are described in Murray C. Bradshaw, *The Falsobordone, A Study in Renaissance and Baroque Music* (Musical Studies and Documents, 34; Stuttgart: American Institute of Musicology/Hänssler Verlag, 1978).

[8] Murray C. Bradshaw, 'Lodovico Viadana as a Composer of Falsobordoni', *Studi musicali*, 19 (1990), 93. Bradshaw describes very well the rationale behind the popularity of *falsibordoni*: '. . . the fullness of sound, the modest polyphony at the two cadences, the clear and flowing declamation of the text during the recitations and the balance and symmetry of the music, would have been a contrast to elaborately set psalm verses or, on the other hand, to simple chanted verses. Falsobordoni were also easy to learn, and, one might add, to embellish. The repetition of the music over several psalm verses would have invited improvised *passaggi* or, at least, smaller ornaments like groppi, trilli, and accenti' (p. 94).

As polyphonic settings of Magnificats became more prominent in the late fifteenth century, a similar practice developed whereby settings were often collected or even composed in cycles of eight—one for each tone.[9] Thus a *maestro di cappella* could select a polyphonic Magnificat in the appropriate tone, just as he could a *falsobordone* psalm setting. Here, too, the absolute pitch standard in performance could be adjusted upwards or downwards according to the convenience of the choir, but now the degree of adjustment was more limited, since settings in *canto figurato*, especially from the early sixteenth century onwards, tended to use most or all of the entire 20–1 note gamut recommended by theorists.[10] Although we cannot know what the limitations in that adjustment were, it is apparent that what governed the limits were the highest pitch the canto could comfortably sing and the lowest possible pitch the bass could accommodate.

The situation with polyphonic psalm settings was somewhat different. When psalms came to be composed regularly in *canto figurato* in the late fifteenth and early sixteenth centuries, the polyphonic psalm setting was typically in one tone only, not all eight. Under this circumstance it became impossible for the mode of the antiphon to determine the selection of the psalm tone, since the tone of the polyphonic psalm was already fixed. Composers were still interested in the tones of psalms in *canto figurato*, however, as demonstrated by the identification of these tones in most sources of polyphonic psalms in the sixteenth century and in many sources of the early seventeenth century as well (Monteverdi did not identify his psalm and Magnificat tones in the Vespers of 1610). But where one might expect a composer to write a polyphonic psalm in a tone that matched the largest number of antiphons with which the psalm could be coupled, this was not at all the case. In fact, collections of polyphonic psalms are frequently ordered by the numerical sequence of the psalms, beginning with Psalm 109, *Dixit Dominus*, and the first several, sometimes eight, psalms in this sequence are simply set in the numerical sequence of tones. Where this psalm number/tone sequence pattern was not followed, there seems to be no identifiable factor determining the tone in which a given psalm is set. What is clear from this circumstance is that the most frequently encountered modes of antiphons for particular psalms had no discernible influence on the choice of psalm tones in *canto figurato* psalmody.[11] Moreover, *canto figurato* psalms, like polyphonic Magnificat compositions, were not as much subject to upward or

---

[9] Sources containing Magnificat cycles from the late 15th to the middle of the 16th century are listed in Winfried Kirsch, *Die Quellen der mehrstimmigen Magnificat- und Te Deum-Vertonungen bis zur Mitte des 16. Jahrhunderts* (Tutzing: Hans Schneider, 1966), 40–1, 52–3.

[10] See Kurtzman, 'Tones, Modes, Clefs and Pitch'.

[11] e.g. the most common mode for antiphons to *Dixit Dominus* is the eighth mode, while the most frequently used tone for polyphonic settings of *Dixit* is the first tone, in keeping with its position as the numerically first psalm in the Vesper sequence.

downward transposition in the selection of a pitch standard as plainchant or even *falsobordone* psalm settings.

What, then, was the relationship between psalm tone and antiphon mode in the performance of a mostly polyphonic vespers? Adriano Banchieri, in *L'organo suonarino* of 1605, provides texted organ basses for each tone in *canto figurato* to be alternated with plainchant in the performance of psalms. Each psalm is preceded by a rubric indicating the feasts for which it is appropriate, and these feasts do indeed have proper antiphons for the specific psalms Banchieri gives in the modes matching the tones of these psalms.[12] Thus, in Banchieri's approach, *canto figurato* psalm settings were limited in the scope of their use by the tones in which they were set. In order to bring the reciting notes of all eight tones into a limited, comfortable range for singers, several of the tones are transposed by means of a one-flat signature, and the fifth tone is transposed by omission of the flat signature, so that all reciting notes fall within the fourth *f–bb*. As a result, the first, fourth, and sixth tones all share the reciting note *a*, the second and eighth tones share *bb*, the fifth and seventh tones share *g*, and the third tone stands alone with its reciting note *f*.[13]

Girolamo Diruta, on the other hand, recommended more intervals of transposition than simply an upward fourth or a downward fifth. While moving the chant up or down would not have meant the use of sharp or flat signatures as far as the singers themselves were concerned, it often forced an accompanying organist to use sharps or flats, and Diruta's transpositions include signatures with as many as two flats in one direction and three sharps in the other. Banchieri, in the *Secondo registro* of *L'organo suonarino*, describes having heard, on a trip to Venice, Giovanni Gabrieli and Paolo Giusto perform all eight psalm tones so that the final chord always fell on D. Banchieri says that these tones 'are either unaltered [untransposed from their usual position, as in the first tone], or use the accidentals of flats and sharps . . .' and then illustrates these tones with musical examples in transpositions with signatures ranging up to two flats and two sharps.[14]

---

[12] pp. 45–57; Eng. trans. Donald E. Marcase as 'Adriano Banchieri, "L'organo suonarino": Translation, Transcription and Commentary' (Ph.D. diss., Indiana University, 1970), 145–6. See the discussion of this passage in Ch. 4. Banchieri also recommends other transpositions that reduce the range of reciting tones to *g–bb*. His transpositions are discussed in Harold S. Powers, 'Mode', in *The New Grove Dictionary of Music and Musicians*, ed. Stanley Sadie (London: Macmillan Publishers Ltd., 1980), xii. 414–15.

[13] Banchieri transposes exactly the same tones as those still recommended by the French organist Jean Denis in 1650 and the Spanish theorist Francisco Valls more than a century later (1742). See Panetta, *Treatise*, 48 and Nelson, 'Alternatim Practice', 245.

[14] *L'organo suonarino*, 43–4. The full passage reads: 'Le intuonationi mostrate di sopra sono veramente le reali nell'Organo per lasciare in voce il Choro, ma si possono però (a chi ne ha intelligenza) trasportare, alte, & basse in diverse corde, si come hò sentito con grandissimo gusto nell'Illustrissima Città di Venetia (mentre ivi son dimorato alcuni giorni per interesse di far stampare questa mia fatica) da gl'Eccellentissimi Musici, & Organisti nella Chiesa di S. Marco, il Sig. Gio: Gabrielli, & Sig. Paolo Giusto. [sic] la dove in questo proposito per mia curiosità, utile & studiosa fia bene vedere, che gl'otto Tuoni, possino havere la corda finale, nella positione D.la, sol, re, & questi per naturalità & accidenti, di

Where a psalm tone has been transposed by means of a signature, whether one flat or several sharps, Banchieri has made it clear that the signature applies to the chant as well as to the organ bass. Therefore, these transpositions of the plainchant are 'real', maintaining the same interval relationships as the untransposed chant.

Further complications, however, are introduced by Banchieri's organ basses for each psalm tone described above. In each of Banchieri's examples, the psalm tone intonation is given for the first verse, and the bass-line of the alternate organ verses is 'figured' with numerous accidentals indicating whether the third above the bass is major or minor (see Ex. 2.1). At the end of each organ verse Banchieri gives a single blackened bass note for each subsequent verse sung by the plainchant choir, presumably for the purpose of providing an opening harmonization and final cadence for the chant verses.[15]

It is Banchieri's 'figured' accidentals in the organ verses that are of most interest. Ex. 2.1 reproduces Banchieri's first tone, in which bass notes on *A*, *d*, and *e* are often figured with a sharp, the resulting C♯, F♯, and G♯ conflicting with the *f* and *g* of the chant. The single blackened bass notes associated with each plainchant verse also have a Picardy third notated above *d*, the F♯ contrasting with the *f* of the chant.[16] If the first tone chant is sung with the traditional b♭, this pitch will conflict with the fifth of the many E major triads built over the bass *e* in the organ verses. Within the organ verses themselves, Banchieri frequently contrasts the B♭ of a G minor triad with the B♮ of an E major triad.

Similar clashes between plainchant and organ verses occur in Banchieri's figuration for the organ basses in all of the other tones; in the third, fifth, and eighth tones there are even chromatic clashes between the reciting note of the chant and harmonies in the organ verses. Nowhere, either in the examples or the text of Banchieri's treatise, is there a suggestion that the intervals and pitches of the plainchant psalm or Magnificat tones would have been adjusted to agree with those in the alternate polyphonic organ verses. In other words, it seems inescapable that Banchieri tolerated, even considered inevitable, pitch clashes

b. b. molli & diesis ## come qui sotto saranno realmente trasportati. Praticati sono gustosi da sonare, & comodi al Choro, ma non praticati niuno si ponghi all'impresa, atteso che potrai dirsi con il Poeta Mantovano Oibovasselli.' Trans. from Marcase, 'Adriano Banchieri, "L'organo suonarino"', 143 (bracketed explanation mine). It is clear from Banchieri's rubrics for each tone that by 'naturalità & accidenti' he is not referring to tonal and real transpositions, but rather to tones that remain in their normal (*naturale*) position and others that are transposed by flats and sharps (*accidenti*).

[15] Banchieri's organ basses are also texted, presumably so that a bass voice (or the organist himself) could sing them to the organ's accompaniment.

[16] The same accidentals occur in the first organ verse *sopra il Re* in Antonio Valente's *Versi spirituali sopra tutte le note* (Naples: Mattio Cancer, 1580) (RISM V34); therefore, alternation of Valente's verse with plainchant in the first tone results in the same pitch clashes as in the Banchieri example. Unlike most collections of organ versets, Valente's is organized according to the notes of the hexachord rather than according to the eight (nine) tones. Three of Valente's verses *sopra il Re* are published in Luigi Torchi, ed., *L'arte musicale in Italia* (Milan: Ricordi, n.d.), iii. 45–8.

between plainchant verses and polyphonic organ verses in *alternatim* performance. The alternative, that Banchieri's clerics would have sung the plainchant verses of Ex. 2.1 with *f♯*, *b♭*, and perhaps even *g♯*, seems far-fetched, especially in the absence of any evidence that this was the case. In polyphonic settings, of course, plainchant cantus firmi were often chromatically altered according to the context, but there is no evidence to indicate that such alterations were common in *alternatim* performance. To summarize the discussion of Banchieri's treatise, plainchant psalm and Magnificat tones may be subjected to transposition, maintaining the integrity of their interval structure, but the alternating

PRIMO SALMO ET TUONO

Questa s'accorda in alternativa al Choro, il giorno dell'Annuntiatione & quello di Santa Caterina

Ex. 2.1. Adriano Banchieri, *L'organo suonarino*, 1605, p. 45

polyphonic organ verses may contain pitches that clash chromatically with the plainchant.

Further evidence of transposition of psalm tones and the occurrence of pitch clashes between plainchant and polyphony can be seen in Giovanni Luca Conforti's *Salmi passaggiati* of 1601–3 (RISM C3498), published in Rome, Viadana's *Cento concerti ecclesiastici* of 1602 (V1360), published in Venice, and Francesco Severi's *Psalmi passaggiati* of 1615, also published in Rome (S2847).[17] Viadana's publication provides a group of solo *falsobordone* settings for each of the four voice registers. As is typical for *falsibordoni*, the voice declaims most of each half-verse on a reciting note before breaking into a long melisma for the mediant and final cadences. Since Viadana supplies text for the second verse only of *Dixit Dominus* in all of his settings, each setting would have to have been preceded by the first verse in plainchant, and it is highly likely that performance of these *falsibordoni* would thereafter have alternated plainchant and *falsobordone* verses. Viadana's first pair of settings for each voice register has the single rubric at its head 'for the first, seventh, and eighth tones'.[18] In each of these settings (see Ex. 2.2), the two half-verses have their own, different, reciting notes. In fact, the reciting notes of the *falsibordoni* are only occasionally related to the reciting notes of the chant in any of the three tones named in the rubric. On the other hand, whatever the reciting notes, all of the settings 'for the first, seventh and eighth tones' in every voice register conclude with a triad on D with Picardy third, indicating in every case the positioning of the psalm chant itself to cadence on D, as in the Banchieri examples of Gabrieli's and Giusto's transposition practice described above.[19] In Banchieri's examples, the first tone remains in its usual

(a)

Di - xit___ Do - mi - nus Do - mi - no me - o   Se - de a dex - tris me - - - is.

Ex. 2.2. *a* First psalm tone

[17] Modern editions: *Giovanni Luca Conforti, 'Salmi passaggiati' (1601–1603)*, ed. Murray C. Bradshaw (Neuhausen and Stuttgart: American Institute of Musicology, Hänssler-Verlag, 1985); *Lodovico Viadana, Cento concerti ecclesiastici opera duodecima 1602: Parte prima: Concerti a una voce con l'organo*, ed. Claudio Gallico (Kassel: Bärenreiter, 1964); *Vesper and Compline Music for One Principal Voice*, ed. Jeffrey Kurtzman (Seventeenth-Century Italian Sacred Music, 11; New York: Garland Publishing, Inc., 1995), 16–23; and *Francesco Severi, Salmi passaggiati (1615)*, ed. Murray C. Bradshaw (Recent Researches in the Music of the Baroque Era, 38; Madison, Wis: A-R Editions, Inc., 1981). Viadana's *falsibordoni* are discussed in Bradshaw, 'Lodovico Viadana as a Composer of Falsobordoni.'

[18] 'Del primo, settimo e ottavo tono'. The other three *falsobordone* pairs are for the 'secondo, terzo e quinto tono', for the 'quarto' tono, and for the 'sesto tono'.

[19] Bernadette Nelson's examination of Spanish organ versets also shows agreement between the root of the final organ chord and the *finalis* of the plainchant. See Nelson, 'Alternatim Practice', 243. In Ex. 2.2, Viadana has given the chant incipits for the seventh and eight tones. The seventh tone, which normally cadences on A, has been transposed up a fourth to cadence on D. Similarly, the eighth tone, whose normal cadence is on G, has been transposed up a fifth to cadence on D.

Ex. 2.2. *b* Lodovico Viadana, *Falsibordoni passeggiati* from *Cento Concerti ecclesiastici*, 1602

position, but the seventh tone, whose normal cadence is on *a*, is transposed a fifth down by a one-flat signature, while the eighth tone is transposed down a fourth by a one-sharp signature. With Viadana's transpositions, the only agreement between the three psalm tone chants and his *falsibordoni* is in the *finalis*; the reciting notes are sometimes quite incompatible between the plainchant and the *falsibordoni*. Moreover, there are even chromatic pitch clashes between the chant and the *falsibordoni* in some cases.[20]

It is evident that Viadana's assignment of these three tones to the same *falsobordone* setting depends on their all having a final of D, as in Banchieri's transpositions reflecting what he had heard in Venice. It is equally clear that the reciting note of the chant is not a determining factor in the relationship between the psalm tone and the *falsobordone*, and that pitch clashes occur between the plainchant and the *falsobordone*, in terms of both the reciting notes of each and the chromatic inflection of some notes in the *falsobordone*. It should also be remembered that Viadana's final of D is itself not an absolute pitch, but may be transposed for the comfort of the singers. The determining factor in pitch placement for the singers, however, is the reciting note, since the singers must negotiate pitches both above and below it.

Viadana's paired solo *falsibordoni* for each of the four voices 'for the second, third and fifth tones' all have a one-flat signature and conclude on G harmonized with a Picardy third. The second plainchant tone had long been commonly transposed by one flat to *g* because of the low notated register of the Hypodorian mode. But transposing the third tone to *g* requires a two-flat signature, while placing the fifth tone final (untransposed = *a′*) on *g* also requires two flats (in addition to the B♭ often found as a fifth mode signature, denoting not a transposition but a customary pitch inflection). These transpositions of the plainchant psalm tones likewise create occasional chromatic conflicts with Viadana's *falsobordone* verses.

Viadana's *falsibordoni* for the fourth tone have two different finals, one on *A* and the other on *e*, reflecting the two levels at which the fourth tone is often

---

[20] e.g. the second *falsobordone* for canto and the first for tenor begin with a reciting note A harmonized by a D major triad, the F♯ of the harmony conflicting with the opening note of the chant in both the first and seventh tones. Even within a *falsobordone* verse itself Viadana sometimes notated radical pitch clashes. Bradshaw, in 'Lodovico Viadana as a Composer of Falsobordoni', 114, provides an example of a five-part *falsobordone* in the first tone from Viadana's 1596 collection of *Falsi bordoni* in which the reciting note *a′* in the first half of the verse is harmonized with a D major triad, cadencing at the mediant on an A major triad, to be followed immediately by an F major triad harmonizing the reciting note *a′* of the second half of the verse (which cadences on a D major triad). Nelson, in 'Alternatim Practice', 246–50, cites chromatic pitch clashes resulting from the psalm tone transpositions recommended by the Spanish theorist Martin y Coll in the early 18th century. Pitch clashes between a *falsobordone* setting and the chant quoted in the *falsobordone* itself appear as early as 1557 in a keyboard *fabordón* by Venegas de Henestrosa. See Murray C. Bradshaw, *The Origin of the Toccata* (American Institute of Musicology, 1972), 20–1.

found in the sixteenth and seventeenth centuries.[21] The transposition to an *A* final requires a one-flat signature in the plainchant. Viadana's sixth tone *falsibordoni* all have finals on *F*, the normal final of this tone.

When the psalm tone transpositions required by Viadana's *falsibordoni* are taken together, one sees that all eight reciting notes (when reduced to a single octave) have been brought to within a minor third, *g–b♭*. The only exceptions are those several *falsibordoni* for the fourth tone with final *A*, which place the reciting note of the chant on *d'*.[22] Viadana's transpositions allow a limited set of *falsibordoni* to serve for all eight tones, notated within a limited pitch range for the convenience of the singers, but they also generate the same kinds of pitch clashes between some of the psalm tones and the polyphonic *falsibordoni* that we have seen in the Banchieri examples. In Ex. 2.2, F♯, C♯, and G♯ all appear in the harmonization, clashing with *f♮'* and *g♮'* of the first psalm tone. Similarly, both *b♮'* and *b♭'* appear in each *falsobordone*. Presumably, the first tone chant would be sung with the customary *b♭'*.

Similar pitch clashes can also be seen in the *Salmi passaggiati* of Conforti. Conforti's solo syllabic recitations are measured rather than unmeasured, and are by no means confined to the psalm tone itself. Rather, the cantus firmus 'is often present only in an "ideal" way, that is by being the impetus for the melodies, harmonies, figurations, and, indeed, for all the musical elements that are present'.[23] Conforti's settings are all *alternatim*, and chromatic clashes of pitch are common between the plainchant verses on the one hand and the solo vocal part and its accompaniment on the other. The setting of the first tone in Conforti's first book, for example, begins with an *f♯'* as the reciting note in the solo voice, harmonized with a D major triad. This *f♯'* conflicts chromatically with the *f♮'* initial note of the first tone plainchant. But even within Conforti's *falsobordone* verse both F♯' and F♮ appear. The juxtapositions are especially striking at the close of the *falsibordoni* verses and the beginning of the next plainchant verse (see Ex. 2.3). The *falsobordone* embellishes the cadential descending fifth of the first tone, using F♮ in both the voice and the accompaniment. But the final chord is a D major triad by virtue of the Picardy third. That this third should be major is clear not only from numerous treatises from the sixteenth and early seventeenth centuries insisting on major thirds at all final cadences, but also from Banchieri's examples of harmonization of the psalm tone where the Picardy third is notated

---

[21] Both *falsibordoni* for the bass conclude with the pitch-class E harmonized by an E major triad, but one cadences on the low *E*, while the other cadences an octave higher on *e*.

[22] The Parisian organist Guillaume-Gabriel Nivers, in his *Dissertation sur le chant grégorien* (Paris, 1683), states that the fourth tone may conclude a fourth higher for the convenience of convent choirs. See Howell, 'French Baroque Organ Music', 112. Viadana provides *falsobordone* settings in the transposed fourth tone for the canto, alto, and tenor voices, but not the bass.

[23] Giovanni Luca Conforti, '*Salmi passaggiati*', ed. Bradshaw, p. xliii.

Ex. 2.3. Luca Conforti, *Laudate pueri*, verse 4, from *Salmi passaggiati*, 1601

in every instance. After this conclusion on a D major triad, the next verse, in plainchant, begins on an F♮'. Conforti's setting from the same book of the third tone has frequent contradictions between G♯ and B♭ in the *falsobordone* and the natural versions of these notes in the plainchant. Similar pitch clashes between *falsobordone* and plainchant occur in all of Conforti's settings except those for the cantus and tenor in the sixth tone.

Conforti's only transpositions are for the second tone, which appears at both a fourth and a fifth above D. As a consequence, the reciting notes of the plainchant verses (not the *falsibordoni*) in all eight tones fall within the fourth *a–d'* (when all are placed in the tenor octave).

Pitch clashes can also be seen in Severi's *Salmi passaggiati*. Severi's settings are mostly *alternatim*, with different *falsibordoni* in different voice ranges for each verse. Aside from clashes between *falsobordone* settings and plainchant verses, the third verse of the first tone *falsobordone* setting, assigned to the alto, has an *f♯'* as the 'reciting note' of the first half-verse and an *f♮'* as the 'reciting note' of the second half-verse. The variety of 'reciting notes' in the *falsobordone* verses is illustrated by the subsequent verses, assigned to the tenor, bass, and canto voices, which have 'reciting notes' on *a, d, f, a', c',* and *d'*.

The finals of Severi's *falsibordoni* place all of the chant reciting notes (when reduced to a single octave) within the compass of a fourth: *g–c'*. The seventh tone is the only one with the lowest reciting note, *g,* but the chant itself has the same *d–b♭* compass as the first tone with its reciting note *a*. Thus Severi's *falsibordoni* also require transposition of the alternating plainchant psalm tones, bringing the tones into a more constrained, and therefore more comfortable, total gamut.

These transpositions of psalm tones, with shared reciting notes between different tones, were clearly widespread in the early seventeenth century and probably much earlier. But they also resulted in an elimination of some of the distinctions between different modes and tones, most particularly their ranges and reciting notes. Bernadette Nelson has traced the concern of Spanish theorists and organists over just this issue in the early eighteenth century.[24] In the discussion above, I have assumed that transpositions of the plainchant in *alternatim* situations were 'real' transpositions, that is, they maintained the interval structure of the untransposed chant. This requirement is stated explicitly by Zarlino and is implied in Banchieri's notation of the eight tones all with finals on D, for he gives all of the signatures necessary to maintain the intervallic integrity of each psalm tone.[25] But Spanish theorists indicate that two or more psalm tones at the same pitch level shared the same scale, thus obliterating the intervallic differences between the tones.[26] The tones that were most frequently combined in this fashion were the second, third, and fifth, precisely those that Viadana combined in his second pair of *falsobordone* settings. Viadana's signature for these *falsibordoni* is a single flat. If the same signature were used for each of the three tones, rather than the 'transposing' signatures given above, then the three psalm tones would not only share the same octave, but the same interval structure. Similarly, Viadana's first paired *falsibordoni*, for first, seventh, and eighth tones, without signature, would have amalgamated these three tones to the same octave and same interval structure. The only remaining distinctions would have been the typical intonation of each tone (in some cases with altered intervals), some of their reciting notes, and their cadence formulas (in some cases with altered intervals). On the basis of the evidence of Banchieri and Severi, however, I am inclined to believe that Viadana too would have expected his chants to be sung in 'real' transpositions, resulting in pitch clashes between the chant and his *falsibordoni*. I know of no discussion of transposition by an Italian theorist from the sixteenth or early seventeenth century that suggests anything other than 'real' transposition.[27] However, it cannot be excluded that Viadana's singers or

---

[24] See 'Alternatim Practice', 247–55. While the theorists Nelson cites date from the early 18th century, many of the organ versets they discuss date from the 17th century. Since the *alternatim* practice was itself very old and conservative in character, these theorists were dealing with the same issues as 16th- and 17th-century organists.

[25] See n. 5 above.

[26] Nelson, 'Alternatim Practice', 250–5.

[27] Nivers, in his *Dissertation sur le chant grégorien*, 109, indicates that the reciting notes of different tones should not always be on the same sounding pitch. The reason is that this would require transpositions in some tones that were not available on organs with mean tone-tuning and a limited number of split keys. In the *Traité* Denis says explicitly that 'organists must never transpose either the *tons* of the church or the modes of music except to the customary notes or keys. Choirmasters must not and cannot force them to do otherwise . . .' See Panetta, *Treatise*, 49–50, 75. French practice, therefore, did not reduce all tones with the same reciting note to a single diatonic scale as Spanish practice apparently did, but rather maintained the intervallic integrity of each tone when transposed or, at the least, the reciting note and the appropriate third above the final. On the other hand, Bates, in 'From Mode to Key', 141–4, cites a transposition by Jean Titelouze (1626) of the seventh tone a fourth down in which the F is not sharped, thereby altering the intervallic structure of the tone. Later French transpositions

other Italian singers may at times have sung each group of three chants according to a single diatonic scale, in the same fashion as that reported by Spanish theorists. It should be remembered, as mentioned above, that in polyphonic settings, plainchants were often altered intervallically, whether by accidentals or by diatonic transposition. Monteverdi's own *Dixit Dominus* from the Vespers illustrates alteration by an accidental, for he replaces the *subtonium* G at the beginning of the psalm tone with the *subsemitonium* G♯.[28]

The harpsichord-builder and organist Jean Denis treats the relationship between plainchant and organ versets in his *Traité de l'accord de l'espinette* of 1650, as does the organist Guillaume-Gabriel Nivers in his *Dissertation sur le chant gregorien* of 1683.[29] Although both these treatises originate in Paris from a period somewhat later than Monteverdi's Vespers, the matters they consider are the same as those discussed above and may shed further light on possible resolutions of these issues. Like Viadana, both Denis and Nivers declare that the singers must relate the *finalis* of their chant to the *finalis* of the organ, and Nivers indicates further that the singers should not search for the tone while the organ is playing:

in churches where the organ is used in the divine service, it is a rule of absolute necessity that the organ should give the *ton* of everything that is sung after the organ by the choir. The first [organ] antiphon must therefore be at the *ton* of the second which is sung by the choir immediately after the organ has played the first, and so on for the others. That is why the singers, without submitting themselves to the bother of rules, need only pay attention to the final of the organ (and nothing beyond that, since the attempt to find the *ton* while the organ is playing is ever one of the principal causes of discord and error), and on this final of the organ, which should always be the final of the antiphon which is to be intoned, [they can] regulate by proportion the first note of the antiphon.[30]

Nivers implies that the organ replaced the antiphon after the psalm, but that the antiphon preceding the psalm was still sung in plainchant, as James Moore has shown was the case at St Mark's in Venice (see Chapter 1). This would follow from Nivers's statement that 'the first [organ] antiphon must therefore be at

of the seventh tone also often used the minor third above the final, sometimes intermingling both minor and major thirds (ibid. 145–6). See n. 33 below for Denis's transpositions of the *tons*.

[28] In Paolo Sabbatini's 1650 publication of psalm tones and versets, *Toni ecclesiastici colle sue intonationi all'uso Romano*, chromatic alterations are made in the psalm tones themselves, very likely reflecting in notation what had been improvised practice for some time. In the first tone, *b* is notated as *b♭* (*fa sopra la*); in the fourth tone the *subsemitonium g♯* is notated; and the seventh tone uses a *subsemitonium f♯*. Sabbatini's print concludes with a brief treatise for beginners for playing the basso continuo, in which the author not only explains the meaning of continuo figures, but also gives a series of clefs and key signatures for transposition, extending as far as two sharps and two flats.

[29] A first version of Denis's treatise appeared in 1643, but without the discussion of the eight church tones, which was added in 1650. Nivers's *Dissertation* is discussed in Howell, 'French Baroque Organ Music', 106–18, and Panetta, *Treatise*, 46–50. French organ versets and their relationship to chant are discussed in Bates, 'From Mode to Key'.

[30] Nivers, *Dissertation*, 111, trans. in Panetta, *Treatise*, 47.

the *ton* of the second which is sung by the choir immediately after the organ has played the first, and so on for the others'. The organ, substituting for the plainchant antiphon after the first psalm (the first organ antiphon) would end on the *finalis* of the plainchant antiphon for the second psalm, so that the choir could take its pitch from the organ for the second antiphon. Since Nivers declares that not all chants should be sung with the same reciting note,[31] it would seem that the organist selected the *ton* and *finalis* of his antiphon substitute following the psalm according to the next plainchant antiphon. This practice also implies that the organ antiphon and its preceding psalm were not necessarily in the same *ton*. In fact, Denis declared that his teacher, Florent le Bienvenu, was once questioned as to why he played the antiphon at the Magnificat in one *ton* and the Magnificat in another. Bienvenue replied 'that he performed the plainchant [verses of the Magnificat] so as to suit the singers'.[32] Because playing the more complicated antiphon substitute at the same pitch level as the plainchant would have required notes unavailable on an organ in mean-tone tuning, Bienvenu played the latter in a different *ton*.[33]

It is clear that by *finalis* of the organ, Nivers refers to the bass note upon which the final chord is built, not the note at the top of the chord. Indeed, Viadana's D major concluding chords have different voicings in different settings, with the

[31] See n. 27 above.

[32] Panetta, *Treatise*, 77.

[33] Later in the *Traité*, Denis lists the notes on which the psalms, the Magnificat, and the Benedictus must 'begin and end according to the *tons* of the antiphons'. The second *ton* receives its standard transposition up a fourth. In the third mode, the antiphon begins on E *mi, la*, and its reciting note is C *sol, ut, fa*. However, for the Magnificat in the third tone, the choir begins on G *re, sol, ut* with reciting note C *sol, ut, fa*, and ends on A *mi, la, re*. 'But for the convenience of the singers it should be played on F *ut, fa* with B♭, its dominant on B *fa*, and ended on G *re, sol, ut*.' Thus the Magnificat would be sung a step lower than its antiphon. Panetta claims that this transposition does not preserve the intervallic integrity of the mode, which begins with a minor semitone. However, I believe Panetta has confused the antiphon mode, beginning and ending on E *mi, la*, with the Magnificat mode, which begins on *g*, ascends to *c* as reciting note (with *d* upper inflection), and concludes on *a*. This Magnificat tone can indeed be transposed down a step to F *ut, fa* preserving its intervallic structure. Denis's fifth tone undergoes modification of the final as well as transposition. While the fifth tone begins on F *ut, fa*, its reciting note is C *sol, ut fa*, and its final is A *mi, la re*, the transposition for the convenience of the choir is by a fourth down, resulting in reciting note G *re, sol, ut* and an altered final of C *sol, ut, fa*, rather than E *mi, la*. Denis has thus accommodated the final of the psalm tone to the final of the mode. It is unclear whether this transposition would be applied to the psalm or Magnificat tone only, not the organ's antiphon, again resulting in different reciting notes and finals between the antiphon and the psalm or Magnificat. The seventh tone is transposed down a fifth, and the organist is instructed to conclude on the reciting note G with a B♭ in order to accommodate the various endings of the seventh *ton*. The eighth *ton* is to be transposed down a step. Denis notes that 'all those who practice it [this science] lack certainty, and even in discussions with the learned there are differences of opinion'. See Panetta, *Treatise*, 84–6. Alteration of the finals of the fifth and sixth tones was already recommended by Pierre Maillart in his treatise *Les tons, ou discours, sur les modes de musique, et les tons de l'èglise, et la distinction entre iceux* (Tournai, 1610). See Albert Cohen, 'Pierre Maillart', in *The New Grove*, xi. 536–7. Alteration of the fifth and seventh *tons* to agree with the modal finals is also indicated in the anonymous *Nouvelle mèthod très facile pour aprendre le plain-chant* of the late 17th century. See Bates, 'From Mode to Key', 21–2. Ibid. 48–84 gives all of the transpositions of the eight *tons* found in French sources of the 17th century.

solo voice concluding on D in either octave or on F♯.[34] Thus the vocal cadence is not the determining factor, but rather the bass note of the chord in the organ. Denis and Nivers also consolidate tones like Viadana, but use different criteria resulting in different groupings. According to Nivers, organ tones should be grouped according to whether the third above the *finalis* is major or minor, and the organ tone *finalis* should be the same as the plainchant *finalis*. Since the *finalis* as a sounding pitch is determined by agreement between the organist and singers, Nivers groups the tones in order to consolidate all of the reciting notes on either A or B♭, giving the key signatures the organist would have to use to attain the appropriate reciting note.[35] Nivers's reciting notes, therefore, are more narrowly constricted than Viadana's or Banchieri's and resemble more closely Spanish practice than Italian practice.[36] Nivers's first, fifth, and seventh tones cadence on D, in contrast to Viadana's first, seventh, and eighth, while his tones with cadences on G are the second and third, whereas Viadana combines second, third, and fifth. Like Viadana, Nivers treats the fourth and sixth tones individually with cadences on E and F.

The discussion to this point has concerned the relationship between transposed psalm tones and polyphony in *alternatim* settings. But the same issues pertain to the relationship between plainchant antiphons and polyphonic psalms and Magnificats, whether *alternatim* or through-composed. The question is, were plainchant antiphons transposed, and if so, were they transposed so that the reciting note of the antiphon matched the reciting note of the polyphonic psalm setting, or so that the final of the antiphon matched the final of the polyphonic setting, as in Viadana's *falsibordoni*? Or were both types of transposition used? Furthermore, if an antiphon were transposed, was the transposition 'real', maintaining the melody as the singers would have known it, producing pitch clashes with the polyphonic psalm, or would it have been simply accommodated to the diatonic scale of the polyphonic psalm, thereby altering the interval structure of the antiphon and obscuring its modal character? Nivers's *Dissertation* treats the transposition of the antiphon as well as the psalm tone. He instructs the singers to settle on a comfortable pitch for the notated dominant (tenor or reciting note) of the antiphon and to determine from that the sounding *finalis* of the mode. That *finalis* is then used by the organist to give the choir its pitch and serve as the *finalis* for organ versets in *alternatim* perfor-

---

[34] The Spanish theorist Pablo Nassarre also indicated that the final chord of an organ verset served as the reference pitch for the choir in determining their reciting note. Bernadette Nelson has found that in Spanish versets the root of the final chord is almost invariably the final of the psalm tone '*differentia* or principal *saeculorum* formula'. See Nelson, 'Alternatim Practice', 242–3.

[35] Denis's consolidation of tones results in reciting notes within the compass G–B♭.

[36] Nivers introduces a further complication, however, in order to eliminate chromatic clashes when tones 5 and 7 follow tones 2, 3 and 8. In these instances, tones 5 and 7 are to be sung a step lower, with reciting note G. See Bates, 'From Mode to Key', 32–7.

mance. Thus the relationship between the plainchant antiphon and the polyphonic organ verset is once again in the *finalis*, not in the reciting note, according to Nivers's Parisian practice of the late seventeenth century. Moreover, it seems evident from Nivers's discussion of key signatures and his examples that he expected the chants to be sung in 'real' rather than diatonic transpositions.[37] With 'real' transpositions of antiphons following organ versets with the same *finalis*, there would be no pitch clashes between antiphons and versets. This result contrasts with the pitch clashes between psalm tones and *falsibordoni* verses in Viadana's settings because the latter fix a single key to serve for three different tones.

The evidence adduced above suggests that different approaches to the adjustments required to match plainchant psalm tones and antiphons with polyphonic organ versets or *falsibordoni* settings were used in different circumstances. Banchieri and Severi bear witness to pitch clashes between chant and polyphonic verses, but Spanish theorists testify to the consolidation of separate tones in a single diatonic scale. Nivers, focusing like the Spanish on a very narrow range of reciting notes, transposes the tones to a wide variety of keys.[38] It is even possible that at any given time in any given location, any of these practices might have been used.[39] The state of our knowledge is insufficient at this point to claim a particular practice for a particular location at a particular time. Indeed, musicians of the seventeenth century may have been just as inconsistent and uncertain as we are in resolving such issues. Jean Denis lamented in 1650:

I have not encountered an author who has written a study of the modes that are sung in the church (and that the organist ought to know), who has been able to clarify the matter of their range for those who wish to learn. . . . It is indeed difficult to write about a science upon which no one else has yet written, concerning which all those who practice it have little certainty, and wherein even in conferring with the most learned, one will find differences of opinion.[40]

The problem, in relation to Monteverdi's Vespers, is further complicated by liturgical matters. Indeed, not a single Marian feast has a set of antiphons that modally matches Monteverdi's psalm and Magnificat tones. Many have argued that Monteverdi's motets in the 1610 print provide the solution to this problem (see the discussion of this issue in Chapter 1). However, if the practice at St Mark's, whereby the antiphon substitute was performed after the psalm but the psalm was still preceded by its plainchant antiphon, was widespread, the problem of matching plainchant antiphons to Monteverdi's psalms still prevails

---

[37] Howell, 'French Baroque Organ Music', 109.

[38] See the tables of matching ten different keys with the eight tones in Howell, 'French Baroque Organ Music', 113.

[39] In 1555, the Spanish theorist Juan Bermudo observed that 'every church had its own way of intoning the psalms and its own distinct chant' ('Cada yglesia tenga su modo en entornar los psalmos, y su canto distincto'). Quoted in Nelson, 'Alternatim Practice', 255 n. 14.

[40] *Traité*, 25–6, trans. in Howell, 'French Baroque Organ Music', 113.

(see the discussion below).[41] Moreover, Monteverdi provided no motet or instrumental piece to serve as an antiphon substitute for the Magnificat. If a seventeenth-century *maestro di cappella* had employed plainchant antiphons in a performance of Monteverdi's Vespers, he, like a modern conductor wishing to use plainchant antiphons, would have had not only to consider whether or not to transpose an antiphon and in what manner ('real' or 'tonal'), but also, perhaps, to make liturgical compromises. This places the director in the position of choosing musical and/or liturgical compromises according to one of two sets of criteria: (1) the maintenance of liturgical propriety, forcing musical compromises, or (2) the maintenance of tonal identity between psalm or Magnificat and antiphon, forcing liturgical compromises. A third option, of course, is compromising both musically and liturgically.

If the *maestro di cappella* were to maintain liturgical propriety, that is, use those plainchant antiphons liturgically appropriate to the Marian feast being celebrated, there might have been three alternatives. The first would have been to perform the antiphons (transposed in the modern sense) so that their reciting notes matched the initial reciting notes of Monteverdi's psalms and Magnificats (Monteverdi transposes the plainchant in the course of the Magnificats and some of the psalms). However, transposition of the plainchant antiphons to accommodate the psalms and Magnificats in many cases would have forced one or the other of two musical compromises: (1) 'real' (exact) transposition resulting in the introduction of several sharps or flats in the antiphon, thereby producing chromatic pitch clashes between the antiphon and the psalm or Magnificat; (2) 'tonal' transposition requiring alterations in the sequence of tones and semitones in the antiphon, altering its modal character, in order to retain the same diatonic pitches as in the psalm or Magnificat. The evidence of the Italian sources cited above suggests 'real' transposition.

The second alternative would have been to perform the antiphons (transposed in the modern sense) so that their finals matched the finals (defined as the root of the final chord) of Monteverdi's psalms and Magnificats. As with matching of reciting notes, 'real' transposition may create chromatic pitch clashes between notes in the antiphon and notes in the polyphonic psalm or Magnificat setting, while 'tonal' transposition would alter the intervallic character of the mode.

The third alternative would have been to perform the plainchant antiphons and the psalms as notated, either at a comfortable pitch level or in modern fixed-pitch terms, ignoring the tonal differences between the antiphons and the psalms. This is the simplest solution, but it ignores the tradition of tonal relationships between antiphons and psalms, which apparently had some residual

---

[41] See Ch. 1 for a discussion of recent recordings that provide plainchant antiphons for each psalm and the Magnificat. See also App. D.

force in the early seventeenth century, since Magnificats were still sometimes published in all eight tones and the tones of polyphonic psalms were still sometimes identified by composers. This solution also ignores the evidence of numerous theoretical treatises, like those of Banchieri, Diruta, Denis, Nivers, and others, that discuss the tonal relationship between plainchant and organ versets.

The only practical evidence I know of pertaining to these three choices regarding polyphonic antiphons stems from a 1619 publication of psalms, motets, hymns, and Magnificats by Paolo Agostini, in which multiple settings of vesper psalms and Magnificats are each followed by polyphonic settings of the liturgically appropriate antiphons, or by polyphonic motets which likely serve as antiphon substitutes[42] (see Chapter 1 and below for more on antiphon substitutes). In this collection the psalm tones are identified but not the modes of the antiphon settings or the motets. In most instances, the polyphonic antiphon or motet has as a central pitch the reciting note of the psalm or Magnificat with which it is associated, or is in the same tonality (but in either the *mollis* or the *durus* version) as its psalm or Magnificat. In some cases, the melodic shape of the antiphon or motet resembles the psalm tone, even though the two pieces are in different tonalities. In other cases the tonality of the psalm and the antiphon or motet are the same, but there is no other particular melodic relationship between psalm tone and motet or antiphon. And in a few cases, there is no pitch or tonal correlation at all between the antiphon or motet and its psalm or Magnificat.[43]

While it is risky to extrapolate from a single example or from these polyphonic relationships to the relationship between plainchant antiphons and polyphonic psalms, the Agostini print at least suggests a continuing interest in matching the antiphons with psalms in terms of reciting note or tonality, but not slavishly. Agostini, rather, has taken a variety of approaches to the relationship between antiphon or motet and its psalm, but has not considered a reciting note or tonal relationship to be imperative. James Armstrong's study of Giovanni Francesco Anerio's *Antiphonae* of 1613 (A1104) also suggests flexibility in the tonal relationship between polyphonic antiphons and psalms, aside from flexibility in the substitution of antiphon texts.[44] Where substitutions were

---

[42] *Salmi della Madonna Magnificat a 3. voci. Hinno Ave Maris Stella, Antifone A una, 2. & 3. voci. Et Motetti Tutti Concertati . . . Libro Primo* (Rome: Luca Antonio Soldi, 1619).

[43] See the list of contents of this print in Ch. 4. The motet *Cantate Domino*, in G *cantus durus*, follows the psalm *Laetatus sum, quarto tono*, harmonized principally in A minor with final cadence on E major, as is typical of the fourth tone. Similarly, *Nisi Dominus, secondo tono*, at the transposed level of G *cantus mollis*, is followed by *Antifona quarta, Iam hiems transijt*, in C *cantus durus* with an opening motif reminiscent of either the third tone or the eighth tone *initium*. The second *Magnificat, secondo tono*, again in G *cantus mollis*, is succeeded by the motet *Ab initio* in C *cantus durus*, which is a setting of the chapter from Second Vespers of the Common of the BVM (also used for the feasts of the Visitation and Nativity of the BVM). See also James Foster Armstrong, 'The *Antiphonae, seu sacrae cantiones* (1613) of Giovanni Francesco Anerio: A Liturgical Study', *Analecta musicologica*, 14 (1974), 148.

[44] Ibid. 89–150.

made for antiphons, whether in the form of polyphonic motets, organ music, or other instrumental music, they seem generally to have come after the psalm (see the discussion below). That this may not always have been the case is revealed by an unusual approach to psalm antiphons described in a note to the reader in the *Motecta quinque tantum vocibus . . . Liber secundus* by Pietro Maria Marsolo from 1614 (M750). In his instructions, Marsolo describes both a common practice and his own approach to psalm antiphons:

> In metropolitan, cathedral, and collegiate [churches] it is customary either before or after each vesper psalm to sing the antiphon that goes with that psalm with one or more voices with organ or another instrument. Because of this the vespers becomes long, nor does it leave room for any instrument [instrumental composition]. To avoid such inconvenience, the author has included in each motet all five psalm antiphons; thus one sings the motet after the last psalm, which satisfies the office, the vesper [service] is less tedious, and if one desires to play an instrument, there is enough room for it.[45]

On the basis of the evidence from the theorists discussed above, the Agostini print, and Anerio's *Antiphonae*, a modern director might choose to transpose some antiphons to match the psalms or Magnificat and not transpose others. Such a mixed approach would allow for transposition of those antiphons that would require no or few alterations in interval structure to bring their reciting notes or finals to the same level as in the psalm or Magnificat. Those antiphons whose transposition would require significant changes in interval structure ('tonal' transposition) or would result in numerous chromatic pitches foreign to the note of the psalm or Magnificat ('real' transposition) could be left untransposed. Such an approach may be unsystematic, but it would be in keeping with the variety of methods we have discovered in the seventeenth century itself as well as with the eminently practical and non-doctrinaire nature of seventeenth-century musicians in dealing with liturgical and musical matters.

If liturgical propriety was not a priority, two other solutions were possible in order to avoid the issue of transposition of antiphons. First, the *maestro di cappella* may have selected a set of plainchant Marian antiphons that tonally matched Monteverdi's psalms. These antiphons would have been appropriate for Marian worship, but would not have coincided with the distribution of specific antiphons among the various Marian feasts in the breviary.[46] James Armstrong's

---

[45] Marsolo gives the instructions in both Latin and Italian. The Italian version is as follows: 'Nelle Metropolitane, Catedrali, & Colleggiate si suole dopò ciaschedun Salmo del Vespro, ò innanti cantare da una ò piu voci nell'Organo ò altro instrumento L'Antifona che corre a tal Salmo, per la qual cosa il Vespro diviene longo, ne si da loco a instromento alcuno, onde acciò non succeda tale inconveniente, hà l'Autore in ciascheduno Motetto abbracciate tutte le cinque antifone di Salmi, qual Motetto si cantarà dopò l'ultimo salmo, che così si sodisfara all'officio, il Vespro sarà meno tedioso, & se alcuno instromento vorra sonare hara loco commodamente'.

[46] This is the procedure followed by Denis Stevens in his edition of the response, psalms, hymn, and Magnificat *a 7* from Monteverdi's 1610 print (Stevens omits the *sacri concentus* as liturgically inappropriate). See *Claudio Monteverdi: Vespers*, ed. Stevens (London: Novello, 1961). Gottfried Wolters also matched the modes of most of his suggested antiphons with Monteverdi's psalms in his edition, *Claudio Monteverdi: Vesperae beatae Mariae virginis* (Wolfenbüttel: Möseler Verlag, 1966).

study of Anerio's *Antiphonae* of 1613 supports such a practice.[47] Armstrong found many discrepancies between the texts of Anerio's antiphon sets for particular feasts and those specified in contemporaneous breviaries. In numerous instances Anerio quite freely shifted antiphons from one position in the psalm *cursus* of a feast to another, or shifted antiphons from one feast to another. Even though Anerio's antiphons are polyphonic, his freedom in the use of texts must have been based on practices originating in plainchant offices.

As a second alternative, plainchant antiphons for the psalms and Magnificat may sometimes have been replaced by motets or instrumental pieces as antiphon substitutes (the celebrant would likely still have spoken the appropriate liturgical text *sotto voce*). In Monteverdi's Vespers, this meant performing the *sacri concentus* that follow each psalm in the order in which they appear in the original print. A plainchant antiphon or antiphon substitute would still have to have been provided from another source for Monteverdi's Magnificat. From the discussion in Chapter 1, it is apparent that motets and instrumental compositions were performed with some frequency between psalms in vesper services in the sixteenth and seventeenth centuries, evidently serving as substitutes for the plainchant antiphons officially sanctioned by the breviary. It has also been demonstrated that substitutions were common for certain sections of the mass.[48] The large numbers of motets published in the second half of the sixteenth century and throughout the seventeenth may bear witness not only to the growth in non-liturgical devotions, but also to widespread use of both liturgical substitutes and interpolations in the office and the mass. A large portion of the instrumental music published in the seventeenth century may have served a similar purpose.[49]

---

[47] 'The *Antiphonae, seu sacrae cantiones*'. Armstrong has demonstrated that while some of Anerio's polyphonic antiphon settings reflect the liturgically appropriate texts in the correct order, many others rearrange the order within a given feast-day, interchange antiphons between first and second vespers, borrow antiphons from other offices or feasts, alter or expand canonical antiphon texts, or utilize texts outside the antiphon repertoire. According to Armstrong, 'Anerio's collection, in its arrangement and in its selection of texts, suggests a much broader interpretation of the term antiphon than has previously been offered in the study of seventeenth-century Vesper music. It is no longer possible to dismiss settings of texts (like those in Monteverdi's 1610 Vespers) that do not conform to the antiphons of the Roman Breviary. Often the Breviary is merely a point of departure for the composer, who alters the antiphons or adds additional text. The order of the antiphons may be changed, and antiphons transposed from another office or even another feast. Short texts may be replaced by longer texts, particularly from Matins and Lauds' (p. 130). Armstrong also notes in those Anerio antiphons that are based on a plainchant a frequent lack of tonal agreement between the mode of the chant and the harmonization of the cantus firmus. Moreover, Agostini's association of polyphonic antiphons with psalms in his 1619 print does not always demonstrate a tonal relationship (pp. 147–8).

[48] For studies that cite contemporaneous references to motets and instrumental compositions as insertions or substitutions in the liturgy see Chapter 1, notes 59–65 and Thomas Noel O'Regan, 'Sacred Polychoral Music in Rome 1575–1621' (D.Phil. dissertation, University of Oxford, 1988), i. 85, 87.

[49] Since only the celebrant can be responsible for the official liturgy, he would likely have spoken the proper antiphon text *sotto voce* during an instrumental interpolation. The same may well have been the case during the performance of a motet: the celebrant would have spoken the liturgically correct antiphon, and the motet could be viewed as a gloss on the liturgical text. See Bonta, 'Liturgical Problems', 103–6.

Whether these substitutes might also have led to dropping plainchant antiphons before psalms is unclear. James Moore, in his study of vespers at St Mark's, cites instructions from the *Caeremoniale Episcoporum* of Clement VIII (1600) and a *Manuale Sacrarum Caeremoniarum, iuxta Ritum S. Romanae Ecclesiae* (1689) indicating that where organ music substituted for the antiphon after the psalm, the antiphon was still supposed to be sung before the psalm.[50] Banchieri's instructions for playing organ music immediately after psalms or an instrumental piece immediately after the Magnificat do not necessarily imply omitting the plainchant antiphon before the psalm or Magnificat.[51] Whether the instructions of the *Caeremoniale* were followed in actual practice is uncertain, however. If they were, then antiphon substitutes did not actually solve the problem of modal match between antiphons and polyphonic psalm settings as Bonta suggests, since the issue would still survive in the relationship between the antiphon before the psalm and the tone of the psalm, as discussed above. Whatever the case, it cannot be stressed sufficiently that despite attempts by the Church to impose uniform liturgies after the Council of Trent, all kinds of unofficial local practices continued and developed throughout Italy (sometimes tolerated and sometimes denounced), so that it is impossible to state just how any particular vesper service would have been performed. In fact, the variety of alterations and interpolations to the official liturgy in the late sixteenth century and throughout the seventeenth century almost certainly indicates an undoctrinaire approach to resolving the issues raised above. It is quite possible that all of the possible solutions I have suggested above were followed at one time or another in one situation or another. A modern choir director interested in performing Monteverdi's Vespers has several options, and, like his or her counterpart in the early *Seicento*, may choose a solution according to aesthetic, liturgical, theoretical, or practical priorities.

[50] See Moore, *Vespers at St Mark's*, 176; id., 'The Liturgical Use of the Organ in Seventeenth-Century Italy. New Documents, New Hypotheses', in Alexander Silbiger, ed., *Frescobaldi Studies* (Durham, NC: Duke University Press, 1987), 357–9.

[51] *L'organo suonarino* (1611), 45, quoted in David Blazey, 'A Liturgical Role for Monteverdi's *Sonata sopra Sancta Maria*', *Early Music*, 18 (1989), 182 n. 19. See also the discussion of Banchieri's instructions in Ch. 1 above.

3

A Brief History of Vespers in the
Sixteenth Century

THE early history of polyphonic music for vespers reaches back before 1430, to the time of Dunstable, Dufay, and Binchois. The surviving vesper music of the entire fifteenth century has been studied in a dissertation by Masakata Kanazawa,[1] but need not detain us here. Suffice it to summarize Kanazawa's findings very briefly in noting that by the middle of the fifteenth century, some of the best-known manuscripts, scattered now throughout Europe and England, included a sizeable repertoire of Magnificat and hymn settings, as well as a few antiphons and the very first, rare settings of psalm texts, almost always the fifth psalm for Sunday vespers, *In exitu Israel*. Thus, considerable quantities of polyphonic settings of items for the liturgy of vespers began to appear in the generation of Dunstable and during the early part of the careers of Dufay and Binchois, with all three of these composers, but especially Dufay, contributing significantly to the repertoire.[2] Manuscripts from the third quarter of the century testify to the increasing emphasis placed on vesper music not only by Dufay and Binchois, but also by numerous anonymous composers of their generation. Dunstable, too, continues to be represented posthumously in several of these manuscripts. During this period we still find a concentration on hymns, Magnificats, and, to a lesser extent, antiphons. Psalm settings remain rare.

It is only in the last quarter of the fifteenth century that we begin to encounter with some frequency settings of psalms alongside the Magnificats, hymns, and antiphons. These early polyphonic psalms are uncomplicated pieces, consisting of simple chordal harmonization of the psalm tone. The psalms are still small in number in most manuscripts, but there are a few important exceptions. The complete *cursus* of five psalms for all seven days of the week

---

[1] 'Polyphonic Music for Vespers during the Fifteenth Century' (Ph.D. dissertation, Harvard University, 1966). See also id., 'Two Vesper Repertories from Verona, *ca.* 1500', *Rivista italiana di musicologia*, 10 (1975), 154–79.

[2] Documentary evidence of polyphonic vesper psalms sung in Santa Maria del Fiore in Florence during the early part of the 15th century has been presented in Frank A. D'Accone, 'Music and Musicians at Santa Maria del Fiore in the Early Quattrocento', *Scritti in onore di Luigi Ronga* (Milan: Ricciardi, 1973), 99–126.

is found in a pair of large choirbooks at Modena, dating from around 1480.[3] Each choirbook contains alternate verses, illustrating that antiphonal singing between choirs, as has been observed many times before, by no means origi-nated in Venice.[4]

Another important manuscript at Verona from near the end of the century preserves a sizeable quantity of psalms, providing settings for feasts of Mary and other virgin saints, for many male saints from the Common and the Proper, and for many feasts from the Proper of the Time.[5] Thus, by the end of the fifteenth century, while the mass and motet dominated sacred composition, there was already beginning to emerge a repertoire of music for the vesper service, some of it written by the most prominent composers of the day.

It is also from the last quarter of the fifteenth century that we have our first evidence of another approach to polyphonic psalm setting in Spain, Portugal, and Italy, the *falsobordone*.[6] *Falsibordoni* consisted of simple chordal harmoniza-tions of the psalm tone in four parts, using root-position triads with the chant often in the top voice. *Falsibordoni* were untexted and frequently appeared in all eight of the psalm tones, sometimes also including the *tonus peregrinus* for the psalm *In exitu Israel*. With such a set of *falsibordoni* a choir could sing whatever psalm text was required for a particular vesper service in the appropriate tone,

---

[3] Kanazawa, 'Polyphonic Music for Vespers', chs. 4–8. See also David E. Crawford, 'Vespers Polyphony at Modena's Cathedral in the First Half of the Sixteenth Century' (Ph.D. dissertation, University of Illinois, 1967); Manfred F. Bukofzer, 'The Beginnings of Choral Polyphony', in *Studies in Medieval and Renaissance Music* (New York: W. W. Norton & Company, 1950), 181–6; Konrad Ruhland, 'Der mehrstimmige Psalmvortrag im 15. und 16. Jahrhundert. Studien zur Psalmodie auf der Grundlage von Faburdon, Fauxbourdon und Falsobordone' (Ph.D. dissertation, University of Munich, 1978). The choirbooks in question are Modena, Biblioteca Estense MSS Alpha M.1, 11–12 (cod. lat. 454–455). These choirbooks also contain a small number of hymns and Magnificats.

[4] See Bukofzer, 'The Beginnings of Choral Polyphony'; Giovanni D'Alessi, 'Precursors of Adriano Willaert in the Practice of *coro spezzato*', *Journal of the American Musicological Society*, 5 (1952), 187–210; Denis Arnold, 'The Significance of "Cori spezzati"', *Music & Letters*, 40 (1959), 4–14; Joan Long, 'The Motets, Psalms and Hymns of Adrian Willaert—A Liturgico-Musical Study' (Ph.D. dissertation, Columbia University, 1971); Victor Ravizza, 'Formprobleme des frühen Coro spezzato', *International Musicological Society, Report of the Eleventh Congress, Copenhagen 1972* (Copenhagen: Wilhelm Hansen, 1974), 604–11; id., 'Frühe Doppelchörigkeit in Bergamo', *Die Musikforschung*, 25 (1972), 127–42; Anthony F. Carver, 'The Psalms of Willaert and his North Italian Contemporaries', *Acta musicologica*, 47 (1975), 270–83; Denis Arnold, 'Cori spezzati', in *The New Grove Dictionary of Music and Musicians*, ed. Stanley Sadie (London: Macmillan Publishers Ltd., 1980), iv. 776; Lewis Lockwood and Jessie Ann Owens, 'Willaert, Adrian', in *The New Grove*, xx. 423–4; Anthony F. Carver, 'The Development of Sacred Polychoral Music to 1580' (Ph.D. dissertation, University of Birmingham, 1980); id., 'Polychoral Music: A Venetian Phenomenon?', *Proceedings of the Royal Musical Association*, 107 (1981–2), 1–24; Gary Spaulding Towne, 'Gaspar de Albertis and Music at Santa Maria Maggiore in Bergamo in the Sixteenth Century' (Ph.D. dissertation, University of California at Santa Barbara, 1985).

[5] Verona, Biblioteca Capitolare, MS 759. This MS also contains a large number of hymns and Magnificats. See Kanazawa, 'Polyphonic Music for Vespers', ch. 8; and id., 'Two Vesper Repertories from Verona'.

[6] For a thorough study of the origins and development of the *falsobordone*, see Murray C. Bradshaw, *The Falsobordone, A Study in Renaissance and Baroque Music* (Musicological Studies and Documents, 34; Stuttgart: American Institute of Musicology/Hänssler-Verlag, 1978). Bradshaw dissociates the *falsobor-done* from the tradition of *fauxbourdon*. See ibid. 21.

that tone being determined by the antiphon for each psalm. *Falsibordoni* thus provided a very simple and useful means of singing polyphony at vespers. Indeed, it is probable that choirs had improvised such chordal polyphony long before any settings were actually composed and notated.

The typical *falsobordone* consisted of unmeasured chords plus a slightly more elaborate cadence for each half of the psalm tone. The chords, like the original reciting note, were merely repeated as many times as necessary to accommodate the number of syllables in each half-verse. By the end of the sixteenth century, the cadences had come to be augmented and elaborated rather strikingly by many composers. In Monteverdi's Vespers, the opening response is nothing more than a *falsobordone* with added instrumental parts and expanded cadences. *Falsibordoni* and their cadential melismas are the main structural feature in Monteverdi's *Dixit Dominus*, and *Laetatus sum* has a brief passage in *falsobordone*.[7] Many other passages in measured chordal recitation are simply slightly more complicated versions in mensural notation of *falsibordoni*.

While no one has yet written a comprehensive survey of vesper music from the first half of the sixteenth century, it is apparent from studies of manuscripts in Modena, Padua, Treviso, Bergamo, and other places that the same traditions which had originated in the fifteenth century continued unabated into the sixteenth.[8] The number of psalms in manuscripts increases, while there is an enduring interest in hymns and Magnificats. Frank A. D'Accone's research in the archives of Santa Maria del Fiore in Florence gives some idea of how polyphony was used there at vespers in the early sixteenth century. One of his documents, dated 26 February 1502, 'lists all the days when vocal polyphony was performed at the Cathedral'.[9] Interestingly, most of the entries are for vespers, where polyphonic performance is indicated for a single psalm, either the first or the last, on the feast-days enumerated. Of particular note is that the mass was sung in polyphony on relatively few occasions, while innumerable feasts required the one polyphonic psalm.

A new stage in the development of the repertoire of polyphonic music for vespers in Italy begins with the first printed books of vesper music, the earliest

---

[7] See the discussions of *Domine ad adjuvandum*, *Dixit Dominus*, and *Laetatus sum* in Ch. 6.

[8] Commentaries on particular repertoires or aspects of vesper music in the first half of the sixteenth century are found in a number of studies. See esp. Carl-Heinz Illing, *Zur Technik der Magnificat-Komposition des 16. Jahrhunderts* (Kieler Beiträge zur Musikwissenschaft, 3; Wolfenbüttel and Berlin: Georg Kallmeyer Verlag, 1936); D'Alessi, 'Precursors'; Crawford, 'Vespers Polyphony'; Ravizza, 'Frühe Doppelchörigkeit'; Winfried Kirsch, *Die Quellen der mehrstimmigen Magnificat- und Te Deum-Vertonungen bis zur Mitte des 16. Jahrhunderts* (Tutzing: Hans Schneider, 1966); Klaus Fischer, *Die Psalmkompositionen in Rom um 1600 (ca. 1570–1630)* (Kölner Beiträge zur Musikforschung, 98; Regensburg: Gustav Bosse Verlag, 1979), 4–27; Anthony M. Cummings, 'Toward an Interpretation of the Sixteenth-Century Motet', *Journal of the American Musicological Society*, 34 (1981), 43–59; and Towne, 'Gaspar de Albertis'.

[9] 'The Musical Chapels at the Florentine Cathedral and Baptistry during the First Half of the 16th Century', *Journal of the American Musicological Society*, 24 (1971), 1–50.

extant examples of which date from 1542.[10] Music printing obviously had a major impact on the performance of music in smaller, less important churches—churches that were not likely to possess or have access to polyphonic music in manuscript form. Before the advent of printed music, smaller and poorer ecclesiastical establishments had probably been confined mostly to the singing of Gregorian chant or simple improvised polyphony. But music printing, whether of masses, motets, vespers, or other offices, would have given smaller churches and poorer monasteries the opportunity to perform more elaborate polyphony. These opportunities may well have stimulated them to alter the size and character of their choirs, to seek better trained choristers, and to obtain choirmasters or organists proficient in the performance of the newly accessible works. But despite the vast expansion of printed music in the second half of the sixteenth century, much vesper music remained in manuscript, especially polychoral music as practised in Rome in the last quarter of the century. The characteristics of this repertoire, gleaned principally from archival sources documenting payments to singers and instrumentalists, have been closely studied by Noel O'Regan and are briefly described in Chapters 1, 4, and 15.

If we compare the quantity of composers of sacred music in Italy whose names we know from the time of Petrucci's first print in 1501 with the number whose names we know from a hundred years later, we not only observe an astonishing increase in quantity, but also see that many of the latter musicians were active in collegiate, parish, or monastic churches less significant than the great cathedral churches, ducal churches, or major pilgrimage centres. The small cities and less prominent churches from which so many publications of the early seventeenth century stem bear witness to the fact that music printing played a major role in expanding the composition and performance of sacred polyphony in a relatively short span of time.

Among the earliest Italian publications were settings of the Magnificat in all eight tones, following the pattern of many earlier Magnificats in manuscripts. The tone of the Magnificat could thus be selected by the singers to match that of the appropriate antiphon for whatever feast was being celebrated (see Chapter 2). The earliest such print of which we have any notice was purportedly one for five voices published by Vincenzo Ruffo in 1539, but Robert Eitner's citation of this collection in Lüneburg, Germany, is followed by a question mark.[11] Whether it ever existed is still an open question, although it seems likely that the citation actually refers to Ruffo's 1559 Magnificats, also not found at Lüneburg.[12]

[10] RISM 1542[9] (M3592) and 1542[11] (W1113). See the more detailed discussion below.

[11] *Biographisch-bibliographisches Quellen-Lexikon* (Leipzig: Breitkopf und Härtel, 1898–1904), vii. 353.

[12] RISM R3052. Lewis Lockwood reports in *The Counter-Reformation and the Masses of Vincenzo Ruffo* (Studi di musica veneta, 2; Venice: Fondazione Giorgio Cini, Universal Edition, 1967), 243 that he was unable to find a 1539 edition of Ruffo Magnificats at Lüneburg, and I have had no luck myself in locating such a print.

Our first surviving Italian prints of music for vespers are two anthologies, published by Scotto in Venice in 1542. One of these contains settings of Magnificats by Morales, Richafort, Jachet of Mantua, Tugdual, and Loiset Pieton.[13] Half of these Magnificats set all twelve verses, while the other half set the even-numbered verses only and are obviously designed for *alternatim* performance, in this case polyphony in alternation with plainchant or with an organ playing harmonized plainchant.

This anthology proved very popular and was reprinted a number of times during the next decade; pieces from it were also published in enlarged German editions. The reprints present a complicated bibliographical problem, since in some of them the complete Magnificat settings were split into settings of odd and even verses, while new settings were also added or substituted for some of the pieces from the 1542 publication. The other 1542 anthology of Scotto's is a collection of hymns by Willaert and other, anonymous, composers, a collection also reprinted later, in 1550.[14]

Like manuscript vesper music of the fifteenth and early sixteenth centuries, published vesper music in the second half of the sixteenth century developed slowly. There survive only two other publications of Magnificats from the decade before 1550, a 1545 set by Morales, reprinting some of those from 1542 and adding a few new ones,[15] and a 1548 set, entitled *Liber secundus Magnificarum*, by Genesius Dominicus de Villena.[16] No trace remains of Villena's *Liber primus Magnificarum*. In 1550 two very well-known composers joined in a publication of polyphonic psalm settings, which included a few pieces by other composers as well. This famous print, by Adrian Willaert and Jachet of Mantua, reissued in 1557, is rather complex.[17] According to the title-page, there are settings of enough vesper psalms to fill the requirements of all the major feasts of the year; the *maestro di cappella* simply had to extract whatever psalms were needed for any feast.[18] There are two separate indexes in the print, one for the Chorus Primus, and the other for the Chorus Secundus. These indexes group the psalms into four categories. The first, *Salmi a versi con le sue risposte ali medesimi numeri*, consists of psalms in which the odd verses are set for the Primus Chorus and the even verses for the Secundus Chorus, that is, in choral antiphony. In these

[13] RISM 1542[9] (M3592). Of eleven Magnificats in this print, five are by Morales. Ed. Higinio Anglés in *Cristóbal de Morales: Opera omnia*, xvi: *Magnificat* (Monumentos de la música española, 17; Barcelona: Consejo Superior de Investigaciones Científicas, 1956).

[14] RISM 1542[11] (W1113) and 1550[3] (W1114).

[15] RISM M3594.

[16] RISM D2115.

[17] RISM 1550[1] and RISM 1557[6]. Ed. Hermann Zenck in *Adriani Willaert opera omnia*, viii (American Institute of Musicology, 1972).

[18] For discussions of this print, see Hermann Zenck, 'Adrian Willaert's "Salmi spezzati"', *Die Musikforschung*, 2 (1949), 97–107; D'Alessi, 'Precursors'; Carver, 'The Psalms of Willaert'; Joan Long, 'The Motets, Psalms and Hymns of Adrian Willaert'; James Armstrong, 'How to Compose a Psalm: Ponzio and Cerone Compared', *Studi musicali*, 7 (1978), 110–15.

settings the odd-numbered verses are ordinarily by one composer and the even-numbered verses by another.

The second grouping consists of *Salmi senza risposte quali sono nel primo choro*, comprising *alternatim* settings in which either odd or even verses are set polyphonically and the alternate verses are to be sung in plainchant or perhaps played on the organ. The third group contains *Salmi spezzadi di M. [Maestro] Adriano*, which are complete settings of all verses for double choir by Adriano himself. Finally, the last group is comparable to the second, consisting of *Salmi senza risposte*, psalms setting only alternate verses, but this time in the Secundus Chorus rather than the first choir.

This collection of Willaert and Jachet illustrates three different methods of psalm composition, methods that would be maintained for another 150 years: (1) the setting of only odd- or even-numbered verses, with alternate verses to be sung in chant or played on the organ; (2) the setting of all verses, but split antiphonally between alternating choirs; and (3) through-composed settings, in this case for *cori spezzati*, but in many other publications for choirs of four or five voices. Even in *cori spezzati* settings the two choirs may overlap.

Not only do the indexes identify compositions by type of setting, but within each of the four categories, the pieces are arranged alphabetically by text incipit, making it easy to find any specific psalm the choirmaster should want. However, the sequence of pieces in the indexes is quite different from the sequence of pieces within the part-books themselves. The succession in the Primus Chorus and Secundus Chorus is as follows, illustrating a different logic from the indexes:

Primus Chorus	Secundus Chorus
Dixit Dominus, Iachet, odd verses	*Dixit Dominus*, Adriano, even verses
Confitebor tibi, Iachet, odd verses	*Confitebor tibi*, Iachet, even verses
Beatus vir, Iachet, odd verses	*Beatus vir*, Adriano, even verses
Beati omnes, Iachet, odd verses	*Beati omnes*, Finot, even verses
Laudate pueri, Iachet, odd verses	*Laudate pueri*, Iachet, even verses
In exitu Israel, Iachet, odd verses	*In exitu Israel*, Adriano, even verses
Laudate Dominum, Iachet, odd verses	*Laudate Dominum*, Adriano, even verses
Dixit Dominus, Iachet, odd verses	*Dixit Dominus*, Finot, even verses
	De profundis, Iachet, odd verses
Laudate pueri, Iachet, odd verses	*Laudate pueri*, Iachet, even verses
Laetatus sum, Iachet, odd verses	*Laetatus sum*, Adriano, even verses
Nisi Dominus, Iachet, odd verses	*Nisi Dominus*, Adriano, even verses
Lauda Ierusalem, Iachet, odd verses	
	Laudate pueri, Iachet, odd verses
Memento, Iachet, odd verses	*Memento*, [anonymous], even verses
Credidi, Iachet, odd verses	*Laetatus sum*, M.Ian, odd verses
In convertendo, Iachet, odd verses	*Nisi Dominus*, M.Ian, odd verses

Laudate pueri, Adriano, *spezzadi*	*Laudate pueri*, Adriano, *spezzadi*
Confitebor tibi, Adriano, *spezzadi*	*Confitebor tibi*, Adriano, *spezzadi*
Lauda Ierusalem, Adriano, *spezzadi*	*Lauda Ierusalem*, Adriano, *spezzadi*
	Dixit Dominus, Iachet, odd verses
Domine probasti me, Scaffen, odd verses	*Confitebor tibi*, Iachet, odd verses
	Beatus vir, Iachet, odd verses
De profundis, Adriano, *spezzadi*	*De profundis*, Adriano, *spezzadi*
Memento, Adriano, *spezzadi*	*Memento*, Adriano, *spezzadi*
Domine probasti me, Adriano, *spezzadi*	*Domine probasti me*, Adriano, *spezzadi*
Credidi, Adriano, *spezzadi*	*Credidi*, Adriano, *spezzadi*
In convertendo, Adriano, *spezzadi*	*In convertendo*, Adriano, *spezzadi*

This ordering of pieces in the part-books is not completely systematic, but it does illustrate an interest in grouping psalms according to their patterns of usage (*cursus*) for various categories of feasts (see Appendix A for the principal and subsidiary vesper psalm *cursus* and the feasts they serve).[19] I have separated various groups with spaces to help clarify the organization. The first three psalms, *Dixit*, *Confitebor*, and *Beatus vir*, comprise the opening psalms for first and/or second vespers on a large number of feasts, such as those for male saints from the Temporale and the Common, Sundays (including major feasts, such as Easter, that occur on Sunday), Christmas, Epiphany, Pentecost, feasts of angels and archangels, Dedication of a Church, SS Agnes and Agatha, and others (see Appendix A).

Beati omnes is simply inserted into the series at this point. It is a far less useful psalm, constituting the fourth psalm on Corpus Christi and at second vespers for the feast of the Sacred Heart. After *Beati* the contents continue with three psalms, *Laudate pueri*, *In exitu*, and *Laudate Dominum*, from which the psalm cycle of many of the feasts listed in the paragraph above can be completed (see Appendix A): Sundays require *Laudate pueri* and *In exitu*; the 'male *cursus*' from the Temporale and the Common concludes with *Laudate pueri* and *Laudate Dominum*. The Dedication of a Church and second vespers for SS Agnes and Agatha and a few 'male' feasts require *Laudate pueri* as the fourth psalm, but conclude with other, separate psalms.

The next group of psalms listed under Primus Chorus comprises the *cursus* for all Marian feasts, feasts of other virgin saints, and the feast of the Circumcision (the 'female *cursus*'). These are, of course, the five psalms set by Monteverdi in 1610. In this group, all except the final psalm have corresponding *risposte* in the Secundus Chorus. But the cycle is interrupted after the first

[19] It is noteworthy that Willaert and Jachet do not include the psalms *Lauda anima mea* and *Laudate Dominum quoniam bonus est*, which, together with *Laudate pueri*, *Laudate Dominum omnes gentes* and *Lauda Jerusalem*, comprise the *Vespero delli Cinque Laudate*, specific to the rite of St Mark's. This 1550 print is obviously addressed to the Roman rite, seeking wide circulation, rather than to the liturgy of Willaert's home church. See James H. Moore, 'The *Vespero delli Cinque Laudate* and the Role of *salmi spezzati* at St Mark's', *Journal of the American Musicological Society*, 34 (1981), 249–78.

psalm in the Secundus Chorus by *De profundis*, which serves as the fourth psalm for second vespers at Christmas and within the octave, as well as the office of the dead. It serves as the fifth psalm for first vespers on the feast of the Sacred Heart.

Following the 'female *cursus*', the Primus Chorus has three psalms, *Memento*, *Credidi*, and *In convertendo*, which combine with psalms already given to complete various cycles. *Memento* is the fifth psalm for several feasts from the Proper of the Time that begin with *Dixit*, *Confitebor*, and *Beatus vir*. *Credidi* also serves the same function, but in addition is used as the third psalm for second vespers in several feasts for male saints and at Corpus Christi (see Appendix A). Parallel to this group in the Secundus Chorus are three additional psalms for the 'female *cursus*', *Laudate pueri*, *Laetatus sum*, and *Nisi Dominus*, interrupted by the even verses of *Memento*, corresponding to the odd verses in the Primus Chorus.

The next group consists of the first three *spezzadi* psalms of Willaert, *Laudate pueri*, *Confitebor*, and *Lauda Ierusalem*, which follow no particular sequence at all, and are employed in a large number of feasts. All three psalms appear in the cycles for the Dedication of a Church and for second vespers on the feasts of SS Agatha and Agnes, but *Confitebor* is the second psalm in this cycle, while *Laudate pueri* and *Lauda Ierusalem* are the fourth and fifth respectively.

The next set of psalms in the Secundus Chorus constitutes the Christmas cycle. The last two of these are *spezzadi* psalms by Willaert, shared with the Primus Chorus. In the meantime, the Primus Chorus has had a setting of the odd verses only of *Domine probasti me* by Henricus Scaffen. This serves as the final psalm in a less frequently used *cursus* for male saints (see Appendix A). As such, it complements *Credidi* and *In convertendo*, the third and fourth psalms in this *cursus*, which appear earlier just before the first three *spezzadi* psalms of Willaert. Perhaps the printer, Gardane, should have positioned *Domine probasti me* directly after *In convertendo*. The association of these three psalms, though in reverse order, recurs in the last group, which consists of the remaining *spezzadi* psalms of Willaert.

Although this ordering of the psalms in the part-books cannot be explained in every detail, it nevertheless appears that the pieces have in large measure been arranged in convenient sequences for a *maestro di cappella* and singers who wished to perform all five psalms in polyphony during a given service. The various cycles or partial cycles allow for the performance of many full *cursus* with a minimum of leafing back and forth through the part-books. In other words, the publisher has taken pains to make it as convenient as he could for performers to sing all five psalms in polyphony, suggesting that by mid-century, this had become a frequent practice, in contrast to the documentary evidence from Florence early in the century.

This collection is also indicative of an important new direction in Italian vesper polyphony, that is, the emphasis on psalms rather than hymns and Magnificats. The user of Willaert's and Jachet's 1550 print had available to him only psalms, and if he wished to perform the vesper hymn and/or the Magnificat in polyphony, he would have had to find them in other sources.

While the decade 1540–9 saw only Magnificat and hymn publications, many prints from the period 1550–9 emphasize psalms. This is illustrated by *Il primo libro di Salmi* of 1555 by Dominique Phinot, also published in Venice by Scotto[20] and reprinted by Gardano in 1563.[21] Although the title-page contains the phrase *con la gionta di dui Magnificat*, there are actually three Magnificats listed in the index:

Vespro Primo		*Vespro terzo della Madonna*	
Dixit dominus domino meo	1	*Dixit dominus domino meo*	1
Confitebor tibi domine	2	*Laudate pueri dominum*	5
Beatus vir qui timet dominum	4	*Letatus sum in his que dicta sunt*	14
Laudate pueri dominum	5	*Nisi dominus edificaverit domum*	16
Laudate dominum omnes gentes	7	*Lauda Hierusalem dominum*	17
Vespro secondo		*Tempore quadragesime et adventus*	
Dixit dominus domino meo	8	*Anima mea dominum Octavi toni*	18
Confitebor tibi domine	9	*Aliis temporibus*	
Beatus vir qui timet dominum	11	*Et exultavit Primi toni*	19
Laudate pueri dominum	12	*Et exultavit Quarti toni*	20
Laudate dominum omnes gentes	14		

This index has a different arrangement from the index of the Willaert and Jachet collection. The psalms are grouped into three sets of five, the first two each comprising the 'male *cursus*'. The third group of psalms, labelled *Vespro terzo della Madonna*, contains the 'female *cursus*'.[22] Last in the index come the three Magnificats, the first setting odd verses and indicated as appropriate for Lent and for Advent, while the two settings for even verses only are suitable for all other times of the year. Once again the actual contents of the collection differ somewhat from the index. In this case, the psalms *Dixit Dominus* and *Laudate pueri* for the Madonna are simply to be drawn from the *Vespro Primo* group, since there are no separate settings of these psalms for the Madonna, as can be seen from the page references in the index. These eight different psalms, therefore, while not covering the entire liturgical year, could still prove quite useful to any choirmaster for a large number of important feasts.

This collection by Phinot is the first to limit its contents to psalm cycles for only the most common feast-days. The final psalm for Sunday vespers, *In exitu*

---

[20] RISM P2022.

[21] RISM P2023.

[22] Stephen Bonta has coined the term 'Regular' to refer to those liturgical items that fall between the Ordinary and the Proper, such as groups of vesper psalms that remain the same for all feasts of a certain category, but do not serve all feasts throughout the year. See Bonta, 'Liturgical Problems', 90.

Israel, is missing, but *Laudate Dominum* seems often to have served as an unofficial substitute for *In exitu* at Sunday vespers. This kind of limitation is significant, for Phinot's print has a different purpose from Willaert's and Jachet's. Whereas the latter publication furnishes multiple settings of all the psalms one would need for major feasts (to be selected by the user according to the demands of the day and the number of psalms he wanted to sing in polyphony), Phinot presents the choirmaster with the core of three integral vesper services. The only major musical portions he has not included are the response, the hymn, and the six antiphons, all of which may well have been sung in plainchant. This kind of collection not only is very convenient for the *maestro di cappella*, but also illustrates the growing interest in vesper celebrations that were predominantly polyphonic, making more and more of the vesper service a musical concert of polyphony.

Providing even more office polyphony is a complex collection by Willaert, likewise from 1555, containing two sets of psalms, serving both Christmas vespers and the 'female *cursus*', together with a hymn, two *alternatim* Magnificat settings, and even a few antiphons.[23] In addition, this collection contains psalms, hymns, antiphons, versicles, and the canticle for compline. In this print we have a single composer providing practically entire polyphonic services for specific vesper feasts as well as for compline:

INDEX PSALMORUM

Vespro Primo		*Benedicamus in lande* [sic] *Iesu*	18
In Nativitate Domini, Ad vesperas		*Ad completorium, Psalmi, Antiphone*	
Psalmi consueti cum suis Antiphonis.		*cum suo Hymno, & versiculis.*	
Dixit dominus domino meo	I	*Cum invocarem exaudivit me deus*	9
Confitebor tibi domine	I	*In te domine speravi non confundar*	10
Beatus vir qui timet dominum	2	*Qui habitat in adiutorio altissimi*	11
De profundis clamavi ad te domine	3	*Ecce nunc benedicite dominum*	12
Memento domine David	4	*Antiphona, Miserere mihi domine*	13
Antiphone. Tecum principium in		*Hymnus*	
die virtutis tue cum reliquis.	15	*Procul recedant somnia & noctium*	13
Hymnus, Tu lumen tu splendor	17	*Versiculi, In manus tuas domine*	13
Ad magnificat Antiphona		*Nunc dimittis servum tuum*	14
Hodie Christus natus est	17	*Antiphona, Salva nos domine*	14
Benedicamus domino	18	*Regina celi letare alleluia*	14
Vespro secondo della Madonna		*Hymnus, Amatorem paupertatis*	18
Dixit dominus domino meo	I	*Hymnus, Respice clemens*	18
Laudate pueri dominum	6	*Tempore Quadragesime, & Adventus*	
Letatus sum in his que dicta sunt mihi	7	*Anima mea dominum Sexti Toni*	19
Nisi dominus edificaverit domum	7		

---

[23] RISM W1123. Repr. 1565 and 1571: RISM W1124 and W1125. See the discussion of this collection in Armstrong, 'How to Compose a Psalm', 118–20.

		Alijs temporibus	
Lauda Ierusalem dominum	8	*Et exultavit spiritus Sexti Toni*	20
Hymnus, Sumens illud ave	15	*FINIS*	

The number of vesper publications from the decade 1550–9 is still rather small; there survive only twelve. Six of these are principally psalm collections, five are Magnificats, and one consists of hymns. Three of these are reprints.[24]

In the next decade we find the number of extant publications containing vesper music increasing to eighteen.[25] Greater variety enters the picture along with the greater numbers. There are collections consisting solely of hymns for the entire liturgical year; there are more collections of Magnificats only; there are collections of psalms with one or more Magnificats added; and there is a 1561 reprint of Willaert's 1555 publication, with music for vespers and compline.[26] One major collection from this period even contains some motets, and another is a publication of motets with one vesper psalm included.[27]

A new kind of print by Simone Boyleau, issued in Milan in 1566, contains not only Magnificats in all eight tones, but also *falsibordoni* in the eight tones as well as the *tonus mixtus* (*tonus peregrinus*) used for the Sunday vesper psalm *In exitu*.[28] This collection provides elaborate versions of the Magnificat, but simple chordal settings for the psalms. Since the *falsibordoni* are untexted, Boyleau's print could serve for vespers for any feast imaginable.

The most unusual print of this decade is the 1565 collection of Diego Ortiz from Toledo, published by Gardano in Venice.[29] Ortiz was *maestro di cappella* at the Neapolitan court, which was ruled by the Spanish. This large publication, in choirbook format, contains an extensive selection of hymns, a series of eight *alternatim* Magnificats, one in each tone (some setting odd verses and some even), the five vesper psalms *Dixit Dominus*, *Confitebor tibi*, *Beatus vir*, *Laudate pueri*, and *Laudate Dominum* (for many feasts of male saints), a polyphonic compline service with alternative versicles of the *Benedictus*, and a series of motets, consisting of the four seasonal Marian antiphons, other motets, and, at the end, a setting of the *Te Deum*. While the music of this print serves many functions, its use for vespers, confined to those feasts of male saints requiring the 'male *cursus*', is more limited than is the case with Phinot's and Willaert's collections.

---

[24] RISM 1550¹, 1550³, 1554¹⁷, 1557⁶, F642, K441, L2320, M3596, P1655, P2022, R3052, W1123.

[25] RISM A1237, B4186, C3541, I109, J22, K442, K443, K444, M3597 (1562¹), M3598, M3599, O135, P865, P2023, P5222, P5402, and W1124 and Paulo Aretino's *Musica cum quatuor, quinque, ac sex vocibus super hymnos* (1565), not listed in RISM.

[26] RISM W1124.

[27] RISM O135 and P5222.

[28] RISM B4186.

[29] RISM O135. For studies of Ortiz, see Robert James Borrowdale, 'The *Musices liber primus* of Diego Ortiz: Spanish Musician' (Ph.D. dissertation, University of Southern California, 1952); and Paul Gene Strassler, 'Hymns for the Church Year, Magnificats and other Sacred Choral Works of Diego Ortiz' (Ph.D. dissertation, University of North Carolina, 1967).

Publications of vesper music continued to increase slowly during the decade of the 1570s, from which some thirty-six prints survive.[30] Some title-pages now call attention to a collection's adherence to the Tridentine musical reforms through such phrases as *secondo l'ordine del Concilio di Trento*. Adherence to the dicta of Trent hardly required radical reform, since much vesper music was already characterized by mostly homophonic textures and syllabic declamation. The great majority of publications from this decade emphasize psalms, although there are nine collections of Magnificats alone. Two of these prints group sets of five psalms according to the feast or category of feast. Cipriano di Rore and Jachet of Mantua's joint publication of *Salmi a quattro voci*, reprinted in 1570 (the original edition is no longer extant), begins with the psalms for Christmas vespers, as did Willaert's 1555 print, and then continues with the five psalms for Sunday vespers. An additional psalm, *Laudate Dominum*, follows, and its substitution for *In exitu* from the Sunday *cursus* yields the full 'male *cursus*'. The collection closes with two *alternatim* Magnificats and two sets of *falsibordoni*.

Bonifacio Pasquale's *I salmi che si cantano tutto l'anno al vespro* of 1576 also groups six psalms into the Sunday and 'male *cursus*' under the heading *In dominicis diebus* and another five into the 'female *cursus*' under the heading *De beata virgine*. The collection is not limited to these feasts, however, since six more psalms and two Magnificats are added under the rubric *In festivitatibus per annum*.

Another type of collection, represented by Ippolito Camatero's *Salmi corista a otto voci* of 1573, simply provides eight psalms. In this instance, the eight supply the five psalms of the 'male *cursus*', the Sunday psalm *In exitu* (also required for Easter Sunday), and the two additional psalms necessary for Christmas, *De profundis* and *Memento Domine David*. Such a collection is small in scope, less expensive than the more complex publications described above, yet useful for many feasts. The only category of feast for which Camatero's *Salmi* will not serve are Marian feasts and feasts of other female saints. Camatero's is one of those prints that recognize the Council of Trent with the phrase *secondo l'ordine del Concilio di Trento* on the title-page. It is also the first to bear witness to the use of instruments by this time in vesper psalms, presumably doubling the voices, with the descriptive phrase 'convenient for voices, accompanied also by every sort of musical instrument'.[31] While such rubrics are uncommon in psalm collections, they do appear from time to time through the end of the century (see the discussion in Chapter 19). Camatero was of Roman origin, and his print

---

[30] RISM 1570², 1575¹ (A2520), 1576⁷ (P973), A2517, A2526, A2532, B3502, C279, C281, C3421, C3542, C3949, D1323, F3, F87, G576, I110, I114, M186, M266, M680, M682, M1266, M3600, R2737, R3056, R3057, R3059, S1605, S3550, T791, V1421, V1427, W1125, and Z1 and Rodio Rocco, *Psalmi ad vespera dierum festorum . . . quae vulgus falso bordone appellat* (1573), not listed in RISM. I am grateful to Murray Bradshaw for the loan of his film of the *unicum* of the latter print in the cathedral archive in Pesaro.

[31] *Comodi alle voci, accompagnate anco con ogni sorte di instrumenti Musicali.*

may well have been influenced by Roman music of the 1570s, by which time double-choir psalms with instrumental accompaniment had been introduced in the Holy City.[32]

In the 1570s, the addition of motets to vesper collections became a significant factor, as in a print by Orazio Faa, published in Venice in 1573.[33] The table of contents places three motets at the end:

TAVOLA delli Salmi & Motetti

Domine ad adiuvandum me festina
Dixit dominus domino meo
Confitebor tibi domine
Beatus vir qui timet dominum
Laudate pueri dominum
Laudate dominum omnes gentes
Credidi propter quod locutus sum
In convertendo dominus
Letatus sum in his
Nisi dominus edificaverit domum
Lauda hierusalem dominum
De profundis

Magnificat

Et exultavit spiritus meus
Anima mea dominum
Et exultavit spiritus meus   A 6
Benedictus dominus deus israel
Regina celi letare alleluia
Alleluia alleluia
Lumen ad revelationem gentium

Motetti

O quam suavis est dominus   A 8
Hec dies quam fecit dominus
Pater noster qui es in celis   A 6

These motets serve various purposes. *O quam suavis est domine* is the Magnificat antiphon for the feast of Corpus Christi, and *Hec dies quam fecit dominus* is a psalm antiphon for vespers on Easter Sunday. The *Pater noster* can have several different functions, including opening the vesper service or preceding the *Confiteor* in compline. Thus Faa has placed in this print two texts suitable for use in particular vesper services of great solemnity and a third for general use at vespers or compline.

---

[32] See Thomas Noel O'Regan, 'The Performance of Roman Sacred Polychoral Music in the Late Sixteenth and Early Seventeenth Centuries: Evidence from Archival Sources', *Performance Practice Review*, 8 (fall 1995), 107–9.

[33] RISM F3.

There are also some pieces subsumed under the heading 'Magnificat' that serve special purposes.[34] The *Benedictus* is the canticle of Zacharia for lauds, usually found paired with the psalm *Miserere mei Deus* in sixteenth-century collections of music for Holy Week. The *Benedictus* is also occasionally associated with compline, as in the Ortiz print discussed above. The *Regina celi letare*, of course, is one of the four seasonal Marian antiphons for compline, but until the present century would also close vespers in the appropriate season unless compline were sung immediately afterwards (see Chapters 1 and 2).[35] The *Alleluia*, like the *Pater noster*, might serve a variety of functions, but is especially prominent as the psalm antiphon for vespers and compline in Paschal Time. *Lumen ad revelationem* has a rubric within the part-books reading *In festo purificationis Beate Marie pro benedictione candellarum*. This text functions as the antiphon to the canticle *Nunc dimittis* in a special candle-blessing service which follows terce and precedes mass on the feast of the Purification of the Blessed Virgin Mary (2 February).[36] Faa's collection, therefore, goes beyond the standard texts normally found in vesper prints, but all of the texts serve some particular function in either vespers or compline.

Polyphonic music for the individual vesper service was expanded in another way by Guglielmo Sitibundo in 1574 with the publication of a series of polyphonic settings of all of the Magnificat antiphons for the liturgical year.[37] When this collection of seventy-four antiphons was used in conjunction with one or more of the other types of publication, a *maestro di cappella* could assemble an even more thoroughly polyphonic vesper service.

In this decade Giovanni Matteo Asola first emerged as a prolific and influential composer, single-handedly contributing more than anyone else to the promotion of a musical vespers simply by publishing collection after collection of vesper music. Four of Asola's vesper publications appeared within the span of just a few years.[38] His 1575 print consists of nothing more than *falsibordoni* in all eight tones for the psalms, together with *falsibordoni* in several tones for hymns in various metres.

Yet another new type of publication containing vesper music appeared in 1576 from the hand of Thomas Lodovico de Victoria.[39] Victoria's collection is

---

[34] A separate heading for these motets may be missing, or Faa may have intended the heading 'Motetti' to be placed before the *Benedictus*.

[35] See Ch. 1 n. 114 for the secondary literature on this subject. See Ch. 2 n. 3 and App. B for the rubrics governing the role of the seasonal Marian antiphons from a 1583 Roman breviary.

[36] This ceremony is found in *The Liber Usualis with Introduction and Rubrics in English* (New York: Desclée Co., 1963), 1356–61.

[37] RISM S3550.

[38] 1574: RISM A2517, repr. in 1582, but not in 1608 as reported in RISM A2519; 1575: RISM A2520 (1575¹), repr. in 1582, in an enlarged edn. in 1584, twice in 1587, and again in 1592; 1576: RISM A2526, repr. in 1581 and 1590; 1578: RISM A2532 and A2538 (Primus and Secundus Chorus of the same edn.), repr. in 1582, 1583, 1586, 1590, 1596, and 1598.

[39] RISM V1427.

a pot-pourri, including five complete masses for four, five, and six voices, several Magnificats in *alternatim* settings, the vesper hymn for Marian feasts, the four seasonal Marian antiphons, several motets, and one vesper psalm. This is a large collection which allowed a choirmaster to select music for the mass, music for vespers, and Marian antiphons for vespers or compline, all from a single print. The only previous publication at all comparable to Victoria's is the one discussed above by another Spaniard, Diego Ortiz, with its hymns, Magnificats, psalms for vespers, music for compline, and motets, but no masses.[40]

Up until the 1580s, psalm and Magnificat settings had more often been *alternatim* than through-composed; that is, only odd or even verses were set to polyphony, and there seems to have been no particular preference for setting odd or even verses. Nevertheless, there are also numerous polyphonic settings of all verses of psalms and Magnificats, beginning with Morales's Magnificats of 1542. In the case of Magnificats, some publications, such as Giovanni Contini's Magnificats of 1571, provide a setting of odd verses and a separate setting of even verses for each of the eight tones. Such compositions could thus be used in two ways, as *alternatim* settings of either odd or even verses, or in combination to provide complete through-composed polyphonic settings.

In the next decade the quantity of published vesper music continued to expand, and the surviving number of publications, seventy-one, is slightly more than double that of the previous ten years.[41] Most of the growth occurred in the second half of the decade, when almost two-thirds of the surviving prints were issued. In this period it became quite normal for collections to include all of the vesper psalms required for feasts throughout the year. Among the new types of prints are vespers for the Office of the Dead, which require a different set of psalms from those employed in the annual cycle of feasts.[42] Of special interest are a few collections containing a mass, music for vespers, and motets. It appears that it was not unusual by this time to celebrate mass and vespers in succession.[43] A publication containing both mass and vesper music could thus serve a single large-scale celebration on an important feast-day. The earliest extant collection of this type is by Giacomo Piccioli, published in Milan in 1587.[44] The index of Piccioli's print reads as follows:

---

[40] See n. 29 above.

[41] The quantity is too large to list the RISM references here.

[42] The cycle of psalms for the Office of the Dead comprises *Dilexi quoniam exaudiet Dominus, Ad Dominum cum tribularer, Levavi oculos meos, De profundis,* and *Confitebor tibi . . . quoniam.*

[43] Instances of vespers following immediately upon the completion of mass are cited in Thomas D. Culley, *Jesuits and Music,* i: *A Study of the Musicians Connected with the German College in Rome during the 17th Century and of their Activities in Northern Europe* (St. Louis: St Louis University, 1970), 81–3; and Graham P. Dixon, 'Liturgical Music in Rome (1605–45)' (Ph.D. dissertation, University of Durham, 1981), 39.

[44] RISM P2218.

Missa: Factum est silentium   I

Magnificat: Primi toni.   7

Magnificat: Secundi toni.   9

Magnificat: Primi toni.   11

Haec dies boni nuntii est   13

Plaudat nunc organis Maria   15

Egressae sunt mulieres   16

Exultate Deo adiutori nostro   17

MEDIOLANI, Apud Michaelem Tinum.

M. D. LXXXVII.

The print contains a mass, three Magnificats, and four motets, but does not include settings of the psalms or hymns; if they were to be performed polyphonically, the *maestro di cappella* would have had to supply them from another publication. The motets might have been inserted into the mass or even the vesper service. This is a rather modest collection, to be followed by much larger ones with more complete music for both services in the following decades.[45]

The increasingly frequent appearances of motets in collections of music for vespers raise the question as to just how and where these motets were to be performed, the liturgical issue already discussed in Chapters 1 and 2 in connection with Monteverdi's 1610 print. But in the 1580s, we also encounter an opposite situation with growing frequency—the appearance of a small number of pieces for vespers, especially Magnificats, in what are primarily motet collections. The earliest such print known to me is an isolated example by Francesco Portinaro dating back to 1568.[46] The next instance I know of is Andrea and Giovanni Gabrieli's famous collection of *Concerti* from 1587, which, in the midst of an enormous quantity of motets and madrigals, contains a solitary Magnificat.[47]

The interpolation of vesper polyphony among motets is significant primarily with regard to the development of style in vesper music. Towards the end of the century, as the early appearance of modern compositional techniques in sacred music began to transform the motet, these same techniques also found their way into the small number of Magnificats and psalms published in motet collections. It seems that the Magnificats and psalms in such prints absorbed modern features of style from the motets with which they were associated.[48]

Victoria was another composer who included vesper music in a collection consisting primarily of motets in this decade,[49] but the vast majority of prints continued in the patterns established earlier, with the greater weight still falling

---

[45] See e.g. the 1590 print of Asola (RISM A2581) discussed below.

[46] RISM P5222. This print contains twenty-three motets *a 6*, two motets *a 7*, one motet *a 8*, and concludes with the single psalm *Laudate pueri a 10*.

[47] RISM G85.

[48] See Ch. 4 for a discussion of this issue.

[49] RISM V1422 (1583) and V1423 (repr. and rev. edn. of 1589). This print contains a large number of motets, identified by feast, and five vesper psalms, but the psalms do not form a single *cursus*. The majority of the motets are reprinted from Victoria's *Motecta* of 1572 (RISM V1421).

on collections emphasizing psalms. Giovanni Matteo Asola flourished in the 1580s, with another thirteen publications of Vesper music of one type or another.[50] Asola, along with a few other composers, was particularly devoted to through-composed rather than *alternatim* settings. Several of his collections were also published with the Primus Chorus and the Secundus Chorus as separate entities. Alternate verses were split between the two choirs, so that either choir could perform odd or even verses in *alternatim* style, or the two choirs could be combined for through-composed settings. In Rome, not only did double-choir psalm settings increase in popularity, but settings for three and even four choirs were also introduced, often with instrumental doubling or substitution.[51]

In the 1590s, the combination of a mass, vesper music, and motets became more common, as in Asola's *Vespertina omnium solemnitatum* from the first year of the decade.[52] The contents of this print are extensive, comprising fifteen vesper psalms, two Magnificats, a mass, a Marian antiphon, and five motets. This sizeable publication is printed in a larger format than usual and set for three choirs.[53] The title even indicates that all types of instruments may be used in performing the music (see Chapter 19). By this time, the combination of a mass and a vesper service had become a major musical event, to be performed on select occasions with large choral and instrumental forces. In the same year Orfeo Vecchi published a collection with a mass, the vesper response, psalms, a Magnificat, two motets, and *falsibordoni*.[54] But Vecchi's collection has only five psalms and is limited specifically to Sunday vespers, as indicated on the title-page. The function of the two motets is not entirely clear; evidently, they may be inserted into the mass or vesper service as desired. This was the first extant collection in over two decades to revive the focus on a specific category of feasts, although the *falsibordoni* would allow for any feast if the choirmaster were satisfied with this less sophisticated form of polyphony. A Roman publication, Asprilio Pacelli's *Motectorum et psalmorum* of 1597, also limits its psalms to five, this time the 'male *cursus*'.[55]

---

[50] 1581: RISM A2527 (repr. of A2526); 1582: A2518 (repr. of A2517), A2521 (repr. of A2520), A2533 (repr. of A2532); 1583: A2539 (repr. of A2538, which forms part of A2532; see n. 38 above); 1584: A2522 (enlarged repr. of A2520); 1585: A2561, A2562; 1586: A2534 (repr. of A2532), A2565 (enlarged and modified in successive reprs. of 1593, 1599, 1603, and 1610); 1587: A2523, A2524 (both reprs. of A2522), A2568 (repr. in 1599). The majority of Asola's vesper publications in this decade are reprints of collections published in the 1570s. In the 1580s his new publications concentrated on masses, music for compline, music for Holy Week, and motets. There is even a collection of psalm settings for terce (A2563).

[51] See O'Regan, 'The Performance of Roman Sacred Polychoral Music', 109–10.

[52] RISM A2581.

[53] I have not taken precise measurements of this volume, but the copy at Bologna, Civico Museo Bibliografico Musicale, is approximately 30 cm. wide × 45 cm. tall.

[54] RISM V1057.

[55] RISM P24.

In this decade, the quantity of surviving prints expands by almost 50 per cent, with slightly more than a hundred currently traceable. By this time, the quantity of through-composed settings of psalms and Magnificats began to exceed *alternatim* settings. Not only did Asola continue to publish with great frequency, but Giovanni Francesco Anerio and Lodovico Viadana also began regularly turning out vesper music. In this period we encounter more frequently collections containing a mass, vesper music, and motets, as well as motet collections with occasional interpolations of vesper music. A few publications add some purely instrumental pieces to the combination, and organ basses were introduced, both novelties appearing in the *Concerti ecclesiastici* of Adriano Banchieri, published in 1595.[56] Banchieri assembled a mass, three Magnificats, nine motets, and three *canzon francesi*, arranged in a seemingly haphazard manner.[57] Another large, complex publication is the *Psalmi integri* of Orfeo Vecchi, published in Milan in 1596.[58] This print contains the vesper response, sixteen psalms, two Magnificats, the four Marian antiphons, and two sets of *falsibordoni*. Two years later an organ part was published for this collection.[59]

These complex publications could easily grow to unwieldy proportions. By the time a composer assembled a complete Mass Ordinary, settings of all the vesper psalms, some five or six motets, two or three Magnificats, *falsibordoni*, and perhaps even four Marian antiphons or some instrumental pieces, his publication had become inordinately large and correspondingly expensive.[60] The practical response to this problem was to reduce the number of psalm settings, leaving just enough to cover most efficiently the largest possible number of feasts. Antonio Mortaro's *Messa, salmi, motetti, et Magnificat, à tre chori*, first published in 1599, illustrates this solution.[61] Mortaro's print contains a parody mass, the vesper response, the same eight psalms that are found in the Phinot print cited above, four motets, two Magnificats (one a parody Magnificat), and a set of *falsibordoni*. In fact, the collection is designed with a multiplicity of practical purposes in mind. Aside from music for mass and vespers, the textless *falsibordoni* provide alternative possibilities for singing all vespers, compline, and other office psalms, and the motets might have been employed in a variety of ways: possibly during the performance of the mass, perhaps in the vesper service, in

---

[56] RISM B799.

[57] On the same page as his *Tavola*, Banchieri also gives instructions *A gli Sig. Organisti* for the creation of the second organ bass: 'Volendo la Spartitura di tutti due Chori, sarà facil cosa accommodarla prestissimo, pigliando la parte acuta & grave del Secondo Choro, & dove in questa dice à 8. lasciarlo, & aggiungendo quella à questa, vi saranno tutt.due: ma l'Autore non l'ha fatta, atteso che l'intentione sua è per concertarla à Chori separati. Intanto vivete felici.'

[58] RISM V1058.

[59] RISM V1059.

[60] A case in point is Asola's *Vespertina omnium solemnitatum psalmodia* of 1590, described above.

[61] RISM M3741.

church on other occasions when their texts were suitable, or even as devotional music in secular surroundings.

Not only does Mortaro's collection possess considerable flexibility in its practical application, but it also furnishes a more complete body of music for a single vesper service than the collections *per tutte le solennità*. In this one publication a *maestro di cappella* had enough music to perform an elaborate polyphonic mass and vespers on the feast of a male saint, a Marian feast, or the feast of a virgin saint. Not only are all the major items supplied, but there are also a polyphonic setting of the response and several motets from which to choose.

Mortaro's collection reveals several related tendencies in sacred music publications around the turn of the seventeenth century. First, the contents illustrate the expansion beyond the homogeneous collections that characterized the 1570s and 1580s. Secondly, this expansion reflects a desire for more flexible practical applications of a single publication. And thirdly, the provision of enough music for an elaborate polyphonic service demonstrates an interest in enlarging the scope of polyphony at vespers. That all three were broad-based historical trends is shown by the fact that during the period 1600–10 more than three times as many such complex publications, often with widely varying contents, appeared than in the last decade of the sixteenth century.

An important new type of collection, emerging for the first time in the late 1590s, contains polyphonic settings of the vesper antiphon texts for the entire liturgical year, as exemplified in a large print by Girolamo Lambardi from 1597.[62] Several such large collections appeared over the next decades, and these prints of polyphonic antiphons, the texts of which differ from one collection to another and differ from the *Breviarium Romanum* as well, may provide us, once someone has had a chance to study all of them thoroughly, with invaluable information about diversity of liturgical practice in an age that was attempting to impose liturgical standardization.[63]

The expansion in number of publications in the 1590s, like that in earlier decades, was accompanied by a further expansion in variety of contents. Through much of the second half of the sixteenth century there had been an obvious tendency to publish collections of separate liturgical genres. We find many prints exclusively of hymns, exclusively of Magnificats, exclusively of

[62] RISM L366.

[63] Aside from Lambardi's 1597 print, there are another by Lambardi from 1600 (RISM L367), a three-volume set of antiphons by Anerio from 1613 (RISM A1104), and four books of antiphons by Cazzati from 1672. Only book i is listed in RISM (as C1661). No copy of book ii survives; books iii and iv are extant in the Bibliothèque G. Thibault, Paris. Two other prints, one by Cifra from 1638 (RISM C2211) and the other by Giamberti from 1650 (RISM G1831), include a significant number of antiphon settings among motets. For a thorough discussion of the Anerio print, see James Armstrong, 'The *Antiphonae, seu sacrae cantiones* (1613) of Giovanni Francesco Anerio: A Liturgical Study', *Analecta musicologica*, 14 (1974), 89–150.

psalms, or even exclusively of antiphons. Some mixing of genres did take place, as has been noted above, but these are exceptions to the general rule of genre-specific publications. By 1595 this discrete separation of genres was clearly beginning to unravel. From the mid-1590s onwards not only did increasing numbers of prints mix psalms and Magnificats under the title *psalmi*, but masses were frequently joined with psalms, a small or larger quantity of motets were often included, a litany might be added, and vesper and compline music might be mixed together with other items in the same print. As we will see in the next chapter, mixed-genre prints began to rival, though not outnumber, the prints devoted primarily to one genre during the period 1600–10.[64]

These printed collections tell us a great deal about what was available to the *maestro di cappella* at various times during the second half of the sixteenth century. What they do not tell us with any specificity is how they were used. Certainly the *cursus* of five psalms for particular categories of feasts was sometimes employed *in toto*, together with a polyphonic Magnificat, on an appropriate feast-day, but such extensive use of polyphony may have been confined to feasts of unusual solemnity, such as patronal feasts, Easter Sunday, a church's consecration anniversary, or some other special feast. At many churches such celebrations might have been limited to one or two feasts per year, while in a cathedral or other prominent church, extended polyphonic services may have been more common. Evidence survives of vesper services with a mixture of polyphony, *falsibordoni*, and plainchant as late as the early *Seicento*. Such mixtures were probably the norm even in prominent churches, considering the large number of feast-days and Sundays throughout a liturgical year, but the prints described above also demonstrate a commerical market for polyphonic music organized to serve single, largely polyphonic vesper celebrations.[65]

This chapter has taken us up to the threshold of the seventeenth century. Chapter 4 will explore the more immediate musical context of Monteverdi's Vespers in the first decade of the new century and attempt to assess Monteverdi's influence on other composers in the decade 1610–20.

---

[64] See Ch. 4. A thoroughgoing analytic study of the more conservative extant vesper psalm repertoire of Rome from the period 1570–1630 can be found in Fischer, *Die Psalmkompositionen in Rom um 1600*. The Roman vesper repertoire of 1605–45 is also surveyed in Dixon, 'Liturgical Music in Rome', 156–90. The most thorough and up-to-date account of Roman vesper polyphony in the last quarter of the 16th century and the first quarter of the 17th is found in Thomas Noel O'Regan, 'Sacred Polychoral Music in Rome 1575–1621; 2 vols. (D.Phil. dissertation, University of Oxford, 1988) and the other studies by O'Regan listed in the Bibliography. Various aspects of the vesper repertoire of the first half of the 17th century are discussed in Jerome Roche, *North Italian Church Music in the Age of Monteverdi* (Oxford: Clarendon Press, 1984).

[65] Colleen Reardon assembles the evidence for a mixture of styles in *Agostino Agazzari and Music at Siena Cathedral, 1597–1641* (Oxford: Clarendon Press, 1993), 68–9. She also assesses the feasts for which the professional choir (the *cappella*) was required to sing polyphony at vespers at a number of Sienese churches in the late 16th and early 17th centuries. See ibid. 68–81.

4

Vesper Publications and Modern Style, 1600–1620: A Comparison of Monteverdi's Vespers with the Contemporaneous Repertoire

I

IN the preceding chapter we witnessed the growth of the published Italian vesper repertoire in the second half of the sixteenth century, a growth which increased dramatically as the century approached its end. In the first decade of the new century, the number of extant prints once again augments by approximately 50 per cent. I have located more than 150 publications from this period, about two-thirds of them issued between 1605 and 1609. From the year 1610 alone, aside from Monteverdi's print, I have been able to trace an additional 25 surviving collections containing vesper music. Of the total of nearly 180 publications from these eleven years, 24 are reprints. By this time, the number of vesper publications has exceeded the number of mass prints from the same period. For the decade 1600–10, Anne Schnoebelen has counted 56 prints of masses only (19 of which are reprints), 21 of masses and motets (including 2 reprints), 12 of masses and psalms (which also count in my vesper calculations), and 22 of masses with other genres (including 3 reprints).[1] The total number of publications containing masses is 111, less than two-thirds the number of publications of music for vespers. It is clear that by the first decade of the century, a major shift in emphasis had taken place in the public services of the Catholic Church in Italy. The vesper service had become a ceremony of major musical importance, not merely rivalling the mass, but actually surpassing it in number of publications and, consequently, in musical significance for the church calendar.

As demonstrated in the previous chapter, a few publications from 1565 onwards reduced the number of psalm settings to only the five vesper psalms for the 'male *cursus*', the 'female *cursus*', or Sunday vespers, placing significant

[1] I am grateful to Anne Schnoebelen for calculating these masses at my request.

limitations on a collection's use during the liturgical year. Such collections, aimed at a specific category of feasts, increased further in the decade 1600–10, culminating in Monteverdi's own Vespers, which is limited to feasts of the Virgin. Thus Monteverdi's combination of a mass, response, vesper psalms for a specific category of feasts, Magnificats, and motets had several recent precedents.[2]

In the first decade of the century, the number of collections consisting principally of motets with a few vesper items also increased significantly. In these collections the few vesper compositions tended to adopt the stylistic character of the motets they accompanied. Since it is through many of these motet books (frequently called *concerti ecclesiastici* or some related title) that modern stylistic features made their first inroads into sacred music, the psalms and Magnificats in them represent the first vesper music to display these characteristics. Monteverdi's adoption of modern textures, ornamentation, and other stylistic features in his motets, psalms, and Magnificats, therefore, had antecedents in the growing repertoire of motet books with occasional vesper compositions. Several of these motet books and their influence on Monteverdi's Vespers will be investigated below.

Collections like Monteverdi's 1610 print supplied music for elaborate public concerts for mass and vespers, lasting as long as two or three hours. Thomas Coryat's famous description of such a large-scale service *qua* concert at the Scuola San Rocco in 1608 has been republished several times and bears witness to the magnificence and variety of such musical events:

The third feast was upon Saint Roches day being Saturday and the sixth day of August, where I heard the best musicke that ever I did in all my life both in the morning and the afternoone, so good that I would willingly goe an hundred miles a foote at any time to heare the like. The place where it was, is neare to Saint Roches Church, a very sumptuous and magnificent building that belongeth to one of the sixe Companies of the citie. . . . This feast consisted principally of Musicke, which was both vocall and instrumental, so good, so delectable, so rare, so admirable, so superexcellent, that it did even ravish and stupifie all those strangers that never heard the like. But how others were affected with it I know not; for mine owne part I can say this, that I was for the time even rapt up with Saint Paul into the third heaven. Sometimes there sung sixteene or twenty men together, having their master or moderator to keepe them in order; and when they sung, the instrumentall musitians played also. Sometimes sixteene played together upon their instruments, ten Sagbuts, foure Cornets, and two Violdegambaes of an extraordinary greatnesse; sometimes tenne, six Sagbuts and foure Cornets; sometimes two, a Cornet and a treble violl. Of those treble viols I heard three severall there, whereof each was so good, especially one that I observed above the rest, that I never heard the like before. Those that played upon the treble viols, sung and played together, and sometimes two singular fellowes played together upon Theorboes, to which they sung also, who yeelded admirable sweet musicke, but so still that they could scarce be heard but by those that were very neare them. These two Theorbists concluded that nights musicke, which

---

[2] RISM M2876, P1036, R1540, S3431, T537, T1013, V2109. See also G267, M3741 (repr. as M3742), and N70, where similar organizational considerations apply.

continued three whole howers at the least. For they beganne about five of the clocke, and ended not before eight. Also it continued as long in the morning: at every time that every severall musicke played, the Organs, whereof there are seven faire paire in that room, standing al in a rowe together, plaied with them. Of the singers there were three or foure so excellent that I thinke few or none in Christendome do excell them, especially one, who had such a peerelesse and (as I may in a manner say) such a supernaturall voice for such a privilege for the sweetnesse of his voice, as sweetnesse, that I think there was never a better singer in all the world, insomuch that he did not onely give the most pleasant contentment that could be imagined, to all the hearers, but also did as it were astonish and amaze them. I alwaies thought that he was an Eunuch, which if he had beene, it had taken away some part of my admiration, because they do most commonly sing passing wel; but he was not, therefore it was much the more admirable. Againe it was the more worthy of admiration, because he was a middle-aged man, as about forty yeares old. For nature doth more commonly bestowe such a singularitie of voice upon boyes and striplings, than upon men of such yeares. Besides it was farre the more excellent, because it was nothing forced, strained or affected, but came from him with the greatest facilitie that ever I heard.[3]

One might think Coryat to have been describing Monteverdi's own Mass and Vespers if the date were not a bit too early. Nor do we have any indication of Monteverdi's sacred music being heard in Venice prior to a trial performance in 1613 of his compositions before the Procurators of St Mark's at the time he was being considered for the post of *maestro di cappella*.[4] In fact, as I have suggested in Chapter 1, it is probable that the stylistic variety of Monteverdi's collection was deliberately intended as an advertisement of the range of his abilities in the hope of attracting the attention of a major ecclesiastical establishment.

If this were indeed the case, a publication containing an old-style mass and a modern vespers would have ideally suited Monteverdi's purposes. And we should not be surprised at the significance assumed by the Vespers in this large and magnificent publication. On the contrary, as I have attempted to demonstrate in Chapter 3 and the beginning of this chapter, Monteverdi's *Vespro* is the consequence of decades of growth and development in the vesper repertoire. This repertoire had become so large and so prominent by the early seventeenth century that nearing the end of its first decade, when Monteverdi was planning his first major publication of sacred music, the most important medium in which he could demonstrate his prowess was the liturgy for vespers. The *Missa in illo tempore* was the vehicle for proving his contrapuntal virtuosity and mastery of the *stile antico*, or, as Monteverdi himself put it, the *prima prattica*.[5] But

[3] *Coryat's Crudities* (London: William Stansby, 1611), 250–3; repr. edn. (Glasgow: James MacLehose and Sons, 1905), 388–91.

[4] See the account of Monteverdi's audition in Ch. 1. For earlier interpretations of the archival documents, see Denis Arnold, 'The Monteverdian Succession at St Mark's', *Music & Letters*, 42 (1961), 208; and a slightly different interpretation in id., *Monteverdi's Church Music* (BBC Music Guides; London: British Broadcasting Corporation, 1982), 33–4.

[5] Detailed discussions of the Mass can be found in Jeffrey G. Kurtzman, 'A Critical Commentary on the "Missa In illo tempore"' in *Essays on the Monteverdi Mass and Vespers of 1610* (Houston: Rice University Studies, 1978), 47–68; Gerhard Hust, 'Untersuchungen zu Claudio Monteverdis

however much effort he put into the Mass, he clearly made his best showing with the *Vespro della Beata Vergine*, and the contrast between his brilliant Vespers and the antiquated and perhaps even occasionally pedantic Mass underscores both the importance of the vesper service in his thinking and his greater comfort with modern styles and techniques. The *Missa*, betraying the labour Casola described, appears as a somewhat uneasy homage to tradition, conservative technique, and a bygone style. The Vespers, on the other hand, constituted the kind of opulent music that had become increasingly prominent in both southern and northern Italy—a brilliant, diverse style that contributed to Monteverdi's eventual success in securing his new post in that most opulent of all Italian cities, Venice.

The *Missa in illo tempore*, although reprinted two years later in Antwerp and cited 166 years later in Giambattista Martini's didactic treatise on counterpoint, proved to be of little contemporary significance.[6] But the grandiloquent Vespers exerted a profound influence on other composers, especially in the Veneto, in the years immediately following its publication. The large-scale *concertato* of Gabrieli's posthumous *Symphoniae sacrae* of 1615 marked the end of this style in Venice, while Monteverdi's Vespers marked the beginning of a new chapter in the history of Venetian sacred music based on smaller forces and greater stylistic variety. Moreover, the complexities and variety of this new *concertato* style became the basis of progress and the sign of modernity in the vesper repertoire for many years to come.

It is one of the paradoxes of musicological research that we generally have become acquainted with a period, a repertoire, or a style through recognized masterworks that are tacitly or expressly assumed to be representative. Yet a 'masterpiece', by definition, is unrepresentative, unusual, and beyond the scope of ordinary musical activity. A more thorough and realistic knowledge of music history must come from a broader and deeper acquaintance with its constituent elements than is provided by a limited quantity of exceptional composers and works. Such an expansion of the range of our historical research has the advantage not only of enhancing our understanding of a given topic, but also of supplying the basis for comparison among those composers and works that have faded into obscurity and the few composers and 'masterpieces' that have sur-

Messkompositionen' (Ph.D. dissertation, Ruprecht-Karl-Universität, Heidelberg, 1970), 31–106; and Lewis Lockwood, 'Monteverdi and Gombert: The Missa *In illo tempore* of 1610', in Peter Cahn and Ann-Katrin Heimer, eds., *De musica et cantu: Studien zur Geschichte der Kirchenmusik und der Oper. Helmut Hucke zum 60. Geburtstag* (Hildesheim: Georg Olms Verlag, 1993), 457–69.

[6] The reprint appeared in Orazio Vecchi's *Missae senis et octonis vocibus* of 1612 (RISM V1009 (1612¹)). This version, like the one in Capella Sistina MS 107, does not include the Bassus Generalis. Giambattista Martini published and discussed the first Agnus Dei of Monteverdi's Mass in the *Parte seconda* of his *Esemplare o sia Saggio fondamentale pratico di contrappunto fugato . . . parte seconda* (Bologna: Lelio dalla Volpe, 1776), 242–50. Martini's comments are reproduced in Paolo Fabbri, *Monteverdi* (Turin: E.D.T. Edizioni, 1985), 158–60. See also Ch. 1 above.

vived to become the primary focus of our attention today. Only in relation to lesser efforts can we fully comprehend the qualities that raise the 'masterpiece' above the common level. Only by comparison can we learn to what degree the master composer has rooted his creation in contemporary currents, or conversely, to what extent original ideas and techniques are responsible for its special features. Similarly, it is only by means of broader investigations that we can detect what specific historical influence the masterwork has had upon contemporaries and younger colleagues, and thereby arrive at judgements about the historical significance of the master composer.

Recent trends in musicology have tended to downplay the importance of the master composer and the masterwork in favour of more broadly based studies of a musical culture. Expansion of our base of knowledge of the general musical culture has been the purpose of the surveys of the vesper repertoire of the sixteenth and early seventeenth centuries in Chapter 3 and in the present chapter. Moreover, the study below of contemporaneous stylistic tendencies as a background to Monteverdi's Vespers represents an effort to place the Vespers in its appropriate historical context. But the result of these efforts is not to reduce the historical significance either of the 1610 Vespers or of Monteverdi as a master composer. His own contemporaries recognized him as a giant in their midst with the sobriquet *il divino Claudio*, and from 1613 to his death, he occupied the single most important and influential musical position in Italy. In addition, the comparative studies below will highlight the many features of Monteverdi's 1610 print that are unique in the surviving vesper repertoire and demonstrate how profound the impact of the Vespers was on many of his contemporaries.

Returning now to a more detailed examination of the contemporaneous vesper repertoire, especially collections that, like Monteverdi's, limit their psalms to specific categories of feasts, I have been able to locate seventeen others from between 1600 and 1620 that limit their psalms to either the 'male *cursus*' or the 'female *cursus*', the latter being in the majority with ten.[7] Several of those with the 'female *cursus*' (including Monteverdi's) are specified on the title-page as pertaining to feasts of the Virgin Mary, though they would also have been suitable for feasts of most other virgin saints.[8] Among other, more unusual

---

[7] For a list of these collections that I had located by 1972 along with their contents, see Jeffrey G. Kurtzman, 'The Monteverdi Vespers of 1610 and their Relationship with Italian Sacred Music of the Early Seventeenth Century' (Ph.D. dissertation, University of Illinois at Urbana-Champaign, 1972), Apps. B and C, 414–25. The following publications may be added to those lists. 'Female *cursus*': Orazio Scaletta, *Messa, et il Vespro della Beatissima Vergine . . . 1615* (RISM S1145), comprising a mass, the five psalms, a Magnificat, and three motets; 'male *cursus*': Filippo Cristianelli, *Psalmi cum primo, & secundo versu . . . 1611* (C4417), comprising the five psalms, a Magnificat, and eight motets; Giovanni Piccioni, *Psalmi sex ternis vocibus . . . 1612* (P2222), comprising the five psalms, a Magnificat, and eleven motets; Giovanni Michiel Scarpa, *Messa, salmi et motetti . . . 1613* (S1219), comprising a mass, the response, the five psalms, a Magnificat, and fourteen motets; Giovanni Piccioni, *Concertus [sic] ecclesiastici . . . 1619* (P2224), comprising the five psalms, a Magnificat, and eleven motets.

[8] Only SS Agnes and Agatha have different *cursus* for both first and second vespers.

publications are Vincenzo de Grandis's *Psalmi ad vesperas et motecta* of 1604 (RISM G3480), with numerous motets, two Magnificats, a litany, and the five psalms (one of them in two settings) for second vespers of the Commons of One or Several Martyrs, All Saints, and a few other martyred male saints.[9] Also unusual are Giacomo Finetti's *Psalmi ad vesperas* of 1611 (F813), containing, in addition to the vesper response and two Magnificats, the five psalms for Corpus Christi. One collection, Agostino Agazzari's *Psalmi sex* of 1609 (A357), is limited to only five vesper psalms plus a Magnificat, but the five do not form a *cursus* for any category of feast, since the crucial psalm *Dixit Dominus* is lacking.[10] Similarly, Giovanni Piccioni's *Salmi intieri* of 1616 (P2223) mixes five psalms from the 'male *cursus*' and the 'female *cursus*' without forming a complete *cursus* for any feast.[11]

Other prints may have more than five psalms, but also contain a distinct grouping of five for the 'male *cursus*', the 'female *cursus*', or Sunday vespers. For example, Vincenzo Gallo's *Salmi del Re David* of 1607 (G267) contains the eight psalms discussed above, but groups them in the 'male *cursus*' followed by a Magnificat, and then adds the three additional psalms as a unit under the rubric *Salmi della Madonna*, plus the response and a polyphonic *Dixit Dominus* intonation under yet another rubric, *Fine delli salmi*. Alessandro Capece's *Davidis cithara psalmorum* of 1615 (C890) presents the 'male *cursus*' followed by a Magnificat and then a second setting of the psalm *Laudate pueri*. Pietro Pace's *Salmi a otto voci* of 1619 (P12) contains the 'male *cursus*' marked *non concertati* plus three additional psalms, *Dixit Dominus*, *Laudate pueri*, and *Lauda Jerusalem*, which are indicated *concertati*. These latter do not complete a 'female *cursus*', however. Pace also provides two Magnificats, one *non concertato* and the other *concertato*. Giovanni Bernardino Nanino's *Salmi vespertini a quatro per le Domeniche, Solennita della Madonna, & Apostoli* of 1620 (N20) comprises, according to the title-page, the 'female *cursus*', psalms for many feasts of male saints, and the Sunday psalms. Since *In exitu Israel* is lacking, this is another print in which *Laudate Dominum* apparently serves as an unofficial substitute for the final psalm at Sunday vespers.

Some collections from this period limit their psalms to fewer than five. Archangelo Borsaro, for example, in one section of his large *Concerti ecclesiastici* of 1605 (B3779), provided a response, a setting of *Dixit Dominus*, a Magnificat, and *falsibordoni* in six of the psalm tones. With this combination, the principal items of a vesper service for male saints, for female saints, for Sundays, or for any

---

[9] The psalms are *Dixit Dominus* (in two settings), *Confitebor tibi, Beatus vir, Laudate pueri*, and *Credidi*. See the table of psalm *cursus* in App. A.

[10] Agazzari's psalms are *Confitebor tibi, Beatus vir, Laudate pueri, Nisi Dominus*, and *Laudate Dominum*. The 'sixth' psalm mentioned in the title is, of course, the Magnificat. This print also contains the psalm, canticle, and hymn for compline. The Magnificat is published in Jeffrey Kurtzman, ed., *Vesper and Compline Music for Three Principal Voices* (Seventeenth-Century Italian Sacred Music, 13; New York: Garland Publishing, Inc., 1998).

[11] Piccioni's psalms are *Dixit Dominus, Confitebor tibi, Laudate pueri, Laetatus sum*, and *Nisi Dominus*.

other feast could be sung, simply by furnishing the *falsibordoni* with the texts of the four remaining psalms. Three collections provide the first four psalms of the 'male *cursus*' and a Magnificat, omitting the short fifth psalm, *Laudate Dominum*. Two of these collections also contain *falsibordoni*, through which *Laudate Dominum* could be sung.[12]

A number of other collections from between 1600 and 1620 feature six psalms. In a few cases, the six psalms form a seemingly random selection of useful compositions without forming a *cursus* for any type of feast, as in Antonio Cifra's *Salmi septem . . . opus decimum* of 1611 (C2188), containing *Dixit Dominus*, *Nisi Dominus*, *Laudate Dominum*, *De profundis*, *Laetatus sum*, *Laudate pueri*, and two Magnificats. Sometimes the combination results in one of the principal *cursus* plus another widely applicable psalm, as in Pompeo Signorucci's *Il secondo libro de concerti ecclesiastici* of 1608 (S3431), where the 'female *cursus*' is joined by *Laudate Dominum*. In other instances, the sixth psalm, when substituted for one of the five (usually the last), forms a complete set for a service that could otherwise have been incomplete. For example, Stefano Nascimbene, in his *Concerti ecclesiastici* of 1610 (N70), added *Memento Domine David* to the 'male *cursus*'; the substitution of this psalm for *Laudate Dominum* provides a full complement of psalms for second vespers on some of the feasts for which it also serves for first vespers.[13] Valerio Bona accomplished a similar enlargement of his print's serviceability by adding *Lauda Jerusalem* to the 'male *cursus*' in his *Messa e Vespro* of 1611 (B3433), as did Domenico Massenzio by adding *Credidi propter quod* to the same *cursus* in his *Psalmi, qui in vesperis* of 1618 (M1313).[14]

These publications all illustrate the narrowing of the liturgical focus, concentrating on the more prominent feasts, of many prints containing vesper music in the first two decades of the seventeenth century. The limitation to the five Marian vesper psalms is one feature shared between some of these collections and Monteverdi's Vespers, but it is not the only grounds for comparison. In several, the remaining contents are also similar, though nowhere identical.

Monteverdi's collection, the reader will recall, begins with the parody mass *In illo tempore*, which is then succeeded by the vesper response, *Domine ad*

---

[12] Sisto Visconte, *Concenti spirituali . . . 1609* (V2109) and Tomaso Cecchino, *Salmi et motetti concertati . . . 1616* (not in RISM). The collection without *falsibordoni* is Tomaso Cecchino, *Psalmi, missa, et alia cantica . . . 1619* (C1675). Colleen Reardon notes that many churches, even prominent ones, often performed vesper psalms 'in a mixture of styles: some in polyphony, some in *falsobordone*, some in chant'. See Reardon, *Agostino Agazzari and Music at Siena Cathedral, 1597–1641* (Oxford: Clarendon Press, 1993), 68–9.

[13] See the table of psalm *cursus* in App. A.

[14] See the table of psalm *cursus* in App. A. Another case in point is Antonio Cifra's *Psalmi septem . . . opus septimum* of 1609, which contains the *cursus* for second vespers of a number of male saints, but is also usable for the dedication of a church, and for second vespers for SS Agnes and Agatha by the substitution of *Lauda Jerusalem* for *Credidi*.

adjuvandum. Next comes the regular alternation between the five psalms and five *sacri concentus*, followed by the hymn *Ave maris stella* and two Magnificats.[15] A 1601 collection by Francesco Terriera (T537) is similar but a little smaller in dimensions: a single mass is succeeded by the five Marian vesper psalms, one Magnificat, and four motets.[16] A 1606 print by Don Serafino Patta (P1036) is somewhat more expansive, with the vesper response inserted between the mass and the first psalm, *falsibordoni* added after the Magnificat, the motets increased to five, and a setting of the Litany of the BVM appended at the end. Giovanni Righi's publication from the same year (R1540) is very similar. The contents follow the same pattern as Patta's, but Righi adds a second Magnificat, includes only four motets, and places the litany and *falsibordoni* last. In 1608, Pompeo Signorucci positioned a mass at the conclusion of his print, added a sixth psalm, *Laudate Dominum*, and incorporated three motets, but did not supply a litany or *falsibordoni*.

These are the only seventeenth-century Marian vesper collections antedating Monteverdi's in the known surviving repertoire. The main differences between Monteverdi's and the others are his interspersal of the motets between the psalms, his inclusion of the Marian vesper hymn, and his omission of anything else not directly obligatory to a vesper service, such as the litany. It is the first of these differences that has given rise to so much controversy over the collection. It has been argued on the one hand that the motets are extraneous to the vesper service, and on the other that they serve as substitutes for the plainchant antiphons normally required by the liturgy, a function indicated by their position between the psalms in the original print.[17]

Persuasive evidence has been gathered on the side of the antiphon substitute theory, but even these arguments have taken limited cognizance of the evidence supplied by comparable contemporaneous collections. The question 'Why were motets included in Monteverdi's publication if they were not to be used in the vesper service?' can also be asked about the other prints just listed, even if the motets come only at the end of each part-book. If these Marian vesper collections, in contrast to those *per tutte le solennità* and those with multiple functions, were designed to provide a greater quantity of polyphonic music for a single category of feast, the reasonable assumption is that the few motets included are also usable as part of the liturgical performance.

More direct evidence of antiphon substitutes is found in the Roman composer Paolo Agostini's *Salmi della Madonna* of 1619 (A411). The succession of compositions in this print is as follows:

---

[15] See the discussion of the contents of Monteverdi's print in Ch. 1.

[16] The contents of this and the following prints mentioned in this paragraph are listed in Kurtzman, 'The Monteverdi Vespers of 1610', 414–16.

[17] See Chs. 1 and 2 for a discussion of this issue and the literature on the subject.

> *Dixit Dominus*, secondo tono
> *Dum esset Rex*, antifona prima
> *Dixit Dominus*, primo tono
> *Sub tuum praesidium*
> *Laudate pueri*, sesto tono
> *Leva eius*, seconda antifona
> *Laudate pueri*, intonatione del sesto tono
> *Virgo prudentissima*
> *Laudate pueri*, intonatione del quarto tono
> *Beata es Virgo*
> *Laetatus sum*, sesto tono
> *Nigra sum*, tertia antifona
> *Laetatus sum*, quarto tono
> *Cantate Domino*
> *Nisi Dominus*, secondo tono
> *Iam hiems transiit*, antifona quarta
> *Nisi Dominus*, ottavo tono
> *Veni in hortum meum*
> *Lauda Hierusalem*, ottavo tono
> *Speciosa facta es*, quinta e ultima antifona
> *Lauda Hierusalem*, primo tono
> *Gaudeamus omnes*
> *Ave maris stella*
> *Ave maris stella*
> *Magnificat*, ottavo tono
> *Beata Mater*, antifona ad Magnificat
> *Magnificat*, secondo tono
> *Ego dormio*
> *Magnificat*, secondo tono
> *Ab initio*
> *Veni de Libano*

The index at the end of each part-book actually obscures this order. Instead of following the succession of pieces, the index groups all compositions in a single genre together, with the motets and antiphons for one, two, and three voices following after the psalms, hymns, and Magnificats.

Agostini's collection is another of those devoted exclusively to vespers of the Virgin, but it differs from all earlier examples in presenting multiple settings of each of the psalms. It is also the only collection besides Monteverdi's to include the hymn *Ave maris stella* (in two settings, one of odd verses, the other of even verses), but most importantly, Agostini follows Monteverdi's precedent in interspersing the antiphons and motets between the psalms. His method is systematic and clearly indicates the liturgical function of the motets. Each psalm in the collection has two settings, except *Laudate pueri*, which has three. The first version of a psalm is followed by a polyphonic composition on the appropriate antiphon text for the feast of Holy Mary of the Snow, the liturgy which became the Common of the BVM. These pieces are labelled *antifona prima*, *antifona seconda*, and so on. However, these antiphon texts are not suitable for all Marian feasts. Those feasts listed in the Proper of the Time each require their own set of six antiphons. Agostini apparently resolved the problem of the proliferation of antiphons by furnishing single substitute texts, set polyphonically and placed after the second version (and the third in the case of *Laudate pueri*) of each psalm in the print. Thus every motet occupies the same position relative to the preceding psalm as does each of the polyphonic antiphon settings derived from the feast of Holy Mary of the Snow.[18] There seems to be no alternative but to accept these motets as antiphon substitutes for use in Marian feasts from the Proper of the Time. The analogy with Monteverdi's collection is obvious and offers further support for performing his *sacri concentus* in place of plainchant antiphons.[19]

A less definitive, but nevertheless suggestive, print with regard to antiphon substitutes is Giovanni Battista Fergusio's *Motetti e dialogi per concertar* of 1612 (F249). Fergusio groups the pieces in his print according to the number of voices, with groupings for each combination from one to nine voices. Each of the first four groups contains seven compositions—the first six are motets, and the last one is a Magnificat. There are no psalms in the print. This unique and systematic approach suggests that the motets may have been intended as antiphon substitutes to precede psalms that might have been sung in plainchant, in *falsibordoni*, or in polyphony (derived from another publication). The sixth motet would then serve as the antiphon substitute for the Magnificat Fergusio himself supplies. This print has a lengthy preface, devoted to matters of performance practice, including the use of instruments in the dialogue motets for seven, eight, or nine voices, but nowhere does Fergusio mention a reason for his systematic ordering of the compositions from one to four voices. Nor would it have been appropriate for him to do so, considering the frequent attempts of church officials to curb the practice of substituting for official liturgical texts.

In 1629, Leandro Gallerano of Brescia published a collection of *Messa e salmi concertati* (G160) with two separate sets of psalms and the Magnificat for the 'male *cursus*'. In the first *cursus*, the psalm *Dixit Dominus* and the Magnificat each have a short motet preceding the official liturgical item. The text incipits of these motets are not given in the table of contents; rather, they are referred to simply as *Introducione*. For *Dixit Dominus*, the table reads: *Dixit con l'Introducione*

---

[18] *Ab initio* is a polyphonic setting of the chapter from this feast, also usable for the Visitation and the Nativity of the BVM. *Nigra sum* and *Ab initio* are published in Jeffrey Kurtzman, ed., *Vesper and Compline Music for Two Principal Voices* (Seventeenth-Century Italian Sacred Music, 12; New York: Garland Publishing, Inc. 1997). *Laudate pueri sesto tono Beata mater*, and the setting of the odd verses of *Ave maris stella* are published in id., ed., *Vesper and Compline Music for Three Principal Voices*.

[19] This is precisely the role claimed by Stephen Bonta for the prolific outpouring of motet and instrumental publications in the 17th century. See Bonta, 'Liturgical Problems in Monteverdi's Marian Vespers', *Journal of the American Musicological Society*, 20 (1967), 104–5.

à 5; the *Introducione* for the Magnificat is listed separately: *Introducione del Magnificat à 5*, and on the next line: *Magnificat à 5*. These motets would appear to be substitutes for the plainchant antiphons, but it is noteworthy that they appear before the liturgical item rather than afterwards, as seems normally to have been the case.[20]

Other evidence regarding the substitution of polyphonic motets, organ music, and other instrumental pieces for plainchant antiphons, especially following psalms, has been presented in Chapter 2. It also appears, from James Armstrong's study of Giovanni Francesco Anerio's *Antiphonae* of 1613 (A1104), that not only could antiphon texts be rather freely rearranged, altered, or substituted, but that the modal relationship between antiphon and psalm was also considerably loosened, perhaps even eventually dissolved through the *canto figurato* settings of both psalms and antiphons or antiphon substitutes (see Chapter 2).[21]

Stephen Bonta, arguing in favour of the antiphon substitute theory, notes that it is impossible to find in the *Liber usualis* liturgically correct plainchant antiphons that fit the tonalities of Monteverdi's five psalms.[22] The same is true when one consults early seventeenth-century liturgical books, and a similar observation may be made regarding all the collections of Marian vespers published between 1600 and 1620. In none of these does the succession of psalm tonalities match the modes of the plainchant antiphons for the feast of Holy Mary of the Snow or for any Marian feast from the Proper. This difficulty, which Bonta suggests was resolved by substituting polyphonic motets that did not have to agree with the psalm in tonality, has implications extending beyond Monteverdi's own Vespers and the Marian vespers of other composers.

The fact is that any *canto figurato* setting of a vesper psalm necessitated a choice of a single tonality, thereby limiting the number of modally compatible plainchant antiphons with which the psalm could be sung if the rule of matching mode and tone were maintained. Since it is the antiphon that is proper to a particular feast-day or group of feasts (as in the Common), the ability of the psalm to match the mode of the antiphon would have been, according to the rule, crucial as to whether or not the psalm could be used for a particular feast. Thus a psalm in *canto figurato* would have been limited to far fewer feasts than its Gregorian counterpart, which could be used at any feast for which its text was

---

[20] For a discussion of the practice in Venice, see James H. Moore, *Vespers at St Mark's: Music of Alessandro Grandi, Giovanni Rovetta and Francesco Cavalli* (Ann Arbor: UMI Research Press, 1981), 175–7. Some of the contemporary references speak of a motet or instrumental piece between the psalms, thereby failing to specify whether it belongs to the psalm preceding it or following it.

[21] Armstrong, 'The *Antiphonae, seu sacrae cantiones* (1613) of Giovanni Francesco Anerio: A Liturgical Study', *Analecta musicologica*, 14 (1974), 146–8.

[22] 'Liturgical Problems', 95–6. Both Denis Stevens and Gottfried Wolters encountered the same problem in preparing their editions, which included plainchant antiphons. See the discussion of this issue in Ch. 1 above.

appropriate. The psalm in *canto figurato*, by contrast, could ostensibly only be sung when the plainchant antiphon happened to be in the same mode. The reader is referred to Chapters 1 and 2 for an extensive discussion of this issue and its possible solutions.

From the evidence presented there it appears not only that antiphon texts could be rather freely rearranged, substituted, or altered, but also that the modal relationship between antiphon and psalm was also considerably loosened, perhaps even eventually dissolved through the *canto figurato* settings of both psalms and antiphons or antiphon substitutes.

II

The music of the *Vespro della Beata Vergine* presents a complex picture, not only in its own right as demonstrated in the analytical portion of this book, but also in comparison with the contemporaneous vesper repertoire. Just as it was essential to examine the historical background of vesper collections in order to obtain a perspective on the contents and organization of Monteverdi's print, it is necessary to investigate the compositional techniques and styles of vesper music, both before and after 1610, to understand the relationship between Monteverdi's work and that of other composers.

A few general points of reference may be established at the outset. First, Monteverdi's is the earliest surviving vesper publication to make extensive use of obbligato instruments. The use of instruments to double or replace vocal lines *ad libitum* had been suggested on the title-pages of many sixteenth-century motet collections, and obbligato instrumental parts appear in a number of early *Seicento* motet books as well as in a few settings of vesper psalms and a Magnificat from the first decade of the century. Ippolito Camatero's *Salmi corista a otto voci* of 1573 (C279) have already been mentioned in Chapter 3 as an early example of a collection calling for *ad libitum* instruments in vesper music (see also the discussion below).

Even more revealing than these title-pages are documentary studies of church, oratorio, and confraternity archives in the late sixteenth and early seventeenth centuries that demonstrate the frequent use of instruments in both the mass and office in Rome as well as in northern Italy. What distinguishes the Monteverdi Vespers is that there are no prior examples of such extensive and decorative orchestration actually notated in the vesper repertoire, and even Monteverdi's optional instrumental ritornellos have no counterparts other than the *sinfonie* of a few of Giovanni Gabrieli's motets. As with many other aspects of the 1610 Vespers, Monteverdi has put into print performance practices that were common throughout Italy for many years, even decades, indicating with far greater precision than his contemporaries his expectations for performance.[23] He has taken these practices into his own hands as a composer, making such matters as ornamentation and instrumentation part of the compositional process rather than relegating them entirely to the performers. This shift in the relative roles of composer and performer quite naturally manifests itself in the musical notation and in Monteverdi's performance rubrics.

A second peculiarity of Monteverdi's collection is the extensive employment of a cantus firmus in the psalms and Magnificats. While cantus firmi do appear sporadically in vesper music of the early seventeenth century, as demonstrated below, they are nowhere as ubiquitous as in Monteverdi's print of 1610.

Thirdly, all of the music of the *Vespro* is composed in an elaborate style. This is true not only with regard to the virtuoso character of much of the vocal and instrumental writing, but also with respect to Monteverdi's large-scale, complicated structures. The psalms and Magnificats are more expansive and possess more internal stylistic contrasts than any known previous examples. The motets are musically more sophisticated than most such contemporary pieces, and *Duo Seraphim* exhibits more virtuosic ornamentation than notated in any other motet from the early *Seicento* I have seen. The *Sonata sopra Sancta Maria* is ampler in both size and sonority than the several models on which it is based. Even the response and hymn are larger and more grandiose than the settings of other composers of the period. Consistent with such complexity and diversity, Monteverdi's is the first collection of vesper music for a single category of feast to vary the number of voices required from one piece to the next.

In sum, we may begin with the general observation that the Monteverdi Vespers are on an unparalleled level of musical sophistication in the complexity of their structures and textures, in the variety of their styles and techniques, and in the magnitude of their individual pieces. Moreover, their notation displays a level of splendour and complexity in ornamentation, in vocal and instrumental colours, and in virtuosity that may have occurred *ad libitum* in large celebratory liturgical performances of the period, but were probably not surpassed. This musical opulence may be traced to a number of sources: Monteverdi's obvious desire to establish himself through this one collection as a pre-eminent composer of sacred music in both the old style (the *Missa in illo tempore*) and almost every new style then in the process of development; the possible origin of at least part of the Vespers as music for a lavish celebration in Mantua; or the personal taste of Duke Vincenzo Gonzaga, reflected in the designation on the title-page *ad Sacella sive Principum Cubicula accommodata*, which suggests the duke's

---

[23] A discussion of the use of instruments in contemporaneous motets and vesper music follows below.

private church and rooms, in contrast to *ad Ecclesiam*, a public church.[24] Whatever the genesis of the stylistic idiosyncrasies of the Monteverdi Vespers, our historical perspective on this collection can be enhanced only by an examination of the precedents upon which Monteverdi drew and enlarged, and by an investigation of the impact of his approach to vesper music in the years immediately following his publication of the work in 1610.

The vesper psalm repertoire of the first decade of the seventeenth century is an extension of the styles and techniques of the late *Cinquecento*. The revolution in secular music and the motet, already in progress at the turn of the century, by 1610 had had only a limited effect on polyphonic psalmody. In one sense this is paradoxical, for psalm settings, which had always relied heavily on a chordal style originating in harmonization of the psalm tone, were by their very nature closer to the newly evolved concepts of homophony and intelligible declamation than were many other forms of sixteenth-century music. In addition, the verse structure of psalm texts automatically divided a composition into discrete sections, both in *alternatim* and through-composed settings. Such sectionalization of large compositions into smaller components, often contrasting in texture, metre, or style, was another of the characteristic developments of the early *Seicento*.

But opposing those aspects of polyphonic psalmody that were compatible with modern trends was the conservative aesthetic view of this liturgical genre, exemplified by the brief remarks of Pietro Cerone in 1613:

> In composing psalms, even to omit imitating the psalmody will be no error, for if one were to imitate the plainsong in all the parts, repeating the motives, the verse would be very long, very elaborate, and overly solemn, solemnity being unsuited to psalmody. . . . Be it further observed that the music should be such as does not obscure the words, which should be very distinct and clear, so that all the parts will seem to enunciate together, no more, no less, as in a falso bordone, without long or elegant passages or any novelty other than ordinary consonances, introducing from time to time some short and commonplace imitation. . . . To conclude, I say that any invention used in the verses of the psalms should be very short, formed of few notes and these of small value, and also that the parts should enter in succession after rests of not more than one, two, three, or sometimes four measures. And this should be observed both to avoid making the verses long and to avoid falling into the style of the three privileged canticles.[25]

Although Cerone reproaches Italian composers for sometimes violating the simplicity of psalmody, his aesthetic orientation is corroborated by countless psalm collections of the time. Whether *alternatim* or through-composed, whether completely homophonic or incorporating polyphonic imitation,

---

[24] See Ch. 1 for a fuller discussion of the old and new styles in the print as well as an assessment of possible performances in Mantua.

[25] Trans. in Oliver Strunk, *Source Readings in Music History* (New York: W. W. Norton & Company, Inc., 1950), 269–70. James Foster Armstrong, in 'How to Compose a Psalm: Ponzio and Cerone Compared', *Studi musicali*, 7 (1978), 103–39, demonstrates Cerone's dependence on Pietro Ponzio's *Ragionamento di musica* of 1588, a source that would have been familiar to Italian musicians.

whether set for a single choir or *cori spezzati*, vesper psalms were not usually the place for a composer to display his prowess. Psalms were normally more functional than decorative; they tended to be unpretentious and lacking in the artifice and solemnity bestowed on masses, motets, and even Magnificats.[26] In many respects, Vesper psalmody represented the ideal type of liturgical music when measured against the concerns of the Council of Trent. The clearly declaimed homophony of psalm settings matched perfectly the Council's requirements for sacred music, though the reformers' main concern was the mass.[27]

Nevertheless, psalms, especially multi-choir psalms, could also function, like masses and motets, as the vehicle for elaborate celebrations through the addition of instruments, an increase in the size of vocal forces, and perhaps even improvised ornamentation or *contrapunto alla mente*.[28] In 1555, the Venetian theorist Nicola Vicentino, in his *L'antica musica ridotta alla moderna prattica*, championed such sonorous music, indicating that to make a large sound (*intonatione*) in spacious churches and other large places, 'one can compose masses, psalms and dialogues and other things to play with various instruments, mixed with voices; and to make a greater sound, one can even compose for three choirs'.[29] In 1573, after the Council of Trent, Ippolito Camatero di Negri, a composer of Roman origin working in Udine, published in Venice his set of double-choir vesper psalms 'according to the order of the Council of Trent, convenient for voices, accompanied also by every sort of musical instrument'.[30] Among the early studies of Denis Arnold was an assemblage of considerable documentation that had been published up to that time regarding the role of instruments for the celebration of especially important ceremonies in churches and confraternities in northern Italy in the late sixteenth and early seventeenth centuries.[31] These

---

[26] 'Solemnity' is a relative term. In Venice, the *salmi spezzati* were reserved for certain especially solemn services. See James H. Moore, 'The *Vespero delli Cinque Laudate* and the Role of *salmi spezzati* at St Mark's', *Journal of the American Musicological Society*, 34 (1981), 249–78.

[27] See the extensive discussion of the Council and the mass in ch. 2 of Lewis Lockwood, *The Counter-Reformation and the Masses of Vincenzo Ruffo* (Studi di Musica Veneta, 2; Venice: Fondazione Giorgio Cini, 1970), 74–135. A text deliberated by the Council, but ultimately considerably shortened as the Council's final canon for the mass, is quoted in Gustave Reese, *Music in the Renaissance* (New York: W. W. Norton and Company, Inc., 1954), 449. The canon finally published says merely, 'They shall also banish from the churches all such music which, whether by the organ or in the singing, contains things that are lascivious or impure.' See Rev. H. J. Schroeder, *Canons and Decrees of the Council of Trent* (St Louis: B. Herder Book Co., 1960), 151.

[28] I am grateful to Tim Carter for the suggestion regarding *contrapunto alla mente*.

[29] (Rome: Barre, 1555; fac. edn. Kassel: Bärenreiter, 1959), ch. 28, fo. 85ʳ.

[30] 'Secondo l'ordine del Concilio di Trento Comodi alle voci, accompagnato con ogni sorte di instrumenti Musicali'. *Salmi corista a otto voci* (Venice: Scotto, 1573) (RISM c279). Cited in Thomas Noel O'Regan, 'Sacred Polychoral Music in Rome 1575–1621' (D.Phil. dissertation, University of Oxford, 1988), i. 155. See also Ch. 3 above.

[31] 'Instruments in Church: Some Facts and Figures', *Monthly Musical Record*, 85 (Feb. 1955), 32–8; id., 'Brass Instruments in Italian Church Music of the Sixteenth and Early Seventeenth Centuries', *Brass Quarterly*, 1 (1957), 81–92. See also id., 'Music at the Scuola di San Rocco', *Music & Letters*, 40 (1959), 229–41.

records show that instrumentalists not only took part in processions and played instrumental music separately from the liturgical music, but also performed 'in motets and other musical compositions'.[32] San Petronio in Bologna had an instrumentalist as a permanent member of its *cappella* as early as 1560 and added several others in the next few decades.[33] The French ambassador to Venice described a vesper service in the church of the Saviour in 1607 accompanied by 'sackbuts, oboes, viols, violins, lutes, *cornetti*, recorders and *flageolets*' in addition to the permanent organ and six portative organs. In the same year at the church of the Frari he heard compline accompanied by 'trombones, spinets, bass viols, treble violins, lutes and oboes' and two years later by two portative organs as well as trombones, theorboes, lutes, cornettos, bass viols and at least one flageolet.[34]

Late in the sixteenth century permanent instrumental ensembles were added to the vocal ensembles of some of the larger northern Italian churches and even confraternities.[35] These permanent ensembles typically comprised violins and trombones, to which cornettos might be added. For major feasts, additional voices and instruments were often employed.[36] Confraternities also sponsored elaborate liturgical performances with instruments in their own buildings or in the churches to which some were attached (see the description by Thomas Coryat above). At the very least, such instruments were used to double voices, but they could also be used to replace them, in addition to playing introductions or conclusions to vocal compositions or performing purely instrumental music, not only at the beginning or end of a service but also between liturgical functions or accompanying liturgical acts.[37]

More recent research has revealed that Rome in the post-Tridentine period did not lag behind northern Italy in the exploitation of instruments as a means for enhancing prominent feasts.[38] Already in the 1570s, one visitor described the variety and magnificence of music in numerous Roman churches, including the use of instruments and the speech-like declamation of chant by a solo bass accompanied by the organ.[39] In the 1580s, polychoral music with instru-

---

[32] Arnold, 'Brass Instruments', 84.

[33] See Marc Vanscheeuwijck, 'Musical Performance at San Petronio in Bologna: A Brief History', *Performance Practice Review*, 8 (1995), 74–5.

[34] Egon F. Kenton, 'The "Brass" Parts in Giovanni Gabrieli's Instrumental Ensemble Compositions', *Brass Quarterly*, 1 (1957), 76. See also Eleanor Selfridge-Field, *Venetian Instrumental Music from Gabrieli to Vivaldi* (New York: Praeger Publishers, 1975), 29.

[35] In addition to the well-known case of San Marco in Venice, Arnold cites the basilica of San Antonio in Padua as well as San Petronio in Bologna. See Arnold, 'Brass Instruments' and 'Music at the Scuola di San Rocco'. See also Nicoletta Billio D'Arpa, 'Amadio Freddi, musicista padovano', *Il Santo. Rivista antoniana di storia dottrina arte*, 27 (1987), 245–7.

[36] See also the discussion of choral and instrumental ensembles in Ch. 15.

[37] See e.g. the discussion of Amante Franzoni's *Apparato musicale* below. See also Ch. 19 for a discussion of doubling instruments in Monteverdi's Vespers.

[38] The principal literature on Roman festal music in this period are O'Regan, 'Sacred Polychoral Music' and several other studies by O'Regan and by Graham Dixon, listed in the Bibliography.

[39] O'Regan, 'Sacred Polychoral Music', i. 6–7.

ments, including music for three choirs, was performed at both mass and vespers.[40] The polychoral idiom was expanded in the 1580s and 1590s to four
choirs and even five.[41] At the Jesuit church of the Gesù, Giovanni Francesco
Anerio even performed a mass for eight choirs in 1616, and Paolo Agostini directed twelve choirs in St Peter's on the Feast of St Peter in 1628.[42]

As in the north, the principal instruments aside from organs were violins,
trombones, cornettos, lutes, and theorboes, with occasional mention of bass
string instruments, bassoons, violas, a spinet, a harpsichord, a serpent, a shawm,
and a transverse flute.[43] Typically an elaborate musical celebration comprised
both first and second Vespers as well as the mass and a procession, though first
vespers seems to have been of less significance since normally fewer singers were
hired for that service.[44] Trumpets, drums, and shawms were the usual proces-
sional instruments, and even artillery was used to heighten the festivities.[45]
During Lent, compline was also performed with elaborate music.[46] In the mass,
polychoral music was limited to motets, either interpolated or as substitutes for
the offertory, the elevation, and the communion. The amount of polyphony
used in vespers varied with the importance of the feast; not all psalms were
necessarily set in polyphony, even in the Sistine Chapel.[47] Those that were not
could be sung in chant, in *falsobordone*, or in *contrapunto alla mente*, whereby
counterpoint was improvised to the liturgical chant.[48]

In many instances, these celebrations were financed by the confraternities
attached to churches, and in some cases elaborate performances took place in
the oratories of the confraternities. The German College was particularly

[40] Ibid. 24–5, 28, 58, 64–5; also id., 'Victoria, Soto and the Spanish Archconfraternity of the
Resurrection in Rome', *Early Music*, 22 (1994), 288–9.

[41] O'Regan, 'Sacred Polychoral Music', i. 66, 89. See also Graham Dixon, 'The Pantheon and Music
in Minor Churches in Seventeenth-Century Rome', *Studi musicali*, 10 (1981), 272.

[42] O'Regan, 'Sacred Polychoral Music', i. 83, 89. See also id., 'The Performance of Roman Sacred
Polychoral Music in the Late Sixteenth and Early Seventeenth Centuries: Evidence from Archival
Sources', *Performance Practice Review*, 8 (fall 1995), 112, and esp. the eyewitness account by André
Maugars of a festal performance in 1639, pp. 137–8; Graham Dixon, 'The Origins of the Roman
"Colossal Baroque"', *Proceedings of the Royal Musical Association*, 106 (1979–80), 119, 121; id., 'Musical
Activity in the Church of the Gesù in Rome during the Early Baroque', *Archivum historicum Societatis
Iesu*, 49 (1980), 334.

[43] See the table of expenditures for extra singers and for instrumentalists by various Roman churches
for specific feasts as well as the summary of instrumental usage in O'Regan, 'Sacred Polychoral Music',
i. 67–71, 77. Instruments are also specifically named in id., 'Victoria, Soto and the Spanish
Archconfraternity', 285–7; and id., 'The Performance of Roman Sacred Polychoral Music', 117–23,
126–8. Notation of obbligato instruments in Roman sources is very rare; it is highly likely that instruments either doubled voices or played some or all of the parts of one or more choirs in polychoral
settings. See O'Regan, 'Sacred Polychoral Music', i. 293.

[44] Ibid. 71–2, 84, 88. *Falsobordone* was the typical form of music in processions. See ibid. 20, 22.

[45] O'Regan, 'Victoria, Soto and the Spanish Archconfraternity', 285–7; id., 'Palestrina, a Musician
and Composer in the Market-Place', *Early Music*, 22 (1994), 558.

[46] O'Regan, 'Sacred Polychoral Music', i. 51–2, 85, 94.

[47] Ibid. 85–7. See the tables comparing the frequency of surviving Roman polyphonic settings of
vesper psalms with their frequency in the liturgy, ibid. 86–7.

[48] Ibid. 43. See also id., 'Palestrina, a Musician and Composer', 560.

known for its music, but the English College also hired musicians for special festivities in the early seventeenth century.[49] As in northern Italy, at least one church, that of San Luigi, included instrumentalists in its permanent ensemble.[50] Instruments were so much a part of important celebrations that oratorios hired instrumentalists during Holy Week, when the organ was officially proscribed in the churches.[51] Easter services could also be occasions for polychoral music with instruments.[52]

While instruments were forbidden in the Sistine Chapel, the choir there did sing double-choir music, and possibly also the three- and four-choir psalm and Magnificat settings published by Soriano in 1616 (53984).[53] Moreover, it used the organ when it performed vespers in the papal apartments on Easter, Pentecost, and the Feast of St Peter.[54] On the other hand, the Cappella Giulia, the choir of St Peter's Basilica, performed polychoral music not only with organ, but also with other instruments. There is documentation of elaborate multi-choir music on a number of different occasions from the turn of the century onwards, as the basilica approached structural completion in 1615.[55]

Most of the music performed in these churches was never published, and the number of manuscript sources is also quite limited, so we cannot know if obbligato instrumental parts were often notated in the scores, but it seems unlikely since obbligato instruments appear only rarely in the surviving manuscripts and not at all in Roman prints of sacred music before the *Psalmi Magnif. cum quatuor antiphonis ad vesperas octo vocib.* of Paolo Tarditi in 1620 (T225) (see below).[56]

While it has been customary to think of early seventeenth-century monody as a particularly Florentine phenomenon, it should be remembered that Caccini first presented his new style in Rome, where he says he had already achieved fame for his solo singing before the turn of the century.[57] In Viadana's preface to the *Cento concerti ecclesiastici* (Venice, 1602, V1360), containing sacred monodies, duets, trios, and four-voice compositions, including a few psalms and Magnificats, the composer similarly mentions that he had written some of these pieces five or six years previously in Rome, and was publishing them be-

---

[49] On the German College, see Thomas D. Culley, *Jesuits and Music*, i: *A Study of the Musicians Connected with the German College in Rome during the 17th Century and of their Activities in Northern Europe* (St Louis: St Louis University, 1970). The German College and English College are also discussed in O'Regan, 'Sacred Polychoral Music'.

[50] These included a cornettist, a trombonist, and a violinist in 1600. See ibid. i. 72.

[51] Ibid. 90–1.

[52] Ibid. 94.

[53] Ibid. 53, 84.

[54] Ibid. 43.

[55] Ibid. 46–53, 73. Two cornettos and two sackbuts are mentioned in 1600 and 'various instruments' in 1620.

[56] MS Vatican Library, Giul. XIII 25 from the 1580s contains a Magnificat by Giovanni Maria Nanino with obbligato violin and cornetto as well as an organ part. See ibid. 114–15.

[57] Strunk, *Source Readings in Music History*, 379.

cause others had imitated them and were already publishing such imitations.[58] In fact, in the early seventeenth century a number of Roman composers published not only few-voiced motets resembling the rather conservative style of Viadana,[59] but also solo motets, psalms, and Magnificats in a highly virtuosic style or in open emulation of Caccini. Two Roman virtuoso singers, Giovanni Luca Conforti and Francesco Severi, published solo psalms with extensive *passaggi*.[60] Ottavio Durante's *Arie devote* of 1608 (D3975) is unabashedly modelled on Caccini's monodies and contains a solo Magnificat in a style similar to the motets. Gerolamo Kapsberger, a celebrated virtuoso of the chitarrone, also published both secular and sacred solo vocal music in a virtuoso style in 1612.[61]

Denis Arnold has cited the pervasive diffusion of the plainchant cantus firmus throughout the psalms and Magnificats of the *Vespro della Beata Vergine* as evidence of Monteverdi's concern for structural cohesion in these expansive and variegated compositions,[62] a concern which is demonstrated below in Chapters 6–10 and in the structural outlines of Appendix C. But the monotony of the psalm tone also posed difficult aesthetic and organizational problems for lesser composers. While harmonization of the psalm chant had been practised with some frequency in the early part of the *Cinquecento*, by late in the century most composers employed the cantus firmus sparingly. The reason is obvious: harmonic and tonal tedium are difficult to avoid. One has only to look at some of the rare instances where the chant was used extensively: Victoria's *Dixit Dominus*, published in 1581, illustrates the harmonic limitations resulting therefrom.[63] The effect is worse in Giovanni Croce's eight-voice, double-choir *Domine probasti me* from his *Vespertina* of 1597.[64] This particular psalm text is of unusual length, and the desire to unify the composition is probably what prompted Croce to employ the chant in the first place. But even though the

[58] Ibid. 421.

[59] Both Agostino Agazzari and Antonio Cifra were somewhat conservative and focused on motets for two voices and continuo. Giovanni Francesco Anerio was more progressive and included solo motets in his first publication of 1609 (A1096). Other Roman composers of solo and few-voiced motets active in the first decade of the century were Girolamo Bartei, Pietro Paolo da Cavi, and Giovanni Bernardino Nanino. See Graham Dixon, 'Progressive Tendencies in the Roman Motet during the Early Seventeenth Century', *Acta musicologica*, 53 (1981), 105–19.

[60] Conforti, *Salmi passaggiati sopra tutti i toni* (1601–3, C3498), *Passaggi sopra tutti li salmi* (1607, C3499, repr. of 1601 vol.); and Severi, *Salmi passaggiati . . . sopra i falsi bordoni* (1615, S2847). See the discussion of these prints in Ch. 2.

[61] Kapsberger's first books of *arie passeggiate a una voce* (K186) and *mottetti passeggiati a una voce* (K185) both date from this year. Fac. ed. Piero Mioli (Florence: Studio per Edizioni Scelte, 1980). Despite the examples of Durante and Kapsberger, the solo motet never gained a strong foothold in Rome during the first twenty years of the century. See Dixon, 'Progressive Tendencies', 115.

[62] 'Monteverdi and the Technique of "Concertato"', *Amor Artis Bulletin*, 6 (Apr. 1967), 7.

[63] Ed. Philippo Pedrell in *Thomae Ludovici Victoria Abulensis: Opera omnia* (Leipzig: Breitkopf & Härtel, 1902–11), vii. 1–10.

[64] Complete transcriptions of this, most of the other unpublished compositions mentioned in this chapter, and additional responses, psalms, Magnificats, hymns, and motets are found in Kurtzman, 'The Monteverdi Vespers of 1610'.

primary texture is relieved by several two-voice sections in the middle of the piece, the monotony of Croce's setting is evident.

Consequently, most composers by the early seventeenth century paid rather limited attention to the psalm tone if they used it at all. In the numerous psalms beginning with a plainchant intonation, the chant often continues in the tenor or soprano once the polyphony starts. Almost invariably, however, the psalm tone is abandoned after the completion of the first verse. Similar treatment may be accorded to interior sections of *alternatim* settings. Here too the plainchant begun in an even or odd verse may continue in one voice in the succeeding polyphonic segment. But this procedure rarely occurs in more than one or two verses in psalms of the late sixteenth or early seventeenth centuries.[65]

Aside from the continuation of the plainchant into a polyphonic texture, the psalm tone may also be confined entirely within a polyphonic segment itself. Most often this takes the form of single verses cast in unmeasured *falsibordoni*. In other instances the method may be harmonization in *canto figurato*. Occasionally the psalm tone appears as a long-note cantus firmus, serves as an imitative subject, or is even treated in canon, as in the *Sicut erat* of *Lauda Jerusalem* from the *Vespertina omnium solemnitatum* of 1602 (G501) by Monteverdi's Mantuan colleague Giovanni Giacomo Gastoldi.

Such sophisticated contrapuntal procedures are exceptional and are normally found in only a single section of a polyphonic psalm or Magnificat. Except for the Croce psalm mentioned above and a work by Giovanni Francesco Capello to be discussed below, Monteverdi seems to have been the only composer in the early seventeenth century to use the cantus firmus as a pervasive organizational device. The discussion in Chapters 6–8 below reveals the imagination and inventiveness with which he was able to achieve both the desired structural cohesion and the harmonic, tonal, textural, and stylistic variety necessary to avoid the monotony threatened by a repeated cantus firmus.

Despite the conservative tendencies of vesper psalmody, a few impulses in the direction of modernity can be witnessed in settings of the first decade of the seventeenth century. The natural subdivision of a psalm into several sections invited contrasts among those sections, and composers in the early *Seicento* gradually began to take advantage of such opportunities. A 1601 through-composed setting of *Nisi Dominus*, from the collection *Tutti li salmi* by Gastoldi (G498), not only utilizes antiphonal, homophonic four-voice choirs in duple time, but also shifts to triple metre three times in the course of the piece and includes a passage of *falsobordone* as well. The block-like exchanges between the two choirs, frequently comprising entire lines of text (see Ex. 4.1), denote a forerunner of Monteverdi's own *Nisi Dominus*, though the latter work employs a plainchant

---

[65] Further discussion of the role of the psalm tone in polyphonic psalm settings is found in James Armstrong, 'How to Compose a Psalm'.

Ex. 4.1. Giovanni Gastoldi, *Nisi Dominus* from *Tutti li salmi*, 1601

cantus firmus throughout and is considerably longer, with its second choir echoing each line sung by the first. Monteverdi's rhythms are also more varied than Gastoldi's and his part-writing is more complex, even though *Nisi Dominus* is the simplest and least progressive of the five psalms of the *Vespro*.[66] This type of antiphonal setting is common in the vesper repertoire, though the dimensions of Monteverdi's version are typically larger.

Contrasting sections within a psalm are more fully exploited by Gastoldi in his 1607 six-voice setting of *Memento Domine David* from his *Salmi intieri* of 1607 (G503). This lengthy text requires considerable variety of treatment in order to maintain musical interest. Gastoldi employs homophonic textures for all six voices, chordal antiphony between the upper three and the lower three, polyphony in varying combinations of parts, *falsibordoni* followed by polyphonic melismas, sections in triple metre, and passages in faster note values than the prevailing rhythms. This may well be the most complex and varied psalm setting published before 1610, but the styles of its component parts are rooted in the past and not comparable to the modern aspects of Monteverdi's even more complex psalms.

Composers outside the Mantuan circle also occasionally contrasted successive sections of a psalm, and there even survive a few compositions from before 1610 with emphasis partly or entirely on ornamented solo voices and the newest vocal styles. Both features are combined with *falsobordone* in a three-voice *Dixit Dominus* published in the *Sacri fiori motetti* of 1606 by Leo Leoni (L1997), employed at the time in Vicenza. Leoni's *Dixit* contrasts the polyphonic texture of its first and last segments with internal sections of unmeasured recitation for one, two, and three voices.[67] The ornamental element consists of melismas following each half-verse in *falsobordone*. The melodic shapes and rhythmic patterns of these melismas are similar to much of the vocal writing in few-voiced motets from Viadana onwards. They are not yet in the faster semiquavers favoured by Monteverdi (see Ex. 4.2).

Another example of the rather rare appearance of solo voices in psalm composition may be found in Don Severo Bonini's compline psalm *Cum invocarem*, published in *Il secondo libro de madrigali, e motetti à una voce sola* of 1609 (B3497).[68] This piece is a monody modelled on those of Bonini's Florentine compatriot Caccini, particularly in the extensive use of the most modern ornaments. As in

---

[66] See Chs. 6 and 15 for further commentary on *Nisi Dominus*.

[67] Many of these passages of unmeasured recitation are labelled *falsibordoni* in the prints themselves, even though they may be for only one voice accompanied by organ continuo. The organist would have had to play a full chordal harmonization of the psalm tone, so the rubric *falsibordoni* in connection with a solo voice is not an inconsistency in terminology.

[68] A complete transcription is published in Jeffrey Kurtzman, ed., *Vesper and Compline Music for One Principal Voice* (Seventeenth-Century Italian Sacred Music, 11).

Ex. 4.2. Leo Leoni, *Dixit Dominus* from *Sacri fiori mottetti*, 1606

Leoni's *Dixit Dominus*, the ornamental passages follow the initial part of each line, which is set in *falsobordone* (see Ex. 4.3).

It is significant that both the Leoni and Bonini psalms were not printed in collections of vesper music, but in books of motets (madrigals and motets in the case of Bonini). As mentioned earlier, the inclusion of occasional vesper psalms and Magnificats in motet books seems to have led to the assimilation by these psalms and canticles of the style of their companion pieces. It is actually in this peripheral part of the vesper repertoire that we find the forerunners of the few-voiced sections of Monteverdi's *Dixit Dominus*, *Laudate pueri*, and *Laetatus sum*. Monteverdi's is thus the first publication of vesper music to amalgamate the full-choir techniques common to psalmody with the newer few-voiced virtuoso style.

Many of the precedents for Monteverdi's separate obbligato and optional instrumental parts in the Vespers also derive from the motet repertoire.[69] A motet from Viadana's *Cento concerti ecclesiastici* of 1602 (V1360), *O bone Iesu*, is scored for tenor solo and two trombones. In Leoni's *Sacri fiori* of 1606, there are two motets for two voices and instruments: *In te Domine speravi* for two altos and two trombones, and *Deus exaudi* for two sopranos or tenors, a trombone, and a *violetta*. A mixed posthumous print of *Concerti per sonare et cantare* from 1607 (R29) by Giulio Radino Padavano, also containing music by other composers, features instrumental pieces as well as instruments in both motets and a Magnificat. The ten-part motet *O Domine Iesu* by Amadio Freddi from Radino's print is texted in all voices, but also has a rubric calling for a trombone in all parts except the cantus. The twelve-part motet *Media nocte* by Orindio Bartolini calls for a

---

[69] See Chs. 18 and 19 for an extensive examination of the role of instruments in the Vespers.

Ex. 4.3. Don Severo Bonini, *Cum invocarem* from *Il secondo libro de madrigali e mottetti*, 1609[2]

trombone in the texted Duodecimus part-book. In each of these pieces, the instrumental parts all seem to be obbligato doubling instruments, since substitutions would likely carry the rubric *si placet* or *à beneplacito*.

A book of *Concerti ecclesiastici* published in 1608 by Arcangelo Crotti of
Ferrara (C4552) includes several pieces for one or two soloists with notated in-
strumental accompaniments, most of which are marked *si placet*. The Milanese
Girolamo Baglioni's *Sacrarum cantionum* of 1608 (B644) contains a setting of
Maria Magdalena & altera Maria for two sopranos, bass, and one unspecified ob-
bligato instrument notated in the G_2 clef. Caterina Assandra, a nun originally

from Pavia, included in her *Motetti* of 1609 (A2637, 1609³) a setting of *O salu-taris Hostia* for soprano and bass supported by a violin and violone in addition to the basso continuo.[70] Viadana provided two trombones *se piace* for the motet for alto and tenor *Repleatur os meum*, as well as for *Benedicam Dominum in omni tempore* for two tenors, in his third book of *Concerti ecclesiastici* of 1609 (V1392). In the midst of the table of contents of Giovanni Battista Dulcino's publication of *Sacrae cantiones octo vocibus* from the same year (D3679), a rubric declares that 'the six following pieces must be performed with the organ and other instruments'.[71] Unfortunately only two part-books of this print survive, but a notated violin part is found in one of these for a single motet, *Cantate Domino*. According to the rubric at the head of the piece, it is 'to be concerted with two violins and two trombones'.[72] Presumably the other five motets had notated instrumental parts in the missing part-books. Dulcino's print is dedicated to Don Bassano Casola, his compatriot from Lodi, who was *vice-maestro di cappella* at Mantua under Monteverdi. Arcangelo Borsaro's *Novo giardino de concerti* of 1611 (B3781) calls for optional substitution of trombones for the two lower voices in each of its twenty motets. While all of these compositions bear witness to the introduction of notated instrumental parts into the sacred repertoire, the instruments nevertheless serve as accompaniment to the voice or voices, or substitutes for voices, and do not play a role in the texture any different from that of voices themselves.

    The most famous examples of obbligato instrumentation in motets are in Giovanni Gabrieli's *Sacrae symphoniae* of 1615 (G87) as well as in a couple of manuscript motets.[73] Since Gabrieli died in 1612, the contents of the *Sacrae symphoniae* antedate its publication by at least three years and in some cases by many more, as determined from concordances.[74] Gabrieli's obbligato instruments play a very different role from those in the motets cited above. Gabrieli uses his ensemble for extensive introductory sinfonias, as interludes in the course of a motet, to reinforce the sonority by doubling voices, to thicken the texture with independent parts while voices are singing, to accompany one, two or three voices, and to play independent counterpoint to the voices, sometimes in imitation of the vocal parts. It is in Gabrieli's music that instruments assumed a truly

---

[70] Biographical information on Caterina may be found in Carolyn Gianturco, 'Caterina Assandra, suora compositrice', in Alberto Colzani, Andrea Luppi, and Maurizio Padoan, eds., *La musica sacra in Lombardia nella prima metà del Seicento* (Como: AMIS, 1988), 115–27.

[71] 'Questi sei seguenti sono di bisogno sonarli con l'Organo, e altri Instrumenti'. The print contains fifteen motets, a litany, and a Magnificat.

[72] 'Per Concertar con doi Violini, e doi Tromboni'.

[73] Ed. Denis Arnold and Richard Charteris in *Giovanni Gabrieli: Opera omnia* (Rome: American Institute of Musicology, 1956–), iii–vi. See Chs. 18 and 19 for discussions of instrumental doubling and substitution in Gabrieli's music and Gabrieli's use of obbligato instruments.

[74] See Egon F. Kenton, *Life and Works of Giovanni Gabrieli* (Musicological Studies and Documents, 16; American Institute of Musicology, 1967), 163–6, 179, 185–8.

significant role in the motet repertoire, in some passages surpassing the voices as the main focus of attention.

Psalms and Magnificats also occasionally called for obbligato instruments. The Magnificat by Giulio Radino mentioned above is texted in all sixteen parts, but four of these are also marked *Choro de Violini*, four as *Choro de Cornetti*, and four as *Choro de Tromboni* in addition to a four-part *Capella*.[75] One of the psalms in Agostino Agazzari's *Psalmi sex* of 1609 (A357) is headed by the rubric: 'first one plays an instrumental sinfonia', though this must be improvised since no music is given.[76] Denis Arnold describes a *Laudate pueri* by the Venetian Giovanni Croce, who died in 1609, in which one of three four-part choirs consists of a tenor and three instruments, 'two of which are specified to be trombones'.[77] The date of this piece is unknown, since its first appearance is in an anthology published in 1630.[78] According to the preface of the Bolognese Girolamo Giacobbi's *Prima parte dei salmi concertati* of 1609 (G1821), the lower choir of these double-choir psalms comprises a contralto 'accompanied by a body of instruments on the remaining parts, such as trombones, violas, or the like'. Moreover, text may also be sung to these remaining parts where indicated in the music. Viadana's *Salmi a quattro chori* of 1612 (V1400) has a lengthy preface in which the composer describes the use of instruments to double voices in the second, third, and fourth choirs.[79]

That notated instrumental parts became significant in sacred music at Mantua at about this time is evident not only from Monteverdi's Vespers, but also from Amante Franzoni's *Apparato musicale* of 1613 (F1813).[80] The mass in this collection, which according to the preface was performed in the ducal church on the feast of Santa Barbara in 1612 and reflected the taste of Franzoni's *Padroni*, contains an instrumental *Entrata* in place of the Introit, an instrumental ritornello to be fitted between the segments of the Kyrie, a *canzona francese* to accompany the Epistle, sinfonias to be inserted between sections of the Offertory, two more sinfonias to precede the Sanctus and Agnus, and a canzona to conclude the ser-

---

[75] The Undecimus part-book is missing, but presumably would have belonged to the *Choro de Tromboni*.

[76] 'Prima si fa una Sinfonia di stromenti'.

[77] 'Giovanni Croce and the "Concertato" Style', *Musical Quarterly*, 39 (1953), 44.

[78] Though not precisely specified by Arnold, the collection in question is Leonardo Simonetti's *Raccolta terza . . . de messa et salmi* of 1630 (SD1630¹). It is devoted to music of Croce and Grandi.

[79] See the discussion of this print in Ch. 19. The preface is translated complete in Jerome Roche, *North Italian Church Music in the Age of Monteverdi* (Oxford: Clarendon Press, 1984), 118–20.

[80] Franzoni had assumed the post of *maestro di cappella* in Santa Barbara in Oct. 1612. See n. 135 below. Franzoni, a Servite, was originally from Mantua and a member of the Accademia Olimpica, so he was returning home to his new employment at Santa Barbara. Recent studies of the *Apparato musicale* are Federico Mompellio, ' "L'Apparato musicale" del Servita Amante Franzoni', *Rivista internazionale di musica sacra*, 14 (1993), 211–69; and Graham Dixon, ' "Behold our Affliction": Celebration and Supplication in the Gonzaga Household', *Early Music*, 24 (1996), 250–61.

vice. As indicated on the title-page, these instrumental pieces could be omitted, and they are not integral elements in any of the mass sections.[81]

Although it is clear that by 1610 Monteverdi had many precedents in the use of instruments in liturgical music and that instruments probably participated with some frequency in celebrations in the ducal church of Santa Barbara, his manner of employing instruments differed considerably from that of most of his contemporaries. In *Dixit Dominus* and *Ave maris stella*, unspecified instruments serve for ritornellos, which are optional in *Dixit Dominus*, and probably also optional in *Ave maris stella*, though Monteverdi is silent regarding the matter. The antecedents for these ritornellos are not in the sacred repertoire, but rather in Monteverdi's own *L'Orfeo*, the *Scherzi musicali* of 1607, and *Il ballo delle ingrate* of 1608. The extensive independent, even virtuoso, instrumental parts in the *Sonata sopra Sancta Maria* are comparable only to the instrumental writing of Giovanni Gabrieli. But even here there are significant differences in style, as described below in the discussion of the *Sonata*. The Magnificat *a 7* utilizes instruments for ritornellos and for independent, often virtuosic roles in pairs of like instruments, as counterparts to the pairs of virtuoso voices. I know of no precedents for this type of instrumental writing in either the sacred or the secular repertoire of the first decade of the seventeenth century.

III

Having established the general background for the music of the 1610 print, we may now turn to the music itself as it relates to this background. The first stage in Monteverdi's compositional process throughout the Vespers consisted in the derivation of relatively simple techniques and formal concepts from a variety of traditional and modern sources (see Chapters 6–10). These diverse materials were then combined in a new synthesis to forge large-scale, elaborate structures whose size and impact far surpass the creations of other composers. Nowhere is this more evident or striking than in the psalm *Dixit Dominus*. The symmetrical structure of this expansive setting may be seen in Fig. 4.1.

Structural symmetry was an important organizational principle for Monteverdi throughout his life, but the sequence of sections outlined in Fig. 4.1 also represents a complex fusion of techniques practised separately by other

---

[81] See also Stephen Bonta, 'The Uses of the Sonata da Chiesa', *Journal of the American Musicological Society*, 22 (1969), 54–84. Carol MacClintock notes the importance of instruments in the services at Santa Barbara during the tenure of Giaches de Wert as *maestro di cappella*. See *Giaches de Wert: Life and Works* (Musicological Studies and Documents, 17; American Institute of Musicology, 1966), 148, 154.

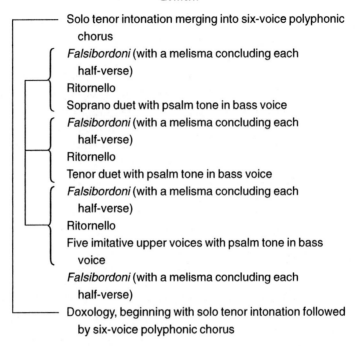

Solo tenor intonation merging into six-voice polyphonic
chorus
Falsibordoni (with a melisma concluding each
half-verse)
Ritornello
Soprano duet with psalm tone in bass voice
Falsibordoni (with a melisma concluding each
half-verse)
Ritornello
Tenor duet with psalm tone in bass voice
Falsibordoni (with a melisma concluding each
half-verse)
Ritornello
Five imitative upper voices with psalm tone in bass
voice
Falsibordoni (with a melisma concluding each
half-verse)
Doxology, beginning with solo tenor intonation followed
by six-voice polyphonic chorus

FIG. 4.1. *Dixit Dominus*, symmetries

composers.[82] The opening imitative chorus employs as its main subject the fourth psalm tone. Such imitation based on the chant was nothing new, though ordinarily it can be found only in the most elaborate and sophisticated psalm settings. The passages of *falsibordoni*, commencing immediately after the opening, are quite common in vesper psalmody, but Monteverdi's concluding melismas are more polyphonically elaborate than usual. Unique is the fact that each of these melismas is a rhythmic and melodic variant of a single basic harmonic pattern.[83] In addition, each of the optional instrumental ritornellos is a varied repetition of the immediately preceding melisma.

In *Dixit Dominus*, the section immediately following the first ritornello exhibits a modern style and texture based upon an old structural technique. Here a typical Baroque trio, consisting of two imitative voices in the same range supported by an independent bass part, makes its first appearance in vesper psalmody. Similar trios are found in *Laudate pueri*, *Laetatus sum*, *Pulchra es*, *Duo Seraphim*, the *Sonata sopra Sancta Maria*, and both Magnificats. While such tex-

---

[82] Structural symmetry in the Vespers is discussed in Chs. 6–8. See also Donald J. Grout, *A Short History of Opera* (New York: Columbia University Press, 1947), 60–8, for a discussion of symmetries in *L'Orfeo*.

[83] See Ex. 6.8*a*, *b*, and *c* below.

tures are common in Monteverdi's madrigals from the Fourth Book onwards, they also occur frequently in the few-voiced motet books beginning with Viadana's *Cento concerti ecclesiastici* of 1602.[84] This underscores once again the influence of the motet repertoire on Monteverdi's collection.

What makes this passage in *Dixit Dominus* of particular interest is the character of the bass-line. At first provided solely by the organ continuo, it is formed primarily from a single sustained chord. But as the second soprano enters in imitation of the first, a bass voice is also added, and the sustained chord in the organ proves to have been a simplification of the measured psalm tone recitation in the bass. This same pattern of imitative upper voices supported by a psalm tone bass recurs after the ritornello in each of the tripartite groups bracketed in Fig. 1. In the first two of these sections the old-fashioned technique of *falsobordone* serves as a foundation for the modern trio texture of the combined parts.

In the structure of *Dixit Dominus* as a whole, it is apparent that aside from the opening and closing polyphonic choruses, the remainder of the work is actually based on the extremely simple and traditional *alternatim* procedure whereby verses in *falsobordone* alternate with plainchant. But the *falsibordoni* are embellished by means of large polyphonic melismas and instrumental ritornellos, while the plainchant is given specific rhythms and elaborated by the addition of imitative upper parts. The overall scope of the setting with its *falsibordoni*, ritornellos, trio textures, imitative choral polyphony, and extended six-voice melismas is so expansive as to obscure the humble origins of this very complex and variegated composition.

The remainder of the psalms in the *Vespro* also draw on a variety of both traditional and modern styles and techniques.[85] *Laudate pueri*, for example, embraces antiphonal writing, imitative polyphony, eight-voice homophony, virtuoso duets in counterpoint with the psalm tone, plainchant accompanied solely by the organ, and a concluding polyphonic melisma. *Laetatus sum*, on the other hand, is built on a series of varying textures unfolding over four separate bass patterns, which are themselves repeated in the sequence abacd, abacd, abd (see Chapter 6). This complicated procedure has its roots in the strophic variations of *L'Orfeo* and the secular works of other early seventeenth-century composers, but is unknown in previous music for vespers. *Nisi Dominus* bears a close relationship to antiphonal psalms by Gastoldi, as already described above. *Lauda Jerusalem* is reminiscent of *Nisi Dominus* in its consistency of texture and absence of few-voiced virtuoso passages. The seven parts form two three-voice choirs around the cantus firmus in the tenor, and the texture is both antiphonal

---

[84] A Magnificat with a trio texture antedating Monteverdi's Vespers is found in *Musica per cantare* of 1607 by Tiburtio Massaini (M1286, 1607[19]). This is another early instance of a modern technique occurring in a publication of motets rather than in a psalm collection.

[85] For a more extended study of the musical organization and structure of the psalms, see Ch. 6.

and polyphonic, with more rhythmic complexity and closer interaction between the vocal ensembles than in *Nisi Dominus.*

In speaking of the context of Monteverdi's psalms, it should be emphasized how little they have to do with the late style of Giovanni Gabrieli, other than their general propensity for magnificence and complexity on a large scale.[86] No vesper psalms by Gabrieli survive at all; the closest he came to psalmody are seven settings of the Magnificat and one of the compline canticle *Nunc dimittis.* All of these compositions are for multiple choirs in *cori spezzati* style, and none employ obbligato instruments. Where Gabrieli relies on massed bodies of sound, frequently in rapid-fire exchanges, perhaps doubled by instruments or even with obbligato instruments in his motets, Monteverdi reflects in his first three psalms the Ferrarese, Mantuan, and Florentine affection for solo voices. In these psalms Monteverdi's contrasts are not between different choirs of voices or voices and instruments, but between a six- or eight-voice choir and soloists in pairs. Gabrieli, on the other hand, uses a single voice part infrequently, and when he does, it does not display the soloistic virtuosity so prominent in Monteverdi.

Even in Monteverdi's antiphonal psalms, *Nisi Dominus* and *Lauda Jerusalem,* the antiphonal exchanges tend to differ from Gabrieli's approach. In *Nisi Dominus* the sections of text and music for each choir are lengthy in comparison with Gabrieli. In *Lauda Jerusalem,* the more frequent exchanges, with considerable overlapping and integration between the two three-voice groupings, are more like some of the passages in Gabrieli's eight-voice motets, but does not approach the antiphonal style of his larger posthumous compositions. Additionally, the pervasive presence of the psalm tone in both *Nisi Dominus* and *Lauda Jerusalem* creates a harmonic framework unlike anything found in Gabrieli's music. Monteverdi's psalms have closer connections with psalm settings by other composers from Mantua and the Veneto than with the motets of Gabrieli. In fact, they are least attractive in these two settings, where Monteverdi is rather restrained in his use of polychoral techniques and antiphonal effects, in contrast to Gabrieli, whose extravagance in such polychoral music forms the basis of his historical reputation.

In Monteverdi's 1610 print, stylistic complexity and diversity is therefore evident not only in each individual psalm but also in the succession of psalms. The variety of sources from which Monteverdi has drawn and the constantly changing manner in which he has combined his materials are truly astonishing. Cohesion and diversity have been brought together in a dynamic synthesis that is one of the most significant factors in the aesthetic impact of these compositions.

[86] Roche also compares and contrasts Gabrieli and Monteverdi in *North Italian Church Music,* 121–2.

The dialectical forces of cohesion and diversity also focus attention on the antithetical tendencies of conservatism and progressiveness. The pervasive cantus firmus is a thoroughly conservative device, which by 1610 was no longer utilized by other composers of vesper psalms. Monteverdi was fully conscious of this, for the Basso continuo part-book is inscribed with the rubric *composto sopra canti fermi*, openly advertising his approach to the psalm tone. On the other hand, the old-fashioned cantus firmus is adorned in the several psalms with the most modern musical styles and textures, emphasizing contrast and heterogeneity, especially in the first three pieces. This dichotomy and tension between the old and the new is another fundamental aesthetic feature of these works.

While many detailed technical differences between Monteverdi's psalms and those of other composers may be cited, the larger issue of comparative aesthetic effect and the elements that create it is an equally important concern, though rather more elusive and difficult to verbalize. Monteverdi's psalms doubtless make a stronger impression on the listener than those of his contemporaries. Although many factors contribute to this, there can be little question that among the most important are the dynamic tensions between cohesion and diversity and between conservatism and modernity described here.

IV

Monteverdi's two Magnificats (one a close variant of the other) are even more unusual than his psalms in comparison with the repertoire of the late sixteenth and early seventeenth centuries.[87] The canticle of Mary has a longer history of polyphonic composition than vesper psalmody, and it was customarily treated in a more elaborate style.[88] Pietro Cerone emphasizes this relationship in his commentary on the three principal canticles: 'As is the custom, the three principal canticles, namely, the Magnificat, the Nunc dimittis, and the Benedictus Dominus Deus Israel, are always made solemn; for this reason, they must be composed in a more lofty style and with more art and more skill than the other canticles and the psalms.'[89]

---

[87] See Ch. 7 for a detailed study of the relationship between the two Magnificats.

[88] The early history of polyphonic Magnificats, hymns, and psalms is treated in Masakata Kanazawa, 'Polyphonic Music for Vespers during the Fifteenth Century' (Ph.D dissertation, Harvard University, 1966). On *Cinquecento* Magnificats see Carl-Heinz Illing, *Zur Technik der Magnificat-Komposition des 16. Jahrhunderts* (Kieler Beiträge zur Musikwissenschaft, 3; Wolfenbüttel and Berlin: Georg Kallmeyer Verlag, 1936) and Winfried Kirsch, *Die Quellen des mehrstimmigen Magnificat- und Te Deum-Vertonungen bis zur Mitte des 16. Jahrhunderts* (Tutzing: Hans Schneider, 1966).

[89] Strunk, *Source Readings in Music History*, 270. Cerone's dependence on Ponzio in his treatment of the Magnificat is discussed in Armstrong, 'How to Compose a Psalm'.

As in psalm settings, the importance of the plainchant cantus firmus in Magnificats gradually subsided as the sixteenth century progressed. In Costanzo Festa's Magnificats from the 1530s, a paraphrase of the Magnificat tone serves as the subject for imitation at the beginning of almost every verse.[90] From time to time the cantus firmus surfaces in longer note values in a single part, usually the topmost. As the chant approaches its cadence, the tone is almost invariably ornamented. Most of Festa's Magnificats have at least one segment in which the Magnificat tone is treated in strict canon between two voices.

Similar techniques are employed in the Magnificats of Morales and Victoria, published in 1545 (M3594) and 1576 (V1427) respectively, although in none of these is the Magnificat tone quite so pervasive as in the works of Festa.[91] The plainchant as cantus firmus is even less significant in the Magnificats of Palestrina.[92] Palestrina typically begins with the *initium* of the chant melody, usually as the imitative subject of his polyphonic texture. In those instances where the chant continues beyond the opening of a verse, it is often so highly embellished as to be virtually unrecognizable; the reciting note appears only occasionally as a single pitch in an active, flowing line. The second half of a verse is generally closer to the Magnificat tone, with the style often becoming more chordal as the reciting note is harmonized homophonically. Some verses of the Palestrina Magnificats show little or no evidence of the Magnificat tone, and only infrequently does it appear as a distinct cantus firmus or the subject of a canon.[93]

Interest in the Magnificat tone cantus firmus in polyphonic verses continued to decline into the seventeenth century. *Alternatim* settings, which constitute perhaps half of all Magnificats from the early *Seicento*, would of course still have had every other verse sung in plainchant in the same manner as *alternatim* psalms. But printed Magnificats having any significant reference to the chant in their polyphonic verses comprise less than half the extant repertoire. Where a Magnificat tone is in evidence, it is normally confined to the continuation of a solo intonation into the first part of the polyphonic setting, similar to the practice in psalmody. In some compositions the *initium* of the Magnificat tone opens a polyphonic verse other than the first, but rarely does the chant appear in this

---

[90] Ed. Alexander Main in *Costanzo Festa: Opera omnia* (American Institute of Musicology, 1962–), ii.

[91] Ed. Higinio Anglés in *Cristóbal de Morales: Opera omnia: XVI Magníficat* (Monumentos de la Música Española, 17; Barcelona: Consejo Superior de Investigaciones Científicas, 1956), and Pedrell in *Thomae Ludovici Victoria Abulensis opera omnia*, v.

[92] Ed. Raffaele Casimiri in *Le opere complete di Giovanni Pierluigi da Palestrina* (Rome: Edizione Fratelli Scalera, 1939–), xvi. The only book of Magnificats published by Palestrina in his lifetime did not appear until 1591. His earlier Magnificats remained in MS only.

[93] For an overview of the Palestrina Magnificats see Jeffrey Kurtzman, 'Palestrina's Magnificats: A Brief Survey', in David Crawford and Grayson Wagstaff, eds., *Encomium musicae: Essays in Honor of Robert J. Snow* (Stuyvesant, NY: Pendragon Press, forthcoming).

manner more than once. The custom of setting the doxology in a canon based on the Magnificat tone survives only marginally.[94] By the time of Monteverdi's Vespers, only vestiges of the earlier significance of the Magnificat chant remained. The chant usages most frequently found in the early seventeenth century do not differ substantially from those encountered in contemporaneous psalmody.

The waning importance of the chant sets in striking relief Monteverdi's highly original approach to the cantus firmus in his two Magnificats of 1610. In his psalms Monteverdi usually gave to the cantus firmus rhythmic values commensurate with those of the other voices. As a result, even though the chant regulates the basic harmony, the tone itself is often absorbed into the larger texture. In the Magnificats, however, the chant is set in long notes and usually stands apart from the other voices and instruments. This type of strict, long-note cantus firmus in all verses is extremely unusual in the history of the Marian canticle, and I know of no other examples in Italy in the early seventeenth century. Monteverdi ignored the traditions of this repertoire and revived instead the oldest cantus firmus technique of the mass and motet, applying it to his Magnificats with great rigour. The result is a continuous series of variations on the Magnificat tone, with the other parts disporting themselves in the most progressive styles.[95] Once again the multiplicity and diversity of Monteverdi's sources is revealed, and once again the virtuosity with which they are combined is unique among his contemporaries.

Monteverdi's utilization of modern techniques is even more pronounced in the canticles than in the psalms, as if his adherence to a conservative, strict cantus firmus required the opposite extreme in the other parts. With the exception of choral textures in the first and last verses of the seven-voice Magnificat and in the first and final two verses of the six-voice setting, the pieces are devoted to solo writing, trio textures, vocal and instrumental virtuosity, dialogues, echo duets, ritornello structures, obbligato instrumental accompaniments, and rapid note values; in short, a dazzling array of the most recently developed techniques, styles and structures, all unified by the severe and unremitting presence of the cantus firmus. The tension between diversity and cohesion, between modernity and conservatism, is even more starkly evident here than in the psalms.

Though one may search vainly in the early seventeenth-century sacred repertoire for anything comparable, adumbrations of a few of Monteverdi's

[94] See e.g. Giovanni Croce, *Magnificat omnium tonorum cum sex vocibus* of 1605, partially transcribed in Kurtzman, 'The Monteverdi Vespers of 1610', 785–7, and the Magnificats by Luigi Mazzi in *Li salmi à cinque voci* of 1610. One of these Magnificats is transcribed in Kurtzman, 'The Monteverdi Vespers of 1610', 788–802.

[95] See Ch. 1 above for Graham Dixon's association of this combination with the ducal church of Santa Barbara.

techniques did appear between 1600 and 1610. In this decade contrasts in sonority, texture, and style among successive verses began to emerge in Magnificats as they did in vesper psalms. Variations in sonority assume importance in an *alternatim* Magnificat from Viadana's *Cento concerti ecclesiastici* of 1602 (V1360). While the polyphonic texture remains three-voiced throughout, the combination of voices changes at several stages along the way. Initially the trio comprises soprano, alto, and bass, but the parts shift to soprano and two altos at the *Et misericordia*; alto, tenor, and bass at the *Deposuit*; soprano, alto, and tenor at *Suscepit Israel*; and then return to the original voicing for the *Gloria Patri*. There are no changes in style in the course of the piece, however, aside from a short passage of *falsobordone* in the *Deposuit*.

On the other hand, contrasts in style are manifest in a five-voice *alternatim* Magnificat by Gastoldi, also published in 1602.[96] Most of the piece is conceived in imitative polyphony, but the *Deposuit* is set in *falsobordone*, the *Et misericordia* employs a reduced number of voices (a long-standing tradition in Magnificat composition), and the doxology deviates to triple metre.

Even greater contrasts may be observed in a four-voice *alternatim* Magnificat by Leo Leoni from 1606.[97] The traditional reduction in number of voices is retained in the *Fecit potentiam* and the *Esurientes*, but the resulting duets for soprano and tenor and for alto and bass display a more embellished vocal line than the four-voice sections (see Ex. 4.4). The other segments rely heavily on *falsibordoni* followed by polyphonic textures, which are sometimes melismatic. There is even a sequential imitative passage very similar to the polyphonic melismas of Monteverdi's *Dixit Dominus* (see Ex. 4.5).

Trio textures and virtuoso solo writing are prominent in a 1607 *alternatim* Magnificat by Tiburtio Massaini, who, like Monteverdi, was in the employ of the Duke of Mantua.[98] In this setting for two voices and organ continuo (the organ part-book is missing from the British Library copy), Massaini writes particularly elaborate parts, amply endowed with ornaments in small note values and modern dotted rhythms. He adheres to custom by reducing the number of voices for two interior sections, but the outcome is a very untraditional florid monody. The duet passages are consistently imitative, and the parts frequently proceed in parallel thirds and sixths after an initial point of imitation, a favourite device of Monteverdi's (see Ex. 4.6).

The first decade of the century witnessed mounting interest in virtuoso writing in Magnificats. Giovanni Luca Conforti's *Salmi passaggiati* of 1601–3 (C3498) and his *Passaggi sopra tutti li salmi* of 1607 (C3499) apply diminutions, often reaching extraordinary proportions, to his Magnificat as well as his psalms

[96] In *Vespertina omnium solemnitatum psalmodia . . . 1602* (G501).
[97] In *Sacri fiori mottetti . . . 1606* (L1997).
[98] In *Musica per cantare . . . 1607* (M1286, SD1607[19]).

Ex. 4.4. Leo Leoni, Magnificat from *Sacri fiori mottetti*, 1606

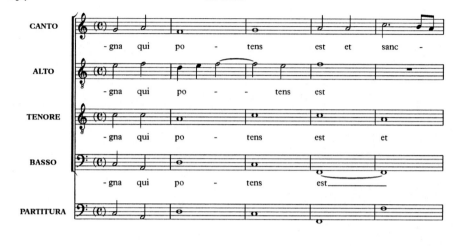

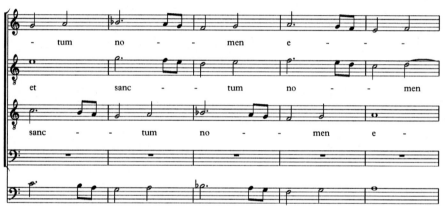

Ex. 4.5. Leo Leoni, Magnificat from *Sacri fiori mottetti*, 1606

(see Ex. 4.7).[99] The two Magnificats in Ottavio Durante's *Arie devote* of 1608 (D3975) are also prolific in their ornamentation, but the embellishments are conceived as an integral part of the melodic line (see Ex. 4.8).

Significantly, all of the few-voiced, virtuoso Magnificat settings described here, with the exception of Conforti's, were published in motet books rather than vesper collections. While vesper psalms appeared only rarely outside prints devoted specifically to vesper music (see the Leoni and Bonini examples discussed above), Magnificats were included not only in psalm and Magnificat publications, but also in books of *mottetti*, *concerti ecclesiastici*, *sacri concentus*, and so on. As a result, several types of Magnificat developed in the early seventeenth

---

[99] Ed. Murray C. Bradshaw as *Giovanni Luca Conforti, 'Salmi passaggiati' (1601–1603)* (Neuhausen and Stuttgart: American Institute of Musicology, Hänssler-Verlag, 1985).

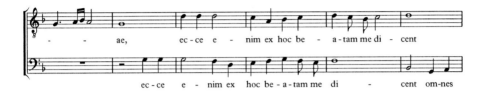

Ex. 4.6. Tiburtio Massaini, Magnificat from *Musica per cantare*, 1607

century. Those canticles incorporated into vesper collections tended to be similar to the psalms with which they were printed, whether the style was homophonic, imitative, or *cori spezzati*. Magnificats in motet books likewise corresponded to the style of the pieces they accompanied. Since the motet was the genre in which few-voiced writing first penetrated into sacred music in the early *Seicento*, Magnificats frequently assumed the new textures by association. As virtuoso embellishments invaded the motet repertoire around 1604, increasing in intensity during the next several years, Magnificats were also affected, as illustrated by those of Massaini and Durante.

These observations demonstrate that in composing his canticles Monteverdi once again took the motet books rather than contemporary vesper collections as his point of departure. It is in the motet repertoire that one finds the precedents for his few-voiced virtuoso writing in the Magnificats and the psalms, even though the inventory of pieces in the *Vespro della Beata Vergine* is modelled on the other Marian vesper publications described in section I of this chapter.

A feature of Monteverdi's Magnificat *a 7* described in Chapter 7 is its structural symmetry. Other composers in the decade 1600–10 also organized their canticles in a symmetrical fashion. The Leoni Magnificat mentioned above frames the two central duets for soprano and tenor and for alto and bass with two polyphonic verses on either side. The Croce Magnificat cited in note 94 displays

Ex. 4.7. Luca Conforti, Magnificat from *Passaggi sopra tutti li salmi*, 1607

a six-voice imitative texture in the first two and last two polyphonic verses, while the central two verses in *canto figurato* comprise high and low duets, each with an optional third voice. A similar organization is found in a 1609 Magnificat from Agostino Agazzari's *Psalmi sex* (A357) in which optional alternative settings for solo soprano may be substituted for the two central verses.[100] Yet these symmetrical structures in *alternatim* settings are quite simple in comparison with the elaborate symmetry of Monteverdi's large-scale Magnificat with instruments.

---

[100] The Agazzari collection is discussed above and in n. 10.

Ex. 4.8. Ottavio Durante, Magnificat from *Arie devote*, 1608

Even Monteverdi's echo effects in the two Magnificats, whether or not marked as *echo*, are not unprecedented in the contemporaneous repertoire. As described below, echo effects are quite common in the motet repertoire of the period, but a Magnificat by Monteverdi's Mantuan colleague Gastoldi from *Tutti li salmi* of 1601 (G498) has an entire second choir responding in echo to the first.

Despite the foreshadowing of some of Monteverdi's techniques in several early seventeenth-century motet books, his Magnificats emerge as even more original compositions than his psalms. The dialectical synthesis of modern styles and an antiquated form of the cantus firmus, the expansive dimensions of both settings, and the extensive use of obbligato instruments in the Magnificat *a 7* are all unparalleled in the previous history of the Marian canticle. While

Monteverdi's psalms employ both traditional and contemporary styles and devices in new and original combinations, his Magnificats are quite unique, exhibiting only minimal connections with the remainder of the repertoire.

V

The *sacri concentus* of the *Vespro della Beata Vergine* comprise the celebrated *Sonata sopra Sancta Maria* and the motets, *Nigra sum*, *Pulchra es*, *Duo Seraphim*, and *Audi coelum*. While similarities between the *sacri concentus* and Monteverdi's secular music have been suggested by earlier writers,[101] it is even more important to note that Monteverdi was not the first to employ the monodic style, virtuoso embellishments, quick dotted rhythms, trio textures, echo effects, rhetorical declamation, affective text expression, and orchestral sonatas in sacred music. All of these procedures and styles can be found in the motet repertoire of the decade 1600–10, most noticeably in the last five years of this period. In fact, all five *sacri concentus* are considerably more representative of main currents in early seventeenth-century sacred music than either Monteverdi's psalms or his Magnificats.

Some of the *sacri concentus* are actually based upon individual models by other composers. The *Sonata sopra Sancta Maria*, with its Litany of the Saints intoned eleven times by the cantus part over a large-scale instrumental sonata, is a more elaborate version of a type of piece cultivated in the second half of the *Cinquecento* and the early *Seicento*.[102] Denis Arnold was the first to locate a forerunner in a collection of *Concerti ecclesiastici* by Arcangelo Crotti of Ferrara published in 1608 (C4552).[103] Crotti's piece is of much smaller scope than Monteverdi's, and the richness of the latter's imagination in varying rhythmic patterns, textures, sonorities, bass-lines, and structural features stands out in comparison with Crotti's pedestrian regularity of phrase lengths, cadences, melodic motifs, appearances of the cantus firmus, and structural repetitions. Nor is Monteverdi's the only such sonata with litany emanating from Mantua. Amante Franzoni, who had been appointed *maestro di cappella* at Santa Barbara

[101] See Leo Schrade, *Monteverdi, Creator of Modern Music* (New York: W. W. Norton & Company, Inc., 1950), 256 and 258; Hans F. Redlich, *Claudio Monteverdi: Life and Works*, trans. Kathleen Dale (London: Oxford University Press, 1952), 127–8; Denis Arnold, *Monteverdi* (London: J. M. Dent and Sons, Ltd., 1963), 142–3; and Guglielmo Barblan, Claudio Gallico, and Guido Pannain, *Claudio Monteverdi* (Turin: Edizioni RAI Radiotelevisione Italiana, 1967), 337. Arnold discusses a few related sacred pieces by other composers in 'Notes on Two Movements of the Monteverdi "Vespers" ', *Monthly Musical Record*, 84 (Mar.–Apr. 1954), 59–66, and 'Monteverdi's Church Music: Some Venetian Traits', *Monthly Musical Record*, 88 (May–June 1958), 83–91.

[102] Structural aspects of the *Sonata* are discussed in Ch. 8 and outlined in App. C.

[103] 'Notes', 60–3. See also the discussion of Crotti's *Sonata* in David A. Blazey, 'The Litany in Seventeenth-Century Italy', 2 vols. (Ph.D. dissertation, University of Durham, 1990), i. 218–23, 231; and Harriet A. Franklin, 'Musical Activity in Ferrara, 1578–1618', 2 vols. (Ph.D. dissertation, Brown University, 1976), i. 174–7 and ii. 497–503 (transcription of the *Sonata*).

in 1612, published a similar work in his *Apparato musicale* of 1613 (F1813).[104] This piece utilizes exactly the same litany as Monteverdi's, repeated four times in the soprano part (with pauses between each statement) against a continuous sonata for four trombones. In the table of contents the composition is entitled *Santa Maria*, 'Concerto *a cinque* to be played with four trombones, that is three basses and one tenor, and the soprano sings throughout'.[105] Like Crotti's sonata, Franzoni's piece is on a much smaller scale than Monteverdi's, with fewer iterations of the chant, fewer instruments, and a simpler style. Nowhere in Franzoni's brief concerto do we find the metric shifts, the colouristic opposition of different instruments, or the variety of textures and styles that characterize Monteverdi's gigantic *Sonata*. Like Monteverdi, Franzoni frequently uses descending scales in the bass, imitated in other parts, interspersed with highly cadential bass patterns. Despite the differences of size, the presence of two such compositions in publications by Mantuan composers just three years apart suggests that intoning a litany over an instrumental sonata may have been a traditional practice at Santa Barbara. Franzoni's *Apparato musicale* also contains a *Duo Seraphim* motet with the same text as Monteverdi's (see the discussions above and below). The Trinitarian orientation of this motet was particularly suited to Santa Barbara because the saint had been martyred for her espousal of the Trinity (see Chapter 1).[106]

These instrumental sonatas with ostinato cantus firmus had their origin in ostinato motets or *laude* where a vocal ensemble accompanied the repeated motif or chant. Such motets can be traced in French sources as far back as the thirteenth century. Petrucci's *Laude libro secondo* of 1504 contains a short piece by 'B.T. & M.C.' (Bartolomeo Tromboncino and Marchetto Cara) on the text *Sancta Maria ora pro nobis*, in which the same Litany of the Saints used by Monteverdi is intoned four times, each time in a different voice, in a four-voice texture.[107] Josquin's *Miserere mei Deus* and the *tertia pars* of his *Salve Regina* use

---

[104] See the discussion of instruments in Franzoni's collection above. According to Franzoni's dedication, the mass in this print was performed on the Feast of Santa Barbara when he first took office as *maestro di cappella*, i.e. in 1612. The motets (called *concerti* by Franzoni in the dedication) were added to accompany the mass with greater dignity (*decoro*) into the *gran Teatro del Mondo*. Franzoni's *Sancta Maria* is also discussed in Blazey, 'The Litany', i. 218–23, 233. Transcriptions of Franzoni's *Sancta Maria* are found in Mompellio, ' "L'Apparato musicale" ', 266–9, and Blazey, 'The Litany', ii. 451–3.

[105] 'Concerto a cinque da suonarsi con quattro Tromboni cioè tre bassi, un Tenore, & il Soprano sempre canta'.

[106] See Graham Dixon, 'Monteverdi's Vespers of 1610: "della Beata Vergine"?', *Early Music*, 15 (1987), 387. Dixon also discusses Franzoni's *Apparato musicale* in ' "Behold our Affliction": Celebration and Supplication in the Gonzaga Household', *Early Music*, 24 (1996), 250–61.

[107] Ed. in Knud Jeppesen, *Die mehrstimmige italienische Laude um 1500* (Leipzig: Breitkopf und Härtel, 1935), 31. Wolfgang Osthoff drew attention to this piece in connection with Monteverdi's *Sonata* in 'Unità liturgica e artistica nei *Vespri* del 1610', *Rivista italiana di musicologia*, 2 (1967), 321. An Italian contrafactum of it appeared in Petrucci's Book IV of *frottole* of 1505. See Ottaviano Petrucci, *Frottole, Buch I und IV*, ed. Rudolph Schwarz, in Theodor Kroyer, ed., *Publikationen älterer Music* (repr. Hildesheim: Georg Olms, 1967), viii, 64.

ostinatos as a structural device.[108] Jean Mouton set a *Sancte Sebastiane ora pro nobis* in Antico's fourth book of motets of 1521. In this piece the litany text is sung to a motto of Mouton's invention, which serves both as a motif for imitation at the beginning as well as a recurring quasi-ostinato in much of the *prima pars* and at the end of the brief *secunda pars*.[109] Ostinato motets are found in the Vallicelliana part-books, compiled in 1530–1.[110] The Litany of the Saints chant, addressed to St Andrew, reappears as an ostinato in Cristóbal de Morales's five-voice motet *Andreas Christi famulus*. In both the *prima pars* and *seconda pars* of this piece the unadorned litany is repeated regularly in the cantus secundus voice, the statements separated by rests of three breves.[111]

Several ostinato motets can also be found in Giovanelli's famous anthology of 1568, *Novi thesauri musici liber primus* (SD1568²), a copy of which was in the Santa Barbara library.[112] Denis Arnold has called attention to Andrea Gabrieli's ostinato motet *Judica me* of 1587 specifically in connection with the Monteverdi *Sonata*.[113] His discovery in the surviving part-books of handwritten suggestions

---

[108] Noted in Cristle Collins Judd, 'Modal Types and *Ut, Re, Mi* Tonalities: Tonal Coherence in Sacred Vocal Polyphony from about 1500', *Journal of the American Musicological Society*, 45 (1992), 456–9. Josquin's *Miserere* is studied in Patrick Paul Macey, 'Josquin's "Miserere mei Deus": Content, Structure, and Influence', 2 vols. (Ph.D. dissertation, University of California at Berkeley, 1985).

[109] RISM 1521⁵. Ed. in Martin Picker, *The Motet Books of Andrea Antico* (Chicago: University of Chicago Press, 1987), 398–407. Picker notes a relationship between Mouton's motif and the first psalm tone. See his commentary ibid. 60–1. See also the discussion of this piece in Reese, *Music in the Renaissance*, 281–2.

[110] Edward E. Lowinsky, 'A Newly Discovered Sixteenth-Century Motet Manuscript at the Biblioteca Vallicelliana in Rome', *Journal of the American Musicological Society*, 3 (1950), 173–232.

[111] Ed. Higinio Anglés in *Cristóbal de Morales: Opera omnia*, ii: *Motetes I–XXV* (Monumentos de la Musica Española', 13; Rome: Consejo Superior de Investigaciones Científicas, 1953), 157–65. A contrafactum of the *prima pars* of this piece has the ostinato text *Sancte N[omen]ora pro nobis* (ibid. 37). Attention to the piece was first drawn by Osthoff, 'Unità liturgica e artistica', 322. Morales composed ceremonial ostinato motets as well. *Jubilate Deo omnis terra*, celebrating the peace treaty between François I and Charles V in 1538, repeats the word *Gaudeamus* as an ostinato throughout, and *Gaude et laetare ferrariensis civitas*, honouring Ippolito II d'Este's elevation to the college of cardinals, repeats an ostinato with the words *Magnificabo nomen tuum in aeternum*. See Robert Stevenson, 'Morales, Cristóbal de', in *The New Grove Dictionary of Music and Musicians*, ed. Stanley Sadie (London: Macmillan Publishers Ltd., 1980), xii. 554. There are several other ostinato motets in Morales's collected works. Aside from the ones mentioned above, see *Tu es Petrus, Exaltata est Sancta Dei Genitrix, Emendemus in melius*, and *Virgo Maria. Tu es Petrus* is in an anthology that formed part of the Santa Barbara library. See Guglielmo Barblan, ed., *Musiche della Cappella di S. Barbara in Mantova* (Florence: Leo S. Olschki Editore, 1972), 96–102 (item 101). Some ninety ostinato motets from the period 1480–*c*.1562 have been studied in Mary Electa Columbro, 'Ostinato Technique in the Franco-Flemish Motet: 1480–ca. 1562' (Ph.D. dissertation, Case Western Reserve University, 1974). Columbro lists thirteen works based on the Litany of the Saints (p. 340), but does not include the Tromboncino-Cara or Mouton examples. Edward E. Lowinsky has also discussed ostinato motets in the Renaissance, beginning with Clemens non Papa's *Fremuit spiritu Jesu*, and noted the popularity of this form in Venice. See Lowinsky, *Secret Chromatic Art in the Netherlands Motet* (New York: Russell & Russell, 1946), 16–26.

[112] Barblan, *Musiche della Cappella di S. Barbara*, 82–95 (item 99). Motets from this collection with one or more ostinato voices are *Veni sancte spiritus* by Giovanni Castiletti and *Hodie nobis de celo, Christus surrexit, Emitte spiritum tuum, Tibi decus et imperium*, and *Hic est panis* by Michael des Buissons. Iain Fenlon suggests that Giovanelli presented this print to Duke Guglielmo because of its dedication to the Emperor Maximilian II, the duke's protector. See Fenlon, *Music and Patronage*, i. 86.

[113] 'Monteverdi's Church Music', 84–6.

for instrumentation in several of the voices establishes a close link between the ostinato motet and the instrumental sonata with litany. The two top parts have annotations for violin and viol, while two other parts are marked for trombone and the bass for violone. There are no instrumental indications for the two canonic voices.[114] It is unclear whether these rubrics were for instrumental doubling or substitution, but if substitution were meant, the resultant sonority would be similar to Monteverdi's *Sonata*, though with no counterparts to the latter's cornettos.

Another Venetian motet, *Beatissimus Marcus*, published by Antonio Gualteri in his *Motecta octonis vocibus* of 1604 (G4791, SD1604⁶), employs the same Litany of the Saints as Monteverdi's work, but addresses *Sancte Marce* instead of *Sancta Maria*.[115] The text of the other voices lauds the martyrdom of the patron of Venice, and the piece therefore functions simultaneously as both a song of praise and a supplication.

The use of an ostinato motif in an instrumental sonata was also practised by Giovanni Gabrieli in a composition first described by Christiane Engelbrecht.[116] It is not clear when this piece, found only in manuscript, was written, though its extensive reliance on a large number of obbligato instruments suggests it is probably a late work. The instrumentation (some of it presumed from the clefs and ranges) is rather close to that of Monteverdi's *Sonata*, including four cornettos, two violins, and eight trombones. But the instruments and voices are grouped in three choirs, the first consisting of one voice in the alto clef, a cornetto, a violin and four trombones; the second of two voices (soprano and tenor) with cornetto, violin and three trombones; and the third of three voices in the alto, tenor, and bass clefs respectively, accompanied by two cornettos and one trombone. Underpinning the entire ensemble is the basso continuo for organ. After a long introduction (as in Monteverdi's *Sonata*), involving the instruments of the first two choirs only, Gabrieli proceeds with the alto and tenor voices from these two choirs intoning, sometimes in canon, the text *Dulcis Jesu patris imago*. The text and its melody are reiterated frequently but

---

[114] Ibid.

[115] This composition was called to my attention by the late Don Siro Cisilino of the Cini Foundation in Venice. See the discussion and transcription in Blazey, 'The Litany', i. 223–4 and ii. 424–41.

[116] 'Eine Sonata con voce von Giovanni Gabrieli', *Bericht über den internationalen musikwissenschaftlichen Kongress Hamburg 1956* (Kassel: Bärenreiter Verlag, 1957), 88–9. This piece is edited by Richard Charteris in *Giovanni Gabrieli: Opera omnia*, vii (Neuhausen and Stuttgart: Hanssler-Verlag, 1991), 111–46. David Douglas Bryant has associated it with the annual thanksgiving celebrations on the feast of the Redeemer marking the end of the plague of 1575–7. See Bryant, 'Andrea Gabrieli e la "musica di Stato" Veneziana', *XLII Festival internazionale di Musica Contemporanea: Andrea Gabrieli 1585–1985* (Venice, 1985), 37. Another instrumental composition with a slow-moving ostinato motif is the *Ricercar con obligo del basso come appare* in Frescobaldi's *Fiori musicali* of 1635. In this piece the four-note ostinato migrates among the various parts and modulates to several different keys. See *Girolamo Frescobaldi: Orgel- und Klavierwerke*, v, ed. Pierre Pidoux (Kassel: Bärenreiter, 1954), 44–5. I am grateful to Stephen Bonta for drawing the piece to my attention.

intermittently, sometimes fragmented into the first and second pairs of words, and sometimes at different pitch levels. Only after three-quarters of the piece has transpired do the third choir and the remaining voices finally enter, to sing additional text accompanied by instruments in the same style as many other late Gabrieli motets with multiple choirs of voices and instruments. Despite the similarities between the first part of this piece and Monteverdi's *Sonata*, Monteverdi's virtuoso instrumental writing in pairs has no counterpart in the Gabrieli motet.

Ostinato motets are also found in the few-voiced motet repertoire from after the turn of the century, as witnessed by two examples in a collection of Ignazio Donati published in his *Sacri concentus* of 1612 (D3379). One of these pieces pits the Litany of the Saints against the text *Beatus vir qui inventus est* sung by a solo vocal quartet, each voice of which is to be positioned in a different part of the church and provided with its own continuo. Donati suits his litany to any saint simply by omitting a specific name and adding the rubric, 'this motet serves for every feast of a male or female saint'.[117] The other motet, which is to be performed in a similar manner, has two ostinato voices continually reiterating the phrase *Vanitas vanitatum et omnia vanitas*. Two other works based on the Litany of the Saints as ostinato, the motet *O quam pulchra es* by Romano Micheli from 1615 and the psalm *Credidi* by Tarquinio Merula from 1640, have also been described by David Blazey.[118]

At this point some general remarks about the relationship between Monteverdi's *Sonata* and the canzonas and sonatas of Giovanni Gabrieli are in order. Gabrieli was the only other composer of the period to create instrumental works on such an extravagant scale, and it is only natural that many writers have claimed that the *Sonata sopra Sancta Maria* reveals his influence.[119] The multi-sectional structure of Monteverdi's piece, characterized by frequent changes of metre, rhythm, and texture, certainly resembles the organization of many of Gabrieli's canzonas from the posthumous *Canzoni e sonate* of 1615.[120] But upon comparison of specific compositional details, Monteverdi's independence from the Gabrieli idiom becomes clear.

---

[117] 'Questo motetto serve per ogni festa di Santo o Santa'. Part of Donati's preface, describing the manner of performance, is translated in Arnold, 'Monteverdi's Church Music', 87. For further discussion and a transcription of this piece, see Blazey, 'The Litany', i. 224–6 and ii. 442–7.

[118] Ibid. i. 218–23, 226–30, ii. 448–9. The Merula psalm is published in Kurtzman, ed., *Vesper and Compline Music for Three Principal Voices*. Yet other pieces with the text *Sancta Maria ora pro nobis* have been located by Graham Dixon in a MS copied in 1613 by a Mantuan, Giovanni Amigone, then resident in Rome. See Dixon, 'Giovanni Amigone, un cantore lombardo del seicento e il suo metodo didattico', *Seicento inesplorato: Atti del III Convegno internazionale sulla musica in area lombardo-padana del secolo XVII* (Como: AMIS, 1993), 329, 333, 336.

[119] See e.g. Redlich, *Claudio Monteverdi*, 127; Schrade, *Monteverdi*, 262; and Arnold, *Monteverdi* (1963), 141.

[120] Ed. Michel Sanvoisin in *Giovanni Gabrieli: Canzoni e sonate* (Le Pupitre, 27; Paris: Heugel & Cie., 1971).

One of the most important differences lies in the character of Monteverdi's melodic lines. Throughout the *Sonata* they tend to be conjunct, based on shorter or longer scale patterns. Their rhythms are comparatively even, normally involving only three adjacent rhythmic levels within a single section. The forward impetus of these smoothly flowing melodic lines is further enhanced by the imitative texture.

Gabrieli, by contrast, usually employs shorter, more angular melodic motifs with much more rhythmic differentiation. His lines tend to end abruptly, through either cadential harmony or antiphonal exchange with another part. A single melodic phrase may also contain several different types of motifs, while Monteverdi maintains much greater motivic consistency, not only within a single phrase, but throughout the entire *Sonata*. This motivic consistency depends upon the repeated use of certain intervals and the universally binding effect of scale motion. How characteristic these features are of Monteverdi can be seen by comparison with Gabrieli, who rarely employs scale patterns in either basses or melodies and whose linear intervals cover a wider range. Canzonas XV and XVIII of Gabrieli's 1615 collection are exceptional in utilizing motifs more like those in the Monteverdi *Sonata*.

Most of Gabrieli's larger canzonas and sonatas are conceived in terms of antiphonal choirs of instruments with frequent, abrupt exchanges of short melodic phrases. Even the smaller canzonas, which rely more heavily on imitative techniques, display their share of antiphonal responses. But Monteverdi uses antiphonal effects rather sparingly; moreover, his interchanges are less clearly articulated than Gabrieli's because of the absence of strong cadential harmony in the bass. Monteverdi's antiphonal passages thus do not beget the sectionalization and discontinuity typical of his famous Venetian contemporary. In addition, Monteverdi's greater interest in melodic and harmonic flow is logically accompanied by more frequent reliance on melodic and harmonic sequences.

Monteverdi's *Sonata*, while scored for eight separate instrumental parts plus basso continuo, has numerous sections in which duets supported by the organ prevail, similar to those in other pieces of the Vespers. Duets of like instruments also occur in many of Gabrieli's canzonas and sonatas, but in a manner consistent with his melodic style, they tend to be short and composed of brief motifs, which are often treated antiphonally. These passages are almost invariably ornamental in conception, frequently involving rhythmic values as small as demisemiquavers. Monteverdi's duets, on the other hand, are more extended and form a more integral part of the structure of his work. Although the *Sonata sopra Sancta Maria* bears a closer relationship to the music of Gabrieli than any other piece in the *Vespro della Beata Vergine*, the foregoing comparisons demonstrate that Monteverdi's style was still very personal, with only its broadest outlines reminiscent of the music of the Venetian master.

Of the four motets in the 1610 Vespers, *Duo Seraphim*, with its clamouring of angels in the first part and evocation of the three witnesses, Father, Word, and Holy Spirit, in the second part, represents by far the most frequently composed text. I am aware of forty-two published settings besides Monteverdi's from the period 1600–20.[121] The popularity of this text goes back at least to Victoria's 1583 version *cum paribus vocibus* (for four high voices).[122] Marc-Antonio Ingegneri, Monteverdi's teacher at Cremona, published a setting in 1589.[123] The text, with its reference to Father, Word, and Holy Spirit, is suitable for the Feast of the Trinity, and this is the rubric at the head of Victoria's setting in the 1583 edition of his motets (V1422). In the 1585 edition, the rubric reads *In festo Sancti Michaelis et Angelorum*.[124] The lack of any connection with the Virgin has disturbed many writers; it is the only motet text in the Monteverdi print that was not traditionally associated with the Madonna.[125] Yet it should be noted that Victoria's motet collection of 1583 is dedicated to the Virgin,[126] and that the

[121] The text is derived from Isa. 6: 2–3 and 1 John 5: 7. For a commentary on the music of Monteverdi's *Duo Seraphim*, see Ch. 10 below. For a list of the publications I had located by 1972 in which settings from the period 1600–15 are found, see Kurtzman, 'The Monteverdi Vespers of 1610', app. D. One particularly interesting version, discovered after that list was compiled, is in Giovanni Francesco Capello's *Cantici spirituali* of 1616. A large number of additional settings have been located by Jerome Roche in the compilation of his 17th-century motet index. I list here by RISM number, where applicable, the collections of 1600–20 not included in app. D in my dissertation: Aglione, Giardino, 1618; Giovanni Mateo Asola, *Divinae Dei laudes*, 1600, A2604; Antonio Badi, *Il primo libro de concerti*, 1610, B626; Fabio Beccari, *Il secondo libro de sacri concenti*, 1611, B1507; Giovanni Francesco Capello, *Cantici spirituali*, 1616 (Cracow, Jagellonian Library); Bernardo Corsi, *Motecta binis ternis, et quaternis vocibus*, 1615, C4137; Giovanni Croce, *Sacrae cantilene concertate*, 1612, C4464; Donato De Benedictus, *Harmonici concentus*, 1614, D1285; Andrea Falconieri, *Sacrae modulationes*, 1619, F84; Amante Franzoni, *Concerti ecclesiastici*, 1611, F1812; Marco da Gagliano, *Missae et sacrarum cantionum*, 1614, G105; Francesco Giuliani, *Sacri concerti*, 1619, G2545; Alessandro Gualtieri, *Motetti*, 1616, G4789; Grammatico Metallo, *Motetti per tutte le solennita dell'anno*, 1610, M2439; Giovanni Nicolo Mezzogorri, *Del primo libro de sacri concerti*, 1611, M2616; Bastiano Miseroca, *I pietosi affeti*, 1618, M2877; Ortensio Polidori, *Mottecta . . . liber primus*, 1612, P5019; Rubini, *Sacrae musicales*, 1614; Bernardo Strozzi, *Sacri concentus*, 1612, S6990; Andrea Bianchi in Bianchi's anthology *Libro primo de motetti*, 1620³. I am grateful to Elizabeth Roche for permission to examine Jerome Roche's index file. Several additional settings, including some by German composers, are found in the second part of Johannes Donfrid's *Promptuarium musicum*, RISM 1623².

[122] Ed. Pedrell in *Thomae Ludovici Victoria Abulensis opera omnia*, i. 36–9.

[123] In *Liber sacrarum cantionum quae ad septem, octo, novem, decem, duodecim, sexdecim voces choris . . . 1589* (I47). See Francesco Bussi, *Piacenza, Archivio del Duomo: Catalogo del Fondo Musicale* (Milan: Istituto Editoriale Italiano, 1967), 59. The motet was reprinted the next year in Nuremberg in Frederick Linder's anthology *Corollarium cantionum sacrarum* (RISM 1590⁵). Ingegneri's setting has the rubric *De Sancta Trinitate*. Other than the text, Monteverdi's version has nothing in common with Ingegneri's.

[124] Ed. Higinio Anglés in *Tomás Luis de Victoria: Opera omnia* (Monumentos de la Musica Española, 31; Rome: Consejo Superior de Investigaciones Científicas, 1968), 12. The ducal church in Mantua possessed a copy of the 1585 edn. See Barblan, ed., *Musiche della Cappella di S. Barbara*, 334–8 (item 270), 475.

[125] See e.g. Schrade, *Monteverdi*, 251–3; Dixon, 'Monteverdi's Vespers of 1610'; and the liner notes to Andrew Parrott's recording (see App. D below, item 21).

[126] See *Thomae Ludovici Victoria Abulensis Opera omnia*, ed. Pedrell, viii, pp. xxxi–xxxii.

psalm *Laetatus sum*, for which *Duo Seraphim* is presumably the antiphon substitute in Monteverdi's 1610 print, also speaks of those who give testimony with the phrase *Testimonium Israel ad confitendum nomini Domini*. Graham Dixon has noted the relationship between the text of *Duo Seraphim* and Santa Barbara herself, since her martyrdom was a direct result of her devotion to the Trinity (see Chapter 1).[127]

This text was especially popular in the decade 1600–10 in the musical circles with which Monteverdi was best acquainted: Mantua, Ferrara, and Bologna. Viadana, *maestro di cappella* at the cathedral of San Pietro in Mantua for a brief time in 1594, included a setting in the *Cento concerto ecclesiastici* of 1602 (V1360), and Arcangelo Crotti, an Augustinian monk of Ferrara, set the first portion of this text in the same 1608 print that contains his *Sancta Maria, ora pro nobis*. From Bologna stem settings by Ottavio Vernizzi in his *Armonia ecclesiasticorum concertuum* of 1604 (V1293) and Adriano Banchieri (first section only) in his *Ecclesiastiche sinfonie* of 1607 (B802).[128]

Several distinctive ways of treating this text, some originating as early as the Victoria example, were repeated, developed, and expanded in subsequent interpretations well into the seventeenth century. The opening phrase, *Duo Seraphim clamabant*, was with rare exceptions set for two voices, even when the setting as a whole was for many more.[129] Similarly, the beginning of the second half of the text, *Tres sunt qui testimonium dant*, was usually cast in three parts.[130] Both traditions were followed by Monteverdi.

The settings by Victoria, Viadana, Leoni, Stefanini, and Gasparini (see note 128) all begin with a slow rising figure similar to Monteverdi's. Monteverdi then plays the two voices against one another in imitative alternation at *clamabant alter ad alterum*. Similar imitative alternation can also be found in almost all of the settings of *Duo Seraphim* cited above.

At *Tres sunt*, Viadana asks the organist to sing as well as play, thus expanding the vocal parts to three. Like Monteverdi, Viadana, Vernizzi, Leoni, Anerio,

---

[127] 'Monteverdi's Vespers of 1610', 387.

[128] Monteverdi's direct connections with Bologna, if any, during the first decade of the century are uncertain. His music was not unknown there, however, for the dialogue in Giovanni Maria Artusi's treatise *L'Artusi, ovvero delle imperfettioni della moderna musica* (Venice: Vincenti, 1600) takes place in Bologna. Banchieri's and Crotti's settings are discussed in Arnold, 'Notes on Two Movements', 64–5. Other settings were composed in this period by Giovanni Ripalta of Modena in 1604 (R1733), Archangelo Borsaro of Reggio in 1605 (B3779), Leo Leoni of Vicenza (L1997), Luigi Balbi of Venice (B748), and Giovanni Battista Stefanini of Milan (first portion of text only) in 1606 (S4728), Felice Gasparini, an Olivetan monk, in 1608 (G454), Catarina Assandra of Pavia in 1609 (A2637, SD1609³), Girolamo Bartei of Arezzo in 1609 (B1062), Giovanni Francesco Anerio of Rome, also in 1609 (A1096), Giovanni Croce of Venice in 1610 (C4449), and Giovanni Piccioni, organist at the cathedral in Orvieto (*Tres sunt* only), in 1610 (P2221).

[129] One of the exceptions is the setting by Monteverdi's teacher, Ingegneri, which pairs off two four-voice choirs in alternation for the opening portion of the text, combining the choirs only at *plena est omnis terra*.

[130] Gasparini retained a two-voice texture in his setting of *Tres sunt*.

Assandra, and Croce all begin the second section of the motet with sustained triads (Victoria proceeds similarly, but begins with an open fifth).

The continuation of the second half, *Pater et Verbum et Spiritus Sanctus*, was often set so that the three witnesses, Father, Word, and Holy Spirit, were named successively, each by a single different voice part (Ripalta, Anerio, Assandra, Croce). Another approach tended to be cumulative, with one or two voices singing *Pater*, one, two or three intoning *Verbum*, and all three following with *Spiritus Sanctus*, sometimes in a more chordal texture (Victoria, Vernizzi, Borsaro, Balbi, and Piccioni). Monteverdi chose the latter method, following precisely the pattern of Victoria, by increasing the texture from one to two to three voices in naming each successive witness.

The succeeding phrase, *et hi tres unum sunt* (and these three are one), was often interpreted symbolically with a shift to triple metre, the new time signature denoting a threefold division of the single tactus (Victoria, Ingegneri, Borsaro, Assandra, Anerio).[131] Many composers brought the phrase to a unison or octave on its final word, *sunt* (Victoria, Viadana, Vernizzi, Ripalta, Balbi, Gasparini, Piccioni, and Croce). Monteverdi, however, sought a more dramatic, affective treatment of this line by presenting the three voices at *et hi tres* as a root-position triad and then having all three voices converge on a repeated unison at *unum sunt*. The entire phrase is subsequently reiterated a step higher for further intensification (Victoria repeats the phrase at the same pitch). Giovanni Francesco Anerio's 1609 setting from his *Motecta singulis, binis, ternisque vocibus* is the only other example to treat these words in a comparable fashion by suddenly reducing the texture from three voices to one, creating an equally dramatic effect.

After the turn of the seventeenth century, when virtuoso ornamentation became a characteristic, at times a *raison d'être*, of some motet collections, the *Duo Seraphim* text with its description of heavenly jubilation often gave rise to a florid style. Although Monteverdi's version is more profusely embellished than any of its counterparts, some of the types of ornamentation he employed do appear in the motet repertoire from 1607 onwards. Melismas in these collections often consist of semiquavers or dotted rhythms of quavers and semiquavers, with some embellishments comprehending as many as fifty or sixty notes. Occasional groupings of demisemiquavers also appear, as well as the cadential ornament Caccini calls a *trillo*, consisting of the rapid reiteration of a single pitch.[132] Both the *trillo* and melismas in small note values are common features of the first motet book of Giovanni Francesco Capello, published in 1610 (see

---

[131] Franzoni shifts to a 3/2 *sesquialtera* proportion at this point in his setting.

[132] See the translations of the foreword to Caccini's *Le nuove musiche* of 1602 in Strunk, *Source Readings in Music History*, 384–9, and in *Giulio Caccini: Le nuove musiche*, ed. H. Wiley Hitchcock (Madison, Wis.: A-R Editions, Inc., 1970), 43–56. See Ch. 21 below for a discussion of this ornament.

Ex. 4.9).[133] It is worthy of note that Capello's *trillo* is on the feminine form of the same word as Monteverdi's *gruppo* (alternating notes, like a modern trill) and *trillo*.

But despite antecedents in the sacred repertoire, it seems clear that the most important precedent for the remarkable ornamentation in *Duo Seraphim* is *Possente spirto* from Monteverdi's own *L'Orfeo*. As in the response *Domine ad adjuvandum*, whose instrumental parts are taken directly from *L'Orfeo*, it is Monteverdi's own theatrical music that has exerted the most significant influence.

The 1613 setting of *Duo Seraphim* by Franzoni mentioned earlier is of special interest, since it stems from Mantua.[134] The setting is for eight voices, but the eight sing together only during the sentence *Plena est omnis terra gloria eius*. Franzoni uses fullness of texture to reflect the words, whereas Monteverdi had reserved his greatest contrapuntal complexity in virtuoso passage-work for this portion of the text. Franzoni begins his setting with two voices, but this opening bears little direct resemblance to Monteverdi's. *Alter ad alterum* is expressed through contrary motion between the two parts rather than the imitation employed by Monteverdi. Both Monteverdi and Franzoni treat *Sanctus, sanctus, sanctus* with embellishment, but Franzoni's simple, short, diatonic melismas bear no relation to Monteverdi's virtuoso use of the modern *trillo* in imitation.

Franzoni's *Tres sunt* begins with sustained triads in three parts followed by imitation, similar to Monteverdi's setting, but then the text *qui testimoniam dant* is repeated in chordal homophony by the second choir, a procedure wholly absent from Monteverdi's version. Franzoni's naming of the witnesses follows the tradition of using a single voice for each witness, whereas Monteverdi proceeds cumulatively. The phrase *et hi tres unum sunt* elicits triple metre from Franzoni as well as a threefold presentation of the phrase. Initially the text is sung in the

Ex. 4.9. Giovanni Francesco Capello, *Sancta et immaculata virginitas* from *Sacrorum concentuum*, 1610

---

[133] This collection and other music by Capello are discussed in Jeffrey Kurtzman, 'Giovanni Francesco Capello, an Avant-Gardist of the Early Seventeenth Century', *Musica disciplina*, 31 (1977), 155–82.

[134] For a transcription, see Mompellio, '"L'Apparato musicale"', 251–65.

three higher voices of the first choir with an immediate sequential repetition a third higher (Monteverdi repeats the phrase a step higher). Franzoni then shifts to the four voices of the second choir for the second statement, this one beginning with a sequential repetition a third lower. Subsequently the text shifts back to the first choir for a varied return of its first statement. Nowhere do the voices come to a unison on the word *sunt*. Franzoni's motet ends at this point, without the reiteration of text from the first part that gives Monteverdi's version its rounded structure.

Franzoni's setting thus seems to have only the most superficial characteristics in common with Monteverdi's. The most noticeable difference is the absence of virtuosity in Franzoni's composition, which may well have to do with the dismissal of so many musicians from the Gonzaga court in the summer of 1612 a few months before Franzoni's arrival in Mantua.[135]

Despite the fact that Monteverdi's *Duo Seraphim* has numerous precedents, this composition is illustrative of his propensity for working on a larger, more complex scale than his contemporaries. His *Duo Seraphim* not only is longer than any other setting of this text, but is also more complicated contrapuntally and makes more extensive use of virtuoso ornamental devices than any other few-voiced motet of the early seventeenth century I have yet observed. Like the psalms, Magnificats, and *Sonata*, *Duo Seraphim* confirms once again Monteverdi's disposition towards musical opulence and extravagance.

While both the *Sonata sopra Sancta Maria* and *Duo Seraphim* have numerous antecedents, there are far fewer settings of the text *Audi coelum*.[136] Echo motets, however, were not uncommon in the early seventeenth century.[137] Viadana's *Cento concerti ecclesiastici* of 1602 (V1360) contains three such pieces, *Memento salutis auctor* for tenor solo, *Exijt sermo inter fratres* for two basses, and *Iam de somno*

---

[135] Franzoni published another *Duo Seraphim*, in his *Concerti ecclesiastici* of 1611, while he was still *maestro di cappella* in the cathedral at Forlì. This piece sets only the first portion of the text, for two tenors and organ. The opening four bars are almost identical to Monteverdi's version, though the two compositions diverge after that. The words *clamabant* and *plena est omnis terra* are set to lengthy melismas, the latter involving a typical early 17th-century imitation in parallel thirds. For the dismissal of musicians in 1612, see Susan Parisi, '"Licenza alla Mantovana": Frescobaldi and the Recruitment of Musicians for Mantua, 1612–1615', in Alexander Silbiger, ed., *Frescobaldi Studies* (Durham, NC: Duke University Press, 1987), 60–2. According to Pierre M. Tagmann, Antonio Tarone, who had served as interim *maestro di cappella* after the death of Gastoldi in Jan. 1609, served again in that capacity in Aug.–Sept. 1612. Franzoni assumed the position in Oct. 1612. See Tagmann, 'La cappella dei maestri cantori della basilica palatina di Santa Barbara a Mantova (1565–1630)', *Civiltà mantovana*, 4 (1969–70), 381–2. Gastoldi's will, drawn up on 3 Jan. 1609, the day before he died, is reprinted in Ottavio Beretta, 'Documenti inediti su Giovanni Giacomo Gastoldi scoperti negli archivi mantovani', *Rivista internazionale di musica sacra*, 14 (1993), 271–3.

[136] A small portion of Monteverdi's text is derived from the Song of Songs. See Ch. 10 for the text and an analysis of Monteverdi's *Audi coelum*.

[137] Theodor Kroyer explored the background of the echo and its relationship to *cori spezzati* and dialogue techniques of the 16th century in 'Dialog und Echo in der alten Chormusik', *Jahrbuch der Bibliothek Peters*, 16 (1909), 13–32. At the end, Kroyer gives a bibliography of secular and sacred echo pieces from 1561–1611.

for four voices.[138] Sometimes the final word of a phrase is echoed piano, at other times only the final syllable or syllables, generating a pun on the echoed word. The *Sacrarum cantionum of* 1608 by Girolamo Baglioni of Milan (B644) contains two echo pieces for solo voice.[139] Viadana published another echo motet, *Ingredere dilecta mea*, for three tenors in his third book of *Concerti ecclesiastici* of 1609 (V1392). Pun echoes also appear in Giovanni Francesco Capello's *Iam de somno* from his *Sacrorum concentuum* of 1610 (C902).[140]

The earliest setting of *Audi coelum* of which I am aware is by Gabriele Fattorini, organist at the cathedral in Faenza, from his *Secondo Libro de Motetti a Otto Voci* of 1601 (F133).[141] Fattorini's publication was organized by the Bolognese Don Donato Beroaldi and dedicated to a nun at the convent of Santa Christina in Bologna. His is one of the relatively few collections of motets from this period to include an instrumental canzona. Fattorini's text for *Audi coelum* is the same as Monteverdi's, the only difference being a transposition of two words in Monteverdi's text, coupled with a change in the verb from the hortatory subjunctive to the present indicative (*cuius invocemus nomen* in Fattorini's setting; *cuius nomen invocamus* in Monteverdi's); the pun echoes of the two settings are identical. Fattorini utilizes the first choir for the main text and the second choir for the echoes. There is no musical relationship between Fattorini's first section and Monteverdi's; indeed, Fattorini writes in the late sixteenth-century polyphonic motet style with mostly syllabic declamation in semibreves, minims, and semiminims, few repeated notes, and brief, non-virtuosic melismas. But in the second section, at *Omnes hanc ergo sequamur* (let us all therefore follow her), Fattorini, like Monteverdi nine years later, shifts to triple metre with minim notation. Fattorini's bass is cadential in much the same manner as Monteverdi's, although Fattorini's much shorter presentation of the text does not leave room for the extended harmonic sequences Monteverdi employs. Fattorini, like Monteverdi, also shifts twice back to duple metre, but at the *consequamur–sequamur* echo rather than at *qua cum gratia*, and the second time at *dulce miseris* rather than at *cuius nomen*. His *Benedicta es* then employs the two choirs in *cori spezzati* exchanges to conclude the motet.

Another eight-voice setting was published in 1609 by Giovanni Battista Dulcino in his *Sacrae cantiones* (D3679). As noted above, Dulcino's print is dedicated to Don Bassano Casola, Monteverdi's *vice-maestro di cappella*, and it seems certain that Monteverdi would have been familiar with this collection.

---

[138] *Memento salutis auctor* ed. Claudio Gallico in *Lodovico Viadana: Cento concerti ecclesiastici, parte prima: Concerti a una voce con l'organo* (Monumenti Musicali Mantovani, 1; Kassel: Bärenreiter, 1964), 84–5.

[139] The echo pieces are in the Sextus part-book.

[140] For a transcription see Kurtzman, 'The Monteverdi Vespers of 1610', iii. 1100–1.

[141] I am grateful to Christopher Wilkinson for drawing this motet to my attention and for supplying me with a transcription. I am also grateful to Craig Monson for lending me his photocopy of this print. Monteverdi's text is given, together with an English translation, in Ch. 10 below.

Dulcino's text is identical to Fattorini's except for Dulcino's insertion of the word *Alleluia*, together with its echo, after the *consequamur–sequamur* echo and just before *Praestet nobis Deus*. Thus Dulcino's text is also the same as Monteverdi's except for the inserted *Alleluia* and the inversion of the phrase *cuius invocemus nomen*, which Dulcino shares with Fattorini.

Dulcino's composition, like Fattorini's, is for eight voices in two choirs (Dulcino's organ part-book is missing), with the second choir or individual voices from the second choir providing the echoes. However, where Fattorini presents the main part of the text in all four voices of the first choir, Dulcino relies mostly on solo voices, shifting from one to another and eventually employing all four from the first choir before the onset of the second section, *Omnes hanc ergo sequamur*. In the use of solo voices, Dulcino's setting is closer to Monteverdi's, but the vocal style is completely different. Whereas Monteverdi's version is for tenor solo only (with tenor solo echoes) in an intense recitative style punctuated by virtuosic melismas in small note values and occasionally dotted rhythms, Dulcino's solo parts resemble single lines from a sixteenth-century polyphonic motet, only rarely utilizing affective intervals or chromaticism. At *per quam mors fuit expulsa* (through whom death was expelled) Dulcino employs a chromatic rise from $c\sharp'$ to e' followed by a sudden drop to $g\sharp$–a, but even a melodic shape like this has its counterpart in many a late sixteenth-century polyphonic motet. Dulcino's melismas, too, are conservative, consisting of groups of smooth quavers of moderate duration. Each echo is by the corresponding solo voice in the second choir. Almost all of these echoes are melismatic and of greater length than Fattorini's very brief echoes, but are shorter and less virtuosic than Monteverdi's. The phrase *Dic nam ista*, which has no echo, is sung by two voices—soprano and bass. Like Fattorini (but unlike Monteverdi), Dulcino shifts to triple metre at *replet laetitia terras, coelos* ([she] fills with joy the earth, heavens [and the seas]); moreover, he further reflects the text in filling out the texture with four part-homophony, while Monteverdi remains in duple metre and his single voice, interpreting the text through extended virtuoso melismas (descending and ascending respectively) on *terras* and *coelos*. Because he has been in four parts, Dulcino's echo of *Maria* at the end of this passage requires the entire second choir. Dulcino also expands from the solo voice to four parts for the brief phrase *Illa sacra & felix porta* (that holy and happy portal).

The second part of Dulcino's motet, beginning at *Omnes hanc ergo sequamur*, also turns to minims in triple metre as in both Fattorini's and Monteverdi's settings. Moreover, the second choir, responding to *omnes . . . sequamur*, joins the first in imitation, just as Monteverdi adds five more voices in an imitative texture at this point. Dulcino, however, combines the two choirs only through the phrase *qua cum gratia*. Two shifts to duple metre likewise occur in the second section, but at *vitam aeternam*, rather than at *qua cum gratia*, and at *cuius invocemus* (as in Monteverdi's setting). Dulcino's *Benedicta es* then proceeds in a *cori spezzati* setting strikingly similar to Fattorini's. Dulcino's *Audi coelum* is among those six motets in his collection, as mentioned above, that fall under a rubric in the index calling for instruments in addition to the organ. Since there is no sign of instrumental parts or indications for instruments within the piece itself, Dulcino likely intended that they double voices *ad libitum*, though certainly only in passages where at least one full choir is singing and perhaps just in the second section beginning at *Omnes*.

The only setting for solo voice with echo I have been able to locate is by Ercole Porta, organist in San Giovanni in Persiceto near Bologna, from his 1609 *Giardino di spirituali concenti* (P5191). Porta's version of this text is shorter than Monteverdi's, omitting the lines *Quae semper tutum est medium inter homines et Deum pro culpis remedium* (echo: *medium*) and *Omnes hanc ergo sequamur qua cum gratia mereamur vitam aeternam. Consequamur* (echo: *sequamur*) and the concluding benediction, *Benedicta es virgo Maria in saeculorum saecula*. Lacking the phrase *Omnes hanc ergo sequamur*, Porta's texture does not burst forth in six-voice polyphony like Monteverdi's, but simply proceeds with the solo soprano at *Praestet nobis*. In all of the lines of text shared by the two pieces, the echo puns are identical.

Musical relationships between the two compositions are of a more general nature. Porta calls for sopranos rather than tenors (the two voices were often considered interchangeable in the early seventeenth century), and Porta, like Monteverdi, reserves the second voice exclusively for the echo. Both settings utilize melismas on specific words, though not always the same words, and Porta's melismas are much more modest than Monteverdi's. Porta, like Fattorini and Dulcino, changes briefly to triple metre at *replet letitia terras*.

Both Porta and Monteverdi employ a quasi-recitative style in the phrase *praedicata a prophetis Ezechiel porta orientalis*, but a comparison of these two passages reveals Monteverdi's much more concentrated sense of melodic direction and rhythmic organization (see Ex. 4.10). Where Porta meanders aimlessly until the sequences at *Ezechiel* (*a*), Monteverdi's setting (*b*) is more truly in recitative style, and his repeated notes in a rising sequence shape an intense, goal-directed phrase. Indicative of the sophistication and complexity of Monteverdi's musical thought is that the brief passage in Ex. 4.10*b* also functions on a larger architectural level. This phrase is only the first in a series of three, each of which is a variation upon the preceding one. Porta, on the other hand, after concluding the phrase in Ex. 4.10*a* anticlimactically, continues on to a new, unrelated melodic idea that rises and falls without a strong sense of purpose. A

(a)

(b)

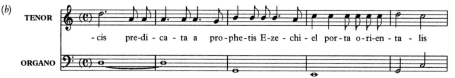

Ex. 4.10. *a* Ercole Porta, *Audi coelum* from *Giardino di spirituali concenti*, 1609; *b* Monteverdi, *Audi coelum*

distinguishing characteristic of Monteverdi throughout the Vespers, indeed throughout his *œuvre*, is his careful integration of details of melody and harmony with broader structural considerations.

Monteverdi's setting also differs from Porta's in the extent of its ornamentation, especially in some of the echoes. Porta's rendering, by contrast, is mostly syllabic and shows little of Monteverdi's interest in appropriate text declamation and affective expression. In *Audi coelum*, as in all of the other compositions from the Vespers examined thus far, Monteverdi's setting is far more expansive and elaborate than any of its forerunners.

The texts of the two remaining motets, *Nigra sum* and *Pulchra es*, are both derived from the Song of Songs. In the case of pieces with the incipit *Nigra sum sed formosa*, so many different verses were assembled for different settings, many bearing little resemblance to Monteverdi's version or to one another, that no specific text traditions or musical traditions of word-setting can be identified. However, Lodovico Victoria had published a six-voice *Nigra sum* with precisely the same text as Monteverdi's in the 1583 collection that also contains his *Duo Seraphim*. The textual identity even extends to the reading *filia Jerusalem* in the first line rather than the Vulgate's *filiae Jerusalem*.[142] In fact, the library of Santa Barbara possessed a copy of Victoria's *Nigra sum* in the 1585 edition of his *Motecta festorum totius anni*, as mentioned above in connection with *Duo Seraphim*, and it seems probable that Monteverdi derived his verses directly from

---

[142] See the discussion of the significance of this change in Ch. 9.

the Spaniard's setting, especially since other, later *Nigra sum* motets have such divergent texts, and only a few versions other than Victoria's and Monteverdi's utilize the form *filia Jerusalem*.[143]

Compositions on the texts *Nigra sum* and *Pulchra es* became fairly popular in the late sixteenth and early seventeenth centuries, especially after the publication of Palestrina's 1583–4 motet collection which he devoted exclusively to settings from the Song of Songs.[144] Motets beginning with the words *Nigra sum* were especially prominent in the years 1608–12, with the publication of eight versions in these five years by the Olivetan monk Felice Gasparini (1608), Serafino Patta of Milan (1609), Adriano Banchieri of Bologna, Giovanni Bernardino Nanino of Rome, and Monteverdi (all 1610), and Antonio Burlini of Venice, the German Girolamo Kapsberger of Rome, and Domenico Massenzio of Ronciglione, north of Rome (all 1612).[145] Of these settings, only those of Massenzio, Nanino, and Kapsberger, all Romans, have texts similar to Monteverdi's. Most of the compositions are for two voices; only those of Patta, Burlini, and Kapsberger, the latter two postdating Monteverdi's, are for solo voice. Thus one can hardly speak of a tradition in the setting of *Nigra sum*, nor of models for or influence on Monteverdi's version. And indeed, no setting of any version of the *Nigra sum* utilizes the recitative style featured in Monteverdi's motet.

Pulchra es amica mea did not inspire as many musical settings, although several composers other than Monteverdi addressed this text, such as Agostino Agazzari of Siena (1606), Lodovico Torto of Chieti (1607), Pietro Paolo Cavi, an Augustinian monk from Cavi (1609), Banchieri (1610), Giovanni Francesco

---

[143] See Barblan, ed., *Musiche della Cappella di S. Barbara*, 334–8, 500. The only early 17th-century settings of which I am aware with this reading are those by Antonio Burlini in his *Riviera fiorita* of 1612 (B5022) and Domenico Massenzio in his *Sacrae cantiones*, also of 1612 (M1309).

[144] *Motettorum quinque vocibus liber quartus* (Rome: Gardano, 1583–4), RISM P716. This collection underwent ten reprints in Italy between 1587 and 1613 as well as one by Phalèse in Antwerp in 1605. A copy of the 1601 edition of Palestrina's motets was in the Santa Barbara library. See Barblan, ed., *Musiche della Cappella di S. Barbara*, 295–6. The specific verses selected by Monteverdi are given in Ch. 9. A shorter version of *Nigra sum* served as the third and fourth psalm antiphons for the Feast of St Mary of the Snow, later transformed into the Common of the BVM. A shorter version of *Pulchra es* forms the fifth psalm antiphon for the feast of the Assumption. For a partial list of publications from 1600–20 in which settings of *Nigra sum* are found, see Kurtzman, 'The Monteverdi Vespers of 1610', app. E. Additional settings from this same period, derived from Jerome Roche's motet index are as follows (RISM numbers, where applicable, follow each date): Gregorio Zucchini, *Harmonia sacra*, 1602, Z360; Orfeo Vecchi, *Motectorum . . . liber primus*, 1603, V1075; Dionisio Bassi, *Sacrarum cantionum*, 1604, B1237; Ottavio Vernizzi, *Caelestium applausus*, 1604, V1296; Leo Leoni, *Sacrarum cantionum liber primus*, 1608, L2002; Bernardino Borlasca, *Scherzi musicali ecclesiastici*, 1609, B3754; Giovanni Valentini, *Motecta . . . liber primus*, 1611, V87; Paolo Quagliati, *Motecta octonis*, 1612, Q8; Giovanni Nicolo Mezzogorri, *La celeste sposa*, 1613, M2618; Michele Malerba, *Sacrarum cantionum*, 1614, M242; Giovanni Francesco Capello, *Cantici spirituali*, 1616 (at Cracow, Jagellonian Library); Giacomo de Civita, *Motetti concertati*, 1616, C2537 (G1827); Giovanni Paolo Caprioli, *Sacrae cantiones*, 1618, C944; Simplicij Tedeschi in *Lilia sacra octo*, 1618[5]; Alessandro Grandi, *Motetti a cinque*, 1620, G3429.

[145] RISM G454, B805, N14, B5022, K185, and M1309 respectively. The Patta print of 1609 is not listed in RISM, though its 1611 reprint is (P1037).

Anerio of Rome (1613), Serafino Patta of Milan (1613), and the Venetian Francesco Usper (1614).[146] In contrast to those of *Nigra sum*, the texts of the majority of the *Pulchra es* motets are virtually identical. A common feature among five of these early seventeenth-century versions is their scoring for two voices, sometimes in the same register, as in Monteverdi's *Pulchra es*, but even more often in different registers. Only Banchieri calls for a pair of sopranos as Monteverdi does. Patta's setting is for solo soprano, Torto's for three voices, and Usper's for six voices. Most of these compositions treat selected words melismatically, and most stress the phrase *me avolare fecerunt* with melismas, increased rhythmic energy, and text repetition. Monteverdi's melismas tend to be more extensive, and he is the only composer to shift to triple metre at *me avolare fecerunt*. A device encountered in many of these compositions, including Monteverdi's, is special harmonic emphasis on the word *suavis* in the opening line. The rendering of this word usually involves some kind of chromatic alteration relative to the first part of the phrase. Monteverdi very likely drew on the Agazzari setting, which was in the library of Santa Barbara,[147] for not only does it begin with a motif quite similar to his own version (see Ex. 4.11), but Agazzari also makes the same *durus* shift to an E-major triad in the phrase *Averte oculos tuos a me* (see Ex. 4.12). Agazzari's setting of *me avolare fecerunt*, though still in duple metre, involves a shortening of note values and sequential treatment of a short motif that is not dissimilar to Monteverdi's sequential treatment of this same phrase of text (see Ex. 4.13). While this relationship is not close enough to suggest modelling on Monteverdi's part, it should be noted that Agazzari and Monteverdi are the only two composers to treat this phrase in a sequential manner.

Vague relationships may also be drawn between Monteverdi's setting and the opening of the version by Cavi (see Ex. 4.14). Banchieri's setting, like those of Cavi, Monteverdi, and Anerio, employs melismas in parallel thirds at *me avolare fecerunt* (see Ex. 4.15).

Monteverdi's *Nigra sum* and *Audi coelum* are especially notable for their utilization of the recitative style. Monteverdi was by no means the first to apply the

---

[146] RISM A340, T1013, C1576b, B805, A1102, P1038, U116. For a partial list of publications from 1600–15 in which settings of *Pulchra es* are found, see Kurtzman, 'The Monteverdi Vespers of 1610', app. F. Additional settings from 1600–20, derived from Jerome Roche's motet index, are as follows (RISM numbers, where applicable, follow each date:) Sisto Galli, *Motecta octo vocum*, 1600, G168; Pompeo Signorucci, *Concerti ecclesiastici*, 1602, S3428; Giovanni Battista Biondi da Cesena, *Motetti a quattro voci*, 1606, B2709 (repr., 1610, B2710); Giacomo Moro da Viadana, *Libro terzo*, 1607; Antonio Badi, *Il primo libro de concerti*, 1610, B626; Bernardo Strozzi, *Sacri concentus*, 1612, S6990; Grammatico Metallo, *Motetti, Magnificat et madrigali spirituali*, 1613, M2442; Giovanni Nicolo Mezzogorri, *La celeste sposa*, 1613, M2618; Gabriello Puliti, *Sacri concentus*, 1614, P5652; Biagio Tomasi, *Quaranta concerti*, 1615, T921; Lodovico Torto, *De sacris*, 1615, T1014; Antonio Brunelli, *Sacra cantica*, 1617, B4649; Aglione, *Giardino*, 1618; Magini de Magis in *Lilia sacra octo*, SD1618[5]; Giovanni Paolo Cima in Calvi, *Symbolae diversorum musicorum*, SD1620[2]; Ecole Porta, *Sacro convito*, 1620, P5194.

[147] See Barblan, ed., *Musiche della Cappella di S. Barbara*, 1–2 (item 1).

Ex. 4.11. *a* Monteverdi, *Pulchra es*, bars 1–5; *b* Agostino Agazzari, *Pulchra es* from *Sacrae cantiones*, 1606

recitative to sacred music, however. Two composers mentioned above who were strongly influenced by Caccini, Ottavio Durante, a Roman, and Don Severo Bonini, a Florentine, both employed recitative in earlier sacred publications.[148] The opening of Durante's *Filiae Jerusalem* may be quoted as an illustration (see Ex. 4.16). Like Monteverdi, Durante did not adhere exclusively to the one style but mixed it with arioso.[149] Durante's collection also features virtuoso ornamentation in such pieces as *Aspice Domine* and *Beata es virgo*, and following the aesthetics of Caccini, these ornaments are carefully applied for expressive

---

[148] Durante, *Arie devote . . . 1608* (D3975) and Bonini, *Il secondo libro de madrigali, e mottetti . . . 1609* (B3497).

[149] Transcription in Kurtzman, 'The Monteverdi Vespers of 1610', iii. 1088–9.

Ex. 4.12. *a* Monteverdi, *Pulchra es*, bars 37–45; *b* Agostino Agazzari, *Pulchra es* from *Sacrae cantiones*, 1606

purpose, for accentuating cadences, and for filling in the gaps between disjunct notes of adjacent harmonies.[150] Underneath ornamental melismas, the bass often consists of a single sustained pitch, as in Monteverdi. Bonini followed much the same practice as Durante, and since he was a Florentine, Monteverdi was probably familiar with his work.

Two other motet books that appeared in the same year as Monteverdi's Vespers deserve attention. These are the first sacred publications of Alessandro Grandi (G3417) and Giovanni Francesco Capello (C902), both of which con-

[150] Transcriptions ibid. 1084–7.

Ex. 4.13. *a* Monteverdi, *Pulchra es*, bars 46–53; *b* Agostino Agazzari, *Pulchra es* from *Sacrae cantiones*, 1606

tain pieces that either closely resemble some of Monteverdi's motets or share a number of distinctive features with them. In the duet for two tenors *In semita iudiciorum*, Grandi, who was employed at the Accademia dello Spirito Santo in Ferrara at the time, uses a declamatory style approaching recitative.[151] Like Monteverdi, he often begins a phrase in imitation and then continues in parallel thirds. Another close parallel with Monteverdi occurs at the very end of this piece, where alternating echoing ornaments closely resemble the conclusion of Monteverdi's *Laudate pueri*. Grandi also shares Monteverdi's preference in duets for voices in the same register. Most other motet composers of the period tend

[151] Transcription ibid. 1090–2.

Ex. 4.14. Pietro Paolo Cavi, *Pulchra es* from *Sacrae cantiones*, 1609

to mix vocal registers in duets. Whether Monteverdi knew Grandi or not at this time, it is likely that the younger composer was familiar with Monteverdi's music, and he was quite possibly influenced by what he knew of the Mantuan's style.[152]

Giovanni Francesco Capello, active in Venice in 1610, was quite modern in his affective treatment of texts and was more inclined towards virtuosity than Grandi.[153] Capello's motets are distinguished by interesting bass-lines frequently outlining cadential harmonies, sequences, and unusual, affective chord progressions. The basso continuo tends to interact imitatively with the upper voices, but employing modern types of figuration and ornamentation rather than the traditional sixteenth-century patterns common in Viadana's *Concerti ecclesiastici*. The upper parts of Capello's motets display significant differentiation in rhythmic patterns and melodic figures, responding expressively to individual words of the text. Particularly akin to Monteverdi's *Nigra sum* is Capello's virtuoso piece *Indica mihi*.[154] The intense, recitative-like character of much of the writing is similar to *Nigra sum*, and the bass moves with a similar tonal purpose, supporting frequent cadences and modulations. What is missing, however, is the sense of melodic direction so important to the Monteverdi piece. Capello concentrates instead on displaying the incredible vocal range of the virtuoso for whom

---

[152] For other discussions of Grandi's 1610 motets see Denis Arnold, 'Alessandro Grandi, a Disciple of Monteverdi', *Musical Quarterly*, 43 (1957), 173–5, and Jerome Roche, *North Italian Church Music*, 63. Grandi later became Monteverdi's *vice-maestro di cappella* at St Mark's.

[153] This Capello collection and other music by Capello are discussed in Kurtzman, 'Giovanni Francesco Capello'.

[154] Ed. Jerome and Elizabeth Roche in *Motets, 1600–1650* (Seventeenth-Century Italian Sacred Music, 24; New York: Garland Publishing, Inc., forthcoming). See also Kurtzman, 'The Monteverdi Vespers of 1610', iii. 1096–7.

Ex. 4.15. *a* Monteverdi, *Pulchra es*, bars 81–6; *b* Adriano Banchieri, *Pulchra es* from *Vezzo de perle musi-cali*, 1610

this piece was composed. The clefs change continually in the part-book, and many passages consist of figures repeated immediately as much as two octaves lower. A long rising melisma on the word *vagar* (to wander) near the beginning ascends through two-and-a-half octaves. Vincenzo Giustiniani mentions by

Ex. 4.16. Ottavio Durante, *Filiae Jerusalem* from *Arie devote*, 1608

name three singers capable of performing pieces of this type,[155] and the virtuosi Puliaschi and Caccini could both negotiate such wide ranges. Capello, working at the time in Venice, was likely writing for someone unknown to modern scholarship; indeed, in the early seventeenth century there may have been a number of singers capable of such vocal feats of whom we have no record.

Capello's use of the *trillo* in a manner closely paralleling Monteverdi's *Duo Seraphim* has already been discussed above. Further similarities with Monteverdi's motets may be seen in Capello's *O Iesu dulcis memoria*.[156] The shape of the melodic line, the ornaments fully integrated into the melodic patterns, the frequent phrases in recitative style, the rapid and varied harmonic motion are all reminiscent of *Nigra sum*, *Pulchra es*, and *Audi coelum*. This piece demonstrates how close the fundamental styles of Capello and Monteverdi are, though Capello is more sparing in his use of virtuoso embellishments.

Parallels with Monteverdi can also be seen in Capello's motets for two voices and basso continuo, exemplified by *Ave virgo gratiosa*.[157] The strong harmonic sequences in the bass, the imitative patterns frequently concluding in parallel

---

[155] Vincenzo Giustiniani, *Discorso sopra la musica*. Eng. trans. Carol MacClintock (Musicological Studies and Documents, 9; American Institute of Musicology, 1962), 69. Although Giustiniani's treatise dates from c.1628, he was describing a new style of singing that began in Rome c.1575 and that included basses singing a range of twenty-two notes. See also Robert Greenlee, '*Disposizione di voce*: Passage to Florid Singing', *Early Music*, 15 (1987), 47–55.

[156] Transcription in Kurtzman, 'The Monteverdi Vespers of 1610', iii. 1098–9.

[157] Transcriptions ibid. 1102–3 and in Kurtzman, 'Giovanni Francesco Capello', 175–7.

thirds, and the close interaction between the two tenors, with voice-crossings and free treatment of dissonance, all reveal a conception of the handling of a duet very similar to Monteverdi's. Capello's music is especially close to Monteverdi in style, yet there is no reason to suppose that this Venetian monk was acquainted with Monteverdi or knew his music, only that there was enough common currency in modern style and technique in northern Italy for unrelated compositions by different composers to share the same features.

Another Venetian composer, Antonio Burlini, published motets in modern style in his *Riviera fiorita di concerti musicale* (B5022) just two years later, testifying further to the presence of the modern idiom in Venetian sacred music.[158] These motets, with separate optional parts for a high and a low instrument, often have long virtuoso melismas, employ motifs sequentially, utilize shifts to triple metre, are sometimes chromatic in melody and harmony, initiate imitative melismas that subsequently proceed in parallel thirds or sixths, and treat solo voices antiphonally with short motifs after the fashion of Gabrieli, but do not include the recitative style or Caccini's typical 'graces', as Capello's motets do. Many of these characteristics resemble those of Monteverdi's motets, but these features had by 1612 spread widely enough in the motet repertoire of northern Italy, including Venice, that it would be problematic to claim direct influence of Monteverdi on Burlini.

VI

The remaining two pieces of the *Vespro*, the response *Domine ad adjuvandum* and the hymn *Ave maris stella*, further confirm Monteverdi's penchant for grandiloquent forms of expression. A number of vesper collections begin with the vesper response, but in the early part of the century it is almost invariably a short, modest piece in keeping with the brevity of its text. *Falsobordone* and measured chordal homophony are frequently-used techniques. Settings by Luigi Roinci of Piacenza, in his *Sacra omnium solemnitatum vespertina* of 1604 (R1957), and Monteverdi's Mantuan colleague Giovanni Giacomo Gastoldi, in his *Salmi intieri* of 1607 (G503), introduce triple metre for the *Gloria Patri*. Only the 1610 setting from Antonio Mortaro's *Secondo libro delle messe, salmi, Magnificat* (M3749) can bear comparison with Monteverdi's in scope; Mortaro's version is for thirteen voice parts in three choirs, each with its own organ. The three choirs play off against one another in antiphonal fashion (sometimes two choirs join against one) until they all combine at the end.

Monteverdi himself draws on the tradition of *falsobordone* in his setting of the response, but when this is superimposed on the adaptation of the toccata from

---

[158] Burlini moved to Siena later in 1612.

L'Orfeo, and the entire structure is enlarged by the addition of triple-metre ritornellos, a much more extended and elaborate composition, with a wholly new aesthetic purpose, ensues. The response becomes a large-scale vocal and instrumental sinfonia, introducing the entire opulent vesper service with its own musical brilliance. As with other pieces of the *Vespro*, Monteverdi has discerned the possibility of combining originally simple types of music with divergent purposes so as to fulfil both the required liturgical function and the need for an appropriately ostentatious introduction to his sumptuous collection.

Hymn settings, in contrast to settings of the response, are extremely rare in publications of vesper music outside collections devoted exclusively or largely to hymns. Monteverdi's inclusion of *Ave maris stella* is an indication of his wish to supply a complete musical service.[159] Lodovico Torto published a short, *alternatim* strophic setting of the even-numbered verses for three voices and organ continuo in his *Missa una, septem divinae laudes* of 1607 (T1013).[160] The style is conservative, with the three voices engaged in either an imitative or a freely polyphonic texture, except for one brief passage of chordal homophony in triple metre. Torto makes no reference to the cantus firmus.

More imposing is a setting by Gaspare Villani of Piacenza from his *Psalmi omnes* of 1611 (V1552).[161] In keeping with the other compositions in this collection, the hymn is for eight-voice double choir (both SATB) singing antiphonally. Verses 1 and 2 are sung to one musical segment; the first phrase presents a paraphrase of the plainchant in imitation in the first choir, but leads quickly to strictly chordal textures in fairly rapid exchanges between choirs with little reference to the chant. A second section, for verses 3 and 4, proceeds similarly, starting with the second choir, and a third section, for verses 5 and 6, is rhythmically livelier, with considerable overlapping between the two choirs after the first phrase. As in verse 1, the beginning of the section paraphrases the plainchant. The seventh and final verse is completely homophonic, but again there are references to the cantus firmus at the beginning. Villani even provides a separate, eight-voice polyphonic *Amen* hinting at the opening phrase of the same cantus firmus, but avoiding the plainchant to which the word *Amen* is sung.

Paolo Agostini, in the 1619 collection of Marian psalms, polyphonic antiphons, motets, and Magnificats described above, also included two settings of *Ave maris stella* for two and three voices and organ continuo.[162] Agostini's settings are *alternatim*, with alternate polyphonic verses in two or three voices according to the following schemes:

---

[159] See Ch. 1.
[160] Transcription in Kurtzman, 'The Monteverdi Vespers of 1610', iii. 1070.
[161] Transcription ibid. 1058–69.
[162] Transcription of odd-verse setting ibid. 1071–5. Ed. Kurtzman in *Vesper and Compline Music for Three Principal Voices*. Yet another setting of *Ave maris stella* is found in Andrea Falconieri, *Sacrae modulationes . . . 1619* (Cracow, Biblioteka Jagiellonska). Falconieri sets each of the seven verses separately.

Ave maris stella (odd verses)

Verse 1 canto I, tenor
Verse 3 canto I, canto II, bass
Verse 5 tenor I, tenor II
Verse 7 canto, tenor, bass (triple metre)

Ave maris stella (even verses)

Verse 2 canto, alto, tenor I
Verse 4 canto, bass
Verse 6 canto, alto, tenor (triple metre)

Agostini's style is imitative and quite conservative in character. Each of his imitative motifs is based on the appropriate phrase of the plainchant. Even the more homophonic final verses in triple metre exhibit elements of imitation.

A strophic format is frequently encountered in hymn collections of the sixteenth century as well, and Monteverdi's version of *Ave maris stella* follows suit. As in the other compositions of the 1610 print based on a cantus firmus, Monteverdi reverts to an old practice, older even than the imitative paraphrases of the hymn tune found in the Villani and Agostini settings just described. Monteverdi sets the cantus firmus, virtually unchanged, in the topmost voice, and harmonizes it with the same basic harmonic scheme in each of the seven verses. But as we have seen so often, he is not content with a simple and unassuming structure and elaborates on this basic plan in an ingenious fashion. The details of his setting are described in Chapter 8, and a structural outline can be found in Appendix C. Here I need only observe that an unpretentious, traditional technique has once again been combined with modern elements to produce a composition of larger than normal dimensions and complexity, despite the many conservative aspects of Monteverdi's setting.

VII

A summary overview of the comparisons made in the preceding sections of this chapter confirms that different aspects of Monteverdi's *Vespro* have different relationships with the contemporary repertoire. The contents of the 1610 print place it within a small group of collections devoted to music for a single category of vesper feasts. These collections are not applicable to as many feasts as the mainstream of vesper publications, but most of them attempt to provide a greater quantity of polyphonic music for the feasts they do serve. Within this specialized repertoire, Monteverdi's is the only collection other than Agostini's Marian Vespers of 1619 to intersperse motets between psalms and to include a setting of an appropriate hymn.

Monteverdi's approach to musical style is considerably more unusual than his selection of pieces for his publication. The psalms and Magnificats draw not only from traditional, even outmoded, procedures in their respective genres, but also from the most progressive tendencies, especially those originating in publications of few-voiced motets. Monteverdi's complex synthesis of highly diverse materials and techniques results in more expansive and variegated compositions than appear anywhere else in the contemporary vesper repertoire. The Magnificats in particular exhibit a unique combination of elements. In sheer musical magnificence, the only published works comparable to Monteverdi's psalms, Magnificats, response, and hymn are the late motets of Giovanni Gabrieli. Gabrieli, however, showed little interest in vesper music and the details of his style differ substantially from Monteverdi's.

The five *sacri concentus*, on the other hand, are more dependent on developments in the motet and instrumental canzona and sonata after the turn of the seventeenth century. But even in his motets and the *Sonata sopra Sancta Maria*, Monteverdi's large dimensions, virtuoso embellishments, structural cohesion, and rhetorical treatment of texts far surpass the achievements of most other composers. Indeed, only *Pulchra es* may be compared in scope with the motets of a few other composers. *Nigra sum* is a uniquely intense monody, effectively utilizing the recitative style in a way I have not seen in any other motet. The lavish and intricate ornamentation in *Duo Seraphim* and *Audi coelum* exceeds that of any other publication of the period, though there are some, such as Kapsberger and Severi, who extend stepwise melismas to enormous lengths. And the *Sonata sopra Sancta Maria* bears comparison only with the larger instrumental canzonas and sonatas of Giovanni Gabrieli.

VIII

The very originality of the *Vespro della Beata Vergine* greatly facilitates a study of the impact and influence of Monteverdi's publication on subsequent vesper compositions. It is probable that any vesper collection from the years immediately after 1610 that exhibits characteristics of Monteverdi's music not found in the repertoire prior to that year has been directly or indirectly influenced by him. The discussion of this material will be limited here to the period 1610–24.[163]

Two collections published in 1611, one by Don Giovanni Flaccomio from Milazzo (F1100) and the other by Don Grisostomo Rubiconi of Padua (R3034), already reveal possible Monteverdian influence.[164] Although only five of nine part-books survive from each collection, they contain enough rubrics

[163] Klaus Fischer suggests possible Monteverdian influence on the Roman composers Micheli Romano and Stefano Landi in *Die Psalmkompositionen in Rom um 1600 (ca. 1570–1630)* (Kölner Beiträge zur Musikforschung, 98; Regensburg: Gustav Bosse Verlag, 1979), 283–98. Jerome Roche also discusses Monteverdi's influence on other composers in *North Italian Church Music*, 64, 70–1, 79, 80, 82, 104, 108, 115, 138.

[164] Flaccomio's is another of the collections containing the psalm *cursus* for the BVM and other virgin saints. The motets in this collection all have rubrics for various virgin saints.

and other indications of style and structure to determine with reasonable accuracy the character of the music. In both publications psalm and Magnificat settings for double choir are subdivided into verses of contrasting sonority, sometimes entailing a soloist or ensemble of two, three, or four voices. The following list illustrates the organization of Rubiconi's *Dixit Dominus* as itemized in the original print.

Dixit Dominus	basso e 2 tenori
Donec ponam inimicos	alto e doi soprani
Virgam virtutis	alto, basso e tenor
Tecum principium	alto e basso
Iuravit Dominus	a 2 canti e a 8
Dominus a dextris tuis	basso e doi tenori
Iudicabit in nationibus	a doi bassi
De torrente	doi bassi e 2 canti
Gloria Patri	a 8
Sicut erat	[a 8]

Rubiconi's reliance on few-voiced textures is even more palpable than Monteverdi's. The full eight-voice choir appears only in a single interior verse and the doxology. In the other verses, the texture is much thinner, and the voices are not always matched in pairs of the same range as with Monteverdi. Rubiconi employs a greater variety of combinations, though at times he pits two soloists in one register against a third in another. In those instances, the lowest part is unrelated to the psalm tone that Monteverdi uses as a bass in trio textures in his own *Dixit Dominus*. The vocal writing in Rubiconi's psalms is ornamented, but does not approach the virtuosity demanded by Monteverdi.

Flaccomio is equally attracted to contrasts in sonority and texture. His *Nisi Dominus*, for example, marked *da concierto*, alternates between odd-numbered verses distributed among soloists from the first choir (descending from soprano through tenor) and even-numbered verses set *a 4* for the second choir. The two verses of the doxology are each assigned to one of the four-voice ensembles. The influence of the *alternatim* technique, at the basis of Monteverdi's *Dixit Dominus*, is also evident here. Flaccomio's solo writing is quite modest and no different from the style employed in the verses *a 4*. Moreover, it seems clear that the psalm tone, if used at all, played only a minor role in this composition. In his Magnificat, Flaccomio adds instrumental colouring, requesting doubling with a cornetto (*cum corneta*) and with a bassoon (*cum basonicco*) in two separate duos.

These extended, sectionalized compositions, with their conspicuous changes in texture and their dependence on solo voices, may well have been directly influenced by Monteverdi's example, since there are no other precedents in the surviving published vesper repertoire. Not all peculiarities of the *Vespro*, however, were equally influential, for neither Rubiconi's nor Flaccomio's extant part-books give any hint of the psalm tone, nor does their solo writing approach Monteverdi's extraordinary virtuosity. As we shall see, the psalm tone played as little a role after 1610 as it had before; indeed, Monteverdi himself never used a psalm tone as a systematic structuring device again.[165] The absence of virtuosity in Rubiconi's and Flaccomio's collections may be attributed to the fact that few places in Italy had the quality of singers available in Mantua and Ferrara. Even in Venice Gabrieli provided comparatively modest parts for his soloists.

A rare instance of the plainchant in a significant role is found in a collection of Lamentations for Holy Week by Giovanni Francesco Capello, published in 1612 (C903).[166] Capello's eight-voice setting of the canticle of Zacharia, *Benedictus Dominus Deus Israel*, accompanied solely by the basso continuo, carries the rubric *Del primo Tono in Sol sopra il Canto fermo*. No other composition I have seen aside from Monteverdi's psalms and Magnificats uses a cantus firmus so extensively as to call attention to the fact in print. The plainchant melody for the canticle closely resembles a psalm tone and is repeated for each verse of the text in the same manner as the psalm chants. A large portion of Capello's piece consists of chordal harmonization of the cantus firmus, which appears successively in different voices and alternately at its initial pitch level and a fourth below.

Many aspects of Capello's music bear a remarkably close relationship to Monteverdi. His motets have already been mentioned, and in his 1612 *Lamentationi*, obbligato instruments are prominently featured. Another composition from this collection, the psalm *Miserere mei Deus*, seems scarcely conceivable without the example of Monteverdi's *Vespro*. This five-voice setting depends heavily on solo writing and an instrumental ensemble comprising a violetta, two violas, a violone, and chitarroni. The sectionalization of Capello's psalm is as pronounced as any of Monteverdi's. Ritornellos are interspersed throughout the piece, and the instrumental ensemble also serves in whole or in part as an accompaniment in several sections. Two imitative duets closely resemble Monteverdi's duet style (see Ex. 4.17). The segments for solo voices approximate the recitative passages of *Nigra sum* and *Audi coelum* (see Ex. 4.18). Virtuoso embellishments are lacking, but they are abundant in other pieces in the *Lamentationi*, as well as in Capello's 1610 collection of motets.

Among the most striking illustrations of Monteverdi's influence are the *Salmi intieri* of 1613 (B5023) and the *Messa, salmi, et motetti concertati* of 1615 (B5025)

---

[165] Monteverdi's *Magnificat à 4 in genere da Capella*, published in the *Selva morale e spirituale* of 1641, employs the Magnificat tone as a cantus firmus in most verses, but without giving it the structural significance it has in the 1610 Vespers. This later Magnificat is in the *stile antico* and resembles the Marian canticles of Victoria. The first *Dixit Dominus* in the *Messa a quattro voci et Salmi* of 1651 also uses the psalm tone as cantus firmus intermittently, and a psalm tone cantus firmus appears a few times in the second *Lauda Jerusalem* of the same print.

[166] See Kurtzman, 'Giovanni Francesco Capello', 161–2. Attention was first called to Capello's *Lamentationi* by Denis Arnold in 'Giovanni Croce and the "Concertato" Style', 42.

Ex. 4.17. Giovanni Francesco Capello, *Miserere* from *Lamentationi, Benedictus e Miserere*, 1612

by Don Antonio Burlini, of Venetian origin, but from some time in 1612 organist at Monteoliveto Maggiore in Siena.[167] The *Salmi intieri* are large-scale,
through-composed, and highly diverse settings of considerable musical interest.
Burlini's four-voice choir is supported not only by an organ continuo but also at
times by separate parts for an *istrumento acuto* and an *istrumento grave*, both *se piace*.
Each verse of a psalm is confined to a distinct section, and these sections are dif-
ferentiated from one another by significant changes of style. Solo and duet textures are frequently encountered, though in these verses all parts may briefly
combine for a four-voice passage. Imitative duets with instrumental accompaniment are also common. *Falsibordoni* and block chordal style appear occasionally, and some passages shift from the prevailing duple metre to triple time.

[167] The compositions from these two collections discussed below are transcribed in Kurtzman, 'The
Monteverdi Vespers of 1610', ii and iii.

Ex. 4.18. Giovanni Francesco Capello, *Miserere* from *Lamentationi, Benedictus e Miserere*, 1612

Within a single section the verse is often split into segments of only a few words, which are repeated several times before the text continues.

Not only is the general character of Burlini's *Salmi intieri* reminiscent of the *Vespro della Beata Vergine*, but there are a few passages that appear to be directly imitative of Monteverdi. The opening of Burlini's *Laudate pueri* employs the same fourth psalm tone as Monteverdi's *Dixit Dominus*, with its characteristic dip to the seventh degree both at the beginning and near the end of the first phrase as well as in the second phrase of the chant. As in *Dixit Dominus*, Burlini's plainsong serves as a subject for imitation, leading to a full-voiced chordal passage (see Ex. 4.19). But Monteverdi's six voices, two of them carrying a countersubject, result in a more complicated texture than Burlini's four. In the *Quia fecit* of Burlini's first canticle, the Magnificat tone emerges in long note values in a solo voice accompanied by the organ and a pair of instruments, a procedure directly comparable to the *Quia respexit* of Monteverdi's Magnificat *à 7* (see Ex. 4.20). Similarly, the *Gloria Patri* of Burlini's setting is a florid echo piece analogous to Monteverdi's.

The second canticle of the *Salmi intieri* is similar in style to the first, although there is more emphasis on the full chorus. The *Et exsultavit* of this piece bears a remarkable resemblance to the *Et exsultavit* of Monteverdi's seven-voice Magnificat. Both versions begin with a melismatic passage in two-voice imitation followed by sequential repetition at a higher level (Monteverdi's sequence

Ex. 4.19. Antonio Burlini, *Laudate pueri* from *Salmi intieri*, 1613

Ex. 4.20. Antonio Burlini, Magnificat from *Salmi intieri*, 1613

rises by a fifth, Burlini's by a fourth). In both settings there is a subsequent slow-ing of the pace at *spiritus meus* succeeded by a short melismatic figure treated imitatively at *in deo*. Although Burlini dispenses with the Magnificat tone and calls for four voices rather than Monteverdi's two, the derivation of his setting of this verse is obvious (see Ex. 4.21).

Despite the parallels between Burlini's and Monteverdi's Magnificats, significant differences are also apparent. Aside from the one verse carrying the Magnificat tone mentioned above, the chant is absent altogether from Burlini's two canticles. Burlini employs his full vocal ensemble (only four voices in com-

Ex. 4.21. Antonio Burlini, Magnificat from *Salmi intieri*, 1613

Ex. 4.21. *Continued*

parison to Monteverdi's seven) much more often, especially as the piece progresses. Burlini's instruments function differently too; their style is less ornamental and, like the voices, they do not approach Monteverdi's characteristic virtuosity. The instruments also perform a sinfonia before the beginning of the first Magnificat, following the example of several motets in Giovanni Gabrieli's *Sacrae symphoniae* of 1615. The Gabrieli collection, of course, postdates Burlini's, but as noted earlier, Gabrieli died in 1612, and since Burlini himself was resident in Venice prior to his removal to Siena in 1612, he undoubtedly would have been quite familiar with Gabrieli's music.[168]

Mention should also be made of Burlini's four-voice setting of the response *Domine ad adjuvandum* from this collection. Burlini's is the only setting from this period besides Monteverdi's to use instruments (the *istrumento acuto* and *istrumento grave*) and display an elaborate style. This composition opens with the cantus part alone intoning *Domine*, imitated by the altus, then shifts to triple metre for a chordal texture resembling *falsobordone*. The duple-metre *Gloria Patri* resorts to modestly virtuosic passages for successive solo voices in naming the Trinity. The *Sicut erat* begins and ends each half-verse with chordal homophony in duple metre, but the interior of the verse is broken up into solo phrases and polyphonic imitation. While there is nothing in this response directly related to Monteverdi's *Domine ad adjuvandum*, the generally elaborate and variegated setting clearly takes its point of departure from Monteverdi.

Burlini's collection of 1615 is somewhat more conservative, while still revealing Monteverdi's influence. The psalms and Magnificat are for two four-voice choirs, one *di concerto* for solo voices and the other *per ripieno*, with homophonic textures and antiphonal effects correspondingly prominent. Nevertheless, there are intervening passages for one, two, three, and four voices in the *concerto* choir, all in a modest vocal style. In addition to the organ continuo, a part for a single obbligato instrument is provided. These pieces, like those of the *Salmi intieri*, are large-scale works of considerable stylistic variety whose overall dimensions reflect the impact of the *Vespro della Beata Vergine*. In contrast with Monteverdi's collection, however, there is no stylistic distinction between Burlini's psalms and his Magnificats in these two prints.

Among Magnificats published in motet books, one from Don Serafino Patta's *Sacrorum canticorum* of 1613 (P1038) displays Monteverdi's influence in its highly varied and complex structure as well as in some individual details.[169] This five-voice piece concentrates heavily on solos and duets in the virtuoso style (see Ex. 4.22), with only a minority of the verses requiring the full ensemble. Some of

---

[168] Burlini's *Riviera fiorita di concerti musicale* (Venice, 1612) names him as *Organista di Santa Elena di Venetia*. However, his *Fiori di concerti spirituali* (also Venice, 1612) indicates that he was now *Organista di Monteoliveto Maggiore di Siena*.

[169] Transcription, Kurtzman, 'The Monteverdi Vespers of 1610', iii. 1003–18.

Ex. 4.22. Serafino Patta, Magnificat from *Sacrorum canticorum*, 1613

the few-voiced sections are cast in *falsibordoni*, but others are reminiscent of the solo writing of Ottavio Durante. The duets tend to be imitative and comparable to Monteverdi's (see Ex. 4.23). The Magnificat tone even appears in long note values at the beginning of the *Deposuit*, while the *Gloria Patri* employs a choral echo.

In 1613 Monteverdi assumed his new post as *maestro di cappella* at St Mark's, and various aspects of his music seem to have had their effect on a few composers in the Venetian state shortly thereafter. The 1614 psalms of Francesco Usper (U116), organist at the church of San Salvatore in Venice, manifest an unusual interest in thin textures. Usper's *Laudate pueri* in particular, marked *concertato senza intonatione*, utilizes its full five voices only at the conclusion of a few sections. Imitative duets prevail instead, and passage-work is frequent.[170]

Much grander in design are the 1616 *Messa vespro et compieta* by Amadio Freddi of Treviso (F1829).[171] An obbligato cornetto and violin accompany the vocal parts in some pieces and perform additional sinfonias in others. The psalm and Magnificat settings emulate Monteverdi in their elaborate style and in their variety of textures, rhythms, metres, and melodic patterns. Change and contrast are almost continuous in these pieces. Short passages of text, sometimes only a few words, are isolated for individual musical treatment. Soloists are juxtaposed with the five-voice tutti, and chordal writing is interchanged with imitation.

---

[170] Usper's psalms constitute the 'male *cursus*'. For a transcription of this psalm and Usper's *Confitebor tibi*, see Kurtzman, 'The Monteverdi Vespers of 1610', 684–701.

[171] Freddi's is another of the collections containing the five psalms for Vespers of the Virgin. For transcriptions of Freddi's *Laetatus sum* and Magnificat, see ibid. ii. 723–46 and iii. 940–68. The entire collection is studied and transcribed in Lee Bryant Bratton, 'Amadio Freddi's "Messa, Vespro, et Compieta" of 1616' (DMA dissertation, University of Texas at Austin, 1986). See also the discussion in Roche, *North Italian Church Music*, 129–32. Two recent articles on Freddi are Billio D'Arpa, 'Amadio Freddi, musicista padovano' and ead., 'Musica sacra tra stile antico e moderno: La Messa, Vespro et Compieta (Venezia 1616) di Amadio Freddi', *Rivista internazionale di musica sacra*, 11 (1990), 287–322.

Ex. 4.23. Serafino Patta, Magnificat from *Sacrorum canticorum*, 1613

Even the psalm tone appears with some frequency, though without the pervasive structural function of Monteverdi. The passages for soloists, however, shun vocal virtuosity.

It was in the collections of Usper and Freddi that the influence of Monteverdi began to supersede that of Giovanni Gabrieli in Venetian music. The antiphonal style shows evidence of yielding to the thinner textures and soloistic passages of St Mark's new *maestro di cappella*, although neither Usper nor Freddi made the extraordinary virtuoso demands that Monteverdi did.

Gabrieli normally confined antiphonal contrasts to his polychoral pieces, while in his works for fewer voices the textures fluctuate in accord with sixteenth-century practice—through the entrance and exit of parts without cadences and without breaking the continuity of the forward motion. The five-voice pieces of Usper and Freddi, however, are much more clearly sectionalized by means of sudden contrasts and deliberate discontinuities. In this respect they follow Monteverdi and arrive at the *concertato* style without indulging in the massed antiphony of Gabrieli. Gabrieli's gigantic polychoral works were rapidly eclipsed with the advent of Monteverdi in Venice, and variety, contrast, and colour became dependent upon factors other than large masses of sound. As a result, Usper and especially Freddi reveal their progressive tendencies not through antiphony, but by their emphasis on thin textures, solo voices and instruments, vocal and instrumental duets, and sudden juxtapositions of contrasting rhythms, textures, and sonorities.

Further possible influence from Monteverdi can be seen in the *Compieta a sei voci* from 1616 of Micheli Romano (M2685), who, despite his Roman origins, had travelled widely in the service of Gesualdo, visiting Naples, Venice, Ferrara, Bologna, and Milan, and subsequently worked in Tivoli, Concordia (near Udine), and Aquileia. Ultimately he settled back in Rome. At the time of the publication of his *Compieta a sei voci*, he was *maestro di cappella* of the cathedral in Concordia.[172] It is therefore appropriate to consider Micheli a northern composer, rather than a Roman one, at least with regard to the *Compieta*.

The modern character of Micheli's collection is advertised on the title-page with the phrase *concertata all'uso moderno*.[173] Among the most notable features of some of these psalms are the frequent changes in texture from one verse to the next, ranging from solo voice to two voices, three voices, four voices, and six voices. Some verses are declamatory in style, others are virtuosic. Some are in *falsobordone*, while others employ triple metre. Micheli uses modern dotted rhythms in small note values, and his duet textures typically begin in imitation

---

[172] Charles M. Atkinson, 'Micheli, Romano', in *The New Grove*, xii. 267.

[173] Much of the following discussion is based on Fischer, *Die Psalmkompositionen in Rom um 1600*, 283–309. Music from the *Compieta* will be published in Kurtzman, ed., *Vesper and Compline Music* (Seventeenth-Century Italian Sacred Music, 17).

followed by parallel thirds over a slower-moving bass—both are features he shares with Monteverdi. Since a similar duet technique is evident in Micheli's *Psalmi ad officium vesperarum* of 1610 (M2682), this approach to two-voice textures is not so much a question of Monteverdi's influence on Micheli, but rather of a parallel development between two composers. The use of rising sequences in single-voice textures, emphasizing individual words or phrases of text, is another technique Micheli has in common with Monteverdi. Micheli's occasional introduction of ornamentation in solo textures is for the purpose of expressing specific words or phrases of text rather than virtuosic display, and his mostly syllabic monodic textures clearly derive their character from Florentine and Mantuan monody.

All of the collections heretofore discussed emanated from northern Italy, where vesper psalms had enjoyed a special prominence throughout the sixteenth century. Rome, on the other hand, had shown less interest in polyphonic psalmody before the Council of Trent, and in the post-Tridentine period, polyphonic and even polychoral psalmody was associated particularly with special feast-days and elaborate celebrations.[174] In relation to northern Italian sources, there are comparatively few vesper psalms in Roman manuscripts and prints of the *Cinquecento*. Only from the 1570s does evidence of increasing Roman interest in polychoral music, including psalms and Magnificats, begin to mount; and much of this music remained unpublished and is lost. It was only in the early seventeenth century that printed collections of vesper music began to proliferate in the Holy City.

In 1620, an unusual collection, containing both conservative and modern settings of psalms and Magnificats, was published by the Roman Paolo Tarditi (T225).[175] The modern compositions are double-choir pieces with the addition of a violin and lute to the first chorus and a cornetto and theorbo to the second. In these works Tarditi's style does not differ significantly from Amadio Freddi's. Despite the division into two four-voice choirs, antiphonal effects are subordinate to such techniques as abrupt contrasts and thin textures. Solo and duet passages, especially duets for voices in the same range, such as at *Rogate quem ad pacem* in *Laetatus sum*, and at the beginning of the doxology of the same psalm, are reminiscent of Monteverdi's duets for like voices. The latter is an echo duet,

---

[174] An extensive study of psalm composition in Rome is found in Fischer, *Die Psalmkompositione*. Polychoral psalmody in Rome is thoroughly discussed in O'Regan, 'Sacred Polychoral Music'.

[175] Tarditi's five psalms in the conservative style form the 'male *cursus*'. For a transcription of Tarditi's *Laetatus sum* and Magnificat, see Kurtzman, 'The Monteverdi Vespers of 1610', 747–65, 969–92. Tarditi's collection is briefly discussed in Dixon, 'The Origins of the Roman "Colossal Baroque"', 120, and the disposition of voices and instruments in Tarditi's *Beatus vir* is outlined in id., 'Roman Church Music: The Place of Instruments after 1600', *Galpin Society Journal*, 34 (1981), 54. O'Regan also describes Tarditi's collection and quotes the composer's preface both in Italian and in English translation in 'Sacred Polychoral Music', i. 244–5. See also id., 'The Performance of Roman Sacred Polychoral Music', 127.

and while echo effects had been prominent in Italian music for some time, this duet bears a striking resemblance in its ornamental style both to Monteverdi's *Audi coelum* and to the *Gloria Patri* of the Magnificat *a 7*. Virtuoso writing is much more in evidence in Tarditi's psalms than in Freddi's compositions, but it still does not approach Monteverdi's extravagance (see Ex. 4.24). Despite these resemblances to Monteverdi and Freddi, the concertato subdivision of psalms and other sacred texts into sections for different musical forces in different styles had become quite common in Rome, so much so that it was referred to by Agostino Diruta, a northern composer, as *concertato alla romana*.[176] Tarditi, therefore, may have been more directly influenced by Roman predecessors and contemporaries than by northerners, though the echo duet in the doxology of *Laetatus sum* suggests his acquaintance with the Monteverdi Vespers.

Klaus Fischer notes the modern characteristics of another Roman publication, Stefano Landi's *Psalmi integri quattuor vocibus* of 1624 (L531).[177] These psalms also frequently change texture, not only from one verse to the next, but sometimes within a verse. Their rapid exchanges of short motifs and frequent sections in triple metre are more reminiscent of Gabrieli than of Monteverdi, but the polyphonic *Amen*s of several psalms resemble closely those of Monteverdi. Landi's monodic textures not only emphasize the recitative style (but without much attention to word expression), but also include ornamental *passaggi* similar to those employed by Monteverdi and other modern composers. By 1624, Landi may represent widespread stylistic tendencies and traditions not necessarily directly traceable to Monteverdi. The ripple effects of the latter's influence in Rome, if any, can only be demonstrated through much broader access to the early seventeenth-century sacred repertoire than we have at the present time.

There is little to be gained by attempting to compare the relative impacts of Monteverdi's psalms and Magnificats, for it is apparent from the collections of Burlini, Freddi, and Tarditi that these composers did not distinguish stylistically between the two liturgical genres as Monteverdi did. The greater consistency of style among their psalms and Magnificats confirms that the character of Monteverdi's unique canticles was not replicated by later composers. These three composers utilize the full ensemble much more often in their Magnificats than Monteverdi did, and their solo writing is more restrained, avoiding his extravagant ornamentation. Although all three employ obbligato instruments, the instruments discharge a more modest function, adding their colour to the total sonority, but assuming very little individuality or idiomatic purpose. The Magnificats of Burlini and Freddi emulate Monteverdi's in their grand and ostentatious manner, based on clearly articulated contrasts, but they do not

---

[176] See Dixon, 'Progressive Tendencies in the Roman Motet', 117–18.
[177] *Die Psalmkompositionen in Rom um 1600*, 291–6, 305–9.

Ex. 4.24. Paolo Tarditi, Magnificat from *Psalmi, Magnif.*, 1620

follow him in his concentration on intimate sonorities and relegation of the chorus to a merely framing role. Tarditi, whether influenced by northern composers or not, follows a path similar to Burlini and Freddi.

Despite the authority exerted by Monteverdi's highly unusual vesper music in the decade after 1610, it must be stressed that the publications revealing this influence are an exceptional few in a large repertoire which continued and developed oblivious to the example of Italy's foremost composer. This conclusion is not unexpected, given the widespread devotion to vesper music and the practical use of vesper collections in surroundings much more humble than the court and ducal church of the Gonzagas or the church of Venice's patron saint. The fact is that few ecclesiastical institutions commanded the vocal and instrumental resources required for such opulent music. In Rome, elaborate music was reserved for special festival days and was principally in the polychoral idiom, often with accompanying instruments, an idiom only modestly represented in Monteverdi's 1610 print. But as the taste for elaborate *concertato* settings grew over the years, so did the ability of many performers and churches to cope with the new styles. The lengthy, varied compositions of Monteverdi, Rubiconi, Flaccomio, Burlini, Patta, Freddi, Micheli, Tarditi, and Landi gradually inspired greater quantities of comparable pieces, and by 1640 extensive vesper psalms and Magnificats employing instruments and soloists permeated the repertoire. After the middle of the century Bologna in particular became a centre for this kind of music under Maurizio Cazzati, the prolific *maestro di cappella* of San Petronio,[178] and the elaborate style travelled as far as Palermo with the publications of the *maestro di cappella* of the Duomo, Bonaventura Rubino.[179]

But while the *concertato* style unquestionably informed a large part of the vesper repertoire and greatly influenced mass composition in the seventeenth century, it did not drive out altogether the older, more conservative styles, which continued unabated alongside the modern. Numerous collections of psalms for five voices or for double choir *per tutte le solennità* testify to the continuation of traditions and techniques of psalmody formulated in the sixteenth century and still practised widely, even if supplemented by the organ continuo. Old-style polyphonic masses continued to be composed as well. The stylistic dichotomy between the old and the new witnessed at the beginning of the *Seicento* by so many theorists and composers, including Monteverdi himself, was still in evidence during the second half of the century.

Nevertheless, the importance of Monteverdi's Vespers in the development of the large-scale sacred *concertato* is apparent. The influence of his music, which at first proceeded slowly, gradually accumulated momentum, especially in northern Italy, as more and more composers and churches in the 1620s and beyond were attracted to the elaborate style. And Monteverdi, of course, made further contributions to the tide with later vesper psalms of his own. But as time went

---

[178] See James Foster Armstrong, 'The Vesper Psalms and Magnificats of Maurizio Cazzati' (Ph.D. dissertation, Harvard University, 1969), and Anne Schnoebelen, 'Cazzati vs. Bologna: 1657–1671', *Musical Quarterly*, 57 (1971), 26–39. An enormous quantity of music for vespers poured from Cazzati's pen. The survival of these collections in many libraries and archives suggests that their use was widespread in the 17th century.

[179] RISM R3040, R3041, and R3042.

on, his influence undoubtedly became less direct, with many composers responding to the stimulus of by-then widespread trends rather than directly to Monteverdi himself. Moreover, the Roman polychoral and *concertato* traditions had their own momentum and influence, often resulting in elaborate music stylistically similar to some of Monteverdi's psalm settings, but probably developing independently of significant influence from Monteverdi himself. This may well have been the case with regard to Micheli in 1616 and Tarditi in 1620.[180] By the 1620s, opulent, *concertato* music, employing multiple styles and requiring instrumentalists and virtuoso singers, represented a general aesthetic outlook shared by many composers writing in all sacred genres. In 1610, Monteverdi's approach to the composition and notation (as opposed to improvised performance) of music for vespers had been quite singular, but the combination of his own influence, of trends already developing, of improvised performance practices, and of the ostentatious Roman polychoral and *concertato* styles led to the broadbased emergence of a new sacred style, quite distinct in the minds of composers and the public alike from the ongoing *stile antico*.

---

[180] Klaus Fischer's discussion of the composers Micheli Romano and Stefano Landi already suggests the difficulty of attributing direct influence to Monteverdi despite many parallels in these composers' music. See Fischer, *Die Psalmkompositionen in Rom um 1600*, 283–309. Jerome Roche also discusses Monteverdi's influence (not just in the Vespers of 1610) on other composers in *North Italian Church Music*, 64, 70–1, 79, 80, 82, 104, 108, 115, 138.

II. THE MUSIC

5

A Preliminary Note on Analytical Method and Terminology

MONTEVERDI'S music has long been considered to span the watershed between the late Renaissance and early Baroque, between the decline of polyphony and the medieval modal system and the beginning of the functional harmonic system and modern tonality that only became fully established in the late seventeenth century. In this sense he has been viewed as a 'transitional' composer, helping to define the criteria of the transition and to move it toward further stages of development. Yet Monteverdi's role in this historical process should not be overestimated. His use of cadentially directed melody and harmony, the scales and ostinatos in his bass-lines, his circle-of-fifths bass movement, his homophonic textures, his melodic and harmonic chromaticism, his variation techniques, and his tonal organization in large structures were shared in some measure or another by the vast majority of composers of his era. Moreover, many of these stylistic features trace their origins well back into the sixteenth century, in some cases as far as the fifteenth century. Cadentially directed melody and harmony, for example, characterize Italian and Spanish dance music and music based on ostinatos like the *passamezzo antico* and *passamezzo moderno* from early in the sixteenth century.[1] Monteverdi's cadences are almost exclusively the same complete, incomplete, 'improper', and evaded cadences described by Zarlino, though Monteverdi's conception of cadences was probably more harmonically oriented than the great theorist's.[2] Homophonic textures were common in secular music of the Renaissance and became

[1] See Edward E. Lowinsky, *Tonality and Atonality in Sixteenth-Century Music* (Berkeley: University of California Press, 1962).
[2] See the Preface above for an explanation of how I use the terms cadence and *clausula* in this book. Zarlino devotes chs. 54 and 55 of the *Terza Parte* of *Le istitutioni harmoniche* (Venice, 1558; fac. New York: Broude Brothers, 1965) to cadences, giving numerous examples. In addition, in the *Quarta Parte*, chs. 18–29, Zarlino discusses cadences in each of his twelve modes. Pt. III trans. Guy Marco and Claude Palisca as *Gioseffo Zarlino, The Art of Counterpoint, Part Three of 'Le istitutioni harmoniche,' 1558* (New Haven: Yale University Press, 1968), 141–53; pt. IV trans. in Vered Cohen, *On the Modes: Part Four of 'Le istitutioni harmoniche', 1558, Gioseffo Zarlino* (New Haven: Yale University Press, 1983), 54–89. See also Siegfried Hermelink, 'Über Zarlinos Kadenzbegriff', *Scritti in onore di Luigi Ronga* (Milan: Riccardo Ricciardi, 1973), 253–73. On the development of the V–I cadence in four-voice sacred music of the 15th century, see Don M. Randel, 'Emerging Triadic Tonality in the Fifteenth Century', *Musical Quarterly*, 57 (1971), 73–86.

increasingly prominent in large-scale sacred works in the last quarter of the *Cinquecento*. Melodic variation was likewise a frequently-used technique in the Josquin period, and formal variation structures were widespread in the second half of the sixteenth century, especially in keyboard music. Melodic and harmonic chromaticism had become increasingly popular after mid-century under the influence of Cipriano di Rore and Orlando di Lasso, and repetitive bass patterns were already known in secular music in the form of the Romanesca, the Ruggiero, and the Folia.

What characterizes the more modern sacred music of the early *Seicento* and Monteverdi's sacred music in particular is not the novelty of its stylistic elements, but rather the infusion into sacred music of features originating in secular music, the development of new combinations and interrelationships among these many elements, and the shift of weight away from the polyphonic style towards a greater emphasis on homophony. Thus cadential direction in melody and harmony becomes more pronounced, and cadences often divide the music into shorter, discrete segments rather than being overlapped by the polyphonic texture. Descending melodic pentachords, from the fifth degree to the *finalis*, become a principal foreground and background linear motion. Melodic and harmonic sequences also take on growing prominence. Chromaticism, rather than appearing exotic and radical, often contributes to the tonal direction of both melody and harmony and becomes an indispensible expressive element in the interpretation of text. The balance between counterpoint and the chords formed from independent voices shifts towards the latter, so that imitation and counterpoint often seem to arise out of chord structures rather than vice versa.

The mix of modal harmony and functional cadential harmony gives the music of this period its peculiar harmonic flavour. Also contributing to the harmonic colour are frequent shifts between major and minor forms of the same triad, shifts between major and minor tonal focuses a third apart, and repetition of entire phrases a fourth or fifth above or below. Tonal shifts tend to appear as discrete blocks in the musical structure, often without establishing hierarchical tonal relationships. In the treatment of text, syllabic declamation becomes the norm; melismas become decorative items appearing only at carefully chosen moments. Composers tend towards the use of ever smaller note values in ornamentation, and jerky dotted rhythms often replace smooth, even quavers and semiquavers. On a structural level, the *concertato* principle prevails, subdividing a composition into discrete segments, each with its own combination of voices and/or instruments, its own rhythmic physiognomy, and its own stylistic character. Monody becomes a principal texture and is mixed with imitative polyphony, with homophony, with *cori spezzati*, and with duet and trio textures. The texture and structure of compositions become variegated and fragmented, allowing for the use of repetitious elements (such as ritornellos) to build more expansive compositions, but also creating problems of cohesion and coherence in large pieces, such as psalms, Magnificats, and mass movements.

The long and complex transition from modally based music to functional harmonic progressions in major and minor tonalities was the achievement of an entire musical culture arching over more than a century. Indeed, it may be that in terms of the transition from a modally based system to functional harmony and tonality Monteverdi had less impact and influence on his contemporaries than in other aspects of musical style.[3] *L'Orfeo*, for example, makes more use of modal harmonies and modal melodic degrees than Jacopo Peri's *Euridice*, which is more oriented towards cadential harmony and frequent complete cadences. It is problematic, therefore, to see Monteverdi as a 'transitional' composer, since the transitional process exceeded his life-span by many decades and was not complete until perhaps sixty years after his death.

Nor should we consider Monteverdi as 'transitional' in the sense of a composer unable to foresee the evolutionary implications of the procedures he uses and therefore unable to apply them as effectively and purposefully as later generations. The esteem in which Monteverdi's music was held by his contemporaries and its lasting power as evidenced by his standing and remarkable popularity among modern musicians and listeners demonstrate that he was fully in command of the medium in which he worked, shaping and adapting it with precision for his expressive purposes. The 'transitional' character of that medium in the retrospective terms of history was not a problem for Monteverdi himself—rather it is a problem for us in understanding, first of all, the characteristics and the nature of his mastery of his own peculiar medium and, secondly, the role of that medium in the long and complex transition to functional harmony and tonality.

The difficulty Monteverdi's music poses for us, hovering as it does between modal and tonal composition, partaking of features of both, is that it does not wholly fit into any of the systems for which scholars have developed various analytical techniques and terminologies. To speak of Monteverdi's music in modal terms is at times valid, at times difficult, and sometimes anachronistic. To describe his music in functional harmonic and tonal terms is also at times appropriate but is often anachronistic. Monteverdi's harmonic language and his sense of tonal direction belie a dichotomy between modal melody and harmony on the one hand and functional harmony and tonality on the other. His melodic and harmonic thinking is often derived from the modal system, but his frequent cadences introduce functional progressions quite regularly into the mix. Moreover, cadential progressions are often found in the middle of phrases. Yet

---

[3] See Ch. 4 sect. VIII for a discussion of Monteverdi's influence in the decade following the publication of the 1610 Vespers.

these cadential progressions are so intermingled with modally based harmony that extended chains of functional progressions rarely emerge. In the cantus firmus compositions of the Vespers, modal plainchants may be accompanied by static harmony or modally based harmony, but also by functional cadential harmony articulating the cadential organization of the plainchants themselves. The cadential progressions, transpositions by a fourth, repetitive basses, and bass motion in circles of fourths and fifths, all hallmarks of later tonal music, do not yet generate tonal hierarchies. While each of the cantus firmus compositions displays a central tonality, other tonalities appear as alternatives to that central focus, not as tension-inducing digressions which can only be resolved by a return to the principal tonality. However, in the few-voiced motets cadential progressions often take clear precedence over modally based harmony and a greater sense of tonal hierarchy emerges, although the degree may depend on each listener's perception.

This problem of understanding Monteverdi's harmonic language and his relationship to the traditional modal system on the one hand and the functional harmonic and tonal system of the next century on the other has challenged Monteverdi scholars ever since serious research on his music began. In the past few decades four principal studies have contributed to a more systematic analytical methodology applicable to his music, though in quite diverse ways: (1) Carl Dahlhaus, *Studies on the Origin of Harmonic Tonality*, originally published in German in 1968,[4] (2) Bernhard Meier, *The Modes of Classical Vocal Polyphony*, originally published in German in 1974,[5] (3) Susan McClary's 1976 dissertation, 'The Transition from Modal to Tonal Organization in the Works of Monteverdi',[6] and (4) Eric T. Chafe, *Monteverdi's Tonal Language*, published in 1992.[7] It will not be the purpose of this chapter to discuss each of these studies

---

[4] Trans. Robert O. Gjerdingen (Princeton: Princeton University Press, 1990. Original title *Untersuchungen über die Entstehung der harmonischen Tonalität* (Kassel: Bärenreiter, 1968). See also Dahlhaus, 'Harmony', in *The New Grove Dictionary of Music and Musicians*, ed. Stanley Sadie (London: Macmillan Publishers Ltd.), viii. 175–88.

[5] Trans. Ellen S. Beebe (New York: Broude Brothers Ltd., 1988). Original title *Die Tonarten der klassischen Vokalpolyphonie* (Utrecht: Oosthoek, Scheltema & Holkema, 1974). Meier has followed this book with another, *Alte Tonarten dargestellt an der Instrumentalmusik des 16. und 17. Jahrhunderts* (Kassel: Bärenreiter, 1992), in which the same modal structures are examined in instrumental music.

[6] (Ph.D. dissertation, Harvard University).

[7] (New York: Schirmer Books, 1992). Aside from these major studies, a number of articles have appeared in recent years analysing individual works of Monteverdi, but without attempting to develop a system of analysis applicable to his entire *œuvre*. See Geoffrey Chew, 'The Perfections of Modern Music: Consecutive Fifths and Tonal Coherence in Monteverdi', *Music Analysis*, 8 (1989), 247–73; id., 'The Platonic Agenda of Monteverdi's *Seconda pratica*: A Case Study from the Eighth Book of Madrigals', *Music Analysis*, 12 (1993), 147–68; Tim Carter, ' "An Air New and Grateful to the Ear": The Concept of *Aria* in Late Renaissance and Early Baroque Italy', *Music Analysis*, 12 (1993), 127–45; Jeffrey Kurtzman, 'A Taxonomic and Affective Analysis of Monteverdi's "Hor che'l ciel e la terra" ', *Music Analysis*, 12 (1993), 169–95; id., 'What Makes Claudio "Divine"? Criteria for Analysis of Monteverdi's Large-scale *Concertato* Style', *Seicento inesplorato, Atti del III convegno internazionale sulla musica in area lombardo-padana del secolo XVII* (A.M.I.S. Como, 1993), 259–302.

in depth, nor even to provide a summary account, but rather to explain briefly the principal points that will contribute to my commentary on the music of Monteverdi's *Vespro* in the five subsequent chapters.

In his effort to understand and define the transition from the modal system to a functional harmonic system, Dahlhaus considered a number of criteria as basic for functional harmony and tonality: that a combination of simultaneous sounds be heard as a chord, that is, as a 'directly perceived unity';[8] that chord inversion be recognized as a repositioning of the root of the chord rather than as placing a sixth above the bass;[9] that complementary intervals (adding up to an octave) be considered 'harmonically identical'; that a major or minor chord comprise a root, third, and fifth, with the root position 'taken as the norm'; that the placement of the chord's third or fifth in the bass be considered an inversion of the root position; that in a major or minor chord the characteristic interval be the major or minor third or sixth; that 'the six-four sonority be considered a consonance if it is understood as an inversion'; that root progression, 'the relationship between chordal roots', be a governing principle for combining sonorities; and that in a given key a hierarchy of primary and secondary chords be formed.[10]

In terms of chord combinations, the subdominant must be understood as a fifth relation to the tonic, its second relation to the dominant must demand resolution to the tonic, and it must be interchangeable with the chord on the second degree.[11] Cadential progressions by themselves, however, do not necessarily generate a sense of functional tonality. Complete cadences in the form of I–IV–V–I, I–IV–I–V–I, and I–ii–V–I are common in music of the sixteenth and seventeenth centuries, but are not based on a broader underlying system of chords: 'The "complete" cadence existed as a compositional topos without being conceived as the founding principle of a chordal system.'[12] The same is true of circle-of-fifths and circle-of-fourths progressions, which typically do not have a fixed beginning or ending point and therefore do not define a functional tonal system.[13]

---

[8] *Studies on the Origin*, 67. Bonnie J. Blackburn traces Pietro Aaron's conception of chord and other 15th- and 16th-century theorists' notions of 'harmony' in 'On Compositional Process in the Fifteenth Century', *Journal of the American Musicological Society*, 40 (1987), 210–84. In analysing Tinctoris's discussion of the making of a *res facta* (a written composition in three or more parts), Blackburn concludes that 'this compositional process is more properly called "harmonic composition," not only because it lays emphasis on vertical sonorities, but mainly because it coincides with contemporary descrptions of harmony as a process of dissonance resolving into consonance' (p. 266). She finds in Renaissance theorists a greater sense of harmony in terms of the movement of vertical combinations than Dahlhaus does.

[9] Dahlhaus, *Studies on the Origin*, 99–100.

[10] Ibid. 112. See also p. 92.

[11] Ibid. 108.

[12] Ibid. 101–2, 111.

[13] Ibid. 103–4.

Dahlhuas warns that 'the stereotyped bass formulas of the early 17th century ought not to be misunderstood as "representatives" of chord progressions', since the bass is still autonomous in relation to the chords that appear above it: 'On the one hand, it can hardly be denied that the bass formulas of the early 17th century prefigure the typical chord progressions of tonal harmony. But on the other hand, upon closer inspection it is the differences from tonal harmony that come to the fore.'[14] Dahlhaus finds four principal differences between music of this period and music of the early eighteenth century: (1) the bass defines a series of tones, not a chord progression; (2) 'the $\frac{5}{3}$ and $\frac{6}{3}$ sonorities are often interchangeable'; (3) 'the "dynamic" factor of tonal harmony, the reciprocal relationship between the whole and its parts, was still foreign to the bass formulas of the early 17th century'; and (4) 'bass formulas lack the "tendency" toward a tonal "center of gravity"'.[15]

Even in monody Dahlhaus found the criteria for functional harmony and tonality incomplete:

For in monody, the conditions that must be present to make a harmonic analysis seem an adequate description of compositional technique—that the bass represents triads or seventh chords, and that the voice part is based on chords and can thus be divided into chord tones and 'nonharmonic tones'—are partially, but not entirely, fulfilled. The seventh still has not merged with the triad to form a seventh chord. And the remaining dissonances cannot always be interpreted as tones appended to chords, but must often be viewed as parts of intervallic progressions. The categories 'chord' and 'non-harmonic tone' are not inappropriate to describe the compositional technique of the early 17th century. But then neither are they fully adequate.[16]

A principal modern feature of monody lies in its dissonance treatment (the very feature that incensed Artusi most about Monteverdi's five-voice madrigals published subsequently in his Fourth and Fifth Books). In contrast to the norms of sixteenth-century polyphony, 'in the modern counterpoint of the 17th century, the correlation breaks down between, on the one hand, a dissonant tone and its reference tone, and on the other, strong and weak beats'.[17] Passing-notes often appear on the strong beat or are unprepared by a preceding consonance. Similarly, suspensions may resolve downwards by leap or upwards by step.[18] Successive dissonances may also occur. Most of these irregular dissonance treatments, however, result not from a chordal conception of the music, but rather from a new view of counterpoint in which the texture has been drastically reduced. Missing voices, which may be realized over the basso continuo, often serve to explain the dissonance in more traditional terms.[19] Nevertheless, many

---

[14] Dahlhaus, *Studies on the Origin*, 139–40.

[15] Ibid. 140–1.

[16] Ibid. 122. I have omitted Dahlhaus's footnote and an extraneous repetition of the word 'are' in the last sentence.

[17] Ibid. 125.

[18] Ibid. 126–7.   [19] Ibid. 126–32.

of these irregular dissonances eventually lead to a chordal conception of the vertical sonority: 'A rigid contrasting of intervallic and chordal composition would be a gross simplification of musical reality. In modern counterpoint, the category of interval progression was not entirely abandoned, but only demoted to the status of a secondary factor.'[20]

In his effort to understand and define the transition from sixteenth-century modal polyphony to a functional harmonic and tonal system, Dahlhaus studied a number of Monteverdi madrigals. He came to the conclusion that Monteverdi did not use a functional harmonic and tonal system according to his criteria.

In Dahlhaus's analysis of Monteverdi, the subdominant and dominant are often reversed in their relationship; similarly, series of stepwise chord progressions and circle-of-fifths or circle-of-fourths progressions are not directed towards specific goals. Moreover, Monteverdi does not often display a conception of the $\frac{6}{3}$ chord as an inversion of a root-position triad; indeed, $\frac{6}{3}$ and root-position chords over the same bass note are often interchangeable and the difference is of no intrinsic significance.[21] While Monteverdi uses complete authentic cadential chord progressions, these are functional only at the cadences themselves, not in the context of a system that encompasses all harmonic progressions. The same is true of other brief passages which may be understood in functional harmonic terms, but do not constitute a goal-directed harmonic system.

Dahlhaus's conclusions regarding Monteverdi's madrigals are also applicable to the 1610 Vespers, though in differing degrees, depending on whether the composition is based on a cantus firmus or is one of the few-voiced motets. In the cantus firmus compositions Monteverdi frequently employs functional cadential progressions, but does not derive them from an underlying functional harmonic system. Outside of cadences, the harmony normally mixes modal harmony with brief V–I, IV–V–I, or VI–V–I progressions. Tonal relationships between different sections of the same piece appear as separate, alternative tonal regions, not as a set of hierarchical tonal areas generating tension toward a specific goal. In the bass, scale patterns and circles of fifths or fourths do not lead towards a predetermined stopping-point apparent to the listener. Other features of Monteverdi's style that reveal their modal origins include the subdivision of the principal octave into pentachord and tetrachord (the reverse in plagal modes); the use of the natural seventh degree in the Dorian and Mixolydian modes (as well as their plagal counterparts); movement back and forth between *fa* and *mi* in the Dorian, Mixolydian, and Aeolian modes (including their plagal counterparts), resulting in shifts between D minor and D major, between G

---

[20] Ibid. 132.   [21] Ibid. 140.

major and G minor, or between A minor and A major; and the facile shift in harmonic focus between C major and A minor, between F major and D minor, and
between G minor and B flat major without the mediation of a strong cadence
(i.e. without modulation in the modern sense).

In the few-voiced motets, the thinner textures, descending-fifth melodic
patterns, freer use of dissonance, and heavy reliance on cadential bass movement
give a stronger impression of tonal direction within any given phrase or section,
though aspects of modal scales, such as the pentachord–tetrachord division and
natural seventh degrees are still evident. Secondary tonal areas in the motets
seem dependent on the principal area, and movement away from the principal
tonality does, at least for this listener, generate a sense of tension and expecta-
tion for return. Dahlhaus describes monody as coming closer to a functional
harmonic and tonal system, and this characterizes Monteverdi's few-voiced
motets as well. Details of all of these aspects of Monteverdi's music in the
Vespers will be discussed in the subsequent chapters.

Bernhard Meier does not concern himself with Monteverdi at all in his
monumental book on the modes of Renaissance polyphony. Nevertheless, he
lays a solid foundation and set of criteria for modal analysis of polyphonic compositions of the Renaissance and early Baroque on the basis of Renaissance theory and the analysis of a wide variety of compositions of the period. While
Meier's description of the modes, their structure, their cadences, and their ethos
are impeccable in terms of Renaissance theory, his own modal analyses have frequently been criticized as 'forced'. Many modern scholars hold that composers
of this period adhered to the definitions of mode and the criteria for modal
composition described by theorists only some of the time, and that in many
instances these criteria were modified, exceeded, or not followed at all. Where
Meier seems to believe that a strict interpretation of the modes lies behind all
Renaissance polyphonic composition, others see these criteria as applicable to
a limited repertoire, with different criteria governing the organization of pitch
in some polyphonic compositions and in other repertoires.[22]

It is only in a recent article discussing the motets in the 1610 Vespers that
Meier has addressed the question of modal organization in Monteverdi's
music.[23] His analysis of mode in these motets is not wholly satisfactory, for

---

[22] Lowinsky's *Tonality and Atonality* was the first major study to emphasize other organizational systems. Harry Powers's several studies of mode, listed in the Bibliography, also recognize that many compositions do not strictly adhere to the modal system. Cristle Collins Judd's essay on Josquin's motets,
'Modal Types and *Ut, Re, Mi* Tonalities: Tonal Coherence in Sacred Vocal Polyphony from about 1500',
Journal of the American Musicological Society, 45 (1992), 428–67, looks at modal practice in polyphony from
a different angle from Meier. Meier's analytical method is discussed in Frans Wiering, 'The Language of
the Modes: Studies in the History of Polyphonic Modality' (Ph.D. dissertation, University of
Amsterdam, 1995), ch. 2.
[23] 'Zur Tonart der Concertato-Motetten in Monteverdis *Marienvesper*', in Ludwig Finscher, ed.,
Claudio Monteverdi. Festschrift Reinhold Hammerstein zum 70. Geburtstag (Laaber: Laaber Verlag, 1986),
359–67.

Monteverdi's mixed modes and the modern aspects of his approach to harmony and tonal centres do not lend themselves comfortably to a strictly modal analysis. For our purposes, the value of Meier's approach is in its definition of basic criteria governing modal composition. Its difficulty is that it seems too much bound to a theoretical system of modes that at times does not accord well with Monteverdi's actual compositional practice. Analysis of Monteverdi's music by Meier's modal criteria therefore must be modified and tempered by other perspectives.

Susan McClary, in her dissertation, sought to incorporate both modal and tonal characteristics in analysing melody, harmony, rhythm, and structure in her overall objective of explaining the transition from modality to tonality in the period 1600–50 through the works of Monteverdi.[24] In contrast to Dahlhaus's emphasis on harmony and counterpoint, McClary viewed Monteverdi's madrigals from a perspective based on the Schenkerian concept of the 5–4–3–2–1 melodic progression, with each note in the sequence functioning differently in the movement towards 1 as *finalis*.[25] Each of these melodic pitches forms a structural point in the overall pentachordal descent, and these structural pitches may be separated by some distance, generating a 'background' melodic structure in contrast to the 'foreground' of the localized melodic motion. The pitches of the descending *diapente* and their structural functions in the melody are supported and interpreted by harmonic collections, but it is the melody that is functional in the sense of giving direction and goals to the entire texture.[26]

These structural pitches provide a means for analysing not only Monteverdi's tonal direction, but also his interruption of the background melodic descent by tonicization of pitches in the descent or by structural interpolations.[27] It is these interpolations, or 'subregions', that lead toward a more 'tonal' organization in Monteverdi's later works.[28] In direct opposition to Dahlhaus, McClary sees the transition to tonal organization as rather abrupt, taking place especially in operatic declamation, where the often widely spaced background structural pitches

---

[24] *The Transition*, 5–6.

[25] In the *diapente* descent, the fifth, third, and *finalis* are the more stable notes (structurally consonant), while the fourth and second degrees are unstable (structurally dissonant) and must eventually descend. The sixth degree serves as an upper auxiliary to the fifth and the leading-note circumscribes the *finalis* (ibid. 33–4). In the Hypodorian, Phrygian, Hypophrygian, Hypolydian, and Hypomixolydian modes the structurally critical fifth degree will be a different pitch from the traditional reciting note. See the discussions of *Nigra sum* and *Pulchra es* in Chs. 9–10 regarding the tension between the fifth degree and the reciting note.

[26] McClary, *The Transition*, 9.

[27] McClary sees the harmonic structure as expandable by means of the temporary tonicization through cadential harmony of any of the notes of the typical *diapente* descent. The stability of the mode depends on cadences on the *finalis*, the third degree, and the fifth degree as well as frequent emphasis on the stepwise *diapente* descent. Instability of mode results from cadences on other notes and octave divisions disrupting the basic pentachord–tetrachord combination (ibid. 30–1).

[28] In McClary's theory of subregions, any of the boundary notes of the pentachord and tetrachord of the mode may be temporarily emphasized as the goals of their own diatonic *diapente* descents (ibid. 56–61). Similarly, 'parenthetical expansion' may elaborate one or more significant pitches of the mode, often pitches other than the pentachord and tetrachord boundaries (ibid. 108–10).

may lead to temporary tonicization and full-scale key areas.[29] In tonally organized music the structural functions that had resided in the melody of modal
music are projected on the harmony; conversely, the structural harmonies now
project the structural melodic pitches.[30]

McClary's analytical method furnishes a valuable means for discussing
Monteverdi's approach to melody in the four motets not based on a cantus
firmus. In the first three of these pieces Monteverdi often relies on the descent
from the fifth to the first scale-degree to give his melody its sense of motion and
tonal direction. The structural tones in this descent play a significant role in the
organization of the melody for large sections or in the motet as a whole, developing a coherent, large-scale melodic structure supported and reinforced by the
underlying harmony and cadences. An analysis of these pieces helps explain
how the *diapente* descent coupled with cadential harmony generates a long-
term sense of direction toward a single tonal centre. The fourth motet, *Audi
coelum*, is based on the authentic octave of the first mode, with the initial note
of its melodic descents as *d'*, the eighth degree of the mode. These descents
therefore lead principally to the reciting note of the mode, *a*, constituting a
descending fourth rather than a fifth. Nevertheless, each of the notes in this
descent are treated as background structural tones in the first, solo part of this
piece.

On the other hand, in the works based closely on a cantus firmus, it is the
psalm and Magnificat tones, with their repetitive reciting notes, and the plainchant hymn tune that serve to define the principal melody. Thus the harmonization of the plainchant and the style, texture, and structure in which the
chant is embedded are the primary focal points for analysis. In these pieces,
McClary's method is less useful.

Eric Chafe's recent book takes its point of departure from Dahlhaus as well as
Renaissance modal theory in attempting to integrate modal theory and modern
concepts of major and minor, key signatures, transposition, and circle-of-fifths
harmonic successions. His conception of Monteverdi's tonal language recognizes and explains Monteverdi's modal thinking as well as those modern features
of the composer's style that parallel many aspects of music of a later period.[31] As

---

[29] In McClary's view, operatic recitative, with many melodic pitches for each structural pitch in the
diapente descent, slowed the rate of structural harmonic change supporting that descent. Consequently,
there was far more room between structural pitches and harmonies for flexibility in both melody and
harmony (ibid. 178–81). Additionally, elaboration of structural pitches by parenthetical circumscrip-
tion could include brief progressions to other key areas within the framework of the broader structural
descent. Progressions of this kind, which briefly establish independent key areas, are functional in the
modern tonal sense, relying mainly on subdominant, dominant, and tonic chords. In such parctheti-
cal elaborations based on these harmonies, the melody may be generated out of the harmony rather
than vice versa (ibid. 194–7).

[30] Ibid. 40–1, 181.

[31] Chafe's position on the relationship between modal theory and tonal theory is summed up in his
preface: 'One premise of this study is that the tonal language of the seventeenth century—and

a consequence, Chafe uses terminology derived from both modal theory and tonal theory, but not without first making clear what aspects implied by modern terminology *do not* apply to Monteverdi. On the 'transitional' character of Monteverdi's music Chafe affirms, 'the music often tended intrinsically toward the future, but was regulated conceptually by the past. The resultant conflict or dialectic of old and new is . . . intimately related to why we perceive the music of the early seventeenth century as transitional'.[32] Despite the interplay between modal and tonal theory, between Renaissance and Baroque aesthetics, Chafe sees Monteverdi's music as rooted in the Renaissance 'modal-hexachordal' system.[33] At the same time, the modern features of the music generate rational structures on the figural surface and hierarchical structures dependent on tonality at deeper levels.[34] The result is both an unpredictability and a perceptible logic in Monteverdi's music, based significantly on the meaning of the words as well as on verbal logic in general and on the particular instances of individual texts.[35] This aspect of Monteverdi's compositional method is summarized in the statement: 'one of Monteverdi's major achievements in the development of the new style was the merging of tonal structure with a kind of narrative logic that derives from the poetic text.'[36] In more general terms: 'Melody determines the sense of continuity in the work that relates seemingly disparate events to a larger framework. The sense of directedness, of goal, leads it to produce the extrinsic effect of a particularized emotional sphere.'[37]

Chafe's discussion is based on the Renaissance and early Baroque distinction between *cantus durus* and *cantus mollis*, that is, compositions without a key signature (therefore using *B-quadro* (B♮) or *durus*) and compositions with a one-flat signature (therefore using *B-rotondo* (B♭) or *mollis*).[38] Within each of these two systems various modes may appear; two finals, G and D, are found in both systems. In the early seventeenth century, Banchieri identified these modes as C,

Monteverdi's perhaps more than any other—combines its past and its future in changing yet balanced proportions, rather than proceeding in a direct line from the one to the other. That past is the modal and hexachordal theory of the sixteenth century, which survived well into the seventeenth century in a form that for convenience I call the "modal-hexachordal" system; the future is, of course, the tonal theory that surrounds the appearance of the circle of major and minor keys in the early eighteenth century. There is no unassailable reason to prefer the past, to give it logical as well as chronological priority. We can choose instead to operate within a larger framework in which past and future exist simultaneously, as they do in our minds' (*Monteverdi's Tonal Language*, pp. xiii–xiv).

[32] Ibid., p. xiv.

[33] Ibid., p. xv.

[34] Ibid. 2–6. Note in the chapters below the distinction I draw between hierarchical relationships in the motets and non-hierarchical 'alternative' tonal regions in the psalms, Magnificats, and hymn.

[35] Ibid. 6.

[36] Ibid. 17.

[37] Ibid. 18. Since Chafe's study is based solely on Monteverdi's secular music, the conservative and restrictive influence of the cantus firmus on melody, harmony, and tonal goals does not come into consideration.

[38] Ibid. 22–4.

G, D, A, and E in the *durus* system and F, G, and D in the *mollis* system.[39] In G and D, shifts can occur back and forth between the *durus* and the *mollis* versions of the scale within a single composition.

Banchieri numbers the modes according to finals a fourth apart (D, G, A, E, C, F, D, G),[40] not by the traditional Greek names nor by the numbering systems of Glareanus or Zarlino, which distinguish between authentic and plagal octave species with the same *finalis*. Banchieri's system is indifferent to octave species, and when Monteverdi employs virtuoso voices in his motets expanding the range well beyond an octave, the distinction between the plagal and authentic versions of a mode tends to disappear as well. The tonality of the composition encompasses both ('mixed modes'), sometimes emphasizing the plagal range, sometimes the authentic range extending a fourth higher.[41] In such cases it makes sense simply to speak, for example, of G *cantus durus* or *mollis* with the ranges *d–g′* or *d′–g″*. References to the Mixoloydian (seventh mode) and Hypomixolydian (eighth mode) may be more appropriately reserved for specific segments of the composition where the range emphasizes one or the other octave species, rather than applying these identifiers to the composition as a whole.

Within the *cantus durus* and the *cantus mollis* systems, the traditional hexachord system may also be discerned. The *cantus durus* contains the natural, soft, and hard hexachords (the second through the use of B♭ as an accidental); the *cantus mollis* contains the natural, soft, and transposed soft hexachords (the latter through the use of E♭ as an accidental).[42] In *cantus durus* the natural hexachord is the central one, in *cantus mollis* it is the soft hexachord.[43] The available cadence harmonies within a given mode are the six chords rooted in the notes of the central hexachord.[44] Harmony in general may also be said to derive from one or another hexachord, since root-position triads based on the notes of the hexachord identify that hexachord, even if other pitches of a chord may fall outside it. Thus, for example, all three hexachords may support an A major triad as dominant of D, since the root A is a pitch contained in all three hexachords, as is the note of resolution, D. Similarly, all three hexachords are capable of supporting

[39] Ibid. 39. Chafe notes that Athanasius Kircher in *Musurgia universalis* also identifies C as overlapping both systems, though Monteverdi rarely uses the *cantus mollis* form of C. See *Monteverdi's Tonal Language*, 48–9.

[40] *L'organo suonarino* (Venice: Amadino, 1605; fac. edn. Amsterdam: Frits Knuf, 1969), 39–41; Eng. trans. in Donald E. Marcase, 'Adriano Banchieri, "L'organo suonarino": Translation, Transcription and Commentary' (Ph.D. dissertation, Indiana University, 1970), 139–42. It should be noted that Banchieri is referring to psalm and Magnificat tones rather than modes *in abstracto*.

[41] See the discussion of the four motets *Nigra sum*, *Pulchra es*, *Duo Seraphim*, and *Audi coelum* in Chs. 9 and 10.

[42] Chafe, *Monteverdi's Tonal Language*, 27.

[43] Ibid. 29.

[44] Ibid. 30.

a G minor triad, but only the soft hexachord can serve as the source of a B♭ major triad.

Transposition may be achieved by shifting from one hexachord to the adjacent one and is related to the modern concept of modulation (since there is change of pitch but not of intervallic structure). Circle-of-fifths and circle-of-fourths harmonic sequences may be viewed as hexachordal transpositions.[45] According to Renaissance theory, shifts should only take place between adjacent hexachords, that is, from soft to natural, from natural to hard, and vice versa, so that movement between the soft and hard hexachords would proceed through the natural hexachord as a pivot. A direct, unmediated shift between soft and hard hexachords is thus quite radical, and Monteverdi employs such shifts rarely in the Vespers and only in situations where there is a striking rationale in the text.[46] In contrast to the 'modulatory' transposition of the hexachord, transposition of the figural surface of the music without changing the scale may result in a temporary shift of mode within the hexachord (a device related to the modern concept of a tonal answer or sequential transposition within a single key).[47]

Chafe associates the *cantus durus* and the *cantus mollis* as well as the movement back and forth among the hexachords with various categories of affect generated by Monteverdi's madrigal and operatic texts. In other words, Monteverdi's modal and hexachordal usage is systematically applied to the expression of the text:

> In the earliest publications . . . the *cantus durus* . . . often bears pejorative associations bound up with ideas of hardness, sharpness, dissonance, and the like. In the fourth book the *durus* idea is connected specifically, though not exclusively, to compositions in the a-minor mode, which is treated as sharper than the other modes. In the fifth and sixth books Monteverdi makes conspicuous *mollis/durus* juxtapositions involving a shift from g to G. . . . In the *Scherzi musicali* of 1607 the predominant mode of G bears the association of light music that it does in much of *Orfeo* and in later pieces such as *Tirsi e Clori*. Yet eventually (from Book Seven on) it becomes linked to a sphere of different, positive qualities that undoubtedly derive from the greater sense of perfection of the major mode.[48]

Hexachordal transposition may also reflect textual ideas. In reference to a madrigal from the Fourth Book, *Cor mio, mentre vi miro*, Chafe observes: 'The

---

[45] Ibid. 29.

[46] Such hexachordal shifts, 'skipping' the intermediate hexachord, are much more common in Monteverdi's madrigals, supporting their often more chromatic harmony.

[47] Ibid. 31. Chafe gives a list of four different types of transposition: (1) exact transposition of all details both of scale and musical surface; (2) 'harmonic' transposition, involving, for example, the chords and bass-line but not the voice-leading and other surface details; (3) transposition of the surface details that is inexact with regard to accidentals, interval relationships, and harmonic content and therefore may not involve hexachordal shift; and (4) 'free' transposition, in which some but not all of the surface details and harmonic events are carried over to another pitch level.

[48] Ibid. 54–5.

intent of all these devices (the high bass, ascending patterns of voice pairing, ascending melodic sequences, and above all, ascending tonal patterns both within each of the two hexachords and from the one-flat to the natural) is unmistakable. Monteverdi conceived of the tonal motion from flat to sharp as an ascent, and he intended it to signify the idea of rebirth as motion from *mortale* to *vitale* . . .'[49] Thus, not only shifts of hexachord in either the flat direction or the sharp direction are used by Monteverdi to underscore changes in concept originating in the text, but shifts towards cadences on the more flat or more sharp degrees of a single hexachord can be used for the same purpose. These shifts within a hexachord are often accomplished by circle-of-fifths or circle-of-fourths bass motion. For example, a series of cadences around the ascending circle of fifths rooted entirely in the natural hexachord (V/F–F, V/C–C, V/G–G, V/D–D, V/A–A), employs harmonies that progressively require more sharps.

In the Vespers of 1610, movements from flat to sharp and increasing degrees of sharpness are also often (but not always) related to a sense of positive religious value, such as exaltation, the rising dawn as a metaphor for Mary, petitions for mercy leading to confidence in mercy, the descent from power followed by ascent to grace, or the passage of winter into spring as a metaphor for the new dispensation of Christ. Such examples will be discussed in further detail in the course of Chapters 6–10.

Even more importantly than text interpretation, Monteverdi's 'modal-hexachordal' system is applied to the coherent structuring of the music. How Chafe describes this system and the terminology he uses depends on the context. There are circumstances where modal terminology seems most appropriate and most accurate; there are also situations where Monteverdi utilizes dominant–tonic cadential formations so consistently that it is valid to speak of major and minor tonalities for such passages, and even of modulation in the modern sense. Chafe uses a mixture of modal and modern terminology throughout his study, an approach which offers flexibility in dealing differently with different contexts and the capability of conveying both the traditional and the modern aspects of Monteverdi's compositional technique.[50]

The difficulty for the analyst, of course, is to know when to use modal or tonal terminology, and that will depend on the analyst's judgement of the context. There are some passages which may be profitably viewed from both perspectives. In the ensuing discussion, my point of departure is principally modal, since that is Monteverdi's apparent conceptual basis in the Vespers, largely be-

[49] Ibid., 64.

[50] Chafe's is a sophisticated and complex theory whose implications and application will need to be tested and perhaps expanded by Monteverdi scholars for some time to come. Its most immediate virtue, aside from offering coherent explanations for important aspects of many specific compositions, is that it provides a systematic basis for examining the melodic, harmonic, and structural features of Monteverdi's music, whether secular or sacred.

cause of the plainchant cantus firmi. However, for the more tonally oriented motets and for occasional passages in the cantus firmus compositions, I will sometimes employ both terminologies, indicating the similarity or equivalence of meaning between one and the other. I also use the expression 'functional cadential harmony' to refer to the complete cadential progressions V–I, IV–V–I, VI–V–I, and ii–V–I, since these do, in my view, have a functional import, regardless of any derivation from the contrapuntal texture.

All of the theoretical approaches briefly reviewed above are concerned with melodic direction and the harmonic support of that direction. Indeed, issues of pitch relationships and melodic and harmonic direction have been the central concern of music theory ever since Rameau's *Traité de l'harmonie* of 1722. Yet many other aspects of musical composition were also of paramount interest to Monteverdi. The large-scale settings of psalm and Magnificat texts and the grand scope of the *Sonata sopra Sancta Maria* all required different structural considerations from the composer's relatively short motets and madrigals. Apart from hexachords and modes, textures, rhythms, sonorities, and metaphorical interpretations of the text were crucial elements in Monteverdi's compositional thought. My discussion of the music of the Vespers, therefore, not only will deal with pitch relationships, harmonic language, and tonal organization, but will also touch upon all of these other compositional features as they prove pertinent to an understanding of particular pieces or of more generalized compositional processes. Since the ten works based on a cantus firmus are all schematically organized in some way, Appendix C contains structural outlines of each of these pieces, together with their Latin texts and English translations. The four motet texts and their translations, on the other hand, accompany the discussions of each of these pieces in Chapters 9 and 10, since the semantics of the texts play a more prominent and decisive role in these works than in the cantus firmus compositions.

It should also prove useful for understanding the following discussion to distinguish between mode and psalm or Magnificat tone.[51] 'Mode' refers to the medieval and Renaissance theoretical system of eight octave species, grouped in pairs of four with finals of *d*, *e*, *f*, and *g*. Each octave is divided into a conjunct pentachord and tetrachord, with their relative positions defining the version of the pair: in the authentic version the pentachord is below, while in the plagal version the tetrachord is below. Each of these eight octave species, or modes, has a principal secondary note, known as the reciting note or tenor. In three of the authentic modes, normally numbered 1, 5, and 7, the reciting note is a fifth above the final. In mode 3, the reciting note is a sixth above the final of *e*. The

---

[51] Zarlino describes the differences between tone and mode in *Le istitutioni harmoniche*, 315–17; trans. in Cohen, *On the Modes*, ch. 15, 46–9. The distinction between antiphon mode and psalm or Magnificat tone is discussed in Ch. 2 above.

reciting notes of the plagal modes, 2, 4, 6, and 8, differ from those of their 'authentic' counterparts: mode 2, *f*; mode 4, *a*; mode 6, *a*; mode 8, *c'*. The authentic and plagal modes differ in range as well, since each plagal mode lies a fourth below its corresponding authentic mode.

In the mid-sixteenth century, the theorists Heinrich Glareanus and Gioseffo Zarlino expanded the modal system to twelve modes by defining 'authentic' and 'plagal' modes with finals on *a* and *c*, reflecting long-standing musical practice. In the late sixteenth century and throughout the seventeenth century, many theorists and other musicians were divided as to whether they supported an octonary or a dodecachordal system.

While 'modes' represent a theoretical system for classifying melodies, 'tones' comprise a set of actual melodies used for the recitation of psalms and canticles.[52] The Church recognized eight principal tones, corresponding to the eight modes in their species of pentachords and tetrachords as well as in the reciting note, but not necessarily concluding with the same final. Moreover, fewer than half the tones begin on the final (only tones 5, 6, 8, and solemn tone 7),[53] and none begin on the lowest note of the plagal tetrachord in tones 2, 4, 6, and 8. But the biggest difference between the modes and tones is that the latter have changeable cadential formulas, or *differentiae*. These cadential formulas are designed to allow the end of a psalm or canticle tone to merge smoothly with an antiphon in a specific mode.[54] Therefore, the *differentia* was chosen according to the Proper antiphon for a particular feast. Nevertheless, there was a single set of standard *differentiae* for the eight tones that were almost invariably used in polyphonic settings of psalms and Magnificats in the sixteenth and seventeenth centuries. These standard cadential formulas present the same finals as the eight modes except in tones 3, 5, and 7, where the finals are all typically *a*.

Psalm and canticle tones are divided into two parts, corresponding to the two halves of each psalm or canticle verse. While the second half concludes with the *differentia* as described above, the first half concludes with a mediant cadence on the reciting note, except in tones 6 and 7, where the mediant cadences are on *f* and *e* respectively.

In addition to the eight psalm tones, there exists a ninth *tonus peregrinus*, specifically for the psalm *In exitu Israel*, with two separate reciting notes, *a* and *g*, for the two halves of the verse. This ninth tone need not concern us in relation to Monteverdi's Vespers.

The distinction between mode and tone does not imply their separation in Monteverdi's music. The psalm and canticle tones are accompanied by modal

---

[52] The psalm and canticle tones can be found in *The Liber Usualis with Introduction and Rubrics in English* (New York: Desclée Company, 1963), 128–218.

[53] The solemn tones are more elaborate Magnificat tones for use on principal feasts of the first and second class. See ibid. 213–18.

[54] See the discussion of this issue in Ch. 2.

harmony and functional cadential harmony, the latter especially at mediant and final cadences of the chant, yielding a rich mixture of tones, modes, and functionally directed cadences. Moreover, in some of the psalms, the tones are embedded in structures that are to some degree independent of the chant and have a tonal organization not wholly determined by the chant.

In the Vespers, the presence or absence of a cantus firmus is a crucial factor not only in the organization of each composition, but also in its relative degree of modernity in melody and harmony. Moreover, it also significantly affects Monteverdi's approach to interpretation of his texts. For that reason, my analytical discussion will be subdivided into two principal segments: (1) compositions based on a cantus firmus, comprising all of the psalms, the response, the Magnificats, the hymn, and the *Sonata sopra Sancta Maria*, and (2) the four motets *Nigra sum*, *Pulchra es*, *Duo Seraphim*, and *Audi coelum*. The commentary on compositions based on a cantus firmus is organized around specific analytical issues which pertain to most or all of those pieces, using a variety of examples to illustrate the central points. In addition, the discussion of the Magnificats will focus on the parallels between verses in the two settings. The motets, on the other hand, will be treated more individually, befitting the unique style and organization of each piece. Those readers who may not necessarily wish to explore the many analytical issues raised in the Vespers, but may find a brief structural overview of a particular composition useful, are referred to Appendix C, which includes structural outlines of each of the ten pieces based on a cantus firmus.

6

Compositions Based on a Cantus Firmus: The Response and Psalms

⟨❦⟩

In the Bassus Generalis part-book, at the head of *Domine ad adjuvandum*, the rubric appears *Vespro della B.Vergine da concerto, composto sopra canti fermi* (Vespers of the Blessed Virgin in concerto, composed on cantus firmi). Of the fourteen compositions aside from the *Missa in illo tempore* in Monteverdi's 1610 print, ten are 'composed on cantus firmi'. These comprise the response, all five psalms, both Magnificats, the hymn *Ave maris stella*, and the *Sonata sopra Sancta Maria*, the latter based on the Litany of the Saints. Only the four few-voiced motets are without a cantus firmus.

The purpose of this and the ensuing two chapters is to examine, first of all, the highly imaginative and variegated ways in which Monteverdi treats the cantus firmus in all of the compositions named above. As a structural scaffolding, the cantus firmus and its text have an enormous influence over the way each composition unfolds. Yet the context in which the cantus firmus is embedded differs dramatically from one composition to the next, and often between separate sections of the same composition. While the cantus firmus constitutes a stable, unifying force, the continually changing surroundings in which it appears form free-flowing variations on the borrowed melody. These chapters will attempt to reveal the remarkable variety in Monteverdi's treatment of the cantus firmus, including subjecting the chant melody itself to transposition and rhythmic variation. A concise outline of the structural organization of each of the compositions based on a cantus firmus may be found in Appendix C.

Secondly, these chapters examine polyphonic cadential formations, whose placement is very often determined by the mediant and final cadences of the cantus firmus. Monteverdi's cadential formations are quite traditional, involving principles of voice-leading that date back at least as far as the early sixteenth century. From cadential formations, the discussion proceeds to harmonic language in general. 'Harmonic language' refers both to the bass-line and the counterpoint and chordal structures built upon the bass. The texture of the upper parts may range from equal-voiced imitative polyphony to solos, virtuoso duets, strictly homophonic chord successions, or even rhythmically complicated reiterations of a single chord. In textures for three or more upper voices, counterpoint and homophony often merge as an inseparable combination. In some instances chords arise out of the combination of contrapuntally independent lines. In other cases, the contrapuntal texture arises out of chords whose parts are rhythmically staggered to appear as separate entities. Descending scale patterns in the bass, frequently employed by Monteverdi, often give rise to upper voices that more or less reflect the bass with their own descending scale patterns.

Where basses contain frequent leaps, especially leaps of a fourth or fifth, the upper parts sometimes produce chord successions which appear to modern ears as tonally functional progressions (see Carl Dahlhaus's criteria for tonally functional progressions in Chapter 5). At other times the chord successions are without functional import except at cadences. Very often, Monteverdi moves freely between brief passages with non-functional chord successions and passages that resemble more modern functional chord progressions. Other aspects of Monteverdi's harmonic language include shifts between major and minor triads over the same bass, shifts of tonal focus by a third (even if only temporary and unaccompanied by a cadential progression), and the relative concentrations of major and minor chords in a given passage.

A further feature of Monteverdi's compositional method discussed in these chapters is his manipulation of texture and style within each cantus firmus composition. Texture and style are important aspects of the contextual variety of the cantus firmus and will be discussed as they bear on that topic, but some of the ways in which Monteverdi deals with textural and stylistic variety are independent of the cantus firmus and will be examined separately.

Finally, the literal and symbolic meanings of the texts of the psalms and Magnificats give rise on occasion to musical interpretation. Unlike the poetry that Monteverdi set in his madrigals and operas, these liturgical texts had not been designed specifically for affective musical treatment; nevertheless, Monteverdi as well as other composers of the early seventeenth century responded to those words and phrases that could be interpreted musically within the prevailing structural and stylistic framework of a psalm or Magnificat setting. In some verses, especially in the Magnificats, the significance of the text determines the stylistic character of the music, while in others, there seems to be little or no relationship between text and musical setting beyond rhythmic declamation and the structure of musical phrases, which follow the structure of the psalm or Magnificat verse.

THE CANTUS FIRMUS, ITS VARYING CONTEXTS, AND ITS ROLE IN THE STRUCTURE OF THE RESPONSE AND PSALMS

Monteverdi's use of the cantus firmus in the response, the psalms, the Magnificats, the hymn, and the *Sonata sopra Sancta Maria* is quite conservative in relation to the practices of many other composers of the late sixteenth and early seventeenth centuries (see Chapter 4). In each of these compositions, the appropriate chant is presented unparaphrased in its entirety, and in most it is repeated complete in one voice or another during much of the piece. Monteverdi usually imitates the tradition of chanted psalmody by limiting the intonation of the psalm tone to the first verse, beginning subsequent verses with the reciting note. Nevertheless, in *Laudate pueri*, *Laetatus sum*, and *Lauda Jerusalem*, there is at least one verse after the first where the intonation is used. In *Nisi Dominus*, the intonation appears at the beginning of every verse.

In all of the psalms as well as the Magnificats, the cantus firmus is transposed from its original pitch level, most often to the fourth above (also to the fifth below), thereby affording greater tonal variety to the psalm as a whole. Monteverdi does not engage, however, in the elaborate chant paraphrases found, for example, in the Palestrina Magnificats, nor does he quote fragments of the chant, such as intonations, inflections, or cadences. It is this faithful quotation of complete psalm and Magnificat tones that not only marks the most conservative element in these pieces, but also serves as a principal organizing force, often determining the structure and harmony of an entire composition.

For this reason, Monteverdi's treatment of the cantus firmus often consists of successive variations on a given melody. For each verse of the response, for every segment of the Magnificats, for most verses of the psalms, for all verses of the hymn, and for much of the *Sonata sopra Sancta Maria*, the cantus firmus appears as a repeated theme in constantly varied surroundings. The cantus firmus itself is subjected to both rhythmic variation and transposition to other pitch levels. Thus an analytical study of the compositions based on cantus firmi must of necessity concentrate first on Monteverdi's concept of variation on the plainchant.

The techniques of variation on the chant in the response and psalms are multiple and complex. In the psalms Monteverdi's challenge in dealing with the cantus firmus is complicated by two factors: rhythmic values applied to the chant that are equivalent to those of the other voices, and the static nature of the psalm tones themselves. The psalm tones, with their constant reiteration of a single pitch, impose severe harmonic restrictions on the composer, and the multiplicity of ways in which Monteverdi resolves this dilemma is remarkable.

In the psalms, the structure of the chant, divided into two half-verses with a mediant cadence and a final cadence, determines the organization of the polyphonic setting of each verse. The overall structure of a psalm similarly depends heavily on the verse structure of the entire psalm text; that is, each psalm is organized in such a way as to traverse the full psalm text and doxology through successive statements of the psalm tone.

In no composition in the Vespers is the cantus firmus subjected to a more elaborate contextual treatment than in the response, *Domine ad adjuvandum*. The chant itself is harmonized simply, with a repeated D major chord in *falsobordone*, such as had been commonly improvised in Italy at least since the fifteenth century. Such *falsibordoni* frequently appear notated in manuscripts and prints of vesper music from the sixteenth century.[1] In Monteverdi's response, the pitches of the six voices singing the *falsobordone* are notated without rhythm; the rhythmic enunciation of the text is indicated only in the Bassus Generalis part-book, where the text is underlaid to the rhythmicized bass-line.

Complicating this simple treatment of the cantus firmus is the superimposition of the instrumental toccata from *L'Orfeo* (also based on static harmony) upon the *falsobordone*, the insertion of triple-metre instrumental ritornellos between the verses of the text, and the abandonment of the chant at the conclusion for an expanded triple-metre *Alleluia* combining voices and instruments. It is only during the ritornellos and the final *Alleluia* that the unremitting D major chord is alleviated by some variety in the harmony.

The toccata from *L'Orfeo* is modified somewhat in its adaptation to its new surroundings through the addition of a second treble part for cornetto and violin and the repetition of its stepwise rising fifths and thirds. The added second part generates an imitative duet with the already existing first part and thereby brings the response into correspondence with the numerous sections throughout the Vespers in which two voices or instruments in the same register are paired in imitation. Duets of voices or instruments in a single register became a trademark of Monteverdi's style in both secular and sacred music from early in the seventeenth century to the end of his long career.

The instrumentation of the original toccata was for trumpets in addition to *tutti li stromenti*, and Monteverdi's performance rubric in *L'Orfeo* notes that the piece, which is written there in C, is to be performed a tone higher through the use of mutes with the trumpets, which raised their pitch by a full step.[2] The

---

[1] The history of *falsobordone* is described in Murray Bradshaw, *The Falsobordone, A Study in Renaissance and Baroque Music* (Musical Studies and Documents, 34; Stuttgart: American Institute of Musicology/Hänssler-Verlag, 1978). See my discussion of *falsibordoni* in vesper music in Ch. 2 above. In Monteverdi's response, the original chant, which is in the simple style of a lection tone, is altered slightly in its *falsobordone* setting, for Monteverdi employs the reciting note only, omitting the occasional movement a step above or half-step below it.

[2] 'Toccata che si suona avanti il levar de la tela tre volte con tutti li stromenti, & si fa un Tuono piu alto volendo sonar le trombe con le sordine'. See Edward H. Tarr, 'Monteverdi, Bach und die

instrumentation of the response omits the trumpets of *L'Orfeo*, but retains cornettos, violins, violas, trombones, a *contrabasso da gamba*, and, of course, the organ, all of which were included (along with other instruments) in the original toccata.[3] In transferring the toccata to the response, the sounding pitch of D is also retained, which calls for transposition of the chant as well as the instruments to D from their notated C.[4]

In each psalm the varying contexts of the cantus firmus help to define the structure of the psalm itself. The simplest organization is found in the *cori spezzati* setting of *Nisi Dominus*, which exhibits a continuous cantus firmus (sixth tone with *finalis f*) in the tenor part of each of the two five-voice choirs. Each statement of the psalm tone begins with its intonation, offering Monteverdi enhanced opportunities for harmonic variety in setting the chant (see Ex. 6.1).

Ex. 6.1. *Nisi Dominus*

Trompetenmusik ihrer Zeit', *Bericht über den internationalen musikwissenschaftlichen Kongress Bonn 1970* (Kassel: Bärenreiter, 1972), 592–6, and Detlef Altenburg, 'Die Toccata zu Monteverdis "Orfeo"', *Bericht über den internationalen musikwissenschaftlichen Kongress Berlin 1974* (Kassel: Bärenreiter, 1980), 271–4. On the transposing effects of trumpet mutes, see Jindrich Keller, 'Antique Trumpet Mutes', *Historic Brass Society Journal*, 2 (1990), 97–103, and Don L. Smithers, 'Baroque Trumpet Mutes: A Retrospective Commentary', *Historic Brass Society Journal*, 2 (1990), 104–11.

[3] See Ch. 18 for a discussion of the instruments used in the response.

[4] For the singers, this is a transposition in notation only, since the absence of a fixed pitch standard meant that the sounding level of any chant could easily be adapted to the accompanying instruments by using the latter to set the pitch.

Although the cadential organization of each verse is similar, the bass underlying each statement of the psalm tone presents considerable variety, as can be seen in Ex. 6.2, which shows, for comparison, the harmonization of the psalm tone in verses 1–4. Continuo figures have been added to Monteverdi's unfigured bass to clarify the harmony of the upper voices.

Ex. 6.2. *Nisi Dominus*, bars 1–122, basso continuo

The chant itself varies rhythmically from long notes to the same shorter notes as appear in the other parts, and a little more than half-way through, at *Sicut sagittae* (verse 5), the tone is transposed up a fourth, allowing harmonization with B♭ major and G minor chords in contrast to the predominating F major and D minor triads of the preceding verses. At the same point, the metre shifts to triple time, introducing a further variant in both the cantus firmus and its polyphonic context.

The varied context of the cantus firmus depends not only on its harmonization and rhythmic organization, but also on the polychoral patterning of the other four voices. Monteverdi's opening verse combines both choirs in a densely imitative texture, but thereafter the two choirs alternate as strict *cori spezzati* (with overlap at verse endings and beginnings) until midway through verse 6, where the choirs rejoin to the end of the psalm. The *cori spezzati* section (verses 2–6) reveals a gradually growing level of rhythmic excitement and ultimately textural density as the two choirs merge.[5]

The doxology of a polyphonic psalm is often set somewhat apart from the psalm proper. In *Nisi Dominus*, Monteverdi not only returns to the original duple metre, but in the *Gloria Patri* also transposes the psalm tone down a fifth (from *d'* to *g*), allowing for harmonization by E♭ major and C minor triads.[6] In many psalms, the *Sicut erat in principio* is a musical pun, reflecting the first verse in keeping with the meaning of the text, and in *Nisi Dominus* Monteverdi returns to F and reiterates the opening verse, giving a rounded structure to the psalm.

A nearly continuous psalm tone cantus firmus (tone 3 with *finalis a*) in the tenor voice also forms the scaffolding for *Lauda Jerusalem*. In the first two verses the chant begins with the intonation, but in subsequent verses it follows the normal pattern of commencing with the reciting note. Transposition of the psalm tone by a fourth occurs in verses 4–6 and again at the beginning of the doxology. Within the tonal areas prescribed by the reciting level of the chant, the harmony fluctuates continually, never establishing a regular pattern. A comparison of the basses underlying three successive statements of the psalm tone with the reciting note *f'* (with continuo figures added to indicate the harmony) suffices to illustrate the variety of harmonic contexts Monteverdi has generated (see Ex. 6.3).

---

[5] Verse 2 alternates between groupings in three minims and two minims (combined into a six-minim phrase), but is otherwise almost stodgy in its declamatory semiminims and minims. Verse 3, whose text produces groupings of four minims throughout, is enlivened through the introduction of dotted rhythms. Verse 4 adds ornamental melismas in canon between the two upper voices to the dotted rhythms. The rhythm is further enlivened with triple metre at the beginning of verse 5 and a truncation of the text by the 'premature' entrance of verse 6, which presses the psalm forwards. Verse 6, for the first time since the opening verse, presents the denser texture of both choirs singing together, at the short canonic interval of one bar; the two choirs finally merge fully at the cadence.

[6] The *Gloria Patri* continues with the combined choirs, but in unison throughout, in effect reducing the one-bar canonic time interval of verse 6 to zero.

Ex. 6.3. *Lauda Jerusalem*, basso continuo: *a* bars 42–4; *b* bars 48–50; *c* bars 56–8

Lauda Jerusalem, like *Nisi Dominus*, is characterized by two choirs in frequent antiphonal responses, but the texture is thinner, comprising only seven parts. The six voices apart from the cantus firmus are subdivided into two equal ensembles of canto, alto, and bass, and the more transparent sonority of these three-voice choirs facilitates more frequent interchanges and greater rhythmic complexity than is exhibited by *Nisi Dominus*. While the overall tonal organization of this psalm is determined by the pitch at which the reciting note appears, structure on a smaller scale is determined, as in *Nisi Dominus*, by antiphony. However, in contrast to the lengthy passages with one choir only that characterize *Nisi Dominus*, the second choir of *Lauda Jerusalem* regularly alternates (sometimes in imitation) with the first choir at the interval of approximately three bars. With verse 5 this interval is reduced by at least half. Finally the two choirs join in verse 7, at the point where the chant returns to its original reciting level, and remain together until the doxology. Although the texture in verses 7–9 is full-voiced and mostly homophonic, it is simultaneously imitative (sometimes only in the outer voices). At verse 9 the time between entries reduces to only a minim or crotchet (depending on the voice), producing a lively mosaic of entrances as pitches and motifs heard in the leading trio reappear almost immediately in the other while the tenor continues to intone the cantus firmus uninterruptedly (see Ex. 6.4). I know of no other example of double-choir music from this period, aside from the first and last verses of Monteverdi's *Nisi Dominus*, that develops such a complex texture from the interplay of two separate groups.

Like *Nisi Dominus*, the doxology is an entirely separate section where the chant for the first time migrates out of the tenor into the top voice, achieving greater prominence. The *Sicut erat*, which in this case does not resemble the opening verse, begins with rhythmicized *falsobordone*, followed by an imitative texture based entirely on the psalm tone. Because the psalm tone comprises principally a repeated pitch, this imitative texture differs from the rhythmicized

Ex. 6.4. *Lauda Jerusalem*, bars 89–106

Ex. 6.4. *Continued*

falsobordone only in its staggered entrances (see Ex. 6.5). In contrast to *Nisi Dominus*, a large polyphonic *Amen*, from which the cantus firmus is absent, concludes *Lauda Jerusalem*. The structural parallels between *Lauda Jerusalem* and *Nisi Dominus* not only relate these two psalms to one another, but separate them from the other three, which, as will be illustrated below, are also related to one another by various means.

The other three psalms make more flexible and complicated use of the cantus firmus. *Dixit Dominus*, for example, after its opening verse, alternates between *falsobordone* settings of the chant (tone 4 with *finalis e*) and imitative textures built over the cantus firmus in the bass. Each *falsobordone* is followed by an optional instrumental ritornello. The doxology then concludes with a solo tenor intonation of the psalm tone and a six-voice polyphonic chorus, balancing the opening verse in a symmetrical construction (see Fig. 4.1 above). Throughout the psalm, only the melismas that conclude each half-verse (typical for *falsibordoni*) and the optional ritornellos are free of the chant.

Within this scheme, Monteverdi varies the context of the chant in several different ways. In the *falsibordoni* themselves, the first half-verse is presented on an A minor chord (A major for verse 6), while the second half-verse is a step

Ex. 6.5. *Lauda Jerusalem*, bars 131–48

Ex. 6.5. *Continued*

lower on a G major triad.[7] In the alternate verses 3, 5, and 7, the chant, trans-
ferred to the bass in minims and crotchets, supports first an imitative duet in the
top two parts, then an imitative tenor duet, and finally an imitative five-voice
texture, creating a series of variations over the bass cantus firmus. The beginning of this latter verse looks very much like measured *falsobordone* and, like Ex.
6.5, illustrates how closely chordal textures in the harmonization of a psalm
tone approximate *falsobordone*, especially when the chant is in the bass, allowing
for very little variety of harmonization (see Ex. 6.6). Even within each of these
verses the principle of variation predominates, since each half-verse repeats the
text, prompting a variation in its setting. Ex. 6.7 shows the third verse, beginning with the cantus alone and then adding the sextus in an imitative texture for
the reiteration of the text. Note that although the chant is not present for the
first statement of the half-verse in the cantus, the bassus generalis still reflects
the psalm tone. In the second half of the verse a subtle colouristic variation
is achieved by shifting the leading role from the cantus to the sextus.

[7] This transposition of the second half of the verse is uncommon, though not unique, in *falsobordone*
psalm passages. Other contemporaneous examples may be found in *Laudate pueri* from Viadana's *Cento
concerti ecclesiastici* of 1602 (RISM V1360), *Laudate pueri* from Luigi Roinci's *Sacra omnium solemnitatum
vespertina* of 1604 (R1957), and *Nisi Dominus* from Viadana's *Il terzo libro de' concerti ecclesiastici* of 1609
(V1392).

Ex. 6.6. *Dixit Dominus*, bars 165–82

180

Ex. 6.6. *Continued*

Even in those passages not based on the cantus firmus the principle of variation prevails. The melismas concluding each half-verse are rhythmic variants of
a single underlying descending sequence (three of eight variants are shown in
Ex 6.8).[8] Each instrumental ritornello is similarly a slightly modified repetition
(transposed up a step) of the immediately preceding melisma, exchanging the
vocal sonority for an instrumental one.

The first verse and the doxology exhibit yet further contextual variants for
the cantus firmus. In the first verse, the psalm tone itself becomes a subject for
polyphonic imitation, joined by a countersubject in a six-voice texture. At the
beginning of the doxology the solo cantus firmus appears in long notes a step
lower on *g* in *cantus mollis*. The *Sicut erat* then presents the chant as a long-note
cantus firmus on *d*, first in the bass, then in the cantus, in a full six-voice texture
of imitative melismatic figures. This *Sicut erat* is unrelated to the first verse of
the psalm, but is reminiscent in its reiteration of the sustained psalm tone on D
(harmonized with D minor) of *Domine ad adjuvandum*.

---

[8] A number of closely related sequences can be found in the *Missa in illo tempore*. See Jerome Roche,
'Monteverdi and the *Prima Prattica*', in Denis Arnold and Nigel Fortune, eds., *The Monteverdi Companion*
(London: Faber and Faber, 1968), 173–4 and 176–8; and Jeffrey G. Kurtzman, *Essays on the Monteverdi
Mass and Vespers of 1610* (Houston: Rice University Studies, 1978), 47–68. Denis Arnold quotes a simi-
lar sequence from the sacred music of Giaches de Wert in his *Monteverdi*, rev. edn. (London: J. M. Dent
& Sons Ltd., 1975), 134. Monteverdi's *Io mi son giovinetta* from the Fourth Book of Madrigals of 1603
has a melisma identical to that concluding the first *falsobordone* verse, as well as the subsequent ritornello.

Ex. 6.7. *Dixit Dominus*, bars 53–68

Laudate pueri is scored for eight voices, but here, in contrast with his technique in *Nisi Dominus* and *Lauda Jerusalem*, Monteverdi rarely divides the ensemble into antiphonal four-voice combinations, preferring instead to pair voices in the same register. Throughout this psalm, Monteverdi is extremely flexible in his treatment of the plainchant. The psalm tone (tone 8 with *finalis g*)

Ex. 6.8. *Dixit Dominus*, melismas: *a* bars 39–45; *b* bars 24–37; *c* bars 145–52

(b)

Ex. 6.8. *Continued*

Ex. 6.8. *Continued*

migrates freely from voice to voice, is transposed several times and is absent altogether in some passages. Nevertheless, each verse of the psalm appears at least once in plainchant.

The treatment of the psalm tone at the beginning of *Laudate pueri* resembles that at the opening of *Dixit Dominus*: after an initial solo intonation in a tenor voice (quintus), the psalm tone combines with a countersubject to evolve a steadily expanding imitative texture (see Ex. 6.9). Even the countersubject is similar to the one at the beginning of *Dixit Dominus*. Whereas this process encompassed the entire first verse in *Dixit*, in *Laudate pueri* only the first half of the verse is traversed, so the process is repeated, with a new countersubject, to complete the first verse.

After the first verse, where *Dixit Dominus* had turned to the tripartite series of *falsibordoni*, ritornellos, and duets, *Laudate pueri* presents a lengthy succession of virtuoso duets for voices in a single register, accompanied by the cantus firmus (see the beginning of the first of these trio textures in Ex. 6.10). In this portion of the psalm (verses 2–5), the psalm tone migrates upwards through the texture from one verse to the next, starting in the quintus and proceeding through the altus, the cantus, and finally the sextus. It is sung both in long notes and in minims and crotchets, but even in its shorter rhythmic values the cantus firmus appears sustained because of the rapid embellishments in the other voices. The movement of the chant out of its bass role in the quintus part permits increased harmonic variety, and successive transpositions of the psalm tone upwards by a fifth (verses 2 and 3 transpose the reciting note to G, verse 4 to D) admit a wider tonal compass as well. Only at verse 5 does the reciting note return to its original C.

The virtuoso duets of verses 2–5 employ the two sopranos (cantus and sextus) in verses 2–3, the two tenors (tenor and quintus) in verse 4, and the two basses (bassus and [octavus]) in verse 5. The gradual descent in register of the duets is mirrored by the gradual ascent of the cantus firmus (quintus, altus, cantus, sextus). The migrations and transpositions of the cantus firmus thus bring the psalm tone from the low register to the top of the vocal texture, paralleling the text of these verses, which begins with man's praise of God and ultimately exalts God above all nations, heaven, and earth in the climactic verses 4 and 5. The phrase *et super coelos gloria eius* is accompanied by *durus* harmonies over the notes of the natural hexachord, cadencing to A major, illustrating Monteverdi's tendency to associate *durus* harmonies with positive textual ideas from this period in his life onwards.[9]

[9] Eric T. Chafe, in *Monteverdi's Tonal Language* (New York: Schirmer Books, 1992), 54–5, links *durus* harmonies and positive textual conceits only from the Seventh Book of Madrigals (1619) onwards, but see the discussion of *Nigra sum* below in Ch. 9.

Ex. 6.9. *Laudate pueri*, bars 1–15

Ex. 6.10. *Laudate pueri*, bars 29–37

For the remainder of the psalm, Monteverdi abandons the few-voiced textures and makes use of all eight voices, with the exception of very brief passages
for reduced forces. The psalm tone has already returned to its reciting note of C
in verse 5, and it remains there for the rest of *Laudate pueri*, including the doxology. Because the chant always appears in an inner voice until it is projected to
the top of the texture in the *Sicut erat*, there is considerable flexibility in its harmonization. Moreover, temporary pauses in the psalm tone allow for even
further harmonic freedom and variety. Indeed, this portion of the psalm is characterized by substantial tonal variety coupled with considerable textural variety,
ranging from homophony to imitation, with the number of participating voices
changing constantly. The rhythmic organization also shifts frequently between
duple and triple metre.

Like *Dixit Dominus*, the doxology shifts tonality. The psalm text itself concludes with a complete cadence to A major, and through circle-of-fifths harmony, a transition is made to G major for the beginning of the *Gloria Patri*. As
in *Dixit Dominus*, the psalm tone is recited by the tenor in long note values, ac-

companied only by the bassus generalis (though interrupted by a four-voice passage). This passage again reminds us of the traditional *alternatim* technique where plainchant verses alternate with polyphony. The *Sicut erat*, with its harmonization of the psalm tone in the top voice, is also somewhat parallel to the same verse in *Dixit Dominus* (*Dixit* places the chant in both bass and top parts). But while the *Sicut erat* of *Laudate pueri* parallels *Dixit Dominus* in style, it is also reminiscent of the final verse and rounded structure of *Nisi Dominus* in closely resembling the opening verse of the psalm.

The final *Amen*, devoid of the psalm tone, constitutes an extended coda based on ascending fifths (see Ex. 6.11). At first the tenor and quintus remain silent in an otherwise full texture, but as that texture gradually thins, they commence singing the same motifs as the other voices, emerging from the other parts to complete the psalm with a lovely imitative duet of their own. As a consequence, *Laudate pueri* ends with a thin texture in the tenor register, as it began. The two voices converge on the unison final *g*, the same note on which the two sopranos will begin their duet an octave higher in the following motet, *Pulchra es*. Indeed, the opening of *Pulchra es* outlines the same ascending fifths with which *Laudate pueri* concludes.[10] The duet concluding the *Amen* is reminiscent of a very similar passage in Giovanni Gabrieli's *Quem vidistis pastores*, published posthumously in his *Symphoniae sacrae* of 1615 (G87).[11]

In *Laudate pueri*, Monteverdi has built a more dynamic form than the symmetrical structure of *Dixit Dominus*. This form proceeds, after the initial polyphonic verse, to a series of trio textures (duets against the psalm tone) before expanding again to the full choir. The length of each verse depends heavily on the character of the musical figures and their working out, and these figures depend in turn much more on the significance of individual words or phrases of the text than do the figures in *Dixit Dominus*. Yet some degree of symmetry is present in the reiteration of the music of the first verse in the *Sicut erat*. It may well have been the absence of other forms of symmetry in *Laudate pueri* that prompted Monteverdi to repeat the opening music for the *Sicut erat* (as in *Nisi Dominus*), whereas *Dixit Dominus*, being governed throughout by a symmetrical organization, did not require a similar return at the end.

Whereas the structure of *Dixit Dominus*, *Laudate pueri*, *Nisi Dominus*, and *Lauda Jerusalem* is centred around reiterations of the psalm tone in each verse, the formal organization of *Laetatus sum* does not depend on the cantus firmus, but rather on the disposition of the text over a series of repeated bass patterns in the sequence abacd, abacd', ab'd', where d' is a variant of d. Each pattern corresponds to one of the eleven verses of the text except c and d (or d'), which

---

[10] See Chs. 1 and 2 for a discussion of the placement of the motets in relation to the psalms.

[11] See *Giovanni Gabrieli: Opera omnia*, ed. Denis Arnold (Rome: American Institute of Musicology, 1969), 14–15 (bars 72–8).

Ex. 6.11. *Laudate pueri*, bars 211–25

Ex. 6.11. *Continued*

combine for a single verse. The *Sicut erat*, concluding the doxology, coincides with the final statement of pattern d'. The psalm tone appears only occasionally in the tenor, altus, or cantus part, though it normally stands out prominently when it does make an appearance.

The first of Monteverdi's structural modules (a) is the famous walking bass frequently cited in the Monteverdi literature (see Ex. 6.12*a*).[12] This bass is repeated exactly in each of its five recurrences, lending *Laetatus sum* a strong sense of harmonic and structural continuity. The other three patterns, whose systematic return tightens the organization even further, have generally escaped notice (see Ex. 6.12*b, c, d*).[13]

The walking bass is both highly repetitive and sequential in its motivic structure. The second bass pattern (b) is similarly repetitive (Ex. 6.12*b*). This pattern is reiterated almost exactly in its second statement, but is simplified in its final version (see Ex. 6.13).

[12] See esp. Denis Arnold's discussion of this bass in 'Formal Design in Monteverdi's Church Music', in Raffaello Monterosso, ed., *Claudio Monteverdi e il suo tempo* (Verona: La Stamperia Valdonega, 1969), 207.
[13] Hugo Leichtentritt has been the only one to outline the complexity of this repetitive structure. See Leichtentritt, *Geschichte der Motette* (Leipzig, 1908; repr. edn. Hildesheim: Georg Olms, 1967), 245. Jürgen Jürgens mentions the repetition of three separate bass patterns in 'Urtext und Aufführungspraxis bei Monteverdis *Orfeo* und *Marien-Vesper*', in Monterosso, ed., *Claudio Monteverdi e il suo tempo*, 284.

Ex. 6.12. *Laetatus sum*, bass patterns

Ex. 6.13. *Laetatus sum*, bars 190–212, basso continuo

The third bass pattern (c) is almost completely static and serves as the support for virtuoso passage-work both times it appears (Ex. 6.12*c*). The only difference between its two statements is in the length of the sustained Gs.

The fourth bass pattern (d) is also repetitious, in that the final eight bars are a sequential replication of the preceding eight (Ex. 6.12*d*). This pattern is shortened through truncation and diminution in its second and third presentations (d′) (see Ex. 6.14).

Patterns a and b each accommodate one verse of the psalm text, while c and d (or d′) combine to present verses 4 and 8. The virtuoso passage-work over pattern c introduces each of these two verses, which then continue with a more normal polyphonic texture over pattern d (or d′). d′ subsequently underlies the entire *Sicut erat*.

Ex. 6.14. *Laetatus sum*, basso continuo: *a* bars 158–72; *b* bars 213–27

Ex. 6.15. *Laetatus sum*, bass relationships

Although these patterns appear on the surface to be very different from one another, there are some important points of similarity among three of the four. A comparison between the beginning of the walking bass (a) and pattern b demonstrates that the latter is a slower-moving variant of the former, particularly in its harmonic outline (see Ex. 6.15). Pattern d also features scale motifs similar to patterns a and b. Only pattern c, which is without any rhythmic or pitch motion at all, is radically different.

The structural sequence of these patterns, as schematized above, gives special prominence to the walking bass (a), which underlies all odd-numbered verses until the doxology, an arrangement reminiscent of the more primitive *alternatim* technique of psalmody. Since the underlying identities of each of the other basses are not obscured despite their varied repetitions, the entire psalm unfolds as a complex series of strophic variations, inspired perhaps by Monteverdi's essays in strophic variations in *L'Orfeo*. In several of these, too, Monteverdi varied the bass-line in each successive strophe.

Monteverdi's ingenuity in writing strophic variations is readily apparent in the manifold ways in which he manipulates the six voices, achieving continuous variety in texture and style as a counterbalance to the repeated bass. A few examples from the walking-bass segments, where each successive statement of the bass supports a progressively larger number of upper parts, illustrate this variety (see Ex. 6.16). Bass pattern b also supports varied textures and styles, ranging

Ex. 6.16. *Laetatus sum*, walking basses: *a* bars 1–17; *b* bars 39–55; *c* bars 173–9

(c)

175

Ex. 6.16. *Continued*

from a solo intonation to paired duets to imitative textures. On the other hand, pattern d (or d') normally underlies a full six-voice sonority, and the sustained pitch of pattern c supports virtuoso *passaggi*.

The sporadic, though prominent, statements of the psalm tone (occasionally transposed down a fourth) occur in connection with all four bass patterns, sometimes in the prevailing rhythms and sometimes as a long-note cantus firmus. In verses 3, 5, and 9 the psalm tone, highly paraphrased, constitutes more an underlying presence than a cantus firmus.

Unlike *Laudate pueri*, *Laetatus sum* does not have an elaborate *Amen*. Rather, there is a simple plagal cadence to G with Picardy third, virtually identical to the plagal cadence concluding *Dixit Dominus*.

Despite their manifest differences, *Dixit Dominus*, *Laudate pueri*, and *Laetatus sum* have various features in common. Each has a sophisticated schematic structure, utilizing as organizing elements the psalm tone, repetitive bass patterns, vocal duets, and variation in styles and textures. All three psalms open with the psalm tone in a single voice, and all three present the psalm tone both as a long-note cantus firmus and in faster rhythmic values, incorporating the chant into the surrounding texture. All three use a descending fifth either as a countersubject to the psalm tone in the imitative texture of the opening verse or, as in *Laetatus sum*, as the imitative subject of verse 2, where the psalm tone is absent. Duets featuring solo voices in the same register are prominent in the early portion of all three psalms. Both *Dixit Dominus* and *Laetatus sum* employ unmeasured *falsibordoni*, and they have virtually identical concluding *Amen*s. All three psalms use the same motif of an ascending or descending fifth in dotted crotchets and quavers as the basis of a full-voiced imitative texture in the doxology. These recurring features, which clearly distinguish the first three psalms of Monteverdi's Vespers from the last two, suggest that *Dixit Dominus*, *Laudate pueri*, and *Laetatus sum* were all composed at about the same time, representing a matrix of related musical ideas and organizational schemes.

As described above, there are also structural parallels between *Lauda Jerusalem* and *Nisi Dominus* which not only relate these two psalms to one another, but distance them from the other three. One might hypothesize on stylistic grounds that these two groups of psalms were composed at different times and joined together for purposes of the 1610 publication. The few parallels between the pair *Nisi Dominus* and *Lauda Jerusalem* on the one hand and the first three psalms on the other suggest that the chronologically prior group may have influenced the composition of the later group in a few particulars. But which group might antedate the other?

There are two forms of evidence suggesting that *Nisi Dominus* and *Lauda Jerusalem* are earlier compositions. The first is their conservative style and relative structural and stylistic simplicity in comparison with *Dixit Dominus*, *Laudate pueri*, and *Laetatus sum*. The rigorous, only modestly varied organization of the two antiphonal psalms not only reflects an older, more traditional style of psalmody, but also bespeaks a less imaginative and less sophisticated compositional technique. The three *concertato* psalms, on the other hand, are quite modern in character and significantly more varied and complex.

An assessment of errors in the 1610 print also provides supporting evidence for an earlier date of composition for *Nisi Dominus* and *Lauda Jerusalem*. Both reveal remarkably few misprints for compositions of their length and number of parts, far fewer than the other three psalms.[14] This suggests that the typesetter had accurate manuscript copies from which to work. The quality of these copies may have resulted from rehearsals and performances through which mistakes in the manuscripts could have been discovered and carefully corrected in clear, accurate final drafts given to the printer. The first three psalms, on the other hand, display a number of problems in their printed notation, possibly resulting from faulty manuscripts prepared in haste with little time to check for errors and make emendations. Perhaps they were composed specifically for the 1610 publication and never rehearsed or performed, or perhaps they stem from the busy years of 1607–08 (see Chapter 1), when Monteverdi was so overwhelmed with writing new music that he would have had little time to correct recently completed compositions.

These five psalms demonstrate seemingly inexhaustible imagination and inventiveness on the part of Monteverdi. The melodically monotonous psalm tone, rather than proving restrictive, stimulated the composer to a multitude of different solutions, most of them rooted in the process of variation on a given theme. In these psalms, variations in vocal style, in texture, in choral and solo sonorities, in antiphonal effects, in rhythm, in melody, and in harmony and tonality all come into play. Yet the psalm tones and the limitations they impose serve as a binding thread for all five compositions, generating aesthetic consistency and cohesion despite the diversity of treatments. The psalms highlight two opposite but complementary facets of Monteverdi's compositional method. He displays not only boundless invention, but also disciplined mastery of formal design. This combination of freedom of imagination and organizational discipline is an artistic achievement of the highest order, palpably distinguishing Monteverdi from his contemporaries.

CADENCES

As described earlier, the psalm tones each outline two cadences, the mediant at the end of the first half of the verse, and the final, defined by the

---

[14] See the critical notes to my Oxford University Press edition of the Vespers for details of these errors as well as those in the other three psalms.

differentia.[15] These cadences are melodic rather than harmonic, and the cadence notes of the psalm tones may be harmonized in various ways when the cantus firmus is not in the bass part itself. In general, at the points where the cantus firmus cadences, Monteverdi creates a cadence in the other parts as well. His cadences in *Lauda Jerusalem*, where the mediant cadence of the psalm tone is on *c* and the final cadence descends to *a*, are representative. The mediant cadences embrace a typical two-part *clausula*, with the second voice forming a sixth or third with the penultimate note of the chant, the sixth expanding to an octave or the third contracting to a unison for the closure. Such cadences are normally supported by a leap in the bass from the fifth degree to the cadence note except where the chant itself or the contrapuntal voice joining it in the *clausula* is in the bass (see Ex. 6.9). In those cadences where the bass has either the chant or the contrapuntal voice of the *clausula*, a cadence is formed without the leap in the bass (see Ex. 6.17). Similar formations occur in cadences to the final of the

Ex. 6.17. *Lauda Jerusalem*, bars 36–7

[15] The *differentiae* are the different cadence formulas for psalm and canticle tones, allowing the cantor to choose an ending that will merge smoothly with the antiphon. In most polyphonic settings of psalms and Magnificats of the 16th and 17th centuries, the most common set of *differentiae* are used, creating a standard cadence for each of the tones.

psalm tone. Where the mediant and final cadences of a psalm tone are on different pitches, as in *Lauda Jerusalem*, a repetitive pattern of varied cadential harmonies is automatically introduced.

When the psalm tone is transposed up a fourth, as in *Lauda Jerusalem*, the cadential patterns also shift by a fourth, closing on an F major triad at the mediant and a D minor triad at the final instead of C major and A minor. Thus two different sets of cadential poles are established, a principal tonal pole with the psalm tone at its original level and a subsidiary tonal pole based on the transposed chant. Yet the subsidiary pole does not engender significant tension by its departure from the original tonal orbit. Rather, it seems to establish its own tonal realm as an alternative to the principal one, generating tonal and harmonic variety for the psalm as a whole. Its subsidiary status is only manifested by the eventual return of the chant to its original level.

Since the doxologies of *Dixit Dominus* and *Nisi Dominus* present the *Gloria Patri* chant transposed down a step, new harmonies and tonalities suddenly become available beyond those characteristic of the psalm proper.[16] Such transpositions, therefore, are one of Monteverdi's principal means of introducing harmonic and tonal variety into his psalms.

The fourth psalm tone (with reciting note *a*), used in *Dixit Dominus*, was traditionally harmonized with A minor (sometimes A major). However, the final, *e*, could not be supported by an authentic cadence with a leap of a fifth or fourth in the bass, since a B major triad was beyond the scope of normal harmony in psalm settings, and a split-key *d♯* was not usually available on organs.[17] Consequently, the final *e* was normally harmonized with an E major triad in the context of A minor or major, sounding to present-day ears like a half cadence. For sixteenth- and seventeenth-century listeners, however, this was the normal cadence for the fourth tone. Since the *differentia* Monteverdi uses does not descend stepwise to the final *e*, but rather falls through the E minor triad, cadences to the final involve parallel triads a third apart, an E major triad being preceded either by a C major or a G major triad. The latter 'progression' is the most common, since the chant is in the lowest voice for several verses (see Ex. 6.18). The same pattern holds true in the doxology, where the psalm tone is transposed. In the *Gloria Patri*, the cadence to the final proceeds from B♭ major to D minor, and in the *Sicut erat*, from F major to A major just before the final E major triad.

Not all cadences in *Dixit Dominus* include the psalm tone, however. Each half-verse of *falsobordone* concludes with an elaborate melisma, appended to the reciting note. The cadences at the ends of the melismas all comprise typical

---

[16] Part of the *Gloria Patri* chant is transposed down a fourth in *Laetatus sum*, without, however, introducing any new harmonic or tonal areas.

[17] See Ch. 22 for a discussion of mean-tone organ tuning and split keys.

Ex. 6.18. *Dixit Dominus*, bars 82–4

Ex. 6.19. *Lauda Jerusalem*, bars 93–4

two-part *clausulae* supported by a leap of a fifth or fourth in the bass—in
modern terms, a perfect authentic V–I cadence. The *falsibordoni* are recited at
two different levels, so the cadences are likewise at two different levels: C major
and A major. The cadence chord is chosen to provide a smooth transition to

what follows, however, rather than being determined by the level of the *fal-sobordone* it concludes.

Monteverdi does not always find it necessary to form a strong cadential context for the mediant cadences of the chant. The other parts may generate a very weak cadence (see Ex. 6.19) or simply sing through the psalm tone cadence without a contrapuntal *clausula* or cadential leap in the bass (see Ex. 6.20). Nor do all cadences in the chant necessarily coincide with cadences in the other parts. In the mediant cadence from the first verse of *Nisi Dominus*, the other voices come to an incomplete close on a D major triad, while the cadential *f* of the chant, harmonized with an F major triad, overlaps the beginning of the second half of the verse in the other parts (see Ex. 6.21).[18]

In *Laudate pueri* and *Laetatus sum*, as well as in *Dixit Dominus*, as described above, there are numerous cadences where the psalm tone is not a factor. In these cadences, Monteverdi typically uses the two-part *clausula* coupled with a

Ex. 6.20. *Lauda Jerusalem*, bars 59–60

[18] A similar overlap, but with a different bass-line, occurs at the mediant cadence of verse 4. Several other verses have no contrapuntal or harmonic cadence at all at the mediant point of the psalm tone.

Ex. 6.21. *Nisi Dominus*, bars 16–21

leap of a fifth or fourth in the bass. Much less frequently, he constructs a *clausula* cadence without bass leap (see Ex. 6.22).

Each of the psalms concludes with a separate *Amen*; in *Dixit*, *Laetatus sum*, and *Nisi Dominus* the setting is very brief and closes with a plagal cadence with bass leap from the fourth degree to the final. In *Laudate pueri* and *Lauda Jerusalem* the *Amen* is quite elaborate and extended, concluding with a perfect authentic cadence.

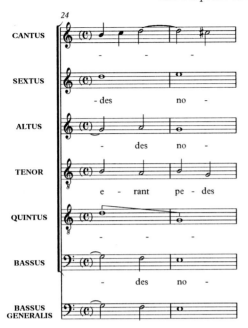

Ex. 6.22. *Laetatus sum*, bars 24–5

HARMONIC LANGUAGE

Harmonic language in the response and psalms is determined in three principal ways: (1) static triadic harmonization of the reciting note or static triadic underpinning for upper-voice virtuoso duets; (2) harmonization, whether homophonic or polyphonic (very often some combination of the two), of a bass that frequently moves by leap, especially a fourth or fifth; and (3) bass movement that consists of scale motion or some elaboration of scale motion, yielding scale-based counterpoint in the upper parts. Imitative textures involving the bass are much less common, characterizing principally the openings of *Dixit Dominus* and *Laudate pueri*. Monteverdi's harmonic language also encompasses shifts of tonal focus by a third (resulting in major–minor juxtapositions) and temporary major–minor triadic shifts through alteration of the third of a chord.

Illustrating the simplest form of harmony is the third bass pattern (c) in *Laetatus sum*, where a single chord supports a lengthy upper-voice duet (see Ex. 6.12c above). Static basses also arise from the placement of the psalm tone in the bass voice, where the reciting note determines the harmony (see Exx. 6.23 and 6.24).

Ex. 6.23. *Dixit Dominus*, bars 61–8

When the chant is not in the bass voice, the reciting note may be harmonized by as many as three different chords. In Ex. 6.3*a* above, the reciting note *f* is harmonized by all three possible triads: D minor, B♭ major, and F major. Thus the harmonic context need not be restricted too severely by the monotony of the reciting note, and transposition of the entire psalm tone by a fourth yields yet another set of potential harmonizations.

Apart from cadences, it is in the chordal harmonizations of the psalm tone (when the tone is not in the bass) that Monteverdi's harmonic successions most nearly resemble tonal chord progressions. In such passages, bass movement is often by fourth or fifth. Yet Monteverdi's basses also frequently move by thirds, and even in movement by step or by fourth or fifth, chord sequences are often the reverse of typical functional progressions (e.g. V–IV instead of IV–V; or II–VI instead of VI–II). Exx. 6.25 and 6.26, from *Dixit Dominus* and *Laudate pueri*, are characteristic of brief chordal progressions harmonizing the psalm tone. Ex. 6.25 begins with a I–V–I progression in A minor (bars 17–19) but concludes with a non-functional cadence to E (bars 21–2). The E is harmonized

Ex. 6.24. *Dixit Dominus*, bars 228–43

Ex. 6.24. *Continued*

Ex. 6.25. *Dixit Dominus*, bars 17–23

Ex. 6.26. *Laudate pueri*, bars 12–15

Ex. 6.27. *Lauda Jerusalem*, bars 20–7, basso continuo

with a major triad, allowing it to function as dominant to A (bars 22–3), where the subsequent *falsobordone* passage begins. Ex. 6.26 concludes with a IV–I–V–I cadence in C, but the IV is preceded by V.

The bass of *Lauda Jerusalem* exhibits a characteristically non-functional chordal succession. In Ex. 6.27, whose cadential goal at the end of the passage is C major, it is apparent that only the II–V–I progression in the second bar and the cadence itself exhibit chord sequences typical of functional harmony; the chord succession of the passage as a whole cannot be considered functional by the criteria Dahlhaus establishes for functional tonal progressions (see Chapter 5 above).

Monteverdi's harmonic language is frequently characterized by shifts between G minor and B♭ major, F major and D minor, or C major and A minor, without a pivotal cadence establishing the new chord as a tonic (though the new chord may be preceded in some circumstances by its dominant).[19] In such situ-

Ex. 6.28. *Nisi Dominus*, bars 141–52

[19] Such shifts were termed 'bifocal tonality' by Jan LaRue, 'combining major and relative minor to form a broader but not indefinite harmonic arena'. See La Rue, 'Bifocal Tonality: An Explanation for Ambiguous Baroque Cadences', *Essays on Music in Honor of Archibald Thompson Davison* (Cambridge, Mass.: Harvard University, 1957), 182. I am grateful to Stephen Bonta for reminding me of this article.

Ex. 6.28. *Continued*

ations, the tonal orientation of the passage may become ambiguous; nevertheless, there is a definite change in the focus of both the harmony and counterpoint in such shifts of emphasis. Whereas G minor harmony is likely to be articulated by voices outlining the G–D fifth or the D–A fifth (supported by a D major triad), a sudden change to a B♭ major harmony will be articulated by a change in the vocal lines to the B♭–F fifth or the F–C fifth (supported by an F major triad) (see Ex. 6.28). The walking bass at the beginning of *Laetatus sum*, beginning with a G minor cadence, soon shifts to B♭ major before returning to G at the end (see Ex. 6.12*a* above).

These shifts of a third, which also entail shifts between major and minor triads, constitute a significant feature of the harmonic colour of Monteverdi's psalm settings. They are suggested by some of the psalm tones themselves, whose mediant cadences are often a third above the final, with the mediant harmonized a third higher than the final (see Ex. 6.29). The bass underlying the first half of this psalm tone is typical of the ambiguity in Monteverdi's tonal direction. The constant *C–f* bass motion may imply to modern ears an F major tonality, but the mediant cadence is V–I in C. Both C major and F major triads, of course, can be used to harmonize the reciting note *c*, without necessarily implying precedence of one over the other. In the second half of the psalm tone, the reciting note is harmonized most often with an A minor triad in preparation for the cadence to A major. Similar harmonizations of the psalm tone by alternating bass notes a fourth apart are found in *Laetatus sum* (see Ex. 6.30).

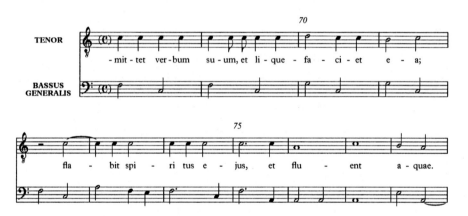

Ex. 6.29. *Lauda Jerusalem*, bars 68–78, tenor and basso continuo

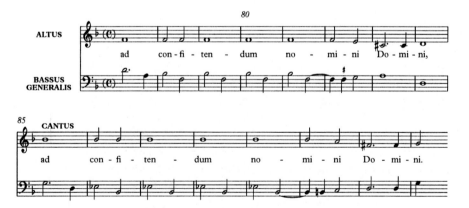

Ex. 6.30. *Laetatus sum*, bars 77–92, altus, then cantus, and basso continuo

Such shifts of a third do not require an interval of a third between the mediant and final cadences of a psalm tone, however. Tone 6f, used in *Nisi Dominus*,
has its mediant and final cadences on the same *f*. Nevertheless, Monteverdi shifts
back and forth by a third in his harmonization of the chant (see Ex. 6.31). The
first phrase of the psalm tone resembles a functional progression; the second
phrase less so.

Another feature characterizing Monteverdi's harmonic language is the juxtaposition of major and minor versions of the same triad, especially at cadences.
While the *cantus durus* or *cantus mollis* system will determine the prevailing character of triads built over the notes of the hexachord in either system, direct juxtapositions of A major and A minor, G major and G minor, or D major and D
minor triads through the use of accidentals are not uncommon. Such shifts in
the quality of chords should not be thought of as changes in the underlying
durus or *mollis* system, or as changes in mode (as in tonal music), for Monteverdi
still thinks of a G minor chord produced by a flat accidental in the *cantus durus*
system as a triad built on either *sol* in the natural hexachord or *ut* in the hard
hexachord. The temporary change in quality of the chord by alteration of its
third is a matter of colouring and affect, not a change in the underlying system,
nor even necessarily a shift in hexachord.[20]

The non-functional character of Monteverdi's bass-lines is revealed most
prominently in their tendency towards scale motion of one kind or another. A
typical pattern, found in madrigals, operas, and sacred music, is the descending
scale in some kind of sequential pattern, usually articulating or implying a series
of alternating thirds. This is the pattern underlying all of the cadential melismas
following the *falsibordoni* in *Dixit Dominus* (see Exx. 6.32*a* and 6.32*b*). The ritornello immediately following the latter melisma simplifies the bass to its most
essential motion (see Ex. 6.33). The initial bass pattern in *Laetatus sum*, mentioned several times already, is also highly dependent on scale motion, as is the

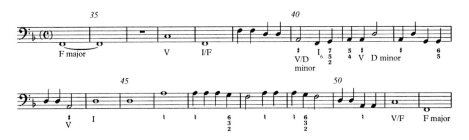

Ex. 6.31. *Nisi Dominus*, bars 34–52, basso continuo

[20] See Chafe's discussion of such chromatic alterations in *cantus durus* and *mollis* as well as in hexachords in *Monteverdi's Tonal Language*, Ch. 2.

second bass pattern (see Ex. 6.12*a* and *b* above). The *Gloria Patri* of *Laudate pueri* likewise relies heavily on scale motion in the bass (see Ex. 6.34).

Other sequential bass patterns are common in Monteverdi's music, but play only a limited role in the psalms because of the restrictions imposed by the psalm tone. Indeed, sequences emerge principally when the psalm tone is absent, as in the *Dixit Dominus* melismas described above. The triple-metre passages at *Suscitans à terra* and *erigens* in *Laudate pueri* consist of ascending sequences, enabled by the temporary absence of the psalm tone (see Ex. 6.35). The concluding *Amen* of *Laudate pueri* is also dependent on sequential bass motion (see Ex. 6.11 above).

VARIATION IN TEXTURE AND STYLE

Various aspects of texture and style have already been touched upon in the preceding discussion, and it is perhaps in these features that Monteverdi's psalms are most remarkable. Textures and styles range from solo intonation of the psalm tone to virtuoso duets in rapid notes, *falsibordoni*, homophony, *cori spezzati*, elaborate polyphonic melismas in many parts, instrumental ritornellos, and fully

Ex. 6.32. *Dixit Dominus: a* bars 24–31; *b* bars 39–45

(b)

Ex. 6.32. *Continued*

Ex. 6.33. *Dixit Dominus*, bars 46–51

imitative textures, sometimes using the psalm tone as principal subject. Tim
Carter has remarked how *Nisi Dominus* resembles the style of Roman
contrapunto alla mente, the practice of two or more voices improvising counterpoint against a cantus firmus.[21]

In all of the psalms except *Laetatus sum*, Monteverdi's tendency is either to
begin with a full texture, as in *Nisi Dominus* and *Lauda Jerusalem*, or to build imitatively from one voice to a full texture, as in *Dixit Dominus* and *Laudate pueri*.

[21] In private conversation.

Ex. 6.34. *Laudate pueri*, bars 155–89

Ex. 6.34. *Continued*

Ex. 6.34. *Continued*

Subsequent verses tend to have thinner textures before Monteverdi returns to his complete complement of voices prior to the doxology. In *Nisi Dominus* and *Lauda Jerusalem* these reduced textures take the form of overlapping *cori spezzati*, which finally merge into a full-voiced sonority. *Laudate pueri* has a series of duets accompanied by the cantus firmus before a fuller (but varying) texture returns at *Suscitans*. Both *Dixit Dominus* and *Laetatus sum* are further complicated by their repetitive structures, which bring similar textures back in a regularly recurring pattern. In *Dixit*, the recurring *falsibordoni* with their cadential melismas and instrumental ritornellos alternate with imitative duets accompanied by the cantus firmus, the last time expanding the imitation to a five-voice texture over the psalm tone. The succession of textures in *Laetatus sum* depends on the succession of bass patterns. Pattern a, the walking bass, supports a solo intonation of the psalm tone at the beginning and a series of few-voiced imitative textures, gradually increasing in number of voices from a duet in its second appearance to all six voices in its last. The static bass, c, on the other hand, supports virtuoso soprano and tenor duets in its two appearances. Bass pattern b, consisting principally of descending scale motion, underlies a six-voice imitative texture, paired duets, a solo intonation of the cantus firmus, and a four-voice imitative texture accompanied by the cantus firmus. Pattern d (or d′) supports a six-voice chordal texture.

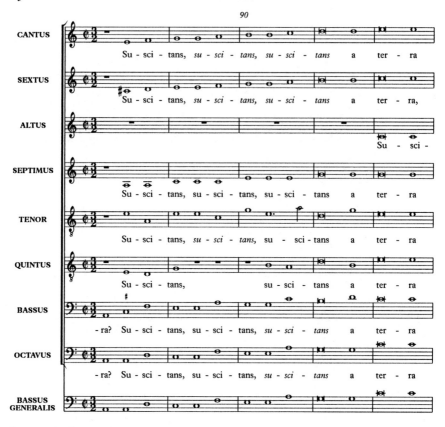

Ex. 6.35. *Laudate pueri*, bars 88–92

As suggested earlier, the doxologies constitute quite separate segments of the psalms, often beginning at a different tonal level and employing their own structural schemes. Only the doxology of *Laetatus sum* utilizes variants of the psalm's previous bass patterns, with the texture ranging from an elaborate, six-voice polyphonic melisma at the beginning of the *Gloria Patri* to homophony and *falsobordone*. The doxologies of *Dixit Dominus* and *Laudate pueri* alternate solo intonation of the plainchant with chordal textures, while *Nisi Dominus* and *Lauda Jerusalem* harmonize the cantus firmus with a full chordal texture throughout. The *Sicut erats* of both *Nisi Dominus* and *Laudate pueri* each comprise a reiteration of the music for verse 1 (somewhat varied in *Laudate pueri*).

Both *Laudate pueri* and *Lauda Jerusalem* have extended polyphonic *Amens*, with imitative melismas based on brief triadic motifs. The imitative figure and its polyphonic unfolding in *Laudate pueri* are remarkably similar to the figure and texture with which the *Gloria Patri* of *Laetatus sum* begins. A survey of Monteverdi's many later published psalm settings reveals that, as in the 1610

Vespers, some close with very short *Amens*, while others have elaborate contrapuntal settings similar in character to *Laudate pueri* and *Lauda Jerusalem*.

INTERPRETATION OF TEXT

By 1610, Monteverdi was well known for powerfully affective musical interpretations of his texts. Already in 1605 and 1607 his brother, Giulio Cesare, had
defended Claudio's madrigals, some dating from even before the turn of the
century, against the attacks of the conservative theorist Artusi on the grounds
that the words had become 'the mistress of the harmony'.[22] Arianna's role in the
opera of that name had been sung in 1608 by an actress, and the famous lament
was reported to have moved all of the women in the audience to tears.[23] Yet in
the psalms of the 1610 Vespers, musical interpretation of the texts seems to have
been of limited interest to Monteverdi. The reasons are not difficult to fathom.
The repetition of the psalm tone for every verse and the large-scale structural
organizations based on the psalm tone often left little room for interpretation of
individual words and phrases of text. Moreover, the limitations on harmonic
language imposed by the reciting note and the tonal coherence of the chant
prohibit the kind of affective chromatic writing found in Monteverdi's secular
output as far back as a few madrigals from the Second and Third Books and
much more prominently in the Fourth and Fifth Books.

Nevertheless, there are passages in the psalms where the texture, the rhythm,
or the harmonic colouring is unquestionably a product of the semantics of
the text. Mention has already been made of a passage in *Laudate pueri* where the
psalm tone successively rises from a tenor voice (quintus) to the altus, the
cantus, and the sextus (another cantus voice) as the text first sings man's praise of
God and then exalts God above all nations, heaven, and earth. Also cited earlier
were the repetition of the music of the first verse of *Nisi Dominus* at the *Sicut erat
in principio* of the doxology and the close resemblance between the *Sicut erat* and
the opening verse in *Laudate pueri*. Such references to the opening verse in the
Sicut erat were already common in the sixteenth century.

Among the most frequent means for emphasizing particular words in both
secular and sacred music of the sixteenth and seventeenth centuries are melismas. In the psalms of the Vespers, words such as *aeternam* (*Dixit Dominus*),
Domine, *Excelsus*, *caelos*, and *gloria* (*Laudate pueri*) are all set to melismas of various lengths. At *Excelsus super omnes gentes Dominus* in *Laudate pueri*, the melisma

---

[22] From the preface to the Fifth Book of Madrigals. See Oliver Strunk, *Source Readings in Music
History* (New York: W. W. Norton & Company, Inc., 1950), 407.
[23] For the account of the court chronicler, Federico Follino, of the performance see Paolo Fabbri,
Monteverdi (Turin: E.D.T. Edizioni, 1985), 133–8.

rises directly through an octave, the voices remaining at the higher register to the end of the half-verse. Similarly, in the same psalm, *in altis* generates an energetic rising melisma, *et humilia* is set to a slow, very simple descending scale, and *respicit in caelo et in terra?* (who cares for heaven and earth?) entails an energetic sequential rise to *caelo* and a melismatic tumbling in dotted rhythms at *in terra*. Not all melismas are necessarily the product of text interpretation, however. In *Laetatus sum*, the most extensive melismas are reserved for the adverb *illuc* (there) and the preposition *propter* (for the sake of). These melismas have nothing to do with the semantics of the words they set; rather they form a notable musical introduction to the two verses to which they belong, perhaps reflecting by their multitude of notes the tribes of the Lord (*tribus Domini*) and the brothers and friends (*fratres meos et proximos meos*) of their respective verses. More obviously, the entire phrase *illuc enim ascenderunt tribus, tribus Domini* (there the tribes went up, the tribes of the Lord) reflects the multiplicity of ascending tribes in the gradual accumulation of voices through the half-verse. These tribes unite in a homophonic and largely homorhythmic texture in bearing witness (*ascenderunt tribus Domini: testimonium Israel*). As the verse continues, the phrase *ad confitendum nomini Domini* (to acknowledge the name of the Lord) is emphasized through copious imitative repetitions.

Solid, chordal textures are used several times in the psalms to convey a sense of stability or stasis. The second half of the first verse of *Dixit Dominus*, *sede a dextris meis* (sit at my right hand) is set homophonically in six voices, creating a firm, stable texture for the Lord's command *sede*. The conclusion of this chordal passage suggests the awe and mystery of Him (Christ, according to an early seventeenth-century exegete)[24] who sits at the right hand of God by means of the juxtaposition of the E major dominant of A, with its G♯, against a short-lived full cadence in C, with its G♮. In *Laudate pueri*, the placement of the poor among princes, *Ut collocet eum cum principibus, cum principibus populi sui* (giving them a place among princes, among the princes of his people), similarly results in a homophonic texture in slow notes, reflecting the new-found dignity of the poor. The change of condition is also highlighted at the beginning of the verse by movement from C major to an unusual half-cadence on an E major triad, the radical harmonic shift signalling the radical change in state of the *pauperem*.

Among the most striking treatments of words in the five psalms is a passage in *Laudate pueri*: *Suscitans à terra inopem, et de stercore erigens pauperem* (who lifts the weak out of the dust and raises the poor from the rubbish heap). The act of raising up the poor (*suscitans* and *erigens*) is expressed through two sets of energetically rising sequences in triple metre that stand out conspicuously from the rest

---

[24] According to Gerard Génébrand (1607), 'Christum ad Patris dexteram sessurum . . .'. See Helmut Hucke, 'Die fälschlich so genannte "Marien"-Vesper von Claudio Monteverdi', *Bericht über den internationalen Musikwissenschaftlichen Kongress Bayreuth 1981* (Kassel: Bärenreiter, 1984), 301.

of the psalm. Shortly thereafter, the joyful mother described in the text *Qui habitare facit sterilem in domo, matrem filiorum laetantem* (who makes the woman in a childless house a happy mother of children) is represented by a dance-like motif in triple metre, treated both imitatively and sequentially. The livelier pace of triple metre is associated in *Nisi Dominus* with the texts *Sicut sigittae in manu potentis ita filii excussorum* (like arrows in the hand of a warrior are the sons of one's youth) and *Beatus vir* (happy is the man). In the second half of this latter verse, the phrase *non confundetur* (he shall not be confounded) is stressed by insistent text repetition and constantly reiterated cadences.

The antiphonal organization and continuous cantus firmus in *Nisi Dominus* and *Lauda Jerusalem* preclude significant musical interpretation of individual words and phrases of the text. In *Lauda Jerusalem*, one can only point to the opening acclamation on the word *Lauda* and the generally festive character of the setting. In these psalms Monteverdi's approach to his texts is objective, concentrating simply on declamation of the psalm verses in rhythmic patterns that accord with the natural accentuation of the words.

7

Compositions Based on a Cantus Firmus:
The Magnificats

⟨⟨❈⟩⟩

THE two Magnificats, printed one after the other in Monteverdi's 1610 publication, deserve separate examination not only because of their unique character *vis-à-vis* the five psalms, but also because of their close relationship to one another. In addition to the cantus firmus and its contexts, cadence types, harmonic language, texture, style, and interpretation of texts, this chapter will explore the relationship between the two canticles. 'Parody' is an appropriate term to describe this relationship, for ten of the twelve verses exhibit similarities, in some instances very close parallels, between the two settings. Much of this chapter will be devoted to a comparison between the individual verses of the two Magnificats, whereby the varying contexts of the cantus firmus in style and texture will also be revealed. Through this process, the reader can observe both Monteverdi's parody technique, as he adapts the setting of the same verse from one Magnificat to the other, and his variation technique, as he resets the same chant in the successive verses of each canticle. Such comparisons not only offer insight into the relationship between Monteverdi's parody and variation techniques; they also offer a fascinating glimpse into the composer's workshop in showing how he takes the material of one setting and recomposes it for the other. These comparisons demonstrate unequivocally that one Magnificat served as prototype for the other, but which one? While this question cannot be answered definitively, I will argue that the second Magnificat in the order of the 1610 print, the setting *a 6*, served as the source for the version *a 7* with instruments.

THE CANTUS FIRMUS

The principal difference between the two Magnificats is in their scoring: the first is for seven voices and six obbligato instruments, while the second is for six voices with no instruments beyond the organ accompaniment. In both canticles Monteverdi has provided registration rubrics for the organist as well as occasional rubrics regarding tempo (see Chapters 13 and 20). The Magnificat tone for both settings is 1d, transposed up a fourth in *cantus mollis* with reciting note D and *finalis* G. However, Monteverdi also frequently presents the tone at its untransposed level, a fourth lower, with reciting note A and *finalis* D, but still in *cantus mollis*.[1] These two levels tend to alternate from one verse to the next, but not consistently. In both Magnificats the transposed version is more common, and as in the psalms, transposition of the cantus firmus enlarges the available harmonic palette. Moreover, because the plainchant always includes its intonation, and is sung in relatively long note values, there is room for greater variety in harmonizing a single statement of the cantus firmus than is often the case in the psalms. Indeed, the bass-lines harmonizing parallel passages of the chant in successive verses of each canticle are remarkably diverse. But despite such variety, certain similarities in the basses of different verses do exist. Virtuoso duets, for example, all tend to be supported by slow-moving, strongly cadential basses, and basses comprising ascending and descending scale patterns are also common.

Also distinguishing the Magnificats from the psalms is the clear separation of the verses of the former into distinct, closed compositions, each with a complete statement of the Magnificat tone and featuring its own style and texture. The cantus firmus appears variously in the cantus, sextus, altus, tenor, and quintus (second tenor) voices, but most often in the altus. The styles and textures of the successive verses encompass simple continuo harmonization of the chant with organ or instrumental ritornellos, virtuoso duets for pairs of voices in a single register, antiphonal polyphonic trios, antiphonal dialogues, virtuoso echo pieces, a full-voiced, melismatic imitative texture (reminiscent of the *Gloria Patri* of *Laetatus sum* and the *Amen* of *Laudate pueri*), and full-voiced chordal harmonization of the Magnificat tone. Further enlivening the variety of styles and textures is the extensive use of obbligato instruments in many verses of the Magnificat *a 7*.

CADENCES

Following the structure of the Magnificat tone, each verse except for the *Sicut erat* comes to some kind of cadence or hiatus in the middle, though these articulations sometimes amount to no more than a half-cadence, a fleeting full cadence, or a shift in texture. Both versions of the final verse of the doxology exhibit so much overlap in the part-writing, however, that there is no definable break at the mediant.

---

[1] Both Magnificats are notated in the high clefs (*chiavette*), almost certainly indicating downward transposition in performance. The typical early 17th-century transposition of music in this notation down a fourth would bring the Magnificat tone right back to its untransposed position on D in *cantus durus*. See the discussion of this issue in Ch. 17.

There is only one final cadence type in the Magnificats: a cadence in which the cantus firmus descends by step to the final while another voice approaches it by a *subsemitonium* and the bass leaps to the final from the fifth degree (in modern terms, a perfect V–I cadence). Mediant cadences, however, are more diverse. Some complete a perfect cadence at the psalm tone mediant, while others consist of interrupted cadences, resolving only at the beginning of the second half of the verse. The mediants of *Quia fecit* from the Magnificat *a 6* and the *Et misericordia* from the Magnificat *a 7* (parallel settings, as described below) as well as that of the *Deposuit* from the larger canticle comprise incomplete cadences to D, with the chant reaching its mediant from below by full step while the bass descends a half-step (from the lowered sixth) to the fifth degree. In the *Quia respexit* of the Magnificat *a 7* a similar mediant cadence is prepared, but resolved unexpectedly in the bass by leap from eb to Bb to allow for continuation of the two trombone parts as an instrumental interlude. Sometimes the mediant of the chant is overlapped by other voices, despite 5–1 bass motion, creating more continuity between the two halves of the verse. In both *Esurientes* settings, the two voices are unaccompanied, even by the bassus generalis, and the Magnificat tone mediant is simply approached in parallel thirds by the second voice.

HARMONIC LANGUAGE

Despite the nearly unremitting presence of the cantus firmus in the two Magnificats, the intonation at the beginning of each verse and the slow movement of the chant permit bass patterns and harmonic motion that are found less frequently in the psalms. For example, extended scale motion appears only sporadically in the psalms, but is more common in the Magnificats (see Ex. 7.1). Similarly, bass sequences are infrequent in the psalms but occur often in the canticles. Many sequences proceed by step, outlining a scale pattern at each stage. (see Ex. 7.2). Transpositions of bass patterns by a fourth or fifth are also more frequent in the Magnificats than in the psalms (see Ex. 7.3).

The most significant distinction between the bass patterns in the psalms and in the Magnificats is the frequent use of repetitive leaps of a fourth or fifth in the latter, often resulting in repetitive cadential progressions. The bass of *Et exsultavit* from the Magnificat *a 6* is a case in point (see Ex. 7.7a below). At the outset, the 5–1 motion in the bass is not accompanied by cadential movement in the voices, nor does the chord on the fifth degree contain a major third. However, from bar 42 onwards, the tonal focus shifts to D, and the raised seventh degree appears regularly in Monteverdi's notation (with the exception of bars 48, 62, and 67). Consequently, the successions of chords in this passage have

Ex. 7.1. Magnificats, basso continuo parts: *a* Magnificat *a* 6, bars 25–30, *Magnificat*; *b* Magnificat *a* 6, bars 73–7, *Quia respexit*; *c* Magnificat *a* 6, bars 425–30, *Sicut locutus est*; *d* Magnificat *a* 6, bars 450–4, *Gloria Patri*; *e* Magnificat *a* 7, bars 330–8, *Suscepit Israel*

Ex. 7.2. Magnificats, basso continuo parts: *a* Magnificat *a* 6, bars 115–21, *Quia respexit*; *b* Magnificat *a* 6, bars 218–21, *Fecit potentiam*; *c* Magnificat *a* 6, bars 285–8, *Esurientes*; *d* Magnificat *a* 6, bars 439–43, *Gloria Patri*; *e* Magnificat *a* 7, bars 385–9, *Sicut locutus est*

(a)

(b)
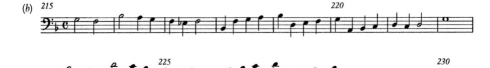

(c)

(d)

(e)

Ex. 7.3. Magnificats, basso continuo parts: *a* Magnificat *a 6*, bars 124–39, *Quia fecit*; *b* Magnificat *a 6*, bars 215–30, *Fecit potentiam*; *c* Magnificat *a 6*, bars 401–6, *Sicut locutus est*; *d* Magnificat *a 7*, bars 208–24, *Fecit potentiam*; *e* Magnificat *a 7*, bars 370–7, *Sicut locutus est*

for the most part the character of functional, tonal progressions. Similar patterns appear in several other verses (Magnificat *a 6*: *Et misericordia*; Magnificat *a 7*: *Et exsultavit*, *Quia fecit*, *Suscepit Israel*).

Other basses also have a strongly cadential orientation. The opening phrase of *Fecit potentiam* from the Magnificat *a 6*, after beginning on a G minor triad, makes a typical shift to a B♭ major tonal focus (strengthened by 5–1 bass motion), and concludes with a return to G minor, effected by a perfect cadence (see Ex. 7.4). The continuation (bars 223–30) transposes the entire first phrase up a fifth, establishing an alternative set of tonal focuses. The third phrase (bars 231–9)

Ex. 7.4. Magnificat *a* 6, *Fecit potentiam*

Ex. 7.4. *Continued*

strongly affirms F as the tonal focus of its mid-point, through a V–I cadential progression, then shifts to D minor with another V–I progression overlapping the begining of the next phrase and the second half of the Magnificat tone. D minor is prolonged in bars 239–42, but from that point onwards, the bass is mostly stepwise and far less cadential in orientation until the final V–I cadence to D. The change in character of the bass motion may well be related to the text, the first part of which describes strong action (He has shown the might of his arm; he has scattered the proud), while the concluding phrase consitutes a far more abstract concept (in the imagination of their hearts).

Despite the example of *Fecit potentiam* from the Magnificat *a 6*, harmonic shifts between G minor and B♭ major and between F major and D minor, encountered with some frequency in the psalms, are less common in the Magnificats. Moreover, when such shifts do occur in the canticles, the new harmony is more often approached by a full cadence, rather than a mere chord shift (see Ex. 7.5).

The strongly cadential directions of many bass-lines in the Magnificats, exemplified by the *Et exsultavit* and *Fecit potentiam* settings in both canticles, tend towards functional progressions and functional tonality, but often reveal roots in older, modally based harmony through the retention of modal seventh degrees until the arrival of the cadence, through non-hierarchical shifts of tonal focus (as in *Fecit potentiam* from the Magnificat *a 6*), and through the absence of a central, unifying tonality with which a verse could begin and could be anticipated to end (again as in *Fecit potentiam* from the Magnificat *a 6*). A simple but characteristic example is provided by the role of the seventh degree in D *cantus mollis* in the second half of this same *Fecit potentiam* (beginning with the cadence to D in bars 238–9). When the seventh degree is C♯, the pitch prepares a perfect

Ex. 7.5. Magnificat *a 7*, *Fecit potentiam*, bars 208–15

cadence in D, but where it is C♮, whether part of a C major, A minor, or F major triad (all three appear), the pitch and its harmony imply a modal orientation. By the criteria that Carl Dahlhaus uses to define functional chord progressions and tonality (see Chapter 5), such passages in the Magnificats do not qualify, but the tendency in that direction is clear. In the intermingling of modally oriented basses and part-writing on the one hand and cadentially oriented progressions on the other that characterizes so much of Monteverdi's music, the Magnificats display an approximate balance between the two. Some passages and verses are quite modal in character, while others, as we have seen, are highly cadential. Yet many passages represent a mixture of both, and one of the characteristics of Monteverdi's compositional style is the frequent oscillation between these older and more progressive vocabularies, often making clear definitions of harmonic style or the nature of tonal direction and tonal focus difficult, if not impossible. It is precisely this ambiguity that gives Monteverdi's harmonic language its distinctive flavour.

RELATIONSHIPS BETWEEN THE TWO MAGNIFICATS

General similarities have been noted in the past between the two Magnificats of the Vespers.[2] Of the twelve verses of the canticle (including the doxology), ten are parallel in some fashion between Monteverdi's two settings. While it is not possible to determine with certainty which Magnificat served as the framework or basis for the other, analysis strongly suggests that the smaller six-voice setting served as a prototype for the larger one with instruments.

The character of the parallels between the two canticles varies from one verse to the next. The polyphonic treatment of the opening word, *Magnificat* (prizes the greatness), based on imitations of the cantus firmus, is very similar in both: the basses of both versions, for instance, have identical pitches; only the rhythms differ slightly. The gradual increase to a full texture in both settings (though more complicated in the Magnificat *a 7*) is clearly associated with the meaning of the word *Magnificat*.

The continuation of the opening verse with *anima mea Dominum* likewise proceeds in parallel settings (see Ex. 7.6). The Magnificat *a 6* presents first a solo soprano in the descending fifth *d″–g′*, then repeats the passage in parallel thirds with a second soprano, generating the same number of bars for the second half of the verse as in the first. Since the larger Magnificat uses only a single soprano, the passage is only half as long, resulting in unbalanced lengths for the two half-verses (see the structural outlines in Appendix C). There are also some important differences between the two canticles in the bass-lines in this passage. Where the bass unfolds in long sweeping scale patterns in the setting *a 6* (Ex. 7.6*a*), it is tightened into shorter motivic units involving frequent sequences in the Magnificat *a 7* (Ex. 7.6*b*).

A different kind of relationship obtains between the two settings of *Et exsultavit*. Both versions place the Magnificat tone, transposed down a fourth in the altus, and both feature a virtuoso tenor duet against the long-note cantus firmus, the highly florid style obviously engendered by the theme of exaltation (see Ex. 7.7). In both settings the initial motif is reiterated a fifth higher. Even though the Magnificat *a 6* is in triple metre and the Magnificat *a 7* in duple time, the basses have nearly identical pitches through *in Deo*. But after that point the smaller

[2] Only Wolfgang Osthoff has called attention to the depth of these similarities. See Osthoff, 'Unità liturgica e artistica nei *Vespri* del 1610', *Rivista italiana di musicologia*, 2 (1967), 323 n. 18. The most extensive study of the Magnificats previously published is in Adam Adrio, *Die Anfänge des geistlichen Konzerts* (Berlin: Junker und Dünnhaupt Verlag, 1935), 57–68. Adrio describes some striking resemblances between the two Magnificats but attributes them to Monteverdi's representation of the text: *dass der gegebene Text eine bestimmte klangliche Vorstellung des Komponisten hervorgerufen habe* . . . (p. 64). Hans F. Redlich briefly notes the relationship in *Claudio Monteverdi: Leben und Werk* (Olten: Verlag Otto Walter, 1949), 146, and describes the Magnificat *a 6* as a 'simplified "pocket edition" of the preceding large Magnificat' in the English edition of this book, *Claudio Monteverdi: Life and Works*, trans. Kathleen Dale (London: Oxford University Press, 1952), 129.

Ex. 7.6. *Anima mea*: *a* Magnificat *a* 6, bars 17–32; *b* Magnificat *a* 7, bars 15–24

(a)

Ex. 7.7. *Et exsultavit: a* Magnificat *a 6; b* Magnificat *a 7*

Ex. 7.7. *Continued*

Magnificat continues and ends with harmonization of the psalm tone principally on D, while the harmonization in the larger Magnificat deviates from D
towards F and an eventual conclusion on G. In both versions, there is a shift from
the flat side to the sharp side in the harmonization as the spirit exults in the Lord.

Interestingly, the tenor parts of the two settings diverge before the bass-lines
do. The paired tenors begin quite similarly, though the melisma of the
Magnificat *a 6* expands to a sixth in contrast to the fifth of the Magnificat *a 7*.
The sequential repetition beginning at the second *et exsultavit* follows the same

Ex. 7.7. *Continued*

pattern in both pieces, but the conclusion of the phrase with *spiritus meus* is different. In the Magnificat *a 7* the text is repeated, the tenors participate in imitative voice-exchange, and there is more complex rhythmic interaction between the voices. After the cadence the vocal parts diverge significantly, even though the bass-lines remain the same. The large Magnificat treats the words *in Deo* with shorter melismatic patterns, which imitate one another at briefer time

Ex. 7.7. *Continued*

intervals (resulting in parallel thirds). These melismatic figures do not have much in common with those of the Magnificat *a* 6. As described above, the harmony changes in the midst of this passage, and *salutari meo* receives more extended and more complex melismatic treatment in the Magnificat *a* 7, introducing imitation near the end, while the Magnificat *a* 6 is restricted exclusively to parallel thirds. Thus the similar openings of the two verses gradually give way to greater and greater divergence until only the general character of both settings remains the same at the end, the two versions even concluding on different triads. As with the setting of the word *Magnificat* in verse 1, the setting of verse 2 of the Magnificat *a 7* is more complicated and sophisticated than that in the smaller canticle. Once again the Magnificat *a 6* reveals an exactly even division of the verse while the larger Magnificat is unbalanced.

We encounter yet another type of relationship in the next verse, *Quia respexit*. In both settings the plainchant is in the tenor, having returned to its original reciting pitch class D, but the obbligato instruments of the Magnificat *a 7* constitute an obvious distinction between the two versions. Nevertheless, both are constructed on the same pattern, consisting of an introductory ritornello in triple metre followed by the unadorned solo psalm tone in duple time, and completed by the return of the triple-metre ritornello accompanying the concluding words, *omnes generationes* (all generations). The organ ritornello of the Magnificat *a 6* shares little with the instrumental ritornello of the larger setting aside from its structural position, metre, and the use of scale patterns in the bass; the two ritornellos even begin with different harmonizations (G minor and D minor respectively), though both verses conclude with a complete cadence to G. The ritornello in the Magnificat *a 6* has unpredictable scale motion in the bass, since there is no hint at a cadence before the chant enters and no way of knowing just when the bass will change direction or assume a different pattern. The ritornello bass in the Magnificat *a 7*, however, while similarly scale-derived, divides into two equal phrases, each cadencing on the same note with which it began. The second phrase is merely a transposition down a fifth of the first. Consequently, the ritornello in the Magnificat *a 7* appears more carefully organized with clearer cadential goals than its counterpart, suggesting, as with *anima mea*, that the Magnificat *a 6* was the antecedent version.

During the verse, where the two settings have the same chant, there are both similarities and significant differences in the bass-lines. At first the basses are identical, but the subsequent successive entrances of paired *pifare*, trombones, and recorders in the Magnificat *a 7*, which result in a sizeable pause between the two halves of the verse, are accompanied by displacements in the harmony in comparison to the Magnificat *a 6*. Corresponding passages between the two settings are still similar, but these passages no longer occur in exactly the same place (see Ex. 7.8).[3] These differences in the bass-lines underlying the plainchant again suggest that the Magnificat without instruments served as the prototype for the Magnificat *a 7*, since several of the differences in the latter were necessitated by the introduction of the obbligato instruments and the corresponding

---

[3] In bars 72–4 of Ex. 7.8*b* the cadence in the bass is extended in comparison with bars 90–1 in Ex. 7.8*a*, giving the *pifare* a brief opportunity to sound alone during the pause in the cantus firmus. Also compare bars 84–9 of Ex. 7.8*b* with 102–7 of Ex. 7.8*a*.

Ex. 7.8. *Quia respexit*: *a* Magnificat *a* 6, bars 85–110; *b* Magnificat *a* 7, bars 67–100

lengthening of the note values of the plainchant.[4] By contrast with the florid melismatic settings of *Et exsultavit*, the confinement of *Quia fecit* to plainchant with organ or instrumental ritornellos reflects an opposite affect, the low estate of the servant described in this verse.

The parallels between the two Magnificats in their first three verses yield to a reversal of styles and performing forces in the next two segments. In the Magnificat *a* 6, verse 4, *Quia fecit*, is set for six voices *in Dialogo*, that is, in alternating groups of three voices. The two trios contrast in sonority, one comprising the three high voices with the plainchant in the topmost part, and the other the three low voices, likewise with the plainchant in the topmost part.

The alternating trios divide the first half-verse into two segments, the first featuring the high trio with reciting note *d″* and the second with the same music transposed down a fourth with reciting note *a*. The shorter second half of the verse is not subdivided, but rather stated three times: (1) in the low trio with reciting note *a*, (2) in the high trio with reciting note *d″*, and (3) homophonically combining both trios with reciting note *d″* so that the bass can cadence in G, as the verse opened. The alternations between high and low trios throughout *Quia fecit* permit the Magnificat tone eventually to appear complete at both

---

[4] See e.g. the interpolations and displacement of the bass in relation to the text in bars 75–81 of the larger Magnificat in comparison with bars 92–7 of the smaller setting.

(b)

Ex. 7.8. *Continued*

Ex. 7.8. *Continued*

the *d″* and *a* reciting levels. Since the general stylistic character of the trios resembles late sixteenth-century polyphony, the setting has a decidedly conservative flavour despite its modern rubric *in Dialogo*. In fact, the rubric designates
nothing more than the old-fashioned *cori spezzati* technique.

This conservative *Quia fecit* is followed in the Magnificat *a 6* by *Et misericordia*
set as a modern imitative duet for two virtuoso sopranos in dotted rhythms concerted against the Magnificat tone in the tenor. In the first half of the verse, the
imitation between the two sopranos is at the time interval of only one bar, but
in the second half, whose text is much shorter, the cantus has a lengthy virtuoso
solo before being joined by the sextus in canonic imitation. As a result, the
second half of the verse, with far less text, is actually several bars longer than the
first half. The jerky dotted rhythms of the exceptionally long melismas setting
timentibus eum (towards those who fear him) are an obvious metaphor for fearful
trembling.

In the Magnificat *a 7* the styles of these two verses are inverted (see the discussion at the end of this chapter for a rationale for this). Here the *Quia fecit* is
the virtuoso duet in dotted rhythms, set for two basses with the alto carrying the
cantus firmus, and the *Et misericordia* is the polyphonic dialogue in six parts. The
Quia fecit employs obbligato instruments in addition to the voices and resembles

the *Et misericordia* of the Magnificat *a 6* only in general character and overall structural outline: both pieces begin imitatively with melismas in dotted rhythms, reach a cadence in declamatory, chordal style, continue with only one of the duet parts (the small Magnificat also has the cantus firmus at this point), and then restore the voice-pairing until the end. On the other hand, the chant is at a different level, with reciting note *a'* instead of the *d'* of the smaller Magnificat's *Et misericordia*.

The obbligato violins of the larger Magnificat's *Quia fecit* serve to expand the sonority as well as to continue the dotted rhythms originating in the voices while the voices themselves momentarily sing in declamatory style or sustained chords. In the second half of the verse, the rapid violin scale passages are reminiscent of the ritornellos in the aria *Possente spirto* from *L'Orfeo*. The strongly accented dotted rhythms of this version of *Quia fecit* (for the Mighty God has done great things for me) seem more appropriate to the text than the more languid, conservative setting of the Magnificat *a 6*. Towards the middle of the verse, at *fecit mihi magna*, the two basses leave off their virtuoso melismas to sing a boldly declamatory motif in repetitive imitation, rising a third to sustained minims on the highest notes of the setting. This climax is followed by a series of solemn semibreve chords in the three voices on the words *qui potens est*. All the while, the violins continue their rapid echo exchanges in dotted rhythms, carrying forward the sense of energy deriving from the beginning of the text. Similarly, in the second half of the verse, the vocal duet slows to mostly semibreves and minims in chordal style for the words *nomen eius* (his name), while the violins continue their even more rapid flourishes and exchanges.

Why Monteverdi calls for a pair of basses in the Magnificat *a 7* and a pair of sopranos in the corresponding verse of the small Magnificat is not completely clear, though the *Quia fecit* is the only bass duet in the large Magnificat while there are none in the Magnificat *a 6*. The Magnificat *a 7*, therefore, has a more even balance among duets in various registers. The four verses based on equal-voiced duets proceed from tenors (*Et exsultavit*) to basses (*Quia fecit*), to sopranos (*Suscepit Israel*), and back to tenors (*Gloria Patri*), while in the Magnificat *a 6* the duets are for tenors (*Et exsultavit*), sopranos (*Et misericordia*), sopranos (*Fecit potentiam*), sopranos (*Deposuit*), and soprano and bass or tenor (*Sicut locutus est*). Moreover, the successive verses *Esurientes* and *Suscepit Israel* in this Magnificat both present the plainchant as a duet in parallel thirds, the *Esurientes* for alto and tenor, the *Suscepit* for sopranos.

In the Magnificat *a 7* the duets are symmetrically placed in the second and fourth verses (tenors, then basses) and the ninth and eleventh verses (sopranos, then tenors). The Magnificat *a 6*, by contrast, has several successive duets bunched in the middle verses, all for sopranos except for the *Esurientes*. In utilizing instruments in the Magnificat *a 7*, Monteverdi has relied less frequently on vocal duets, has spread them more evenly among the vocal registers, and has placed them carefully in the overall structure of the composition. Once again, the implication is that the Magnificat *a 7* is the later version.

Not only are the types of settings reversed between *Quia fecit* and *Et misericordia* in the two Magnificats, but in the six-voice dialogues, the positions of the trios are exchanged as well. The high trio comes first in the Magnificat *a 6*, but the low trio does so in the Magnificat *a 7*. Similarly, while the high trio initiates the *Quia fecit* of the smaller Magnificat with reciting note *d''*, the *Et misericordia* of the larger Magnificat begins with reciting note *a*.[5] As in the smaller Magnificat, the alternating trios permit complete presentation of the Magnificat tone on both reciting notes.

Despite the close parallels in style and structure between the *Quia fecit* of the Magnificat *a 6* and the *Et misericordia* of the Magnificat *a 7*, there are only rare correspondences between the two settings in the vocal and continuo parts themselves: occasional similarities in the individual voices and the bass-lines are observable when comparing one trio with its counterpart in the other

Ex. 7.9. *a* Magnificat *a 6*, *Quia fecit*, bars 124–32; *b* Magnificat *a 7*, *Et misericordia*, bars 160–71

[5] The text is divided somewhat differently from the *Quia fecit* of the smaller Magnificat: the beginning of the first half-verse, *Et misericordia eius*, is sung by the low trio, and the text is echoed by the high trio with the reciting note transposed up a fourth to *d''* (bars 160–71). The low trio then continues with *a progenies* with reciting note *a* (bars 171–9), and the high trio responds with the same text and music transposed up a fourth (bars 179–88). As a result of this more symmetrical arrangement, the high trio is able to imitate precisely the low trio at a fourth above throughout the half-verse. This regular alternation thus permits a regular alternation between D minor as the opening harmony for the low trio and G minor for the high trio. At the end of the half-verse the high trio repeats the last two words of text in order to modulate from the cadential G to D to prepare the second half of the verse, which begins on D minor (bars 189–91). The second half of the verse, with a much shorter text than the first half, is consequently treated in a briefer fashion than the second half of the *Quia fecit* of the smaller Magnificat. The words *timentibus eum* begin in the low trio with reciting note *a* (bars 191–9), and then both trios combine to repeat the text with reciting note *d''* (bars 199–207). The second half of the verse thus begins on D minor and concludes on G.

(b)

Ex. 7.9. *Continued*

Magnificat (see Ex. 7.9). While the concepts and structures of the two *Quia fecit–Et misericordia* pairs are mirror images of each other, the details differ considerably, and the parallel verses are not so closely related to one another as some of the other verses described elsewhere in this chapter.

In the succeeding verses intriguing parallels again emerge between the two canticles. Verse 6, *Fecit potentiam*, features the cantus and sextus in a modest vocal style in the Magnificat *a* 6, the altus intoning the transposed cantus firmus with reciting note *a'* (see Ex. 7.4). The bass supporting this trio texture consists of patterns repeated sequentially a fifth higher or fourth lower, and can be characterized, for frequent stretches, as a walking bass in even crotchets (see the discussion of this bass under 'Harmonic Language' above).

At first sight this setting would appear to bear little relation to the other *Fecit potentiam*, which is for three string instruments and cantus firmus. Moreover, the rendering in the Magnificat *a* 7 is in triple metre while that in the Magnificat *a* 6 is in duple time. As in the *Quia respexit* settings, the version with obbligato instruments is a more extended piece. But once again the bass-lines reveal a relationship, with substantial portions of the Magnificat *a* 7 parallel to passages

Ex. 7.10. *Fecit potentiam*, bass-lines

of the Magnificat *a 6*. This is illustrated in Ex. 7.10, which distributes the bass
from the larger Magnificat below that of the smaller one.

Once it is observed that the lowest of the three instruments in the Magnificat
a 7 merely doubles the continuo part, it becomes evident that the two violins
play an analogous role to the two sopranos from the Magnificat *a 6*. The violin
parts are entirely different from the vocal lines, but they serve the same function
in relation to the plainchant in the altus. The structure of the two settings is also
parallel at their openings. The Magnificat *a 7* version commences with the ritornello alone, analogous to the solo continuo opening of the Magnificat *a 6*.
This ritornello is then transposed up a fifth in anticipation of the entrance of the
Magnificat tone, just as the organ bass is in the Magnificat *a 6*.

A similar substitution of instruments for voices is manifest in the two *Deposuits*.
The Magnificat *a 6* again employs paired sopranos against the cantus firmus,
which this time appears in the tenor voice with reciting note *d'*. The sopranos
engage in virtuoso ornamentation, alternating with one another over the continuous cantus firmus *in echo*, according to Monteverdi's rubric (see Ex. 7.11*a*).

Ex. 7.11. *Deposuit: a* Magnificat *a 6*, bars 259–65; *b* Magnificat *a 7*, bars 253–7

Ex. 7.11. *Continued*

The melismas on *Deposuit* (he has brought down) and *de sede* (from their thrones) appropriately descend, just as the figures for *potentes* (the mighty) and *exaltavit* (raised on high) ascend (though the latter eventually descends). The musical interpretation of the word *potentes* is independent of its meaning in context, since the half-verse *Deposuit potentes de sede* speaks of the putting down of the mighty. This is an example of Monteverdi creating a musical metaphor for an individual word that is actually opposed to the significance of that word in its complete phrase or sentence. The first half of the verse, with its emphasis on *deposuit*, consistently adds eb'', generating harmony (C minor) further to the flat side in the transposed soft hexachord, but the second half-verse, emphasizing *exaltavit*, does not use eb'', except as possible *musica ficta* when the *exaltavit* melismas turn downwards towards the final cadence.

This verse in the Magnificat *a 7* employs at first two cornettos and subsequently two violins instead of the sopranos of the Magnificat *a 6*, but features the instruments in echo, similar to the treatment of the voices (see Ex. 7.11*b*). Close parallels in the upper parts may be seen in comparing *a* and *b*, though Monteverdi does not pursue such parallels systematically. The instrumental parts of the Magnificat *a 7* are even more florid than the virtuoso vocal parts of the Magnificat *a 6*, and once again are reminiscent of the ritornellos of the aria

Ex. 7.12. *Deposuit* basses in relation to Magnificat tone

Ex. 7.12. *Continued*

Possente spirto from *L'Orfeo*. Moreover, the instruments ascend and descend according to their own patterns, the direction unrelated to words such as *Deposuit*, *de sede*, *potentes*, and *exaltavit* in the chant they accompany. On the other hand, the text-related shift away from the flatter side of the transposed soft hexachord at *et exaltavit* witnessed in the Magnificat *a 6* (where *et exaltavit* is repeated) is also evident in the larger canticle. The harmonic similarities and differences between the two settings are illustrated by a comparison of their basses, aligned according to their relationship with the Magnificat tone (see Ex. 7.12).

The two versions of *Esurientes* are another instance where an organ ritornello in the small Magnificat is paralleled by an instrumental ritornello in the larger one. The vocal parts of both settings consist simply of the plainchant duplicated in parallel thirds below, sung by altus and tenor in the Magnificat *a 6* and by the cantus and sextus in the Magnificat *a 7*. The Magnificat *a 6* maintains triple metre throughout, while the Magnificat *a 7* alternates between triple-metre ritornellos and chant in duple metre. The ritornellos themselves are quite different, but in both versions the verse appears without continuo accompaniment until near the end, apparently in response to the words *Esurientes* (the hungry) and *inanes* (empty).

The ritornello of the Magnificat *a 6* is to be improvised over the bass, the only part notated by Monteverdi. This bass consists of a five-bar pattern, alternating with the unaccompanied voices until near the end. It appears in both its original form and in transposed inversion (see Ex. 7.13).

Esurientes in the Magnificat *a 7* has an analogous structure in its alternation between a ritornello for three cornettos and viola and the unaccompanied chant (accompanied by the instruments at the end). Repetitions of the ritornello feature the bass transposed, but without inversion. As in several other parallel verses, the level of the Magnificat tone is different in the two settings (reciting note *a'* in the Magnificat *a 6*; *d''* in the Magnificat *a 7*), and the voices in the

Ex. 7.13. Magnificat *a* 6: *Esurientes*, bars 285–99, basso continuo

Magnificat *a* 7 present the complete half-verse rather than dividing the text into two segments as in the smaller Magnificat. In the second half of the verse (Magnificat *a* 7), at the last word (*inanes*, empty), Monteverdi ornaments the Magnificat tone with a descending third figure cast in descending imitative sequences, a mournful expression of the condition of the 'rich sent away empty'. This is the earliest example known to me of a conceit in interpreting this word that reappears in much more elaborate form in the Magnificat of J. S. Bach. Rather than end the verse with this affect, however, Monteverdi repeats the text, concluding with the simpler chant in parallel thirds accompanied by the ritornello. This conceit, absent from the Magnificat *a* 6, points to the greater sophistication of the larger Magnificat, as does the ritornello bass, which is once again more organized and directed than the simple sequence of the Magnificat *a* 6.

Although the two Magnificats have displayed rather close parallels in their first eight verses, the next verse, *Suscepit Israel*, is subjected to two completely different treatments. The small Magnificat, as mentioned earlier in the discussion of duets, follows the pattern of the preceding *Esurientes*. The unaccompanied cantus firmus is in parallel thirds again, this time in duple metre for two sopranos, and the organ performs a walking-bass ritornello (appearing in two different octaves, and once transposed down a third) that joins the voices only for the last two words of the text.

Suscepit Israel of the large Magnificat also employs two sopranos, but in a virtuoso duet in duple metre over a tenor cantus firmus. There is no ritornello structure, and the basso continuo of this version bears no relationship to the bass of the other. The cantus and sextus are in strict canonic imitation for most of the verse, suggesting a possible association with the text *Suscepit Israel puerum suum* (he has supported Israel, his servant), both in the use of the two high voices (*puerum*) and the canonic imitation of the sextus, which follows after and supports the leading cantus voice. The second half of the verse terminates the canon and slows for a more sustained homophonic style at the word *misericordiae* (mercy) with emphasis on a C minor triad, a tradition in the setting of this word dating at least as far back as Dufay's funeral motet

Ave regina coelorum.[6] Virtuoso style returns for the final cadence, and the cantus and sextus interact in alternation in a manner similar to the tenor and quintus duet at the conclusion of *Laudate pueri*. As suggested above, this soprano duet functions as a counterbalance in the overall structure of the canticle to the bass duet of *Quia fecit* and seems to have been specially composed for this purpose, which would explain its lack of reference to the *Suscepit Israel* of the Magnificat *a 6*.

With verse 10, *Sicut locutus est*, a relationship between Monteverdi's two settings emerges once again. As in *Fecit potentiam* and *Deposuit*, instruments appear in the large Magnificat where there are voices in the smaller one. The Magnificat *a 6* is set for five parts, with four of the voices arranged *in dialogo* between a soprano-bass pair (cantus and bassus) and a soprano-tenor pair (sextus and tenor), the latter echoing precisely the phrases of the former. It is evident that the dialogue technique was stimulated by the phrase *Sicut locutus est ad patres nostros* (as he spoke to our fathers).

The middle register is occupied by the alto voice intoning the Magnificat tone transposed down a fourth with reciting note a'. The version with instruments in the Magnificat *a 7* juxtaposes a pair of violins with a pair of cornettos (the organ bass is also doubled alternately by a viola and a trombone), but the cantus firmus is still in the alto voice with reciting note a', and there is a strong resemblance between the bass-lines of the two settings (see Ex. 7.14). An especially rapid exchange in the dialogue of the small Magnificat even finds a parallel in the instrumental dialogue of the other version (see Ex. 7.15). In this passage, too, a similarity between the two basses may be noted.

Ex. 7.14. *Sicut locutus est*, basses: *a* Magnificat *a 6*, bars 398–409; *b* Magnificat *a 7*, bars 364–75

[6] Ed. Heinrich Besseler in *Guillelmi Dufay: opera Omnia* (Rome: American Institute of Musicology, 1966), v. 124–30.

Ex. 7.15. *Sicut locutus est: a* Magnificat *a* 6, bars 420–3; *b* Magnificat *a* 7, bars 390–3

The vocal style in the Magnificat *a* 6 is modest, with short, unpretentious melismas at *locutus* (spoke) and *patres* (forefathers), and longer, more modern melismas in dotted rhythms at *Abraham* and *saecula* (for ever) in the second half of the verse. The instrumental pairs in the Magnificat *a* 7 are similarly in a modest style. In the first half-verse of the Magnificat *a* 6, the exchanges between pairs of voices reduce in time: the first and second exchanges are after three bars, then subsequent exchanges are at one bar's distance or a little more until the pairs join for the mediant cadence. Not only do these opening exchanges reveal a harmonic pattern in common with the *Et exsultavit* and *Fecit potentiam* of the same Magnificat, where the opening motif is likewise subsequently transposed up a fifth, but the thematic material itself is also closely related to *Fecit potentiam* (see Ex. 7.16).

In the second half of the verse, the time interval of the exchanges proceeds in reverse direction, commencing with one-bar intervals expanding to two and two-and-a-half bars, and shortening to two bars before the voices all join. In this second half-verse, the bass becomes a walking bass in crotchets, at times

Ex. 7.16. Magnificat *a* 6: *a* bars 215–22, *Fecit potentiam*; *b* bars 398–400, *Sicut locutus est*

repetitive in the manner of an ostinato. The gradually expanding scope of the descending scales in the bass is directly reflected in the vocal melismas, whose descents expand from a fourth to a sixth to a tenth.

In the first half-verse of the Magnificat *a 7*, the exchanges between pairs occur at regular two-bar intervals rather than the reducing intervals of the Magnificat *a 6*, and there is no transposition of the opening figure by a fifth. The bass motif of this figure, however, does later reappear as the top part of both instrumental groups. As in the Magnificat *a 6*, the second half of the verse has a walking bass in crotchets, but this time the scales ascend in sequential one-bar units around the circle of fifths, rather than descending in progressively longer groupings. The conclusion of the verse brings the two pairs of instruments together in descending imitative parallel thirds in a dotted rhythm familiar from *Dixit Dominus*, *Laudate pueri*, and *Nisi Dominus*.[7] In these two *Sicut locutus* settings, like earlier instances of bass scale patterns in parallel verses, the patterns in the Magnificat *a 7* are organized into clearer, more coherent groupings, again suggesting that the small Magnificat was reworked to create the larger one.

In the first verse of the doxology, the *Gloria Patri*, we encounter for only the second time an absence of parallel conceptions between the two Magnificats. Though both versions are highly melismatic, the smaller Magnificat employs the full six-voice chorus in an imitative texture based on the same dotted rhythm noted at the end of the preceding paragraph. In fact, the version used here is very closely related to two of the melismas concluding *falsibordoni* in *Dixit Dominus*.[8] The cantus and sextus of the *Gloria Patri* are identical to the sextus of the first of these *Dixit* melismas, and the *Gloria Patri* has the same bass transposed a fifth up (see Ex. 7.17). The sequence in all parts comprises a series of descending fourths, each one a step lower than the last.

This imitative texture, which functions as a vocal ritornello, is interrupted by the solo chant (quintus voice) presenting the verse, accompanied only by a walking bass. As in other verses with ritornellos in the Magnificats, the last few words (in repetition) are joined with the ritornello.

The *Gloria Patri* of the Magnificat *a 7*, by contrast, comprises another virtuoso duet, this time for two tenors, the second responding in echo to the first. The slow-moving Magnificat tone appears in the cantus voice. This duet symmetrically corresponds to the tenor duet *Et exsultavit* and exhibits the most virtuosic vocal writing found in either Magnificat. The solo tenor opens the verse with an extraordinarily long and florid flourish on the single word *Gloria*, as if to announce boldly the significance of its message.

Whereas the first half of the verse began with the solo tenor, the second half begins with the unadorned plainchant, the tenor and quintus only continuing

---

[7] See *Dixit*, bars 228–54; *Laudate*, bars 211–20; and *Nisi*, bars 1–8, 21–30, 176–83, and 196–205.
[8] See bars 154–7 and 200–4.

Ex. 7.17. *a* Magnificat *a* 6, bars 439–43, *Gloria Patri*; *b Dixit Dominus*, bars 154–8

their echo duet during a repetition of the text. In that respect, the structure of the second half of the verse bears a resemblance to the same portion of the *Gloria* in the Magnificat *a 6*. Where the word *et* serves as the basis of long melismas in the Magnificat *a 6* (and short melismas in the Magnificat *a 7*), in the duet version the first syllable of *sancto* is stretched out to the extraordinary length of seven bars through the constant echoing of short fragments between the two tenors.

In the final verse, the *Sicut erat*, the two Magnificats once again resemble each other closely. Both employ a full polyphonic texture with the cantus firmus in the top part. There are several passages where the bass-lines are similar, but the setting *a 7* is more extended, both in the verse itself and the concluding *Amen*. The larger Magnificat also calls for full instrumental doubling of the voices, forming a colourful, sumptuous conclusion to the entire composition as well as to the main portion of the Vesper service.[9]

In the Magnificat *a 6*, the setting consists of a slow homophonic harmonization of the Magnificat tone at its original level with the reciting note in canon and then in parallel thirds between the cantus and sextus. The reciting note is harmonized for the first eleven bars with a sustained G minor chord, constituting a kind of measured *falsobordone*. The final, brief *Amen* begins immediately at the end of the verse with imitative descents of a fifth, culminating in a plagal cadence to G. The *Amen* is related in thematic material and character not only to that of the Magnificat *a 7*, but also to the *Amen*s at the end of *Nisi Dominus* and *Lauda Jerusalem*.

The Magnificat *a 7* likewise features the Magnificat tone in canon between the cantus and sextus, but with a more rhythmically complicated and varied texture. The first nine bars are again harmonized with a sustained G minor chord, creating the same kind of measured *falsobordone* as in the Magnificat *a 6*. The *Amen* forms an extended, separate segment. The texture is imitative in short note values (dotted crotchets and quavers), like the *Amen* of *Laudate pueri*, and the motif is based on a perpetually descending scale, once displaced by an octave. The *Amen* is without cantus firmus and concludes with a plagal cadence to G very similar to that of the Magnificat *a 6*.

The variety and ingenuity displayed in Monteverdi's employment of similar structures, textures, and styles in the parallel verse settings of the two canticles are impressive. Although he has maintained basic similarities in ten of the twelve sections, each of the verses has been modified in a substantial manner. A comparative overview of the relationships between these ten pair of verses reveals that modifications of texture and structure are Monteverdi's principal means of adapting a setting from one Magnificat to the other. The parallel between pairs

---

[9] See Ch. 19 for further discussion of instrumental doubling in the Magnificat *a 7*.

of verses may be limited to the virtuoso duet texture, as in *Et misericordia* of the Magnificat *a 7* and *Quia fecit* of the Magnificat *a 6*, or to the dialogue technique for two three-voice ensembles, as in *Quia fecit* of the larger Magnificat and *Et misericordia* of the smaller one. Similarly, the structural combination of a ritornello juxtaposed to unaccompanied chant with a second voice in parallel thirds is found in both *Esurientes* settings, and both *Fecit potentiam* verses accompany the chant in the altus with two parts in the high register: violins in the Magnificat *a 7* and sopranos in the Magnificat *a 6*. In all of these verse pairs there is little or no similarity of compositional detail between one and the other—the parallels reside in the fundamental concept behind each pair. The remaining verse pairs, on the other hand, exhibit not only basic conceptual similarities, but also considerable parallels in compositional detail, though in every case Monteverdi has altered the original setting in significant ways. Many of these detailed alterations suggest that the original versions were those of the Magnificat *a 6*; the Magnificat *a 7* displays more sophisticated treatment of the same materials, and amorphous bass patterns in the Magnificat *a 6* are often reorganized or recomposed to provide more coherent phrase structures and tonal direction in the Magnificat *a 7*. A comparison of the basses of the two *Quia respexit* settings suggests that alterations were made in the Magnificat *a 6* version in order to accommodate the obbligato instruments of the Magnificat *a 7*.

Monteverdi's procedure is unquestionably parodistic, but since each of the Magnificat segments is based on the same plainchant cantus firmus, there is sometimes little conceptual difference between the compositional process of parodying the same verse from one Magnificat to the other and the process of variation on the cantus firmus as it unfolds in the successive verses of a single Magnificat. The transformation of a virtuoso soprano duet with cantus firmus in one Magnificat into a duet for instruments with cantus firmus in the other (*Deposuit*) is essentially the same procedure as accompanying the cantus firmus with a virtuoso tenor duet in one verse of a canticle (*Et exsultavit* in both Magnificats) and accompanying it in another verse of the same composition with a virtuoso soprano duet (*Et misericordia* in the Magnificat *a 6*), or a bass duet with paired violins (*Quia fecit* in the Magnificat *a 7*). However, these correspondences between different verses of the same Magnificat are not as frequent as resemblances between parallel settings in the two canticles; Monteverdi's parody technique generates closer relationships than his variation technique. The difference between parody and variation in the Magnificats is thus an issue of similarity between two compositions (parody) versus variety within a single canticle (variation). In the former, textual identity is the underlying cause, while in the latter, it is the constancy of the cantus firmus. Nevertheless, by describing the details of Monteverdi's parody process, most aspects of his variation technique within each Magnificat have also been revealed.

In addition to the evidence from the parallel verses between the two canticles suggesting that the Magnificat *a 6* is the antecedent composition, a comparison of the placement of vocal duets in the two Magnificats demonstrates a deliberate concern for symmetry in the Magnificat *a 7*, not only in terms of which verses were treated in this manner, but also with regard to voice register. Monteverdi even composed a new *Sicut locutus est* for this Magnificat to ensure both types of symmetry. The Magnificat *a 6*, on the other hand, seems quite haphazard and unbalanced in both the registers and the distribution of its duets.

Contributing further to the impression that the small Magnificat was the prototype for the large one is the apparent rationale for reversing the settings of two successive verses from one Magnificat to the other. We have already seen how Monteverdi generated symmetrical balance in the Magnificat *a 7* through the placement of duets. With the exchange of styles between *Quia fecit* and *Et misericordia* and the newly composed settings for *Suscepit Israel* and *Gloria Patri*, the verses of the Magnificat *a 7* fall into a mostly symmetrical ordering on the basis of style and the employment of obbligato instruments (see Fig. 7.1).[10] Only *Et misericordia*, which is unique in character, and *Esurientes*, which bears a distant relationship to *Quia respexit* with its triple-metre ritornello, do not contribute to the symmetry. By contrast, the verses of the Magnificat *a 6* proceed with a judicious eye for variety of texture and style, but without any overall structural pattern clearly determining succession (see the structural outline in Appendix C). Therefore it seems that Monteverdi, in basing one Magnificat upon the other, also sought to impose a more balanced, large-scale structural organization on his second effort. While definitive proof is still lacking that the Magnificat *a 7* is the later composition, the cumulative evidence makes such a conclusion probable. If this is correct, it was Monteverdi's tendency in parodying pre-existing compositions, as seen in both *Domine ad adjuvandum* and the Magnificats, to elaborate and expand upon his sources rather than to reduce them. This inclination to enlargement can be observed on the smaller level of individual passages and sections as well as on the larger level of entire pieces.

Throughout the discussion of each verse I have alluded to Monteverdi's interpretation of individual words or phrases of the text or to settings whose style and vocal or vocal and instrumental forces seem appropriate to the significance of the entire verse. Yet, as in the psalms, these musical metaphors are limited in number and in scope, and in many cases the musical metaphor is not especially striking nor so closely allied to the text that some other, quite different metaphor might not have served as well. Monteverdi often seems more interested in the musical figure associated with each verse and its working out in a cohesive structure than he is in interpretation of the text. The most obvious

---

[10] For a similar diagram, but with comparisons made on the basis of number of voices only, see Denis Stevens, 'Where are the Vespers of Yesteryear?', *Musical Quarterly*, 47 (1961), 330.

Magnificat	Chorus followed by solo soprano
Et exsultavit	Virtuoso duet for tenors
Quia respexit	Ritornello structure and paired obbligato instruments
Quia fecit	Virtuoso duet for basses with two obbligato violins
Et misericordia	Two vocal trios in dialogue
Fecit potentiam	Duet for violins
Deposuit	Echo duets for cornettos and violins
Esurientes	Ritornello structure with Magnificat tone in parallel thirds in two voices
Suscepit Israel	Virtuoso duet for sopranos
Sicut locutus	Dialogue between paired obbligato instruments
Gloria Patri	Virtuoso duet for tenors
Sicut erat	Chorus

FIG. 7.1. Magnificat *a 7*, symmetries

example of this attitude is the exchange of styles between *Quia fecit* and *Et misericordia* in the two canticles. The desire for symmetrical structuring in the Magnificat *a 7* clearly overrode any text associations Monteverdi might have had in mind when he was composing the settings of these two verses for the Magnificat *a 6*.

This discussion of the handling of the cantus firmus and the character of the harmonic language has uncovered some of the differences between Monteverdi's Magnificats on the one hand and his five psalms on the other. The Magnificat tone, complete with intonation in every verse, serves as a slow-moving structural scaffolding around which the many different compositional styles and techniques of the canticles are woven. Each verse is treated as a separate composition, unrelated in character to the one preceding it and the one following it. The long-note cantus firmus actually permits more variety of styles and more variety in harmonic language and bass patterns, including passages forming functional chord progressions, than the treatment of the cantus firmus in the psalms, where the chant functions much more often as an integral part of the texture. Additional differences between the psalms and the Magnificats include the much greater prominence of virtuoso duets, ritornello structures, dialogues, and echo techniques in the latter. There is no counterpart in the psalms for the significant role accorded to obbligato instruments in the Magnificat *a 7*.

Monteverdi's Magnificats, therefore, are stylistically dissimilar in many important respects to his psalms. It is highly unusual, in fact, for psalms and canticles in the same publication to be so different in character. I know of no other collection of seventeenth-century vesper psalms and canticles where the difference is so pronounced. Moreover, as already seen in Chapter 4, Monteverdi's

Magnificats from the 1610 Vespers stand alone in style and structure amidst the entire Magnificat repertoire of the early *Seicento*. On the other hand, their vir-tuoso vocal duets derive from the motet repertoire of the period, as discussed in Chapter 4. In this aspect of their syle they bear a close relationship to *Pulchra es* and *Duo Seraphim* from the 1610 print. Indeed, basses oscillating between notes a fourth or fifth apart and other cadentially oriented basses supporting the vir-tuoso duets in the Magnificats reappear in Monteverdi's motets. Thus the long-note cantus firmus in the Magnificats has left Monteverdi enough ma-noeuvering room for his basses to generate many patterns usually associated with music not based on a cantus firmus. The virtuosity with which he has combined the rigid, conservative structure of the cantus firmus with the most modern techniques and styles of harmony, melody, rhythm, and texture is once again astonishing.

8

Compositions Based on a Cantus Firmus:
The Hymn and the *Sonata sopra Sancta Maria*

AVE MARIS STELLA

The Cantus Firmus and the Strophic Structure of the Hymn

THE treatment of the cantus firmus in the hymn *Ave maris stella* is quite different from its use in the psalms and the Magnificats. In the hymn, the plainchant always appears in the topmost part as the principal melody, harmonized in an essentially chordal fashion. This manner of setting the *Ave maris stella* melody can be traced all the way back to Dunstable's *alternatim* version, which adds a modest degree of ornamentation to the plainchant.[1] Monteverdi, however, adheres strictly to the notes of the chant itself, which is a first-mode melody evidently derived not from the Roman rite, but from the liturgy of Santa Barbara in Mantua, prepared specifically for the Gonzaga ducal church in the late sixteenth century.[2]

Monteverdi sets each of the seven verses either in vocal polyphony or as accompanied monody, subjecting the borrowed melody in successive verses to a series of variations in texture, sonority, and metre.[3] Separating verses 2–6 is a ritornello for five unspecified instruments.[4] The overall setting is conservative in character, even in its notation, which is principally in semibreves and minims under a ¢ mensuration.[5] The only modern elements are the insertion of the ritornello and the reduction of the texture to a solo voice with continuo accom-

---

[1] See *John Dunstable: Complete Works*, ed. Manfred F. Bukofzer (Musica Britannica, 8; London: Stainer and Bell, Ltd., 1953), 95.

[2] Poala Besutti, 'Ricorrenze motiviche, canti dati e "cantus firmus" nella produzione sacra di Claudio Monteverdi'. Paper delivered at Convegno, Claudio Monteverdi: Studi e prospettive, Mantua, 21–4 Oct. 1993, published as ' "Ave Maris Stella": La tradizione mantovane nuovamente posta in musica da Monteverdi' in Paola Besutti, Teresa M. Gialdroni, and Rodolfo Baroncini, eds., *Claudio Monteverdi: Studi e prospettive, Atti del Convegno (Mantova, 21–24 ottobre 1993)* (Florence: Olschki, 1998), 57–78. For a discussion of the association of *Ave maris stella* with the rite of Santa Barbara, see Ch. 1 above.

[3] See Ch. 20 for a discussion of the tempo relationship between duple and triple metre in the hymn.

[4] For discussions of performance of this ritornello, see Chs. 18 and 19 below.

[5] See Ch. 20 for the meaning of this mensuration in relation to performance tempo in the hymn.

paniment in verses 4–6. Nowhere is there an attempt to interpret individual words of the text, a difficult proposition in the strophic setting of a hymn in any event.

The successive variations in texture, sonority, and metre are organized around both symmetrical and asymmetrical principles (see Fig. 8.1). The first and last verses comprise identical eight-voice, double-choir polyphonic settings. The second and third verses reset the cantus firmus in triple metre and are identical except that they alternate four-voice choirs, thereby varying the sonority (see Ex. 8.1 for a comparison of the duple and triple versions of the melody). The fourth, fifth, and sixth verses retain the triple-metre version of the melody, but are performed by a solo voice with only basso continuo support. The solo voice itself changes from verse to verse: the fourth verse is sung by a soprano from the first choir (cantus), the fifth by a soprano from the second choir (sextus), and the sixth by a tenor from the first choir (tenor). Thus there is a regular alternation between first and second choirs in verses 2–7. Throughout all seven verses the harmonization of the plainchant remains unchanged.

The ritornello, in triple metre, is identical in each repetition, and bears no melodic relationship to the hymn tune. It does, however, bear a structural relationship to the verses in triple metre and the tonal structure of the vocal harmonization. Like the triple-metre verses, the ritornello comprises four phrases of five bars each, and several phrases begin and end with the same har-

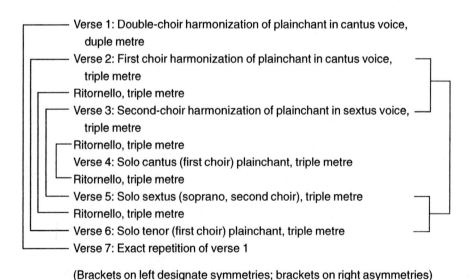

Verse 1: Double-choir harmonization of plainchant in cantus voice, duple metre
Verse 2: First choir harmonization of plainchant in cantus voice, triple metre
Ritornello, triple metre
Verse 3: Second-choir harmonization of plainchant in sextus voice, triple metre
Ritornello, triple metre
Verse 4: Solo cantus (first choir) plainchant, triple metre
Ritornello, triple metre
Verse 5: Solo sextus (soprano, second choir), triple metre
Ritornello, triple metre
Verse 6: Solo tenor (first choir) plainchant, triple metre
Verse 7: Exact repetition of verse 1

(Brackets on left designate symmetries; brackets on right asymmetries)

Fig. 8.1. *Ave maris stella*, symmetries and asymmetries

mony as the verses (though sometimes substituting a major or minor chord for its opposite).[6]

This ritornello is symmetrically deployed in the hymn: it does not appear until after the second verse, and according to Monteverdi's rubric, it is to be omitted between the sixth and seventh verses. There are therefore paired verses at the beginning and end not separated by the ritornello; otherwise, the ritornello alternates with each verse. Likewise, the deployment of the hymn tune is arranged symmetrically between the two choirs. On the other hand, the varying textures and varying parts carrying the hymn tune are organized asymmetrically. As a result, Monteverdi, in his customary fashion, creates a structure based on simple principles, but not at all simple in its realization (see Fig. 8.1).

Harmonic Language

Monteverdi's harmonization of the hymn tune intermingles cadentially oriented chord progressions with non-cadential triadic successions and juxtapositions of unrelated chords that mitigate against a single tonality. The first phrase of the hymn, for example, establishes a G major tonal focus at the outset through a V–I progression, which, after prolonging the I, moves to IV in bar 6 (see Ex. 8.2). The end of the phrase then suddenly shifts, without pivot, to a V–I–V–I cadential progression in A major. Thus Monteverdi has employed cadential harmony in this phrase, but the shift from a G major tonal focus to a cadence in A demonstrates that he does not deploy his cadential harmony to generate a functional tonal progression in Carl Dahlhaus's terms (see Chapter 5). The tune itself would easily have permitted a functional harmonization in G major. The opening *d'* could have been harmonized with I instead of V, and the tune would

Ex. 8.1. *Ave maris stella*, hymn tune, duple- and triple-time versions

[6] The ritornello and the verse both begin with a D chord (major in the verse, minor in the ritornello), and the end of the first phrase of both is harmonized with an A major triad. The second phrase of the ritornello begins with an A major chord, the verse with A minor, and the end of this phrase differs between verse and ritornello. The beginning of the third phrase also differs in the two versions, but both ritornello and verse conclude their phrases with a full cadence to C major. The last phrases of both ritornello and verse begin on C major and conclude with a full cadence to D major.

Ex. 8.2. *Ave maris stella*, hymn tune and figured bass

have enabled Monteverdi in bars 7–10 to continue harmonization in G, closing
the phrase on a D major dominant triad.

The next phrase opens with a non-cadentional chord succession. The opening A minor triad not only contrasts with the A major chord concluding the previous phrase, but is itself succeeded by another A major triad, which may be
viewed as a dominant of the following D minor. The D minor triad, however,
is succeeded in bars 13–14 by C major and G minor chords, devoid of any cadential relationships. The harmony finally becomes cadential in bars 15–18, establishing a series of repetitive V–I motions in D. While the D is minor at first,
the phrase closes in D with a major third. Thus only the cadence of bars 15–18
comprises a functional progression.

The third phrase, beginning with a minor-chord juxtaposition similar to that
at the end of the preceding prase (D minor in relation to phrase 2's cadence on
a D major triad), proceeds non-functionally to a C major chord. The phrase
then continues with what appears to be a functional progression in C (I–VI
[VII$_6$/V]–V), but the functional sense is disrupted by the motion V–IV in bars
24–5. Cadential motion towards C then continues with a IV–V–I progression.

The final phrase begins in C where the last phrase left off and seems as if it is
directed towards a confirming cadence on C (I–VI–V) until the second half of

bar 30, where V becomes III. This non-functional E minor triad is succeeded by an equally non-functional A minor chord. Only with the shift to A major in bar 32 is a functional cadential progression in D established. As in the second phrase, D is at first minor and turns to major only at the end.

A survey of the harmonic and cadential movement of the hymn as a whole reveals what motivated Monteverdi's choices. In each phrase he has harmonized the final note of the hymn tune with a major triad built on that note, each time utilizing a complete cadence to lead to that chord. Where the note is A or D, the final triad, made major by the typical Picardy third, has been preceded by its minor version. Thus the cadential succession A major–D major–C major–D major is simply generated by the hymn tune itself. Since the hymn begins on *d'*, Monteverdi has harmonized that note with a D major triad as well. Therefore although the hymn begins and ends on a D major triad, D is clearly not the 'tonality' of the harmonization in the sense of a reference point for all other harmonic motion: the four phrases together do not add up to a tonally oriented sequence of progressions. D is, in fact, incidental in the opening phrase, appearing only once, where it serves as the dominant of G. While D is the cadential goal of the second and fourth phrases, those phrases do not begin by establishing it. The phrases cadencing on A and C do not generate any hierarchy of tensions in relation to D; indeed, they seem, when they occur, to have equal weight with D and with one another. Where D receives its priority in the scheme of the hymn as a whole is through its cadential role at the end of each stanza and its correlation with the Dorian mode of the chant. This priority is insufficient, however, given Monteverdi's harmonization of the hymn tune, to establish it as the 'tonality' of the hymn in any functional sense of the term.

SONATA SOPRA SANCTA MARIA

The Cantus Firmus and its Contexts

The only remaining composition in the Vespers employing a repeated cantus firmus is the *Sonata sopra Sancta Maria*. This work borrows the opening phrase from the Litany of the Saints (see Ex. 8.3) and reiterates it in the soprano voice eleven times over a sonata for eight instruments.[7] In general, the structive of the *Sonata* resembles, on a very large scale, that of a typical late sixteenth-century instrumental canzona, comprising a series of loosely related sections with repetition of the opening material at the end.[8] As with the adaptation of the *L'Orfeo*

---

[7] The Litany of the Saints is found in *The Liber Usualis with Introduction and Rubrics in English* (New York: Desclée Company, 1963), app. II, p. 2*. Monteverdi transposes the chant a full step up and occasionally adds a sharp to the last *c''*.

[8] See Ch. 4 for a discussion of antecedents of the *Sonata*.

San - cta   Ma - ri - a   o - ra   pro   no - bis

Ex. 8.3. Litany of the Saints, opening phrase

toccata to *Domine ad adjuvandum*, a liturgical chant is superimposed on the
instrumental composition, which could easily stand alone.

The cantus firmus does not begin until well into the piece, and its successive
statements are altered rhythmically and separated by rests of varying durations.
The instrumental sonata supporting the cantus firmus unfolds in ten overlapping sections, the first one restated at the end in the manner of a da capo (see the
structural outline in Appendix C). As in the Magnificats, the separate sections of
the *Sonata* differ in style and texture, and the metre shifts between duple and
triple time with some frequency. In contrast to the Magnificats, the sections do
not correspond exactly with the restatements of the plainchant, since the opening segment is without cantus firmus and another section supports two intonations of the chant melody.

The lengths of the ten separate sections comprising the *Sonata* vary considerably—the longest is three-and-a-half times the length of the shortest. Yet
despite these many irregularities, there are some elements of symmetry in the
structure of the composition, even if the piece is not as schematic as the psalms,
Magnificats, and hymn. The *Sonata* is framed by the opening section and its da
capo at the end; only the final plagal cadence with the last statement of the cantus firmus lies outside this frame. Sections 2–4 concentrate on virtuoso, dotted-
rhythm scale patterns and ornamented versions of these patterns in the
cornettos and violins. These sections are entirely in duple metre until the introduction of a series of four-bar interpolations in triple metre at the very end. The
central segment of the *Sonata*, section 5, is a brief passage notated in blackened
triplets, still under duple mensuration. This passage merges with the succeeding
large segment comprising four subgroups (sections 6–9), all in triple metre.

Thus the outward frame encloses an only slightly off-balance symmetry of
sections 2–4 and 6–9, the former in duple metre, the latter in triple metre, which
surround the central segment in black notation. This middle segment is not
perfectly centrally located, however, since it is the concluding cadence of this
section, in bar 142, that articulates the mid-point of the 285–bar composition.[9]

---

[9] Roger Bowers attempts to make a case for his interpretation of the tempo of the black notation on
the basis of number symbolism. I do not find his number symbolism convincing, but ironically, if the
black notation is understood as blackened semibreves and minims, his numbers are the same regardless
of the tempo relationship. See Bowers, 'Some Reflection upon Notation, and Proportions in
Monteverdi's Mass and Vespers of 1610', *Music & Letters*, 73 (1992), 391–5, and my 'Correspondence',
Music & Letters, 74 (1993), 490.

The variation concept applies not only to the differing contexts of the reiterated litany, but also to portions of the *Sonata* where the chant is absent. The first two sections, for example, are formed from the same music, first in duple metre, then reorchestrated and recast in triple time, a procedure frequently encountered in dance pairs of the sixteenth and seventeenth centuries (see Ex. 8.4).[10]

A later figure, played by the violins in duet, is presented in several melodic and rhythmic variants, even in its first appearance: a scale in dotted quavers and semiquavers is embellished with an extra semiquaver and then continues in a sequence of ornamented broken thirds (see Ex. 8.5).

The scale pattern, in both melody and bass, is a fundamental motif in the *Sonata* and appears in a variety of guises (see Exx. 8.5 and 8.6). While variation procedures may be at the root of some of these similarities, others may be attributed to a basic motivic consistency throughout the composition. The figure shown in Ex. 8.6*d* not only involves scale motion, but also is closely related by inversion to the opening motif of the *Sonata*, quoted in Ex. 8.4*a*. In fact, the section based on this motif functions as a transition between the scale forms of Ex. 8.6*a* and *b* and a new triple-metre section whose main motif bears a strong resemblance to the opening figure (see Ex. 8.7). An affinity with the turning figure of Ex. 8.5 may also be discerned.

The motif in Ex. 8.7 undergoes several metamorphoses in the course of this extended section (bars 142–247), but all its forms are sufficiently related to one another and to the opening motif in their use of conjunct and disjunct thirds to render perfectly natural and convincing the da capo return of the opening passage (bars 248–79) following the conclusion of this section.

These techniques in the *Sonata* illustrate the close relationship between Monteverdi's concept of melodic and rhythmic variation and sixteenth-century methods of motivic development. Although the motifs quoted in Exx. 8.4, 8.5, and 8.7 are typical of the early seventeenth century in the strength and regularity of their rhythms and the time intervals of their imitations, the metamorphosis of one motif out of another by means of expansion, contraction, inversion, retrogression, and alteration of rhythmic values is the same process found in innumerable *ricercari* and canzonas of the second half of the *Cinquecento*. It is only in those passages where greater identity of material is maintained, such as Ex. 8.4*a* and *b*, that one can speak of variation in the form-building sense rather than as thematic development. Yet the distinction between the two in the *Sonata sopra Sancta Maria* is largely a matter of degree, although it has significant structural implications. The techniques of thematic

---

[10] See Ch. 20 for a discussion of the tempo relationship between duple and triple metres in the *Sonata*.

Ex. 8.4. *Sonata sopra Sancta Maria*: *a* bars 1–6; *b* bars 17–22

(*h*)

Ex. 8.4. *Continued*

Ex. 8.5. *Sonata sopra Sancta Maria*, bars 45–57

development facilitate the construction of large continuous sections, which maintain a certain sense of homogeneity despite alterations in the melodic material. The process of formal variation, on the other hand, through its retention of a basic and readily perceptible morphological identity, tends to subdivide the music into comparatively short, discrete sections where first one variation technique is exposed and then another. This is apparent in the first half of the *Sonata* (bars 1–142), which relies more on the process of variation and is more clearly

Ex. 8.6. *Sonata sopra Sancta Maria*, basso continuo: *a* bars 41–50; *b* bars 99–110; *c* bars 127–9; *d* bars 130–4

Ex. 8.7. *Sonata sopra Sancta Maria*, bars 142–8

sectionalized than the portion depending on sixteenth-century methods of motivic development (bars 142–246).

The passage in blackened triplets concluding the first half of the *Sonata*, section 5 (bars 130–42), has given rise to a variety of interpretations of its rhythmic relationship to the surrounding sections. My reading of this passage allows for a single tactus to be used throughout the *Sonata*, and all the bars in my edition of this piece are of equivalent length in performance.[11]

---

[11] See Ch. 20 for a detailed discussion of this passage and the controversy surrounding it.

Harmonic Language

The bass in the *Sonata sopra Sancta Maria* consists of two types of patterns. The first of these, evident at the very opening, comprises a cadential progression in G major with bass movement by leaps of a fourth or fifth. The progression is then repeated sequentially at the levels of A minor and C major (modified) before the original G major level is repeated (see Ex. 8.8).

Sequential cadential chord successions also characterize the harmony of the central passage in black notation. The passage begins and ends in G, but G serves as dominant of C at the opening, and until the return to G at the end, the passage makes sense as a functional chord series in C major (V–I–V/VI–VI–V/II–V/V–V–I–IV–I–V–I–V–V/V–V = I/G) (see Ex. 8.9). It is telling, however, that the passage begins with G major, established by its own dominant, and closes with a cadence to G major, the intervening chord progression thereby not establishing as tonic the focal note around which the series is organized. The question then becomes, 'In what terms is the progression functional?' We may certainly hear the chord succession as functional, but the D minor and F major chords mitigate against our interpreting the series as functional in terms of the opening and closing G.

Another passage with bass movement principally by fourths and fifths may be viewed in similar terms (see Ex. 8.10). This passage likewise begins with a V–I cadence in G, with the G then serving as dominant to C, and also concludes

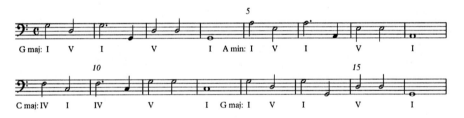

Ex. 8.8. *Sonata sopra Sancta Maria*, bars 1–16, figured bass

Ex. 8.9. *Sonata sopra Sancta Maria*, bars 130–42, figured bass

Ex. 8.10. *Sonata sopra Sancta Maria*, bars 156–76, figured bass

Ex. 8.11. *Sonata sopra Sancta Maria*, bars 142–55, figured bass

with a cadence in G. However, like the passage in black notation, everything in between is focused around C major. Once C is reached in bar 158, the progression proceeds as I–IV–V–I–II–V–VI–II–V/VI–VI–V/V–V–I–IV–V–I–I–V/V–V = I/G. Since the passage again begins and ends with perfect cadences to G rather than the C that serves as the focal point, the progression must be considered functional only in terms of its localized reference and not in terms of its cadential goal.

After the two opening sections (the same music in duple, then triple metre), the first half of the *Sonata* is characterized by extended scale motion in the bass, the second type of bass pattern found in this piece. These basses include leaps of a seventh, which are nothing more than octave displacement of the continuing scale motion (see bars 45–50, Ex. 8.6*a*). Scale patterns can also serve as the basis of sequences (see Ex. 8.6*d*). Such patterns permeate the lengthy segment (sections 2–4) preceding the central section in black notation. In these passages the bass and upper parts are in scale-based counterpoint with one another, the chord succession simply being determined by the notes of the scale sounding at the beginning or at the beginning and middle of each bar. In some cases, this leads to nothing more than a series of parallel triads (see bars 99–106, Ex. 8.6*b*). A similar series of non-functional chords results from a sequential, scale-based pattern in the segment immediately following the central black-notation section (see Ex. 8.11).

Thus, the *Sonata sopra Sancta Maria* mixes non-functional bass patterns and chord successions with progressions that come much closer in character to modern functional harmony. The tonal focus of the *Sonata* is clearly G in *cantus durus*, since not only is G the opening and closing focal point of the piece, but every section except the fourth begins on G major as the completion of a perfect cadence initiated at the end of the preceding section. What prevents our referring to the tonality of the entire *Sonata* as the key of G major are the scale-oriented sections where F♮ is the normal seventh degree, changing to F♯ only for cadences.

With the *Sonata sopra Sancta Maria* we conclude the discussion of compositions based on a cantus firmus. Monteverdi's different ways of dealing with the cantus firmus in different pieces and with the repeated cantus firmus within each composition are remarkable in their variety and ingenuity. The cantus firmus imparts to each of these works a schematic organization, but the variety of organizational schemes is as varied as the treatments of the cantus firmus itself. Yet symmetry, even if at times unbalanced in some of its elements, is often at the heart of Monteverdi's process of construction in these large-scale compositions.

The compositions based on a cantus firmus do not lend themselves to sophisticated musical interpretation of the text. In some pieces, such as the hymn and the *Sonata sopra Sancta Maria*, the meaning of the text is irrelevant to the musical setting. Even in the psalms and Magnificats, where individual words are sometimes singled out for particular treatment, or a word or phrase may stimulate the character of the musical setting of a verse, there is just as often little correlation between the significance of the text and the music. The text–music relationship in many instances is more one of syllabic declamation and appropriate rhythmic accentuation than one of semantic interpretation. While the modern features of these pieces have sometimes prompted commentators to refer to them as *seconda prattica* compositions, they actually have little to do with the *seconda prattica* as defined in the preface to Monteverdi's *Scherzi musicali* of 1607. These are not compositions where the 'words are the mistress of the harmony', even though some aspects of the music are clearly stimulated by the words. The phrase *seconda prattica* has sometimes been used by scholars much more loosely than was intended by Claudio's brother, Giulio Cesare, in 1607, to mean any style of modern music.[12] By *seconda prattica* the Monteverdi brothers were referring to the more limited issue of irregular dissonance treatment en-

---

[12] See e.g. Hans F. Redlich, 'Monteverdi's Religious Music', *Music & Letters*, 27 (1946), 209 (where the *seconda prattica* and *concertato* style are equated); id., *Claudio Monteverdi: Leben und Werk* (Olten: Verlag Otto Walter, 1949), 130–4; and *Claudio Monteverdi: Vespro della Beata Vergine*, ed. Jürgen Jürgens (Vienna: Universal Edition, 1977), p. viii. Leo Schrade, who discusses the Vespers extensively in his book *Monteverdi, Creator of Modern Music* (New York: W. W. Norton & Company, Inc., 1950), 247–62, says much about modern style but does not bring the terms *prima prattica* and *seconda prattica* into the discussion at all. More recent writers, such as Denis Arnold, Claudio Gallico, and Paolo Fabbri have been circumspect about applying these terms to the Vespers.

gendered by the words of the text, not to modern style in general.[13] Such dissonance treatment is not found in the cantus firmus compositions of the Vespers; these works are modern in style, structure, and some of their harmonic features, but not in terms of the irregular dissonances, chromatic harmony, or modal combinations in the madrigals of Books Four and Five that provoked Artusi. Even those elements of the Vespers derived from *L'Orfeo*, such as the opening toccata and the virtuoso vocal and instrumental technique of *Possente spirto*, are not representative of the *seconda prattica*.

The cantus firmus compositions of Monteverdi's 1610 Vespers display a balance between conservative and modern characteristics. The continuous presence of a cantus firmus was in itself a conservative element in psalms and canticles by the early seventeenth century, as was the *cori spezzati* technique and the harmonization of an unadorned hymn tune. The modern side of these compositions is revealed, on the other hand, in the *concertato* style of the response, psalms, Magnificats, and *Sonata*, wherein large pieces are subdivided into contrasting sections, employing continually varying textures and changing metres, as well as emphasizing few-voiced virtuoso writing and, in some pieces, virtuoso obbligato instruments. Even the hymn displays elements of modern style in its varying textures, its shift of metres, and its instrumental ritornellos.

The four few-voiced motets in the 1610 publication are quite different from the cantus firmus compositions, not only in their lack of plainchant, but also in their manner of responding to the text. These works more nearly reflect the *seconda prattica*, and it is to them that we now turn.

---

[13] While Giulio Cesare employs the phrases 'modern usage' and 'modern music' in this preface, the definition of the second practice is given as follows: 'he [Claudio] has called it "practice," and not "theory," because he understands its explanation to turn on the manner of employing the consonances and dissonances in actual composition' ('ha detto prattica e non Theorica perchioche intende versar le sue ragioni intorno al modo di adoperar le consonanze e dissonanze nel atto prattico'). See Domenico De' Paoli, *Claudio Monteverdi: Lettere, dediche e prefazioni* (Rome: Edizioni de Santis, 1973), 399. Eng. trans. from Oliver Strunk, *Source Readings in Music History* (New York: W. W. Norton & Company, Inc., 1950), 409. I have discussed this distinction further in 'What Makes Claudio "Divine"? Criteria for Analysis of Monteverdi's Large-Scale *Concertato* Style', *Seicento inesplorato, Atti del III convegno internazionale sulla musica in area lombardo-padana del secolo XVII* (Como: AMIS, 1993), 259–302; 'A Taxonomic and Affective Analysis of Monteverdi's "Hor che'l ciel e la terra"', *Music Analysis*, 12 (1993), 169–95; and 'Monteverdi's Changing Aesthetics: A Semiotic Perspective', in Thomas J. Mathiesen and Benito V. Rivera, eds., *Festa musicologica, Essays in Honor of George Buelow* (Stuyvesant, NY: Pendragon Press, 1994), 233–55. See also Tim Carter, 'Artusi, Monteverdi, and the Poetics of Modern Music', in Nancy Kovaleff Baker and Barbara Russano Hanning, eds., *Musical Humanism and its Legacy: Essays in Honor of Claude V. Palisca* (Stuyvesant, NY: Pendragon Press, 1992), 171–94.

9

Compositions not Based on a Cantus Firmus:
Nigra Sum

ᘒ❦ᘐ

THE remaining four pieces of the Vespers, the motets *Nigra sum, Pulchra es, Duo Seraphim,* and *Audi coelum,* are all in the modern solo or few-voiced style and are without any dependence on a *cantus prius factus.* Nevertheless, an examination of these works demonstrates once again that, as in the psalms, hymn, Magnificats, and *Sonata,* variation techniques are a principal feature of Monteverdi's compositional process.

Amid Monteverdi's correspondence there survive several letters written between 1618 and 1627 discussing various operatic projects. In these letters Monteverdi repeatedly stressed his need for adequate time in order to compose well rather than sloppily. Compositions completed in haste and performances insufficiently rehearsed troubled him greatly.[1] Indeed, it is becoming increasingly apparent to twentieth-century scholars that one of the main distinctions between the music of Monteverdi and that of his contemporaries is the carefully planned construction of his works, including even operatic recitatives. In his *stile rappresentativo* as well as in other monodies and few-voiced compositions, Monteverdi carefully adhered not only to the rhetorical expression and semantics of his texts but also to the necessities and requirements of purely musical logic. The power of his writing lies not in the predominance of one approach to composition over the other, but rather in the marriage of the two interests—interpretation of the text and musical logic—in a coherent whole.

The musical coherence of Monteverdi's *seconda prattica* compositions has often been overlooked by taking too literally his brother Giulio Cesare's famous declaration that in the new style 'it has been his intention to make the words the mistress of the harmony and not the servant'.[2] Monteverdi and his brother, for

---

[1] See esp. letters of 21 July, 1618, 9 Jan. 1620, 16 Jan. 1620, 1 Feb. 1620, 28 Mar. 1620, 4 Apr. 1620, 10 May 1620, and 1 May 1627 in Domenico De' Paoli, *Claudio Monteverdi: Lettere, dediche e prefazioni* (Rome: Edizioni de Santis, 1973) and Eva Lax, *Claudio Monteverdi: Lettere* (Florence: Leo S. Olschki Editore, 1994); Eng. trans. in Denis Stevens, *The Letters of Claudio Monteverdi* (Cambridge: Cambridge University Press, 1980).

[2] The theory of the *seconda prattica* is propounded by Giulio Cesare Monteverdi in the famous *Dichiaratione* printed in the *Scherzi musicali* of 1607. The *Dichiaratione* is cast in the form of extensive glosses upon the phrases of a *Lettera* that Claudio had printed in the Fifth Book of Madrigals of 1605

the sake of argument and without enough time to develop the thesis at greater length, oversimplified the issue in the *Dichiaratione* of the 1607 *Scherzi musicali*. While Monteverdi certainly took the text as his point of departure as well as the ultimate rationale for many features of his madrigals, motets, and dramatic compositions, he never became a slavish imitator of words nor an ingenious inventor of musical metaphors, even though madrigalisms are readily apparent in his music.

The balanced union of textual and musical considerations took different forms in the *stile rappresentativo* and the polyphonic and *concertato* madrigals and motets. Moreover, the relationship between text and music took on a different aspect in each individual composition. But whatever the style or character of the piece, Monteverdi never ignored the demands of musical logic and coherence. Conversely, it is often this musical coherence that gives the primary force to the expression of the text, for in the absence of a powerful musical logic, the addition of tone to word is likely to prove fleeting, superficial, and unconvincing.

Despite the success of his two early operas and the widespread popularity of the Lament of Arianna, Monteverdi did not write many independent monodies, preferring instead the trio texture of two equal voices with basso continuo. Of the pieces he did compose for solo voice, the majority are sacred rather than secular monodies, and the earliest of these is *Nigra sum* from the 1610 Vespers. Another motet from the 1610 print may also be considered a monody: *Audi coelum*, whose second tenor (quintus) serves merely an echo role, mimicking the ends of phrases of the tenor. *Audi coelum* is further complicated by the participation of a six-voice chorus in its concluding section.[3]

The other two motets from the Vespers, *Pulchra es* and *Duo Seraphim*, are for two and three voices respectively. In fact, the order of the five *sacri concentus* of the Vespers (including the *Sonata sopra Sancta Maria*) matches the increasing number of parts employed (see Chapter 1). The monody *Nigra sum* comes first, then the duet *Pulchra es* and the trio *Duo Seraphim*; *Audi coelum* calls for six vocal parts in its final section, and the *Sonata sopra Sancta Maria* has eight separate instrumental parts aside from the single vocal part and the continuo. The present chapter is devoted to a study of *Nigra sum*; the other three motets will be examined in Chapter 10.

Nigra sum is an extraordinary composition, exceptionally fascinating in its melodic shape, chromatic writing, formal organization, and textual allusions.

announcing his intention to publish a theoretical treatise explaining the rationale behind his 'second practice'. A modern edition of the *Dichiaratione* is found in De' Paoli, *Claudio Monteverdi: Lettere, dediche e prefazioni*, 394–404; Eng. trans. in Oliver Strunk, *Source Readings in Music History* (New York: W. W. Norton & Co., Inc., 1950), 405–12. For the passage quoted here see ibid. 406, but Giulio Cesare restates the same idea several times with different wording.

[3] See Ch. 10 for a more extended discussion of *Audi coelum*.

Of all the pieces in the Vespers, it is perhaps the richest and most rewarding to explore in depth. For that reason, the analysis that follows is much more detailed than I have offered for other compositions from the 1610 print.

Nigra sum   *Motetto ad una voce* (motet for one voice); includes adaptation of Song of Songs 1: 4; 2: 10–12 and the third and fourth antiphons for vespers on feasts of the BVM *per annum*[4]

> Nigra sum, sed formosa filia Jerusalem.
> Ideo dilexit me Rex
> et introduxit me in cubiculum suum,
> et dixit mihi: surge, amica mea, et veni.
> Iam hiems transijt,
> imber abijt et recessit,
> flores apparuerunt in terra nostra,
> tempus putationis advenit.

> I am the dark but lovely daughter of Jerusalem.
> Therefore the king loved me
> and brought me into his chamber,
> and said to me: 'Arise, my love, and come.
> Already the winter is past,
> the rains are over and gone;
> flowers have appeared in our land,
> the time of pruning comes.'

The Song of Songs canticles represent at times a female speaker, at times a male speaker, and at times a group of speakers, interpreted from early in the Christian era as *sponsa*, *sponsus*, and male and female *Chorus* respectively.[5] The significance of these speakers was the subject of a variety of allegorical interpretations from medieval times onwards. The Song of Songs became especially popular as a source for motet texts after the publication of Palestrina's cycle based on these canticles.[6] In *Nigra sum*, the *sponsa* begins the motet with a first-person com-

---

[4] Because the texts of the motets are adaptations from various sources and the original spellings in Amadino's 1610 print sometimes differ from the Vulgate and 17th-century liturgical books as well as from modern Latin spellings, I have adopted Monteverdi's orthography for all four motets. Monteverdi's spellings sometimes reveal important textual significance, as in *Nigra sum*. To obtain the text for *Nigra sum*, Monteverdi adapted the Vulgate text by slightly rearranging it and mixing it with the third and fourth antiphons for vespers on feasts of the BVM (perhaps even relying on earlier musical settings as sources; see Ch. 4). These antiphons had themselves originally been adapted from the Song of Songs.

[5] Robert L. Kendrick, '"Sonet vox tua in auribus meis": Song of Songs Exegesis and the Seventeenth-Century Motet', *Schütz-Jahrbuch*, 16 (1994), 99–118. I am grateful to Prof. Kendrick for sharing a copy of this article prior to publication.

[6] Ibid. 99–100. The Palestrina publication is his *Motettorum quinque vocibus liber quartus* (Rome: Alessandro Gardano, 1583–4), RISM P716. That Palestrina viewed these texts in an allegorical light is clear from his dedication to Pope Gregory XIII: 'Therefore I have both already labored on those poems which have been written of the praises of our Lord Jesus Christ and his Most Holy Mother the Virgin Mary [Palestrina's first book of spiritual madrigals from 1581], and at this time chosen those which contain the divine love of Christ and his spouse the soul, indeed the Canticles of Solomon.' Eng. trans. from Strunk, *Source Readings in Music History*, 323–4.

mentary, after which she directly quotes the *sponsus*. Thus both female and male are represented, but the only speaker is the *sponsa*.

Monteverdi, like Victoria and a few composers in the early seventeenth century, substituted the singular *filia* for *filiae* in the first line, thereby causing *filia Jerusalem* to refer back to the female speaker as a predicate nominative rather than serving the function of a vocative addressed to the female chorus as in the Vulgate's *filiae Jerusalem*. This change also brings the reference to *filia Jerusalem* into line with that in *Pulchra es* (see text).[7]

Monteverdi's designation of the tenor voice for *Nigra sum* may seem odd in view of the first-person, feminine orientation of the text. However, if the motet were to be sung in church as part of a liturgical service, it would have had to have been performed by a male singer, whatever the register in which it was composed.[8] The choice of a tenor may in fact have been dictated by the specific singer Monteverdi had available for the initial performance of the piece. Two other motets in the 1610 print, *Duo Seraphim* and *Audi coelum*, are also for virtuoso tenors.

On the other hand, if *Nigra sum* were to be sung outside of church, in 'chapels or chambers of princes' according to one possibility suggested on Monteverdi's title-page, a female singer might well have performed it. If so, Monteverdi's designation of a tenor would have proved no barrier to performance by a woman, since it was common practice in the early seventeenth century to treat the tenor and cantus voices as interchangeable. Countless published motets of the period display the rubric *canto ovvero tenore*, and such substitutions may be assumed feasible even if the composer or printer did not bother to indicate them.

The brief duration of *Nigra sum* belies its melodic, rhythmic, and harmonic complexity (see Ex. 9.1). The motet begins and ends with a G major triad, defining a *finalis* of G, but Bernhard Meier has described the mode of this piece as somewhat difficult to recognize and has analysed it in terms of both the eighth mode and the sixth mode (or twelfth mode transposed to G), depending on the use or absence of F♯.[9] In the first part of the composition (bars 1–9) the vocal line encompasses the octave *d–d'*, divided plagally, that is, with a tetrachord below and a pentachord above its finalis of *g*. The plagal *d–d'* octave also appears in bars 27–34 (combined with the authentic octave in bars 27–31—see

[7] I am grateful to Robert Kendrick for calling the change in the text to my attention.

[8] The exception, of course, would have been performance in a female convent. There is evidence, however, of Vittoria Archilei of Florence singing in liturgical services. See H. Wiley Hitchcock, 'Vittoria Archilei', in *The New Grove Dictionary of Music and Musicians*, ed. Stanley Sadie (London: Macmillan Publishers Ltd., 1980), i. 551, and Claude Palisca, 'Emilio de' Cavalieri', in *The New Grove*, iv. 20–3.

[9] 'Zur Tonart der Concertato-Motetten in Monteverdis *Marienvesper*', in Ludwig Finscher, ed., *Claudio Monteverdi. Festschrift Reinhold Hammerstein zum 70. Geburtstag* (Laaber: Laaber-Verlag, 1986), 361. Meier's analysis seems to me anachronistic and fallacious in its rigid definition of mode according to interval structure.

Ex. 9.1. *Nigra sum*

Ex. 9.1. *Continued*

the discussion below). From bar 34 to the end, however, the tenor voice has an ambitus of *e–f'* and a clear emphasis on the pentachord *g–d'*, suggesting the authentic mode 7 rather than the plagal mode 8. But it is the passage in bars 10–26, with cadences to A minor and to C major that significantly complicates the modal picture, and this is precisely where F♮ is prominent in both the voice and the bass.

However, it is not clear that the distinction between F and F♯ was meaningful to Monteverdi in 1610 in terms of defining the mode of the piece.[10] It seems more likely that he conceived the motet as in the mixed seventh and eighth modes on G. When G is presented as the goal of a cadence, F♯ will appear; when other steps of the mode become points of cadential arrival, F♮ will be used, and

---

[10] Chafe notes that 'the minor triads of the hexachord can be altered to major without affecting their ability to represent particular hexachordal degrees'. See Eric T. Chafe, *Monteverdi's Tonal Language* (New York: Schirmer Books, 1992), 26–7. In other words, the fluctuation between *f♮* and *f♯* does not change the hexachord on which a D triad is built. Similarly, *f♮* and *f♯* do not affect the *finalis*, the ambitus, or the octave species (division into pentachord and tetrachord) that define modes 7 and 8.

one may speak at these points of temporary changes in the mode (see below) that do not alter the principal mode of the composition. This way of viewing the two forms of F is close to the modern concept of modulation, whereby there are temporary changes of tonality in the course of a piece which depend on alterations of one or more pitches of the principal tonality in cadential progressions.

Susan McClary's method of dealing with tonality in Monteverdi's music calls for an examination of the principal linear descents to the *finalis* and the tension engendered by emphasizing either the fourth or the fifth degree, since these two focal pitches are in tension with one another in relation to the *finalis*.[11] From this standpoint, with the tonality centred on G, we can anticipate structural linear descents from both the fifth degree, *d*, and the fourth degree, *c*. If these descents reach all the way to *g*, they complete a cadence, but if they stop short of *g*, on *a*, then the cadence is incomplete and we can expect it to be completed at some later structural point in the composition.

Analysing *Nigra sum* from this perspective confirms the usefulness of McClary's method in several respects. The *finalis g* serves as the cadential note for the pentachord above (*d'* descending to *g*). While much of the composition is in a tessitura above *g*, the tetrachord below also receives emphasis at the beginning (bars 1–2 and 8–9). The total range of the voice, however, extends from *C* to *g'*, so the *d'* which defines the pentachord above *g* is itself exceeded several times by a third as well as by the tetrachord *d'–g'* (bars 29–30). In terms of the total range of the vocal part, both the plagal and authentic forms of the *tetradus* G modes (modes 8 and 7 respectively) are combined (mixed modality). Once again, the centrality of *g* as *finalis* is confirmed regardless of the modal interpretation. This combination of plagal and authentic octaves, however, establishes two possible reciting notes: *c'* for the plagal octave *d–d'*, and *d'* for the authentic octave *g–g'*.

In the first phrase of the motet (bars 1–7), the pentachord descent is initiated by the opening leap from *d* to *d'* and then accomplished twice by largely stepwise descent in bars 4–5. However, the attainment of *g*, while supported by a V–I harmonic progression, only serves as the springboard for further melodic motion, eventually culminating on the sustained *a* in bar 7, an incomplete cadence on the second degree of the mode supported in the bass by the fifth degree. This opening phrase establishes the plagal octave, whose reciting note is *c'*, yet the *diapente* descent has as its starting-point and upper limit *d'*, the reciting note of the authentic octave. It is the tension between this *d'* and the anticipated but absent *c'* that leads to the incomplete cadence and the alterations in the mode immediately to follow. In other words, a measure of uncertainty is

---

[11] Susan McClary, 'The Transition from Modal to Tonal Organization in the Works of Monteverdi' (Ph.D. dissertation, Harvard University, 1976). See esp. ch. 2.

established at the outset because of the inherent tension between d' and c' and because of the incomplete cadence, and this uncertainty quickly leads to further modal instability through cadences on other degrees of the scale.

The second phrase (bars 8–14) repeats a similar process to the first, but d' is accented by its upper sixth degree (bars 10–11), and the stepwise descent never reaches g, once again settling on a. The a, however, is now supported by A in the bass, approached by its own fifth, e, in a V–I cadence. In this phrase the pitch a has been reinterpreted as its own temporary *finalis*, and the descent from e' to a is now in retrospect the *diapente* descent in an A mode. In Renaissance terms, there has been a complete cadence on the second degree of the principal mode using $g\sharp$ as its *subsemitonium modi*. In modern terms, this constitutes a brief modulation to A minor.

The next phrase (bars 15–23) leads to two melodic cadences on c' (bars 20, 23), the fourth degree of the prevailing G mode, both supported by V–I harmonic cadences. This phrase, which begins on g (with C in the bass), therefore emphasizes the tetrachord above g, rather than the pentachord. The note c' is itself reached by melodic descent from a tetrachord above, extending the overall vocal range to f' (bars 18–20, continuing to bar 23). The c', which is the reciting note of the plagal octave of the G mode, is thus emphasized in the context of the authentic range of the mode (mode 7, g–g'), like the emphasis on d' (bars 3–5) in the plagal octave (mode 8). The central pitch in each phrase, therefore, contradicts the reciting note of the modal octave in which it is embedded.

In Renaissance terms, there has been a complete cadence in bar 23 on the fourth degree of the mode; in modern terms, there has been another modulation, this time to C major. Once the cadence on c' has been reached, it is confirmed by a tetrachord ascent from g to c' (bars 24–6). If c' is taken as a temporary *finalis*, then the passage in bars 15–26 defines the plagal form of the c mode with tetrachord (g–c') below and incomplete pentachord (c'–f') above.[12]

This analysis assumes that the f' in bar 18 falls short of the upper g' of the pentachord and that the f of bar 24 falls one note below the lowest note of the modal octave. However, the entire passage could also be viewed as an authentic octave of the f mode (mode 5), with range f–f' divided at the fifth by the cadences on the reciting note of the mode (c'). However, it is highly unusual to find the F mode without $b\flat$, and it is unlikely that Monteverdi would have thought of this passage as defining the Lydian mode.[13]

The ambiguities attendant on a modal analysis of this passage illustrate the problems that arise in approaching Monteverdi's procedures from just one perspective. In fact, the strength of the cadences on c', which give no hint of being

---

[12] Meier views this passage as confirming mode 8. See 'Zur Tonart der Concertato-Motetten', 362.

[13] Meier, in 'Zur Tonart der Concertato-Motetten', 361, suggests that the entire motet could be considered as in the sixth mode, or in the twelfth mode transposed.

subordinate to any other *finalis*, as well as the strictly cadential character of the bass from the very beginning of the piece, justify viewing this passage in harmonically functional, tonal terms. The passage in bars 15–26 may be seen simply and unambiguously as in the tonality of C major, and modal theory has limited relevance to it except with regard to the role of the note *c'* in the overall modal context of the piece.

To summarize the melodic motion thus far in *Nigra sum*, the pentachordal descent from *d'* to *g*, fundamental to the tonal construction of the work, has been left unfinished, first by an incomplete cadence on *a* (bar 7), then by a complete cadence on *a* (bar 14), and finally by a series of complete cadences on *c'* (bars 20, 23, 26).

While the tenor's melodic line, to the point of its first cadence on *c'* in bar 20, has consisted entirely of descending patterns, it now assumes an exclusively ascending physiognomy in accord with the word *surge* (arise).[14] It is just at this point that the entire ambitus of the vocal line, *c–g'*, is presented in one long sweep (bars 27–30), passing through both the plagal and the authentic octaves of the *tetrardus* before cadencing on *d'* in bar 31, the same note where the original pentachordal descent began in bar 3. But this time the *d'* has been reached by means of the ascending scale of bars 27–30 rather than the simple octave leap of bars 2–3. At this point the reciting note of the authentic octave (*d'*) has become the cadential degree, or, in modern terms, there has been a modulation to D minor. As if to remind us, however, that the *finalis* of the composition is *g*, an abbreviated version of bars 27–31 presents the ascent a fifth lower, cadencing finally onto *g* (bars 32–4). This *g*, however, has been reached by ascent from below, not by completing the descent of the pentachord above, and it comes much too quickly and easily to create a strong sense of closure after so many lengthy disruptions in the original descending motion towards the cadential *g*.

In the subsequent extended passage (bars 34–46) the principal melodic motion comprises an ascent of the pentachord *g–d'*, spending much of its time circulating around *d'* by as much as a third above and below (bars 38–46). This *d'* is itself somewhat unstable, however, since it is first overshot by leap to *e'* after *g* has been altered to *g♯* (bar 36), and *d'* is itself altered to *d♯'* as leading-note to *e'* (bars 39–40). The bass in bars 38–44 frequently presents the altered note *g♯*, which makes *a* a cadential tone, the *a* finally serving as dominant to D, where both the voice and the bass finally settle at the end of the phrase (bars 45–6). In harmonically functional terms, this second cadence in D minor has been preceded by its dominant and secondary dominant (V/V–V–I).

If the passage just completed destabilized *d'*, bars 47–54 do just the opposite.

---

[14] The long ascent on *surge* is anticipated by the brief ascent to *c'* in bars 22–3 and the longer ascent in bars 24–5.

Here d' is reiterated six times by the voice in semibreves, with an added breve at the end, supported by a stable progression in the bass whose cadential goal is G. And indeed, that G cadence accompanies the tenor's completion of the opening melodic descent from d' to a, the culminating g quickly reached in bars 55–6. As if to underscore the relationship between this cadence and the opening incomplete cadence, Monteverdi does not descend stepwise from d' to g; rather, he picks up in bar 55 precisely where he left off in bar 7, with a. But like the g cadence in bar 34, this one also comes too quickly and easily to constitute the *finalis* of the composition. Monteverdi therefore avails himself of one of the most ubiquitous forms of the sixteenth and seventeenth centuries (ABB) and repeats the passage from bars 34–56, his only significant changes comprising the diminution by half of most of the reiterated d's of bars 47–54 and the accompaniment of these notes by a lengthy descending scale in crotchets in the bass (bars 69–74). The reiteration of this entire section of the composition, including the cadence of bars 55–6, finally makes the arrival at g complete and convincing.

Whereas the first part of the piece emphasized the plagal octave $d–d'$, making only occasional incursions into the $d'–g'$ tetrachord above, from bar 34 to the end the melodic motion is centred around the authentic $g–d'$ pentachord. The pentachord recedes somewhat into the structural background in bars 34–46, with their chromatic alterations, several escapes to e', and one foray to f' (bar 40), but emerges triumphantly into the foreground in bars 47–55. What differentiates the use of d' as reciting note from bar 38 to the end from its role at the beginning of the motet as the starting-note for pentachord descents is that d' is now the appropriate reciting note for the authentic octave of the *tetrardus*. In other words, the initial tension in the use of d', contrasting with the expected eighth-mode reciting note of c', has been resolved. The newly found stability of d' is emphasized strikingly through its multiple repetitions in semibreves in bars 47–54.

This type of analysis outlines the overall melodic and cadential direction of *Nigra sum*, but as yet does little to explain the relationship between text and music other than to note the correlation between rising scales and the word *surge*. Moreover, by focusing on large-scale structural direction, it tends to turn our attention away from details of word-music relationships in favour of uncovering the melodic schema for the motet. Therefore it is to Monteverdi's interpretation of the text that I now turn my attention.

Robert Kendrick has approached *Nigra sum* from the standpoint of the allegorical significance of the text and its reflection in Monteverdi's modal usage.[15] In Kendrick's analysis, the female spouse (*sponsa*) at the opening (bars 1–26)

[15] 'Sonet vox tua'.

outlines mode 8 (*d–f′*) and cadences on the reciting note *c′*.[16] With the shift in the text to quotation of the male spouse by the *sponsa* (*et dixit mihi:*), Monteverdi introduces mode 7 (based on a *c–c′* ambitus, although he also includes the upper pentachord, *c′–g′*, (in bars 29–30). The emphasis on *d′* in bars 31–46 is an emphasis on the reciting note of mode 7 (see above), an emphasis highlighted even further by the sustained series of *d′*s in bars 47–73.[17] Kendrick notes a further distinction between the words of the *sponsa* and the words of the *sponsus* in bars 35–45, where there is 'a far more *durus* pitch content, with notated *c♯*, *g♯* and even *d♯* in the vocal part', a passage which is repeated, as noted above.[18] The musical division marked by the shift from mode 8 to mode 7 and the introduction of the many sharps in the latter coincides with the 'two literary voices', making of *Nigra sum* a

dialogue a 1, a form not unknown in both the secular and sacred repertory of the early Seicento.[19] But the explicit gender-based division of the dialogue's voices—the Sponsa's words with a more *mollis* pitch content and in the plagal cofinalis of the *tetradus*, while the Sponsus is allotted a more *durus* spectrum and is set in the authentic mode—reveals Monteverdi's sensitivity to both literary voice and the associations of sexual roles.[20]

Kendrick interprets the repeated, sustained *d′* as an emphasis on the allegorical interpretation of the words *tempus putationis advenit*. According to Kendrick,

This phrase was taken in contemporary exegesis as referring to the passing of the old Law and the coming of the new Law through the Incarnation of Christ (in Marian terms, the Annunciation).[21] In this sense, Monteverdi's highlighting of the *tempus putationis* phrase by its suspension on the recitation tone of the mode (over a descending bass) is analogous to the public

---

[16] It may also be noted here that the rising harmonic sequence (described below) reaches its climax in bar 23 with the second cadence on C at the words *et introduxit* [*me Rex*] *in cubiculum suum*. This phrase was commonly interpreted by biblical exegetes to refer to ascension into the heavenly kingdom. See Martin Del'Rio Antverpiense, *In Canticum Canticorum Salomonis commentarius litteralis, et catena mystica* (Lyons: Cardon, 1611), 33.

[17] Kendrick, 'Sonet vox tua', 108–11. Note the correlation with the focus on *c′* (bars 17–26) while still in mode 8, and the reciting note *d′* (bars 31–73) while in mode 7.

[18] Ibid. 109.

[19] Ibid., n. 40: 'For some monodic secular dialogues, see John Whenham, *Duet and Dialogue in the Age of Monteverdi* (Ann Arbor: UMI Research Press, 1982), 1: 181–2. Several pieces (*Si bona suscepimus, Quid agit Domine?*) in Ignazio Donati's *Secondo libro de motetti a voce sola* (Venice: Vincenti, 1636) are essentially dialogues a 1.'

[20] Kendrick, 'Sonet vox tua', 109 n. 41: 'For some theoretical reflections of male/female dichotomies in the Monteverdi–Artusi controversy, viewed in a classically structuralist and biologically reductionist framework, see now Suzanne G. Cusick, "Gendering Modern Music: Thoughts on the Monteverdi–Artusi Controversy", *Journal of the American Musicological Society*, 46 (1993), 1–25.'

[21] Kendrick's n. 39: 'See Ghisleri's [Michael Ghisleri(us), *Commentarii . . . in Canticum Canticorum Salomonis*, Venice 1609] explication, redolent of the vocabulary of the canticle itself, *Commentarii*, 332–33 ('Exposition IIII, De Tertia Sponsa, quae est B. Maria'): "*Surge*, neve moreris venire, quo te voco, instat enim partus eijs, quem gestas in ventre: iam legis *hiems transiit, imber* doctrinae Prophetarum *abit, & recessit*, cum primum, quod intra te est, Verbum carnem assumpsit . . . iamque & flos campi, ac lilium convallium in te progemmavit Christus filius Dei: *Adventi* iam *& tempus putationis*, quo per eundem Dei filium universi a mundo resecentur errores, & redemptione omnia amputentur peccata."'

proclamation and ritual re-creation of the Incarnation and Redemption, namely the Elevation of the Host at Mass. The repetition of the melodic gesture . . . is of course paralleled by the double Elevation (of the bread and the wine) during the Canon of the Mass.[22]

Kendrick goes even further in his association of this passage with the mass to suggest that 'Perhaps *Nigra sum* was originally conceived, not as a Vespers item (antiphon substitute) but rather as an Elevation piece to accompany the six-voice Mass'.[23] Kendrick's analysis attempts to interpret the motet on contemporary grounds—the long-standing and widespread practice of explicating biblical texts allegorically. This method is wholly appropriate and may well bring us closer to understanding Monteverdi's conception of text–music relations. The difficulty is that all allegorical interpretations must remain hypothetical unless there is a direct statement by the composer of his intentions. While the musical features of *Nigra sum* correlate with the text in the manner described by Kendrick, the meaning of that correlation can only be suggested and never determined definitively. The allegorical meaning Kendrick proposes may have been a common one in the seventeenth century, but it also shares the stage with the literal significance of the text and with other allegories yielding different possibilities.[24] For example, Helmut Hucke has offered an allegorical interpretation of *Nigra sum* based on a 1604 edition of Martin Del'Rio's *In Canticum Canticorum Salomonis commentarius litteralis, et catena mystica*, a different source from those consulted by Kendrick.[25] Hucke's discussion focuses on the text and includes only limited commentary on the relationship between the textual allegory and the music.

According to Hucke, Del'Rio interprets the *sponsa* as Mary, the king (*Rex*) as Christ, and the king's chamber as heaven, making of the first part of the text an allegory for the ascension of the Virgin into heaven.[26] Del'Rio also offers alternative interpretations. Taking the phrase *iam hiems transijt* to refer to the passing of the winter of sin and the departure of the stormy wrath of heaven, the earth becomes the Blessed Virgin, who gives forth fruit from the shoot of Jesse in the form of Jesus.[27] This interpretation then alters the significance of the first part of the text so that *introduxit me [Rex] in cubiculum suum* refers to Mary's conception of Jesus.[28] Del'Rio also gives two different exegeses for the phrase *tempus putationis*. The first takes its point of departure from a reported apostolic

---

[22] Kendrick, 'Sonet vox tua', 109.

[23] Ibid. The mass cited is the *Missa in illo tempore*, published with the Vespers in 1610.

[24] Ibid. 103–5.

[25] (Ingolstadt, 1604). See Hucke, 'Die fälschlich so genannte "Marien"-Vesper von Claudio Monteverdi', *Bericht über den internationalen musikwissenschaftlichen Kongress Bayreuth 1981* (Kassel: Bärenreiter, 1984), 295–305.

[26] Del'Rio even offers several explanations from patristic writers as to why the Virgin is depicted as *nigra* (*In Canticum Canticorum*, 50).

[27] Ibid. 128; Hucke, 'Die fälschlich so genannte "Marien"-Vesper', 301.

[28] Ibid.

discussion of whether a heathen converted to Christianity must be circumcised. The decision of the Apostles is that the heathen who turns to God need undergo no further burdens, since salvation through Christ has abrogated the old law. The second interpretation takes its origin from John 15: 1–2: 'I am the true vine and my Father is the husbandman. Every branch in me that beareth not fruit he taketh away: and every branch that beareth fruit, he purgeth it, that it may bring forth more fruit'.[29] According to Hucke, 'the text of the first *concerto* therefore represents with words of the Song of Songs the salvation Mary has brought to the world through the birth of Christ. . . . The manner in which Monteverdi composes *tempus putationis* shows how impressed too his consciousness was with the vanity of the world, the sinfulness of man and the anticipation of the Last Judgement.'[30]

Did Monteverdi have one of these contemporaneous allegories in mind, or was he more concerned with the literal semantic significance of his text? Or are both approaches present simultaneously, as is, in fact, the very premiss of allegory? All of these possibilities require further consideration. Kendrick's additional suggestion that *Nigra sum* may originally have been conceived as an Elevation motet is fascinating and provocative, though more speculative than his initial allegorical interpretation because it is based on two levels of allegory— the assumed allegorical liturgical function of a presumed text-music allegory. Nevertheless, his suggestion is not implausible and is worthy of consideration.

In addition to the musical analysis offered above and the allegorical interpretations of Kendrick and Hucke, it is also informative, as I have just suggested, to view *Nigra sum* in terms of the literal significance of the text before making an allegorical exegesis, relying on an allegorical interpretation only where a literal one seems absent. It is obvious from Monteverdi's sacred and secular works throughout his career that the surface meaning of his texts, even in the most immediate significance of a single word isolated from its context in a phrase or sentence, often elicited specific musical metaphors. Therefore, my analysis, after establishing a principal conception for the piece, will proceed through the motet step by step, dealing with each feature as it presents itself, postponing until the end my suggestion as to the significance of these steps in the perspective of the entire piece.

---

[29] Hucke, 'Die fälschlich so genannte "Marien"-Vespe', 301–2. The Vulgate Latin reads: 'Ego sum vita vera, et Pater meus agricola est. Omnem palmitem in me non ferentem fructum, tollet eum; et omnem qui fert fructum, purgabit eum, ut fructum plus afferat'.

[30] 'Der Text des ersten *Concerto* stellt also mit Worten des Hohen Liedes dar, daß Maria durch die Geburt Christi die Erlösung in die Welt gebracht hat. . . . Die Art und Weise, wie Monteverdi das "Tempus putationis" vertont, zeigt, wie sehr auch er von diesem Bewußtsein der Nichtigkeit der Welt, der Sündigkeit des Menschen und der Erwartung des Gerichts geprägt war'. See Hucke, 'Die fälschlich so genannte "Marien"-Vesper', 302. Hucke, ibid. 305, also affirms the multiplicity of possible allegorical interpretations of sacred texts.

The central semantic concept in the text of *Nigra sum*, as Monteverdi interprets it melodically and harmonically, is embodied in the word *surge*. The command 'arise' establishes the fundamental character and direction of the melodic and harmonic structure throughout the composition. At the very outset of the piece this rising concept is expressed in its simplest and most elemental form by means of an octave leap from the lower *d* to the higher *d'* (bars 1–3). The lower *d*, with its dark vocal colouring, is suitable for the first enunciation of the phrase *Nigra sum*.[31] Monteverdi relieves this sudden, energetic opening leap with a pair of descending motifs in bars 3–4 and 4–7, first by a descent to *g* and then by a more leisurely descent to *a* (using the *g* as lower neighbour-note), but stopping short of resolution on an incomplete cadence. The contrast between the low-pitched, slow pronunciation of the words *Nigra sum* and the higher-pitched, rhythmically and melodically lively presentation of *sed formosa filia* highlights the textual contrast introduced by the conjunction *sed*. The *a* at the end of the phrase not only constitutes the incomplete cadence noted above, but marks the incomplete sentence, lacking its final word, *Jerusalem*. It is noteworthy that Monteverdi has altered the text from the Vulgate's vocative *filiae Jerusalem* to the predicate nominative *formosa filia Jerusalem* as noted above. Monteverdi's association of the word *formosa* with *filia* and their separation from *Jerusalem* in this first musical phrase demonstrate that the change in text was purposeful, with the altered significance deliberately exploited in the incomplete first phrase. This incompleteness requires that a significant structural articulation immediately follow.

The energy originating from the first leap is at this point increased by a yet larger leap in bars 9–10 designed to enhance the upward thrust not only by its greater interval, but by arriving at a note dissonant to the initial pitch. This *e'* in bar 10 also serves to announce the second stage of the rising sequence from G to A minor and to C major, encompassing bars 1–23. The cadence to A minor in bars 11–14 not only gives a sense of temporary closure to the pitch *a*, which was left unresolved in bar 7, but also serves to bring the text to the conclusion of its sentence with an ornamental flourish on *Jerusalem* (bars 13–14).

Now that the upward surge has been extended beyond pitch and register to the domain of sequential cadential goals, the third phrase completes the process by beginning at a higher pitch level with *Ideo* in bar 15 and rising to the highest note yet, the *f'* in bar 18, before continuing with the familiar short descending motif. This new pitch level coincides with the third stage of the sequence, which now cadences to C major. The appearance of *Ideo* a fourth higher than the corresponding notes for *Nigra sum* and the sequential repetition of *Ideo* a

---

[31] Noted by Meier, 'Zur Tonart der Concertato-Motetten', 361.

fourth higher still on *c'* highlight the second stage of the argument. The sentence beginning with *Ideo* is the logical consequence of the first sentence, and is therefore appropriately emphasized by its higher pitch level and sequential repetition. The phrase mentioning the king's love, *dilexit me Rex*, begins on *f'*, the highest pitch yet (bar 18). The continuing phrase, *et introduxit in cubiculum suum*, whereby the *sponsa* is brought to a new place, leads correspondingly to a cadence in a new location, the fourth degree of the eighth mode.[32]

The initial three phrases of *Nigra sum* have thus established the generally upward direction of the motet, first in an abrupt fashion with the opening leap and then more deliberately by the rising sequence of phrases passing from G major to A minor and finally to C major.[33] In the analysis above it was noted that the *d'* of the opening was in contradiction with the *c* reciting note of the plagal eighth mode. This contradiction underscores the contradiction in the first phrase of the text that is signalled by its conjunction, *sed*: *Nigra sum sed formosa*.

The opening section of the motet does not conclude at this point, but is extended by a short *codetta* to accommodate the conjunctive phrase that introduces the next portion of the text: *et dixit mihi*. This codetta in bars 24–6 also serves as a melodic link between the two sections, diatonically filling the leap from *g* to *c'* with which the preceding phrase began (bars 15–17). The embellishment also anticipates the next section, which begins in bar 27 with the even more extended ascending scale.

The second section commences at bar 27 with the word *surge* itself; it is repeated several times, accompanied by a variety of upward thrusts in the melody. At first the scale rises easily through a twelfth from the low *c* to the high *g'*, but then it turns back upon itself to settle on *d'* in bar 31. This phrase constitutes a stepwise subdivision of the opening octave leap of the motet, expanded to a larger compass. The span between the *c* and *d'* at the beginning and end of the phrase effects a modulation back from the C major in which the first section closed to the dominant of G, which was the harmony underlying *d'* in bar 3. The upward drive of this phrase is also enhanced by the continuo, following immediately behind the voice in imitation (bars 28–9).

Just as the octave rise at the outset of *Nigra sum* was accomplished deceptively simply with respect to its weighty significance in the composition as a whole, the ascent from *c* to *d'* in bars 27–31 has also occurred without great effort, even overshooting the mark by a fourth before resolving back to the principal pitch *d'*. Monteverdi therefore retreats in bar 32 to the original *d* to attack the ascent more vigorously and systematically. First he repeats the rising scale, this time beginning on *d*, climbing only as far as *a*, and then settling on *g* (bars 32–4). The *g*

---

[32] The allegorical significance of this point of arrival is described in n. 16 above.

[33] It should be noted that the pitch sequence *g–a–c* comprises the intonation of the eighth psalm tone. Moreover, the upper inflection of the eighth tone is *d*.

next serves as the point of departure for a series of short sequential leaps reaching as high as e' in bar 36 before quickly coming back down again. This last phrase has brought the melody once more to the region of the upper d', and in bar 38 Monteverdi begins his next phrase on d' itself, hovering around this note throughout the recitative of the next eight bars. This circling ascends as high as f' on the command *veni* (come) in bar 40, which was also the highest pitch at the climax of the sequence in the first section (bar 18). The prominence of d' is underscored by its repetition in bars 43–4 and the closure on d' in bar 46. The passage from bars 34–46 is the most unstable in the motet, with its interpolations of $g\sharp'$, $c\sharp'$, and $d\sharp'$, as described above, reflecting the unstable passage of the seasons articulated in the text. The rhythmic organization is also irregular, with syncopations and dotted rhythms at different levels. Only with the arrival of spring flowers (*flores apparuerunt in terra nostra*) do the melody and harmony finally settle unambiguously on D, as the rhythmic organization also becomes more settled and regular. Referring once again to Kendrick's allegorical interpretation, the striking shift of hexachord to one based on two sharps (treating $g\sharp$ as *subsemitonium modi* to a) and the radical introduction of $d\sharp'$ as *subsemitonium modi* to e' (bars 39–40) may serve to emphasize the shift in dispensation from the old law to the new, symbolized in the text by the change of seasons. The arrival of spring signals the arrival at the new dispensation.[34]

The entire passage from bar 27 to bar 46 can now be seen as a purposeful, methodical extension from the low d to the upper d', a series of events foreshadowed in simple form in bars 1–3.[35] Once the high d' has been attained in this systematic manner, Monteverdi emphasizes it decisively by the repetition of long sustained notes in bars 47–54. There is no immediately obvious reason based on the semantics of the text why this passage should consist of repeated semibreves (a pun on the word *tempus* would have required breves). Kendrick compares these repeated notes with a public proclamation of the new law. It may also be that Monteverdi interpreted the *tempus putationis* as a time of simplification, of pruning away the accretions and complications of the old law, or

[34] That such an interpretation was both venerable and widespread is demonstrated by Bede's sermon *In dedicatione templi* and by the service of the Recollection of the Virgin composed by the Dean of the Cathedral of Cambrai, Gilles Carlier, in 1457, reported in Craig Wright, 'Dufay's *Nuper rosarum flores*, King Solomon's Temple, and the Veneration of the Virgin', *Journal of the American Musicological Society*, 47 (1994), 411–12, 434. Bede describes winter (*hiems*) as a metaphor for the asperity of the Jews, and Carlier's ninth lesson at matins declares, 'Now when the winter under the law and the prophets had passed, flowers of virtue appeared in our virgin land, from which truth arose.' (*Iam hyems sub lege et prophetis abierat quando flores virtutum apparuerunt in terra nostra virginea, de qua orta est veritas.*). According to Chafe, in Monteverdi's earlier work the *cantus durus* 'also often bears pejorative associations bound up with ideas of hardness, sharpness, dissonance, and the like'. See *Monteverdi's Tonal Language*, 54.

[35] Chafe notes that 'flat-to-sharp motion [in this case the natural hexachord to the hard hexachord] highlighted by transposition can be used to intensify arrival at the dominant . . . thereby projecting a strong sense of direction' (*Monteverdi's Tonal Language*, 35).

even the errors of the past.[36] From a strictly melodic point of view, this recitation on *d'* fulfils and confirms the melodic goal of the entire composition. But
to conclude at this point would have been unsatisfactory, for Monteverdi, in his
continual upward drive, has constructed a powerful force and tension which are
by no means resolved by the cadence in bars 55–6.

Monteverdi's solution to this dilemma is ingenious. He returns to bars 34–5
in the second section, repeating the sequential upward surge almost verbatim,
reaching the high *d'* a second time. But in repetition this passage sounds slightly
anticlimactic. Once the *d'* is attained again the bass begins an unprecedented
downward scale, which is carried in a pair of sequential segments through
almost two octaves (bars 69–74). This descent has the effect of quickly deflating
and dissipating the accumulated energy and tension of the carefully calculated
upward motion of the voice and now permits a satisfying closure almost identical in form to the unsatisfying cadence of bars 55–6. Repetition of the last segment of a madrigal or solo song, as noted above, is very common in music of the
sixteenth and early seventeenth centuries, but Monteverdi has turned a traditional structural practice into a dramatic resolution of the tensions and drives
that he has engineered throughout the composition.

Nigra sum thus exemplifies a balanced union between poetry and music. Not
only does Monteverdi carefully follow the rhythmic accents of the words and
interpret their rhetorical inflections with corresponding inflections of pitch,
but he has also conceived a unifying melodic structure for the motet as whole,
pursued with relentless musical logic and yet derived from and in perfect accord
with the central concept of the text in both its literal meaning and its apparent
allegorical significance. It is little wonder that Monteverdi wished to 'go slow'
with his compositions in order that they be written well, for the marriage of
poetic and musical meaning demonstrated here is the result of a deeply thought-
ful process in which the composer has brought his greatest intellectual concentration and musical imagination to bear on the compositional and interpretive
challenges of his art.

---

[36] Kendrick quotes the commentary of the 17th-century exegete Michael Ghisleri on this passage:
'*Advenit* iam & *tempus putationis*, quo per eundem Dei filium universi a mundo resecentur errores, & redemptione omnia amputentur peccata.' See Kendrick, 'Sonet vox tua', 109 n. 39. Ghisleri, therefore,
considers *tempus putationis* as the time of cutting away error and sin, which would tend to support my
suggestion. The two interpretations of *tempus putationis* cited by Hucke above also support this view.

Compositions not Based on a Cantus Firmus: *Pulchra es, Duo Seraphim, Audi coelum*

THE three remaining motets from Monteverdi's 1610 print, *Pulchra es, Duo Seraphim*, and *Audi coelum*, exhibit many of the same methods of construction uncovered in *Nigra sum* in the last chapter. Therefore, my discussion of these pieces will be more limited, confined to salient points unique to each motet, and the interested reader may explore these compositions further in terms of their modal implications, octave species, and reciting notes. Some of these features, especially as they pertain to interpretation of the text, will be described below, but not as systematically as in my analysis of *Nigra sum*.

Pulchra es   *A due voci* (for two voices); Song of Songs 6: 3–4

> Pulchra es, amica mea,
> suavis, et decora filia Ierusalem;
> Pulchra es, amica mea,
> suavis, et decora sicut Ierusalem;
> terribilis ut castrorum acies ordinata.
> Averte oculos tuos à me,
> quia ipsi me avolare fecerunt.

> You are beautiful, my dearest,
> lovely daughter of Jerusalem;
> You are beautiful, my dearest,
> lovely as Jerusalem;
> terrible as an army arrayed in camp.
> Turn your eyes away from me;
> for they have made me flee.

The soprano duet *Pulchra es*, whose text, like that of *Nigra sum*, is closely related to a vesper antiphon for a Marian feast, is somewhat less complicated than the solo motet.[1] Monteverdi's text is identical to the Vulgate in lines 3–7. His first two lines are derived from the antiphon. Palestrina's version in the Song of Songs motets of 1583–4 (RISM P716) is taken exclusively from the Vulgate, so that Palestrina begins with the second iteration of *Pulchra es* above, thereby not

---

[1] Fifth antiphon for the feast of the Assumption of the BVM, 15 Aug.: 'Pulchra es et decora, filia Jerusalem: terribilis ut castrorum acies ordinata'. Note the antiphon's substitution of *filia* for *sicut*.

including Monteverdi's and the antiphon's phrase *decora filia Jerusalem* (contrasted with *decora sicut Ierusalem* of the fourth line).[2] I have found only one early seventeenth-century *Pulchra es* setting other than Monteverdi's, by Lodovico Torto in his *Missa una septem divinae laudes* of 1607 (RISM T1013), that uses the phrase *filia Hierusalem*, although Torto does not reiterate the opening lines, thereby omitting the Vulgate version *sicut Jerusalem*. Monteverdi's alterations of the Vulgate text in both *Nigra sum* and *Pulchra es*, in order to refer to the *sponsa* or the Virgin as the daughter of Jerusalem, establish a connection between these two motets.[3] As we shall see, his use of both the antiphon and Vulgate versions of the opening lines in *Pulchra es* is also significant in terms of the structure of his setting.

The speaker in *Pulchra es* is the *sponsus*, who metaphorically describes his beloved as well as his own reaction to her awe-inspiring beauties. These beauties were frequently associated with the virtues of Mary, who may also be considered the personification of the Church, especially because of the comparison the text makes between the *sponsa* and Jerusalem, the Holy City.[4] The contrasting description of the *sponsa*, as *terribilis ut castrorum acies ordinata*, was interpreted by the seventeenth-century exegete Martin Del'Rio in terms of the Apocalypse, whereby the 'army' of the Song of Songs represented the heavenly hosts on Judgement Day.[5] Del'Rio also interpreted this phrase as referring to the armies of the Church, consisting of martyrs, confessors, virgins, and other just people, arrayed against the devil and heretics.[6] According to Del'Rio, *Averte oculos tuos à me* warns humanity against attempting to look directly upon God, for the sight of God is fatal. Human beings should seek to understand God through the Scriptures and his visible creations.[7] Del'Rio typically gives several different

---

[2] A copy of Palestrina's motets was available to Monteverdi in the Santa Barbara library. See Ch. 4 n. 144.

[3] See also the connection with *Audi coelum* below, where the word *pulchra* likewise appears, and the *porta Orientalis* has traditionally been associated with Jerusalem. Helmut Hucke has noted the direct and indirect references to Jerusalem in *Laetatus sum*, *Nisi Dominus*, and *Lauda Jerusalem*. See Hucke, 'Die fälschlich so genannte "Marien"-Vesper von Claudio Monteverdi', *Bericht über den internationalen musikwissenschaftlichen Kongress Bayreuth 1981* (Kassel: Bärenreiter, 1984), 300.

[4] Ibid. 302. *Pulchra, suavis*, and *decora* are all characteristics of the Church, imitating the soul. The Church is even superior in these characteristics to Jerusalem itself, but Jerusalem may also be taken as referring to the heavenly Jerusalem of God. See Martin Del'Rio Antverpiense, *In Canticum Canticorum Salomonis commentarius litteralis, et catena mystica* (Lyons: Cardon, 1611), 436–7. Michael Ghisleri, in *Commentaria in Canticum Canticorum Salomonis* (Antwerp: Keerbergium, 1619), 799, sees *suavis* as the foundation of grace in the Virgin, as Jerusalem is the foundation of Zion.

[5] Hucke, 'Die fälschlich so genannte "Marien"-Vesper', 302–3.

[6] *In Canticum Canticorum Salomonis commentarius*, 433–41. Ghisleri, *Commentaria*, 797, remarks that both Jerusalem and the Church are at peace because Jerusalem itself possesses walls and towers and armies and the Church has many defenders, called the army of the Lord God, with Christ at its head. Ghisleri gives additional interpretations of this phrase as referring to the gravity and majesty of the soul at peace with God (ibid. 798) and to the strength of the Virgin (ibid. 799).

[7] 'Vide ne hic maiestatem meam videre quaeras. . . . Doch mein Angesicht kannst du nicht schauen, denn kein Mensch kann mich schauen und dabei am Leben bleiben. . . . Itaque averte oculos tuos a me, quia dum in carne constituta peregrinaris a prennibus bonis, me perfecte cognoscere non poteris. Igitur

interpretations for each word or phrase. His literal interpretation of *Averte oculos tuos a me* refers to the humility of the *sponsa*, who should not look upon the *sponsus*, while another allegorical interpretation comprises a request to the Virgin to turn her maternal eyes away from the speaker in order that he may look upon her as a friend and *sponsa*. *Quia ipsi me avolare fecerunt* then refers to the eyes of the Virgin drawing the *sponsus* after her to heaven.[8] Ghisleri suggests that the more one understands of God, the further away He flies. Other interpretations ask God to turn His eyes away since the body cannot withstand the divine light, or ask God not to bestow too many blessings, lest the speaker should learn to love his prosperity less.[9]

Monteverdi's setting is for cantus and sextus—male singers if performed in church, but possibly women if sung in 'chapels or chambers of princes' (see Chapter 9). *Pulchra es* is principally a virtuoso duet, filled with lively dotted rhythms and ornamentation. Whereas Monteverdi used monody infrequently outside opera, duets for voices in the same register, responding to one another in imitation quickly leading to parallel thirds, are very common in the Monteverdi canon as well as in the secular and sacred literature of the early seventeenth century in general.[10] In both segments of *Pulchra es*, the cantus introduces the first sentence by itself, and is only then joined by the sextus for a continuation or repetition of the text. The second segment of the motet, with its reference to 'fleeing', is partly in triple metre.[11]

Like *Nigra sum*, *Pulchra es* is in *cantus durus* with G *finalis*, and the vocal lines similarly suggest both the seventh and eighth modes.[12] In the first portion of the piece (bars 1–23), the principal octave $d'-d''$ is subdivided plagally as in the eighth mode (see Ex. 10.1). The word *suavis* by itself is emphasized through the dissonant modal seventh degree (bars 6 and 21, creating cross-relations with the F♯ in an inner part of the continuo in bar 5 and the sextus in bar 20), chromatic inflections being a very common means of interpreting this word in the late sixteenth and early seventeenth centuries. The second adjective describing the *amica*—*decora*—is appropriately ornamented with a melisma.

Since Monteverdi's second sentence is nearly identical to the first, he underscores this similarity by repeating in the sextus voice the same melody that he has

in via perenne praemium non quaeras, quod non dabitur alicui viventium nisi in patria.' [p. 316]. Quoted in Hucke, 'Die fälschlich so genannte "Marien"-Vesper', 303. See also Del'Rio, *In Canticum Canticorum Salomonis commentarius*, 445.

[8] 'Hoc est, propter ipsos avolavi a te: ut avertas oculos illos tuos maternos a me, ascendens in coelum avolavi a te, ut a me in meos transferes teneritudinem maternae pietatis'. Ibid. 444.

[9] *Commentaria*, 802–4.

[10] For a study of duets in this period, see John Whenham, *Duet and Dialogue in the Age of Monteverdi*, 2 vols. (Ann Arbor: UMI Research Press, 1982).

[11] See Ch. 20 for a discussion of the relationship between triple and duple metre in *Pulchra es*.

[12] See the modal analysis by Bernhard Meier, 'Zur Tonart der Concertato-Motetten in Monteverdis *Marienvesper*', in Ludwig Finscher, ed., *Claudio Monteverdi. Festschrift Reinhold Hammerstein zum 70. Geburtstag* (Laaber: Laaber Verlag, 1986), 360–1.

Ex. 10.1. *Pulchra es*, bars 1–29

Ex. 10.1. *Continued*

already notated on the upper stave of the Bassus Generalis at the beginning as an
ornamented variant of the cantus. The cantus itself sings an embellished version
of its opening phrase at this point (bar 15), following the sextus in imitation in
bar 17. The analogy between the loveliness of the daughter of Jerusalem and
Jerusalem itself are thus expressed in the parallels between the two voices. The
relationship between the duet (bars 15–29) and the original melodic statement
of the cantus (bars 1–14) is indicated in Ex. 10.1 by asterisks. This portion of the
composition may be structurally described as AA', the addition of the sextus co-
inciding with the beginning of the harmonic repetition and melodic variation.

The final description of the *amica*—*terribilis ut castrorum acies ordinata*—is of a
sharply contrasting character to *suavis, et decora*. Already with the concluding
sicut Jerusalem of the fourth line, the vocal range is extended upwards, frequently
exceeding the pentachord of the *d'–d''* octave by rising to *e''*, once to *f''*, and
once in each voice to *g''*. This extension of the range by another tetrachord
above *d''* creates the same mixture of seventh and eighth modes we encountered

in *Nigra sum*, encompassing both the plagal octave (*d'–d''*) and the authentic octave (*g'–g''*). And just as *Nigra sum* exploited this extension of the range to cadence on *c'*, *Pulchra es* has a series of full cadences on *c''* in the phrase *terribilis ut castrorum acies ordinata*, forming a codetta to the first segment of the motet.

As in *Nigra sum*, the emphasis on *d''* as the upper limit of the *g'–d''* pentachord in the first part of the piece is in contradiction with the *c''* reciting note of the eighth mode. Similarly, in the phrase *terribilis ut castrorum acies ordinata*, the cadential *c''* is in tension with the reciting note *d''* of the seventh mode. In *Nigra sum* these tensions and contradictions appeared to be related to the contradiction in the opening phrase of the text, articulated by the conjunction *sed*. The contradiction in the text of *Pulchra es* is between the second set of attributes of the *sponsa*—*terribilis ut castrorum acies ordinata*—which are opposite in character from *suavis, et decora*, whether considered in their literal meaning or in the allegorical terms of the virtues of Mary on the one hand and the Apocalyptic vision of the heavenly hosts on Judgement Day on the other. These opposing sets of attributes are therefore set respectively in the plagal eighth mode with *g' finalis* and the authentic seventh mode with *c''* as *cofinalis*.

Melodic organization in the second part of the piece focuses on the *g'–d''* pentachord, and as in *Nigra sum*, the melodic emphasis on *d''* now confirms rather than contradicts the reciting note of the authentic octave. The reaction of the *sponsus* to the attributes of the *sponsa* is one of fear and flight: *Averte oculos tuos à me, quia ipsi me avolare fecerunt*. The turning of the eyes results initially in a turning away from the predominant modality of the piece.[13] The command *Averte* is pronounced through the unusual downward leap *e''–g♯'*, abruptly establishing an E major triad over a sustained *e* in the bass which contrasts with the previous C major chord (see Ex. 10.2). This E major triad is the principal harmony for several bars until the bass moves around the descending circle of fifths to cadence on G at *quia ipsi*, rupturing the grammatical unit of the text. For Monteverdi, the importance of generating a new musical metaphor for the word *avolare* clearly outweighed the syntactic integrity of the final line of the text. The reference to fleeing (*me avolare fecerunt*), instead of resulting in another change of mode, leads to a quickened pace through a shift to triple metre and sequential transposition of the passage up a fifth in the solo cantus. Monteverdi even creates a second musical metaphor for *avolare* in the succeeding passage in duple metre, where the word is set to a lengthy melisma in dotted rhythm (see Ex. 10.3). From the beginning of the triple metre, the melodic motion is centred in the upper pentachord *g'–d''*, continuing the authentic seventh mode first introduced at *sicut Jerusalem*. Thus the plagal eighth mode is associated with the

---

[13] See the modal analysis by Bernhard Meier, 'Zur Tonart', 361.

Ex. 10.2. *Pulchra es*, bars 37–45

Ex. 10.3. *Pulchra es*, bars 54–9

charms of the *amica*, and the authentic seventh mode with 'terrible as an army' whose eyes have 'made me flee'.

As in the first segment of *Pulchra es*, where the solo cantus was eventually joined by the sextus in varied repetition, the sextus now also joins the cantus for reiteration of the final sentence of the text, repeating almost exactly the music of the cantus in parallel thirds. If the codetta concluding the first part of the motet is designated B, then the second portion of *Pulchra es* may be structurally described as CC′ and the organization of the entire motet as AA′BCC′. Although the first sentence of the text is substantially longer than the second, Monteverdi reverses this proportion in his musical setting, where the second musical segment is considerably longer than the first. His structural weight and emphasis is on the impact of the attributes of the *amica* on the *sponsus*, not on the celebration of her charms; in other words, on a psychological interpretation of the text rather than a descriptive interpretation.

Duo seraphim   *Tribus vocibus* (for three voices); adapted from Isaiah 6: 3 and 1 John 5: 7

> Duo Seraphim clamabant alter ad alterum:
> Sanctus, sanctus, sanctus Dominus Deus sabaoth.
> Plena est omnis terra gloria eius.
> Tres sunt qui testimonium dant in coelo:
> Pater, Verbum, et Spiritus sanctus.
> Et hi tres unum sunt.
> Sanctus, sanctus, sanctus Dominus Deus sabaoth.
> Plena est omnis terra gloria eius.
>
> Two Seraphim called to one another:
> Holy, holy, holy is the Lord of Hosts:
> the whole earth is full of his glory.
> There are three who bear witness in heaven:
> the Father, the Word, and the Holy Spirit;
> and these three are one.
> Holy, holy, holy is the Lord of Hosts:
> The whole earth is full of his glory.

Duo Seraphim has caused more controversy over its putative role in a vesper service than any other composition in Monteverdi's 1610 print. The text, a combination of verses from the Book of Isaiah and freely written lines, was traditionally associated with the feast of the Holy Trinity in the sixteenth and seventeenth centuries.[14]

---

[14] Victoria assigns this motet to the feast of the Trinity in the first edition of his *Motecta festorum totius Anni* of 1583, but to the feast of St Michael the Archangel in the 1585 edition. See Ch. 4 nn. 121–4. See also the discussion of the liturgical role of *Duo Seraphim* and antecedents to Monteverdi's setting in Chs. 1 and 4 above. Del'Rio, in commenting on the text *Pulchra es* in his *In Canticum Canticorum Salomonis commentarius*, 437, refers to the acclamations of the Seraphim in proclaiming the heavenly Jerusalem. Thus, through exegesis, the Trinitarian motet *Duo Seraphim* may also be connected with the many allusions in Monteverdi's other motets and his psalms to the heavenly Jerusalem.

The motet is divided into two parts, corresponding to the Old Testament text from Isaiah and the reference to the Trinity of the New Dispensation. In the first part of the piece, two tenors take the role of the *Duo Seraphim*, while in the second, three tenors represent the Father, Word, and Holy Spirit who give testimony. With the repetition of the Isaiah text after the second sentence, much of the music of the first part of the motet is repeated in the second part, recast for three voices.

Bernhard Meier identifies the mode of *Duo Seraphim* as the second mode transposed a fourth up to *g* by means of the single-flat signature.[15] Another way of describing it is *cantus mollis* with *finalis g*, the *finalis* agreeing with those of *Nigra sum* and *Pulchra es*, which are in *cantus durus*. As in the other two motets, the vocal lines reveal a plagal division of the *d–d'* octave, though the octave is exceeded by as much as a third at both ends. A change of mode occurs at the passage *Pater, Verbum, et Spiritus sanctus*, where the same *d–d'* octave is subdivided at *a*, with *d* as its temporary *finalis*, thereby defining the untransposed first mode. This change of mode is underscored by a repeated V–I cadential progression in the bass to D (the continuo player might well fill out the open fifth cadence with a Picardy rather than a minor third). Thus *Duo Seraphim*, like *Nigra sum* and *Pulchra es*, mixes both the authentic and plagal versions of its mode, each being associated with a different aspect of the text.

At the opening, the rising melodic line of the two voices quickly splits into alternating imitations of the word *clamabant*, graphically illustrating the phrase *alter ad alterum* (see Ex. 10.4). The interaction between the two seraphim culminates in a series of dissonant suspensions followed by a spontaneous outburst of virtuoso ornamentation. Since the text is an incomplete third-person narration, the descending fifth *d'–g* stops on *a*, short of its goal, concluding on a half-cadence and setting the stage for quotation of the seraphim themselves in the next passage.

For the remainder of the first section, this suspended *a* will serve to subdivide the plagal *d* octave not at the *finalis g*, but rather at the second degree, maintaining the tension of the incomplete cadence, which does not arrive at its final resolution until the very end of the first section of the piece. The suspended *a* as the melodic focal point is especially obvious in the virtuosic imitative setting of the *Sanctus* acclamations (see bars 20–3, Ex. 10.4).

The concluding sentence of the quotation from Isaiah, *Plena est omnis terra gloria eius*, receives fulsome melismatic treatment until the pace slows for the final cadence to the long-delayed *g*. Throughout this passage Monteverdi has

---

[15] 'Zur Tonart der Concertato-Motetten', 359–67. According to Meier, numerous composers of the 16th century set this text in the second mode as a numerically symbolic representation of the two seraphim.

Ex. 10.4. *Duo Seraphim*, bars 1–29

Ex. 10.4. *Continued*

maintained the tension between *a* and *g* as focal pitches, the tension only being resolved in the final unison *g* of the cadence.

The second part of *Duo Seraphim* adds the third tenor to represent the three witnesses. As at the beginning of the motet, the first phrase is a third-person narration, leading to the enumeration of *Pater, Verbum, et Spiritus sanctus* one by one, cumulatively adding each voice. The theological crux of the text is the unification of the witnesses in a single entity: *Et hi tres unum sunt*. Monteverdi powerfully achieves this unification in sonic terms through triadic recitation resolving to a unison (IV–I bass motion) at *unum sunt*; the passage is then intensified by sequential repetition a step higher (see Ex. 10.5). Monteverdi characteristically created an audible representation of unification in contrast to the numerically symbolic metaphor of a $\frac{3}{1}$ rhythmic proportion used by many

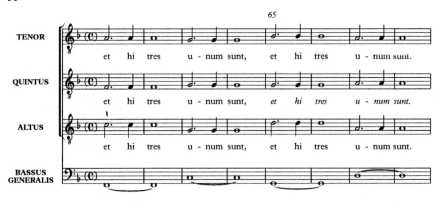

Ex. 10.5. *Duo Seraphim*, bars 61–8

composers in setting this text.[16] The sequential repetition of this passage leaves the tenors on a unison *a*, the principal pitch of the incomplete fifth descent of the first section of the piece, setting the stage for repetition of the *Sanctus* acclamations and the remainder of the text and music from the first part, expanded to a three-voice texture. The addition of the third voice to the repetition significantly complicates the counterpoint, texture, and sonority, effectively representing the phrase *Plena est omnis terra gloria eius* as the climax of the piece. In *Duo Seraphim* we have an even more sophisticated version than we have already seen in *Pulchra es* of the technique of varying and complicating a passage through the addition of another voice. The overall structure of *Duo Seraphim* may be described as ABCB′, with B representing the acclamations of the seraphim.

Audi coelum   *Prima ad una voce solo, poi nella fine à sei voci* (At first for one solo voice, then for six voices at the end); portion of text based on Songs of Songs 6: 9.[17] Remainder of text is non-biblical and non-liturgical.

> Audi coelum verba mea
> plena desiderio, et perfusa gaudio. (Echo: Audio.)
> Dic quaeso mihi quae est ista
> quae consurgens ut aurora rutilat ut benedicam. (Echo: Dicam.)
> Dic, nam ista pulchra ut luna
> electa ut sol replet laetitia

---

[16] See Ch. 4.

[17] 'Quae est ista quae progreditur, quasi aurora consurgens, pulchra ut luna, electa ut sol, terribilis ut castrorum acies ordinata?' This text was also adopted, with minor changes, for the antiphon at the Benedictus for lauds on the feast of the Assumption of the BVM: 'Quae est ista quae ascendit sicut aurora consurgens: pulchra ut luna: electa ut sol, terribilis, ut castrorum acies ordinata'. Note not only the common association of this text and *Pulchra es* with the feast of the Assumption, but also the identity of the last attribute of *Quae est ista* and that of the antiphon *Pulchra es* (fifth line of Monteverdi's motet).

terras, coelos, maria. (Echo: Maria.)
Maria, virgo, illa dulcis
praedicata à prophetis Ezechiel
porta Orientalis. (Echo: Talis.)
Illa sacra, et foelix porta
per quam mors fuit expulsa introducta autem vita. (Echo: Ita.)
Quae semper tutum est medium inter hominem et Deum
pro culpis remedium. (Echo: Medium.)
Omnes hanc ergo sequamur
qua cum gratia mereamur
vitam aeternam consequamur; (Echo: Sequamur;)
praestet nobis Deus Pater hoc et Filius et mater
cuius nomen invocamus dulce
miseris solamen; (Echo: Amen;)
benedicta es virgo Maria
in seculorum secula.

Hear, O Heaven, my words,
full of longing, and steeped in joy. (Echo: I hear.)
Tell me, I entreat: who is she
who, rising, shines like the dawn, that I may bless her? (Echo: I shall tell.)
Tell me, for she, lovely as the moon,
chosen as the sun, fills with joy
the earth, heavens, and the seas. (Echo: Maria.)
Mary, that sweet virgin
foretold by the prophet Ezekiel,
the portal of the rising sun? (Echo: That very one.)
That holy and happy portal
through which death was expelled and eternal life brought in? (Echo: Just so.)
She who is always the secure mediator between man and God,
the remedy of sins? (Echo: The mediator.)
Let us all, therefore, follow her
through whose grace we shall pass
to eternal life. Let us follow. (Echo: We shall follow.)
Grant us, O God, this Father, Son and Mother,
whose name we sweetly invoke,
comfort to the distressed. (Echo: So be it.)
Blessed are you, Virgin Mary
in all ages.

Various references in this text were interpreted by biblical exegetes of the sixteenth century and early seventeenth century in various ways. Interpretations typically equate the Virgin Mary with the Roman Catholic Church. The word *pulchra*, as in *Pulchra es*, was often taken to refer to the Second Temple, the Temple of Solomon, but also to the Roman Church. The Church, like Mary, came out of the East, out of Jerusalem, the *porta Orientalis*, whose beauties sparkled like the sun (*electa ut sol*). The Church is identified with the light that dispels darkness (*pulchra ut luna*), which shines like the rising dawn (*consurgens ut aurora rutilat*) and illuminates the world that it may call her blessed (*ut benedicam*). The Church is the mediator through whom sin is forgiven (*semper tutum est medium inter hominem et Deum pro culpis remedium*); it is the Church whom the populace should follow (*Omnes hanc ergo sequamur*), and through whom eternal life is attained (*qua cum gratia mereamur vitam aeternam consequamur*).[18] From an allegorical point of view, the text refers to both Mary and the Church simultaneously, but it makes no difference to Monteverdi's setting which way the words are understood. Monteverdi treats the text of *Audi coelum* in its obvious significance as a prayer to heaven regarding and ultimately celebrating the virtues and role of the Virgin Mary (whose name Monteverdi reiterates several times), but the Virgin herself is equatable to the Roman Catholic Church by a simple metaphorical transfer.

Audi coelum is the most structurally complicated of Monteverdi's four motets. The first portion of the text, up to *pro culpis remedium / medium*, is set as a dialogue in duple metre between a solo tenor and a second tenor (quintus) functioning as an echo to the ends of the first tenor's phrases. The echo normally omits the initial one or two letters or syllables of the word it reiterates, thereby generating a semantic pun on the principal text. At the words *Omnes hanc ergo sequamur* the motet, reflecting the text, expands to six-voice polyphony, mostly in triple metre, although the two solo tenors emerge twice from the larger texture for further echo effects.[19] *Audi coelum* therefore divides into two distinct sections of vastly different style and character. While the second section is longer than the first by nearly one-third in terms of bars, its quicker pace tends to equalize the actual duration of the two sections.[20]

Audi coelum is the only one of the four motets whose *finalis* is not G. D is clearly established as the *finalis* from the outset, and the *d–d'* octave is divided at *a* by the reciting note, defining the first mode.[21] Although the lack of a signature indicates *cantus durus*, the mode is frequently inflected by a notated *b♭* (*fa supra la*), as is common in first-mode pieces of the sixteenth and seventeenth centuries as well as in the first psalm and Magnificat tones.

The beginning of the motet is an invocation to heaven, *Audi coelum*, which is followed by a series of questions regarding the Virgin Mary, posed by the tenor, and answers, provided by the quintus through the echo puns. When this dia-

[18] See Gilbert Génébrand, *Canticum Canticorum Salomonis versibus et commentariis illustratum* (Paris: Gorbinum, 1585), fos. 77ᵛ–82ᵛ. Del'Rio, *In Canticum Canticorum Salomonis commentarius*, 468–71, interprets the phrase *pulchra ut luna electa ut sol replet laetitia terras, coelos, maria* as describing both the personal history of the Virgin and the history of the Church's progress. Ghisleri, *Commentarius*, 813, also sees this passage as describing the progress of the Church from Paul, through the martyrs, to Constantine. The Church shines like the light of noon amidst the darkness of heresy. The same passage can refer to the progress of the just soul.

[19] See Ch. 20 for a discussion of the relationship between duple and triple metre in *Audi coelum*.

[20] In my edition, the first section comprises 84 bars, the second 109 bars.

[21] See Bernhard Meier, 'Zur Tonart der Concertato-Motetten', 363–5.

logue has been completed, a conclusion drawn from the answers calls upon all to follow the Virgin, asks her for comfort, and offers at the end a blessing to the Virgin. It is this conclusion, calling upon everyone to respond, that brings forth the six-voice polyphonic ensemble.

The echo puns make an essential contribution to the significance of the text in providing the responses to the invocation and questions. For example, while the opening prayer calls upon heaven to listen, the melismatic echo responds to the command *audi* with the affirmation *audio* (echoing *gaudio*). With heaven listening, the way is paved for the supplicant's inquiries. The first of these begins with another command, *dic*, and the echo responds with the affirmation *dicam*, echoing *benedicam*.

The uncertainty expressed in the series of questions leads to harmonic instability, the bass cadencing at various times on F, G, A, and c. The varying cadential bass motions also define varying melodic outlines, which are no longer confined to the pentachord and tetrachord of the first mode.

Yet underlying this melodic and harmonic variety, a background tetrachord descent may be perceived in the melody (see Ex. 10.6). This leads from *d'* in the third bar of the piece (governing the entire first segment, bars 1–16), through *c'* in bars 18–20, supported by an F major harmony, and *b* in bars 23–9, supported by an E major triad as dominant of A, and finally to *a* in bars 30 ff., resolving the dominant E major to A minor. The pitch *a* then serves as the focal point for much of the remainder of the solo section of the motet. This stepwise background descent represents the working-out on a large scale of the quick *d'–a* foreground descent in bars 3–7.

Particularly striking in this melodic and harmonic structure is the introduction of melodic g♯s generating E major triads as cadential dominants to A. This melodic and harmonic turn is associated with Mary, first as the rising dawn (brightening the world), then when she is first identified by name, and finally as the sweet virgin.[22] Words such as *consurgens*, *aurora*, and *coelos* lead to long rising melismas, while *terras* is sung to a lengthy descending melisma. The naming of Mary results from an echo pun on *maria* (seas), and reiterations of her name in a series of echoes occupy a central portion of the opening section.

Once Mary has been identified by the echo, the tenor is able to continue with more specific attributes. In the next phrase she is described not only as the sweet virgin, but also as the gate of the East who was foretold by the prophet Ezekiel. The continuing description of Mary is cast in a more narrative style than has predominated in the first portion of the piece; no further melismas appear until *Omnes*, the first word of the next section of the text. The sweetness of Mary (*dulcis*) is emphasized not only by the aforementioned harmonic shift to an E

---

[22] *Durus* harmonies have already been associated with positive conceits and positive change in *Laudate pueri* and *Nigra sum*. See Chs. 6 and 9.

Ex. 10.6. *Audi coelum*, bars 1–33

Ex. 10.6. *Continued*

Ex. 10.7. *Audi coelum*, bars 55–61

major triad, but also by a chromatic rise from c' to $c\sharp'$, and d' for the cadential return to the *finalis* (see Ex. 10.7).

The first section of *Audi coelum* concludes with a continuing enumeration of the attributes of the Virgin in rather dry, repeated-note recitative in stepwise rising sequences, leading to a full cadence on c. In order to effect a transition back to d as well as to the six-voice chorus, Monteverdi, after a pause, presents the word *omnes* in the solo tenor with a descending and rising melisma up to d'. The arrival at the *finalis* is the signal for the other five parts to enter, reiterating and confirming the word *omnes*. As the text continues, the metre shifts to triple for an imitative texture based on a brief, dance-like motif clearly reflecting the joy of recognition of Mary as the mediator for remission of sins and the means to eternal life. The imitative texture itself is a representation of the many who shall follow her. The bass supporting this series of imitations is constructed from descending fourths, first around the circle of fourths, then in a stepwise descending sequence of fourths (see Ex. 10.8). This pattern, which underlies much of the six-voice chorus, is the most extensive sequence of harmonic motion by fourths or fifths in the Vespers.

The first polyphonic segment concludes at *qua cum gratia* with a return to duple metre and a more homophonic texture. The energy of the imitative triple

Ex. 10.8. *Audi coelum*, bars 87–109, basso continuo

metre and bass sequences is thereby quickly dissipated, better to express the grace that Mary, the sweet virgin, offers. From this passage emerge the two tenors for an echo pun, as in the first part of the piece. The command to follow Mary is echoed by the second tenor with a confirming declaration.

The next sentence of the text (*praestet nobis Deus*) is set to a repeat of the entire preceding segment, including the echoing tenors at the end. *Praestet nobis Deus* is neither structurally nor semantically related to the previous sentence, yet Monteverdi seizes upon the parallel between the trio Father, Son, and Mother as the sources of comfort to the distressed on the one hand and Mary as the means to eternal life on the other to create a directly parallel musical structure, merely altering the rhythm to match the syllables and accentuation of the new text. Finally this complex motet closes with a textual and musical coda blessing the Virgin. The structure of the polyphonic segment of *Audi coelum* is thus ABAB + coda.

Like *Nigra sum*, *Pulchra es*, and *Duo Seraphim*, *Audi coelum* is constructed in part from the repetition of material. Not only is there reiteration of the same music at *praestet nobis* that has served for *Omnes hanc ergo*, but there are echo repetitions between the quintus and the tenor in both sections of the motet. Moreover, the last portion of the first section is characterized by slightly varied repetitions of a rising sequential pattern. Such varied repetition, whether through expansion of sonority, changes in rhythm, or alterations of melodic and harmonic details, is one of Monteverdi's most fundamental compositional techniques. We have already seen how variations on the cantus firmus form the structural basis of the works composed on cantus firmi, and the motets without cantus firmus simply confirm the importance of varied repetition to Monteverdi's creative process. And like the cantus firmus compositions, the motets display an inexhaustible imagination in manner and techniques of variation.

What is easily overlooked is that many of these concepts and processes of variation were, as far as we know, new to Monteverdi in the years 1607–10. No earlier large-scale sacred compositions, such as psalms, Magnificats, or masses survive.[23] The much smaller genre of the madrigal made fewer structural demands, although even in the madrigals up to Book Five (1605) Monteverdi demonstrates an avid interest in musical structure, often varying the thematic material or an entire passage in some way by altering the harmony, the rhythm, the sonority, the texture, the contrapuntal relationship among the parts, or any combination of these. The historical importance of *L'Orfeo* and the *Vespro della Beata Vergine*, therefore, lies partly in the new architectural challenges these large works posed. Monteverdi's cognizance of these challenges and his success in finding ever new and aesthetically convincing solutions not only testify to his ingenuity and inventiveness, but also justify and reinforce his stature as a composer of extraordinary historical significance in the development of Western music.

In returning to the issue of the *seconda prattica* with which the discussion of the few-voiced motets began, we can now better understand Monteverdi's conception of the term in practice rather than in theory. In examining the four motets, we have seen how individual words give rise to particular melodic, rhythmic, and harmonic forms of expression, how rhetorical nuances of the text are translated into musical rhetoric, and how the underlying emotional tone may be reflected in the metre and general style of a passage. But we have also seen how the semantics of the text may affect structural considerations, as in the contradictions between pentachord limits and reciting notes in *Nigra sum* and *Pulchra es*, the numbers of voices employed in the two sections of *Duo Seraphim*, or the expansion of texture from one to six parts in *Audi coelum*. The words do serve as the 'mistress of the harmony' in the sense that they stimulate not only primary decisions regarding voicing and structure, but also details of harmony, melody, and rhythm. But the words never serve as the 'mistress of the harmony' in the sense of determining or dominating the music independently of musical considerations. Monteverdi's marriage between text and music always allows the music to pursue its own logic, and the analyses offered above illustrate both that musical logic and its relationship to the text. The *seconda prattica* might better have been described as text and music walking hand in hand, each interacting with and affecting the other in fundamental ways, but with music never yielding its primacy. Whereas Monteverdi sometimes violates the structure and syntax of the text for musical purposes, he does not violate musical logic for textual purposes. Interpretation of the text is always somehow incorporated into and expressed through his musical logic.

---

[23] Monteverdi refers to now unknown masses and motets, which were never published, in his first extant letter of 28 Nov. 1601. See Domenico De' Paoli, *Claudio Monteverdi: Lettere, dediche e prefazione* (Rome: Edizioni de Santis, 1973), 17, and Eva Lax, *Claudio Monteverdi: Lettere* (Florence: Leo S. Olschki Editore, 1994), 13. Eng. trans. in Denis Arnold and Nigel Fortune, eds., *The Monteverdi Companion* (London: Faber and Faber, 1968), 22–3; and Denis Stevens, *The Letters of Claudio Monteverdi* (Cambridge: Cambridge University Press, 1980), 37.

III. PERFORMANCE PRACTICE

11

A Philosophical Note on Historical Performance Practice

PERFORMANCE of the Monteverdi Vespers, whether of individual pieces or as a complete vesper service, raises numerous problems that every ensemble director must address and resolve in one way or another. The final part of this volume is devoted to an exploration of historical performance practices as they are applicable to the Vespers and to assisting performers in approaching this music in an informed way.

Our knowledge of seventeenth-century performance practice is incomplete; moreover, the performance practice of Monteverdi's day was itself quite variable. This variability can be seen in comments by seventeenth-century writers who disagreed with the methods of performance advocated by others (especially in the areas of ornamentation and continuo realization); in instructions for performance included in numerous music publications and theoretical treatises, often suggesting various options or demanding the capacity to improvise on the part of performers; and in eyewitness descriptions of performances or even paintings, which may alert us to the use of vocal and instrumental resources or the spatial distribution of performers not indicated in the published or manuscript sources. As Eleanor Selfridge-Field has aptly remarked: 'Our historical perception of the period 1600 to 1750 as a unified whole has encouraged us to search for all-embracing answers where (for the most part) none exists, and where greater aesthetic value is attached to variety than to consistency.'[1]

The role of scholarship in studying performance practice is to discover not only whatever specific information we can, but, even more importantly, to reveal the general framework within which earlier musicians operated, and to present that framework for modern performers to increase their understanding of historical performance practices and to enable them to select what best suits their needs. Indeed, varying the methods of performance according to what best suited their circumstances and needs was precisely the way in which seventeenth-century musicians themselves functioned.

---

[1] 'Introduction', in Howard M. Brown and Stanley Sadie, eds., *Performance Practice: Music after 1600* (New York and London: W.W. Norton & Company, 1989), 3.

While a wide range of performance possibilities existed in the early seventeenth century, there were also limits to that range, both absolute limits and limits appropriate to the particular occasion and location of a performance. We can never be certain about either of these types of limits, but in many parameters of performance there is enough information to suggest what they might have been. Nevertheless, it should be emphasized that even with the plethora of detailed performance practice studies published in the last twenty-five years, many questions remain open, and controversy still enlivens the pages of musicological journals and books. This combination of information, controversy, and uncertainty does not suggest, however, that performers should throw up their hands in despair and simply disregard what is known; at the same time it mitigates against dogmatism with regard to any single solution to performance questions, no matter what the documentary support for that solution.

Questions about performance practice in the Monteverdi Vespers may be approached from three interlocking and overlapping perspectives. The first comprises an attempt to determine as far as possible what Monteverdi himself envisaged for performances of his music. The principal means for understanding Monteverdi's personal expectations are the performance rubrics printed primarily in the bassus generalis part-book. These rubrics are more extensive and explicit than those in any other contemporary music print. They specify organ registration for the two Magnificats and the use of solo voices in some pieces. Other aspects of performance are implied by the rubrics, even if they are not stated directly or in a manner that is clear to us today. But there are also many more performance issues that receive no mention in Monteverdi's rubrics—nor could they, since performance of any major work is a complicated process, and even the most detailed written instructions cannot describe everything that performers must take into account.

Monteverdi, of course, was working within the framework of his own contemporary performance practice, so there was much that he could take for granted about the character and limits of vocal style, choir size, tuning, ornamentation, continuo instruments, and so on. Modern scholarship attempts to rediscover this character and these limits. But because they are wider than could be indicated by Monteverdi's rubrics and cover a broader range of possibilities than Monteverdi himself may have envisaged, we must recognize that other seventeenth-century musicians may have performed the Vespers somewhat differently from the composer. The second perspective on performance practice, then, comprises the range of possibilities that seventeenth-century musicians might have brought to bear on performances of the Vespers. This range is often difficult to discover, and the boundaries can never be precisely determined, leaving many decisions to be based on the modern director's experience, taste, and judgement.

The principal sources for discovering the framework of possibilities envisaged by seventeenth-century musicians are the writings of contemporary theorists, composers' prefaces to music prints, letters of musicians and non-musicians, descriptions of performances actually heard, and paintings or engravings of actual performances. In the chapters that follow, all of these sources will be considered, but especially the writings of theorists of the late sixteenth and early seventeenth centuries, which often treat performance matters *in extenso*. One of the most important of these theorists is Michael Praetorius, a German resident of Wolfenbüttel, from whom I quote in many different contexts. The question has often been raised as to how familiar Praetorius was with Italian musical practice and how valid his comments on Italian style are. As I have examined one performance practice issue after another, I have found that Praetorius repeatedly reflects or summarizes, sometimes even plagiarizes, the views and comments of a number of Italian writers of his generation. From his discussions of actual music, it is also apparent that Praetorius had detailed knowledge of a substantial quantity of the repertoire itself. His remarks in *Syntagma musicum*, volume 3, about the performance of Monteverdi's *Ave maris stella* (see Chapter 15) illustrate how up to date his knowledge of repertoire was, for only a few years could have elapsed between Monteverdi's publication in the autumn of 1610 (which must have reached Praetorius in 1611 at the earliest) and the completion of Praetorius's lengthy manuscript, which was published in 1619. Hans Lampl, who has translated volume 3 into English, has compiled a list of Italian composers and theorists cited by Praetorius.[2] The list is remarkably inclusive, containing 108 names, mostly of composers active in the early seventeenth century, and vastly outnumbers the German composers that Praetorius mentions. In general, therefore, I have found that Praetorius is a valuable and reliable resource for early seventeenth-century Italian performance practice. The one area where he clearly reflects a more German than Italian outlook is in his recommendations for the use of instruments, detailed in *Syntagma musicum*, volume 2, *De organographia*. Consequently, I have treated Praetorius's suggestions for instrumentation with caution, weighing them against what can be determined about Italian instrumental practice from other sources.

The third perspective on the Monteverdi Vespers is that of the modern performer. Modern musicians have practical realities to contend with that are different from those of the seventeenth century. The ubiquitous contemporary use of women's voices in sacred music, even among permanent ensembles specializing in early music, is only the most obvious of a host of differences between modern conditions and those of the seventeenth century. To name just a few: voice-production is different, the size of choirs ranges more widely, modern

[2] 'A Translation of *Syntagma musicum III* by Michael Praetorius' (DMA dissertation, University of Southern California, 1957), app. III, 421–8.

instruments may be the only ones available, organs have different sonorities, tuning systems are often different, and performances almost invariably take place in the context of concerts rather than liturgical services (even when a seventeenth-century vesper service is reconstructed in a church).

The overlap among these three perspectives on performance practice is apparent. If modern musicians are not to ignore altogether what has been learned of seventeenth-century performance practice, then they must first take into account Monteverdi's rubrics and what they tell us about his own expectations; they must then consider the general parameters of seventeenth-century performance practice, which may permit a wider range of possibilities than Monteverdi himself would have employed; and finally they must interpret and adapt this information to the exigencies of each modern performance, including the capabilities and practical needs of the performing ensemble and the acoustics and physical space where the performance is to be given.[3]

Much debate has taken place in recent years about the validity and goals of historical performance practice, the role of original instruments, and the reliance on contemporaneous theoretical sources treating performance issues.[4] The phrase 'historically informed performance' has generally come to replace the earlier, outdated formulation, 'authentic performance'. Lewis Lockwood has made several cogent remarks on the subject that not only are similar to my own views, but are useful in helping performers keep their options and objectives in perspective:

the question of which instruments are being used is secondary when compared with the performer's ability to translate for his listeners not merely the outer shell of sonority of a given work but its inner structure, its deeper qualities—in short, not only its text but the complexities of musical thought and expression that the composer built into it.

I will . . . agree that the entire enterprise of 'early music performance' runs a permanent risk of being dead on arrival in the concert hall in the hands of performers who have thought about the music in no other terms than those they may have derived abstractly and literally from ornamentation treatises and the like without having deepened their grasp of the individuality of the work being presented—its structure, genre and artistic shape, the presumed intricacy and subtlety of its form and expression; in short, all the ramifications that modern musicians have learned to value in music of any period, not simply the remote past.

. . . the performer has a basic obligation to remember that there *is* a body of material that seems to retain . . . a sort of 'privileged status'. But its privileges stem from our realization that it authentically represents the composer's conception of his piece . . . Not that these [historical source materials] are 'definitive' in helping us to understand the celebrated and elusive 'intentions' of the

---

[3] A first-hand account of the effects on tempo of physical spaces and their acoustics is given in Denis Stevens, 'Claudio Monteverdi: Acoustics, Tempo, Interpretation', in Raffaello Monterosso, ed., *Performing Practice in Monteverdi's Music: The Historic-Philological Background* (Cremona: Fondazione Claudio Monteverdi, 1995), 11–22.

[4] See e.g. the series of essays in Nicholas Kenyon, ed., *Authenticity and Early Music: A Symposium* (Oxford: Oxford University Press, 1988).

composer; but they are a great deal better than impassioned guesswork on the part of performers who wish to know as little as possible about them.[5]

To summarize the matter as succinctly as possible: there is no performance practice that can be determined to be truly 'authentic'; there *is* a framework of performance possibilities that can be ascertained from historical sources; historical sources do not provide definitive answers for 'historically informed performance'; and the ultimate aesthetic value and success of a performance are based on musical understanding, interpretation, and expression that are not guaranteed by adherence to a historical performance framework. Performances with modern mixed choirs and modern instruments can be quite satisfying in aesthetic value, even if they do not reproduce the sound-world of the seventeenth century as we understand it. Studying that sound-world, however, can help us understand some of the particular possibilities for interpretation, expression, and aesthetic value at the disposal of *maestri di cappella*, singers, and instrumentalists of that era and can assist modern singers and instrumentalists in developing an approach to the music that illuminates and reveals its essential features and expressive possibilities rather than obscures them.

The comments offered in the succeeding chapters on the principal aspects of performance practice in the Monteverdi Vespers are based on the types of sixteenth- and seventeenth-century sources mentioned above as well as on a large number of studies by many different modern scholars. I have attempted to apply this information to the problems that any ensemble director will inevitably encounter in preparing a performance of the Vespers. My goal has been to establish a performance practice context for directors and other performers to make their own decisions, though in some cases I have also made specific suggestions for resolving certain issues. The text of each chapter discusses the principal issues, while details, including differing opinions among various scholars, can be found in the footnotes. Questions regarding the order or the selection of pieces to perform, as well as the potential for performing a vesper service without instruments other than continuo, have already been addressed above. Recent theories on the order of pieces, with which at the time of this writing I differ, are discussed in Chapter 1. The principal topics covered in the succeeding chapters are: Chapter 12, continuo instruments; Chapter 13, organs and organ registration; Chapter 14, continuo realization; Chapter 15, voices and choirs; Chapter 16, vocal style; Chapter 17, pitch and transposition; Chapter 18, obbligato instruments; Chapter 19, instrumental doubling and substitution for vocal parts; Chapter 20, metre and tempo; Chapter 21, vocal and instrumental ornamentation; Chapter 22, tuning and temperament; and Chapter 23, historical

---

[5] 'Performance and "Authenticity"', *Early Music*, 19 (1991), 502–4. Similar views are expressed by Nikolaus Harnoncourt in *Baroque Music Today: Music as Speech*, trans. Mary O'Neill (Portland, Oreg.: Amadeus Press, 1988), 16–18.

pronunciation of Latin. Questions regarding *musica ficta* are considered in my Oxford University Press edition and its critical notes.

The bibliography at the end of this volume lists many detailed studies of performance practice, the voice, and instruments. Many of these sources are also cited in footnotes in the ensuing pages. It may prove useful to readers, however, to refer here to a limited number of books and journals that specialize in performance practice and are the most readily accessible and widest-ranging sources for basic information on the late Renaissance and early Baroque. Readers should be aware, of course, that much new information has emerged in recent years and that the views and practices of contemporary early music performers have changed as well. The older sources listed below may be out of date in some respects, but still contain much useful information. Readers may wish to compare commentaries on specific subjects in older and more recent sources.

JOURNALS

Basler Jahrbuch für historische Musikpraxis
Chelys: The Journal of the Viola da Gamba Society
Early Music
Galpin Society Journal
Historic Brass Society Journal
Journal of the American Musical Instrument Society
Journal of the Lute Society of America
Performance Practice Review

BOOKS

Howard M. Brown and Stanley Sadie, eds., *Performance Practice: Music before 1600* (New York and London: W.W. Norton & Company, 1989).
—— *Performance Practice: Music after 1600* (New York and London: W.W. Norton & Company, 1989).
Stewart Carter, ed., *A Performer's Guide to Seventeenth-Century Music* (New York: Schirmer Books, 1997).
Mary Cyr, *Performing Baroque Music* (Portland, Oreg.: Amadeus Press, 1992).
Robert Donington, *A Performer's Guide to Baroque Music* (New York: Charles Scribner's Sons, 1973).
—— *The Interpretation of Early Music* (London: Faber and Faber, 1963; rev. ed. New York: St. Martin's Press, 1974; corrected ed. London, Faber and Faber,

1975; new rev. ed. New York and London: W.W. Norton & Company, 1989, 1992).

Jeffery T. Kite-Powell, *A Practical Guide to Historical Performance—The Renaissance* (New York: Early Music America, 1989).

——ed., *A Performer's Guide to Renaissance Music* (New York: Schirmer Books, 1994).

Timothy J. McGee, *Medieval and Renaissance Music: A Performer's Guide* (Toronto: University of Toronto Press, 1985).

Frederick Neumann, *Performance Practices of the Seventeenth and Eighteenth Centuries* (New York: Schirmer Books, 1993).

Elizabeth V. Phillips and John-Paul Christopher Jackson, *Performing Medieval and Renaissance Music: An Introductory Guide* (New York: Schirmer Books, 1986).

12

Continuo Instruments

THE normal continuo instrument for music in church was the organ.[1] Harpsichords were used on rare occasions, such as when organs were in disrepair,[2] or during Holy Week, when the use of the organ was proscribed.[3] Occasionally one finds evidence of the employment of both organs and harpsichords in large-scale, multi-choir works; the harpsichord may in some instances have been the sole keyboard continuo instrument for one of the choirs, but there is also evidence of organ and harpsichord serving simultaneously as continuo instruments for one or more choirs in polychoral compositions.[4] In any case, the descriptions make clear that these were special events employing unusually large vocal and instrumental resources. Even with the combination of organ and harpsichord, there is no evidence known to me that suggests the alternation of the two instruments in the same composition other than between separate choirs of polychoral works. Many prints of polychoral compositions have a separate continuo line to accompany each choir, but Roman double-choir publications typically have only one continuo part, and documentary evidence indicates that Roman polychoral works were usually accompanied by

---

[1] See Peter Williams, 'Continuo', in *The New Grove Dictionary of Music and Musicians*, ed. Stanley Sadie (London: Macmillan Publishers Ltd., 1980), iv. 690. Patrizio Barbieri has shown that notated organ bass parts in Rome may date back as far as 1585. It has generally been assumed that organs accompanied vocal polyphony in church from much earlier in the 16th century, perhaps playing from intabulations of the vocal parts. See Barbieri, 'On a Continuo Organ Part Attributed to Palestrina', *Early Music*, 22 (1994), 587–605.

[2] See Anne Schnoebelen, 'The Concerted Mass at San Petronio in Bologna: ca. 1660–1730. A Documentary and Analytical Study' (Ph.D. dissertation, University of Illinois, 1966), 327–8.

[3] See the *Caeremoniale Episcoporum*, bk. i, ch. 28. See also Eleanor Selfridge-Field, *Venetian Instrumental Music from Gabrieli to Vivaldi* (New York: Praeger Publishers, 1975), 11; and James H. Moore, *Vespers at St Mark's: Music of Alessandro Grandi, Giovanni Rovetta and Francesco Cavalli* (Ann Arbor: UMI Research Press, 1981), i. 84.

[4] See Adriano Banchieri, *Conclusioni nel suono dell'organo . . . opera vigesima* (Bologna: Rossi, 1609; fac. edn. Bologna: Forni Editore), 49–51. Eng. trans. Lee R. Garrett as *Adriano Banchieri: Conclusions for Playing the Organ (1609)* (Colorado Springs, Colo.: Colorado College Music Press, 1982), 45–6. Also see Alexander Silbiger, 'The Roman Frescobaldi Tradition, c.1640–1670', *Journal of the American Musicological Society*, 33 (1980), 46; Thomas Noel O'Regan, 'Sacred Polychoral Music in Rome 1576–1621' (D. Phil. dissertation, University of Oxford, 1988), i. 77; id., 'Victoria, Soto and the Spanish Archconfraternity of the Resurrection in Rome', *Early Music*, 22 (1994), 285–7; and Barbieri, 'On a Continuo Organ Part', 597. Not all such large-scale performances employed harpsichords in addition to organs. For a description by Banchieri of an eight-choir liturgical service where only organs are mentioned, see Donald E. Marcase, 'Adriano Banchieri, "L'organo suonarino": Translation, Transcription and Commentary' (Ph.D. dissertation, Indiana University, 1970), 343.

one organ fewer than the number of choirs 'implying that two choirs shared one organ and platform'.[5] For the Monteverdi Vespers the organ is clearly the most suitable continuo instrument for the strictly liturgical items, that is, the response, the psalms, the hymn, and the two Magnificats. Indeed, the Magnificats both have specific organ registration rubrics for each of the twelve verses.

Other continuo instruments or bass-doubling instruments were also used in church. The violone (a term variously used for (1) bass viola da gamba, or bass viol; (2) bass *viola da braccio*, or bass violin; and (3) contrabass *viola da braccio*, or contrabass violin) is frequently mentioned in sources. Bass violas (bass *viole da braccio*, or bass violins), trombones, bassoons, lutes, theorbos, citterns, and harps are all mentioned in documents and on the title-pages of various sacred collections.[6] Such instruments were not in daily use, however, but employed primarily for special feasts when elaborate music, beyond normal fare, was provided. The Monteverdi Vespers constitute just such elaborate music. These instruments must be viewed, therefore, as either additions to or substitutes for the normal continuo instrument, the organ.

The ways in which these instruments were used were not random, but fell under specific criteria. The bass string instruments, trombones, and bassoons seem to have doubled bass-lines only when there was equivalent doubling or instrumentation of the upper parts, as can be seen in Monteverdi's own orchestration for *Domine ad adjuvandum* and the *Sonata sopra Sancta Maria*. In other words, a trombone might double the bass line when cornettos and trombones were used to double other parts, or a bass string instrument might double the bass-line when violas and violins doubled upper parts. The strings and brass might even be combined, as in Monteverdi's response. Bassoons seem to have been employed on bass-lines whether the upper-part doublings were strings or brass. The question of bass-line doubling in the other pieces of Monteverdi's 1610 print, therefore, would depend on whether or not instruments were used to double the voice parts (see Chapter 19). In large, festal performances, a

---

[5] O'Regan, 'Sacred Polychoral Music', i. 75–6.

[6] The nomenclature of the low string instruments is particularly problematic. Conflicting views on the meaning of the word 'violone' may be found in Alexander Planyavsky, *Geschichte des Kontrabasses* (Tutzing: Hans Schneider, 1970); Francis Baines, 'What Exactly is a Violone? A Note towards a Solution', *Early Music*, 5 (1977), 173–6; Tharald Borgir, *The Performance of the Basso Continuo in Italian Baroque Music* (Ann Arbor: UMI Press, 1987); Stephen Bonta, 'From Violone to Violoncello: A Question of Strings?', *Journal of the American Musical Instrument Society*, 3 (1977), 64–99; id., 'Terminology for the Bass Violin in the 17th-Century', *Journal of the American Musical Instrument Society*, 4 (1978), 5–42; and id., 'Corelli's Heritage: The Early Bass Violin in Italy', in Pierluigi Petrobelli and Gloria Staffieri, eds., *Studi Corelliani IV: Atti del Quarto Congresso Internazionale*, Fusignano, 4–7 Sept. 1986 (Florence: Leo S. Olschki Editore, 1990), 217–31. Bonta's studies are the most thorough and penetrating. 'Theorbo' and 'chitarrone' are two names for the same instrument. I will use the more universal and long-lived term, 'theorbo'. The word 'chitarrone' was a humanistic adaptation from the Greek *kithara* used almost exclusively in Italy during the first thirty years of the 17th century. See Kevin Mason, *The Chitarrone And its Repertoire in Early Seventeenth-Century Italy* (Aberystwyth, Wales: Boethius Press, 1989), 3–7.

number of instruments seem to have combined to form the continuo, including multiple lutes and theorbos.[7] Nevertheless, care should be taken not to shift the balance of sonority too heavily to the bass. In early seventeenth-century Italy, the quantity of bass instruments depended on the acoustics of the performing space, but in general, the bass did not yet carry the weight it did by the early eighteenth century. Performers should take care that the bass-line is an integral part of the ensemble without overpowering the upper parts.

Lutes, harps, harpsichords, and theorbos were used not only for increasing the sonority in especially elaborate performances, but also for accompaniment of few-voiced motets, such as *Nigra sum*, *Pulchra es*, *Duo Seraphim*, and *Audi coelum*.[8] The organ was still the principal continuo instrument for such compositions, but plucked instruments or a plucked keyboard were commonly employed, especially if the motets were performed as devotional music outside the confines of a church or chapel.[9] However, some combinations of these instruments were apparently more appropriate than others. An organ might well be joined by a theorbo, but much less often by a plucked keyboard instrument. Changes of continuo instrument in the course of a motet were probably also avoided. The only exception in Monteverdi's collection might be *Audi coelum*, where the change of texture and style from solo echo motet to six-voice polyphony could suggest a change of continuo instrument as well as doubling of the vocal parts in the latter section. In festive ceremonies where large vocal and instrumental forces were used, a variety of instruments might be added to the organ, but especially lutes and theorbos. Monteverdi's response and psalms and the ensemble verses of the hymn might also include multiple plucked instruments in the continuo, depending on the size of the ensemble and the acoustics of the performance space. A finger-plucked instrument and a plucked keyboard, however, may have been a problematic combination because of difficulty in co-ordinating the sharp attacks of both instruments.

There is a widespread misconception that any bass-line in seventeenth-century music, even the bass-lines of monodies and few-voiced compositions, should be doubled by a bass string instrument. While such doubling may have

---

[7] Paul O'Dette, 'Plucked Instruments', in Jeffery T. Kite-Powell, ed., *A Performer's Guide to Renaissance Music* (New York: Schirmer Books, 1994), 144–5.

[8] See e.g. the description by Thomas Coryat of a service performed at the Scuola San Rocco in Venice in Ch. 4 above. For a good, brief introduction to lutes and theorbos, see O'Dette, 'Plucked Instruments', 139–53. A more extensive study of the theorbo is Mason, *The Chitarrone and its Repertoire*; the use of theorbos in sacred music is treated on pp. 60–76 and 141–6.

[9] In secular monody (and presumably in few-voiced compositions as well), the theorbo was considered more appropriate for accompanying the tenor voice and the harpsichord for accompanying sopranos, apparently because the theorbo lacked a treble register. Since Monteverdi's motets can be used as devotional chamber music apart from any function within a liturgical service, a harpsichord may be the more appropriate instrument for *Pulchra es* in such circumstances, while the theorbo would be more suitable for *Nigra sum*, *Duo Seraphim*, and *Audi coelum*. Neither instrument would have been combined with another continuo instrument in monodies or few-voiced works. See ibid. 34–6.

been a more common practice in the eighteenth century, it was not typical in the *Seicento*.[10] There is evidence that a violone may have been used at times in St Mark's to reinforce the bass-line when a small organ or a theorbo was the primary continuo instrument, but this seems not to have been the standard practice in Italy.[11] The wisdom of this tradition has been confirmed for the author in numerous performances of the Monteverdi Vespers and other early seventeenth-century music. Where a doubling bass string instrument has been used, the weight of the bass-line almost invariably detracts from the voice. In music of the early seventeenth century it is the voice that is paramount, carried above a light and unobtrusive accompaniment which only supports the singer or singers without calling attention to itself.

[10] Several scholars have demonstrated that doubling of the continuo bass with a string or other bass instrument was not the normal practice in Italian music before about 1670. See e.g. Peter Allsop, 'The Role of the Stringed Bass as a Continuo Instrument in Italian Seventeenth Century Instrumental Music', *Chelys: The Journal of the Viola da Gamba Society*, 8 (1978–9), 31–7; Graham Dixon, 'Continuo Scoring in the Early Baroque: The Role of Bowed-Bass Instruments', *Chelys: The Journal of the Viola da Gamba Society*, 15 (1986), 38–53; and Borgir, *The Performance of the Basso Continuo*, 5–9.

[11] See Moore, *Vespers at St Mark's*, 83, 97.

13
Organs and Organ Registration

ᘓᕶᘔ

ITALIAN organs of the sixteenth and early seventeenth centuries, most often comprising a single keyboard with a compass of thirty-eight to fifty-three keys, were rather simple in comparison with the larger instruments of northern Europe. Approximately fifty to fifty-three keys were common, but the lowest octave was usually a short octave, devoid of chromatic half-steps and often containing even less than a full diatonic octave. Many eight-foot organs had their top note as f'' or a'', but some reached as far as c''' or even f'''.[1] Available stops normally consisted of a principal chorus, one or more flutes, and a limited variety of other solo stops. Pedals, if present at all, were also limited in number and primarily served as a means to pull down keys in the lowest octave of the keyboard. They did not ordinarily have their own stops, though pedal boards on some large sixteenth-century organs did.[2] Nevertheless, Italian organ music 'offers hardly any evidence of the use made of the pedals ... in the 16th and 17th centuries'.[3] A limited number of organs had two

[1] Luigi Ferdinando Tagliavini, 'Considerazioni sugli ambiti delle tastiere degli organi italiani', in Friedemann Hellwig, ed., *Studia organologica: Festschrift für John Henry van der Meer zu seinem fünfund-sechzigsten Geburtstag* (Tutzing: Hans Schneider, 1987), 453–60. Tagliavini cites an exceptional twenty-four-foot organ built for St John Lateran, Rome, in 1597–1600 whose keyboard was extended to sixty-six notes, including split keys.

[2] For general and specific descriptions of Italian organs, see the articles and books in the Bibliography by Joseph Horning, Renato Lunelli, Arnaldo Morelli, and Peter Williams. Much important information about northern Italian organs of the late 16th and early 17th centuries is found in the treatise of Costanzo Antegnati, *L'arte organica di Costanzo Antegnati organista del duomo di Brescia* (Brescia: Francesco Tebaldino, 1608), repr. and Ger. trans. by Renato Lunelli and Paolo Smets (Mainz: Rheingold-Verlag, 1958). Antegnati's registration for the Brescian cathedral organ and his instructions for the use of registration during the mass are given in Barbara Owen and Peter Williams, *The New Grove: Organ* (The Grove Musical Instruments Series; New York: W. W. Norton & Co., 1980), 255–6.

[3] Luigi Ferdinando Tagliavini, 'The Art of "not Leaving the Instrument Empty": Comments on Early Italian Harpsichord Playing', *Early Music*, 9 (1983), 299. Both Girolamo Diruta and Adriano Banchieri, writing in the late 16th and early 17th centuries respectively, discuss fingering methods for the organ, and Diruta describes other aspects of good organ technique as well. See Diruta, *Il Transilvano* (pt. I, Venice: Giacomo Vincenti, 1593; pt. II, Venice: Alessandro Vincenti, 1609, repr. 1622); Eng. trans. Murray C. Bradshaw and Edward J. Soehnlen as *Girolamo Diruta: The Transylvanian* (Ottawa: Institute of Mediaeval Music, 1984), 2 vols. Diruta's discussion of organ technique and fingering is in pt. II, pp. 4–8. Banchieri's rules for fingering are given in *L'organo suonarino . . . opera ventesima quinta* (Venice: Amadino, 1611); fac. ed. Giulio Cattin (Amsterdam: Frits Knuf, 1969), 42 (the 2nd edn. of *L'organo suonarino*). Eng. trans. in Donald E. Marcase, 'Adriano Banchieri, "L'organo suonarino": Translation, Transcription and Commentary' (Ph.D. dissertation, Indiana University, 1970), 448–52. For a brief introduction to Diruta's and Banchieri's fingering methods, see Mark Lindley, 'Renaissance Keyboard Fingering', in Jeffery T. Kite-Powell, ed., *A Performer's Guide to Renaissance Music* (New York:

keyboards.[4] It has even been speculated that some northern Italian organs may have had transposing keyboards for automatic transposition down a step or even a fourth or fifth, though none survive.[5]

Italian organ registration in this period was somewhat restricted and seems to have been fairly consistent throughout Italy. The sound of Italian organs of the Renaissance and early Baroque was frequently described in terms such as 'soft', 'sweet', 'mild', and 'delicate'. The primary timbre was produced by the principal register of open pipes. Although the timbre of the principal chorus differed from organ to organ, the principals were in general warmer, more transparent, and less intense, though not thinner, than northern European principals. A major contributor to this quality of sound was the absence of ears on Italian organ pipes. In the upper register the sound was clear and bright and more similar to northern principals, since northern upper registers also did not have ears. Most Italian principal choirs consisted, in addition to the principal itself, of an *ottavo* (octave, or 4 foot), *decimaquinta* (15th, or 2 foot), *decimanona* (19th, or $1\frac{1}{3}$ foot), and *vigesimaseconda* (22nd, or 1 foot). The addition of a *vigesimasesta* (26th, or $\frac{2}{3}$ foot) and *vigesimanona* (29th, or $\frac{1}{2}$ foot) was common. Some of the large eight-foot organs extended the principal chorus as far as a *trigesimaterza* (33rd, or $\frac{1}{3}$ foot) or even *trigesimasesta* (36th, or $\frac{1}{4}$ foot). In a large sixteen-foot organ, all notes sounded an octave lower. While many organs omitted the *duodecima* (12th, or $2\frac{2}{3}$ foot), it was employed in some instruments; at times the principal and *ottava* had double pipes to intensify the sound. Some instruments also had a 'split' principal (*principale spezzato*) that was divided in the middle of the keyboard.

The principal registers constituted the basic *ripieno* of Italian organs of this period. According to the celebrated organ-builder Costanzo Antegnati, organist in the cathedral of Brescia, the *ripieno* comprised the main principal stops (*principale primo, ottava, quintadecima, decimanona, vigesima seconda, vigesima sesta, vigesima nona*, and *trigesima terza* on the cathedral organ of Brescia) but omitted the *flauti* and other stops or combinations of stops with specific timbres that were appropriate 'to play in the concerted style and make various sorts of sonorities'.[6] Antegnati designated the *ripieno* for all intonations, introits, and

Schirmer Books, 1994), 194–5; and Lindley and Maria Boxall, *Early Keyboard Fingerings: A Comprehensive Guide* (Mainz: Schott, 1992). Banchieri also deals briefly with articulation and horizontal connections. As with so many other aspects of performance practice of this period, Diruta's and Banchieri's fingering recommendations contradict one another.

[4] A list of two-keyboard organs is given in Arnaldo Morelli, 'Basso Continuo on the Organ in Seventeenth-Century Italian Music', *Basler Jahrbuch für Historische Musikpraxis*, 17 (1994), 31 n. 3.

[5] Personal communication from Willard Martin. See Ch. 17 n. 13 for information on English transposing organs and on Austrian and German organs of the 17th and 18th centuries with sliding keyboards or separate registers activated by stops for transposition by a major second or minor third. I know of no hard evidence for transposing organs in 17th-century Italy, but that does not mean such instruments did not exist.   [6] *Per concertar, & far diverse sorti d'armonie. L'arte organica*, 62, 64.

other introductions as well as for the *Deo gratias*, and declared that it should be played slowly and legato. Luigi Ferdinando Tagliavini describes the Italian *ripieno* as 'an instrumental interpretation of a choral ensemble' and its character as 'a silvery and light sound that is never aggressive . . . due to the particular voicing of its pipes, voicing that is lively and sweet at the same time'. According to Tagliavini, 'The ideal of sound of the pipes is in one sense a stylization of the spoken word; thus the Italian organ ideally reflects the pronunciation of the Italian language, richer in vowels than in consonants, while the prominent chiff of the northern organ really interprets the rich consonants of the German language.'[7]

To this fundamental chorus other stops were added on individual organs. Most common were one or two flute stops, consisting of a *flauto in ottavo* (4 foot), a *flauto in duodecimo* ($2\frac{2}{3}$ foot), or a *flauto in quintadecima* (2 foot). Other additional stops tended to be associated with particular locales or dependent on certain builders and their followers. The *fiffaro* (*piffaro*), also called the *voce humana*, based on an acoustical tremolo (similar to a modern celeste stop), was favoured by the Antegnati family in the Po Valley region. This stop was not the same as the modern vox humana, but resulted rather from the combination of the *fiffaro* stop and the principal; the *fiffaro* was tuned slightly sharp in relation to the principal, producing the acoustical tremolo.[8] According to Arnaldo Morelli, a reed stop with a short resonator was also called a *voce humana*.[9] Monteverdi calls specifically for the *principale & Fifara* in the *Fecit potentiam* of the Magnificat *a 6*, and for *Principale & registro delle zifare ò voci humane* in the *Fecit potentiam* of the Magnificat *a 7*. Morelli assumes that Monteverdi meant the reed version of the *voce humana*, because of the vigorous character of the music in these two verses, but Monteverdi's registration actually lists the two stops required to produce the acoustical tremolo.[10]

The *tremolo*, which was fairly widespread in Italy, differed from the *voce humana* in being a mechanical effect produced by a regular pulsation or undulation in the air flow. There were two different types of tremulant stop, activated by different mechanisms: the louder 'open' tremulant and the softer, sweeter

---

[7] 'The Old Italian Organ and its Music', *Diapason*, 57/2 (Feb. 1966), 14.

[8] According to Lunelli, 'Un trattatello', 136, the organs of St Mark's did not possess a *voce humana* in this period, and the stop is not mentioned directly (though the *pifaro* in conjuction with the *principale* is) in the conservative 1652 treatise of Antonio Barcatto, an organ-builder in Padua and the environs of Venice.

[9] Morelli, 'Basso Continuo on the Organ', 32.

[10] Ibid. 36. In support of his case, Morelli cites the organ in Sant'Andrea in Mantua, whose *voce humana* must have been a reed register because of the large number of pipes it contained. See also id., 'Monteverdi and Organ Practice', in Raffaello Monterosso, ed., *Performing Practice in Monteverdi's Music: The Historic-Philological Background* (Cremona: Fondazione Claudio Monteverdi, 1995), 131–8.

'closed' tremulant.[11] The latter was probably more widely used in Italian organs of the late sixteenth and early seventeenth centuries.[12] Both types of *tremolo* produced pitch variation corresponding to the undulations in the air flow.[13] The mechanical *tremolo* was combined with the *principale* and even the acoustical vibrato of the *voce humana* to generate a sound suitable for slow passages and sad affects.[14] Antegnati recommends the use of the *tremolo*, but warns that in employing it one must play *adaggio* and *senza diminuire* (without making diminutions).[15] Girolamo Diruta also associates the *tremolo* with mournful affects, indicating that 'the principal register with tremolo will make this effect, or some flute stop'.[16] Monteverdi calls for the *principale & tremolare* midway through the *Quia respexit* of the Magnificat *a 6*, at the point where the text reads *humilitatem ancillae suae ex hoc beatam me dicent*, underscoring the 'lowness of his servant; because of this [all generations] will call me blessed'. The rubric *priniçpale & tremolare* appears only at the end of the word *humilitatem* because of an incomplete cadence followed by a pause in the bassus generalis at the beginning of the word. The initial emphasis of the affective sonority, therefore, falls on 'his servant', and the affect is further highlighted by its contrast with the rubric for the final words of the Latin sentence, *omnes generationes: principale ottava & quintadecima & la voce canta forte* (principal, octave, and fifteenth, and the voice sings loudly).

Antegnati also suggests the *tremolo* in combination with the *principale* for the accompaniment of motets in few voices, 'playing delicately . . . but slowly and without diminutions'.[17] If an organ is used as the accompanying instrument for Monteverdi's few-voiced motets, such a registration might be suitable for the opening of *Nigra sum* (up to bar 26), for the first section in duple metre of *Pulchra es* (if the organist avoids doubling the vocal embellishments), and for the first section of *Audi coelum*. The character of *Duo Seraphim*, with its extraordinary embellishments and its evocation of angels exclaiming the praises of God and celebrating an earth filled with His glory, is contrary to the affect cited by Diruta and Antegnati as appropriate for the *tremolo*. In the early seventeenth

[11] Williams, *The European Organ*, 294, describes the open tremulant as 'a device opening a sprung flap in the main wind-trunk which opened and closed in the force of the wind, and which therefore affected all chests fed by the trunk'. The closed tremulant was 'a gentle shaking-stop or device attached to the chest, or part of a chest, of a secondary manual'.

[12] Stewart Carter, 'The string tremolo in the 17th century', *Early Music*, 19 (1991), 46. Carter bases his conviction on 'descriptions of their sound and from the voicings with which they were used'. See ibid. 57, n. 18.

[13] Ibid. 48.

[14] Ibid. 47.

[15] *L'arte organica*, 66, 70.

[16] Quoted in Carter, 'The String Tremolo', 47. See Diruta, *Il Transilvano*, pt. II, bk. iv, 22; trans. in Bradshaw and Soehnlen, *Girolamo Diruta: The Transylvanian*, ii. 154.

[17] *L'arte organica*, 68–9.

century reed stops, such as the *cornamuse, tromba, tromboncino,* and *zampogna* were also beginning to be incorporated into various organs, but were more appropriate for solo playing than for accompanying voices (see discussion above for the reed version of the *voce humana*).

Aside from Antegnati's brief 1608 treatise, the principal treatise discussing organ registration from this period is the much more comprehensive one of 1609 by Girolamo Diruta, by then organist of the cathedral in Gubbio.[18] Diruta's recommendations are focused on intabulations of choral polyphony and playing over a cantus firmus *alternatim* with the choir, the mainstays of organ playing in the mass and office of the sixteenth and seventeenth centuries.[19] His registrations are conservative and reflect the need to combine the sound of the organ with that of the choir, whether accompanying or substituting for voices or alternating with them. Diruta's suggestion for opening and closing the service is similar to Antegnati's: 'At the beginning and also at the end of the Divine Offices, the organist ought to play all of the *ripieno* of the organ, taking care not to draw ranks other than the usual ones on an organ. One ought not to draw flute stops and other unusual instruments with the organ *ripieno* because this does not make a good blend.'[20]

The primary impetus behind Diruta's recommendations for registration comprises the ethos of the twelve church modes, derived from Zarlino (in his earlier numbering), with each registration designed to underscore a particular mood (see Table 1).[21] Diruta's registrations are based on the Renaissance ideal of consistency throughout a single composition; aside from the *ripieno*, he suggests a maximum of three stops at a time and includes only octave ranks, avoiding the colouration of the fifths.[22] This concentration on the octaves readily provides for doubling of choral parts or support of solo vocal lines without calling attention to the timbre of the organ by the addition of the fifths.[23] Although Diruta does not discuss basso continuo playing in few-voiced motets, it seems likely from his characterizations of the modes that the correspondence between registrations and ethos would apply to the ethos of the text of a motet as well. By the early seventeenth century, mode was not as important in few-voiced motets as in psalms, canticles, and masses, but concern for the proper expression of the character of the text certainly was.

---

[18] See *Il Transilvano*, pt. II, bk. iv, 22–3; trans. in Bradshaw and Soehnlen, *Girolamo Diruta: The Transylvanian*, ii. 153–6.

[19] See Edward J. Soehnlen, 'Diruta and his Contemporaries: Tradition and Innovation in the Art of Registration *c* 1610,' *Organ Yearbook*, 10 (1979), 15–33. This article usefully compares Diruta's and Antegnati's registrations.

[20] Bradshaw and Soehnlen, *Girolamo Diruta: The Transylvanian*, ii. 153.

[21] Soehnlen, 'Diruta and his Contemporaries', 17.

[22] Ibid. 25.

[23] Ibid.

TONE	MOOD	REGISTRATION
I	serious, pleasant	Pr + Oct + Oct Fl; Pr + Oct + 15th
II	melancholy	Pr + tremolo
III	moves to lamentation	Pr + Oct Fl
IV	mournful, sad, sorrowful	Pr + tremolo;Oct Fl
V	joyful, simple, delightful	Oct + 15th + Oct Fl
VI	devout, serious	Pr + Oct + Oct Fl
VII	gay, delicate	Oct + 15th + 22nd
VIII	charming, delightful	Oct Fl; Oct Fl + Oct; Oct Fl + 15th
IX	gay, sweet, resonant	Pr + 15th + 22nd
X	somewhat melancholy	Pr + Oct; Pr + Oct Fl
XI	lively, full of sweetness	Oct Fl; Oct Fl + 15th; Oct Fl + 15th + 29th; Oct + 15th + 22nd
XII	sweet, lively	Oct Fl + Oct + 15th; Oct Fl

TABLE 1[24]

Monteverdi's registration rubrics in each verse of his two Magnificats show some correspondence with Diruta's recommendations. Monteverdi avoids the flutes and adds the *voce humana* and the *tremolante* on only two occasions calling for particular expressiveness (the *Fecit potentiam* of both Magnificats and the middle of the *Quia respexit* of the Magnificat *a 6*).[25] His registrations are carefully calibrated to the volume of sound produced by the voices and instruments: *principale solo* for softer sonorities, *principale* and *ottava* for middle-level sonorities, and *principale, ottave*, and *quintadecima* for louder sonorities. The *ripieno* is required only for the *Sicut erat* of the Magnificat *a 7*. Monteverdi's obvious interest in balancing his transparent organ registration with the sonorities and expressiveness of the voices and instruments reflects the ideals of Diruta.

Antegnati's treatise contrasts with that of Diruta in its focus on the needs of solo organ playing and the newer *concertato* styles of vocal composition. Nevertheless, his comments also bear comparison with Monteverdi's

---

[24] Reproduced from ibid. 21, with the kind permission of the Institute of Mediaeval Music.
[25] Ibid. 29.

registration.[26] Antegnati offers a number of specific recommendations for registering an organ containing the principal choir and the most common additional stops (flute stops and the *fiffaro* or *voce humana*). Aside from the *ripieno* described above, he also suggests a *quasi un mezzo ripieno* (almost a half-ripieno), consisting of the *principale, ottava* (4 foot), *vigesimanona* ($\frac{1}{2}$ foot), *trigesimaterza* ($\frac{1}{3}$ foot), and *flauto in ottava*. Additional registrations include the *principale* and *flauto in ottava*, or the *principale, ottava*, and *flauto in ottava*, or the *ottava, decimanona* ($1\frac{1}{3}$ foot), *vigesimaseconda per concerto* (a second *vigesimaseconda* (1 foot) on Antegnati's Brescian organ), and *flauto in ottava*. According to Antegnati, this latter combination resembles a *concerto di cornetti*. For purposes of playing diminutions and *canzoni alla francese*, he recommends the *ottava* together with the *flauto in ottava*.[27] Other registrations are also described; for playing quickly and with diminutions, the *principale* and *flauto in quintadecima* (2 foot) may be used, and the *ottava* may be added to these. Both the *principale* and the *flauto* may be played as solo stops. These registrations are more varied and colourful than those of Diruta, reflecting the celebrated organ-builder's more contemporary aesthetic sensibility, and they are more suitable for solo organ music, such as might be played before or after the performance of the Monteverdi Vespers, than for accompanying the voices. Banchieri suggested in his *Conclusioni nel suono dell'organo* of 1609 that the organist should play something (*suoni in ripieno*) before the versicle *Deus in adjutorium* and should play a *canzona francese* or motet at the conclusion of the Magnificat.[28]

Monteverdi's registrations in the two Magnificats correspond to some of Antegnati's simpler registrations without the addition of flutes. An overview of Monteverdi's rubrics shows five combinations in addition to the *ripieno*: (1) *principale solo*, (2) *principale e ottava* (4 foot), (3) *principale, ottava e quintadecima* (2 foot), (4) *principale e voce humana*, (5) *principale e tremolare*.[29] The most frequently used of these is the *principale solo*, mostly to support a solo voice or two parts in virtuoso duets, whether of voices or instruments. As noted above, the *principale e ottava* support thicker textures and the *principale, ottava e quintadecima* are used for the thickest textures and other situations where Monteverdi wanted a bigger

[26] See Gianfranco Spinelli, 'Confronto fra le registrazioni organistiche dei *Vespri* di Monteverdi e quelle de *L'arte organica* di Antegnati', in Raffaello Monterosso, ed., *Claudio Monteverdi e il suo tempo* (Verona: La Stamperia Valdonega, 1969), 479–88.

[27] On many old Italian organs, including some built by members of the Antegnati family, the pipes for the *ottava* and *flauto in ottava* are in close proximity to one another at the front of the windchest. As a result, using both stops simultaneously would cause them to draw wind from one another, leading to serious intonation problems. Antegnati evidently had in mind organs, including some built by members of his family, that were large enough for the *flauto in ottavo* to be at the rear of the windchest and therefore more distant from the *principale* rank. I am grateful to Carl Smith for these observations.

[28] *Conclusioni nel suono dell'organo . . . opera vigesima* (Bologna: Rossi, 1609; fac. edn. Bologna: Forni Editore, 1968), 20; Eng. trans. Lee R. Garrett as *Adriano Banchieri: Conclusions for Playing the Organ (1609)* (Colorado Springs, Colo.: Colorado College Music Press, 1982), 16.

[29] Derived from Spinelli, 'Confronto fra le registrazioni', 481.

sound. The addition of the *fifara* or *tremolante* to the *principale* underscores the expression of particular texts. On the other hand, Monteverdi avoided Antegnati's more complicated registrations, those which Antegnati says are especially suited to soloistic playing, as in *canzoni alla francese* and organ diminutions, or which are suitable for dialogues or have special colouring, as in the registration resembling a *concerto di cornetti* or the *mezzo ripieno*.

In contrast to Diruta, Antegnati recommends varying the registration from time to time so as not to fatigue or annoy the listeners. Monteverdi does indeed vary the registration in the course of some of the Magnificat verses in order to increase organ sonority as the vocal texture increases, or for expressive purposes, as in the *Quia respexit* of the Magnificat *a 6*, which has four different registrations in its brief duration.

The *Sicut erat* of the Magnificat *a 7* is marked by Monteverdi *A organo pieno*, and according to the recommendations of both Diruta and Antegnati, the *ripieno* comprises the principal chorus only, without flutes.[30] But Monteverdi's *Sicut erat* is unique in the contemporary literature in being also accompanied by violins, cornettos, and a bass violin. Reflecting this colour, the organ *ripieno* might include, in addition to the principal, all registers of *flauti* as well.[31]

Practical comments by other composers also provide guidelines for the organist in Monteverdi's psalms and few-voiced motets. Viadana, in the preface to his four-choir psalms of 1612, says that 'The organist shall take care to register at the right time and place, and on finding the words Empty [*Voto*] or Full [*Pieno*], shall register empty and full. When the choir is singing with one, two, three, four or five voices, the organist shall play simply and sincerely without diminishing and without playing any passages. He shall play as he likes in the filler parts [*ne' ripieni*], because that is his moment.'[32] Bastiano Miseroca calls for additional registers when the ripieno choir joins the solo choir (1609), while Marcantonio Negri requires the full organ when the ripieno choir sings (1613).[33] Giovanni Ghizzolo in 1619 called upon the organist to increase or lessen the registration in psalms with an optional second choir according to whether or not the second choir was singing and whether or not it consisted of solo voices or the *ripieno* choir (see Chapter 15 below for a discussion of chorus versus soloists in double-choir compositions).[34] For few-voiced motets, however, both Viadana and

---

[30] Soehnlen, 'Diruta and his Contemporaries', 29.

[31] Luigi Ferdinando Tagliavini follows Antegnati in recommending the principal chorus only. See his 'Registrazioni organistiche nei Magnificat dei "Vespri" Monteverdiani', *Rivista italiana di musicologia*, 2 (1967), 368–70.

[32] Quoted in Morelli, 'Basso Continuo on the Organ', 37, from Viadana's *Salmi a quattro chori* (Venice: Vincenti, 1612) (RISM V1400). See also id., 'Monteverdi and Organ Practice', 138–40.

[33] See Morelli, 'Basso Continuo on the Organ', 38–9.

[34] Quoted in Spinelli, 'Confronto fra le registrazioni', 480, from Ghizzolo's *Messa salmi lettanie B. V. falsibordoni et gloria patri concertati a cinque*, 1619. Ghizzolo indicates changes of registration and the *ripieno* by means of *Forte*, *F.*, and *Piano*. See also Morelli, 'Basso Continuo on the Organ', 38–9, and id., 'Monteverdi and Organ Practice', 140–1.

Ercole Porta caution against adding registers to create the *ripieno*, and recommend adding more notes in the hands and feet instead.[35]Similar cautions relating the number of notes in the organ to the number of voices singing are offered by Agazzari and Micheli Romano.[36] These criteria are clearly applicable to the organ accompaniment for all of Monteverdi's psalms, the response, and the hymn.

Diruta makes a sage comment at the conclusion of his discussion of registrations for the twelve modes:

One cannot give a fixed rule for these registrations because organs are not all the same. Some have a few stops and others have many of them. It is enough for you to know the musical effect each tone needs and with your judgment practice finding it . . . Not only may one join together the customary registers that produce the musical effect sought for in each tone, but there are also other stops of various instruments so that one may imitate not only the musical effect of the tones but also every other instrument and even the human voice.[37]

For a modern organist, the matter is complicated by the paucity of Italian-style organs in other countries. A useful guide to the imitation of Italian sonorities on modern organs, using several American instruments as models, can be found in Joseph Horning, 'The Italian Organ, Part II: Registrations'.[38]

[35] Quoted in Spinelli, 'Confronto fra le registrazioni', 480. See also Morelli, 'Basso Continuo on the Organ', 35.
[36] Ibid. 34–5.
[37] Bradshaw and Soehnlen, *Girolamo Diruta: The Transylvanian*, ii. 154.
[38] *American Organist*, 25/9 (Sept. 1991), 69–70.

14
Continuo Realization

THE role of accompanying foundation instruments and the realization of continuo parts were much less consistent in the early seventeenth century than they came to be after many decades of development and gradual standardization. Manuscript and printed accompanying parts were not limited to the single bass-line which eventually became the norm, but ranged from full scores, duplicating precisely the polyphonic texture of all the vocal or instrumental parts, to short scores with bass and one upper part or more, tablatures with bass-line and upper parts arranged according to the capacities of a particular type of instrument, and single bass-lines either derived from one or more of the vocal or instrumental parts or independent of these parts.[1] Each of these types of manuscript and printed accompanimental parts poses different problems in its execution and realization, and all, with the exception of tablature, are represented in the bassus generalis of Monteverdi's Vespers. In my edition of the Vespers, all of the parts printed in the bassus generalis have been included in a separate appendix.

A simple bass-line, mainly following the lowest sounding part at any given moment, is printed in the bassus generalis for *Dixit Dominus*, *Nisi Dominus*, *Lauda Jerusalem*, the second part of *Audi coelum*, the *Sonata sopra Sancta Maria*, *Ave maris stella*, and both Magnificats. Short scores, providing both the bass and a reduced version of the upper voices, are found for *Domine ad adjuvandum*, *Laudate pueri*, *Laetatus sum*, and short segments of the *Sonata sopra Sancta Maria*. Full scores appear for *Nigra sum*, *Pulchra es*, *Duo Seraphim*, the first part of *Audi coelum*, the *Deposuit* of both Magnificats, and the *Gloria Patri* of the Magnificat *a 7*.

The realization of the basso continuo in my edition follows varying principles, depending on the character of each individual composition or

[1] See Otto Kinkeldey, *Orgel und Klavier in der Musik des 16. Jahrhunderts* (Leipzig: Breitkopf and Härtel, 1910; repr. edn. Hildesheim: Georg Olms, 1968), 187–215; Hans Heinrich Eggebrecht, 'Arten des Generalbasses im frühen und mittleren 17. Jahrhundert', *Archiv für Musikwissenschaft*, 14 (1957), 61–82; Imogene Horsley, 'Full and Short Scores in the Accompaniment of Italian Church Music in the Early Baroque', *Journal of the American Musicological Society*, 30 (1977), 466–99; Peter Williams, 'Continuo', in *The New Grove Dictionary of Music and Musicians*, ed. Stanley Sadie (London: Macmillan Publishers Ltd., 1980), iv, 685–99; and John Walter Hill, 'Realized Continuo Accompaniments from Florence *c* 1600', *Early Music*, 11 (1983), 194–208.

segment of a composition. Monteverdi did not assist the continuo player with numerals, and only occasionally are notated flats for upper parts found in the bass-line.[2]

A number of sections of the hymn and the psalms as well as the second section of *Audi coelum* resemble sixteenth-century polyphonic style. My continuo realization for these sections adopts the common late sixteenth-century and early seventeenth-century practice of the organ *partitura*, that is, duplication of the vocal polyphony by the organ to the extent that the fingers and keyboard conveniently allow. In other sections of the psalms a principally homophonic texture prevails, sometimes enlivened by rhythmic disjunction among the parts. In these passages it is usually a simple task for the continuo player to reproduce the full vocal texture. However, in contrast to the norms of sixteenth-century imitative polyphony, the homophonic vocal idiom often uses repeated notes in declamation. There is no reason for an organist to repeat such chords, especially when the declamation of the text is rapid. A suitable accompaniment, therefore, may consist of a single sustained chord, whereby the organist reproduces faithfully the harmonic disposition of the voices, but not their rhythmic declamation. In some situations, however, the repetition of a chord on an important syllable or beat may further enliven or clarify the texture. Monteverdi's own bass-line is, in fact, carefully notated in this regard, sometimes indicating repeated harmonies, sometimes sustained chords.

Monteverdi's short scores in two or three parts are designed to give the continuo player the essentials of the harmony and texture of the composition without going to the length of a full score. There is no reason to assume that a keyboard player would have performed only the notes of the short score, any more than he would have played only the bass-line in those pieces where the continuo consists of but a single line. Rather, the short score would have been used as a point of departure for a fuller accompaniment, and in my edition, the continuo realization again follows the entire vocal texture as far as is convenient for two hands. That this is an appropriate realization of the short score is obvious from the example of *Domine ad adjuvandum*, whose bassus generalis consists of the bass-line and the highest instrumental part (see Ex. 14.1). It would be unsuitable to double the instrumental part, replete with semiquavers and dotted rhythms, with the more sluggish, sustained, and less articulate sound of the organ. The upper part of the bassus generalis is designed, rather, to keep the

---

[2] Figuring of bass-lines was still quite sporadic in the early 17th century and was associated particularly with the Florentine monodists. Peter Williams notes that 'the composer has sometimes required his soloist to "contradict" the implied harmonies, giving rise to a harmonically ambiguous situation. Monteverdi's *Vespro della beata vergine* and *Orfeo* bristle with examples of these problems . . .' See Williams, 'Continuo', 687. My solutions to ambiguous harmonies are detailed in the critical notes to my edition of the Vespers.

Ex. 14.1. *Domine ad adjuvandum*, bars 1–8, bassus generalis

Ex. 14.2. *Laudate pueri*, bars 54–7, bassus generalis

continuo player abreast of the rapidly moving instrumental line while simulta-neously providing him with the information he needs to play the correct chords, in this case a simple matter because of the *falsobordone* style of the voice parts. Similarly, the highly embellished vocal lines that sometimes appear in the upper parts of the short scores of *Laudate pueri* and *Laetatus sum* are clearly not to be doubled in all their detail by the continuo player, but serve as a guide for the harmony and essential notes of each passage (see Ex. 14.2).

The passages in two-part score for the *Sonata sopra Sancta Maria* have a some-what different function. These occur only when there is a violin or cornetto duet in quick notes. The bassus generalis is a rhythmic simplification of the two parts in the same treble register and evidently should be reproduced by the continuo player just as written, without further harmonic embellishment. In this way the continuo doubles the essential notes of both instrumental parts, and the texture is deliberately thin (see Ex. 14.3).

Ex. 14.3. *Sonata sopra Sancta Maria*, bars 41–50, bassus generalis

Paradoxically, it is where Monteverdi provides a full score, in his motets and a few sections of the Magnificats, that the continuo player should follow the vocal parts least closely. The full scores function primarily as detailed guides to the continuo player in those pieces or sections where the vocal parts are most elaborate and rhythmically complicated. These are also the passages in which the singers are most free to shape their expression and rhythmic performance according to the affections of the text, making it essential for the continuo player to be able to follow the vocal parts in detail.

Since the continuo player should not simply duplicate the upper parts of the bassus generalis in these compositions, the question of what to play is more complicated. The relationship between the accompaniment and the voice is treated in general terms in the writings of a number of early seventeenth-century composers. Typical is Viadana's comment that 'the organist is bound to play the organ part simply, and in particular with the left hand; if, however, he wants to execute some movement with the right hand, as by ornamenting the cadences, or by some appropriate embellishment, he must play in such a manner that the singer or singers are not covered or confused by too much movement.'[3]

---

[3] From the preface to the *Cento concerti ecclesiastici . . . opera duodecima* (1602), trans. in Oliver Strunk, *Source Readings in Music History* (New York: W. W. Norton & Company, Inc., 1950), 421.

Galeazzo Sabbatini recommended in 1628 that the parts of the accompaniment be distributed so that the left hand normally played either the single bass note or the bass plus a single consonance, that is, an octave, fifth, sixth, or third. The remaining note or notes of the chord would then fall to the right hand. This distribution had the effect not only of keeping the right hand low-pitched, but also of controlling the intensity of sound of the principal register so as not to overpower the voice.[4]

Pietro Lappi also warns the organist to play as softly as possible so as not to cover the *passaggi*, accents, and gracefulness of the voice.[5] Viadana, Lappi, and Sabbatini are laying down the most basic principle of early seventeenth-century continuo accompaniment of few-voiced music: the accompanist is to play simply and softly, providing a supportive rather than a contrapuntal role. Early seventeenth-century documents make it clear that rhythmic movement and embellishment were the province of the voice or solo instruments, not the continuo. Even embellishment at cadences, which is sanctioned only with caution by Viadana, must be adjusted to the movement of the voice or voices. Cadential embellishment by the continuo is appropriate only when the voice or voices are sustained and lack movement of their own. If a singer embellishes the cadence, then the continuo player should not. The same principle applies to passages between cadences, where the continuo player should only add motion if it is lacking in the other parts. My edition provides a very simple harmonic accompaniment in the few-voiced motets and the Magnificats, avoiding embellishment altogether. The continuo player may add discrete embellishments where appropriate, keeping simplicity as a suitable guide.

The disposition of the harmony is also discussed by many seventeenth-century writers. Agazzari is especially instructive in this regard in a passage which also echoes the points made by Viadana and Lappi above:

An instrument that serves as foundation must be played with great judgment and due regard for the size of the chorus; if there are many voices one should play with a full sound, increasing the registers, while if there are few one should decrease them [the registers] and use few consonances [thinner chords, with few doublings], playing the work as purely and exactly as possible, using few passages and few divisions, occasionally supporting the voices with low notes and frequently avoiding the high ones which cover up the voices, especially the sopranos or falsettos. For this reason one is warned to avoid as much as possible touching or diminishing with a division the note which the soprano sings, in order not to duplicate it or obscure the excellence of the note itself or of the passage which the good singer executes upon it; for the same reason one does well to play within a rather small compass and in a lower register.

---

[4] *Regola facile e breve per sonare sopra il basso continuo nell'organo manacordo & altri simile istrumento* (Venice: Salvadori, 1628). See Arnaldo Morelli, 'Basso Continuo on the Organ in Seventeenth-Century Italian Music', *Basler Jahrbuch für historische Musikpraxis*, 18 (1994), 42–4.

[5] *Partitura per l'organo dlle* [sic] *messe ad otto, et nove voci . . . libro secondo. 1608.*

I say the same of the lute, harp, theorbo, harpsichord, etc., when they serve as foundation with one or more voices singing above them, for in this case, to support the voice, they must maintain a solid, sonorous, sustained harmony, playing now piano, now forte, according to the quality and quantity of the voices, the place, and the work, while, to avoid interfering with the singer, they must not restrike the strings too often when he executes a passage or expresses a passion.[6]

Agazzari also calls for plucked instruments to fill an ornamental role, in addition to their foundational one, in order to 'make the harmony more agreeable and sonorous'.[7] In this role the ornamenting instruments

must make the melody flourishing and graceful, each according to its quality, with a variety of beautiful counterpoints . . . the player must compose new parts above the bass and new and varied passages and counterpoints. . . . For this reason, he who plays the lute (which is the noblest instrument of them all) must play it nobly, with much invention and variety, not as is done by those who, because they have a ready hand, do nothing but play runs and make divisions from beginning to end. . . . Sometimes, therefore, he must use gentle strokes and repercussions, sometimes slow passages, sometimes rapid and repeated ones, sometimes something played on the bass strings, sometimes beautiful vyings and conceits, repeating and bringing out these figures at different pitches and in different places; he must, in short, so weave the voices together with long groups, trills, and accents, each in its turn, that he gives grace to the consort and enjoyment and delight to the listeners. . . . And what I say of the lute, as the principal instrument, I wish understood of the others in their kind, for it would take a long time to discuss them all separately.[8]

Regarding the register of the accompaniment, different writers have somewhat different suggestions. For example, Viadana comments that 'When one wants to sing a concerto written in the four equal parts [*a voce pari*], the organist must never play high up, and, vice versa, when one wants to sing a concerto of high pitch, the organist must never play low down, unless it be in cadences in the octave, because it then gives charm.'[9]

Francesco Bianciardi recommends adjusting the accompaniment according to affect and the need for a full sonority: 'However, many times, because of the words, one seeks a fulness of voice, and in exclamations, the assistance of the high notes; when the material is cheerful, stay in the high register as much as you can; with sad material, stay in the low register; at cadences play the octave below

---

[6] *Del sonare sopra'l basso con tutti li stromenti e dell'uso loro nel conserto* (Siena: Domenico Falcini, 1607; fac. Bologna: Forni Editore, 1985). Eng. trans. from Strunk, *Source Readings in Music History*, 427. Agazzari's treatise was republished the next year in his *Sacrarum cantionum . . . liber II, opus V* (Venice, 1608) (RISM A353), thereby clearly establishing its reference to sacred music (which is also mentioned in the text). The major study of Agazzari is Colleen Reardon, *Agostino Agazzari and Music at Siena Cathedral, 1597–1641* (Oxford: Clarendon Press, 1993).

[7] Strunk, *Source Readings in Music History*, 424.

[8] Ibid. 428–9. For a discussion of the types of embellishments Agazzari mentions, see Ch. 21.

[9] *Cento concerti ecclesiastici*, preface; transl. adapted from Strunk, *Source Readings in Music History*, 422–3.

the bass, avoiding thirds and fifths in the lowest notes because they make the harmony too heavy, offending the ear.'[10]

Another aspect of harmonic disposition is the formation of cadences. This is a topic on which Viadana is explicit:

Let the organist be warned always to make the cadences in their proper position: that is to say, if a concerto for one bass voice alone is being sung, to make a bass cadence; if it be for a tenor, to make a tenor cadence; if an alto or soprano, to make it in the place of the one or the other, since it would always have a bad effect if, while the soprano were making its cadence, the organ were to make it in the tenor, or if, while someone were singing the cadence in the tenor, the organ were to make it in the soprano.[11]

The harmony played by the organ was not subject to all the rules of voice-leading demanded in multiple vocal parts. Viadana, for example, says that 'the organ part is never under any obligation to avoid two fifths or two octaves, but those parts which are sung by the voices are'.[12] Other writers echo Viadana's remarks, and indeed, the positioning of the vocal part or parts and the bass-line in early seventeenth-century music at times makes it impossible to avoid parallel fifths and octaves in the accompaniment unless parts of the harmony are omitted altogether. In my edition they are avoided wherever possible, but they do appear in instances where there is no feasible alternative.

Early seventeenth-century sources present varied opinions regarding the doubling of vocal lines by the continuo, especially when a vocal line is highly ornamented. Agazzari, as quoted above, argues against duplicating the *passaggi* of singers and even suggests avoiding doubling, and especially ornamenting, a pitch sung by a soprano or falsetto. Elsewhere he makes a similar comment about the accompaniment by instruments, whether organ, harpsichord, theorbo, or lute, suggesting that the accompaniment be kept distant from the other parts, keeping it 'close and low so that the high register is left more for the voices and other instruments'.[13] Other composers, such as Giovanni Paolo Cima and Domenico Brunetti, were more amenable to discrete doubling of an ornamented soprano or alto vocal line, which could be played in a more

[10] *Breve regola per imparar'a sonare sopra il basso con ogni sorte d'istrumento* (Siena: Enrico Zucchifice, 1607).
[11] *Cento concerti ecclesiastici*, preface; transl. adapted from Strunk, *Source Readings in Music History*, 422. By 'make the cadence' Viadana is referring to a melodic cadence in the voice, consisting in the most common 17th-century formulation of raised seventh and final followed by another raised seventh and final. Viadana admonishes the organist to double this cadence in the same register as the voice, obviously to avoid doubling the raised seventh in another octave. His advice is ignored in a number of surviving contemporary continuo realizations. See Hill, 'Realized Continuo Accompaniments', 204.
[12] Strunk, *Source Readings in Music History*, 422.
[13] From a letter pub. in Adriano Banchieri, *Conclusioni nel suono dell'organo . . . opera vigesima* (Bologna: Rossi, 1609; fac. edn. Bologna: Forni Editore, 1968), 68; Eng. trans. Lee R. Garrett as *Adriano Banchieri: Conclusions for Playing the Organ (1609)* (Colorado Springs, Colo.: Colorado College Music Press, 1982), 58.

simplified form; the continuo could also play harmony notes above solo tenor and bass parts.[14]

The doubling of dissonances in the vocal parts by the continuo is a related issue, requiring considerable judgement on the part of the player. In Monteverdi's full scores all dissonances can be seen clearly by the reader of the bassus generalis. In the music of the Florentine monodists, dissonances are usually indicated by the precise figuring of the bass. Yet it is not at all certain that these dissonances were reproduced in the accompaniment, especially when they occurred against the background of a sustained chord. The figured dissonance may at times have been meant only to alert the continuo player to the movement of the voice, not to the duplication of that movement on his own instrument. There are numerous passages in music of this period in which dissonances are more pungent and expressive if the voice is allowed to sound against a sustained note or chord in the accompaniment. Indeed, slavishly playing in the continuo the dissonances of the voice frequently robs them of their full expressive power. At the end of the seventeenth century Werckmeister specifically advised against the accompanist blindly following the figures without considering their expressive effect.[15] In my edition, the doubling of vocal lines and of dissonances by the continuo has been approached cautiously; in many instances the doubling of dissonances has been avoided. Accompaniments of bass and tenor solos or duets usually rise above the vocal line, but are still kept in a low register. Accompaniments of soprano duets frequently double the primary rhythmic and harmonic notes when the voices are in a low or middle register, but generally do not double the voices when they are in a higher register.

The principles governing the accompaniment of Monteverdi's motets and those segments of the two Magnificats that are in full score in the bassus generalis also apply to those portions of the psalms, the *Sonata sopra Sancta Maria*, and the Magnificats that are in a modern soloistic style but only have a single continuo line in the bassus generalis part-book. In general these sections and passages are not as rhythmically complicated or flexible as the motets and those segments of the Magnificats with full score. Apparently either Monteverdi or Amadino judged that a full score in these passages was unnecessary and not worth the extra expense. However, the same methods of doubling and the same considerations of register and of disposition of the harmony are

---

[14] See e.g. the instructions to the reader in Giovanni Paolo Cima, *Concerti ecclesiastici a una, due, tre, quattro voci* (Milan, 1610) (RISM C2229, SD1610⁴), quoted in Luigi Ferdinando Tagliavini, 'Registrazioni organistiche nei Magnificat dei "Vespri" Monteverdiani', *Rivista italiana di musicologia*, 2 (1967), 366–7.

[15] See F. T. Arnold, *The Art of Accompaniment from a Thorough-Bass as Practised in the XVIIth & XVIIIth Centuries* (Oxford: Oxford University Press, 1931; repr. edn. New York: Dover Publications, Inc., 1965), i. 39–40 n. 4.

pertinent, and my edition treats these passages and sections in the same manner as the pieces and sections notated in full score in the bassus generalis.[16]

In two of Monteverdi's psalms, *Dixit Dominus* and *Laetatus sum*, there are passages of unmeasured *falsibordoni*. While I know of no discussion in Italian sources regarding continuo accompaniment for *falsibordoni*, Heinrich Schütz did address the subject in the preface to his Resurrection History. There, in the instructions for the chorus of evangelists, he directs that

> It is for the organist . . . to remember that as long as the *falsobordone* lasts on a single tone, he should always on the organ or instrument [Schütz prefers that four violas da gamba, if available, substitute for the organ] make decorative and appropriate runs or *passaggi* under it [the *falsobordone*], which gives to this work as well as all other *falsobordone* the correct style; otherwise they do not have their proper effect. . . . One of the several violas [da gamba] may also perhaps play *passaggi*, as is customary in *falsobordone* and makes a good effect.[17]

Such *passaggi* accompanying *falsobordone* are in fact provided by Monteverdi himself in the response *Domine ad adjuvandum*, where the vocal *falsobordone* is performed against the instrumental toccata adapted from *L'Orfeo*. In the response, the *passaggi* are in the upper register, scored for cornettos and violins, rather than in the bass. It is certainly possible that Monteverdi expected the type of *passaggi* described by Schütz or the type he himself supplied for the response in the *falsobordone* sections of *Dixit Dominus* and *Laetatus sum*.

---

[16] The theoretical statements about continuo realization described in this section may be usefully compared with actual surviving realizations from Florence around the turn of the 17th century. See the summary of eleven Florentine MSS in Hill, 'Realized Continuo Accompaniments', 194–208. Many aspects of the theoretical literature are confirmed by the realizations in these MSS. An account of several intabulated theorbo realizations from the early 17th century is found in Stanley Buetens, 'Theorbo Accompaniments of Early Seventeenth-Century Italian Monody', *Journal of the Lute Society of America*, 6 (1973), 37–45. A detailed manual for continuo realization on plucked string instruments, based on 17th- and 18th-century theoretical and practical sources, is Nigel North, *Continuo Playing on the Lute, Archlute and Theorbo* (Bloomington, Ind.: Indiana University Press, 1987).

[17] *Historia der frölichen und Siegreichen Aufferstehung unsers einigen Erlösers und Seligmachers Jesu Christi* (Dresden: Gimel Bergen, 1623); ed. Walter Simon Huber in *Heinrich Schütz: Neue Ausgabe sämtlicher Werke*, iii: *Historia der Auferstehung Jesu Christi* (Kassel: Bärenreiter-Verlag, 1956). Attention was first drawn to this passage in connection with Monteverdi's Vespers by Hans Redlich in 'Editions of Monteverdi's Vespers of 1610', *Gramophone*, 31 (1954), 503.

15

Voices and Choirs

THE most important feature distinguishing church choirs of the sixteenth and seventeenth centuries from modern choirs was, of course, the exclusive use of male singers, resulting in altogether different sonorities from those of the modern mixed choir.[1] Soprano parts were sometimes sung by boys, at times by adult males singing falsetto, and at times by castrati. Alto parts were sung by adult falsettos or castrati; boys may also have sung alto parts on occasion, although documentary evidence is lacking. The sonority and balance of the choir was therefore affected by whether boys, falsettos, or castrati sang the upper parts.

The ranges of vocal parts in this period also differed from the ranges of a modern choir. The highest note normally found in late sixteenth- and early seventeenth-century sources, as well as in Monteverdi's 1610 Vespers, is a''. But in the Monteverdi print as well as in most other sources of the same period, the a'' appears only when the voices are notated in the *chiavi alte* (*chiavette*), indicating downward transposition in performance (see Chapter 17). Monteverdi's highest note in the *chiavi naturali* in the Vespers is g''.[2] As far as can be determined, this g'' was approximately one half-step higher than modern pitch. Michael Praetorius says that well-trained boys could sing as high as a'', and it seems that this a'' was approximately a half-step higher than the modern pitch.[3] He gives

---

[1] Female choirs existed, of course, in convents, and sang in convent chapels and churches, though males and females were never mixed. For studies of music in female convents in Milan and Bologna, see Robert L. Kendrick, 'Genres, Generations and Gender: Nuns' Music in Early Modern Milan, c. 1550–1706' (Ph.D. dissertation, New York University, 1993); id., *Celestial Sirens: Nuns and their Music in Early Modern Milan* (Oxford: Clarendon Press, 1996); and Craig A. Monson, *Disembodied Voices: Music and Culture in an Early Modern Italian Convent* (Berkeley: University of California Press, 1995). The virtuoso singer Victoria Archilei is also recorded at the end of the 16th century as having sung Emilio de' Cavalieri's *Lamentations* and *Responsi* in the church of San Nicolò at Pisa, where the Florentine court celebrated Easter. See Claude V. Palisca, 'Emilio de' Cavalieri', in *The New Grove Dictionary of Music and Musicians*, ed. Stanley Sadie (London: Macmillan Publishers Ltd., 1980), iv. 22. She is also mentioned after 1610, along with Giulio Caccini's daughters, as a singer of sacred music on 'special court occasions in Florence and Pisa'. See H. Wiley Hitchcock, 'Vittoria Archilei', in *The New Grove*, i, 551. It is not clear that these were actually liturgical services, but in any event, the practices of the Florentine court would have been exceptional and not repeated in ordinary services in parish, monastic, collegiate, or cathedral churches.

[2] This is also the highest note in *chiavi naturali* in Books Four, Five, and Six of Monteverdi's madrigals.

[3] *Syntagmatis musici . . . tomus tertius* (Wolfenbüttel: Elias Holwein, 1619); fac. ed. Wilibald Gurlitt (Kassel: Bärenreiter, 1958), 157–8; Eng. trans. in Hans A. Lampl, 'A Translation of *Syntagma musicum III*

the same maximum note for castrati and falsettos.[4] Nevertheless, such high pitches were used infrequently in actual musical practice.

Monteverdi's highest soprano pitch in *chiavi naturali* is not problematic for modern choirs, but his lowest soprano pitch, the lowest alto pitch, and both extremities of the tenor range do pose difficulties. In *chiavi naturali* the soprano drops as low as *a* and the alto as low as *e*, while the tenor extends from *A* to *a'*. These ranges scarcely coincide with modern ranges; rather, they were dependent on the distribution of voice parts in the all-male choir as well as the use of the falsetto register in parts other than the soprano. Monteverdi's alto, extending in *chiavi naturali* from *e* to *bb'*, coincides much more closely with a modern tenor than with a modern alto, and we can assume that an alto part would have been sung in the seventeenth century by what today would be called a tenor. Monteverdi's tenor, on the other hand, approximates a modern baritone, except that the highest few notes are beyond the reach of most baritones. It is probable that a seventeenth-century tenor, when he encountered pitches above his normal range, simply sang them falsetto.[5] The bass voice in Monteverdi's *chiavi naturali* falls within the customary range of the bass, although there were basses in Monteverdi's day capable of encompassing three octaves, the upper octave or octave-and-a-half obviously in falsetto.[6]

The sounding ranges of the three pieces in Monteverdi's Vespers notated in *chiavi alte* depends not only on the pitch standard chosen, but also on the degree

by Michael Praetorius' (DMA dissertation, University of California, 1957), 267. See Ch. 17 n. 16 regarding the probable frequency range of Praetorius's *a''*.

[4] *Syntagmatis musici . . . tomus secundus de organographia* (Wolfenbüttel: Elias Holwein, 1619); fac. ed. Wilibald Gurlitt (Kassel: Bärenreiter, 1958), 20; Eng. trans. Harold Blumenfeld as *The Syntagma Musicum of Michael Praetorius: Volume Two, De Organographia, First and Second Parts* (New York: Da Capo Press, 1980), 20; and David Z. Crookes, *Praetorius Syntagma Musicum II: De Organographia, Parts I and II* (Oxford: Clarendon Press, 1986), 35. The highest note on many Italian organs of the period is also *a''*. See Luigi Ferdinando Tagliavini, 'Considerazioni sugli ambiti delle tastiere degli organi italiani', in Friedemann Hellwig, ed., *Studia organologica: Festschrift für John Henry van der Meer zu seinem fünfundsechsigsten Geburtstag* (Tutzing: Hans Schneider, 1987), 453–60.

[5] The first musician to discuss the problems of switching from natural voice to falsetto was Pier Francesco Tosi in 1723 in his *Opinioni de' cantori antichi e moderni, o sieno osservazioni sopra il canto figurato*. Though published more than a century after the Monteverdi Vespers and referring to the soprano register, Tosi's comments are still pertinent to the issue faced by Monteverdi's (and today's) tenors: 'A diligent Master, knowing that a [male] *Soprano*, without the *Falsetto*, is constrained to sing within the narrow Compass of a few Notes, ought not only to endeavour to help him to it, but also to leave no Means untried, so to unite the feigned and the natural Voice, that they may not be distinguished: for if they do not perfectly unite, the Voice will be of divers Registers, and must consequently lose its Beauty.' Quoted by Ellen T. Harris from a 1742 English translation in 'Voices', in Howard Mayer Brown and Stanley Sadie, eds., *Performance Practice: Music after 1600* (New York: W.W. Norton & Co., 1989), 102. For a thorough discussion of voice registers and the relationship between head-voice and falsetto, see Sally Allis Sanford, 'Seventeenth and Eighteenth Century Vocal Style and Technique' (DMA dissertation, Stanford University, 1979), 23–50.

[6] See the description of three such basses in *Vincenzo Giustiniani: Discorso sopra la musica*, trans. Carol MacClintock (American Institute of Musicology, 1962), 69–70; and a bass motet with a two-and-a-half octave range in Jeffrey Kurtzman, 'Giovanni Francesco Capello, an Avant-Gardist of the Early Seventeenth Century', *Musica disciplina*, 31 (1977), 159.

of downward transposition. In my edition, *Lauda Jerusalem* and the two Magnificats are presented not only at their originally notated levels, but also transposed a fourth down for the convenience of choirs. In these transpositions, the highest note for the soprano voice is *e″*, while the lowest note for the bass is *D*. Thus the sounding ranges of compositions notated in *chiavette* are lower than those of compositions notated in *chiavi naturali*, and it is the lower portion of each voice's register that poses the greater difficulties for modern singers.

For the soprano voice, falsettos and boys were most commonly used, especially for polyphony or psalmody. Castrati were probably rarer, even for few-voiced motets, except in the Papal Chapel, St Mark's, and other major churches and courts that could afford them.[7] Castrati were also employed at times as altos, since seventeenth-century virtuoso styles sometimes demanded higher pitches than male altos could reach.[8] Viadana comments in the preface to his *Cento concerti ecclesiastici* of 1602 that 'falsettos will have a better effect than natural sopranos; because boys, for the most part, sing carelessly, and with little grace . . . there is, however, no doubt that no money can pay a good natural soprano; but there are few of them'.[9] Alto and tenor parts were sometimes performed by the same singers.[10]

Because there were chronic difficulties in the seventeenth century in obtaining good soprano and alto voices, it was quite common to substitute a voice in a register one octave above or below in few-voiced pieces. The most common substitutions were of tenors for sopranos as well as vice versa, but basses could also substitute for altos. Altos could replace basses without disrupting the harmony only in solo pieces or duets for bass and soprano. Although the motets in Monteverdi's Vespers were obviously composed for virtuosi, probably specific singers who were present at Mantua when they were composed, it is nevertheless within the framework of seventeenth-century performance practice to make such substitutions. Thus *Nigra sum*, *Duo Seraphim*, and the first part of *Audi coelum* could legitimately be sung by sopranos, while *Pulchra es* could be performed by a pair of tenors. It would be inconsistent with Monteverdi's own practice, however, to mix voice ranges in a single motet, such as two tenors and a soprano in *Duo Seraphim* or a soprano and tenor in *Pulchra es*. Voice substitu-

---

[7] Thomas Noel O'Regan in 'Sacred Polychoral Music in Rome 1575–1621' (D.Phil. dissertation, University of Oxford, 1988), 75, demonstrates that in Rome boys were often mixed with adult sopranos (whether falsettos or castrati is not indicated) in many churches, but that boys were not used in the larger musical establishments. The Sistine Chapel began replacing falsettists with castrati in the late 16th century. See Helmut Hucke, 'Die Besetzung von Sopran und Alt in der Sixtinischen Kapelle', *Miscelánea en homenaje a Monseñor Higinio Anglés*, i (Barcelona: Consejo Superior de Investigaciones Científicas, 1958–61), 379–96.

[8] Ibid. 388–93.

[9] Oliver Strunk, *Source Readings in Music History* (New York: W. W. Norton & Company, Inc., 1950), 422.

[10] O'Regan, 'Sacred Polychoral Music', 75.

tion in the virtuoso sections of the two Magnificats and the psalms is undesirable, however, since Monteverdi has written virtuoso passages in these pieces for all the voices except altos with the clear objective of displaying each vocal range separately. Especially in the Magnificats, Monteverdi has paid very close attention to vocal, instrumental, and organ colour, and any tampering would corrupt his intended sonorities.

The size of choirs is an important issue in reconstructing the legitimate framework for performance of seventeenth-century music. Perhaps the only definitive statement that can be made about choir size is that it fluctuated according to economic conditions, the interest and support of a church's or chapel's governing body or patron, the performance traditions of particular churches or chapels, the health and personal affairs of the choir's members, and the religious and civic importance of a particular feast for which extra singers and instrumentalists might be employed.

The smallest possible choir, of course, consisted of a single voice for each register. However, it is clear that at times multiple singers were used for each part. The Venetian theorist Nicola Vicentino, in championing sacred music for multiple choirs in *L'antica musica ridotta alla moderna prattica* of 1555, says that 'in churches and other spacious places, music for four voices is heard very little [any longer], even if it is sung by many singers per part'.[11] It seems that the Sistine Chapel choir and other churches in Rome often sang with one voice per part in the sixteenth and seventeenth centuries, but there is also evidence of two singers per part in the Cappella Giulia (the choir of St Peter's Basilica) and of two or more singers per part in at least one choir of multiple-choir music in specific performances for which archival records have been found.[12] The regular *cappella* of the church of Santa Maria Maggiore in Rome comprised four boy sopranos, two altos, two tenors, and two basses in the first half of the seventeenth century, though it was augmented for special performances on major feasts.[13]

Jerome Roche's studies in the archive of the church of Santa Maria Maggiore

---

[11] (Rome: Barre, 1555); fac. ed. Edward E. Lowinsky (Kassel: Bärenreiter, 1959), ch. 27, fo. 85[r].

[12] Jean Lionnet, in 'Performance Practice in the Papal Chapel during the 17th Century', *Early Music*, 15 (1987), 4–15, claims, not entirely convincingly, that the Papal Chapel choir as well as other church choirs in Rome nearly always sang with only one voice per part. Richard Sherr, in 'Performance Practice in the Papal Chapel during the 16th Century', *Early Music*, 15 (1987), 453–62, suggests that there may have been variety in performance practice, including three or even four voices per part on occasion. O'Regan, in 'Sacred Polychoral Music in Rome', 71, 73–4, 81, 84, 97 n. 8, demonstrates that in Roman polychoral music one singer per part was common, but that there were also times when two singers, and occasionally perhaps even more, were assigned to particular parts or to entire choirs. See also id., 'Victoria, Soto and the Spanish Archconfraternity of the Resurrection in Rome', *Early Music*, 22 (1994), 287–9; and id., 'The Performance of Roman Sacred Polychoral Music in the Late Sixteenth and Early Seventeenth Centuries: Evidence from Archival Sources', *Performance Practice Review*, 8 (fall 1995), 108, 117–23, 137.

[13] John Burke, *Musicians of S. Maria Maggiore Rome, 1600–1700*, supplement to *Note d'archivio, nuova serie*, 2 (Venice: Fondazione Levi, 1984), 69.

in Bergamo, an important musical centre in the first third of the seventeenth century, reveal a choir ranging between four singers at the minimum (an unusual circumstance—otherwise about eight) and sixteen at the maximum.[14] In addition, there were one or two string players and two or three wind players on the payroll during most of this period.[15] The more recent and more detailed studies of Maurizio Padoan confirm the approximate maximum size of the vocal ensemble, which in most years between 1601 and 1626 ranged from fourteen to eighteen.[16] Padoan has also found that the instrumental ensemble was much larger than estimated by Roche, often comprising twelve to fourteen players, giving a total ensemble ranging between twenty-four and thirty-two in the period before 1616. In the more fallow period (1620–6) following a crisis in 1617, the number of singers was reduced to a range of nine to fifteen and the instrumental ensemble decreased to a consistent five.

Depending on economic conditions and the availability of singers, the number of voices in each range at Santa Maria Maggiore fluctuated considerably. While one singer per part represented an unusual circumstance, the distribution varied from four sopranos, five altos, six tenors, and two basses, and one voice of unknown register in 1603 to two sopranos, three altos, five tenors, four basses, and two voices of unknown register in 1610.[17] Such imbalances in the numbers for each register were normal. On special feast-days the permanent choir could be augmented by additional singers and instrumentalists for a more sumptuous musical celebration. According to Roche, a choir of seven sopranos, eight altos, eight tenors, and five basses was used for one feast, and nine sopranos, six altos, seven tenors, and six basses for another. The Assumption Day celebration in 1627 featured 'twenty-eight singers, two cornetts, one violin (doubling trombone), two trombones, two bassoons, two *violoni*, four organs, and two conductors'.[18] Assumption Day in 1628 utilized fifty-seven musicians, probably two-thirds of whom would have been singers.

At the basilica of St Anthony in Padua, the salaried choir in 1594 consisted of three basses, three tenors, three altos, and one soprano, supplemented by boys from the attached convent, while the instrumental ensemble comprised two trombonists, a cornettist, and a violinist. In the period 1606–8, the basilica attempted to keep the choir at sixteen singers, distributed evenly among the four registers. A trombonist was used to double the bass-line and a cornettist would

[14] Jerome Roche, 'Music at S. Maria Maggiore, Bergamo, 1614–1643', *Music & Letters*, 47 (1966), 296–312. Some of the figures are revised in id., *North Italian Church Music in the Age of Monteverdi* (Oxford: Clarendon Press, 1984), 18.

[15] Ibid.

[16] *La musica in S. Maria Maggiore a Bergamo nel periodo di Giovanni Cavaccio (1598–1626)* (Como: AMIS, 1983), 75–91, 158–73.

[17] Ibid. 76.

[18] Ibid. 142.

reinforce the soprano line if the voices were not strong enough. The basilica frequently had two violinists and two cornettists on the payroll; a chitarrone was added in 1606, a violone and a *viola da basso* were hired in 1608 and 1611 respectively, and three more trombonists also joined the ensemble on some occasions.[19] Modena Cathedral in 1615 possessed a choir of approximately fifteen singers, a cornettist, and a trombonist, in addition to the organist.[20] An Assumption Day celebration in 1619 at the cathedral in Parma featured twenty-one singers as well as cornettos and trombones.[21]

The permanent choir at St Mark's in Venice ranged from thirteen in the mid–1590s to eighteen in 1597, approximately twenty in the decade 1601–10, thirty-five in 1643, and about forty in 1653.[22] As at Santa Maria Maggiore in Bergamo, extra singers were employed for more elaborate celebrations. At the vespers on the Vigil of the Ascension in 1604 the choir was augmented to thirty-five singers. In a postscript in his 1627 collection of vesper psalms, the Venetian composer Francesco Usper declares that two or three voices per part plus appropriate instruments are customary in Venice.[23]

Information about musicians at the ducal church of Santa Barbara in Mantua in the early seventeenth century is unfortunately sketchy. Duke Vincenzo Gonzaga (reigned 1587–1612) increased the size of both the court and chapel musical establishments (the two organizations were separate).[24] Nevertheless, only five or six singers can be documented in the chapel of Santa Barbara during the reign of Duke Vincenzo, and five appears to have been the number in 1610. It is apparent, however, that for major musical events the chapel was supplemented by singers from the court, and vice versa.[25] Musicians were also imported from elsewhere for grand court festivities, such as weddings, and these events would have required special religious festivities as well, presumably employing the visiting performers in addition to the full resources of the chapel and the court.

Not all of the singers employed in a large celebration would necessarily have

---

[19] Nicoletta Billio D'Arpa, 'Amadio Freddi, musicista padovano', *Il Santo. Rivista antoniana di storia dottrina arte*, 27 (1987), 245–7. See also Roche, *North Italian Church Music*, 22.

[20] Ibid. 19.

[21] Ibid. 25.

[22] James H. Moore, *Vespers at St Mark's: Music of Alessandro Grandi, Giovanni Rovetta and Francesco Cavalli* (Ann Arbor: UMI Research Press, 1981), 75–7, 80, 89, 103, 246, 345.

[23] *Salmi vespertini per tutto l'anno . . . opera quinta* (Venice: Gardano, 1627) (RISM U117). 'Avertimento sopra li Salmi notati Alla Breve Al Provido Cantante. Potrà benissimo compiacersi il Cantore intendente di cantar i presenti Salmi alla Semibreve, cioè, alla battuta ordinaria; ma avverta però, che riusciranno e più armoniosi, e più melodici se seranno cantati alla Breve con duplicate, & triplicate voci con i suoi proporzionati Stromenti sopra ogni parte, come s'usa nell'inclita Città di Venetia.'

[24] Susan Parisi, 'Ducal Patronage of Music in Mantua, 1587–1627: An Archival Study' (Ph.D. dissertation, University of Illinois at Urbana-Champaign, 1989), i. 122. See also Pierre M. Tagmann, 'La cappella dei maestri cantori della basilica palatina di Santa Barbara a Mantova (1565–1630): Nuovo materiale scoperto negli archivi mantovani', *Civiltà mantovana*, 4 (1969–70), 385.

[25] Parisi, 'Ducal Patronage of Music', 517–32; Tagmann, 'La cappella dei maestri', 390.

taken part in all of the music performed. The larger forces would have performed polychoral works and the *ripieno* parts of concerted works, while the
virtuoso soloists would have sung solo and few-voiced motets as well as the solo
and few-voiced sections of compositions in the *concertato* style. Documents from
St Mark's demonstrate that in double-choir works, one choir consisted of
soloists while the other constituted the *ripieno* choir with multiple singers per
part; the same may have been true in Rome.[26] It is not clear whether the solo
choir or the *ripieno* choir took the lead in echo-like *cori spezzati* singing, but in
all the descriptions of processions, the *ripieno* choir preceded the solo choir.

Monteverdi's only *cori spezzati* psalm in the 1610 Vespers is *Nisi Dominus*.
Following the practice at St Mark's, one choir could consist of five soloists and
the other of multiple singers on a part.[27] Since the second choir echoes the first
through much of the psalm, an obvious approach would be to constitute the
first choir as the *ripieno* and have the second sung by soloists. However, following Praetorius's description of this practice (see the paragraph below), the
opposite may also be possible.

Monteverdi's *Ave maris stella*, which is set for double choir, could also be performed by a choir of soloists and a *ripieno* choir. The two choirs sing together in
verses 1 and 7, but separately in verses 2 and 3. If one of the choirs were to be a
solo ensemble, the choice of which one would depend on whether the director
wished verse 2 (sung by the first choir) or verse 3 (sung by the second choir) to
be performed by soloists. Placing the soloists in the second choir would effect a
gradual transition in sonority from double choir in verse 1 to *ripieno* choir in
verse 2, solo choir in verse 3 and soloists in verses 4–6. Praetorius mentions this
piece specifically; in his account the first verse is sung by both choirs (as
Monteverdi indicates) and the second verse by four *concertato* voices in the first
choir. After the ritornello, the third verse follows in the second choir with
single voices.[28]

---

[26] Moore, *Vespers at St Mark's*, 32–3, 98–9, 270–1, 350; Sherr, 'Performance Practice in the Papal
Chapel', 456. O'Regan, on the other hand, finds 'no evidence from Roman music for a contrast between a large choir or "cappella" and a "coro (or cori) favoriti", made up of soloists, as is found in
Venetian music'. See 'Sacred Polychoral Music', 75. The one situation where O'Regan does find such
a distinction in Rome is in the use of two choirs in processions, one with eight to twelve singers and
the other with four. These choirs were separated at the head and tail of a procession. See O'Regan,
'Palestrina, a Musician and Composer in the Market-Place', *Early Music*, 22 (1994), 557–8.

[27] See James H. Moore, 'The *Vespero delli Cinque Laudate* and the Role of *salmi spezzati* at St Mark's',
Journal of the American Musicological Society, 34 (1981), 275–6; David Douglas Bryant, 'The *cori spezzati* of
St Mark's: Myth and Reality', *Early Music History*, 1 (1981), 168–9; and Richard Charteris, 'The
Performance of Giovanni Gabrieli's Vocal Works: Indications in the Early Sources', *Music & Letters*, 71
(1990), 336–7.

[28] Praetorius, *Syntagmatis musici . . . tomus tertius*, 128 (*recte* 108). Praetorius refers to these voices as
Concertat-Stimmen. In the previous section of the chapter, entitled *Parti vel voci concertate: Voces concertatae*
(pp. 126–7, recte 106–7; trans. Lampl, pp. 177–8) Praetorius makes it clear that *Concertat-Stimmen* refers
to solo voices in contrast to the *Ripieni* and *Plenus Chorus*. Praetorius's text is reproduced, followed by
an Italian translation, in Paolo Fabbri, *Monteverdi* (Turin: E.D.T. Edizioni, 1985), 168.

The size of the vocal ensemble for Monteverdi's response, psalms, hymn, the second section of *Audi coelum*, and the opening and closing verses of the Magnificats should be determined according to the musical style of each piece and the ability of the ensemble to project its musical texture clearly. For *Laudate pueri*, Monteverdi calls for eight solo voices in a rubric in the bassus generalis part-book. The other pieces lack rubrics, however. In the hymn, the polyphonic style of the first and last verses requires an ensemble small enough to make the interplay of parts perfectly clear and keep the texture from becoming heavy and lugubrious.

In *Domine ad adjuvandum*, with its choral *falsobordone*, clarity of texture poses no difficulty. Here the problem is to keep a suitable balance in sonority between the solo obbligato instruments and the choir. A choir of six soloists could prove quite satisfactory, especially if early instruments, with their softer sonorities, are employed. Modern instruments, with their brighter, more penetrating timbres, may require a somewhat larger choir.

Similar criteria apply to *Dixit Dominus*. Here the instrumental ritornellos (which are optional) are interspersed between verses of the psalm, so the choir is not in a position to overshadow the instruments as in *Domine ad adjuvandum*. Nevertheless, a significant discrepancy between the volume of the choir and the volume of the instrumental ritornellos should be avoided in order to keep the ritornellos from sounding weak in comparison to the choir. This psalm could be sung with as few as six voices (one voice per part), especially if the ritornellos are played on early instruments, but as many as three voices per part could also prove satisfactory. If the choir is much larger than this, there is a danger that the intricate melismas at the end of each *falsobordone* might become ponderous. If more than one singer per part is employed, the verses *Virgam virtutis* and *Juravit Dominus* might well be sung by soloists, although the style of these passages is not sufficiently virtuosic to make solo voices absolutely necessary. Following the pattern of *Virgam virtutis* and *Juravit Dominus*, the verse *Judicabit in nationibus* might also be sung by soloists. The measured plainchant of the *Gloria Patri*, however, might be performed by multiple voices rather than a tenor soloist, in order to suggest the *alternatim* performance of plainchant by the clerical choir, which was separate from the *cappella* of professional singers specializing in polyphony.

Laudate pueri is the only psalm for which Monteverdi himself has limited the size of the choir with his rubric *à 8 voci sole nel Organo* (for 8 solo voices with the organ). This rubric also implies that other continuo instruments and instrumental doubling of voices should be avoided (see Chapter 19). Despite Monteverdi's instruction, it is surprising how many modern choirs and even early music ensembles perform this psalm with multiple singers per part for the thicker textures (the virtuoso duets obviously require solo voices).

Laetatus sum, whose texture is based on homophony and is unburdened by complex polyphony, could be performed successfully by a fairly sizeable ensemble, although any ensemble greater than five or six voices per part will be larger than early seventeenth-century standards. This psalm could, of course, be sung by six soloists, and the virtuoso passages at *Illuc enim* and *Propter fratres* should be sung by soloists regardless of the size of the choir. In addition, the non-virtuosic duet at *Jerusalem quae aedificatur*, the trio at *Quia illic*, and the double duet at *Rogate ad pacem* might all be sung by soloists, even though the vocal style does not require it. As in *Dixit Dominus*, the solo plainchant following the *Rogate* double duet might well be sung by multiple voices unless the entire psalm is sung with only one voice per part.

Laude Jerusalem is structured with two choirs, each consisting of soprano, alto, and bass parts, which are separated by a single tenor part intoning the plainchant in measured rhythms. In my edition the voices have been placed in score so that the distinction between the two choirs, separated by the tenor in the middle, is clear on the page. Despite the division of the voices into two choirs with identical distribution of registers, *Lauda Jerusalem* is not a *cori spezzati* composition in the same sense as *Nisi Dominus* or *Ave maris stella*. From the middle of *Lauda Jerusalem* to the end, the two trios are closely integrated through imitation at very brief time intervals. Therefore, if there were more than one voice per part, an equal balance between the two choirs would be appropriate (though the tenor could easily have more or fewer singers than the other parts). However, it is also possible to treat this psalm in the same fashion as suggested for *Nisi Dominus*, with one choir serving as a *ripieno* and the other as a choir of soloists. There is no virtuoso passage-work demanding solo voices.

The second section of *Audi coelum* carries the rubric *Qui entrano le altre cinque parti à cantare* (here the other five voices begin singing), and the musical style changes from the virtuosity of the preceding echo duet to imitative polyphony. Since the first section of this motet employs a solo tenor and its echo, Monteverdi's rubric for the second section implies five more solo voices.[29] Whether another seventeenth-century *maestro di cappella* might have used more than one voice to a part in this second section, giving a double interpretation to the text *Omnes hanc ergo sequamur* (Let us all, therefore, follow her), cannot be determined. If more than one voice is assigned to each part in a modern performance, the choir should still be kept small in order to avoid an exaggerated contrast between the solo tenors and the choral section. With several voices per register, the two brief echoes for the tenors in the second section should revert to solo voices.

---

[29] I am grateful to Joshua Rifkin for this observation.

The two Magnificats are principally for virtuoso soloists. However, in both settings, the opening *Magnificat* of the first verse as well as the entire final verse could be sung with more than one voice per part, the larger choir thereby framing the internal solo sections. Throughout both Magnificats the verses for solo voices are accompanied by the plainchant as cantus firmus, and in several verses a solo voice is specified for the cantus firmus. If Monteverdi's rubrics were consistent, we could assume that where a solo voice were not indicated, vocal doubling was intended. But just the reverse is true. The rubrics are inconsistent, sometimes being more detailed and sometimes more general. The rubrics indicating a solo voice for the cantus firmus as well as for other vocal parts make it apparent that solo voices are appropriate throughout both Magnificats; the only reasonable exception, other than the opening *Magnificat* and closing *Sicut erat*, is the *Gloria Patri* of the Magnificat *a 6*, whose polyphonic texture could conceivably be sung with several voices per part.

The size of early seventeenth-century choirs contrasts greatly with many modern choirs, which may comprise 60–120 voices or more. The remarks above are intended to explain the scope of choral practice in Monteverdi's time and are not intended to discourage large modern choirs from attempting performances of Monteverdi's Vespers. Choirs of such size, however, can easily sound muddy and ponderous when performing the intricate, transparent, and delicate textures of the seventeenth century. Conductors should therefore always remain attentive to clarity of texture and lightness of sonority, whatever the size of the ensemble undertaking a performance of music of this period.

16
Vocal Style

෴

IN late sixteenth- and early seventeenth-century Italy, singing was the most highly prized musical art.[1] Castrati and other virtuoso singers were avidly recruited by courts and churches, and the new Roman and Florentine monody was developed principally by singers. Singing style also figures prominently in the writings of theorists and musicians of this period, although their remarks are often of a general nature rather than furnishing details of vocal training and voice-production.[2] Nevertheless, it is possible to obtain from contemporaneous authors a reasonable idea of Italian preferences in singing style.[3]

Lodovico Zacconi, taking his point of departure from Baldassare Castiglione's *Book of the Courtier*, captures the general aesthetic of vocal style valid for the entire sixteenth and seventeenth centuries:

---

[1] General surveys of vocal style and vocal performance practice in the seventeenth century can be found in Sally Allis Sanford, 'Seventeenth and Eighteenth Century Vocal Style and Technique' (DMA dissertation, Stanford University, 1979); Ellen T. Harris, 'Voices', in Howard Mayer Brown and Stanley Sadie, eds., *Performance Practice: Music after 1600* (New York: W. W. Norton & Company, 1989), 97–116; and Nigel Rogers, 'Voices', in Julie Anne Sadie, ed., *Companion to Baroque Music* (New York: Schirmer Books, 1991), 351–65. Renaissance vocal technique is concisely discussed in Andrea von Ramm, 'Singing Early Music', *Early Music*, 4 (1976), 12–15, and in Jean Edwards, 'The Experience of Early Music Singing', *Continuo*, 8 (1984), 2–5, as well as in essays by Ellen Hargis, Alexander Blachly, and Alejandro Planchart in Jeffery T. Kite-Powell, ed., *A Performer's Guide to Renaissance Music* (New York: Schirmer Books, 1994), 3–38, and by Sally Sanford and Julianne Baird in Stewart Carter, ed., *A Performer's Guide to Seventeenth-Century Music* (New York: Schirmer Books, 1997), 3–42.

[2] A survey of the major treatises discussing Renaissance and early Baroque singing is found in Bernhard Ulrich, *Concerning the Principles of Voice Training during the A Cappella Period and until the Beginning of Opera (1474–1640)* (Ph.D. dissertation, Leipzig, 1910), trans. John W. Seale (Minneapolis: Pro Musica Press, 1973). Nigel Fortune provides an excellent compendium of commentaries on singing by late 16th- and early 17th-century composers and theorists in 'Italian 17th-Century Singing', *Music & Letters*, 35 (1954), 206–19. Other useful sources are Mauro Uberti and Oskar Schindler, 'Contributo alla ricerca di una vocalità Monteverdiana: Il "colore"', in Raffaello Monterosso, ed., *Monteverdi ed il suo tempo* (Verona: La Stamperia Valdonega, 1969), 519–37; Uberti, 'Vocal Techniques in Italy in the Second Half of the 16th Century', *Early Music*, 9 (1981), 486–95; Robert Greenlee, 'The Articulation Techniques of Florid Singing in the Renaissance: An Introduction', *Journal of Performance Practice*, 1 (1983), 1–18; id., '*Dispositione di voce*: Passage to Florid Singing', *Early Music*, 15 (1987), 47–55; and Richard Wistreich, '"La voce è grata assai, ma . . .": Monteverdi on Singing', *Early Music*, 22 (1994), 7–19.

[3] Sally Sanford distinguishes two schools of singing in the 17th century: French and Italian. The Italian style was also adopted in Germany and England, and German treatises are a principal source of information about Italian singing. See Sanford, 'Seventeenth and Eighteenth Century Vocal Style and Technique', p. v.

In all human actions, of whatever sort they may be or by whomever they may be executed, grace and aptitude are needed. By grace I do not mean that sort of privilege which is granted to certain subjects under kings and emperors, but rather that grace possessed by men who, in performing an action, show that they do it effortlessly, supplementing agility with beauty and charm. . . .

It is not, therefore, irrelevant that a singer, finding himself from time to time among different people and performing a public action, should show them how it is done with grace; for it is not enough to be correct and moderate in all those actions which might distort one's appearance, but rather one must seek to accompany one's acts and actions with beauty and charm.[4]

The interpenetration of musical styles, performers, and performance practices between court and chapel in the early seventeenth century suggests that similar criteria are appropriate for solo and perhaps small ensemble (few-voiced) singing in both church and chamber. However, in church, solo singing and ensemble singing could be considered separate skills, as is apparent from audition records indicating that prospective choir members had to demonstrate both.[5] The sources discussed in this chapter, therefore, will encompass comments on both ensemble and solo singing, as well as commentaries referring to secular chamber music as well as sacred music. While much of the discussion of solo singing style in the early seventeenth century is associated with secular monody, prefaces such as those to Ottavio Durante's *Arie devote* of 1608,[6] Giovanni Domenico Puliaschi and Giovanni Francesco Anerio's *Musiche varie à una voce* (containing both secular and sacred music) of 1618,[7] and Ignazio Donati's *Secondo libro de' motetti à voce sola* of 1636[8] illustrate that the principles that Caccini expounded for secular music were applicable to sacred monody as well. Likewise, Francesco Rognoni's examples of vocal graces and *passaggi* in his treatise *Selva de varii passaggi* of 1620 are all underlaid with Latin texts.[9] In Monteverdi's Vespers, issues regarding ensemble singing are pertinent to the response, psalms, hymn, and six-voice section of *Audi coelum*, while questions of solo singing style are relevant not only to the four solo and few-voiced motets, but also to the two Magnificats, the solo verses of the hymn, the *Sonata sopra Sancta Maria*, and the soloistic passages of *Dixit Dominus*, *Laudate pueri*, and *Laetatus sum*.

Even though there is no record of Michael Praetorius ever having visited Italy, his knowledge of Italian music was profound, and his descriptions of

---

[4] *Prattica di musica*, i (Venice: Girolamo Polo, 1592; fac. Bologna: Forni Editore, 1967), fo. 55[v]; trans. in Bruce Dickey, 'Ornamentation in Early-Seventeenth-Century Italian Music', in Stewart Carter, ed., *A Performer's Guide to Seventeenth-Century Music* (New York: Schirmer Books, 1997), 246–7.

[5] See Wistreich, '"La voce è grata"', 11.

[6] RISM D3975. Preface and trans. in Donald C. Sanders, 'Vocal Ornaments in Durante's *Arie devote* (1608)', *Performance Practice Review*, 6 (1993), 70–6. I disagree with a few details of Sanders's translation (see Chapter 21).

[7] RISM SD1618[14]. Preface in Gaetano Gaspari, *Catalogo della Biblioteca del Liceo Musicale di Bologna* (Bologna: Romagnoli dall'Acqua, 1893), iii. 156.

[8] RISM D3403. Preface ibid. ii. 417.

[9] See Ch. 21 below for discussion of Rognoni's treatise.

Italian techniques and practices were often corroborated by Italian authors. In some cases Praetorius even quoted directly from Italian writers. Because of the comprehensive nature of his treatises, he often gives us more detail than the Italian authors themselves. Praetorius notes several requisites for a good singing voice in his discussion of vocal instruction for choirboys:

a singer must have a pleasantly vibrating voice [*zittern- und bebende Stimme*] (not, however, as some are trained to do in schools, but with particular moderation) and a smooth round throat for singing diminutions; second, he must be able to maintain a steady long tone, without taking too many breaths; third, he must choose one voice, such as cantus, altus, or tenor, etc., that he can sustain with a full and bright sound without falsetto (which is a half and forced voice).[10]

Pietro Cerone also preferred the chest register,[11] while Giulio Caccini objected to the falsetto for solo singing (see the quotation below). Nevertheless, falsettos were clearly common in church choirs (see Chapter 15).

In 1592 Lodovico Zacconi, in a section of his *Prattica di musica* devoted to systematic instruction in singing, had already spoken in more detail, though still vaguely, about what he calls a *tremolo*:

the *tremolo*, that is the trembling voice, is the true gate to enter the passages and to become proficient in the *gorgia* [ornaments]: because the boat moves with greater ease when it is first pushed . . . The *tremolo* should be short and beautiful, for if it is long and forceful, it tires and bores. And it is of such a nature that those who employ it must always use it, so that it becomes a habit. The continual movement of the voice aids and voluntarily pushes the movement of the *gorgia*, and admirably facilitates the beginnings of the passages. This movement I am speaking of should only be made with proper speed, and lively and vehemently.[12]

Zacconi is unclear about what he means by a *tremolo*, though he sees it as a method for facilitating *passaggi* and *gorgie*. Zacconi's term has been the subject of much debate; some have identified it with pitch vibrato and others with intensity vibrato and/or the ornament known as a *trillo*, comprising the rapid reiteration of a single pitch. Greta Moens-Haenen considers Zacconi's *tremolo* to be a vibrato, apparently because of his reference to the continual movement of the voice.[13] According to Ellen Harris, Zacconi is referring to a throat vibrato.[14] H. Wiley Hitchcock suggests that Zacconi is referring to the *trillo*, which, accord-

---

[10] *Syntagmatis musici . . . tomus tertius* (Wolfenbüttel: Elias Holwein, 1619); fac. ed. Wilibald Gurlitt (Kassel: Bärenreiter, 1958), 231. Trans. adapted from Carol MacClintock, *Readings in the History of Music in Performance* (Bloomington, Ind.: Indiana University Press, 1979), 164 (bracketed German text inserted by author). Praetorius's remarks were repeated nearly verbatim by Johann Andreas Herbst in his *Musica practica sive instructio* of 1642. Sanford interprets the *zittern- und bebende Stimme*, used with moderation, as meaning either 'using a relatively narrow amplitude of vibrato or using vibrato only selectively'. See Sanford, 'Seventeenth and Eighteenth Century Vocal Style and Technique', 8–9.

[11] Ibid. 34. According to Sanford, 17th-century sources do not generally discuss vocal registers (p. 35), but most of the German and Italian sources that do equate the head-voice with falsetto (p. 48).

[12] *Prattica di musica*, fo. 60ʳ. Eng. trans. from MacClintock, *Readings*, 73, where the treatise is incorrectly dated 1596.

[13] *Das Vibrato in der Musik des Barock* (Graz: Akademische Druck- und Verlagsanstalt, 1988), 18.

[14] 'Voices', *Performance Practice: Music after 1600*, 105.

ing to Caccini, is produced by throat articulation.[15] Sally Sanford agrees with Hitchcock's interpretation.[16] David Galliver sees the term as meaning both: 'emphasizing the distinctive timbre of sound initiated in the larynx, as well as the role of this technique for "cantare con la gorga"'.[17] Greenlee interprets Zacconi's vibrato as an ornament rather than a method of voice-production.[18] The confusion over Zacconi's meaning may be due in part to an earlier passage in his treatise: 'The tremolo is not necessary in music; but in making it, it not only demonstrates sincerity and ardor, it also makes the melodies more beautiful.'[19] Here Zacconi seems to be speaking of the *tremolo* as an embellishment with an aesthetic purpose rather than as an aspect of vocal technique. Even if he meant something different from vibrato by his term *tremolo*, the two are 'clearly related concepts' according to Moens-Haenen: 'The biggest difference between the two is that the tremolo, as a larger segment, shows a certain continuity, which is not the case with a normal vibrato. The difference in sound between the two, aside from the measurement of the tremolo, is not always very large or clear.'[20] If Zacconi is referring to vibrato, then it must be an intensity vibrato, for Sanford indicates that 'the mechanism to produce pitch fluctuation vibrato is in direct conflict with the mechanism to produce throat articulation. They cannot be used simultaneously.'[21] This physical incompatibility must therefore mean that Hitchcock is close to the mark in equating Zacconi's *tremolo* with the *trillo*, for it is throat articulation that would lead directly into the *trillo* and other ornaments. Frederick K. Gable also sees this same passage as referring to an intensity vibrato, 'since the intensity vibrato could lead directly into note repetition (*trillo*) and then into a kind of articulation for fast notes. A possible scale of accelerrating [*sic*] intensity fluctuations from slow, measured tremolo, to vibrato, to *trillo*, to *passaggi* could have existed. These would all have been produced in the same way and have differed only in speed and application.'[22] Zacconi's own vague comments about the *tremolo* are not only confusing; many modern writers, in using the term 'vibrato', do not distinguish between an intensity vibrato and a pitch vibrato, which are produced by different means.

---

[15] Giulio Caccini, *Le nuove musiche* (Florence: I Marescotti, 1601 [recte 1602]); fac. ed. Piero Mioli (Florence: Studio per Edizioni Scelte, 1983); ed. Hitchcock (Madison, Wis.: A-R Editions, Inc., 1970), 51 n. 32.

[16] Personal conversation.

[17] See Galliver, '"Cantare con la gorga": The Coloratura Technique of the Renaissance Singer', *Studies in Music*, 7 (1973), 17.

[18] Greenlee, '*Dispositione di voce*', 55 n. 53.

[19] *Prattica di musica*, fo. 55ʳ.

[20] *Das Vibrato*, 279.

[21] Personal correspondence. See also her comments on throat articulation in 'A Comparison of French and Italian Singing in the Seventeenth Century', *Journal of Seventeenth-Century Music*, 1 (1995), ¶ 7.1 [http://rism.harvard.edu/jscm/].

[22] 'Some Observations concerning Baroque and Modern Vibrato', *Performance Practice Review*, 5 (1992), 94.

Among some other seventeenth-century theorists, the word *tremolo*, when applied to the voice, referred to an ornament slower than a vibrato, comprising measured repetition of two or more notes.[23] Some theorists describe the vocal *tremolo* as something similar to an organ tremolo, which was produced mechanically by rhythmic impulses in the otherwise steady flow of air.[24] These rhythmic impulses in the air supply produced undulations in pitch as well.[25] References to *tremolo* for various instruments suggest still other interpretations (see Chapter 21 below). Indeed, not only did the word *tremolo* have various meanings in the sixteenth century and early seventeenth century, but it has also changed in meaning over time, contributing even further to the difficulty twentieth-century musicians have in trying to assess accurately its usage during the Renaissance and early Baroque.

Both the *tremolo* and the *trillo* were generally regarded by theorists as specific types of ornament rather than as elements of basic vocal technique, and in fact, most theorists discuss the various techniques that have been grouped by modern scholars under the term 'vibrato' as various kinds of ornamentation. Discussion here will be limited therefore, to vibrato as a characteristic of vocal sonority, while treatment of vibrato as an embellishment will be postponed to Chapter 21.

The most extensive modern treatment of the problematic subject of vocal vibrato in the Baroque is by Greta Moens-Haenen, whose study is based on contemporaneous theoretical and practical sources.[26] According to her, the term 'vibrato' did not even exist in the Baroque, nor, as we have already seen with regard to Zacconi's *tremolo*, was there a uniform conception of the vibrating or trembling voice: 'By way of summary one can say that the vibrato is not an unequivocal, determinable concept, but rather a thematic complex, whose meaning has changed several times over the course of time.'[27] Moens-Haenen discusses two principal aspects of vibrato: fluctuation and periodicity, which can occur separately or be combined to produce a pitch vibrato, an intensity vibrato, and/or a change in timbre. Moreover, periodicity can not only be regular, but also accelerating or decelerating.[28] 'The oscillation of a vibrato was not steady, but could be fast, slow, or accelerating. A balance between intensity and pitch vibrato was not implicitly intended. There was no standard in pitch fluctuation and a pitch vibrato could merge into a trill.'[29] Frederick Gable notes the aural

---

[23] Moens-Haenen, *Das Vibrato*, 129–31.
[24] Ibid. 129. An extensive discussion of the tremolo in vocal and instrumental music is found on pp. 253–70. For further discussion of the organ tremolo, see Ch. 13 above.
[25] Stewart Carter, 'The String Tremolo in the 17th Century', *Early Music*, 19 (1991), 48.
[26] *Das Vibrato*.
[27] Ibid. 12, 275.
[28] Ibid. 10.
[29] Ibid. 278.

similarity of the two types of vibrato (intensity and pitch) but distinguishes between the physical means of production:

To the listener, the two types of vibrato may sound similar (unless pitch vibrato becomes rather wide), even though they are generated by different physical means. Intensity vibrato is produced by movement of the diaphragm or by the wind passage in the throat or mouth. Pitch vibrato, on the other hand, is created by the vocal cords or folds. To be sure, a vocal intensity vibrato results in some pitch fluctuation as well, but it is normally very slight and less apt to become wide and uncontrollable.[30]

Seventeenth-century writers do not describe methods of producing a vibrato with any precision, but two general types are distinguished in German and French sources: a throat vibrato and a vibrato controlled by the breath with a slight participation of the throat. The throat vibrato is described only in German sources and is condemned by French writers.[31] Italian sources are silent on the subject of how to produce a vibrato.

Praetorius seems to have been referring to a small intensity vibrato, which improved the quality of the vocal sound and aided the agility of the voice, but was imperceptible as a fluctuation in pitch. Sanford considers the word 'bebende' to refer to a 'variation in volume or intensity, not just a fluctuation in pitch'.[32] According to her, it is the intensity vibrato, even in a 'straight' sound, that 'gives the sound pitch focus and yet vitality, glow, shimmer, overtones'.[33] Moreover, 'there is no evidence from the seventeenth and eighteenth century treatises to support the exclusive use of a colorless or "white" sound'.[34] Such a natural vibrato, in contrast to a modern vocal vibrato, might well be viewed as vibrato-free; in fact, the normal vocal sonority was thought of as vibrato-free in the seventeenth century.[35] Christoph Bernhard, in *Von der Singkunst oder Manier* of 1650, favours a steady voice, considering the *tremulo* a defect of elderly singers. Here he seems to be referring to the *tremulo* as an uncontrolled wavering of the voice. Bernhard also declares that the *tremulo* is not used by the foremost singers except in *ardire*, which is a *tremulo* on the last note of a cadence. Bernhard also suggests that the *tremulo* is most appropriate on long notes, except in the case of basses, who can use it sparingly on short notes as

[30] 'Some Observations', 94.
[31] Moens-Haenen, *Das Vibrato*, 24–5. Bénigne de Bacilly, in his *Remarques curieuses sur l'art de bien chanter*, 2nd edn. (Paris, 1689), seems to allow for 'proper throat pulsation when necessary (and the omission of this technique when it is not called for)'. See Sanford, 'Seventeenth and Eighteenth Century Vocal Style and Technique', 1.
[32] Ibid. 71.
[33] Personal correspondence.
[34] Sanford, 'Seventeenth and Eighteenth Century Vocal Style and Technique', 16.
[35] See Moens-Haenen, *Das Vibrato*, 23–4, 271. Andrea von Ramm declares that 'the so-called natural vibrato does not exist. Vibrato is an interaction of breathing muscles and throat muscles and can be controlled.' Her statement is not necessarily inconsistent with the notion of a light, imperceptible vibrato, however. See von Ramm, 'Singing Early Music', 12–13.

well.[36] In making these recommendations, Bernhard must mean a more controlled *tremulo* than what he condemned in elderly singers.

Frederick Neumann argues that Zacconi and Praetorius refer to a natural
pitch vibrato and that vibrato was in continuous use in one degree or another
throughout the seventeenth and eighteenth centuries.[37] The crux of his argument is the acoustical concept of *sonance*, which Neumann describes as 'the
fusion of the vibrato oscillation above a certain threshold of speed (ca. 7 cycles
per second) into an aural sensation of richer tone, while the perception of the
oscillation is minimized and that of the "wrong" pitches *disappears altogether*. On
strings the combined range of the oscillation above and below the focal pitch is
about a quarter tone; whereas for the voice it averages a half-tone'.[38] While an
imperceptible pitch vibrato (in addition to an intensity vibrato) may have been
characteristic of seventeenth-century singing style, Neumann's fluctuation of a
half-step is excessive. There is a wide range of possible pitch fluctuations
between a so-called 'white sound' and a half-step; Neumann's half-step would
destroy the subtleties of intonation and ornamentation that are so critical to
early seventeenth-century style. His own interpretation of his sources, however,
does not negate the perception of vibrato as something to be used in moderation, at appropriate points in the melodic line.[39]

Modern early music performers and scholars hold varying views on the application of vibrato in solo as opposed to ensemble performance. In reference to the
solo voice, Ellen Hargis proclaims: 'Thankfully, after years of "straight-tone"
singing being the ideal, it is now generally accepted that a gentle vibration of the
voice is natural and expressive, and an inherent part of a healthy singing voice.
. . . The only vibrato that is really completely inappropriate to Renaissance
music is one with a wide pitch variation, or any vibrato that cannot be
consciously altered by the singer.'[40] Sanford, however, disagrees and feels that a
pitch vibrato should be used only in appropriate circumstances, and avoided in
others. For example, she prefers to avoid a pitch fluctuation where precision of
tuning is important, as in mean-tone thirds, perfect fifths, cadential seconds, and
final unisons or octaves. Particular words, such as *freddo* (cold) or *gelo* (ice), may
also suggest an avoidance of both pitch and intensity vibrato. On the other hand,
words such as *fiero* (proud, cruel) or *ardire* (boldness) invite the use of both types.[41]

---

[36] See Walter Hilse, 'The Treatises of Christoph Bernhard', *Music Forum*, 3 (1973), 14, 20; and
Sanford, 'Seventeenth and Eighteenth Century Vocal Style and Technique', 71–2. See also Harris,
'Voices', 104.

[37] 'The Vibrato Controversy', *Performance Practice Review*, 4 (1991), 14–27.

[38] Ibid. 15.

[39] Neumann's critique of other scholars' views on vibrato tends to pigeon-hole them into 'either-or'
positions, glossing over their own citations of ambiguous and contradictory statements in the sources.
Gable, in 'Some Observations', 99–100, also criticizes Neumann's vibrato as much too wide.

[40] 'The Solo Voice', *A Performer's Guide to Renaissance Music*, 5.

[41] Personal conversation.

Recently Sanford has published practical advice to performers on breathing and vibrato in Italian singing of the seventeenth century.[42] She notes a fundamental difference between Italian and French singing stemming 'from the fact that Italian is a qualitative language while seventeenth-century French was quantitative.'[43] Italian vocal music is brought to life chiefly through the expressivity given to the vowels, while in French music the emotional expression rests chiefly in the highly nuanced inflection of the consonants.'[44] From the resultant differences in text declamation, Sanford extrapolates to two different approaches to breathing:

the Italian approach to breathing can be described as one that varied air pressure, air speed and air volume according to the dramatic and emotional declamation of the text, and to some extent according to the size of the space in which one was singing. Even though the air pressure fluctuated, the Italian breath system during the seventeenth century generally used less pressure than we associate with modern operatic singing today.[45] A variable air stream gives a dynamic shading, a chiaroscuro, to the vowels that corresponds to the accentuation and declamation of the text. The text itself thus provides a dynamic plan and shape for the vocal line that should be observed by the singer and reflected in the accompaniment.[46]

An example of how such an approach, where text expression takes precedence over musical function, affects a performance

is an implied descrescendo [*sic*] for the resolution of what we might call a V–I cadence . . . based on the dynamic stress pattern of the Italian *verso piano*, in which the final accent lies on the penultimate syllable.[47] It is often so ingrained in musicians to give a dynamic accent to the arrival of the tonic that we instinctively give such cadences a dynamic shape opposite to that implied by the text, even when we understand intellectually that the resolution of the cadence has an unstressed syllable.[48]

According to Sanford, the Italian approach to breathing was also the foundation of vibrato as well as expressive declamation:

The lower air pressure (compared to modern singing) that we find in both French and Italian breath systems meant not only that the laryngeal setup used did not have vibrato as a constant presence, but also that the vocal tract could be quite relaxed. A more relaxed vocal tract in turn allows for the likelihood that singers used speech mode a good deal. Speech mode is a laryngeal setup that employs a relaxed vocal tract and extends speech production into singing, an indispensable technique for singing in the *stile recitativo*, for example.[49]

---

[42] 'A Comparison of French and Italian Singing'. This on-line article contains audio examples comparing French and Italian styles of breathing, declamation, and singing.

[43] Author's n. 2 omitted here.

[44] Ibid. ¶ 1.1.

[45] Author's n. 5 omitted here.

[46] Ibid. ¶ 2.2.

[47] Author's n. 7: 'See Tim Carter's discussion of Italian versification in *The New Grove Dictionary of Opera*, s.v. "Versification" '.

[48] Ibid. ¶ 2.3.

[49] Ibid. ¶ 4.1.

The appropriate tone of seventeenth-century Italian singing is therefore not produced by decreasing the amount of vibrato in a modern operatic style of voice-production:

The principal reason that vibrato is perceptible as a constant in the vocal tone of modern singing is because of the greater air pressure used. When there is a change in air pressure or in the size of the air stream, the larynx will automatically respond differently. Using a lower pressure (compared to modern operatic singing) avoids the need to control vibrato through mechanical suppression in the vocal tract. Such constriction can lead to uncessary tension and fatigue. This can understandably alarm voice teachers when their students start 'straightening' their sounds for singing early music. Using a laryngeal set-up that is unconstricted, with a breath pressure that will allow for vibratro [*sic*] to be used at the singer's discretion, is a common denominator between Italian and French singing in the seventeenth century; what differs is the variable versus steady state air stream. Vibrato would have been consciously added by the singer when desired and was not a natural by-product of the voice production.[50]

There are two different ways of producing vibrato, one produced with breath pressure . . . and the other produced in the throat. . . . Both types of vibrato mechanism were used during the seventeenth century. The different mechanisms produce a difference in sound for these two types of vibrato—somewhat subtle . . . The French would most likely have used a throat-produced vibrato, a mechanism very similar to their trill technique, in order not to disturb their steady air stream. The Italians most likely used a breath-produced vibrato as their norm, since they were using a variable air stream already, with throat vibrato reserved perhaps for more special effects. No seventeenth-century source addresses this issue, although Johann Adam Hiller in the late 18th century regarded throat vibrato as the more difficult of the two types of vibrato. This suggests to me that the 18th-century Italo-Germanic School used throat vibrato less often than breath vibrato.[51]

With reference to ensemble singing, Gable laments that Moens-Haenen speaks little about vibrato in ensemble performance, due to a lack of early sources. Gable considers that 'The use of vibrato in the ensemble singing and playing of "earlier" music is one of the most abused practices today. . . . solo parts can admit more vibrato, but it should be minimized in ensembles, to allow the audience to hear the notes themselves.'[52]

In determining the degree of vibrato, it should be kept in mind that many of the ornaments described in Chapter 21, as well as the gradual rise of a chromatic semitone described by Ottavio Durante and discussed in Chapter 21, are delicate and subtle features of performance style that can easily be obscured and rendered ineffective by an excessive pitch or intensity vibrato. Andrea von Ramm has declared that 'to apply vibrato on the virtuoso repertory of the . . . Italian solo madrigals of the 16th [*sic*] century would spoil the effect of precision and accuracy. Even the long notes between the fast passages should be taken as a con-

---

[50] Ibid. ¶ 3.1. Author's n. 12 omitted here.
[51] Ibid. ¶ 3.2. Author's n. 13: Johann Adam Hiller, *Anweisung zum musikalisch-zierlichen Gesange* (Leipzig: Johann Friedrich Junius, 1780), 75.
[52] 'Some Observations', 96.

trast to the fireworks of fast notes. That means they should be sung without vibrato. The beats of the vibrato should not interfere with the speed of the virtuoso scales.'[53] In the late seventeenth century, the Englishman Roger North drew in his autobiography a diagram for students of three types of notes: 'plaine', 'waived', and 'trillo', illustrating fluctuations in volume for 'plaine' and 'waived' and in pitch for 'waived' and 'trillo'.[54] North's comments on his diagram are as follows:

Then next I would have them [students] learne to fill, and soften a sound, as shades in needlework, *insensatim*, so as to be like also a gust of wind, which begins with a soft air, and fills by degrees to a strength as makes all bend, and then softens away againe into a temper, and so vanish. And after this to superinduce a gentle and slow wavering, not into a trill, upon the swelling the note; such as trumpetts use, as if the instrument were a litle shaken with the wind of its owne sound, but not so as to vary the tone, which must be religiously held to its place, like a pillar on its base, without the least loss of the accord. . . . The latter [item in the diagram] is the trill, which, as you see, breaking the tone and mixing with another, is dangerous for a scollar to medle with, till he hath the mastery of the sound, else it will make him apt to loose the principall tone; and that spoiles all.[55]

As Gable notes, 'These sorts of expressive distinctions cannot be made if the tone continuously contains a wide pitch vibrato . . .'[56] Moreover, Sanford has noted the incompatibility between pitch-fluctuation vibrato and the throat articulation required for the singing of *passaggi*.[57]

The only major distinction made by sixteenth-century and early seventeenth-century writers between chamber and church singing concerned volume. Zarlino distinguished between the fuller sound required for singing in church and the softer voice suited to private chambers.[58] Lodovico Zacconi claimed that 'he who says that one makes a voice by crying out loud is deceived . . . because many learn to sing softly in *camere*, where (loud singing is abhorred) and are not constrained by necessity to sing in churches and in *cappelle* where paid singers sing.'[59] Similarly, Cesare Crivellati indicated that 'in churches you sing differently from music-rooms: in churches with a loud voice, in music-rooms with a subdued voice.'[60] Yet in noting the distinction between chamber and church singing, Zacconi also warned about excessive force in the latter:

[53] 'Singing Early Music', 14.
[54] The page is reproduced in John Wilson, ed., *Roger North on Music* (London: Novello and Company Ltd, 1959), pl. II (facing p. 20). The diagram alone is reprinted in Gable, 'Some Observations', 92.
[55] Wilson, ed., *Roger North on Music*, 18.
[56] 'Some Observations', 92.
[57] See above.
[58] Gioseffo Zarlino, *Le istitutioni harmoniche* (Venice, 1558; fac. New York: Broude Brothers, 1965), 204; Eng. trans. in Guy A. Marco and Claude V. Palisca, *The Art of Counterpoint, Part Three of 'Le istitutioni harmoniche', 1558* (New Haven: Yale University Press, 1968), 111.
[59] *Prattica di musica*, fo. 52ᵛ, trans. from Uberti, 'Vocal Techniques', 493. Zacconi repeatedly warns against *il gridar* (shouting) and *il gridar forte* (shouting loudly).
[60] *Discorsi musicali, nelli quali si contengono non solo cose pertinenti alla teorica, ma eziandio alla pratica* (Viterbo: Agostino Discep., 1624); Eng. trans. from Rogers, 'Voices', 353.

'When singing in church . . . singers must intone the ornaments with suitable force and rather vehemently, but not so forced as to become coarse and that the effort is noticed.'[61] Similarly, the virtuoso singer Puliaschi advised in 1618 that in both soft and loud singing the 'voice should not lose its sweetness'.[62] Francesco Severi likewise advised in 1615 that the slow intonations of his *Psalmi passaggiati* be sung 'with a firm and sweet voice'.[63] The breath pressure and volume used today for singing in large spaces would certainly have been considered excessive in the seventeenth century, especially since the projection of a modern vibrato was not part of the vocal style. What constitutes a full and loud sound depends, of course, not only on vocal technique and the character of the music being sung (sustained or florid), but also on the size and acoustics of the performance space. There is also a distinction to be made between 'full and loud' on the one hand and forced (Zacconi's *il gridar*) on the other. Aside from distinguishing between loud singing in church and softer singing in the chamber, sixteenth-century and early seventeenth-century writers generally do not mention other desirable vocal characteristics for singing in one location versus the other.

Louder and softer singing was also related to the position of a pitch in the singer's range. Dynamics, in general, depended on register, with higher pitches sung lightly and lower ones more loudly. In the mid-sixteenth century Hermann Finck had declared that 'the higher a voice rises the quieter and lovelier should the note be sung; the more it descends, the richer the sound'. Finck had also warned, 'It should be seen to that the discantus and the alto not rise higher than they should, or that no singer strains his voice.'[64] In the early eighteenth century Tosi was still saying that 'the higher the Notes, the more it is necessary to touch them with Softness'.[65] The practice of singing crescendo–diminuendo on sustained notes (*messa di voce*) is discussed in Chapter 21 below. According to Ellen Harris, 'The modern practice of sometimes maintaining individual phrases at a single dynamic level, or "terraced dynamics", . . . has no sanction in the theoretical sources.'[66]

One of the most comprehensive characterizations of solo vocal style in the late sixteenth and early seventeenth centuries is by Vincenzo Giustiniani, who described the singing style of the ladies at the courts of Ferrara and Mantua in his *Discorso sopra la musica* of 1628:

---

[61] *Prattica di musica*, fo. 78ᵛ, trans. from Uberti, 'Vocal Techniques', 494. Uberti describes the physiological similarities and differences between chamber and church singing on pp. 494–5.

[62] See note 7 above. Also quoted in Fortune, 'Italian Seventeenth-Century Singing', 212. This preface has a lengthy and wonderfully detailed description of the style of *recitar cantando*.

[63] Ed. Murray C. Bradshaw as *Francesco Severi: Salmi Passaggiati (1615)* Madison, Wis.: A-R Editions, Inc., 1981), p. xxiii.

[64] *Practica musica* (Wittenberg: Georg Rhaw, 1556; fac. Hildesheim: Georg Olms Verlag, 1971), bk. v; trans. in MacClintock, *Readings*, 62–3.

[65] Quoted by Harris in 'Voices', 103.

[66] Ibid. 107.

The ladies of Mantua and Ferrara were highly competent, and vied with each other not only in regard to the timbre and training of their voices but also in the design of exquisite passages [*passaggi*] delivered at opportune points, but not in excess (Giovanni Luca of Rome, who served also in Ferrara, usually erred in this respect). Furthermore, they moderated or increased their voices, loud or soft, heavy or light, according to the demands of the piece they were singing; now slow, breaking off with sometimes a gentle sigh, now singing long passages legato [and] detached, now groups [*groppi*], now leaps, now with long trills, now with short, and again with sweet running passages sung softly, to which sometimes one heard an echo answer unexpectedly. They accompanied the music and the sentiment with appropriate facial expressions, glances and gestures, with no awkward movements of the mouth or hands or body which might not express the feeling of the song. They made the words clear in such a way that one could hear even the last syllable of every word, which was never interrupted or suppressed by passages and other embellishments.[67]

Much of what Giustiniani describes lies within the framework of the sixteenth-century technique of *passaggi*. But even before the turn of the century the emphasis on ornamentation had begun to shift away from an almost exclusive reliance on *passaggi* towards smaller, briefer ornaments, often called 'graces' (*grazie*), which were intended to vary the expression in the smaller time-frame of just a few notes or a single beat (see Chapter 21 below for a discussion of specific graces). *Passaggi* were still essential to the vocal style, but they were often shorter in length and more varied in rhythm than in the late sixteenth century. This shift in emphasis from *passaggi* to *grazie* is especially associated with the Florentine monodists, although it should be remembered that Giulio Caccini trained in Rome and performed his monodies there before bringing them to Florence.

Caccini, Peri, and others writing in the Florentine solo style were quite conscious of the unique aspects of their performing technique, resulting in numerous prefaces explaining vocal technique and performance style. But listeners were also aware that significant changes had taken place in the manner of singing. Many years afterwards, Pietro della Valle, a Roman, commented on these differences in recalling a performance in Rome of Emilio de' Cavalieri's *Rappresentatione di Anima et di Corpo*:

However, all of these [singers of the old school], beyond *trilli*, *passaggi* and a good putting forth of the voice, had in singing no other art, such as the piano and forte, gradually increasing the voice, diminishing it with grace, expressing the *affetti*, supporting with judgement the words and their sense, cheering the voice or saddening it, making it merciful or bold when necessary, and other similar gallantries which nowadays are done by singers excellently well. At that time no one spoke about it, nor at least in Rome was news of it ever heard, until Sig. Emilio de' Cavalieri in his last years brought it to us from the good school of Florence, giving a good example of it, before

---

[67] Trans. Carol MacClintock as *Vincenzo Giustiniani: Discorso sopra la musica* (American Institute of Musicology, 1962), 69. MacClintock places 'or' where I have put 'and' in brackets. The bracketed identifications of 'passages' as *passaggi* and of 'groups' as *groppi* are also mine. Greenlee translates this phrase: 'now running long passages well ensuing and detached'. See Greenlee, '*Dispositione di voce*', 54 n. 25.

anyone else in a small representation at the Oratorio della Chiesa Nuova, at which I, quite young, was present.[68]

It has been assumed by modern singers of early seventeenth-century repertoire that this style of expressive monody resulted in changes in vocal technique in the late sixteenth and early seventeenth centuries.[69] Sanford, for example, has suggested that 'how Jacopo Peri sang differed in some important respects from how the three ladies of Ferrara sang. Peri likely used the new approach to breathing (a flexible breath-stream approach) with a laryngeal set-up based more purely on a speech mode than the three ladies of Ferrara used. This affects the degree of relaxation in the vocal tract and influences the resultant sound quality.'[70]

While Giustiniani's remarks on the ladies of Ferrara and Mantua describe the virtuoso ornamental tradition rooted in sixteenth-century *passaggi*, he also mentions aspects of performance style and types of ornamentation that figure significantly in Caccini's preface to *Le nuove musiche* of 1602. Caccini instructs that the method of performing the rapid repeated note called the *trillo* is 'to begin with the first quarter-note, then re-strike each note with the throat on the vowel *à*'.[71] Caccini, like Zacconi, saw mastery of the *tremolo* and the *trillo* as the first stage in learning to sing *passaggi* and other ornaments. According to Giovanni Battista Bovicelli, the notes of the *passaggi* were to be clearly articulated: 'The demisemiquavers thus . . . must be enunciated well.'[72] However, they were also sung so rapidly that contrapuntal dissonances passed without offence.[73] Regarding *passaggi*, Caccini's Florentine contemporary Antonio Brunelli declared that 'quavers [*crome*] should be sung dotted, and beaten with the throat, not with the mouth as many do. . . . semiquavers [*semicrome*], because of their speed, are not sung dotted, but one should beat them with the throat distinctly one upon the other in order that the passage becomes convin-

---

[68] Quoted in Giovanni Battista Doni, *De' trattati di musica . . . tomo secondo* (Florence, 1763; fac. edn. Bologna: Arnaldo Forni Editore, 1974), 255–6; ed. in Angelo Solerti, *Le origini del melodramma* (Turin, 1903; repr. edns. Hildesheim: Georg Olms, 1969, and Bologna: Arnaldo Forni Editore, 1983), 162–3. Eng. trans. adapted from Bruce Dickey, 'Ornamentation in Early-Seventeenth-Century Italian Music', 246.

[69] According to John Potter, 'vocal shifts have occurred when a previous technique or style has become unable to express the text in a way appropriate to the prevailing aesthetic. There are obvious points at which we can see this kind of change happening: around 1600 with the development of the new monodic style and the conscious reduction of polyphonic artifice . . .' See 'Reconstructing Lost Voices', in Tess Knighton and David Fallows, eds., *Companion to Medieval and Renaissance Music* (New York: Schirmer Books, 1992), 312.

[70] Personal correspondence.

[71] *Le nuove musiche*, ed. Hitchcock, 51.

[72] *Regole, passaggi di musica* (Venice: Giacomo Vincenti, 1594); fac. ed. Nanie Bridgman (Documenta musicologica, ser. 1:2; Kassel: Bärenreiter, 1957), 14: 'Le biscrome poi . . . devono esser spiccate bene . . .' Cited in Rogers, 'Voices', 355. See also the similar remarks by Zacconi and Praetorius cited in Greenlee, '*Dispositione di voce*', 48–9, and the instructions by Severi quoted above in the text and in note 76 below.

[73] Noted by Sylvestro Ganassi and Nicola Vicentino. See Greenlee, '*Dispositione di voce*', 48.

cing. For the whole basis of the placing of the voice [*disposizione*] consists in this beating in the throat . . .'[74]

Francesco Rognoni of Milan, in a somewhat convoluted way, confirmed the same technique and contrasted it with chest articulation, which he ridiculed:

everyone who wants to learn the said *trillo* or *groppo* should take and rebeat each note with the throat on the vowel *a* . . . There are certain singers, who at times have a certain way of singing ornaments (in Moorish style), striking the *passaggio* in a certain way, displeasing to all, singing *a-a-a*, which seems as if they are laughing. Those [singers] could resemble those Ethiopians or Moors who . . . during their ceremonies sing in this manner, so that it seems as if they are laughing, showing how many teeth they have in their mouths. From this learn that the ornament should come from the chest, and not the throat.[75]

Rognoni's final sentence seems to be a contradiction of his instruction to articulate the *trillo* and *groppo* with the throat. Richard Wistreich has attempted to resolve this contradiction by interpreting Rognoni's last sentence as referring not to the articulation of the ornament, but rather to the source of breath support: 'if we accept that *gorgie* are ornaments articulated in the throat, Rognoni would appear to be saying that the sound itself must "come from the chest" or, in other words, be generated and supported from there. Unsupported throat articulation does indeed sound like goatish "a a a" bleating.'[76] Sanford, on the other hand, has suggested that Rognoni may be referring to the placement or resonance of the voice, rather than the source of breath support.[77] Sanford also finds that 'throat articulation was the principal technique used in passages and ornaments requiring vocal agility.'[78] However, 'the use of throat

---

[74] *Varii esercitii . . . per i quali si potrà con facilità aquistare la dispositione per il cantare con passaggi* (Florence: Zanobi Pignoni e Comp., 1614), *Avvertimenti* (preface), ed. Richard Erig as *Antonio Brunelli, Varii esercitii, 1614* (Zurich: Musikverlag zum Pelikan, 1977). Preface repr. in Claudio Sartori, *Bibliografia della musica strumentale italiana* (Florence: Olschki, 1952), 202–3. Eng. trans. adapted from Rogers, 'Voices', 355. See also Fortune, 'Italian Seventeenth-Century Singing', 216. Greenlee cites numerous other theorists on the subject of beating with the throat. See Greenlee, '*Dispositione di voce*', 50–2.

[75] *Selva de varii passaggi secondo l'uso moderno per cantare, & suonare con ogni sorte de stromenti* (Milan: Filippo Lomazzo, 1620), fac. ed. Guglielmo Barblan (Bologna: Arnaldo Forni, 1978), *Avvertimenti* (my trans.). For a discussion of Rognoni's treatise, including a translation of his preface, see Stewart Carter, 'Francesco Rognoni's *Selva de varii passaggi* (1602): Fresh Details concerning Early-Baroque Vocal Ornamentation', *Performance Practice Review*, 2 (1989), 5–33.

[76] '"La voce è grata"', 15. According to Zacconi, 'Two things are necessary to whoever wishes to practise this profession, that being chest and throat; chest, so that a great variety and number of tones can be carried through to the end; throat, in order to sing with facility' (*Prattica di musica*, i, fo. 58ᵛ; trans. from Greenlee, '*Dispositione di voce*', 52). Uberti's interpretation of this passage is the same as Wistreich's interpretation of Rognoni—'the term *petto* ("chest") seems clearly to refer to the singer's respiratory capacity'. See Uberti, 'Vocal Techniques', 494. Francesco Severi, in his *Psalmi passaggiati*, also refers to enunciation of rapid *passaggi* from the chest: 'Quinto: Che le semicrome si cantino con vivacità et presto il più che sara possibile purche siano spiccate dal petto e non dalla gola come alcunni fanno, che in cambio di dar gusto all'orecchio, generano confusione, e disgusto.' (Fifth: that the semiquavers be sung as livelily and quickly as possible, provided that they be enunciated from the chest and not from the throat as some do, which, instead of giving pleasure to the ear, engenders confusion and disgust'; my trans.). See *Francesco Severi: Psalmi passaggiati*, ed. Bradshaw, pl. III.

[77] Personal conversation.

[78] 'Seventeenth and Eighteenth Century Vocal Style and Technique', 62.

articulation does not mean that the muscles of the throat should be constricted. On the contrary, in order for the pulsations in the glottal region to occur rapidly and naturally, the throat and tongue must be relaxed.'[79]

In the early seventeenth century the solo voice was supposed to have the same effect as an orator, that is, to impart the feeling of the text to the listener. Praetorius's comments concisely summarize this aesthetic:

Just as an Orator's concern is not only to adorn his oration with attractive, beautiful, and lively words and splendid figures, as well as to pronounce correctly and to move the emotions by his speech, now raising his voice, now allowing it to fall, now louder, now soft, now with full voice; so must a musician not only sing, but sing with art and grace, thereby moving the heart and affections of the auditors and permitting the song to accomplish its purpose.[80]

Italians, such as Caccini, Peri, Cavalieri, and Marco da Gagliano, were the sources of Praetorius's remarks. Emphasis on the expression of the text and the grace with which it is sung are mainstays of their writings. According to Gagliano:

where the sense does not demand it, leave aside every ornament, so as not to act like that painter who knew how to paint cypress trees and therefore painted them everywhere. Instead, try to pronounce every syllable distinctly so the words are understood, and let this be the principal aim of every singer whenever he sings. . . . I will say that no one can fully appreciate the sweetness and the power of his airs who has not heard them sung by Peri himself, because he gave them such a grace and style that he so impressed in others the emotion of the words that one was forced to weep or rejoice as the singer wishes.[81]

In the same vein, Caccini declares that 'to compose and sing well in this style, understanding of the [poet's] conception and sensitivity to the text (plus imitating them through affective music and expressing them through affective singing) are much more useful than counterpoint'.[82]

The affect of the text also had a significant impact on volume and tempo. Christoph Bernhard describes performance of the recitative style thus: 'In the recitative style, one should take care that the voice is raised in moments of anger, and on the contrary dropped in moments of grief. Pain makes it pause; impatience hastens it. Happiness enlivens it. Desire emboldens it. Love renders it alert. Bashfulness holds it back. Hope strengthens it. Despair diminishes it. Fear keeps it down. . . .'[83]

---

[79] Ibid. 61. See also p. 56.

[80] *Syntagmatis musici . . . tomus tertius*, 229; trans. in MacClintock, *Readings*, 163.

[81] *La Dafne* (Florence: Christofano Marescotti, 1608), preface, quoted in Solerti, *Le origini del melodramma*, 78–89; trans. in MacClintock, *Readings*, 188–9.

[82] *Le nuove musiche*, ed. Hitchcock, 51.

[83] *Von der Singkunst oder Manier* (1650), ed. Joseph Maria Müller-Blattau in *Der Kompositionslehre Heinrich Schützens in der Fassung seines Schülers Christoph Bernhard*, 2nd edn. (Kassel: Bärenreiter, 1963), 39; Eng. trans. quoted from Hilse, 'The Treatises of Christoph Bernhard', 24. The character of the text had also been crucial in determining tempo and the character of expression in the contrapuntal style of the 16th century. Lanfranco, Ganassi, Vicentino, and Zarlino all speak about tempo and vocal style in

According to Ottavio Durante, the various forms of expressing the words should not lead to distorting facial gestures or bodily movements: 'Be advised not to make gestures with the body or with the face while you sing, and if nevertheless you wish to make a few, it is necessary to do it with grace and corresponding to the sense of the words, but don't do it excessively.'[84]

The rhetorical, expressive approach to singing could also be achieved through very soft dynamics, even in liturgical music. The English traveller Thomas Coryat, in describing a service at the Scuola San Rocco in Venice in 1608, remarks, 'and sometimes two singular fellowes played together upon Theorboes, to which they sung also, who yeelded admirable sweet musicke, but so still that they could scarce be heard but by those that were very neare them'.[85] This passage, together with evidence cited above distinguishing between ensemble and solo singing in church, suggests that the louder singing normally associated with performances in church (the grand hall of the Scuola San Rocco is as large as many churches) may not necessarily have applied to solo or few-voiced compositions. Such music may have been performed in a more intimate style than compositions for a full choir of four or more parts.

Another aspect of the style of solo singing in the early seventeenth century was an air of freedom in performance, called *nobile sprezzatura* by Caccini. Caccini describes this quality differently in three different sources, but it seems to imply a certain charming carelessness in adhering to the rules of composition and notation. This *nobile sprezzatura* permits transgression of the rules of counterpoint, especially allowing dissonances over a sustained bass. It also implies a relaxed approach to the performance of notated rhythms, whereby the singer is not only permitted flexibility, but may even cut note values in half, the better to interpret the text (see Chapter 20).[86] The object of such freedom or 'nonchalance' is to approximate in music the expressive character of speaking, a concept also espoused by Jacopo Peri.[87]

Caccini's summary of the solo style of singing, while referring to secular

relation to the mood of the text. For pertinent passages from each of these theorists, see Federico Mompellio, '"Un certo ordine di procedere che non si può scrivere"', *Scritti in onore di Luigi Ronga* (Milan: Ricciardi, 1973), 367–88.

[84] *Arie devote*, preface (my trans.). For a slightly different trans., see Sanders, 'Vocal Ornaments', 75.

[85] For the full passage from which this quotation is drawn, see Ch. 4.

[86] Caccini, *Le nuove musiche*, preface; and *Nuove musiche e nuova maniera di scriverle* (Florence: Zanobi Pignoni e Compagni, 1614), fac. ed. Piero Mioli (Florence: Studio per Edizioni Scelte, 1983), preface. Eng. trans. of *Le nuove musiche* preface in Strunk, *Source Readings in Music History*, 377–92; and *Le nuove musiche*, ed. Hitchcock, 43–56. Eng. trans. of 1614 preface in Caccini, *Le nuove musiche e nuova maniera di scriverle*, ed. H. Wiley Hitchcock (Madison, Wis.: A-R Editions, Inc., 1978), pp. xxxi–xxxiii. Rhythmic flexibility in Baroque music is stressed by Harris in 'Voices', 108–10, where several sources from throughout the Baroque era are quoted to emphasize the necessity of rhythmic freedom and variations in tempo to express more effectively the meaning of the words.

[87] *Le musiche . . . sopra l'Euridice . . .* (Florence: Marescotti, 1600), preface. Eng. trans. in Strunk, *Source Readings in Music History*, 373–6; and Jacopo Peri, *Euridice*, ed. Howard Mayer Brown (Madison, Wis.: A-R Editions, Inc., 1981), pp. xliii–xlv.

music, is nevertheless useful in understanding the way in which he might well have approached and taught solo and few-voiced sacred music:

Just as there are many effects to be employed for the greatest refinement of this art, so also is a good voice very essential, especially as regards breath control, to make use of them as needed. In this connection it will be useful to note that when he who professes this art is to sing alone to the arch-lute or some other stringed instrument without being constrained to accommodate himself to others, let him choose a key in which he can sing with a full, natural voice, avoiding falsetto, in which—or at least in a register where one must strain to sing—one must waste breath trying not to expose the tones too much (since for the most part they usually offend the ear). Rather must one use [the breath] to give more spirit to vocal crescendos-and-decrescendos, *esclamazioni*, and all the other effects we have demonstrated: let one make sure not to fall short in a pinch. From the falsetto voice no nobility of good singing can arise; that comes from a natural voice, comfortable through the whole range, able to be controlled at will, [and] with the breath used only to demonstrate mastery of all the best affects necessary for this most noble manner of singing.[88]

Caccini is speaking of individual pieces, detached from any particular context; nevertheless, this passage suggests that keys might be chosen for Monteverdi's motets to suit the singers. The range of keys in which early seventeenth-century music was notated was quite restricted (see Chapters 2, 17, and 22), but since pitch standards were variable and could be adjusted to suit the individual singer, it may be unnecessary to maintain in modern pitch the keys in which Monteverdi's four motets were written. The matter is complicated, however, by such issues as the concluding unison of *Laudate pueri*, which is the same note, an octave lower, as that on which *Pulchra es* begins. On the other hand, there is no special tonal relationship between *Dixit Dominus* and its following motet, *Nigra sum*. Obviously the circumstances of any particular performance and the performer's judgement as to the importance of pitch relations will determine whether Monteverdi's notated keys are retained or transposed. In the other compositions of the 1610 Vespers, the choice of pitch may be affected by obbligato instruments, the selection of doubling instruments, and the clefs in which compositions are notated. The issues of pitch and transposition are treated in detail in Chapter 17.

Not all songs or sections of songs composed in the early seventeenth century are in the recitative style. Caccini also discussed 'airy pieces or dance songs', principally in triple metre, which required a sprightly style of singing, 'with no affect smacking of lethargy',[89] and Thomas Ravenscroft explicitly associated triple metre in sacred music with lively secular dances.[90] While Ravenscroft was

---

[88] *Giulio Caccini: Le Nuove Musiche*, ed. Hitchcock, 55–6. For other writings on breath control, see Sanford, 'Seventeenth and Eighteenth Century Vocal Style and Technique', 79–92. Sanford gives a table of criteria for proper breath control on pp. 91–2.

[89] *Le nuove musiche*, ed. Hitchcock, 50.

[90] *A Briefe Discourse of the True (but Neglected) Use of Charact'ring the Degrees . . .* (London: Edward Allde, 1614; fac. edn. New York: Broude Brothers Ltd., 1976), 12. See the further discussion of Ravenscroft in Ch. 20 below.

far removed from northern Italy, triple-metre passages in the sacred music of Giovanni Gabrieli, Monteverdi, and numerous other northern Italian composers often resemble dance music in their predominantly homophonic textures and their use of short sequential melodic patterns. These observations are especially pertinent to the triple-metre sections in Monteverdi's *Pulchra es* and *Audi coelum* as well as to those in the response, the psalms *Dixit Dominus* and *Laudate pueri*, the *Sonata sopra Sancta Maria*, and the two Magnificats. Only the ritornello of *Ave maris stella* might require a slightly more restrained style.

Although much of what has been discussed here refers specifically to monody and solo singing in few-voiced compositions, the more generalized aspects of these comments are also relevant to the other compositions in Monteverdi's 1610 print. Especially applicable are the descriptions of 'good singing style', involving breath control, a sustained and steady tone, a full but unforced sound, and clear enunciation of the text.

Ellen Hargis has recently summarized the vocal characteristics needed for good Renaissance singing, characteristics which remained applicable in the early seventeenth century, even if there were some changes in technique occasioned by monody and the recitative style: 'Renaissance music calls for purity of tone, a focused, clear sound without excessive vibrato, the ability to sing lightly and with agility, and the command of a wide range of dynamics: loud singing, particularly for church music, and medium to soft singing, to most accompanying instruments. . . . Essential elements include good breath support, well-formed resonant vowels, and focused sound.'[91] These characteristics and the others described above should produce a vocal quality not only consistent with what is known of early seventeenth-century vocal style, but also capable of performing successfully the many different types of ornamentation discussed in Chapter 21 below.

My discussion has focused on what singers should do in performing seventeenth-century music. But Christoph Bernhard also devoted several lines at the end of *Von der Singkunst oder Manier* (1650) to a humorous (from a modern point of view) description of what singers should not do:

a singer should not sing through his nose. He must not stammer, lest he be incomprehensible. He must not push with his tongue or lisp, else one will hardly understand half of what he says. He also should not close his teeth together, nor open his mouth too wide, nor stretch his tongue out over his lips, nor thrust his lips upward, nor distort his mouth, nor disfigure his cheeks and nose like the long-tailed monkey, nor crumple his eyebrows together, nor wrinkle his forehead, nor roll his head or the eyes therein round and round, nor wink with the same, nor tremble with his lips, etc.[92]

---

[91] 'The Solo Voice', 4.
[92] Ed. Müller-Blattau in *Der Kompositionslehre Heinrich Schutzens*, 39; Eng. trans. quoted from 'The Treatises of Christoph Bernhard', 25.

17
Pitch and Transposition

⟨ᎨᎣ⟩

FOR sixteenth- and seventeenth-century music the question of pitch standards is complex, and reliable information is limited.[1] The only certainty is that there was no uniform pitch standard from country to country, from city to city, and not necessarily even between two organs in the same church.[2] To quote Arthur Mendel:

It is clear that absolute pitch could have had relatively little importance to the musician before the late 18th century. . . . To musicians before 1750, the notes on the staff, and the names by which they were referred to, represented degrees in a gamut that had no permanent anchor at a standard pitch level, but was freely movable up and down according to the nature of the voices or instruments involved on any given occasion.[3]

As late as 1713 Johann Mattheson declared, 'Now whether or why this or that tone is called *a* or *b*, chamber, choir, or opera pitch—this is a matter of no basic importance.'[4] The gamut, therefore, was a series of intervals, not fixed pitches, and where the first note of the gamut was located depended on the characteristics and capabilities of the singers or instruments engaged in any particular performance.

Nevertheless, problems of range and tuning gave impetus to the desire for a uniform pitch standard, especially when organs and other instruments were

---

[1] The subject of pitch and transposition of psalm tones and plainchant antiphons is treated in Ch. 2. Tuning and temperament are discussed in Ch. 22.

[2] By far the most thoroughgoing study of pitch is the recent dissertation by Bruce Haynes, 'Pitch Standards in the Baroque and Classical Periods', 2 vols. (Ph.D. dissertation, University of Montreal, 1995). See also id., 'Pitch in Northern Italy in the Sixteenth and Seventeenth Centuries', *Recercare*, 6 (1994), 41–60. Prior to Haynes's dissertation, the two most basic articles on this subject were by Arthur Mendel: 'Pitch in the 16th and Early 17th Centuries', *Musical Quarterly*, 34 (1948), 28–45, 199–221, 336–57, 575–93; and 'Pitch in Western Music since 1500, a Re-Examination', *Acta musicologica*, 50 (1978), 1–93. For a concise summary of recent views on Renaissance and early Baroque pitch, but prior to Haynes's dissertation, see Herbert Myers, 'Pitch and Transposition', in Jeffery T. Kite-Powell (ed.), *A Performer's Guide to Renaissance Music* (New York: Schirmer Books, 1994), 248–56.

[3] 'Pitch in the 16th and Early 17th Centuries', 28–9. Haynes has demonstrated that the freedom of pitch described by Mendel was exaggerated by Mendel's failure to study original instruments and understand the practical exigencies of different instruments playing together. See Haynes, 'Pitch Standards', i. 18–19.

[4] *Das neu-eröffnete Orchestre* (Hamburg, 1713); Eng. trans. from Mendel, 'Pitch in the 16th and Early 17th Centuries', 29.

combined with voices, as in much sacred music of the seventeenth century. The combination of various instruments and voices forced a circumscribed range of fairly specific pitch standards on musicians. Woodwind and brass instruments in particular had relatively stable and invariable pitch built into them by their makers, and since woodwind manufacture, especially of cornettos, was centred in Venice, from where instruments were shipped all over Europe, Venetian cornettos tended to set pitch standards for mixed ensembles everywhere.[5] Similarly, the most prized brass instruments came from Nuremberg, and the pitch standard of these instruments served as a reference point as well. Moreover, since Venetian cornettos often played in consort with Nuremberg sackbuts, the same tuning was required for both.[6] In order to accommodate varying pitch standards, woodwind and brass instruments came in various sizes and also could be modified in size by exchangeable joints or crooks to vary the tuning within finer gradations.[7]

Once an organ was built and tuned, its pitch standard was also relatively fixed, although variation in pitch could be caused by seasonal temperature differentials. This was particularly problematic with regard to permanently installed organs, whose pitch set the standard for performances in which they were used as continuo instruments. Cary Karp reports that a temperature differential of 20 °C in an unheated church could alter the pitch of an organ in the middle register by some 20 Hz (the example given is a fluctuation between $a' = 450$ Hz at the lower temperature and $a' = 470$ Hz at the higher).[8] Moreover, repeated tuning of organs over time gradually raised their pitch, eventually requiring 'shifting the pipes up one position and making a new largest pipe for each voice'.[9] As organs came to be used more frequently with other instruments, especially woodwinds, the latter instruments tended to set the pitch standard for organs.[10] The tuning of organs from the late sixteenth century onward was frequently referred to as *cornet-ton*.[11]

String instruments, too, were built with an optimum sounding pitch

---

[5] Haynes, 'Pitch Standards', i. 11, ii. 414–28. Haynes also charts the frequencies of surviving 16th- and 17th-century Italian curved cornettos in 'Pitch in Northern Italy', 53, and inventories surviving cornettos and their pitches in 'Pitch Standards', ii. 421–8. Pitch-pipes were another means of achieving a consistent tuning. See ibid. ii. 540–7.

[6] Haynes, 'Pitch Standards', i. 36–7, 154–5, 158–9.

[7] The principal groups of tuning for cornettos were a semitone apart, at $a' = c.470$ Hz, called *mezzo punto*, and $a' = c.443$ Hz, called *tutto punto*. The semitone relationship was especially useful, since transposition by a semitone in mean-tone tuning is not feasible, whereas transposition by a full step or a minor third is. See Haynes, 'Pitch Standards', i. 51–6, 71, 161–2. On the use of tuning joints to lower (and raise by removal) the pitch of cornettos, see ibid. 27.

[8] 'Pitch', in Howard Mayer Brown and Stanley Sadie, eds., *Performance Practice: Music after 1600* (New York: W. W. Norton & Co., 1989), 149. See also Haynes, 'Pitch Standards', ii. 486–92. The maximum fluctuation constituted almost a half-step.

[9] Karp, 'Pitch', 149.

[10] Haynes, 'Pitch Standards', i. 12, 58–62, 66, ii. 383, 419–20, 478–80. See also n. 16 below.

[11] Haynes, 'Pitch in Northern Italy', 41–7, 56–7, 180–2.

standard, though changing strings and retuning could change the pitch within as much as a minor third.[12] Vocal ranges were also limited, and transposition up or down by only a half-step could make considerable difference in the comfort level of a choir.

Each instrument or combination of instruments, once tuned, imposed its own pitch standard on a given performance. At that point the notated pitches determined not only interval relationships, but unique placements of the fingers. Where wind instruments were concerned, the notated pitches also implied specific forms of control of the embouchure and breathing. After an instrument had been tuned, changing the relative highness or lowness of a composition in performance meant transposition, the term being understood as a shift in the placement of the fingers or the position of a slide.

Voices, in contrast to instruments, had no relationship between finger or slide position and a note on the page. As a consequence, music performed solely by voices could be sung at any pitch level that was comfortable, regardless of the notation, a fact attested to by numerous Renaissance theorists. Notated pitches, therefore, defined for singers only interval relationships, not particular frequencies or specific degrees of highness and lowness as they did for instruments.

When voices were combined with instruments, either the voices were forced to adhere to the pitch standard set by the instruments, or the instruments were forced to adopt a comfortable vocal pitch standard, or transpose (in terms of finger position, etc.) in order to accommodate the range of the singers. The burden of accommodating singers in church music fell most heavily on the organist. There were three primary means used to adjust the organ pitch to meet the needs of singers: (1) the provision of multiple organs in a church, or more than one keyboard on an organ—in both cases the keyboards were tuned differently, so that analogous keys sounded different sets of pitches; (2) mechanical devices that shifted the tuning upwards or downwards by small intervals;[13] and (3) transposition, which gradually became more and more important towards the end of the sixteenth century. Numerous theorists in the late sixteenth and early seventeenth centuries discussed the necessity for organists to be able to

[12] Since pitch on string instruments is related to open strings, it was often more practical to retune a string instrument than to transpose, although retuning affected the quality of sound of the instrument. See Haynes, 'Pitch Standards', i. 72. String instruments also may have fallen into two sizes with a basic resonance a semitone apart. See ibid. ii. 391.

[13] Mendel, 'Pitch in Western Music', 39. Haynes cites a 1621 contract for an organ in Bressanone (Brixen), that could be shifted from *ChorThon* (*tuona corista*) to *CornetThon*. Other Austrian and German organs of the 18th century contained similar transposition slides. One or more separate registers activated by stops or separate keyboards could also be installed for transposition. See 'Pitch Standards', i. 185, 192, 354 and ii. 496–9. Transposing organs were prominent in England in the 16th and 17th centuries. See J. Bunker Clark, *Transposition in Seventeenth Century English Organ Accompaniments and the Transposing Organ* (Detroit Monographs in Musicology, 4; Detroit: Information Coordinators, Inc., 1974). These instruments were evidently connected with the much higher English choral pitch. See Myers, 'Pitch and Transposition', 251.

transpose by many different intervals in order to play in a range comfortable for the singers.

Despite fluctuating and varying pitch standards, enough common standards for instruments seem to have existed for both Praetorius and Giambattista Doni to have made generalizing comparisons about pitch levels in different countries or in different cities. For example, Doni claimed that 'the organ pitches of Naples, Rome, Florence, Lombardy and Venice form a series ascending by semitones'.[14] On the basis of documents and surviving instruments, Mendel has estimated that pitch in the period in question ranged from approximately a half-step to a minor third higher than modern pitch, and that in northern Italy the pitch standard may have been up to a half-step higher than modern pitch (an early seventeenth century notated *a* would have sounded at a modern *b*♭).[15] Praetorius's discussion of Italian organ pitch places it at $a' = 445\text{--}60$ Hz, probably more towards the higher range,[16] and recent studies of surviving wind instruments suggest a pitch standard in northern Italy of about $a' = 460\text{--}70$ Hz.[2] Herbert Myers notes that many Venetian recorders and cornettos from the seventeenth century are tuned at about $a' = 460$ Hz.[17] Bruce Dickey accepts $a' = c.466$ Hz as an average pitch for seventeenth-century instruments.[18] Henry George Fischer's study of several surviving Renaissance sackbuts places a number of tenor instruments, whose notated fundamental was *A*, at near a modern *B*♭. The instruments he actually measured ranged from $a' = 440$ Hz (a single example) to $a' = 452.4$, 455, and 460 Hz (three examples).[19] Douglas Kirk, on

---

[14] *Annotazioni sopra il compendio* (Rome, 1640), 181–2; Eng. trans. from Mendel, 'Pitch in Western Music', 12. Haynes, 'Pitch Standards', i. 73–97, discusses in detail the pitch differences among these Italian cities and regions.

[15] See the table of pitch approximations for north Italian organs, 'Pitch in Western Music', 32. Mendel warns against taking this information too literally, however (p. 26).

[16] Mendel's interpretation of Praetorius's pitch standard was challenged by W. R. Thomas and J. J. K. Rhodes in 'Schlick, Praetorius and the History of Organ-Pitch,' *Organ Yearbook*, 2 (1971), 58–76, and in their article 'Pitch, §§ 3–4' in *The New Grove Dictionary of Music and Musicians*, ed. Stanley Sadie (London: Macmillan Publishers, Ltd., 1980), xiv. 782–5. However, the careful discussion in 'Pitch' by Cary Karp in Brown and Sadie, eds., *Performance Practice: Music after 1600*, 151–9 sets Praetorius's organ pitch 'in the interval between $a' = 445$ and $a' = 460$ with some bias towards the upper end of this range, since it has been observed in a number of surviving instruments' (p. 157). The views of Thomas and Rhodes have been disputed by Herbert W. Myers in 'Praetorius's pitch', *Early Music*, 12 (1984), 369–71; id., 'Pitch and Transposition', in Jeffery T. Kite-Powell, ed., *A Practical Guide to Historical Performance—The Renaissance* (New York: Early Music America, 1989), 157–63.

[17] Ibid. 159. Bob Marvin, in 'Recorders & English Flutes in European Collections', *Galpin Society Journal*, 25 (1972), 41–2, had already noted a number of recorders pitched about a half-step higher than $a' = 440$. Recorders were especially stable in pitch. See Haynes, 'Pitch Standards', ii. 385–6, 429–31, 451. Questions about Myers's methods and conclusions are raised by Ephraim Segerman in 'Praetorius's Pitch?', *Early Music*, 13 (1985), 261–3. Myers's conclusions were confirmed, however, in Bruce Haynes, 'Johann Sebastian Bach's Pitch Standards: The Woodwind Perspective', *Journal of the American Musical Instrument Society*, 11 (1985), 87–8. For Myers's most recent remarks on pitch see his 'Recorder', in Kite-Powell, ed., *A Performer's Guide to Renaissance Music*, 47 and 'Pitch and Transposition', in ibid., 248–56.

[18] 'Cornett and Sackbut', in Stewart Carter, ed., *A Performer's Guide to Seventeenth-Century Music* (New York: Schirmer Books, 1997), 102.

[19] *The Renaissance Sackbut and its Use Today* (New York: The Metropolitan Museum of Art, 1984), 4, 8, 43–4.

the basis of cornettos presumably manufactured by members of the Bassano family, confirmed a pitch for Venice in the range $a' = 450$ Hz and $a' = 470$ Hz.[20] Kirk later revised his figures for lower-pitched cornettos to about $a' = 469$ Hz, on the basis of the pitch distinction between cornettos *tutto punto* and *mezzo punto*.[21] Bruce Haynes, on the other hand, identifies two principal pitch groups of cornettos, the higher at about $a' = 470$ Hz and the lower a half-step below at about $a' = 443$ Hz (Haynes also cites a few instruments at various levels above $a' = 484$ Hz). While Kirk considers the highest instruments to be those indicated by the term *mezzo punto* and the middle group to be identified as *tutto punto*, Haynes has made a convincing argument that *mezzo punto* refers to the middle group at about 470 Hz. These instruments, because of their stability and reliability, often served as the tuning reference for organs in northern Italy.[22]

The organ installed in the ducal church of Santa Barbara in Mantua in 1565 was pitched *tutto punto*, which Douglas Kirk has suggested was about $a' = 469$, but which Haynes has subsequently shown to be about 443.[23] This pitch is a semitone lower than the many organs tuned to *mezzo punto*. The lower pitch was more convenient for singers, for whom *mezzo punto* was considered too high. The comfortable pitch for choirs (*tuono chorista*) is described as a full step or even a minor third below *mezzo punto*. In general, instruments were pitched higher than was convenient for voices, often necessitating transposition.[24]

Antonio Barcotto of Padua, in his treatise on organ-building of 1652, remarks that the pitch of organs was different in every city; those of Rome were the lowest in Italy, while those of Venice were among the highest, and said to be in the pitch of cornettos. On the other hand, portative organs in Venice, Padua, Vicenza and other cities [of the Veneto] were a full step lower, pitched for the human voice, and called *corristi*.[25] Studies of voice ranges used by modern com-

---

[20] 'Cornetti and Renaissance Pitch Standards in Italy and Germany', *Journal de musique ancienne*, 10 (1989), 16–22.

[21] 'Cornetti and Renaissance Pitch Revisited', *Historic Brass Society Journal*, 2 (1990), 203–5.

[22] 'Cornetts and Historical Pitch Standards', *Historic Brass Society Journal*, 6 (1994), 84–109; and id., 'Pitch Standards', i. 67–71.

[23] For the designation of the instrument as *tutto ponto* [*sic*], see Iain Fenlon, *Music and Patronage in Sixteenth-Century Mantua* (Cambridge: Cambridge University Press, 1980), i. 188, doc. 48. See also Douglas Kirk, 'Cornetti and Renaissance Pitch Revisited', 204, and Haynes, 'Cornetts and Historical Pitch Standards', 90–1. In personal conversation (June 1996), Douglas Kirk has indicated that he now thinks Haynes is correct in associating *mezzo punto* with a pitch range $a' = c.465$–70 Hz and *tutto punto* with $a' = c.440$–3 Hz.

[24] See Haynes, 'Pitch Standards', i. 62–6, 143–7, 227–8. John Caldwell, in a record review entitled 'Historic Organs in Italy, Denmark and Switzerland', *Early Music*, 22 (1994), 341, indicates that the two organs in San Petronio in Bologna had a pitch of $a' = c.470$ Hz in the 16th century.

[25] Renato Lunelli, 'Un trattatello di Antonio Barcotto colma le lacune dell' "Arte Organica"', *Collectanea historiae musicae*, 1 (1953), 153. For an English translation of this passage, see Haynes, 'Cornetts and Historical Pitch Standards', 94; and id., 'Pitch Standards', i. 66.

posers confirm the range observations of sixteenth- and seventeenth-century theorists and suggest a notational differential of approximately a half-step to a minor third between the earlier period and the present, assuming that the most natural and comfortable ranges of singers have not changed physiologically in the intervening centuries (the ranges of trained singers, of course, have widened).[26]

Two principal sets of clefs were most often used to notate pitch relationships in the sixteenth and seventeenth centuries, the so-called *chiavi naturali*, consisting of canto (soprano)—C_1, alto—C_3, tenor—C_4, and bass—F_4; and the equally common *chiavi alte*, also known by the more recent term *chiavette*, comprising canto (soprano)—G_2, alto—C_2, tenor—C_3, and bass—C_4 or F_3. Much controversy has arisen over the meaning and purpose of the set of high clefs, but evidence has accumulated in recent years to demonstrate convincingly that voices notated in these clefs were normally transposed (in the modern sense of the term) downwards, the interval depending on the comfort range of the singers. When voices were joined by instruments, even if only a continuo instrument, the transposition was most often by a fourth or fifth. The continuo, of course, determined the pitch standard for the voices, and the *chiavi alte*, therefore, served as a means of notating the voices higher on the staff than they were meant to be sung relative to the normal placement of the fingers on the continuo. For this reason the continuo player might be required by rubrics to transpose the part downward or the part itself was notated lower. The rationale for notating voices in the *chiavi alte* in the first place are complicated. Although earlier literature on the subject of *chiavette* was filled with controversy, in the past decade the literature has consistently confirmed the transposition thesis, especially for situations when voices are joined with instruments.[27] Stephen Bonta even demonstrates that by the early seventeenth century, downward transposition of vocal parts in *chiavette* was so common, even tacitly understood, as to require a warning not to transpose when a composer wrote in *chiavette* but wanted a composition to be performed at the notated level for some special reason. His summary, with which I agree, is that 'Available evidence, both positive and negative, from music prints and theorists from the 1590's on, suggests that by that time downward

---

[26] Mendel, 'Pitch in Western Music', 47–8; see also Caroline Anne Miller, '*Chiavette*, A New Approach' (MA thesis, University of California at Berkeley, 1960), 3–55, and Jeffrey Kurtzman, 'Tones, Modes, Clefs and Pitch in Roman Cyclic Magnificats of the 16th Century', *Early Music*, 22 (1994), 641–64.

[27] The most comprehensive articles on the subject are Patrizio Barbieri, '*Chiavette* and Modal Transposition in Italian Practice (*c.* 1500–1837)', *Recercare*, 3 (1991), 5–79; Anne Smith, 'Über Modus und Transposition um 1600', *Basler Jahrbuch für Historische Musikpraxis*, 6 (1982), 9–43; Andrew Parrott, 'Transposition in Monteverdi's Vespers of 1610: An "Aberration" Defended', *Early Music*, 12 (1984), 490–516; id., 'Monteverdi's Vespers of 1610 Revisited', in Raffaello Monterosso, ed., *Performing Practice in Monteverdi's Music: The Historic-Philological Background* (Cremona: Fondazione Claudio Monteverdi, 1995), 163–74; and Kurtzman, 'Tones, Modes, Clefs and Pitch'.

transposition of pieces using *chiavette* was an all but universal practice whenever the organ was used.'[28]

The issue of *chiavette* is complicated by the ranges of modes and psalm tones as well as pitch standards and tuning of instruments. However, if we assume the approximate pitch standard cited in this chapter for both voices and instruments, these matters do not affect the discussion of transposition of those pieces from Monteverdi's 1610 Vespers notated in *chiavette* (see below). Suffice it to say for our present purposes that the *chiavi alte* originated in the first half of the sixteenth century principally to avoid leger lines or complicated flat or sharp signatures for singers when the range of particular modes or transposed modes lay higher than the comfortable range of the voice. Compositions in *chiavi alte* that have been transposed downwards often have sounding ranges a bit lower than the sounding ranges of untransposed pieces in *chiavi naturali*, even though the original notation of pieces in *chiavi alte* looks higher.[29]

Most of the compositions in Monteverdi's 1610 publication are notated in *chiavi naturali*. Two, *Domine ad adjuvandum* and the *Sonata sopra Sancta Maria*, are notated in mixed clefs, but the vocal parts are all in *chiavi naturali*, with the G_2 clef added merely for the convenience of the high-ranging instruments. Four compositions are notated in the *chiavi alte*: the entire *Missa in illo tempore*, *Lauda Jerusalem*, the Magnificat *a 7*, and the Magnificat *a 6*. The *Missa in illo tempore* only concerns us here because of a manuscript organ partitura of uncertain date for this piece, containing all of the vocal parts as well as the bassus generalis. In this partitura, obviously prepared for an actual performance, all of the parts have been transposed down a fourth, placing the Mass in the tonality of G rather than its notated C and confirming the meaning of the *chiavi alte* described above.[30] As late as 1774–5, Giambattista Martini still understood Monteverdi's *chiavi alte* as signifying transposition, since his scoring of the first Agnus Dei from the *Missa in illo tempore* in his counterpoint treatise shows all voices notated in *chiavi naturali* a fourth lower with a key signature of one sharp.[31] *Lauda Jerusalem*, like the Mass, should also be transposed downwards, most probably by a fourth, to bring its vocal ranges within the normal ambitus of each voice for most music of this

---

[28] 'Clef, Mode, and Instruments in Italy, 1540–1675' (unpublished paper). I am grateful to Prof. Bonta for providing me with a copy of his paper. Barbieri's conclusions in 'Chiavette and Modal Transposition' agree with Bonta's. Bonta is less sure about downward transposition of Monteverdi's Magnificat *a 7*, with its obbligato instruments, but Parrott, in 'Monteverdi's Vespers of 1610 Revisited', 164–8, shows that Bonta's reservations are unnecessary.

[29] The situation was different with instrumental compositions notated in *chiavette*, which were normally performed untransposed at the higher pitch. See Stephen Bonta, 'The Use of Instruments in the Ensemble Canzona and Sonata in Italy, 1580–1650', *Recercare*, 4 (1992), 23–43.

[30] The undated partitura, by one Lorenzo Tonelli, is appended to a copy of Monteverdi's print lacking the bassus generalis from the archive of the cathedral at Brescia, now housed at the church of San Giuseppe in Brescia.

[31] *Esemplare osia Saggio fondamentale pratico di contrappunto sopra il canto fermo* (Bologna: Lelio della Volpe, 1774–5), ii. 242–50.

period and to avoid the shrillness resulting from singing at the very top of the register that invariably accompanies performances at the originally notated pitch.[32]

The two Magnificats are intended for virtuoso voices; nevertheless, they too seem to require transposition to place them in a comfortable register. The use of *chiavette*, as well as the notated transposition of the chant up a fourth at the beginning of each Magnificat, again suggest downwards transposition by a fourth in performance. Transposition also renders the instrumental parts of the Magnificat *a 7* much more comfortable.[33]

Further confirmation of the desirability of transposing *Lauda Jerusalem* and the two Magnificats comes from Praetorius's remarks on Italian singing and transposition:

Some Italians quite rightly take no pleasure in high-pitched singing: they maintain that it is devoid of any beauty, that the text cannot be clearly understood, and that the singers have to chirp, squawk, and warble at the tops of their voices, for all the world like hedge-sparrows. Thus sometimes they will perform in the Hypoionian mode of *C* (transposed down a 5th to *F* and then a 3rd down again on *D*), together with organs, positives, and doubling instruments.[34]

In my edition, which is designed to serve for both study and performance, *Lauda Jerusalem* and the two Magnificats appear at both their originally notated levels and transposed down a fourth for the convenience of performers.

---

[32] Readers wishing to hear *Lauda Jerusalem* transposed down a fourth may consult item 21, 24, 28 (down an augmented fourth), 30, or 34 in Appendix D. In items 36 and 37 *Lauda Jerusalem* is transposed down a full step.

[33] Bonta is equivocal on the need for transposition of Monteverdi's Magnificat *a 7* (see n. 28 above), giving arguments on both sides of the question. However, I believe that he has not considered the fact that the Magnificat *a 7* is based on the Magnificat *a 6* (see Ch. 7 above) nor that the range limitations of the cornetto evidently necessitate transposition downwards. Alan Lumsden notes that the normal range of the cornetto, which is obbligato in the *Deposuit*, is *a–a''*. According to Lumsden, 'Fingering charts (e.g. Mersenne, 1636, and Bismantova, 1677) give a range up to *d'''* but in the solo literature *c'''* is rarely and *d'''* never used . . .' See Alan Lumsden, 'Woodwind and Brass', in Brown and Sadie, eds., *Performance Practice: Music after 1600*, 92. Monteverdi's untransposed notation in the Magnificat *a 7* frequently gives the pair of cornettos *d'''*. The Magnificat *a 7* is transposed down a fourth in items 21, 24, 30, and 34 in Appendix D.

[34] *Syntagmatis musici . . . tomus secundus de organographia* (Wolfenbüttel: Elias Holwein, 1619); fac. ed. Wilibald Gurlitt (Kassel: Bärenreiter, 1958), 16; Eng. trans. in David Z. Crookes, *Praetorius, Syntagma Musicum II: De Organographia Parts I and II* (Oxford: Clarendon Press, 1986), 32.

18

Obbligato Instruments

ͼϾ✣Ͽͼ

In three compositions of the 1610 Vespers, *Domine ad adjuvandum*, the *Sonata sopra Sancta Maria*, and the Magnificat *a 7*, Monteverdi calls for specific obbligato instruments, while in two others, *Dixit Dominus* and *Ave maris stella*, notated instrumental parts are provided for ritornellos without any indication of what instruments might be used.[1] The obbligato instruments are as follows:

DOMINE AD ADJUVANDUM

2 violins (*violini da brazzo*) notated in G_2 clef
2 cornettos notated in G_2 clef
1 viola (*viuola da brazzo*) notated in C_1 clef
1 viola (*viuola da brazzo*) notated in C_3 clef
1 viola (*viuola da brazzo*) notated in C_4 clef
1 bass violin (*viuola da brazzo*) notated in F_4 clef
1 trombone notated in C_3 clef
1 trombone notated in C_4 clef
1 trombone notated in F_4 clef
1 double bass (*contrabasso da gamba*) notated in F_4 clef

SONATA SOPRA SANTA [*sic*] MARIA ORA PRO NOBIS

2 violins (*viuolini da brazzo*) notated in G_2 clef
2 cornettos notated in G_2 clef
1 trombone notated in C_4 clef
1 trombone or viola (*viuola da brazzo*) notated in C_4 clef (part has a single *B* below the low *c* of a modern viola)
1 bass violin (*viuola da brazzo*) notated in F_4 clef
1 contrabass trombone (*trombone doppio*) notated in F_4 clef

---

[1] The diverse instrumentation for these five pieces as well as the inconsistent distribution of the same instruments in different part-books for different pieces has been cited as evidence that the various compositions in the Vespers had diverse origins. See Peter Holman, '"Col nobilissimo esercitio della vivuola": Monteverdi's String Writing', *Early Music*, 21 (1993), 584–5.

MAGNIFICAT À SETTE VOCI & *SEI INSTRUMENTI* (ORIGINAL, UNTRANSPOSED NOTATION)

2 violins (*violini*) notated in G_2 clef

3 cornettos notated in G_2 clef

1 large cornetto notated in C_2 clef (in *Sicut erat* only)

1 bass violin (*viuola da brazzo*) notated in F_3 clef

2 transverse flutes (*fifare*) or shawms (*pifare*) notated in G_2 clef (in *Quia respexit* only; see below for discussion of these terms)

2 recorders (*flauti*) notated in G_2 clef (in *Quia respexit* only)

1 trombone notated in C_3 clef (in *Quia respexit* only)

1 trombone notated in F_3 clef (in *Quia respexit* and *Sicut locutus est* only)

In *Dixit Dominus* and *Ave maris stella*, each unspecified instrumental part is associated with a particular clef:

DIXIT DOMINUS

2 parts in C_1 clef

1 part in C_3 clef

2 parts in C_4 clef

1 part in F_4 clef

AVE MARIS STELLA

2 parts in C_1 clef

1 part in C_3 clef

1 part in C_4 clef

1 part in F_4 clef

These ritornellos can easily be performed with the same instruments required for the response, the *Sonata*, and the Magnificat *a 7*. Assuming downward transposition by a fourth for the Magnificat *a 7* and the use of only one instrument per part, the total instrumentation required for a complete performance of the Vespers is as follows:

2 violins (*violini da brazzo*)

3 cornettos

1 large cornetto (required only in the *Sicut erat* of the Magnificat *a 7*)

3 violas (tenor *viuole da brazzo*)

1 bass violin (bass *viuola da brazzo*: lowest string C)

1 double bass (*contrabasso da gamba*)

3 trombones in tenor range

1 contrabass trombone (*trombone doppio*)

2 recorders (*flauti*) in the tenor range

2 transverse flutes (*fifare*) or shawms (*pifare*) in the tenor–alto range (see explanation below)

Most of these instruments are rather clearly described in late sixteenth- and early seventeenth-century theoretical sources, though nomenclature is often inconsistent and confusing. The *viuole da brazzo* comprised the entire range of the violin family, from bass to treble. In the early seventeenth century, this family consisted primarily of four types of instrument, the violin, the alto viola, the tenor viola, and the bass viola (bass violin), sometimes called the violone, later evolving into the violoncello.[2] In the 1610 Vespers, Monteverdi labelled the high *viola da braccio* either *viuolino da brazzo* or *violino*, leaving the term *viuole da brazzo* itself to the middle- and low-range members of the family.[3]

These 'arm' violas contrasted with the *viola da gamba*, or 'leg' viola (from the Renaissance viol family), even though the bass *viole da braccio* were also actually played between the legs. Praetorius and Zacconi give tunings for *viole da braccio* of varying sizes. Praetorius lists two four-string bass *viole de braccio*, the lower one with the bottom string tuned to *C* as on the modern cello, and the higher one with the bottom string tuned to *F*.[4] Lodovico Zacconi's two bass instruments have their bottom strings as *FF* and *F* respectively.[5] Adriano Banchieri indicates a single bass violin with lowest string *G*.[6] The higher instruments tuned in *F* and *G* were also known as tenor violins, although Praetorius reserves this term for the instrument tuned to *c*.[7]

---

[2] See Praetorius, *Syntagmatis musici . . . tomus secundus de organographia* (Wolfenbüttel: Elias Holwein, 1619); fac. ed. Wilibald Gurlitt (Kassel: Bärenreiter, 1958), 48; and David Boyden, 'Monteverdi's *violini piccoli alla francese* and *viole da brazzo*', *Annales musicologiques*, 6 (1958–63), 387–401. For a concise history of the violin family and of viols up to the early 17th century, see Peter Holman, *Four and Twenty Fiddlers: The Violin at the English Court 1540–1690* (Oxford: Clarendon Press, 1993), 1–31. On the bass violin and the evolution of the violoncello, see Stephen Bonta, 'From Violone to Violoncello: A Question of Strings?', *Journal of the American Musical Instrument Society*, 3 (1977), 64–99; id., 'Terminology for the Bass Violin in the 17th-Century', *Journal of the American Musical Instrument Society*, 4 (1978), 5–42; id., 'Corelli's Heritage: The Early Bass Violin in Italy', in Pierluigi Petrobelli and Gloria Staffieri, eds., *Studi Corelliani IV: Atti del Quarto Congresso Internazionale*, Fusignano, 4–7 Sept. 1986 (Florence: Leo S. Olschki Editore, 1990), 217–31; and id., 'The Use of Instruments in Sacred Music in Italy, 1560–1700', *Early Music*, 18 (1990), 519–35.

[3] See Holman, ' "Col nobilissimo esercitio" ' for a study of Monteverdi's string instruments and their usage.

[4] *Syntagmatis musici . . . tomus secundus*, 26; Eng. trans. in Harold Blumenfeld, *The Syntagma Musicum of Michael Praetorius: Volume two De Organographia, First and Second Parts* (New York: Da Capo Press, 1980), 26; and David Z. Crookes, *Praetorius, Syntagma Musicum II: De Organographia Parts I and II* (Oxford: Clarendon Press, 1986), 39.

[5] *Prattica di musica* (Venice: Girolamo Polo, 1592; fac. Bologna: Forni Editore, 1967), fo. 218[v].

[6] *Conclusioni nel suono dell'organo . . . opera vigesima* (Bologna, Rossi, 1609; fac. Bologna: Forni Editore, 1968), 55; Eng. trans. Lee R. Garrett as *Adriano Banchieri: Conclusions for Playing the Organ (1609)* (Colorado Springs, Colo.: Colorado College Music Press, 1982), 48.

[7] See n. 4. According to Peter Holman, the tenor viola 'may have existed for a short period', and he suggests that such an instrument 'may . . . have been used for the "Trombone, overo Viola da brazzo" part with the range *B–f'* in Monteverdi's *Sonata sopra Sancta Maria'*. See Holman, 'Col nobilissimo esercitio', 581–2. Agnes Kory suggests that the use of the tenor violin may have been more widespread

In *Domine ad adjuvandum*, Monteverdi uses five different clefs for instruments of the *viuola da brazzo* family: G_2, C_1, C_3, C_4, and F_4. The extra clef is the C_1 clef for a part labelled *viuola da brazzo* rather than *violino da brazzo*. This may be for another alto viola; the part itself ranges from *d'* to *e''*, and the frequent *d'* and *a'* could be played on the open D and A strings. The *e''* would still fall in first position on the A string. Agnes Kory, on the other hand, argues that the five-part ritornellos of *L'Orfeo*, which all have one part with a C_4 clef (the final *Moresca* uses the same clef combination as *Domine ad adjuvandum*) imply 'two violins, one viola, one tenor violin and a bass violin'.[8] Monteverdi's original notation of the Magnificat *a 7* enables the use of either higher or lower bass *viole da braccio*, but when transposed down a fourth, as recommended in Chapter 17, requires the lower one.

The Vespers call for only a single instrument of the *viola da gamba* family, a *contrabasso da gamba*, which appears solely in *Domine ad adjuvandum*. It is virtually certain that Monteverdi intended an instrument requiring transposition of the part an octave down.[9]

Among 'brass' instruments, cornettos and trombones are the types normally encountered in church ensemble music of the early seventeenth century. Praetorius describes two types of cornettos—a straight instrument and a curved one. He further subdivides the straight cornettos into two types, one with a removable mouthpiece, known as the *cornetto diritto*, and one with an undetachable mouthpiece lathed directly onto the instrument. The latter was known as the *cornetto muto*, was pitched lower, and produced a very soft, quiet tone.[10] No preference for one or the other has been discerned from sixteenth- and early seventeenth-century documents, although the softer *cornetto muto* may normally have played with strings and harpsichords, while the standard cornetto, whether of the straight or curved variety, was often paired with trombones.[11]

than previously suspected and proposes that the small bass violin, i.e. the tenor violin, survived well into the 18th century and became generally known as a violoncello [sometimes called the violoncello piccolo—a smaller instrument than the violoncello tuned to C] by the late 17th century. See Kory, 'A Wider Role for the Tenor Violin?', *Galpin Society Journal*, 47 (1994), 123–53.

[8] See ibid. 132. Holman notes that the 'two-soprano scoring is not known to have been applied to violin consorts until the first decade of the 17th century, when it is found in several printed sources from Monteverdi's Mantuan circle'. See ' "Col nobilissimo esercitio" ', 582. Stephen Bonta suggests that even pieces that could have been played on the higher of the bass violins (the tenor violin) were probably most often played on the lower one in order to make use of the highest string. See his 'From Violone to Violoncello', 68, 73–7.

[9] An opinion also held by Bonta in 'Terminology for the Bass Violin in the 17th-Century', 11 n. 22. See also Holman, ' "Col nobilissimo esercitio" ', 585.

[10] *Syntagmatis musici . . . tomus secundus*, 35–6; trans. Blumenfeld, pp. 35–6; Crookes, pp. 46–7. For a discussion of surviving *cornetti muti* see Bruce Haynes, 'Cornetts and Historical Pitch Standards', *Historic Brass Society Journal*, 6 (1994), 84–109. Haynes provides a graph of the pitches of these instruments in the 16th and 17th centuries on p. 92.

[11] See Douglas Kirk, 'Cornett', in Jeffrey T. Kite-Powell ed., *A Performer's Guide to Renaissance Music*. (New York: Schirmer Books, 1994), 79–80; and Bruce Dickey, 'Cornett and Sackbut', in Stewart Carter, ed., *A Performer's Guide to Seventeenth-Century Music* (New York: Schirmer Book, 1997),

The normal-sized cornetto had a range virtually identical to that of the violin (though the cornetto is more limited in the extreme upper register), and the two instruments were often used interchangeably.[12] Monteverdi calls for cornettos and violins to share the same treble parts in *Domine ad adjuvandum*. In the *Sonata sopra Sancta Maria*, the violins and cornettos often imitate or echo one another. In the Magnificat *a 7*, they share identical parts or exchange roles, as for example in the *Deposuit*. Numerous seventeenth-century sources identify a treble instrumental part as *violino o cornetto*. Since the *cornetto muto* was a lower-pitched instrument, Monteverdi must have intended the treble cornetto for his obbligato parts. However, if the Magnificat *a 7* is transposed down a fourth, the third cornetto part descends too low for the treble instrument, and a lower-pitched cornetto is required.[13]

The trombones of the early seventeenth century, often called sackbuts, were softer and mellower than modern trombones.[14] The tenor trombone was by far the most ubiquitous, and the combination of tenor trombones playing alto, tenor, and bass parts with cornettos on treble parts formed one of the most common consorts of sixteenth- and early seventeenth-century instrumental music.[15] The combination of trombones and cornettos is frequently encountered in early seventeenth-century church ensembles.[16] If Monteverdi's Magnificat *a 7* is transposed down a fourth, the lowest note in the first trombone part of *Quia respexit* and the trombone part of *Sicut locutus est* is D. This pitch was probably playable by skilled instrumentalists, but could also have been played by inserting a tuning crook into a tenor trombone or by using a lower-pitched instrument.

In addition to the three tenor trombones required by Monteverdi's orches-

98–115. Dickey includes a brief description of 16th-century tonguing techniques. See *Basler Jahrbuch für historische Musikpraxis*, 5 (1981) for an entire issue devoted to studies of the cornetto, its repertoire, and treatises discussing methods of playing the instrument. This issue also includes an essay on Renaissance trombones. For a modern cornetto 'tutor', see Christopher Monk, 'First Steps towards Playing the Cornett', *Early Music*, 3 (1975), 132–3, 244–8.

[12] See Sandra Mangsen, '*Ad libitum* procedures in Instrumental Duos and Trios', *Early Music*, 19 (1991), 29–31 and Eleanor Selfridge-Field, 'Instrumentation and Genre in Italian Music, 1600–1670', *Early Music*, 19 (1991), 63.

[13] See Douglas Kirk, 'Cornett', 81. A *cornetto muto* might be used, but Bruce Dickey reports the survival in museums of more than thirty-five lower-pitched cornettos, often referred to as *cornetto torto* or tenor cornetto, testifying to widespread use in Italy and Germany. See Dickey, 'Cornett and Sackbut', p. 102.

[14] A short monograph describing the physical characteristics of a number of surviving sackbuts is Henry George Fischer, *The Renaissance Sackbut and its Use Today* (New York: The Metropolitan Museum of Art, 1984). An introduction to the sackbut can be found in Stewart Carter, 'Sackbut', in Kite-Powell, ed., *A Performer's Guide to Renaissance Music*, 97–108; and in Dickey, 'The Cornett and Sackbut in the 17th Century'.

[15] See Carter, 'Sackbut', 98–9; James Tyler, 'Mixed Ensembles', in Kite-Powell, ed., *A Performer's Guide to Renaissance Music*, 221; and Dickey, 'The Cornett and Sackbut in the 17th Century'.

[16] See e.g. James H. Moore, *Vespers at St Mark's: Music of Alessandro Grandi, Giovanni Rovetta and Francesco Cavalli* (Ann Arbor: UMI Research Press, 1981), 81–2.

tration, the *Sonata sopra Sancta Maria* also calls for a contrabass trombone (*trombone doppio*). The *trombone doppio* is identified by Praetorius with the octave trombone, which transposes down one octave.[17] As with the *contrabasso da gamba*, Monteverdi notates the contrabass trombone in the F_4 clef rather than the F_3 clef recommended by Praetorius. Praetorius describes two different constructions for this instrument, one which is twice the length of a tenor trombone without crooks, and another which is not quite so long, but has wider tubes as well as crooks to produce its lower pitch.[18] He seems to suggest that the latter was in more common use. Monteverdi normally requires this instrument to play only as low as notated G (sounding GG). But in bars 236–8 of the *Sonata sopra Sancta Maria*, a descending scale is continued beyond notated G all the way to C (sounding CC). Examples of transposing notation reaching this far down into the low register of the contrabass trombone are included in Praetorius's treatise.[19]

Flauti are required in the Vespers for only twelve bars as accompaniment to the cantus firmus in *Quia respexit* of the Magnificat *a 7* (bars 91–102). *Flauto* was the sixteenth- and seventeenth-century Italian term for recorder, and by the early seventeenth century the instrument existed in a variety of sizes.[20] Both parts in *Quia respexit* can be played on a tenor recorder in C, assuming downward transposition of the parts by a fourth. Recorders in the sixteenth and seventeenth centuries sounded an octave higher than written, so in relation to Monteverdi's notation, the *flauti* are transposing instruments.[21]

For ten bars (bars 70–9) *Quia respexit* also requires two *fifare* or *pifare* (differently labelled in the alto and tenor part-books). It is highly unlikely that two different instruments are meant, since Monteverdi invariably used pairs of like instruments and voices in this period. If *fifare* are intended, it is clear that a pair of transverse flutes is appropriate. Praetorius describes and pictures such a flute,

[17] *Syntagmatis musici . . . tomus secundus*, 20, 32, 46; trans. Blumenfeld, pp. 20, 32, 46; Crookes, pp. 35, 43, 54.

[18] Only the length of the tubing, not its diameter, affects its pitch. See the discussion of brass instruments in Arthur H. Benade, *Fundamentals of Musical Acoustics* (New York: Oxford University Press, 1976), 391–430. Praetorius's wording is ambiguous as to whether he thought wider tubing was necessary for the lower pitch, or only the crooks. See *Syntagmatis musici . . . tomus secundus*, 32; trans. Blumenfeld, p. 32; Crookes, p. 43.

[19] *Syntagmatis musici . . . tomus tertius* (Wolfenbüttel: Elias Holwein, 1619); fac. ed. Wilibald Gurlitt (Kassel: Bäenreiter, 1958), 160–1. Eng. trans. in Hans A. Lampl, 'A Translation of *Syntagma musicum III* by Michael Praetorius' (DMA dissertation, University of Southern California, 1957), 271–2. In *Syntagmatis musici . . . tomus secundus*, 46, trans. Blumenfeld, p. 46; Crookes, p. 54, Praetorius recommends writing out the part for an octave transposing contrabass violone or contrabass trombone an octave higher in the F_3 clef.

[20] Praetorius, *Syntagmatis musici . . . tomus secundus*, 33–5, pl. IX; trans. Blumenfeld, pp. 33–5, pl. IX; Crookes, pp. 44–6, pl. IX. See Herbert Myers, 'Recorder', in Kite-Powell, ed., *A Performer's Guide to Renaissance Music*, 41–55.

[21] Praetorius, *Syntagmatis musici . . . tomus secundus*, 21; trans. Blumenfeld, p. 21; Crookes, p. 36. See also Myers, 'Recorder', 45–6. Myers is a good source of information about Renaissance and Baroque recorders as well as practical matters regarding modern performance on recorders.

which bore the Italian names of *travers* or *fiffaro*, and, like the recorder, sounded an octave higher than notated. Praetorius's tenor-alto *fiffaro* will encompass Monteverdi's range, even in transposition down a fourth.[22]

It is less likely that Monteverdi intended two *pifare*. The term *piffaro* is ambiguous in early seventeenth-century usage; *piffari* had a generic meaning in late sixteenth- and early seventeenth-century Venice, where the term referred to the doge's ceremonial wind band as well as other similar ensembles. The *piffari e tromboni* of the doge consisted of cornettos and trombones.[23] Other *piffari* bands were rather common in Venice and at various times included cornettos, trombones, natural trumpets, shawms, drums, bagpipes, recorders, viols, and transverse flutes.[24] But in this usage, *pifara* would have been a meaningless, generic term in Monteverdi's score, insufficiently specific and inconsistent with the detailed naming of instruments throughout the Magnificat *a 7*. However, Praetorius used the Italian term *piffaro* to refer specifically to the descant shawm.[25] It is difficult to know whether he was using the term correctly according to Italian practice or whether he may have mistaken a generic term for one of the instruments often found in the *piffari* ensembles. If Praetorius's identification of the *piffaro* with a discant shawm is correct, then it is possible that Monteverdi intended two shawms rather than two transverse flutes. However, there is no evidence of shawms having been played in the ducal church of Santa Barbara or in the court at Mantua.[26] Shawms and recorders were employed in some churches in Venice, but seem never to have been used in instrumental ensembles at St Mark's.[27] Two of the descant shawms listed by Praetorius have ranges adequate for Monteverdi's parts, even when transposed down a fourth.

---

[22] Praetorius, *Syntagmatis musici . . . tomus secundus*, 22, 35, pls. IX, XXXVIII; trans. Blumenfeld, pp. 22, 35, pls. IX, XXXVIII; Crookes, pp. 36, 46, pls. IX, XXXVIII. Praetorius depicts several sizes of six-hole flutes. All are without a key, must have had a cylindrical bore, and, except for the largest size, are in a single piece. Confusions and contradictions in Praetorius's comments about flutes in *Syntagma musicum*, vols. ii and iii, are discussed in Bernard Thomas, 'The Renaissance Flute', *Early Music*, 3 (1975), 2–10. For useful introductions to the Renaissance flute, see Herbert Myers, 'Renaissance Flute', in Kite-Powell, ed., *A Performer's Guide to Renaissance Music*, 56–62 and Anne Smith, 'The Renaissance Flute', in John Solum, *The Early Flute* (Oxford: Clarendon Press, 1992), 11–33. See also Filadelfio Puglisi, 'A Survey of Renaissance Flutes', *Galpin Society Journal*, 41 (1988), 67–82. The Baroque flute, which was in more than one piece, was conically bored, and possessed at least one key, was a development of the second half of the 17th century. See Jane Bowers, 'New Light on the Development of the Transverse Flute between about 1650 and about 1770', *Galpin Society Journal*, 3 (1977), 5–56, and Solum, *The Early Flute*, 34–49.

[23] Moore, *Vespers at St Mark's*, 81.

[24] See Eleanor Selfridge-Field, *Venetian Instrumental Music from Gabrieli to Vivaldi* (New York: Praeger Publishers, 1975), 13–15; and ead., 'Bassano and the Orchestra of St Mark's', *Early Music*, 4 (1976), 153. The term *piffari* was also used for civic wind bands in many other north Italian cities.

[25] *Syntagmatis musici . . . tomus secundus*, 22, 37; trans. Blumenfeld, pp. 22, 36–7; Crookes, pp. 37, 47–8.

[26] Personal communication from Susan Parisi.

[27] Selfridge-Field, *Venetian Instrumental Music*, 17, 29, 32; ead., 'Bassano', 158.

On the other hand, the typically loud sound of the shawm seems out of place in the rather delicate texture of *Quia respexit*, especially as a foil to the pair of recorders.[28]

The obbligato instruments from *Domine ad adjuvandum*, the *Sonata sopra Sancta Maria*, and the Magnificat *a 7* may also be employed in varying combinations for performance of the ritornellos in *Dixit Dominus* and *Ave maris stella*. Monteverdi's own orchestration demonstrates that the sixteenth-century concept of consorts of similar instruments no longer holds. Monteverdi freely mixes strings, trombones, and cornettos. Praetorius still suggests a variety of unmixed consorts, depending on the clefs in a given choir, but the many possibilities he lists for substitutions or other combinations virtually obliterate the concept of a uniform consort altogether.[29]

An important consideration in the scoring of the ritornellos is variation in tone colour between reiterations. Praetorius and others stress repeatedly the delight early seventeenth-century musicians took in varying the tone colour, in contrast to the monotony of retaining the same sonority throughout.[30] The ritornellos in *Dixit Dominus*, with two parts in the C_1 clef, 1 part in the C_3 clef, two parts in the C_4 clef, and one part in the F_4 clef, can be played by various string and brass instruments. The two upper parts could be played by violins, three tenor violas (simply violas if modern instruments are used) could take the mid-range parts, and the bottom line could be assigned to a bass viola (cello in modern terms), thereby forming a pure consort. A consort of brass could similarly be created from three cornettos and three trombones. For mixed consorts, higher and lower instruments might be employed in various combinations, including strings and brass in all registers. In mixing instruments performers should maintain Monteverdi's own strict principle of two like instruments playing the two upper parts, whether these instruments play alone or are doubled by another pair. An ensemble of strings alone on the upper parts and brass alone on the middle and lower parts, or vice versa, would be less consistent with the combinations described by Praetorius or used elsewhere by Monteverdi.

One might also wish to use the recorders or transverse flutes (or shawms) from the Magnificat *a 7* for the upper two parts in these ritornellos. It should not be forgotten that the organist might well play a ritornello by himself, provided

---

[28] For recordings that use shawms in this verse, see App. D, items 22 and 31.

[29] Praetorius, *Syntagmatis musici . . . tomus tertius*, 152–68; trans. in Lampl, 'A Translation of *Syntagma musicum III*', 259–82. See also Howard Mayer Brown, *Sixteenth-Century Instrumentation: The Music of the Florentine Intermedii* (American Institute of Musicology, 1973), 79–81.

[30] Praetorius, *Syntagmatis musici . . . tomus tertius*, 130 (recte 110); trans. Lampl, pp. 187–8. Further discussion of instrumentation in ritornellos is found in Gloria Rose, 'Agazzari and the Improvising Orchestra', *Journal of the American Musicological Society*, 18 (1965), 385–8.

that he could actually manage all of the parts, possibly with the help of pedals for the bass-line.[31]

Instrumentation of the ritornello in *Ave maris stella* should follow the same principles. Since the vocal sonority of the verses of the hymn varies from one stanza to the next, it may prove desirable to select an instrumentation for each successive ritornello that takes into account the sonority of either the preceding or following verse.

The number of instruments to be employed, whether they are obbligato or *ad libitum*, as discussed in the next chapter, is uncertain. The largest ensembles described in contemporary documents range from approximately sixteen to twenty-two players, although it has been suggested that the normal St Mark's contingent of sixteen instrumentalists may have alternated for feasts, with only eight playing at a time.[32] However, the lists of players employed for special feasts make it clear that, at least on some occasions, as many as twenty-two players participated.[33] Evidently, an instrumental part was normally played by only one of a given instrument, although it might in rare instances be shared by two instruments of different kinds (such as violin and cornetto or viola and trombone, as in Monteverdi's *Domine ad adjuvandum*).[34] However, on special feasts, when extra instrumentalists were employed, one or more lines may have been doubled to reinforce the sonority.

In Monteverdi's Vespers, the largest number of obbligato instruments is required in *Domine ad adjuvandum* and the Magnificat *a 7*, each of which name twelve different instruments. The Magnificat is principally a work for solo voices and instruments, where the virtuoso character of the vocal and instrumental lines requires only one singer or player per part. Only the opening and closing verses of the Magnificat could be performed with multiple singers on a part (see Chapter 15), and in these two verses, more than one instrument could conceivably play each of Monteverdi's notated obbligato instrumental parts, so long as the voices and instruments were in satisfactory balance. The ritornello of the verse *Quia respexit* might also employ doubling of lines, especially since the performance rubric calls for 'six instruments, which will play as loudly as they can' (*sei instrumenti li quali si soneranno con più forza che si può*). However, the

---

[31] It should be remembered that many 17th-century Italian organs had pull-down pedals for the lowest notes of the keyboard, enabling the organist to play these pitches with the feet rather than the fingers. See Ch. 13 above.

[32] Selfridge-Field, 'Bassano', 156.

[33] Denis Arnold, *Giovanni Gabrieli and the Music of the Venetian High Renaissance* (London: Oxford University Press, 1979), 140.

[34] See Holman, ' "Col nobilissimo esercitio" ', 585. Holman notes the possible doubling of string parts in *L'Orfeo*, *Questi vaghi concenti*, and *Il ballo delle ingrate* as unusual in Monteverdi's œuvre; see pp. 582, 584. According to Peter Walls, 'in the 1660's works by Stradella would have been performed with single players on ripieno and concertino parts. The practice of using more than one player for ripieno parts was introduced in the 1670s.' See Walls, 'Strings', in Howard Mayer Brown and Stanley Sadie, eds., *Performance Practice: Music after 1600* (New York and London: W. W. Norton & Company, 1989), 78 n. 47.

fifare, trombones, and recorders that alternate as obbligato instruments in this verse during the singing of the cantus firmus by a solo tenor should be played with only one instrument per part.

The ritornellos of the *Esurientes* might also be performed with more than one instrument per part, although care must be taken that the last word of the verse, where the two voices and the instruments join, is not overshadowed. In *Fecit potentiam* only three instruments should be employed, since the cantus firmus sings against the instruments during much of the verse. Moreover, the organ registration for this verse, with its *voce humana*, is quite soft (see Chapter 13), suggesting the need for solo instruments. In all the remaining verses of the Magnificat, including *Sicut locutus*, only single instruments should play the obbligato parts.

In the response, *Domine ad adjuvandum*, Monteverdi himself calls for doubling of five of the six obbligato instrumental lines by instruments of different families. This is a fairly large ensemble, but could be increased further within the framework of early seventeenth-century practice. Instruments of the same types could be added to several or all of the lines, depending on the resulting balance of instrumental and vocal sonorities. Other types of instruments could also be added, such as a pair of recorders to play the top two lines and a dulcian (bassoon) to double the bass, but it should be noted that here, as in the Magnificat *a 7* and the *Sonata*, Monteverdi has been far more detailed in his orchestration than any of his contemporaries, and this fact alone should inhibit modern performers from deviating from his original specifications without careful consideration.

The *Sonata sopra Sancta Maria* should be performed with only one instrument per part. The two pairs of treble parts are for virtuoso players and are wholly unsuited to doubling. The two mid-range instruments should prove adequate to fill out the sonority, especially since they are also supported by the continuo. Even the middle and bass instruments, with the exception of the *trombone doppio*, play in virtuoso style for portions of the *Sonata*. The continuo line is often doubled by both the *trombone doppio* and a *viuola da brazzo*, both parts notated separately by Monteverdi. During the passage in black notation (bars 130–41), the pair of violins and the pair of cornettos alternate with one another, each supported by a different pair of lower-pitched instruments. The cornettos are supported by a trombone and the trombone *doppio*, while the violins are supported by one part labelled at the outset of the piece *Viuola da brazzo* and another labelled *Trombone overo Viuola da brazzo*. It seems clear that in order to maintain the string–wind alternation, the viola must be chosen for the latter part.

The ritornellos in *Dixit Dominus* and *Ave maris stella* present opposing pictures. The *Dixit* ritornellos feature considerable polyphonic complexity, and are therefore best played by only one instrument per part. The homophonic ritornello of the hymn, however, could quite suitably be played, in at least one of its repetitions, with two or even three instruments on some or all of its five parts, depending, of course, on the size of the choral ensemble performing the choral verses. Praetorius suggests, as one of his instrumental choirs, an ensemble of plucked string instruments, consisting of several types.[35] Thus the lute, theorbo, and double harp might be used alone or in various combinations in one or more of the ritornellos in *Dixit Dominus* and *Ave maris stella*, as well as for doubling in other pieces as discussed both above and in the next chapter.

[35] *Syntagmatis musici . . . tomus tertius*, 168; trans. Lampl, pp. 281–2.

19

Instrumental Doubling and Substitution
for Vocal Parts

THE practice of doubling voices with instruments and/or using instruments to substitute for voices in both secular and sacred music was widespread and well established in Italy long before the turn of the seventeenth century.[1] Although the evidence is more ubiquitous for masses and motets than it is for psalmody in the sixteenth century,[2] there is also firm evidence for instrumental doubling in vesper psalms. The Venetian theorist Nicola Vicentino had declared as early as 1555 that to make a large sound (*intonatione*) in spacious churches and other large places, 'one can compose masses, psalms, and dialogues and other things to play with various instruments, mixed with voices'.[3] The title-page of Ippolito Camatero's *Salmi corista a otto voci* of 1573 describes the contents as 'convenient for the voices, accompanied as well with every sort of musical instrument'.[4] The first collection of Magnificats to refer to instruments is Orazio Colombani's *Li dilettevoli Magnificat* of 1583, whose title-page indicates that the canticles are 'suitable for singing and playing *in concerto*.[5] Similarly, the title-page of Giovanni

---

[1] For a good, brief survey regarding instruments in sacred music, see Stephen Bonta, 'The Use of Instruments in Sacred Music in Italy, 1560–1700', *Early Music*, 18 (1990), 519–35. Instruments in the 17th-century mass are discussed in Anne Schnoebelen, 'The Role of the Violin in the Resurgence of the Mass in the 17th Century', *Early Music*, 18 (1990), 537–42. Instruments function in similar capacities in all genres of liturgical music from this period.

[2] The earliest collection of motets I know of that was published in Italy and specifically alerts the user to the possibility of instrumental substitution or doubling is Orlando Lasso's *Sacrae cantiones . . . liber secundus* of 1566 (RISM L794). Lasso's title-page describes the motets as 'very appropriate for voices or all sorts of instruments' ('Tum viva Voce tum omnis generis Instrumentis cantatu commodissimae'). Lasso's *Sacrae cantiones* went through several later editions, all of which retain the same rubric. Pietro Giovanelli's large and prominent anthology of motets, the *Novi thesauri musici liber primus* of 1568 (RISM SD1568²), describes its contents on the title-page: 'which are sung in the Holy Catholic Church on the highest and most solemn feast-days, [and] are suitable for all types of musical instruments' ('quae in sacra Ecclesia catholica, summis solemnibusque festivitatibus, canuntur, ad omnis generis instrumenta musica, accommodata'). The most famous motet collection mentioning instruments before the turn of the century is the anthology *Concerti di Andrea, et di Gio: Gabrieli* of 1587 (RISM G85, SD1587¹⁶).

[3] *L'antica musica ridotta alla moderna prattica* (Rome: Barre, 1555); fac. ed. Edward E. Lowinsky (Kassel: Bärenreiter, 1959), ch. 28, fo. 85ʳ.

[4] *Comodi alle voci, accompagnate anco con ogni sorte di instrument Musicali* (RISM C279). See Chs. 3 and 4 above.

[5] 'Accomodati per cantar: & sonar in concerto' (RISM C3423). Andrea Gabrieli's *Psalmi Davidici . . . poenitentiales*, also of 1583 (RISM G56), are 'tum omnis generis Instrumentorum, tum ad

Mateo Asola's *Vespertina omnium solemnitatum psalmodia* of 1590 for three choirs instructs that the third chorus may include instruments,[6] and Asola's *Completorium romanum* of 1599, also for three choirs, is described as 'to be performed with all types of instruments'.[7] In 1591 Lucrezio Quintiani, a Cistercian monk in Cremona, had published a Magnificat cycle 'suitable to be performed either with all sorts of instruments or with voices'.[8] Similar rubrics appear on the title-pages of a number of early seventeenth-century prints containing vesper music.[9] The archival evidence of instruments in performances of polychoral vesper music in Rome in the late sixteenth and early seventeenth centuries, described in more detail in Chapter 4, may refer to doubling of vocal parts, substitution for vocal parts, a mixture of vocal and instrumental parts in one or more choirs, or even entire choirs comprising instruments alone.[10]

Monteverdi's *Vespro della Beata Vergine* and other vesper music published shortly afterwards testify further to the rapid introduction of instruments into vesper services during this period.[11] In 1612, Viadana issued a set of psalms for four choirs with a detailed preface on how they could be performed. The *capella* choir could be doubled by instruments, while the third, four-part choir consisted of a soprano part played by cornetto, or violin, a second soprano part to be sung 'by up to three good soprano voices', an alto part to be 'performed by several voices, with violins and curved cornetts', and a tenor to be 'sung by several voices, with trombones, and with violins and organ an octave higher than usual'. In the fourth choir, a low choir, 'the top part is a very low alto sung by several voices, with violins and curved cornetts an octave higher; the next part is in a comfortable tenor register, sung by a number of voices with trombones; the third part is a baritone—again this should have good voices or trombones, with violins. The bass is always low, so it should be sung by deep voices

vocis modulationem accommodati' (suitable for performance either with all sorts of instruments or with voices). In 1587, Michele Varotto published a set of Lamentations of Jeremiah with virtually the same rubric (RISM V989).

[6] 'Omnia Duodenis Vocibus. Ternis variata Chorus, ac omni Instrumentorum genere modulanda' (RISM A2581).

[7] 'Ac omni instrumentorum genere modulanda' (not listed in RISM).

[8] 'Tum omnis generis Instrumentorum, tum ad vocis modulationem accomodata' (RISM Q115). In the same year, Francesco Ramella of Novara published a collection of motets, a mass, and a Magnificat (R195) with the phrase 'Tum vivae voci, tum omnibus Musices Instrumentis aptissimae' on the title-page. Other Italian prints before the turn of the century calling for instruments, always in conjunction with eight or more voices, are Ippolito Baccusi's *Psalmi omnes* of 1597 (RISM B34), Giovanni Gabrieli's *Sacrae symphoniae* of 1597 (RISM G86), Francesco Stivori's *virginis Mariae canticum modulationes super omnes tonos* of 1598, (RISM S6451), and Agostino Zineroni's *Missa, Beatae Virginis cantica, sacraeque cantiones* of 1599 (RISM Z240).

[9] Prints from the first decade of the century with such rubrics are RISM B2607, C68, G4803, M3732, N10, N732, S1084, S3429, S3431, S6928, V1368, V1369. The title-pages are given in full in App. E.

[10] This evidence appears in the several publications by Thomas Noel O'Regan cited in the Bibliography.

[11] See Ch. 4 for a discussion of instruments in vesper music in the first twenty years of the century.

with trombones, double-bass viols [*violoni doppi*], and bassoons, with organ an octave lower than normal'.[12]

Psalm publications in the early seventeenth century also began to specify obbligato instruments, further suggesting that doubling instruments or instrumental substitution for voices had already been fairly common in this repertoire.[13] It is an open question whether Monteverdi himself would have used *ad libitum* instrumental doubling in his Vespers, but even if he would not have done so, it is quite possible that his contemporaries, following the common practice of the period, would have doubled or replaced voices with instruments. In fact, Monteverdi may well have anticipated that they would.[14] The modern performer, therefore, may choose to follow Monteverdi's notated instrumentation explicitly, but may also feel justified in supplying additional instrumental doubling or instrumental substitution for voices. If the latter is preferred, what instruments may be employed?

In addition to the obbligato instruments named in Monteverdi's Vespers, other instruments commonly used in sacred music were the lute, theorbo, double harp, bassoons, shawms, and recorders. Also occasionally mentioned are such instruments as the harpsichord, the cittern, the large cittern, the *lirone*, horns, and trumpets.[15] Theoretically, virtually any instrument could be brought

---

[12] Preface repr. in Federico Mompellio, *Lodovico Viadana: Musicista fra due secoli* (Florence: Leo S. Olschki, 1966), 163–5; Eng. trans. from Jerome Roche, *North Italian Church Music in the Age of Monteverdi* (Oxford: Clarendon Press, 1984), 118–19.

[13] See Ch. 4 for a discussion of obbligato instruments in the early seventeenth-century motet and psalm repertoire. See also David Bryant, 'The *cori spezzati* of St Mark's: Myth and Reality', *Early Music History*, 1 (1981), 178, 180–1. James H. Moore's documentation of instruments and instrumentalists at St Mark's in the early 17th century does not reveal whether they were used in vespers or compline beyond the performance of purely instrumental music and obbligato instrumental parts. See Moore, *Vespers at St Mark's: Music of Alessandro Grandi, Giovanni Rovetta and Francesco Cavalli* (Ann Arbor: UMI Research Press, 1981), i, 81–2.

[14] Peter Holman, on the other hand, considers it 'unlikely that Monteverdi wanted his instrumentalists to double the vocal parts in numbers where they are not specified, as happens routinely in modern performances; there are no doubling parts in the partbooks, and *Laudate pueri* is specifically described as "a 8 voci sole nel organo" in the *bassus generalis* part'. See Holman, ' "Col nobilissimo esercitio della vivuola": Monteverdi's String Writing', *Early Music*, 21 (1993), 585. Yet the rubric for *Laudate pueri* that Holman cites may actually indicate that Monteverdi would otherwise have anticipated instrumental doubling—hence the need for the rubric. Richard Charteris shows that instrumental doubling and/or substitution in Giovanni Gabrieli's vocal music is actually called for by Gabrieli's rubrics in one case and is implied in many others, and cites documentary evidence of widespread instrumental doubling and substitution in the performance of Gabrieli's vocal works in Germany and Austria. See Charteris, 'The Performance of Giovanni Gabrieli's Vocal Works: Indications in the Early Sources', *Music & Letters*, 71 (1990), 336–51. Documentary evidence from the basilica of St Anthony in Padua indicates that a trombone was regularly used to double the bass in the late 16th and early 17th centuries, and that a cornetto sometimes doubled the soprano line if the voices were weak. See Nicoletta Billio D'Arpa, 'Amadio Freddi, musicista padovano', *Il Santo. Rivista antoniana di storia dottrina arte*, 27 (1987), 246.

[15] See Agostino Agazzari, *Del sonare sopra'l basso con tutti li stromenti e dell'uso loro nel conserto* (Siena: Domenico Falcini, 1607; fac. Bologna: Forni Editore, 1985), 3; Eng. trans. in Oliver Strunk, *Source Readings in Music History* (New York: W. W. Norton & Company, Inc., 1950), 424–5. Flutes, trumpets, trombones, and horns in sacred music are the subject of a complaint by a Veronese musical reformer as early as 1529. See Christopher A. Reynolds, 'Sacred Polyphony', in Howard M. Brown and

into the church for playing in sacred music, although different churches had their preferred ensembles. St Mark's, for example, relied most heavily on members of the violin family, cornettos, trombones, bassoons, and theorbos. Violas da gamba, recorders, and shawms are not mentioned, at least during the period surrounding Monteverdi's Vespers.[16]

Praetorius gives elaborate and extravagant suggestions for instrumental doubling and substitution in sacred music. Some of the instruments he recommends were not usually found in Italy, and his suggestions in many cases may reflect the adaptation of Italian practices to the instrumental ensembles common in Germany.[17] Nevertheless, his frequent references to Italian composers, theorists, and genres demonstrate that he was well acquainted with contemporary Italian style and practices.[18] Indeed, he bases many of his recommendations on the music of Giovanni Gabrieli and Monteverdi, and even if he is not always consistent with the documentary evidence from St Mark's, his suggestions for the use of cornettos, violins, violas, violas da gamba, trombones, and bassoons are all feasible within the framework of known Italian instrumental resources. Praetorius also permits octave doubling of parts, both above and below, but with the caveat that doubling in the lower octave must not obscure the harmonic foundation.[19]

Praetorius clearly favours a large-scale, colourful ensemble for the multi-choir music of Gabrieli. His suggestions are based on multiple three-, four-, and five-part choirs, each usually with a different set of clefs. Basic to his concept is that at least one of the parts in each choir must be sung; the voice may carry that part alone or may be doubled by an instrument.[20] In general, Praetorius recommends unmixed instrumental choirs, such as a choir of violas da gamba, a choir of violas, or a choir of trombones. However, his allowances for instrumental substitutions may produce choirs in which cornettos, recorders, or transverse flutes play upper parts, while trombones or trombones and bassoons play lower parts. Similarly, in a choir of violas, or violas da gamba, a trombone or a bassoon may take the bottom part. Other combinations may mix a cornetto with violas, a violin with a cornetto, and trombone, or a recorder, violin, trombone, and

---

Stanley Sadie, eds., *Performance Practice: Music before 1600* (New York: W. W. Norton & Company, 1989), 193.

[16] These instruments, along with lutes, spinets, and flageolets, do appear in early 17th-century documents from other Venetian churches, however. See Eleanor Selfridge-Field, *Venetian Instrumental Music from Gabrieli to Vivaldi* (New York: Praeger Publishers, 1975), 26–33.

[17] *Syntagmatis musici . . . tomus tertius* (Wolfenbüttel: Elias Holwein, 1619); fac. ed. Wilibald Gurlitt (Kassel: Bärenreiter, 1958), 152–228; Eng. trans. in Hans A. Lampl, 'A Translation of *Syntagma musicum III* by Michael Praetorius' (DMA dissertation, University of Southern California, 1957), 259–366.

[18] See esp. *Syntagmatis musici . . . tomus tertius*, pt. II, ch. 12, and pt. III, chs. 1–7 (pp. 91–168); trans. Lampl, pp. 156–282.

[19] *Syntagmatis musici . . . tomus tertius*, 92–100, 137–8 (recte 117–18), 161; trans. Lampl, pp. 158–9, 162–71, 202, 204, 272.

[20] *Syntagmatis musici . . . tomus tertius*, 152–4; trans. Lampl, 259–63.

bassoon.[21] Cornettos, recorders, and violins are virtually interchangeable for upper parts and may be mixed in combinations such as two violins and one cornetto, and one violin, one cornetto, and one recorder. But despite Praetorius's view of the interchangeability of treble instruments, he still prefers cornettos to be supported by trombones, and violins to be supported by violas.

Praetorius's recommendations, while wider in scope than our current picture of Italian resources and practices, nevertheless reflect the experience of a practical musician, not a mere theoretician. He is invariably concerned with the immediate sound effect of a particular selection of instruments, and many of his suggestions concern practical ways to improve that sonority. Although modern instruments or modern reproductions of early instruments do not necessarily bring with them all of the practical problems encountered by musicians of the early seventeenth century, the spirit of Praetorius's comments should be kept in mind. Orchestration is not to be chosen on the basis of hard and fast theories, but on the underlying principles of seventeenth-century instrumentation with a keen ear for what is suitable for the voices employed and effective in the acoustical space where a performance is to take place.

Italian sources of the early seventeenth century corroborate some of Praetorius's suggestions for Gabrieli's music. Several motets in Gabrieli's posthumous *Symphoniae sacrae* of 1615 specify instruments, even if they are marked *si placet*.[22] *Suscipe clementissimae Deus* from this collection has a choir of six voices and another choir of six trombones playing together throughout. In *Jubilate Deo*, not only is there an optional sinfonia for two cornettos, five trombones, bassoon, and organ, but seven of the eight instrumental parts have the rubric *Cornetto* [or other instrument] *e Voce si placet*. The rubric is simply missing from the eighth instrumental part, since it, like all the other parts except the organ, is fully texted. The implication of these rubrics is that any combination of doubling and/or substitution is possible.[23] *Surrexit Christus*, on the other hand, has eight separate parts for instruments alone (two cornettos, two violins, four trombones, and organ) and three parts for voices in the C_3, C_4, and F_4 clefs respectively. The instruments not only play an initial sinfonia and a purely instrumental interlude, but also occasionally double the vocal parts; but mostly they play independent counterpoint to the voices throughout much of the composition. *Quem vidistis pastores* has a lengthy introductory sinfonia (not marked *si placet*), and after an extended section for single voice parts plus a brief duet, the instruments (two cornettos, three trombones, three unspecified

---

[21] *Syntagmatis musici . . . tomus tertius*, 156–8; trans. Lampl, pp. 266–9.

[22] Ed. Denis Arnold in *Giovanni Gabrieli: Opera omnia*, iii–v (Rome: American Institute of Musicology, 1962–9).

[23] I agree with the interpretation of Richard Charteris on this point. See Charteris, 'The Performance of Giovanni Gabrieli's Vocal Works', 338–9.

instruments in the F₁ and F₃ clefs, and the organ) join them, the instruments often doubling the voices at the unison or octave, for the remainder of the piece. The well-known *In ecclesiis* calls for three obbligato cornettos, a violin, and two trombones (in addition to the organ), which play an internal sinfonia, reinforce the voice parts in homophonic *alleluias*, occasionally double voices, and play intricate, independent parts of their own. The instruments Gabrieli specifies in these motets are those found in the payment records of St Mark's, reported by Moore: cornettos, trombones, violins, and occasionally a bassoon. The notated instrumental parts *si placet* also suggest the possibility of instrumental doubling and substitution for voices where not specified, and Richard Charteris has found ample indications that this was often the practice.[24] In contrast to the motets, the three Magnificats in Gabrieli's *Symphoniae sacrae*, the only vesper items in the print, do not have any notated obbligato or optional instruments, although this would not necessarily preclude the use of *ad libitum* orchestration.

It is also apparent that instruments were used in the Gonzaga ducal church of Santa Barbara in Mantua in the early seventeenth century. While instrumentalists other than organists were never on the payroll at Santa Barbara or in the nearby cathedral of San Pietro, court musicians could be utilized in the ducal church and presumably in the cathedral, Sant'Andrea, and other Mantuan churches as well.[25] Instrumentalists employed at the court in the early seventeenth century included organists, harpsichordists and spinet players, lutenists, theorbists, harpists, Spanish guitarists, a player of the *lira*, string players, cornettists, trombonists, and a trumpeter.[26] The one composition in the 1610 Vespers that has been connected with the ducal church is the hymn *Ave maris stella*, whose chant is close to the variant unique to the rite of that institution.[27] *Ave maris stella* calls for a ritornello of five unspecified instruments, although the ritornello could conceivably have been omitted. One printed collection of music among the surviving sources from Santa Barbara, Amante Franzoni's *Apparato musicale di messa, sinfonie, canzoni, motetti, & letanie della Beata Vergine* of 1613, con-

---

[24] I agree with the interpretation of Richard Charteris on this point.

[25] Pierre M. Tagmann, 'The Palace Church of Santa Barbara in Mantua, and Monteverdi's Relationship to its Liturgy', in Burton L. Karson, ed., *Festival Essays for Pauline Alderman* (Provo, Ut.: Brigham Young University Press, 1976), 56, 58; and id., 'La cappella dei maestri cantori della basilica palatina di Santa Barbara a Mantova (1565–1630)', *Civiltà mantovana*, 4 (1969–70), 377. See also the list of musicians employed at Santa Barbara and at the cathedral in Susan Helen Parisi, 'Ducal Patronage of Music in Mantua, 1587–1627: An Archival Study' (Ph.D. dissertation, University of Illinois at Urbana-Champaign, 1989), 517–39.

[26] See the detailed account of individual musicians at court in ibid. 399–517. It is not always known what instrument or instruments a musician employed at court played.

[27] Paola Besutti, 'Ricorrenze motiviche, canti dati e "cantus firmus" nella produzione sacra di Claudio Monteverdi' (paper delivered at Convegno, Claudio Monteverdi: studi e prospettive, Mantua, 21–4 Oct. 1993, published as ' "Ave maris stella": La tradizione mantovane nuovamente posta in musica da Monteverdi' in Paola Besutti, Teresa M. Gialdroni, and Rodolfo Baroncini, eds., *Claudio Monteverdi: Studi e prospettive, Atti del Convegno (Mantova, 21–24 ottobre 1993)* (Florence: Olschki, 1993), 57–77. See the discussion of this matter in Ch. 1 above.

tains a short introductory instrumental piece for the Introit, ritornellos for the Kyrie, instrumental canzonas and sinfonias for various portions of the mass Ordinary and Proper, and a concerto for soprano and four trombones.[28] The concerto is a setting of the same Litany of the Saints, addressed to Mary, that appears in Monteverdi's more elaborate concerto for soprano and instruments, the *Sonata sopra Sancta Maria*.[29] In his dedication, Franzoni indicates that his mass was performed in the ducal church on the feast of Santa Barbara and represented 'that sort of music that is to the taste of my masters and that I judged suitable for such an important day'.[30] It should be noted that there was a separate altar to the Virgin in the church of Santa Barbara.[31]

The obbligato instruments in Monteverdi's *Domine ad adjuvandum* and the larger Magnificat, as well as the unspecified instrumental ritornellos in *Dixit Dominus* and *Ave maris stella*, all point to significant use of instruments on important liturgical occasions in Mantua, possibly in Santa Barbara, but perhaps also in the cathedral, in Sant'Andrea, and in other churches of the city. If obbligato and optional instruments figure prominently in the Vespers, it is probable that *ad libitum* instruments were used to double and/or substitute for voices in Mantuan sacred music on many occasions where they are not specified in the musical sources. It should be remembered that Monteverdi's 1610 print is the most detailed sacred publication of its age in terms of performance instructions, notated ornamentation, and notated instrumentation, and that other sacred music, both in Mantua and elsewhere, was possibly performed at times just as elaborately without such performance details having been notated in either manuscripts or prints.

Monteverdi's orchestration in his sacred music allows for the free mixing of instruments across registers, but he does not mix two different timbres in the same register unless one pair of instruments doubles another. Thus he may call for two violins and two cornettos to play the same pair of lines, but he never specifies one violin and one cornetto on two different treble parts, or the mixture of violin, cornetto, and recorder suggested by Praetorius. Monteverdi also

[28] Listed in Gugliemo Barblan, ed., *Musiche della Cappella di S. Barbara in Mantova* (Florence: Leo S. Olschki Editore, 1972), 153–5. According to Franzoni's title-page, the instruments represent *un novo ordine*. Franzoni had only recently become the *maestro di cappella* of Santa Barbara (see Chs. 1 and 4). See also Graham Dixon, '"Behold our Affliction": Celebration and Supplication in the Gonzaga Household', *Early Music*, 24 (1996), 250–61.

[29] See Ch. 4 for a discussion of similar pieces and their relationship to Monteverdi's *Sonata*.

[30] 'quella sorte di Musiche che ed' al gust de' Padroni, ed' alla grandezza d'un tanto giorno guidicai più convenevole'. The *Apparato musicale* (RISM F1813) also contains a motet, *Duo Seraphim*, for eight voices, with exactly the same text as Monteverdi's *Duo Seraphim*. As Graham Dixon has demonstrated, the Trinitarian text *Duo Seraphim* was particularly suited to Santa Barbara, who was martyred for her belief in the Trinity. See Dixon, 'Monteverdi's Vespers of 1610: "della Beata Vergine"?', *Early Music*, 15 (1987), 386–9. See Ch. 4 above for a discussion of the role of the motet *Duo Seraphim*.

[31] See Paola Besutti, 'Ceremoniale e repertorio liturgico della basilica palatina di Santa Barbara in Mantova' (thesis, University of Parma, 1984–5), 16.

sometimes displays Praetorius's predilection for choirs of like instruments; for example, a number of compositions in the *Selva morale e spirituali* of 1641 call for optional doubling by four trombones or violas (*viole da braccio*).

Praetorius's discussion of orchestration in multiple choirs is directly applicable to only two of Monteverdi's compositions in the 1610 Vespers: *Nisi Dominus* and *Ave maris stella*. However, the division of *Lauda Jerusalem* into two overlapping vocal ensembles may suggest similar treatment. Where these *cori spezzati* compositions differ from those described by Praetorius is in their distribution of voices. Praetorius's concept of orchestration is based on the assumption that different choirs are in different registers, an arrangement often found in Gabrieli. But in each of these three pieces Monteverdi's two choirs are in the same register, with an identical combination of clefs. Thus Praetorius's contrast of high and low instruments of opposing timbres, such as recorders and trombones, is not suited to the disposition of Monteverdi's voices. Moreover, Monteverdi's orchestration elsewhere in the Vespers does not reveal such contrasts; rather, he mixes sonorities so that the upper parts may consist of violins and cornettos and the lower parts of violas and trombones. This suggests that if instruments are to be used to double or substitute for vocal parts in both choirs of *Nisi Dominus, Ave maris stella,* or *Lauda Jerusalem,* the two choirs should be orchestrated alike, just as their voices are distributed equally.

In deciding whether to employ instruments at all in these three pieces, especially in the clearly *cori spezzati* works *Nisi Dominus* and *Ave maris stella,* it is well to recall James H. Moore's caution that instruments do not seem to have been used in performances of *cori spezzati* psalms (and perhaps *cori spezzati* hymns as well) at St Mark's (see Chapter 15 above), where *cori spezzati* psalmody served a special religious function.[32] However, instrumental doubling or substitution in polychoral music was common in Rome and dated well back into the sixteenth century in northern Italy as well, as evidenced by the 1573 print of Camatero cited at the beginning of this chapter. Considering that *cori spezzati* psalms were performed at St Mark's and perhaps elsewhere with solo voices in one of the choirs and with vocal doubling in the other, it may be appropriate to double or substitute with instruments only in the *ripieno* choir, thereby creating an even greater sonorous contrast between the *cori spezzati.*

Praetorius's commentary on Monteverdi's *Ave maris stella* (see Chapter 15 above for his remarks on the use of a solo choir and the *capella*) recommends that 'in the seventh [last] verse both choirs with instruments [utilized for the ritornellos] and voices perform together'.[33] This procedure enhances further the climactic double-choir setting of the last verse, especially since Praetorius does not

---

[32] 'The *Vespero delli Cinque Laudate* and the Role of *salmi spezzati* at St Mark's', *Journal of the American Musicological Society*, 34 (1981), 249–78.

[33] *Syntagmatis musici . . . tomus tertius*, 128 (recte 108); trans. Lampl, pp. 184–5.

mention instrumental doubling for any other verse. Praetorius's recommendation thus offers a rationale for Monteverdi's omission of the ritornello between the sixth and seventh verses: if the ritornello instruments double the final verse, an instrumental ritornello following the sixth verse will prove superfluous.

In *Dixit Dominus*, the other composition with ritornellos, the ritornello instruments could well be used for doubling of some verses. However, instrumental doubling would be inadvisable for the verses in *falsobordone* and those scored for a duet of voices over the psalm tone bass (*Virgam virtutis* and *Juravit Dominus*). The verse *Judicabit in nationibus*, because of its analogy to *Virgam virtutis* and *Juravit Dominus*, should probably also be spared doubling. Like the verses in duet, the *Gloria patri*, for tenor alone, would be better left without instrumental participation. In addition, the polyphonic melismas following each *falsobordone* verse should be performed by voices alone in order for the subsequent ritornellos, which resemble the melismas, to provide an effective tonal contrast.

The rubric for *Laudate pueri*, 'for 8 solo voices with the organ' (*à 8 voci sole nel Organo*), implies an injunction against instrumental doubling or substitution in this piece. If instruments were to participate, the eight solo voices would lose their intimacy and unique sonority. Moreover, Monteverdi's phrase *nel Organo* implies that the continuo is to consist of the organ alone, without additional foundation instruments.

Laetatus sum might well be subject to instrumental doubling, particularly in its denser passages. If so, the organ bass-line, with its repetitive walking bass pattern in several sections, could be supported by a bassoon and/or bass violin (cello in modern terms), depending on the amount and character of doubling in the upper parts. If trombones are used with the voices, the bassoon would be a particularly appropriate doubling instrument for the bass according to Praetorius's criteria. A combination of violins, cornettos, violas, and trombones would be comparable to the orchestration Monteverdi requires in *Domine ad adjuvandum*, where there are also six separate parts. The virtuoso duet textures in *Laetatus sum*, which require solo voices, should be left without doubling, as should the virtuoso passage at *Propter* (bars 147–57). In the other duet textures, which are not virtuosic in character, doubling may depend on whether or not soloists are employed. Multiple singers on a part could be supported by doubling instruments, but soloists are better left without doubling.

Monteverdi's four motets in the 1610 Vespers are all for virtuoso soloists, and are therefore inappropriate for instrumental doubling. Only in *Audi coelum* does instrumental doubling seem feasible, in the section *omnes hanc ergo*, where the texture expands to six-voice polyphony (see the discussion of this section in Chapter 15 above). The issue of doubling in these motets impinges principally on the role of the continuo, since doubling of the voice by the continuo realization requires careful consideration (see discussion of this question in Chapter 14 above).

The response, *Sonata sopra Sancta Maria*, and Magnificat *a 7* all have detailed orchestration notated in Monteverdi's print. As a consequence, these pieces should be left as they are, without disturbing the combinations of timbre and the balances of sonority Monteverdi has so carefully annotated.

This discussion of *ad libitum* instruments has focused primarily on doubling of vocal parts, although it is clear from the sixteenth- and seventeenth-century sources noted above, as well as many others, that instruments sometimes replaced voices. Such substitutions are infrequent in modern performances of the Monteverdi Vespers, which often take the original notation as literally as possible. Nevertheless, it is obvious that substitutions were quite common in the sixteenth and seventeenth centuries, perhaps even the rule.[34] Modern performers may commendably wish to adhere to the version presented in Monteverdi's original notation, but they should also be aware of the possibilities for substitution and the frameworks within which they may be justifiably applied.

Note should also be taken that polyphonic instruments normally associated with the continuo can also be employed for instrumental doubling or substitution for vocal parts in the same manner as single-line instruments. The lute, theorbo, and double harp thus offer even further sonorities that might be utilized in Monteverdi's psalms, without these instruments necessarily functioning as continuo.[35]

[34] See e.g. Howard Mayer Brown, *Sixteenth-Century Instrumentation: The Music of the Florentine Intermedii* (American Institute of Musicology, 1973), 73–4.

[35] On the use of these instruments for doubling or substitution see Agazzari, *Del sonare sopra'l basso.* Eng. trans. in Strunk, *Source Readings in Music History*, 427. See also Gloria Rose, 'Agazzari and the Improvising Orchestra', *Journal of the American Musicological Society*, 18 (1965), 382–93. Agazzari's treatise was republished in his *Sacrarum cantionum . . . liber II, opus V* (Venice, 1608) (RISM A353), thereby clearly establishing its reference to sacred music (which is also mentioned in the text).

20

Metre and Tempo

QUESTIONS of metre, of mensural proportions, and of their relationship to tempo in the second half of the sixteenth century and the first half of the seventeenth century are among the thorniest issues faced by musicology and performance practice studies of this period. Conflicts and inconsistencies among theorists, diversity in notational practice, variety in the interpretation of notation in performance, changing styles, new genres, and variability in predominant note values all contribute to a sometimes bewildering picture of rhythmic notation, metric signatures, and their significance for tempo.[1]

The present chapter attempts to sort out the most pertinent threads from Renaissance and early Baroque theory and practice that bear on an understanding of Monteverdi's notation in the 1610 Vespers and how we might interpret it. 'Interpret' is the key word in this endeavour, for there can be no real proof of what tempos Monteverdi conceived for his various compositions, nor of what tempo relationships (if any) he may have intended between sections of pieces in duple metre and sections in triple time (notated in three different ways).[2] The examination of sources below highlights consistencies and trends in the

---

[1] A recent detailed study of mensuration signs and proportions in theoretical treatises from the late middle ages to the mid-16th century (but including some commentary on later writers) is Anna Maria Busse Berger, *Mensuration and Proportion Signs: Origins and Evolution* (Oxford: Clarendon Press, 1993). Even more recently, proportions in the 16th century have been re-examined in Ruth I. DeFord, 'Tempo Relationships between Duple and Triple Time in the Sixteenth Century', *Early Music History*, 14 (1995), 1–51. DeFord has studied Zacconi's writings on this subject in 'Zacconi's Theories of *Tactus* and Mensuration', *Journal of Musicology*, 14 (1996), 151–82. A discussion of 17th-century mensural practices according to theorists is found in George Houle, *Meter in Music, 1600–1800: Performance, Perception, and Notation* (Bloomington, Ind.: Indiana University Press, 1987), 1–34. A comprehensive study of Italian rhythmic and metric notation in the period 1571–1630 is Uwe Wolf, *Notation und Aufführungspraxis: Studien zum Wandel von Notenschrift und Notenbild in italienischen Musikdrucken der Jahre 1571–1630*, 2 vols. (Berlin and Kassel: Verlag Merseburger, 1992).

[2] Roger Bowers, in 'Some Reflection upon Notation and Proportions in Monteverdi's Mass and Vespers of 1610', *Music & Letters*, 73 (1992), 347–98, attempts to interpret proportions in the Mass and Vespers strictly according to the mathematical theory of proportions. His conclusions often result in tempos that are much too slow for sections in triple metre. Bowers's approach to questions of proportion ignores complications introduced by smaller note values than those envisaged by the theory of proportions, the practical issues of beating the tactus in the *concertato* style, new notational means for indicating tempo relationships, stylistic criteria as determinants of tempo, contemporary theorists' accounts of proportions, and the voluminous secondary literature addressing this complicated subject. See the correspondence on this issue between Bowers and myself in *Music & Letters*, 74 (1993), 487–95, and 75 (1994), 145–54. More recently, Bowers has applied the same approaches to *Orfeo*; see his

theoretical literature, leading to a consistent and coherent interpretation of Monteverdi's notation. It would be foolish, however, to claim that my interpretation is definitive. The sources are, in the end, too vague and sometimes even self-contradictory, and there are multiple ways of understanding these sources, as well as many other theorists whose writings have not been brought into the discussion.[3] In order to keep the main body of the text as unencumbered as possible by the complexities of the arguments, I have relegated more detailed commentary on the theoretical sources and on the secondary literature interpreting these sources to the footnotes. As a consequence, this chapter may be read as comprising a relatively brief summary of my conclusions in the main body of the text, and a more detailed gloss, further explaining the arguments, in the footnotes.

In the last segment of this chapter I offer my recommendations for tempo ranges and tempo relationships between successive sections in different metres for each composition in the Vespers. Where it proves helpful in understanding these recommendations, I have provided a brief explanation of my choices. Readers should consider these informed interpretations rather than definitive rulings, and every choir director or solo singer undertaking a performance of some or all of this music must ultimately decide personally what will work best in the anticipated performance circumstances.

Several writers in the Renaissance and early Baroque related tempo to the rhythm of the human pulse, which, with the body at rest, may range from approximately sixty to as many as one hundred beats per minute.[4] Thus the mid-

---

'Proportional Notations in Monteverdi's "Orfeo"', *Music & Letters*, 76 (1995), 149–67. See also his highly problematic article on Banchieri, 'Proportional Notations in Banchieri's Theory and Monteverdi's Music', in Raffaello Monterosso, ed., *Performing Practice in Monteverdi's Music: The Historic-Philological Background* (Cremona: Fondazione Claudio Monteverdi, 1995), 53–92. The same controversy over proportions in the Vespers, though pursued in less detail, appeared simultaneously in a German journal. See Roland Eberlein, 'Die Taktwechsel in Monteverdis Marienvesper', *Music und Kirche*, 62 (1992), 184–9; and the response by Uwe Wolf, 'Monteverdi und die Proportionen: Eine Entgegnung auf Roland Eberleins Aufsatz "Die Taktwechsel in Monteverdis Marienvesper"', *Musik und Kirche*, 63 (1993), 91–5.

[3] A completely different interpretation of the meaning of early 17th-century proportions from that of Bowers and Eberlein is found in Paul Brainard, 'Proportional Notation in the Music of Schütz and his Contemporaries', *Current Musicology*, 50 (1992), 21–46. Brainard argues that triple proportional mensurations were then taking on implications of tempo rather than proportions, much as $\mathircal{C}$ and C already had, both in theory and practice. See also Gordon Paine, 'Tactus, Tempo, and Praetorius' in Gordon Paine, ed. *Five Centuries of Choral Music: Essays in Honor of Howard Swan* (Stuyvesant, NY: Pendragon Press, 1988), 167–216. A particularly interesting study of early 17th-century mensurations and tempo relationships, applicable in some respects to Monteverdi's Mass and Vespers, is Étienne Darbellay, 'Tempo Relationships in Frescobaldi's *Primo libro di capricci*', in Alexander Silbiger, ed., *Frescobaldi Studies* (Durham, NC: Duke University Press, 1987), 301–26. Darbellay's interpretations of Frescobaldi's mensural practice and its tempo implications parallel many of my own for Monteverdi. Wolf, however, rejects Darbellay's analysis of Frescobaldi's notation, though not Darbellay's conclusions about tempo relationships. See Wolf, *Notation*, i. 101.

[4] These figures, which vary from one individual to another, have been provided by medical personnel.

range is approximately 75–85 beats per minute. The unit of musical measure was related by Bartolomeo Ramis de Pareia in the late fifteenth century to 'an even moment between the diastole [dilation] and systole [contraction] of a body. . . . therefore, when a singer wishes to sing accurately and equally, let him activate the equivalent of his pulse by striking a foot, hand, or finger on some surface while singing.'[5] A few years later Franchinus Gaffurius drew a relationship between the semibreve and the pulse, like Ramis, dividing his unit into 'diastole and systole, or arsis and thesis, which are mutually opposed and the smallest parts of a pulse'.[6] However, it is clear from Gaffurius's three different statements regarding this relationship that he considered the single pulse to encompass both the diastole and systole and to fall on the semibreve.[7] The smallest principal note value described by both Ramis and Gaffurius is the minim, and Gaffurius's own music is notated principally in semibreves and minims, with semiminims (hereafter, crotchets) reserved mostly for ornamental notes devoid of text.[8] A tempo of semibreve = MM 60–70 works well in Gaffurius's music, though it produces a livelier pace than some ensembles and audiences may be accustomed to in Renaissance music. It should be understood, of course, that a tempo range such as this is only an approximation, and that some compositions or individual mass movements might well profit from a somewhat slower or faster tempo. Nevertheless, the range of the human pulse serves as a reasonable point of departure.

---

[5] *Musica practica* (Bologna, 1482), pt. III, Tractatus 1, chs. 1 and 2; ed. Johannes Wolf (Leipzig: Breitkopf und Härtel, 1901), 77, 83; Eng. trans. Clement A. Miller as *Bartolomeo Ramis de Pareia, Musica practica* (Neuhausen and Stuttgart: Hänssler Verlag, American Institute of Musicology, 1993), 137–8, 144–5 (bracketed passages mine). Ramis declares that 'we must know through diverse signs on which notes we should place a complete measure'. He subsequently describes the note value on which the pulse occurs in different mensurations, resulting in the placement of the pulse variously on the breve, the semibreve, or the minim. It is not quite clear from Ramis's description whether he considers the pulse to equal the diastole and systole individually or in combination. His reference to the measure or bar (*tempus*) as the 'interval which comprises an even moment between the diastole and systole' suggests that there are separate pulses for the diastole and the systole.

[6] *Practica musice* (Milan, 1496; fac. edns. Westmead: Gregg Press Ltd., 1967, and New York: Broude Brothers Ltd., 1979), bk. ii, chs. 1 and 3 and bk. iii, ch. 4; Eng. trans. Clement A. Miller as *Franchinus Gaffurius, Practica musicae* (American Institute of Musicology, 1968), 70, 75, 129. Gaffurius describes the normal pulse as equal, but the pulse of fevered persons as unequal, thereby relating the pulse to both duple and triple time.

[7] These three statements are quoted in Dale Bonge, 'Gaffurius on Pulse and Tempo: A Reinterpretation', *Musica disciplina*, 36 (1982), 167–74. Bonge has attempted to dissociate the semibreve from the pulse rate in his reading of Gaffurius's three pertinent passages, but I do not find his argument convincing. Carl Dahlhaus has argued that Gaffurius's reference to the pulse is an intellectual analogy and is 'not to be understood as a description of the rhythmic character of mensural music'. See 'Zur Theorie des Tactus im 16. Jahrhundert', *Archiv für Musikwissenschaft*, 17 (1960), 26. Ramis, however, in the statement quoted in n. 5 above, drew a direct relationship between the pulse and beating time in music. In a recent article, Ephraim Segerman gives an interpretation of Ramis and Gaffurius in accord with mine, adding evidence from Johannes Vetulus (*c*.1350) and Michaele Savanarola (*c*.1440). See Segerman, 'A Re-examination of the Evidence on Absolute Tempo before 1700—I', *Early Music*, 24 (1996), 227–31.

[8] Gaffurius describes smaller, ornamental note values as well in *Practica musice*, bk. ii, ch. 4. His music is found in Franchinus Gafurius, *Collected Musical Works*, 2 vols., ed. Lutz Finscher (Rome: American Institute of Musicology, 1955).

In 1533, Giovanni Maria Lanfranco described the beat (*battuta*) as 'a certain sign formed in imitation of the motion of the healthy pulse by whoever leads raising and lowering his hand', declaring that it may be placed on the breve, the semibreve, or the minim, depending on the mensuration (the minim beat would have been under the mensuration of major prolation designating augmentation, C).[9] Shortly after mid-century, Gioseffe Zarlino recommended that the beat of the hand 'be regulated in its movement like the human pulse'.[10] Zarlino's conception of the pulse (following Galen) was that it consisted of 'a certain broadening and tightening, or . . . a rising and falling of the heart and of the arteries'.[11] Zarlino then equated the systole and diastole with the downward and upward motion of the conductor's hand (the tactus), which rests between each motion.[12] Zarlino, like many other theorists of the sixteenth century, indicated that the tactus was frequently beaten on the semibreve, reflecting predominant rhythmic movement in semibreves, minims, and crotchets.[13] However, the *note nere* madrigal of the mid-sixteenth century utilized minims, crotchets, and quavers (fusae) as principal values, and one of the authors of a *note nere* madrigal in these values directs that it should be sung to a minim beat.[14] Such short note values became common alongside the more traditional void notes in the secular repertoire of the second half of the century.[15] Moreover, the fusae that had constituted ornamental notes in the *note nere* madrigal eventually came to be frequent bearers of their own syllables in the more declamatory

[9] *Scintille di musica* (Brescia: Britannico, 1533); fac. ed. Giuseppe Massera (Bologna: Forni Editore, 1970), 67; Eng. trans. from Barbara Lee, 'Giovanni Maria Lanfranco's *Scintille di musica* and its Relation to 16th-century Music Theory' (Ph.D. dissertation, Cornell University, 1961), 149. On the minim beat in perfect prolation, see Berger, *Mensuration and Proportion Signs*, 96–103, 110–12.

[10] *Le istitutioni harmoniche* (Venice, 1558; fac. New York: Broude Brothers, 1965), 207; Eng. trans. in Guy A. Marco and Claude V. Palisca as *Gioseffo Zarlino, The Art of Counterpoint, Part Three of 'Le istitutioni harmoniche', 1558* (New Haven: Yale University Press, 1968), 117.

[11] *Le istitutioni harmoniche*, 207; trans. in Marco and Palisca, *Gioseffo Zarlino, The Art of Counterpoint*, 117.

[12] Ibid. Zarlino refers to the downward motion of the hand as *Positione, overo il Battere* and the upward motion as *a Levatione*.

[13] *Le istitutioni harmoniche*, 208. See also Dahlhaus, 'Zur Theorie des Tactus im 16. Jahrhundert', 31–2. In 1540 Seybald Heyden, in his influential *De arte canendi*, proposed a semibreve tactus for all music written under O and C. Ȼ and ₵ were signs of diminution and required a breve tactus, while O and C were signs of augmentation and required a minim tactus. The semibreve tactus served as the central reference point for these proportions. See Heyden, *De arte canendi* (Nuremberg: Joh. Petreium, 1540); Eng. trans. Clement A. Miller (American Institute of Musicology, 1972), 10, 20–2, 53–4, 97–102. Heyden's emphasis on the semibreve tactus as a reference ensures that proportions are actually proportional, in contrast to the practice about which he complains, whereby changing tactus speed when changing mensurations garbled the proportions. While Heyden does not mention any relationship between tactus and pulse or beat, Miller recommends that MM 36 is a suitable tempo for the semibreve tactus in Heyden's music examples, giving MM 72 for the minim, or each separate motion of the hand.

[14] The composition is by Thomaso Cimello from his *Libro primo de canti* of 1548. See Alfred Einstein, *The Italian Madrigal*, 2nd edn. (Princeton: Princeton University Press, 1971), i. 404–5. Cimello was also a theorist and in his single surviving treatise stressed the minim beat in perfect prolation. See Berger, *Mensuration and Proportion Signs*, 96.

[15] See James Haar, 'The *note nere* Madrigal', *Journal of the American Musicological Society*, 18 (1965), 35.

madrigals of the last decade of the sixteenth century. This changing role of the fusa can be readily observed in Monteverdi's first five books of madrigals. By the latter part of the sixteenth century, at least one theorist had described a minim tactus under the mensuration C.[16]

The downward shift in the note values of the tactus, or unit of beat, must also have meant a shifting of the pulse to smaller note values.[17] As a consequence, compositions with different predominant note values would all have tended to fall within a single, but fairly broad, range of pacings, contradicting the notion that a composition in note values one level smaller than another (though quite possibly under the same mensuration) necessarily moved twice as fast.[18]

Near the end of the sixteenth century Lodovico Zacconi continued to equate the movement of music with the pulse, but noted that singers determined that movement from the values of the notes in the composition.[19] Adriano Banchieri, writing in the early seventeenth century, was more vague, simply indicating that 'some say that it [the *battuta*, i.e. the tactus] is produced by the systole and diastole, which means the human pulse'.[20] Banchieri's Roman

[16] Eucharius Hoffmann in his *Musica practicae praecepta* (Wittemberg, 1572), ch. 10. See Martin Ruhnke, *Joachim Burmeister* (Kassel: Bärenreiter-Verlag, 1955), 80–1; and Carl Dahlhaus, 'Zur Entstehung des modernen Taktsystems im 17. Jahrhundert', *Archiv für Musikwissenschaft*, 18 (1961), 225. An interpretation of Hoffmann's discussion of tactus is given in Hans Otto Hiekel, 'Der Madrigal- und Motettentypus in der Mensurallehre des Michael Praetorius', *Archiv für Musikwissenschaft*, 19–20 (1962–3), 51–2, but is contradicted in Carl Dahlhaus, 'Zur Taktlehre des Michael Praetorius', *Die Musikforschung*, 17 (1964), 169. A *tactus alla minima* was earlier associated with mensurations indicating augmentation. See n. 5 above and Dahlhaus, 'Zur Theorie des Tactus im 16. Jahrhundert', 31–3. Such augmentation bears an analogy to the use of smaller note values in the early 17th century—in both instances smaller notes in the notation require that the tactus be beaten on smaller note values.

[17] See Hiekel, 'Der Madrigal- und Motettentypus', 52, for a demonstration of how this is reflected in 16th-century theory. Segerman, 'A Re-examination', 232–9, quotes a number of 16th-century and 17th-century writers who describe the maximum number of notes various instrumentalists can play in a second or other fixed period of time, thereby determining a slower beat or shifting of the pulse to a smaller note value in order to accommodate the rapid notes.

[18] Some modern writers have promoted the theory of a uniform tactus in the Renaissance. This view derives from Seybald Heyden's attempted reform of the mensural system in his *De arte canendi* of 1540. Dahlhaus has shown, however, that practice before the middle of the century was otherwise, though Heyden found many sympathizers in the second half of the century. Heyden's conception of a uniform tactus, however, contradicted the traditional mensural and proportional system, leading to a reinterpretation of the meaning of proportion signs. See Dahlhaus, 'Zur Theorie des Tactus im 16. Jahrhundert', 22–39. J. A. Bank has demonstrated that many other theorists from the middle of the century onwards did not accept the notion of a uniform tactus. See Bank, *Tactus, Tempo and Notation in Mensural Music from the 13th to the 17th Century* (Amsterdam: Annie Bank, 1972), 211–21. See also Haar, 'The *note nere* Madrigal', 22–7.

[19] *Prattica di musica* (Venice: Girolamo Polo, 1592; fac. Bologna: Forni Editore, 1967), fos. 20[r–v], 24[r]–25[v]. The passage on fos. 24[r]–25[v] comes at the conclusion of a discussion of why composers should notate music with the mensuration C instead of ¢ when the predominant note values are minims and crotchets. Zacconi explicitly equates the semibreve tactus under C with the pulse. Like Praetorius in the next century, Zacconi notes that a shift of tactus from the breve to the semibreve entails a slowing of the tactus. Moreover, Zacconi warns against taking too slow a tactus and recommends instead shifting the tactus to a smaller note value to assist the singer in reading the music. See DeFord, 'Zacconi's Theories of *Tactus* and Mensuration', 158–9.

[20] *Cartella musicale nel canto figurato, fermo, & contrapunto . . . terza impressione* (Venice: Vincenti, 1614); fac. ed. Giuseppe Vecchi (Bologna: Forni Editore, 1968), 33. Eng. trans. in Clifford A. Cranna, Jr.,

contemporary Agostino Pisa gave specific evidence of the practical use of a minim tactus, even though he disapproved of it. Pisa was a conservative theorist, arguing against many contemporary practices, and in a concluding catalogue of errors, criticized those who beat a complete tactus on the minim.[21] Such an admonition would have been unnecessary if a minim tactus had not been practised by the very musicians whom Pisa saw as his adversaries; indeed, Pisa acknowledged that there were practical musicians who did use a minim tactus.[22] Another early seventeenth-century writer who mentioned a minim tactus (*cantar doppio*) in connection with triple time notated in minims was Giovanni Battista Olifante, whose brief comments on perfection, imperfection, and proportions were appended in 1611 to Rocco Rodio's *Regole di musica* of 1609.[23] A minim tactus is frequently mentioned alongside the tactus on the breve and semibreve, as if it were nothing out of the ordinary, by Cesare Crivellati of Viterbo in his *Discorsi musicali* of 1624.[24] However, in the middle of the century, Athanasius Kircher still equated the semibreve tactus with the pulse, but noted that pulse rates differed significantly according to age and in

'Adriano Banchieri's *Cartella musicale* (1614): Translation and Commentary' (Ph.D. dissertation, Stanford University, 1981), 126 (bracketed passages mine).

[21] *Battuta della musica dichiarata* (Rome: Zannetti, 1611); fac. ed. Walther Dürr as *Agostino Pisa, Breve dichiarazione della battuta musicale* (Bologna: Forni Editore, 1969), 134 n. 30. On pp. 32–3 Pisa is explicit in placing theory above practice and declaring that practical musicians must be ruled by theorists. On p. 24 Pisa mentions not only Zarlino's concept of the tactus (see above), but also quotes the theorist Fior Angelico: 'secondly, we consider the measure of time, divided into two motions measured by the human pulse, that is, one rising and the other falling, which is called systole and diastole by those knowledgeable of the body, and arsis and thesis by musicians. Diastole signifies lifting in Latin, systole the opposite.' Note that in drawing the parallel between the systole and the diastole of the heart, Fior Angelico first relates them to rising and falling, but in defining the Latin terms, reverses the parallel. Pisa goes on to discuss the contradiction between speaking of arsis and thesis in that order when describing the voice, and speaking of downward motion followed by upward when describing the beat (Zarlino has a similar order in speaking of a 'broadening and tightening' of the pulse, but indicated a downward and upward motion of the hand. See n. 12 above). A principal thrust of Pisa's treatise is the demonstration that the beat (*battuta*) begins with the raising of the hand, not with the *battere* at the end of the downward motion. For a discussion of Pisa's treatise, see Walther Dürr, 'Auftakt und Taktschlag in der Musik um 1600', in Georg von Dadelsen and Andreas Holschneider, eds., *Festschrift Walter Gerstenberg zum 60. Geburtstag* (Wolfenbüttel: Möseler Verlag, 1964), 26–36. A brief summary of the issues Pisa addressed is found in Houle, *Meter in Music*, 6.

[22] That Pisa was explicitly arguing for the superiority of conservative and speculative theory over contemporary musical practice is demonstrated in Dürr, 'Auftakt und Taktschlag'. Dahlhaus, who had cited Eucharius Hoffmann's *tactus alla minima* (see n. 16 above), argued in 1974 against a minim tactus in the 17th century. See Dahlhaus, 'Zur Geschichte des Taktschlagens im frühen 17. Jahrhundert', in Robert L. Marshall, ed., *Studies in Renaissance and Baroque Music in Honor of Arthur Mendel* (Kassel: Bärenreiter, 1974), 117–23. However, Dahlhaus does not mention Pisa, nor does he consider monody in small note values.

[23] *Trattato brevissimo intorno alle proportioni cantabili, composte dalli prattici musici, nelle loro Messe, Mottetti, Madrigali, & altre opere* (Naples: Carlino, 1611), appended to Rocco Rodio, *Regole di musica* (Naples: Carlino e Vitale, 1609; fac. Bologna: Arnaldo Forni, 1981), 93–9.

[24] *Discorsi musicali, nelli quali si contengono non soló cose pertinenti alla teorica, ma etiandio alla pratica* (Viterbo: Agostino Discep., 1624).

relation to both temperature and humidity.[25] Kircher's Roman contemporary Pier Francesco Valentini drew no association between mensurations and pulse rates, arguing 'that there are as many pulse rates as people'.[26] Unlike Kircher, Valentini recognized beats on smaller values than semibreves; indeed, 'any musical note' could serve as the basis of a beat.[27]

In the early seventeenth century many compositions in modern style display note values smaller than those common in the late sixteenth century, and it seems likely that in pieces where crotchets, quavers, and even semiquavers (semifusae) predominate, musicians would indeed have shifted the tactus from the semibreve to the minim. The purpose would have been the same as that which many theorists gave for shifting the tactus from the breve to the semibreve in the sixteenth century—compositions in smaller note values were too difficult to direct and sing when the tactus was retained on the larger value. That Monteverdi thought of the minim as a structural unit from his earliest madrigals is demonstrated not only by numerous complete cadences on the second half of a semibreve, but perhaps even more significantly, by structural repetitions of entire passages that are displaced by a minim in relation to their first appearance. But whether a musician would beat such compositions on the minim or on the semibreve, the pace of the music was nevertheless determined by the smaller note values, and even with a slow semibreve tactus, the underlying pulse in such music tends to shift to the minim.

The beating of the tactus and its relationship to the pulse are imprecise measurements of time, especially in the notational environment of the early seventeenth century, when such diverse ranges of rhythmic values were used in different compositions and sometimes even in a single composition. Michael Praetorius, in order to provide more precise practical information for the Kapellmeister wishing to know the approximate duration of pieces in Praetorius's own *Polyhymnia caduceatrix*, published a table of the number of breves (*tempora*) in given spans of time at a moderate tempo.[28] Praetorius's

[25] *Musurgia universalis*, 2 vols. (vol. i, Rome: Corbelletti; vol. ii, Rome: Grignani, 1650; fac. Hildesheim: Georg Olms Verlag, 1970), i. 279, ii. 52, 416–19. The latter passage is discussed in Franz Jochen Machatius, *Die Tempi in der Musik um 1600* (Laaber: Laaber Verlag, 1977), 40–1.

[26] Margaret Murata, 'Pier Francesco Valentini on Tactus and Proportion', in Silbiger, ed., *Frescobaldi Studies*, 333. See also n. 92 below.

[27] Ibid. 334, 349 nn. 16 and 17. See also Houle, *Meter in Music*, 7, for a passage in which Valentini says that proportions make it possible for any note to serve as the basis of the tactus. Marin Mersenne also related the musical beat by analogy to the systole and diastole of the heart and pulse, but indicated that musicians do not follow the systole and diastole of the heartbeat, sometimes hurrying the tempo and sometimes taking it rather slowly. See *Harmonie universelle contenant la théorie et la pratique de la musique*, 3 vols. (Paris 1636; fac. Paris: Centre National de la Recherche Scientifique, 1963), ii. 324.

[28] *Syntagmatis musici . . . tomus tertius* (Wolfenbüttel: Elias Holwein, 1619); fac. ed. Wilibald Gurlitt (Kassel: Bärenreiter, 1958), 87–8; Eng. trans. in Hans Lampl, 'A Translation of *Syntagma musicum III* by Michael Praetorius' (DMA dissertation, University of Southern California, 1957), 149–50. Praetorius

calculations, when applied to the characteristic minim and crotchet pace of the *Polyhymnia*, yield a tempo of crotchet = MM 85, near the middle of the range of the normal pulse, as described above.[29] However, even though Praetorius's relationship between number of *tempora* and performance time implies some precision in tempo, his formulation must not be taken too literally. Firstly, his figures serve as a practical reference point to give the Kapellmeister an idea of the duration of particular compositions so that he can choose pieces appropriate to the timing of the other elements of the liturgical service, including the sermon. This does not mean that all compositions in the *Polyhymnia caduceatrix* were intended to proceed at exactly the same pace. Substantial differences in predominant rhythmic values and in the use of *passaggi* between one motet and another preclude that all motets were paced alike. Moreover, Praetorius uses both $\math3C$ and C, and mixes both duple mensurations with 3 $\binom{3}{1}$ and $\frac{3}{2}$ signatures in the *Polyhymnia*. If all *tempora* were to have exactly the same duration, then there would be no distinction in significance between $\math3C$ and C, and 3 $\binom{3}{1}$ and $\frac{3}{2}$ would have identical meanings, the latter simply notated with the rhythmic values halved.[30] Yet Praetorius's *Syntagma musicum* goes to considerable lengths to distinguish the meanings of these mensurations, as described below. Clearly, his crotchet = MM 85 is only a central reference point, and the Kapellmeister could approximate his timings on this basis, depending on how much faster or slower than a 'moderate tempo' he anticipated performing individual pieces and separate sections of the same piece.[31]

While MM 60–100 may be taken as the range of a general pulse standard for the sixteenth and early seventeenth centuries (the note value of the pulse depending on the central note values of the composition), numerous other factors affected a performer's choice of tempo. The mensuration signs not only defined the duple or triple subdivision of notes, but also suggested faster or slower

introduces his table as follows: 'Denn weil ich nothwendig *observiren* müssen wie viel *tempora*, wenn man einen rechten mittelmässigen *Tact* heit in einer viertel Stunde *musiciret* werden können:'.

[29] Praetorius's sentence quoted in n. 28 demonstrates that the 'mittelmässigen Tact' is not the breve, which serves only as a unit of time-span, but rather the minim, which equals MM 42–3, giving a crotchet motion equatable with the human pulse. Ephraim Segerman, in 'Tempo and Tactus after 1500', in Tess Knighton and David Fallows, eds., *Companion to Medieval and Renaissance Music* (New York: Schirmer Books, 1992), 337–44, calculates crotchet tempos from a variety of late 17th-century sources. These fall in the range MM 60–85.

[30] Praetorius also complains in the preface that his mensurations have been garbled in the publication. There are so many inconsistencies in mensurations in the *Polyhymnia* that it is impossible to know what Praetorius actually intended. See Paine, 'Tactus, Tempo, and Praetorius', 190–2.

[31] Hiekel, in 'Der Madrigal- und Motettentypus', takes the opposite view, on the assumption of a single, uniform breve duration, which would give the same tempo to all passages under either $\math3C$ or C, regardless of the predominant note values, and would remove any tempo distinction between $\frac{3}{1}$ and $\frac{3}{2}$. It would also make Praetorius's *sextupla* equal to his $\frac{3}{2}$, despite the description of the *sextupla* as *tactus trochaicus diminutus* in *Syntagma musicum*. See n. 109 below. Hiekel's position is refuted in Dahlhaus, 'Zur Taktlehre des Michael Praetorius' and Paul Brainard, 'Zur Deutung der Diminution in der Tactuslehre des Michael Praetorius', *Die Musikforschung*, 17 (1964), 169–74. Brainard, like me, argues that Praetorius's *tempora* durations are approximations.

tempos and traditionally implied proportional tempo relationships between separate sections of a piece in different mensurations. Signs of diminution, such as ₵ or ₡, implied faster tempos, but the precise proportions were a point of contention among theorists. According to some theorists, a sign of diminution meant a 2 : 1 reduction in note values (or a doubling of the tempo when all parts had the same signature), but some northern European theorists recommended a tempo increase of only one third,[32] while others simply declared that the tactus was beaten more quickly.[33] By the early seventeenth century ₵ had become associated, according to Praetorius, with motets and, according to Adriano Banchieri, with 'serious and easy compositions, as in the Masses, Vespers and Motets of Giovanni Matteo Asola and others'.[34] Pieces in ₵ were supposedly beaten on the breve (two semibreves per tactus), although Banchieri grumbled that the majority of singers sang to the semibreve instead.[35] Indeed, many theorists of the late sixteenth and early seventeenth centuries declared that the breve tactus was no longer in practical use.[36]

The mensuration C, on the other hand, was associated by Praetorius with madrigals, which 'have an abundance of semiminims and fusas',[37] and by Banchieri with compositions that 'use black notes and fast ones, as in the Masses, Vespers, and Motets of Giulio Belli and others'.[38] But despite the stylistic distinctions still drawn by theorists (and some composers) between the two

[32] See Dahlhaus, 'Zur Theorie des Tactus im 16. Jahrhundert', 32–9, and Alejandro Enrique Planchart, 'The Relative Speed of "Tempora" in the Period of Dufay', *Research Chronicle*, 17 (1981), 33, 35–6. In the most comprehensive treatment of this question, Berger demonstrates that it was only northern theorists who suggested diminution by one-third, on the basis of a misunderstanding of Jean de Muris. Italian theorists consistently advocated diminution by half. See Berger, 'The Myth of *diminutio per tertiam partem*', *Journal of Musicology*, 8 (1990), 398–426, and ead., *Mensuration and Proportion Signs*, 120–48.

[33] Tinctoris described the slash, whether in C or O, as an *acceleratio mensurae*. See Rob C. Wegman, 'What is "Acceleratio Mensurae"?', *Music & Letters*, 73 (1992), 515–24. For similar descriptions of a quicker tactus by Glareanus, Hoffmann and a number of minor theorists, see Bank, *Tactus, Tempo and Notation*, 215–21 and 235–6, and DeFord, 'Tempo Relationships', 4, 27–8, 35–6.

[34] *Conclusioni nel suono dell'organo* (Bologna: Rossi, 1609; fac. Bologna: Forni Editore, 1968), 35; Eng. trans. in Lee R. Garrett, *Adriano Banchieri: Conclusions for Playing the Organ (1609)* (Colorado Springs, Col.: Colorado College Music Press, 1982), 30.

[35] Ibid. The practice of singing to a semibreve tactus under ₵ was already long established in the 16th century. See Berger, *Mensuration and Proportion Signs*, 152.

[36] See n. 13 above. Wolf, *Notation*, i. 27–30, cites comments by G. B. Rossi, Zacconi, Brunelli, Banchieri, and Botazzi to demonstrate that the breve tactus was scarcely in use any more by the late 16th century.

[37] *Syntagmatis musici . . . tomus tertius*, 50; trans. Lampl, p. 104. Paine, 'Tactus, Tempo, and Praetorius' is a clear, coherent exposition of Praetorius's writings on mensural signs and their meanings, together with a survey of their practical usage in Praetorius's music.

[38] *Conclusioni*, 35; trans. in Garrett, *Adriano Banchieri: Conclusions*, 30. A discussion, including statistical analysis, demonstrating the rapidly decreasing separation between motet style and madrigal style in the late 16th and early 17th centuries is found in Wolf, *Notation*, i. 40–4. Wolf finds that *c*.11 per cent of motets from the period 1590–9 use the mensuration C, associated by theorists with madrigal style (see below), whereas *c*.60 per cent from the next decade are notated in C. Along with the shift in mensuration, of course, come other aspects of style, such as note values, ways of treating text, and tempo implications.

mensurations, Uwe Wolf has found that in practice, these differences were increasingly lost in the very early seventeenth century, and that composers used the signs virtually indiscriminately, without regard to genre, style, or note values.[39] Moreover, the simultaneous use of the two different signatures in two different voices in a 2:1 proportional relationship had ceased by this time, except in very rare instances.

According to Banchieri and Praetorius as well as others, compositions in C were normally beaten on the semibreve (two minims per tactus). Nevertheless, Banchieri noted that both signatures had come in his time to be beaten in the same way; the only distinction was in the speed of the beat: 'It is true that nowadays, by way of a misuse converted into usage, both have come to be executed in the same way, singing and resting according to the value of the semibreve, and beating the Major Perfect [¢] fast (since it has white notes) and the Minor Perfect [C] slow, since it has black notes . . .'.[40] Praetorius, summarizing Italian prefaces and theoretical writings, likewise asserted that pieces in ¢ were beaten more quickly than those in C, but explained that the latter were actually faster-paced because they had so many smaller note values. The different speeds of the beat were 'necessary in order to achieve a mean between two extremes, otherwise the slower speed will annoy the listeners' ears or the faster speed lead to disaster'.[41] Although both Banchieri and Praetorius made a clear theoretical distinction between the two signs, Praetorius lamented the inconsistency in their usage by Italian musicians, an inconsistency confirmed by Wolf in his examination of a large quantity of sources. Praetorius did observe, however, that Monteverdi employed ¢ for compositions in the motet manner and C for compositions with more black notes than white ones.[42] This distinction shows Monteverdi to have been more discriminating and perhaps more conservative in the use of mensural signs than many of his contemporaries.

[39] *Conclusioni*, i. 42–3. Wolf, ibid. 104–5, accurately sums up the situation found in music prints of the period with regard not only to mensuration signs, but also to all other aspects of notation: 'a uniform notational system, as it perhaps had persisted, even if to a limited degree, in the sixteenth century, did not exist in the early seventeenth century' (trans. mine).

[40] 'Vero è che al giorno d'oggi, per modo d'abuso convertito in uso, vengono amendui praticati l'istesso cantando, & pausando sott'il valore della Semibreve, & battendo il perfetto maggiore presto (per essere di note bianche) & il minor perfetto adagio essendo di note negre . . .'. *Cartella musicale*, 29; trans. (bracketed passages mine) adapted from Cranna, 'Adriano Banchieri's *Cartella musicale* (1614)', 115. The passage is also quoted in Wolf, *Notation*, i. 30.

[41] *Syntagmatis musici. . . tomus tertius*, 50; trans. Lampl, p. 104. Franz Jochen Machatius interprets Praetorius's faster and slower tactus in quite precise metronomic terms: ¢ = MM 72 and C = MM 60. These tactus rates are based on Machatius's much-too-precise designation of the human pulse rate as MM 72. See Machatius, 'Dreiertakt und Zweiertakt als Eurhythmus und Ekrhythmus', in Dadelsen and Holschneider, eds., *Festschrift Walter Gerstenberg zum 60. Geburtstag*, 88–97. I see no grounds for assigning such precise speeds to the tactus; indeed, this runs contrary to the spirit of much else that Praetorius says about tempo.

[42] *Syntagmatis musici . . . tomus tertius*, 51; trans. Lampl, p. 105. Praetorius's assessment of Monteverdi's mensural usage is generally accurate, except for the composer's very early publications.

Recognition that pieces in ¢ seem nearly always to have been sung to a semi-breve tactus, especially if smaller note values were frequent, suggests that pieces in C may well have been sung to a minim tactus (slower than the normal semi-breve tactus under C) when even smaller note values, such as crotchets, quavers, and even semiquavers, predominated.[43] The practical possibility of a minim tactus has important implications for the performance of those pieces of the Monteverdi Vespers and other music of Monteverdi that display many small note values, not only in terms of tempo, but also with regard to the relationship between duple- and triple-time sections (see the discussion below).[44] In the two Magnificats of the Vespers, the organ registration rubrics include instructions in three separate verses (Magnificat *a 7*: *Et exultavit*, *Quia fecit*; Magnificat *a 6*: *Et misericordia*) that they should be performed slowly because of the many *crome* and *semicrome* (quavers and semiquavers). In another verse of the Magnificat *a 7*, *Suscepit Israel*, Monteverdi requires a slow tempo because of an echo. A minim tactus is a distinct possibility not only in these verses, but also in others where similar note values or echoes likewise imply a slow tempo, even though Monteverdi has not mentioned it in his rubrics.

Both ¢ and C were beaten with the *tactus aequalis*, or equal tactus; that is, with downward and upward hand strokes of equal duration. The only matters to be decided were the speed of the total down-and-up stroke and the note value—breve, semibreve, or minim—to which it applied.

Triple metre was principally designated by proportional signatures inherited from the sixteenth century.[45] Although a variety of such signatures can be found in music of the first half of the *Seicento*, they normally had one of two meanings according to theorists: *tripla*, or a 3 : 1 proportional ratio; and *sesquialtera*, or a 3 : 2 ratio. Banchieri, however, declares that the 3 : 2 ratio is not a true *sesquialtera*,

---

[43] In the 15th century, major prolation had sometimes been beaten on the minim. See Berger, *Mensuration and Proportion Signs*, 96, 99, 101, 103. German theorists of the second half of the 16th century mention a minim tactus, but the only Italian theorist to do so is Agostino Pisa, who considers such a tactus incorrect, but acknowledges that practical musicians use it (see n. 21 above). Wolf, *Notation*, i. 69–70, draws what I think is the wrong inference from Pisa's comments, stating in n. 290 that there is no theoretical evidence from Italy proving the use of a minim tactus. On the other hand, Wolf. i. 13–14, also notes that theory in this period often has little to do with rapidly evolving practice. For evidence of a minim beat in Italy, see my discussion of Pisa and Valentini above.

[44] Wolf notes the inevitable slowing of the tactus as smaller note values came to predominate in duple metre. See ibid. 73.

[45] In examining notational practice, Wolf, ibid. 37, finds that in 16th-century music 3 is the usual triple mensuration under ¢, while $\frac{3}{2}$ is typical under C. Nevertheless, on pp. 87–8, he notes that $\frac{3}{2}$ may be used with either of the duple mensurations. Under ¢, $\frac{3}{2}$ is usually notated in semibreves, under C, usually in minims. Some prints, however, use both forms indiscriminately. Those prints using both forms of $\frac{3}{2}$ (in semibreves or in minims) under a single duple mensuration sign rise from 7 per cent of the sampled repertoire in 1591–1600 to 17 per cent in 1601–10 to 44 per cent in 1621–30. Wolf describes the theoretically incorrect use of various signs for triple metres in Italian prints of the early 17th century on pp. 106–12. $\frac{3}{2}$ as a free-standing signature at the beginning of a piece or section also becomes confused with *sesquialtera*, which suggests a proportion within a piece or section. Bowers, in 'Some Reflection', has usefully drawn a clear distinction between the two in the Monteverdi Vespers.

which can only result from simultaneous duple and triple mensurations, but rather a proportion of equality.[46] Banchieri's terminology reflects the conception and terminology of Nicola Vincentino and is traceable as far back as Heinrich Glareanus.[47] Praetorius, on the other hand, treats the triple metres both as proportions under prevailing duple metre and as independent mensurations for entire pieces. However, his discussion of the latter emerges directly out of his explanation of the former, thereby easily confusing the two. In addition, he refers to $\mathbb{C}^3_2$ as *tempus perfectum maius* and C^3_2 as *tempus perfectum minus*, both of which are *sesquialtera* proportions, the former at the semibreve level and the latter at the minim level. Praetorius would like to banish $\mathbb{C}^3_2$ and use only $\frac{3}{1}$ or 3 to designate *tripla* (triple groups of semibreves) and $\frac{3}{2}$ to indicate *sesquialtera* (triple groups of minims). He does not indicate that the signs $\mathbb{C}$ or C should precede the numerical fractions.[48] Praetorius sees the usefulness of his *tripla* and *sesquialtera* signatures in enabling performers 'to distinguish more easily between certain types of compositions. Thus *tripla* should be retained in motets and *concerti*; but *sesquialtera* in madrigals, and particularly in galliards, courantes, voltas, and other compositions of this nature, in which a faster *tactus* is necessary.'[49] His comments can only refer to these signatures as the principal metres of such compositions and not merely internal passages in proportional notation. Confusing, though, is his association of the *tripla* with motets and *concerti* and the *sesquialtera* with madrigals and dances. Praetorius had earlier made the same distinction with regard to the role of $\mathbb{C}$ and C for the motet style and the madrigal style, but with opposite tempo implications: $\mathbb{C}$ (motet style) was to be beaten faster than C (madrigal style) because the latter had so many more small note values, actually producing a faster pace than motets, even though beaten with a slower tactus (see above).[50] Praetorius eventually clarified these relationships in

---

[46] See *Conclusioni*, 36–7; trans. in Garrett, *Adriano Banchieri: Conclusions*, 32–3; and *Cartella musicale*, 29–30; trans. in Cranna, 'Adriano Banchieri's *Cartella musicale*', 116–18.

[47] See DeFord, 'Tempo Relationships', 31–3.

[48] Carl Dahlhaus, in 'Zur Entstehung des modernen Taktsystems', 232–3, assumes he does, and Paul Brainard, in 'Proportional Notation', 22, also assumes so by conflating the passage in question with Praetorius's preceding description of signatures that are commonly used but which he would like to eliminate.

[49] *Syntagmatis musici . . . tomus tertius*, 53; trans. Lampl, p. 110.

[50] *Syntagmatis musici. . . tomus tertius*, 50; trans. Lampl, p. 104. The discrepancy between a slow tactus in C and a fast tactus in $\frac{3}{2}$ is discussed in Dahlhaus, 'Zur Entstehung des modernen Taktsystems', 232–3; Brainard, 'Proportional Notation', 21–46; and Paine, 'Tactus, Tempo, and Praetorius', 184–96. Dahlhaus explains the discrepancy by assuming a breve tactus for *tripla* and a semibreve tactus for *sesquialtera*, producing a faster tactus for the latter, while both $\mathbb{C}$ and C utilized a semibreve tactus, resulting in the slower tactus for C described above. Thus there is no contradiction in Praetorius's recommendations, despite the easy conflation and confusion of separate parts of his discussion. Brainard, 'Proportional Notation', 24–5, finds that in music of both Praetorius and Schütz 'this 3 : 1 proportion of semibreves . . . operates . . . whenever *tripla* notation is used in alternation with common time'. Furthermore, 'Rest counts, tempora totals, tactus demarcations, and occasional mensural overlaps all confirm that the three semibreves of Praetorius's *tripla* are at least the "counting" equivalent of one tactus, i.e., one semibreve under duple mensuration'. However, this proportional relationship in terms

a diagram, illustrating clearly that C and $\frac{3}{1}$ have the slower tactus, while ₵ and $\frac{3}{2}$ have the faster tactus.[51] Despite all this theoretical discussion of the difference between *tripla* and *sesquialtera*, numerous theoretical and practical sources of the 16th century already indicated that many musicians understood the two as having identical meaning. Moreover, since *sesquialtera* was often introduced not only by $\frac{3}{2}$, but also by a simple 3, it was often confused with the *tripla*, which was signed by either $\frac{3}{1}$ or 3.[52]

Like duple proportions, the simultaneous use of two different triple mensurations, or of duple and triple mensurations, had almost completely disappeared by the early seventeenth century, and the only relationship of concern in the Monteverdi Vespers is that of tempos between successive sections of a composition.[53] Monteverdi does not use either the *tripla* or the *sesquialtera* signature as the principal metre of any composition in the Vespers, although triple mensurations do occur as the principal metres of the central verses and the ritornello of the hymn *Ave maris stella* and of several verses in the two Magnificats.

Triple metres were also beaten to a twofold tactus according to seventeenth-century theorists, but the down-stroke was held twice as long, and the up-stroke was made on the last third of the tactus, constituting the *tactus inaequalis*. The same theorists who relate the *tactus aequalis* to the pulse also speak of an uneven pulse, which they relate to the *tactus inaequalis*.

In addition to employing the mensurations discussed above, Monteverdi and others notated very brief changes from duple to triple subdivisions by means of blackened notes, termed *hemiola* by most theorists (designated in my edition by interrupted brackets).[54] *Hemiola,* or the reduction of note values by one third so that three blackened notes equaled two void ones, could be at the level of the breve and semibreve under ₵ (*hemiola maior*) or at the level of the semibreve and minim under C (*hemiola minor*). *Hemiola* might occur in all parts simultaneously,

---

of counting notes does not necessarily mean an exact tempo proportion in performance: 'That they are the exact durational equivalent as well—that the tactus speed remains constant at the change from duple to triple and vice versa—can be proved only in the comparatively rare case of overlaps between them . . .'.

[51] *Syntagmatis musici . . . tomus tertius*, 79; trans. Lampl, p. 134. The diagram is reproduced in Brainard, 'Proportional Notation', 21, and Paine, 'Tactus, Tempo, and Praetorius', 184.

[52] See DeFord, 'Tempo Relationships', 11–26.

[53] Frescobaldi still occasionally used different mensurations simultaneously in his *Capricci* of 1624. See Darbellay, 'Tempo Relationships in Frescobaldi's *Primo libro di capricci*', 316. In 15th- and 16th-century treatises, the temporal relationships indicated by these proportional signs referred to their simultaneous use with duple mensurations, and no theorist speaks expressly of successive relationships. As Berger emphasizes, 'different rules might apply to vertical and horizontal relationships'. See Berger, *Mensuration and Proportion Signs*, 51, 91. See also DeFord, 'Tempo Relationships', 30–9. Given the virtual disappearance of simultaneous proportional relationships by the early 17th century, practical musicians and theorists such as Banchieri and Praetorius must have been referring to linear relationships when they described *tripla* and *sesquialtera*.

[54] *Hemiola* is very easily confused with colouration. The former creates triple groupings in duple time, the latter duple units in triple time.

but could also appear in one voice while the others proceeded in duple time. The *hemiola* in blackened notes, therefore, was the means by which seventeenth-century composers notated simultaneous triple and duple subdivisions in different parts.[55] *Hemiola* had the same meaning as triple time in comparable note values, and is equated with triple metres in white notation by most theorists. Its principal advantage over white notation was in notating syncopations and 'Lombard' rhythms, since the rules of perfection, imperfection, and alteration did not apply to the blackened notes of the *hemiola*.

Another triple notation found in the works of Monteverdi and others is the *meliola*, or triple groupings of blackened minims and smaller note values with the numeral *3* inserted within each group.[56] *Meliola* could be used not only to generate the same effect as *hemiola minor*, but also to create triple patterns in note values smaller than minims. The *meliola* actually appears as a diminution, since the blackened minim is visually indistinguishable from a semiminim, and the next smaller note employed is the quaver (*croma*), which may be understood as a diminished crotchet (semiminim). The indistinguishability between a normal *croma* and a quaver as a diminished crotchet (and by extension, the normal *semicroma* from a diminished *croma*) created confusion among theorists and has confused modern interpreters as well.[57] In the Vespers, the single instance of *meliola* does indeed indicate diminution, as will be explained below where tempo and proportional relationships in the *Sonata sopra Sancta Maria* are discussed.

Some theorists recommended the *tactus inaequalis* for *meliola*, while others suggested a *tactus aequalis* in two groups of three notes each. Brunelli and Valentini both designated the *tactus inaequalis*, while Praetorius grouped two such triplets into a compound duple metre (sometimes notated under $\frac{6}{4}$) to be beaten as *tactus aequalis* in order to avoid 'incessant hand and arm movements'.[58] Giovanni Battista Buonamente in 1627 also described two sets of blackened

---

[55] Wolf, *Notation*, i. 108, cites early 17th-century examples of incorrect *hemiola* notation where blackened notes are treated as perfect notes.

[56] See Antonio Brunelli, *Regole utilissime per li scolari che desiderano imparare a cantare, sopra la pratica della musica* (Florence: Volemar Timan, 1606), 29. Much of Brunelli's treatise is translated and discussed in Putnam Aldrich, *Rhythm in Seventeenth-Century Italian Monody* (New York: W. W. Norton & Co., 1966), 26–40. See also Praetorius, *Syntagmatis musici . . . tomus tertius*, 73; trans. Lampl, pp. 124–5; and Margaret Murata, 'Pier Francesco Valentini', 335–9, 349. Not all theorists used the term *meliola* for blackened triplets; many discussed this notation as *hemiola*. Triplets could also be notated with void notes. See Wolf, *Notation*, i. 115, 127–8.

[57] Giovanni Luca Conforti, in his *Breve e facile maniera d'essercitarsi ad ogni scolaro non solamente a far passaggi . . .* (Rome, 1593; fac. New York: Broude Brothers, 1978), fo. 2 of the *Dichiaratione* (note to readers), referred to the blackened minims of *hemiola minore* as semiminims (crotchets). See Wolf, *Notation*, i. 120. Wolf outlines the confusion between *hemiola minore* and triplet crotchets among theorists, especially Zacconi, on pp. 128–30. Neither theorists nor composers are consistent in their understanding and notation of *hemiola*, *meliola*, or triplets in this period.

[58] *Syntagmatis musici . . . tomus tertius*, 73–4; trans. Lampl, pp. 125, 129. See Paine, 'Tactus, Tempo, and Praetorius', 194–6.

triplets as equal to a $\frac{6}{4}$ metre and proposed a *tactus aequalis*.[59] Monteverdi's *meliola* in the Vespers is similarly grouped in pairs of triplets, facilitating a larger *tactus aequalis*. To conduct triple metres, as with duple metres, the *maestro di cappella* had to determine what note value was the basis of the full tactus as well as how fast to beat the tactus, especially in relation to sections in duple metre.[60]

Banchieri designates the relationship between triple and duple sections as follows:[61]

$Ȼ_2^3$ means that three semibreves under $Ȼ_2^3$ = two semibreves under $Ȼ$ (*sesquialtera*).

C_2^3 means that three minims under C_2^3 = two minims under C (*sesquialtera*).

C_1^3 means that three semibreves under C_1^3 = one semibreve under C (*tripla*).

Banchieri's proportions, like those of other theorists, relate equivalent principal note values on either side of the mensuration change; that is, under $Ȼ$, the principal note values are semibreves, and the proportional signature $Ȼ_2^3$ has semibreves as its principal note values. Similarly, C has minims as principal values, while its proportional signature, C_2^3, likewise has minims as the principal notes. Banchieri complains about composers who did not understand or use the proportions correctly, 'indicating the numbers indifferently'.[62] He cites by name only composers who exemplify the correct use of proportions, but he does give an example of incorrect usage in which movement in minims under C is followed by a $\frac{3}{2}$ signature with movement in groups of three semibreves.[63] This example, in fact, parallels Monteverdi's notation in *Dixit Dominus* as well as in *Quia respexit* of the Magnificat *a 7*. Whether Banchieri meant to include Monteverdi

---

[59] See Wolf, *Notation*, i. 94 n. 399. Orazio Scaletta, in his *Scala di musica* of 1657, gives the same instruction for beating $\frac{6}{4}$. See Aldrich, *Rhythm in Seventeenth-Century Italian Monody*, 35.

[60] In the preface to his *Terpsichore* of 1612, Praetorius relates the tempo of branles gay (a lively group dance) and voltas (an energetic couple dance) to a combination of mensuration sign and principal note values. *Tripla* notated as C3 with principal motion in semibreves and minims is designated fast, while *tripla* notated under C3 with principal motion in semibreves and minims is designated very slow. At the other end of the spectrum are the mensurations $Ȼ$ and $Ȼ$, the former in semibreves and minims, the latter in minims and crotchets, both with the rubric *alla breve* and indicated as very fast and fast respectively. Praetorius places the signature $\frac{3}{2}$, which he labels *sesquialtera*, between the extremes, but does not give a verbal indication of tempo. The implication is that his *sesquialtera* falls in between the tempo of *tripla* and that of the diminution signatures. Praetorius indicates that many triple-metre dances, especially quick dances such as branles gay and voltas, were beaten with a *tactus aequalis*, the tactus encompassing two triple units. See Praetorius, *Terpsichore* (1612), ed. Günther Oberst in *Gesamtausgabe der musikalischen Werke von Michael Praetorius*, xii (Wolfenbüttel: Georg Kallmeyer Verlag, 1929), pp. xi–xiii.

[61] Banchieri, *Conclusioni*, 36; trans. in Garrett, *Adriano Banchieri: Conclusions*, 32.

[62] 'Then there are others who achieve marvelous success in their compositions, but who commit great abuses in the proportions, indicating the numbers indifferently. We see some who contradict themselves within the same work.' See Banchieri, *Cartella musicale*, 168; trans. in Cranna, 'Adriano Banchieri's *Cartella musicale*', 355.

[63] *Cartella musicale*, 169; trans. in Cranna, 'Adriano Banchieri's *Cartella musicale*', 357. Complaints about this same issue extend as far back as Pietro Aaron's *Thoscanello de la musica* of 1523. See DeFord, 'Tempo Relationships', 7–13.

among those composers who did not use the proportional system correctly is unknown, but Artusi openly criticized Monteverdi's understanding of it, since he had notated different levels of rhythmic values under the same C_2^3 mensuration in separate pieces of the 1607 *Scherzi musicali*:

> But what should be said about these Scherzi Musicali? One discovers that he does not understand the tempo [the C mensuration] nor the signs he has placed after the tempo [the $\frac{3}{2}$ proportion], knowledge of which is so necessary; and in particular in the three songs, O Rosetta, Damigella, and Clori amorosa. All of these [songs] have the same tempo and numbers [C_2^3], but have different note values in the vocal parts.[64]

Artusi's complaint is that the first two pieces are notated in crotchets and quavers, while the last one is notated in semibreves and minims. He declares that *Clori amorosa* is notated properly but that O *Rosetta* and *Damigella* demonstrate that Monteverdi 'doesn't understand anything of the aforesaid proportions'.[65]

Praetorius described the relationships between the most common contemporary mensurations in a similar but more complicated manner than Banchieri and lamented the indiscriminate use of triple-metre signatures by Italian musicians.[66] In his diagram illustrating the principal signatures under *tactus aequalis* and *tactus inaequalis*, Praetorius refers to the *tripla*, indicated by 3 or $\frac{3}{1}$ and notated in semibreves as slower (*tardior*), and the *sesquialtera*, indicated by $\frac{3}{2}$ and notated in minims as faster (*celerior*).[67] Thus, while C is beaten faster than C because of the many smaller note values of the latter, *tripla* ($\frac{3}{1}$) is beaten more slowly than *sesquialtera* ($\frac{3}{2}$). The reason for this seeming reversal is not hard to fathom. The principal note values under C in relation to C are often two rhythmic levels smaller, while the note values under $\frac{3}{2}$ are only one level smaller than under $\frac{3}{1}$. This diagram suggests that the triple metres may not only be related proportionally to duple metres, as described in Praetorius's text, but may also lead an independent life from duple metres, requiring their own separate tempos.[68]

Banchieri, Praetorius, Brunelli, and other theorists of the early seventeenth

[64] My translation. 'Ma che cosa si dirà di questi scherzi Musicali? si scuopre che non intende il tempo; ne gli segni posti da lui doppo il tempo; la cognitione di cui è tanto necessaria. Et in particolare nelli tre canti, ò Rosetta, Damigella, & Clori Amorosa; Hanno questi tutti il tempo e le zifre numerali ad un modo istesso; ma hanno le figure cantabili diverse.' See *Discorso secondo musicale di Antonio Braccino da Todi, per la dichiaratione della lettera posta ne' Scherzi Musicali del Sig. Claudio Monteverde* (Venice: Vincenti, 1608), 7, pub. in fac. with *L'Artusi overo delle imperfettioni della moderna musica*, ed. Giuseppe Vecchi (Bologna: Forni Editore, 1968). I am grateful to Massimo Ossi for reminding me of this passage. According to Wolf, *Notation*, i. 89–90, the use of smaller note values in duple time while maintaining the traditional larger values of triple time caused an 'uncoupling' of the proportional relationship between duple and triple in practice. Wolf notes that this 'uncoupling' is not described by theorists, who keep repeating old, outdated theories.

[65] *Discorso secondo musicale di Antonio Braccino da Todi*, 7.

[66] *Syntagmatis musici . . . tomus tertius*, 51; trans. Lampl, pp. 105–6.

[67] See n. 51 above. This relationship is the same as that described in the preface of Frescobaldi's *Primo libro di capricci* of 1624.

[68] This is the position taken by Brainard in 'Proportional Notation'. See nn. 50 and 51 above and nn. 75 and 78 below. See also DeFord, 'Tempo Relationships', 26–39.

century all understood proportions in terms of equivalent note values on either side of a proportional mensuration sign (2 semibreves = 3 semibreves; 2 minims = 3 minims). However, the modern styles of Monteverdi, Frescobaldi, and others generated difficulties in this theoretical proportional system, since their frequent use of smaller note values under C (minims, crotchets, quavers, and semiquavers) slowed the pace of semibreves, and maintenance of strict proportions with sections in C_2^3, still utilizing minims as their principal note values, would result in a slowing, sometimes a drastic slowing, of the pace under C_2^3.[69] In several pieces in the Vespers, Monteverdi uses $\frac{3}{2}$ signatures with semibreves or minims as the predominant note values where the primary rhythmic movement under C is in minims, crotchets, and quavers.

The difficulties caused in the old proportional system by the new rhythmic levels in duple time coupled with unchanged rhythmic values in triple metre have resulted in confusion and differing interpretations of Monteverdi's tempo relationships among modern scholars and performers.[70] Monteverdi frequently uses $\math₵_2^3$ signatures in the bassus generalis where he uses C_2^3 in the vocal parts. In the same place in different part-books one can find the signatures C_2^3, $\frac{3}{2}$, or even C3 and 3. Bowers has shown, however, that the bassus generalis signatures with $\math₵$ all occur in pieces or passages with larger principal note values, requiring a faster beat by the *maestro di cappella*.[71] Since the bassus generalis would have served as a 'conductor's score' as well as the organist's score, Monteverdi simply did not bother to make the distinction between C and $\math₵$ for the vocal parts except where $\math₵$ is used to indicate a possible diminution (*Laudate pueri*; see the discussion below). Complicating matters further is the fact that in the vocal parts Monteverdi sometimes notates triple time in $\math₵_2^3$ with semibreves, sometimes in C_2^3 with minims, and in *Dixit Dominus*, in C_2^3 with semibreves. It is unclear whether there is any significant difference in the meaning of all these different notations of triple time.[72]

---

[69] See the articles by Darbellay, Brainard, Murata, and DeFord cited above and in the Bibliography. The variety of Frescobaldi's mensuration signs and the apparent absence of proportional relationships among many of them is outlined in Frederick Hammond, *Girolamo Frescobaldi* (Cambridge, Mass.: Harvard University Press, 1983), 215–19. Wolf, *Notation*, i. 88 describes the preservation of traditional note values in triple time while duple-time values decreased by half in the early 17th century. My own suggestions regarding relationships between triple and duple time in the Vespers result in equivalencies between note values of different sizes on either side of the mensuration change.

[70] The most recent conflict of interpretations can be seen in Bowers, 'Some Reflection', and the correspondence between Bowers and myself in *Music & Letters*, 74 (1993), 487–95; and 75 (1994), 145–54, as well as a similar exchange in *Musik und Kirche*, cited in n. 2 above. Only Bowers and Roland Eberlein in 'Die Taktwechsel' have claimed that Monteverdi's proportional system is consistent and follows the traditional proportional theory. Bowers's approach frequently results in tempos for triple-metre passages that many modern scholars and performers consider too slow and that even appear to contradict the sense of Monteverdi's texts. The many different gramophone recordings of the Vespers also illustrate a variety of tempo relationships between duple and triple metres.

[71] 'Some Reflection', 363, 389–91.

[72] DeFord, in 'Tempo Relationships', 6–26, demonstrates convincingly that throughout much of the 16th century some composers, in a prevailing metre of C, used three semibreves in triple time, treating

There is another way of considering the proportional question, however, that takes into account the practical problem of relating triple time in old, larger note values to duple time in new, smaller note values. This is an approach not discussed by either Banchieri or Praetorius, but implied by Zacconi, by Olifante in his addendum to Rocco Rodio's treatise, and in Crivellati's 1624 *Discorsi musicali*.[73] According to the traditional manner of dealing with *sesquialtera*, the principal note value (the breve or the semibreve) in duple metre was beaten in *tactus aequalis*, and the same principal note value in triple metre (the breve in *sesquialtera maior* and the semibreve in *sesquialtera minor*) was beaten in *tactus inaequalis*, that is, the total up-and-down beat was of equal duration across the proportion, but the up-beat occurred at a different point in the two metres. Where Monteverdi used small note values in duple metre, however, the pulse and the tactus would likely have shifted to the minim from the semibreve, so that each crotchet received a down- or up-stroke.[74] Since the equivalence of the tactus had been the practical means for effecting the *sesquialtera* proportion in performance, it is quite possible that it remained the vehicle for generating the proportion in Monteverdi's new notation, with the difference that now the tactus was on the minim in duple time and the semibreve in triple time. As a result, the tactus could still be proportional in the traditional sense: an unequal tactus of three notes replaced an even tactus of two notes, but the mathematical relationship between note values had changed. Mathematically, the *sesquialtera* had become a *tripla*, but in performance it was still a *sesquialtera* with regard to the tactus.[75]

them in the same way as three minims, thereby making no distinction between the two forms of triple notation.

[73] See nn. 23 and 24 above.

[74] See the discussion above regarding theoretical evidence for a minim tactus. While Olifante's *cantar doppio* with the beat on the minim refers to triple metres, there is no reason why the same principle should not have applied to duple time, as Agostino Pisa's lament implies. Carl Dahlhaus suggested the use of a *tactus alla minima* from about the middle of the 16th century, on the basis of the *note nere* madrigal as well as on comments by Eucharius Hoffmann in *Musicae practicae praecepta* (Wittemberg, 1572). See Dahlhaus, 'Zur Entstehung des modernen Taktsystems', 224–9. Brainard, in 'Proportional Notation', 37–9, suggests a minim tactus for the music of Schütz that is notated predominantly in small note values.

[75] Brainard's solution to the proportion question in Praetorius is somewhat different, though it still suggests faster tempos for the triple metres than the 16th-century proportional system would. Brainard holds that Praetorius no longer sees triple metres as dependent upon the norm of duple metres, but as independent mensurations in their own right. He thus proposes a new set of relationships in Praetorius: '(1) in accordance with long-standing tradition, ₡ (in conjunction with larger note values) calls for a quicker minim pulse than C (in conjunction with smaller note values); (2) in relation *to each other*, tripla (three semibreves to the tactus) and *sesquialtera* (three minims to the tactus) connote slower and faster tempos, respectively; and (3) these tempo connotations exist without regard to the "horizontal" dimension. Where duple and triple mensurations alternate with each other, they may be, but are not necessarily, related to one another by conventional proportion. "Slow" duples may be joined not only with "slow" triples (**C○-³₁○○○**) but also with "faster" ones (**C○-³₂ ♩♩♩**). Only in the former case (or its "fast-fast" counterpart) does the tactus duration remain constant. The combination of a "slow" duple with a "fast" triple or vice versa presumes a change of tactus speed and hence rules out strict proportional equivalence.' See Brainard, 'Proportional Notation', 26. See also nn. 50–1 above.

This practical way of beating time and relating duple- and triple-metre sections is actually very simple and natural for a conductor. The only issue is determining when duple metre should be beaten on the minim and when on the semibreve. In the Vespers, the matter seems unambiguous. Most duple-metre compositions and passages should be beaten on the minim, but *Nisi Dominus*, *Ave maris stella*, the second section of *Audi coelum*, and some segments of the Magnificat *a 7* (*Magnificat*, *Quia respexit*, *Et misericordia*, *Esurientes*, *Sicut erat*) and the Magnificat *a 6* (*Magnificat*, *Quia respexit*, *Quia fecit*, *Fecit potentiam*, *Suscepit Israel*, *Sicut erat*) are notated principally in semibreves, minims, and crotchets, with only ornamental use of quavers, and should, with a few possible exceptions, be beaten to a semibreve tactus; many of them are notated with ¢ in the bassus generalis part-book. In *Nisi Dominus*, *Audi coelum*, and *Quia respexit* of the Magnificat *a 6*, where these passages rub shoulders with triple metre in perfect semibreves, a traditional semibreve *sesquialtera* is in effect, maintaining the same tactus for duple and triple time. In *Ave maris stella* and some segments of the Magnificat *a 7* (*Quia respexit*, *Esurientes*) and the Magnificat *a 6* (*Esurientes*, *Suscepit*), the triple-metre passages are notated in perfect breves. When the tactus is beaten on the semibreve in duple metre and the same tactus is beaten unequally for the perfect breves in triple metre, a *tripla* mathematical proportion once again results in terms of note values, but a *sesquialtera* in terms of the tactus beat.[76]

In several pieces in the Vespers, Monteverdi appears to have used the barring in the bassus generalis part-book as an indicator of the note values to be equated on either side of a mensuration change, much as Frescobaldi systematically used barlines to clarify tempo relationships among the complex mensurations of his *Capricci* of 1624.[77] In addition, it should be noted that Monteverdi's passages and

---

[76] My interpretation of Monteverdi's notation in the Vespers, like Brainard's, allows for the combination of triply grouped semibreves in the context of a prevailing C with a semibreve tactus, but sees Monteverdi as more interested in actual proportional temporal relationships than Brainard considers Praetorius to have been. Brainard's interpretation of Frescobaldi's notation of his *Cento partite* in its second edition of 1637 parallels my interpretation of Monteverdi's in assuming a proportional comparison of notes of different sizes (in the Frescobaldi example, three minims = two semibreves); see 'Proportional Notation', 27–9. Margaret Murata interprets a change from C, with predominant motion in crotchets and quavers, to $\frac{3}{2}$ in semibreves in a fantasia of Frescobaldi's by means of a shift of tactus from the semibreve to the breve, but with a slower tempo for the triple time. Although one duple breve under C = one triple breve under $\frac{3}{2}$, thereby maintaining a mathematical *sesquialtera* in terms of the notation of semibreves, the result in performance of shifting the tactus from the semibreve under C (two tactus per duple breve) to the breve under $\frac{3}{2}$ (one tactus per triple breve) is a slowing of the tempo of the breve by a 4 : 3 ratio; if one examines the relationship between semibreves, however, the $\frac{3}{2}$ signature results in a *tripla*, that is, three semibreves under $\frac{3}{2}$ = one semibreve under C. Valentini's explanation of this signature confirms that three notes replace one. Frescobaldi's Canzona V from *Il secondo libro di toccate* requires tactus shifts between breves and semibreves under different mensurations. See Murata, 'Pier Francesco Valentini', 339–43.

[77] See Darbellay, 'Tempo Relationships in Frescobaldi's *Primo libro di capricci*'. Darbellay (pp. 303–6) demonstrates that some of Frescobaldi's tempo relationships involve a shift of tactus from one note level to another. This problem of shifting tactus from one note level to another as the result of a mensuration change and change in size of predominant note values was discussed by Pietro Aaron as early as 1523, and by others following after Aaron. See n. 63 above. Praetorius used small strokes on the stave starting

sections in triple metres, with their frequent reliance on short, symmetrical phrase structures, sequential thematic patterns, and homophonic textures, are stylistically related to contemporaneous triple-metre dances, suggesting a relatively quick dance-like character, as described in the quotations from Giulio Caccini and Thomas Ravenscroft cited below.

Among the forms of triple subdivision indicated by blackened notes, the *hemiola* poses no problems of interpretation and performance in the Monteverdi Vespers, since its meaning is clear from the context each time it appears. The *meliola*, however, which occurs only once, in an extended passage of the *Sonata sopra Sancta Maria*, has proved more problematic for modern performers. This passage will be discussed below in connection with the entire *Sonata*.

The discussion of metre and tempo in individual compositions of the 1610 Vespers at the end of this chapter is based on the assumption of a proportional relationship between passages in triple time, whatever the means of notation, and adjacent passages in duple time. Such proportional relationships, in my experience, probably also obtain in Monteverdi's later music. Yet there is, within the scope of our present knowledge, no way to prove that this was the case. Indeed, prefaces and theoretical writings from Praetorius onwards suggest that during the first half of the century a somewhat different, non-proportional understanding of triple notations was developing. Triple notations gradually coalesced into three principal levels: (1) triple time notated in breves and semibreves, (2) triple time notated in semibreves and minims, and (3) triple time written in black notation, variously called *hemiola* or *meliola*, but implying a diminution in note values, since black minims cannot be distinguished from crotchets in *integer valor*. Thus an apparent crotchet may actually be a diminished minim, as in Praetorius's *tactus trochaicus diminutus* (see the discussion of diminution by blackening above and of the *tactus trochaicus diminutus* below). The only way to distinguish the black minim from a semiminim is by the presence of black semibreves in the notation. The signatures for these three levels of triple time may vary; in all three, 3 ($\frac{3}{1}$) or $\frac{3}{2}$ may be found, either alone or preceded by C or ₵. In black notation there may be a mensuration sign, the numeral *3* may appear in the midst of triple groupings, or the black notation itself may suffice to indicate the triple units. Black triple groupings may also be compounded under larger duple groups with a mensuration of $\frac{6}{4}$, $\frac{6}{2}$, or $\frac{6}{1}$.

According to some prefaces and treatises from the 1620s onwards, the relative speed of the triple group depended on the note values employed in conjunction with the mensuration sign. Thus triple time in breves and semibreves moved more slowly than triple time in semibreves and minims, and triple time in black notation had the quickest tempo of all. This relationship is expressed clearly in

with his *Musae sionae*, bk. vii, of 1609 to indicate the beginning of a tactus and to facilitate recognition of the type of tactus. See Paine, 'Tactus, Tempo, and Praetorius', 196–7.

the preface to Frescobaldi's *Il primo libro di capricci* of 1624: 'in the *trippole* [patterns in triple proportion] or *sesquialtere* [patterns in $\frac{3}{2}$ proportion]; if they are major [i.e. a three-semibreve pattern] one must play adagio; if they are minor [a three-minim pattern], somewhat more allegro; if [the pattern consists of] three semiminims, more allegro; if there are six [semiminims] against four one must take their tempo with an allegro beat [*battuta*]'.[78]

Frescobaldi's instructions loosen considerably the relationship between mensurations and tempos—all tempos except the last are described in terms of their note values rather than in terms of their mensuration signs, even though the mensuration signs are implied by the note values. Frescobaldi's general temporal relationships are confirmed in writings of the 1630s by Marin Mersenne and the Dutch theorist Joan Albert Ban, who was in contact with Giovanni Battista Doni.[79] The question is whether this conception of tempo relationships in triple time applies to Monteverdi, especially as early as 1610. My own estimation is that it does not. Monteverdi's triple mensurations and their principal note values are complicated by the use of small subdivisions in both breve- and semibreve-based triple time in various pieces, while other pieces and sections do not employ subdivisions beyond the notes defining the triple group. Furthermore, triple time, whether based on breves or semibreves, is sometimes notated with ₵ and sometimes not. The use of the slash, with the possible exception of *Laudate pueri*, seems to imply quicker tempos and is usually (but not always) associated with passages that do not subdivide the principal notes into smaller, ornamental values. In addition, there are factors internal to each composition (see below) that suggest the character of the relationship between duple and triple time. Therefore, I believe that Monteverdi's triple-metre passages cannot be subsumed under a single system implying a single set of tempo relationships, and that the role of the tactus, as described above, is the most important factor in determining the relationship between duple and triple metres in each individual piece. In the recommendations for tempos and tempo relationships given below, the relevant factors guiding each case will be mentioned.

Aside from mensuration signs and the level of principal note values, other factors affected tempo, including the size of the smallest note values employed. In the mid-sixteenth century Nicola Vicentino had discussed tempo in terms of

---

[78] 'Nelle trippole, o sesquialtere, se saranno maggiori, si portino adagio, se minori alquanto più allegre, se di tre semiminime, più allegre[,] se saranno sei per quattro si dia il lor tempo con far caminare la battuta allegra.' Original text from *Girolamo Frescobaldi: Il primo libro di capricci*, ed. Étienne Darbellay in *Girolamo Frescobaldi, opere complete*, iv (Milan: Edizioni Suvini Zerboni, 1984), p. xlv; trans. from Paine, 'Tactus, Tempo, and Praetorius', 315.

[79] See the discussion in Helmut Hell, 'Zu Rhythmus und Notierung des "Vi ricorda" in Claudio Monteverdis *Orfeo*', *Analecta musicologica*, 15 (1975), 125–7; and Brainard, 'Proportional Notation', 29–35. Both Mersenne and Ban, who were in close contact, prescribe mathematically proportional relationships in contrast to the more general relationships described verbally by Praetorius and Frescobaldi.

the size of note values, equating the slowest tempos with the largest notes (*massime*) and the fastest tempos with the smallest notes (*semicrome*).[80] Zarlino also related quick movement to minims and crotchets.[81] But as seen in the discussion of Zacconi, Banchieri, and Praetorius above, by the early seventeenth century the quick movement of smaller note values required a slower tactus.

   The concentration of major or minor thirds and sixths in a composition could also be a determiner of tempo, but the meaning of the text is the most frequently cited reason for hurrying or slowing the speed.[82] Numerous theorists from the middle of the sixteenth century onwards spoke of varying the tempo according to the affect of the text.[83] Praetorius summarized the remarks of many Italian composers and theorists in his comments on tempo, which also touch upon dynamics and cadential *ritardandi*:

It is most necessary to sustain quite a slow, stately pace in *concerti* involving several choirs. But since in such *concerti* madrigal and motet styles are found in frequent alternation, one has to modify the beat accordingly.[84]

The tempo of a performance must not be hurried, or even the most delightful ensemble will sound confused. With a slower beat, however, the music is more agreeable and can be grasped better. . . . But to use, by turns, now a slower, now a faster beat, in accordance with the text, lends dignity and grace to a performance and makes it admirable.

   Besides, it adds to the loveliness of an ensemble, if the dynamic level in the vocal and instrumental parts is varied now and then . . .

   Some [authorities] do not want to allow the mixture of motet and madrigal styles in any one composition. But I cannot accept their opinion; especially since it makes motets and *concerti* particularly delightful, when after some slow and expressive measures at the beginning, several quick phrases follow, succeeded in turn by slow and stately ones, which again change off with faster ones. In order to avoid monotony one should thus, where possible, vary the pace, in addition to a careful use of dynamic changes.

   Furthermore, it is not very commendable and pleasant when singers, organists, and other instrumentalists from habit hasten directly from the penultimate note of a composition into the last note without any hesitation. Therefore I believe I should here admonish [those] who have hitherto observed this [as performed] at princely courts and by other well organized choirs, to linger somewhat on the penultimate note, whatever its time value—whether they have held it for four, five or six *tactus* [for example]—and only then proceed to the last note.[85]

---

[80] *L'antica musica ridotta alla moderna prattica* (Rome: Barre, 1555; fac. ed. Edward E. Lowinsky, Kassel: Bärenreiter, 1959), fo. 42^{r-v}.

[81] *Le istitutioni harmoniche*, 340; Eng. trans. in Vered Cohen, *On the Modes: Part Four of 'Le istituione harmoniche', 1558, Gioseffo Zarlino* (New Haven: Yale University Press, 1983), 96.

[82] *L'antica musica*, fos. 81^{v}–82^{r}, associates major and minor consonances with affect and tempo, as does Zarlino, *Le istitutioni harmoniche*, 156; Eng. trans. in Marco and Palisca, *Gioseffo Zarlino, The Art of Counterpoint*, 21–2.

[83] See Vicentino, *L'antica musica*, fos. 43^{r}, 81^{v}–82^{r}; Zarlino, *Le istitutioni harmoniche*, 204, 340. For Italian prefaces from the early 17th century that discuss tempo, including fluctuating tempos 'now slow, now fast', see Wolf, *Notation*, i. 51–60.

[84] *Syntagmatis musici . . . tomus tertius*, 51; trans. Lampl, p. 104.

[85] *Syntagmatis musici . . . tomus tertius*, 79–80; trans. Lampl, pp. 135–6. I have omitted Lampl's footnotes. Very similar comments by earlier German theorists (from whom Praetorius clearly drew) about adjusting the tempo according to the text are given in Carl Dahlhaus, 'Über das Tempo in der Musik

All of Praetorius's comments on metre and tempo, including his remarks on *concerti* and the madrigal style, concern either polyphonic music for four or more voices (sometimes for multiple choirs) or dance music in the French style, as contained in his own *Terpsichore*.[86] With the development of monody and the few-voiced *concertato* at the end of the sixteenth century, new forms of rhythmic organization emerged, employing breves and semibreves at one end of the spectrum and ranging as far as demisemiquavers at the other.[87] In such music a composer's choice of rhythms and their interpretation by performers depended on the rhetorical and emotional implications of the text. Performance technique stressed the ability to move the affections of the audience through a highly expressive delivery of the words. Caccini included rhythm among the factors in what he called 'a certain noble negligence of song' (*una certa nobile sprezzatura di canto*): 'Whence may appear that noble manner (as I call it), which, not submitting to strict time but often halving the value of the notes according to the ideas of the text, gives rise to that kind of singing with so-called "negligence"'.[88]

Tempo also depended on the text: 'As for the measure or tempo to be taken in these airs: the most important consideration on which it depends is a choice made in conformity with the expression of the words.'[89] While Caccini was referring to secular music, the use of modern styles in sacred music and the mixture of madrigal and motet styles, as described by Praetorius, suggest that the same considerations governed music for church and private chapel.[90] In the preface to his *Sacrae laudes* of 1603, Agostino Agazzari declared that

this style requires, in addition to unerring singers, a very slow beat, especially when there are *esclamazioni* or emotionally charged words. The beat can sometimes be quickened in the middle of a work, when a metre change is indicated or when two choirs toss the same motif back and forth. One then returns to the original beat and in this way, more expression is bestowed on the music and more force is given to the words without losing the gravity required in church . . .'[91]

des späten 16. Jahrhunderts', *Musica*, 13 (1959), 768. Praetorius gives a very similar instruction regarding cadential *ritardani* at the conclusion of the motet *Lob sei dem allmächtigen Gott* in *Polyhymnia caduceatrix*, ed. Wilibald Gurlitt (Wolfenbüttel: Georg Kallmeyer Verlag, 1933), ii. 403.

[86] See n. 60 above.

[87] See the examples of rhythmic notation in this period in Wolf, *Notation*, ii. 27–98.

[88] *Le nuove musiche*, preface. Eng. trans. in *Giulio Caccini: Le nuove musiche*, ed. H. Wiley Hitchcock (Madison, Wis.: A-R Editions, Inc., 1970), 55. See the discussion of Caccini's concept in Ch. 16 above.

[89] Caccini, *Le nuove musiche e nuova maniera di scriverle*, preface. Eng. trans. in *Giulio Caccini, Le nuove musiche e nuova maniera di scriverle*, ed. H. Wiley Hitchcock (Madison: A-R Editions, Inc., 1978), p. xxxi. The idea that the character of the text affected the tempo reaches back to the first part of the 16th century. Lanfranco, Ganassi, Vicentino, and Zarlino all speak about tempo and vocal style in relation to the mood of the text. For pertinent passages from each of these theorists, see Federico Mompellio, 'Un certo ordine di procedere che non si può scrivere', in *Scritti in onore di Luigi Ronga* (Milan: Ricciardi, 1973), 367–88.

[90] See the statistics of Wolf, cited in n. 38 above, regarding the widespread tendency during the first decade of the 17th century towards change in the notation of the motet style in favour of the mensuration C with its smaller note values.

[91] Trans. from Colleen Reardon, *Agostino Agazzari and Music at Siena Cathedral, 1597–1641* (Oxford: Clarendon Press, 1993), 87.

Frescobaldi applied similar principles of flexible tempo to his organ music: 'First, this manner of playing need not be subject to the beat. As in the case with modern madrigals, no matter how difficult they may be, they are made easy by means of the conductor's beat, sometimes slow, sometimes fast, or evenly sustained, according to the affect or sense of the words'.[92] Frescobaldi also echoed Praetorius in recommending a cadential *ritardano*: 'Cadences, even when they are written in rapid note values, should be suitably sustained. When coming to the end, play the passage or cadence more slowly.'[93]

The freedom of the beat in madrigals mentioned by Frescobaldi is confirmed in numerous prefaces to publications of solo music and in theoretical writings of the early seventeenth century. Both the Puliaschi and Donati prefaces mentioned in Chapter 16 above and cited in note 7 there refer to 'various speeds of the beat' (Puliaschi) and even to ignoring a beat altogether (Donati). Valentini also declares that 'airs' (*arie*) are sung without a beat.[94]

Another factor affecting tempo was the presence of ornamental *passaggi*. The Roman composer Paolo Quagliati recommended in 1608 that when singing *passaggi*, by 'suspending the beat, one sings in conformity with the disposition of the singer . . . always slowing somewhat the voice at the end of the *passaggio*'.[95] In his *Salmi passaggiati*, however, Giovanni Luca Conforti, a singer in the Sistine Chapel, declared that the rhythmically notated recitations should be performed freely but that the *passaggi* at the cadences must be sung according to a strict beat.[96] Francesco Severi, another singer there, who published his own *Salmi passaggiati* in 1615, instructed that the *passaggi* in semiquavers should be sung as fast as possible.[97]

These *passaggi* of Severi are preceded by typical unmeasured *falsobordone* recitations of the psalm text, much as found in Monteverdi's *Dixit Dominus* and

---

[92] *Opere complete, II: Il primo libro di toccate d'intavolatura di cembalo e organo, 1615–1637*, ed., Étienne Darbellay (Milano: Edizioni Suvini Zerboni, 1977), p. xxvii. Eng. trans. in Ruth Halle Rowen, *Music through Sources and Documents* (Englewood Cliffs, NJ: Prentice-Hall, Inc., 1979), 170. Similarly Valentini described the beat as 'sometimes slow, sometimes quick, and sometimes between quick and moderately slow, according to the styles of compositions and the indication of the words'. See Houle, *Meter in Music*, 7.

[93] Frescobaldi, *Opere complete, II*, p. xxvii; trans. in Rowen, *Music through Sources and Documents*, 171. The Roman theorist Pier Francesco Valentini also recommended 'lengthening the penultimate note in a cadence when it is ornamented'. See Murata, 'Pier Francesco Valentini', 331.

[94] Ibid. 333. See also n. 92 above.

[95] 'Suspendosi la Battuta si cantano conforme alla dispositione del Cantante . . . rallentandosi sempre aliquanto la voce nel fine del Passaggio.' Quoted in Wolf, *Notation*, i. 56 n. 212.

[96] See the note to readers in Conforti's three books of *Salmi passaggiati* of 1601–3, trans. in *Giovanni Luca Conforti, 'Salmi passaggiati' (1601–1603)*, ed. Murray C. Bradshaw (Neuhausen and Stuttgart: American Institute of Musicology, Hänssler-Verlag, 1985), p. xci.

[97] 'E semicrome si cantino con vivacità et presto il più che sarà possibile'. Ed. Murray C. Bradshaw as *Francesco Severi: Salmi Passaggiati (1615)* (Madison, Wis.: A-R Editions, Inc., 1981). Bradshaw is a little too conservative in his translation of this passage: 'sung in a lively and quick way' (p. xxiii).

Laetatus sum, except that Severi was writing for a single voice. Severi also commented on how the *falsibordoni* are to be sung: 'if when singing the verses it should happen that there are many words on a single note [during recitations], they should be sung gracefully, always holding the first syllable and passing quickly over the second one, and so on with every two syllables. Take care to hold the last syllable of a word.'[98]

The style of a piece or section of a piece also affected tempo. Caccini spoke specifically about 'airy pieces or dance songs': 'It follows that in airy pieces or dance songs instead of these affects [*esclamazioni*] one should rely on the sprightliness of song, as usually conveyed by the air itself; although occasionally some *esclamazione* may occur, the same sprightliness should be maintained, with no affect smacking of lethargy introduced.'[99] Many of the pieces to which Caccini was referring were in some form of triple metre, and although Caccini was again speaking about secular music, the Englishman Thomas Ravenscroft explicitly connected the character of sacred music in triple metre with lively secular dances: 'The use of this *Perfect Prolation* is, in *Service Divine* for *Iubilees* and *Thanksgivings*, and otherwise for *Galliards* in *Revellings*.'[100] In his 1638 treatise on ecclesiastical music, Agostino Agazzari complained about the use of triple-metre dance music (*spagnolette* and *gagliarde*) as well as *arie profane* for the setting of sacred texts.[101]

Since Monteverdi's notation varies among the pieces in the Vespers, implying diverse origins for several of these compositions,[102] recommendations for dealing with each of his proportional relationships will be given below in tabular form along with general tempo suggestions. Proportional relationships between duple and triple metre are suggested where appropriate, but, as indicated above, considerable latitude in tempo relationships was normal by the early seventeenth century.

DOMINE AD ADJUVANDUM

C: Minim = MM 50–60.

$\frac{3}{2}$: Barring of bassus generalis equates semibreve under C with two perfect semibreves under $\frac{3}{2}$. This results in three minims under $\frac{3}{2}$ = one minim under C, achieved by changing the duple *tactus aequalis* to a *tactus inaequalis* under $\frac{3}{2}$.

---

[98] Ibid.: 'Che quando nel cantare li Versetti occorrerà che si recitino molte parole sopra una Nota, si dicano con grazia fermandosi sempre sopra la prima sillaba, e si passi presto la seconda, e cosi di due in due sillabe, con avvertire anco di fermarsi sul ultima sillaba della parola'.

[99] *Le nuove musiche*, preface; trans. from *Le nuove musiche*, ed. Hitchcock, 50.

[100] *A Briefe Discourse of the true (but neglected) Use of Charact'ring the Degrees . . .* (London: Edward Allde, 1614; fac. New York: Broude Brothers Ltd., 1976), 12.

[101] Reardon, *Agostino Agazzari*, 156 n. 74, 192–3.

[102] See the discussion of this possibility in Ch. 1. See also Peter Holman, '"Col nobilissimo esercitio della vivuola": Monteverdi's String Writing', *Early Music*, 21 (1993), 585.

Dixit Dominus

C: Tempo may differ for different sections in different styles. Range: minim = MM 58 to 72–6.

$\frac{3}{2}$: Unmeasured *falsibordoni* before and after each $\frac{3}{2}$ section obviate the need for any direct proportional relationship with the prevailing C of the psalm as a whole. The polyphonic melismas in C following the closing *falsobordone* of each $\frac{3}{2}$ passage reiterate in duple metre a version of the melodic and harmonic pattern of the passages in $\frac{3}{2}$. It is reasonable to assume that the tempo of these patterns would remain constant in $\frac{3}{2}$ and C.[103] Consequently, a perfect breve (dotted breve = one bar) under $\frac{3}{2}$ = one minim (half-bar) under C for the melismas in bars 24–45 and 86–108 and the corresponding optional ritornellos in bars 46–52 and 109–13.[104] Note that subsequent melismas (bars 145 ff. and 200 ff.) in structurally equivalent positions are in C throughout, confirming the relationship between $\frac{3}{2}$ and C suggested here. Minim = MM 76–84 under C; perfect breve (one bar) = MM 76–84 under $\frac{3}{2}$.

Nigra sum

Flexible tempo to be determined by speed of smallest note values and changing affects of text.

Laudate pueri

C: Tempo may differ for different sections in different styles. Opening tempo: minim = MM 70–80. Virtuoso duets beginning at *Sit nomen Domini* require a somewhat slower tempo.

$\mathbb{C}^{3}_{2}$: This is the only notation of $\mathbb{C}^{3}_{2}$ in the vocal parts of the Vespers. The principal note value is the semibreve, but the principal note values under C are the minim, crotchet and quaver, creating unequal levels of notes on either side of the proportion. Most early seventeenth-century theorists do not allow for the pairing of $\mathbb{C}^{3}_{2}$ with C. The use of $\mathbb{C}$ suggests a faster tactus, as both Banchieri and Praetorius describe, but because of the obvious need for a proportional relationship of some kind between bars 87–8, 92–3, 97–8 and 101–2, it seems probable that Monteverdi's use of $\mathbb{C}$ here displays its ancient significance of a 2:1 diminution in note values.[105] Barring in the bassus gen-

[103] Wolf, *Notation*, i. 92–3, does not see motivic repetition between duple and triple time as establishing a 'classical' proportional relationship, but does consider that some kind of inexact relationship must have been maintained.

[104] Wolf, ibid. 102, comes to a similar conclusion about the proportional relationship between perfect breves in triple time and minims in duple time in analogous circumstances in Frescobaldi. The basis for Wolf's equivalencies is the assumption that the smallest ornamental notes in triple metre (pairs of crotchets) relate to the smallest ornamental notes in duple metre (semiquavers).

[105] Wolf, ibid. 109, notes a few publications where the succession C, $\mathbb{C}^{3}_{2}$ (in semibreves) merely indicates that the composer or printer recognized that $\frac{3}{2}$ in semibreves normally was associated with $\mathbb{C}$, not C.

eralis suggests that one perfect breve under $\mathbb{C}_2^3$ equals a single semibreve under C, but when diminution is applied, a perfect breve (dotted breve = 1 bar) under $\mathbb{C}_2^3$ = minim under C. Another way to achieve the same result is with an equal minim tactus under C, which simply changes to an unequal breve tactus under $\mathbb{C}_2^3$. A similar relationship can be maintained in the mensuration changes at bars 130–1, 153–4, 161–2 and 189–90, but is not required because a cadence or potential break precedes each change.[106]

PULCHRA ES

C: Flexible tempo to be determined by speed of smallest note values, relation to $\frac{3}{2}$ sections, and affect of text.

$\frac{3}{2}$: Notation in minims is at a different level of note values from notation in crotchets, quavers, and semiquavers under C. Bassus generalis barring is in two semibreves under $\frac{3}{2}$ and generally in breves under C, but for the few bars before and after the $\frac{3}{2}$ sections, barring is in semibreves, suggesting that three minims under $\frac{3}{2}$ = one minim under C.[107] An equal minim tactus under C, changed to an unequal semibreve tactus under $\frac{3}{2}$ will produce the appropriate relationship. Note Caccini's remarks above about the 'sprightliness' of 'airy pieces or dance songs' and Thomas Ravenscroft's identification of triple time in the divine service with galliards. Perfect semibreve (one bar) = MM 60–70. Tempo chosen for $\frac{3}{2}$ sections may set the pace for the prevailing C.

LAETATUS SUM

C: Tempo may differ for different sections in different styles. Opening tempo: minim = MM 70–80. Slower tempo will be necessary for sections with virtuoso *passaggi*.

DUO SERAPHIM

C: Tempo will be determined by smallest note values. The tempo must be fast enough to keep this piece from bogging down in the dotted rhythms and rapid repeated notes, which must be sung lightly enough and

---

[106] Roger Bowers maintains that three semibreves under $\mathbb{C}_2^3$ equal one semibreve under C. He also claims that the text in the $\mathbb{C}_2^3$ passages prompts Monteverdi to choose 'a gentler character and tempo'. See Bowers, 'Some Reflection', 373–7. Bowers's interpretation, however, contradicts his own account of Monteverdi's $\mathbb{C}$ as indicating a faster beat. Moreover, the texts of the passages in question consist of words and concepts that are typically treated with greater rhythmic energy or faster tempos in the late 16th and early 17th centuries.

[107] Bowers, ibid. 381–5, suggests that a perfect semibreve under $\frac{3}{2}$ equals an imperfect breve under C, which is the mathematically theoretical proportion, but this interpretation ignores Monteverdi's bassus generalis barring and creates a musical oxymoron between the words 'they have made me flee' and a slowing of the tempo.

with enough sense of rhythmic direction to sound graceful rather than heavy-footed.

NISI DOMINUS

C: Minim = MM 60–80 for opening verses and doxology. Minim = MM 100–20 from *Nisi Dominus custodierit civitatem* to doxology. Tempo choices within these ranges will depend on number of singers per part and resonance of performing space. Semibreve tactus.

$\frac{3}{2}$: *Sesquialtera* at the level of the minim, confirmed by barring of bassus generalis. Predominant note values are at same rhythmic level under both C and $\frac{3}{2}$, indicating a traditional proportion: three minims under $\frac{3}{2}$ = two minims under C, again achieved by a simple change from an equal to an unequal tactus. Perfect semibreve (dotted semibreve) = MM 50–60.

AUDI COELUM

First section

C: Flexible tempo to be determined by speed of smallest note values and changing affects of text.

Second section (Omnes hanc ergo)

C: Polyphonic style in larger note values (Praetorius's 'motet' style). Semibreve tactus. Note values are much larger than in first section, where principal motion is in crotchets, quavers, and semiquavers. No tempo equivalency between first section and second section required. Banchieri and Praetorius both suggest a slower tactus for C, which, because of the prevailing motion in semibreves and minims, would produce a moderate pace. Semibreve = MM 50–66.

$\frac{3}{2}$: Sequential thematic patterns in minims suggest fairly rapid tempo. Note Caccini's remarks above about the 'sprightliness' of 'airy pieces or dance songs' and Thomas Ravenscroft's identification of triple time in the divine service with galliards. Perfect semibreve (one bar) = MM 66–76. No proportional relationship required between C of first section and at beginning of second section and $\frac{3}{2}$, or between C and $\frac{3}{2}$ within second section, because the $\frac{3}{2}$ passages are preceded by sustained chords and close with full cadences before the subsequent passages in C begin. A *sesquialtera* relationship is possible, however, although a slowing of the two brief echo duets may be desirable. In such a proportion, a perfect semibreve under $\frac{3}{2}$ (one bar) = an imperfect semibreve under C (one bar), achieved by changing an equal tactus to an unequal tactus. An appropriate tempo would be semibreve = approximately MM 66.

LAUDA JERUSALEM

C: Minim = MM 70–82. Because of greater consistency of style, a steadier tempo can be maintained than in other psalms, although some fluctuations are possible.

SONATA SOPRA SANCTA MARIA

C: Minim = MM 80–90.

$\frac{3}{2}$: *Sesquialtera* at the level of the minim, confirmed by barring of bassus generalis. Three minims under $\frac{3}{2}$ = two minims under C, achieved by changing the equal tactus to an unequal tactus. Because the thematic material of the first $\frac{3}{2}$ section is the same as the opening C section, but in triple metre, the proportional relationship allows the harmonic rhythm to proceed at exactly the same pace in both sections. Whereas *sesquialtera* usually entails a hastening of the principal note values by one third, in the *Sonata* the sections in $\frac{3}{2}$ are actually slowed in relation to C because the principal movement in duple time is in minims, crotchets, and quavers rather than semibreves, minims, and crotchets.[108]

Blackened triplets (*meliola*): Six black minims under C = four crotchets (two minims) under C (one bar of C *meliola* = one bar of C without *meliola*). This relationship allows for continuation of the tactus equivalence among all sections in C and in $\frac{3}{2}$. Consequently, six blackened minims of *meliola* = three minims under $\frac{3}{2}$, and the *meliola* represents a diminution (minims becoming the equivalent of crotchets grouped in triplets). In this particular passage an equal tactus would prevail, expressing the compound duple organization of the thematic patterns (2 × 3). Praetorius calls this notation *sextupla*, or *tactus trochaicus diminutus*.[109] Buonamente describes it as being equivalent to $\frac{6}{4}$, to be beaten with a *tactus aequalis*.[110] The diminution created by blackening

[108] Franz Jochen Machatius proposes a different temporal relationship for dance-based music that reiterates a duple-time passage in triple time. Citing a statement from Martin Agricola, *Musica figuralis deudsch* (1532), which calls for a lengthening (and thereby slowing) of the tactus from two minims to three when the *Proporcientact* appears in all parts in dance music, he argues that triple-time passages under duple metre in canzonetta style should be lengthened by half instead of maintaining an equal tactus. See Machatius, 'Über mensurale und spielmännische Reduktion', *Die Musikforschung*, 8 (1955), 139–51. Arthur Mendel, however, in 'Some Ambiguities of the Mensural System', in Harold Powers, ed., *Studies in Music History: Essays for Oliver Strunk* (Princeton: Princeton University Press, 1968), 141–8, has demonstrated the bewildering inconsistencies and confusions in Agricola's treatise, including the passage cited by Machatius as the basis of his argument. Machatius's proposal seems inapplicable to the *Sonata*, since the resultant further slowing of the $\frac{3}{2}$ passages is unlikely.

[109] *Syntagmatis musici . . . tomus tertius*, 73–5; trans. Lampl, pp. 124–30. Banchieri also discusses blackened minims grouped in triplets by means of the numeral *3*, but for the purpose of creating a true *sesquialtera* in relation to C. See Banchieri, *Cartella musicale*, 31; trans. in Cranna, 'Adriano Banchieri's *Cartella musicale*', 121–2.

[110] See Wolf, *Notation*, i. 94 n. 399. This type of mensural and temporal relationship is described in relation to a secular aria of Domenico Visconti (1616) in Aldrich, *Rhythm in Seventeenth-Century Italian Monody*, 51–2.

minims, to which Praetorius refers, is confirmed by the cantus part-book, which contains both the vocal part and the basso continuo.[111] In this particular statement of the litany only, the cantus part is notated in rhythmic values one level larger than in all other statements. The diminution brings the note values of this statement into line with all the others. The resulting quick pace for the *meliola* seems confirmed by Sigismondo d'India's comments on the *battuta presta* of $\frac{6}{4}$.[112] Brunelli and Valentini, in contrast to Praetorius and Buonamente, indicate an unequal tactus for the *meliola*, each tactus containing one triple grouping, although Valentini also recognizes a $\frac{6}{4}$ grouping of crotchets as a compound duple metre requiring an equal tactus.[113] While Monteverdi's notation could be beaten with an unequal tactus, twice as fast as the tactus of the rest of the *Sonata*, it seems unnecessary to subdivide the measure, and the same tactus can be maintained throughout.[114]

AVE MARIS STELLA

C: Bassus generalis has ₵, suggesting a fast beat. Minim = MM 80–90. Semibreve tactus. The older style and larger note values of the hymn have often misled conductors into performing this piece too slowly. But Praetorius, Banchieri, and many other theorists of the late sixteenth and early seventeenth centuries make it clear that the older style, usually notated in ₵,

---

[111] The vocal part remains in C. As Wolf, *Notation*, i. 121–2, notes, the only means available in the early 17th century to notate the duple mensuration of the cantus firmus with triple time in the other parts was by means of blackened triplets in the latter.

[112] See the preface to d'India's *Le musiche e balli a 4 voci* (1621), quoted in Wolf, *Notation*, ii. 14. Wolf, ibid., 118 n. 495, cites the few theorists who regard *hemiola* as faster than *tripla* or *sesquialtera*; practical examples cited on p. 119 n. 504.

[113] See Murata, 'Pier Francesco Valentini', 335–9, 349–50. Murata translates Valentini's description of the *meliola* as follows: 'Of a certain proportion called by some with the name *Meliola*, which according to the quality of the signs under which it appears, can be of different sorts of proportions'. According to Murata, Valentini equates the *meliola* with the *emiola minore* following the mensuration C. This relationship would make each triplet of Monteverdi's *meliola* equivalent to two minims under C instead of one, and would not account for the augmentation in the cantus part. Monteverdi's usage, as well as his organization of the triplets into compound duple groupings through melodic and harmonic sequences, seems to accord more with Valentini's description of $\frac{6}{4}$, which, like Praetorius's *sextupla*, replaces four crotchets with six in a compound duple metre.

[114] Monteverdi's barring in the bassus generalis and the cantus part-books is inconclusive with regard to the metric relationship between the *meliola* and the other signatures, but his sequential thematic and harmonic patterns are more revealing. These sequential patterns most frequently occupy one bar under C and $\frac{3}{2}$, especially in the portion of the piece in question, and presumably should also occupy one bar under C in *meliola*; otherwise there would be a sudden and inexplicable augmentation not only of the litany in the voice, but of the accompanying patterns as well. Interpreting the *meliola* as coloured minims would also make the *meliola* notation indistinguishable from the $\frac{3}{2}$ section that immediately follows the *meliola*, rendering the *meliola* meaningless in musical terms. Bowers suggests an unconvincing number symbolism as the rationale behind Monteverdi's *meliola*, but ironically, his number symbolism is actually independent of whether or not the *meliola* is treated as diminution. See Bowers, 'Some Reflection', 391–5, and my correspondence in *Music & Letters*, 74 (1993), 490. Anna Maria Vacchelli also argues for performing this passage without diminution. See Vacchelli, 'Monteverdi as a Primary Source for the Performance of his own Music', *Performing Practice in Monteverdi's Music*, 35–9.

requires a somewhat faster beat precisely because of the larger note values and because such pieces must not proceed too slowly (see Praetorius's comments above). For recordings at a somewhat faster tempo than most, readers are referred to Appendix D, items 35 and 36.

C_2^3: Bassus generalis has $\mathcal{C}_2^3$, suggesting a fast beat. These verses are independent and need not necessarily have a directly proportional relationship with the verses in C. The thematic material is a variant of the thematic material of the opening verse in C, but rhythmic values are not always parallel, and the style changes from polyphony in the first verse to homophony for the triple-metre verses. The harmonic rhythm of the triple-metre verses takes only half as many bars as in duple metre. There is no barring in the bassus generalis to serve as a guide to tempo relationships, and a true *sesquialtera* would result in a very slow tempo for the verses in triple metre. Rather, their simple, homophonic style seems to require a faster pace. Since the beat in duple time would be on the semibreve and the beat in triple time on the breve, keeping the same tactus from duple to triple metre would produce a proportion whereby three semibreves under C_2^3 were equivalent to one semibreve under C (one bar of C = one bar of C_2^3 in my edition).

MAGNIFICAT *A 7*

Verse 1, *Magnificat*

C: Bassus generalis has $\mathcal{C}$, suggesting a fast beat and semibreve tactus. Minim = MM 80–90.

Verse 2, *Et exsultavit*

C: Crotchet = MM 70–80. Monteverdi warns the organist 'to play slowly because the two tenors sing in semiquavers'.

Verse 3, *Quia respexit*

C_2^3: Bassus generalis has $\mathcal{C}_2^3$, suggesting a fast beat. Perfect breve (dotted breve = one bar) = MM 45–50.
C: Bassus generalis has $\mathcal{C}$, suggesting a fast beat and semibreve tactus. Minim = MM 90–100. Proportional relationship between the triple-metre ritornello and vocal section in C is required because of overlap of the ritornello and vocal parts at the end of the verse, but pairing of perfect breve units in triple metre with minims and crotchets in duple metre is an incorrect use of proportions according to Banchieri.[115] Barring in bassus generalis suggests an equivalence between bars of $\mathcal{C}_2^3$ and C, as does the notation of the vocal part

---

[115] See n. 62 above. Banchieri's objection is based on mathematical proportions in note values, but if the proportion is based on the tactus, then the difference between a tactus on larger note values and a tactus on smaller note values is irrelevant.

at the end of the verse (perfect breve of Magnificat tone under $Ȼ_2^3$ equivalent to semibreve under C), resulting in the metronome suggestions given above. Maintaining the same tactus between $Ȼ_2^3$ (dotted breve = one tactus) and C (semibreve = one tactus) yields the same proportion. *Quia respexit* in the Magnificat *a 6* (see below) is structured similarly with a varied version of the same bass in the C section, but with a triple mensuration of C_2^3 in perfect semibreve units, creating a true *sesquialtera* proportion. The proportion in the Magnificat *a 6* therefore confirms the interpretation of the proportion given here for the Magnificat *a 7*.

Verse 4, *Quia fecit*

C: Minim = MM 60–72. Monteverdi warns the organist 'to play slowly because the parts sing and play in quavers and semiquavers'.

Verse 5, *Et misericordia*

C: Bassus generalis has $Ȼ$, suggesting a fairly rapid pace and semibreve tactus. Minim = MM 70–80. The polyphonic style and relatively large note values often mislead conductors into performing this verse too slowly.

Verse 6, *Fecit potentiam*

$Ȼ_2^3$: Bassus generalis has $Ȼ_2^3$, suggesting a fast pace. Semibreve = MM 84–114. The range of prevailing note values permits a wide range of tempos.

Verse 7, *Deposuit*

C: Crotchet = MM 64–74. The tempo should not drag, but should not be too fast for the cornettists to play the semiquavers and demisemiquavers.

Verse 8, *Esurientes*

C_2^3: Bassus generalis has $Ȼ_2^3$, suggesting a fast beat. Perfect breve (dotted breve = one bar) = MM 50–60, a little faster than *Quia respexit*, whose ritornello also has semibreves and minims as principal note values.

C: Bassus generalis has $Ȼ$, suggesting a fast beat and semibreve tactus. Semibreve = MM 50–60 because of large note values. No barring in bassus generalis, which has only rests for sections in C. Proportional relationship between triple-metre ritornello and vocal section in C required because of overlap of ritornello and vocal parts at end of verse. Ritornello is barred with six semibreves per bar, as in *Quia respexit*, so that if a similar proportion is maintained between triple and duple metres in *Esurientes* as in *Quia respexit*, three semibreves (dotted breve = one bar) under C_2^3 = one semibreve (one bar) under C. Maintaining the same tactus between C_2^3 (dotted breve = one tactus) and C (semibreve = one tactus) yields the same proportion.

Verse 9, *Suscepit Israel*

> C: Minim = MM 56–66. Monteverdi warns the organist to 'play slowly because the two sopranos sing in echo'.

Verse 10, *Sicut locutus est*

> C: Minim = MM 70–80.

Verse 11, *Gloria Patri*

> C: Crotchet = MM 60–70. The rhapsodic melisma at the opening should be treated quite freely, as if it were an ornamental improvisation. Only when the chant has entered do the groups of notes in the tenor and the quintus echo organize themselves into short and sufficiently regular patterns to require a steady tempo.

Verse 12, *Sicut erat*

> C: Bassus generalis has ₵, suggesting a fairly rapid tempo and semibreve tactus. Minim = MM 70–84. A fast enough tempo will keep the *Sicut erat* from dragging too much. This tempo also permits the lively *Amen* to be performed at the same pace. The verse, with its massed sonorities, should be imposing and stately, and the ultimate choice of tempo should depend upon the size of the vocal and instrumental ensemble as well as the resonance of the performance space. Conductors are often misled by the polyphonic texture and large note values to perform this verse too slowly.

MAGNIFICAT *A 6*

Verse 1, *Magnificat*

> C: Bassus generalis has ₵, suggesting a fast beat and semibreve tactus. Minim = MM 80–90.

Verse 2, *Et exsultavit*

> C_2^3: Minim = MM 84–94.

Verse 3, *Quia respexit*

> C_2^3: *Sesquialtera* at the level of the minim. Perfect semibreve (dotted semibreve = one bar) = MM 60–70.
> C: Semibreve = MM 60–70. Possible semibreve tactus. Two minims (imperfect semibreve = one bar) under C = three minims (perfect semibreve = one bar) under C_2^3.

Verse 4, *Quia fecit*

> C: Minim = MM 70–80. Possible semibreve tactus. The polyphonic style and relatively large note values often mislead conductors into performing this verse too slowly.

Verse 5, *Et misericordia*

C: Minim = MM 60–72. Monteverdi warns the organist to 'play slowly because the sopranos sing in quavers'.

Verse 6, *Fecit potentiam*

C: Minim = MM 70–80. Possible semibreve tactus.

Verse 7, *Deposuit*

C: Crotchet = MM 60–72. Embellishments in small note values require a slower pace than other verses.

Verse 8, *Esurientes*

C_2^3: Bassus generalis has ₵3, suggesting a fast beat. Perfect breve (dotted breve) = MM 50–60.

Verse 9, *Suscepit Israel*

C: Possible semibreve tactus. The cantus firmus might well be sung at the same pace as the preceding *Esurientes*: semibreve = MM 50–60. This would create a *tripla* proportion between the *Esurientes* and this verse, or a *sesquialtera* if the ₵3 mensuration of the bassus generalis in the *Esurientes* is taken as a sign of diminution in relation to this verse.

Verse 10, *Sicut locutus est*

C: Minim = MM 62–72.

Verse 11, *Gloria Patri*

C: Minim = MM 66–76. There should be a lively sense of movement, and the thick texture must not obscure the staggered entries of the voices, or the rhythmic vitality will be lost in the density of sound. An appropriate tempo will depend on the size of the chorus and the resonance of the performance space.

Verse 12, *Sicut erat*

C: Minim = MM 70–84. Possible semibreve tactus. Conductors are often misled by the polyphonic texture and larger note values of this verse to perform it too slowly.

21

Vocal and Instrumental Ornamentation

THE practice of improvising ornaments to written melodic lines was centuries old by the time of Monteverdi's Vespers.[1] The earliest period from which we have detailed information about such embellishments is the sixteenth century, when many theorists were occupied with examining thoroughly all aspects of composition and performance, including the art of improvised ornamentation. Other sources of information from this period include instrumental transcriptions of vocal music, which often contain substantial ornamentation not found in the original versions. Until late in the sixteenth century there was no real distinction between vocal and instrumental ornamentation; in fact, instrumentalists were often advised to imitate the voice as closely as possible.[2]

Two principal forms of ornamentation are described in the theoretical treatises and found in practical sources. The first of these are *passaggi*, comprising rapid scale formations that frequently incorporate turning figures (*passaggi* were normally written in even notes, either quavers or semiquavers, for most of the sixteenth century), and they either fill out the time and pitch intervals between longer notes or elaborate a brief melodic phrase with runs up and down the scale touching on the written notes of the melody. Only in the late sixteenth century did dotted rhythms begin to appear to any significant degree; by the

---

[1] See Ernest T. Ferand, *Improvisation in Nine Centuries of Western Music* (Anthology of Music, 12; Cologne: Arno Volk Verlag, 1961). Andrew Waldo has published a practical guide for instrumentalists wanting to learn how to play *passaggi* in 'So you Want to Blow the Audience Away; Sixteenth-Century Ornamentation: A Perspective on Goals and Techniques', *American Recorder*, 27 (1986), 48–59. Some aspects of vocal technique and style in relation to ornaments has already been discussed in Ch. 16 above.

[2] Sylvestro Ganassi, Jerome Cardan, and Girolamo dalla Casa all stress the importance of imitating the voice on both wind and string instruments. See Ganassi, *Opera intitulata Fontegara* (Venice, 1535; fac. Milan: La Musica Moderna, 1934); Eng. trans. Dorothy Swainson as *Sylvestro Ganassi: Opera intitulata Fortegara* (Berlin and Lichterfelde: Robert Lienau, 1956), ch. 1; *Hieronymus Cardanus, Writings on Music*, trans. Clement A. Miller (American Institute of Musicology, 1973), 69; Dalla Casa, *Il vero modo di diminuir, con tutte le sorti di stromenti* (Venice: Angelo Gardano, 1584); fac. ed. Giuseppe Vecchi (Bologna: Arnaldo Forni, 1976), bk. i, 'Del cornetto'. Cardan is the most detailed in his comments: 'The things that are true for the recorder are true for all instruments, but they are even more appropriate for this instrument. A particular property is imitation of the human voice, not simple imitation (for as we will show, this is common to all instruments) but rather exact imitation is proper to the instrument. This happens by using a relaxed tone in laments, a strong tone in excitement, a smooth, connected tone in serious moods, and so forth concerning the other emotions . . .'.

early seventeenth century, dotted rhythms in *passaggi* became just as common as even rhythms.[3]

Cadential ornaments constitute the second form of embellishment. These, too, often include scale motion, usually culminating with a *groppo* or a *trillo* (see below for descriptions of these ornaments) just before the final note.[4]

By the late sixteenth century instrumental ornamentation had become even more elaborate than vocal ornamentation, extending over a wider pitch range and employing more leaps. Moreover, a new style of vocal ornamentation, emerging from the development of monody with its rhetorically expressive mode of performance, was joined with the old. In addition to the traditional *passaggi* and *cadentie* (ornamented cadences), late sixteenth- and early seventeenth-century singers cultivated what Caccini called *grazie*, or graces— various means of enhancing the expressive character of individual notes and short phrases.[5] A variety of specialized graces developed after 1590 and received their most detailed codification by Francesco Rognoni in 1620.[6] Many of these ornaments emerged directly from the vocal technique of the early seventeenth century, so that a clear distinction cannot always be made between vocal style and ornamentation. Consequently, some features of singing style that might also be considered ornaments are discussed in Chapter 16, and the discussion of vocal ornamentation in the present chapter should be read in conjunction with the earlier chapter.

There is not space in this brief survey for a detailed account of the many forms of *passaggi*, cadences, and graces described by sixteenth- and seventeenth-century composers, performers, and theorists. The quantity and variety of writings on the subject demonstrate the interest of practical musicians in subtle nuances and details of expression through ornamentation. Examples and descriptions of the appropriate manner of performing them may be found in the numerous books and facsimile editions as well as the many articles dealing with ornamentation in this period.[7] Discussion will be restricted here to

---

[3] See Howard M. Brown, *Embellishing Sixteenth-Century Music* (London: Oxford University Press, 1976), 17–30; and Richard Erig, *Italienische Diminutionen* (Zürich: Amadeus Verlag, 1979). The transition can be clearly seen in Giovanni Battista Bovicelli, *Regole, passaggi di musica* (Venice: Giacomo Vincenti, 1594); fac. ed. Nanie Bridgman, Documenta musicologica, ser. 1 : 12 (Kassel: Bärenreiter, 1957).

[4] See Brown, *Embellishing Sixteenth-Century Music*, 1–16; and Erig, *Italienische Diminutionen*.

[5] Bernard Thomas, in 'Divisions in Renaissance Music', in Tess Knighton and David Fallows, eds., *Companion to Medieval and Renaissance Music* (New York: Schirmer Books, 1992), 346, stresses the 'mannered, almost erratic style' of the new irregular rhythms found in ornamentation of the late 16th and early 17th centuries 'that contrasts dramatically with the smooth flow of typical Renaissance divisions'.

[6] Francesco Rognoni, *Selva de varii passaggi secondo l'uso moderno per cantare, & suonare con ogni sorte de stromenti* (Milan: Filippo Lomazzo, 1620; fac. ed. Guglielmo Barblan, Bologna: Arnaldo Forni, 1978).

[7] For the most important literature on this subject, see the articles, books, and editions in the Bibliography by Murray C. Bradshaw, Nanie Bridgman, Stewart Carter, Tim Carter, Friedrich Chrysander, Bruce Dickey, Ernest T. Ferand, H. Wiley Hitchcock, Imogene Horsely, Max Kuhn, Carol MacClintock, Gloria Rose, Donald C. Sanders, Sally Allis Sanford, and Oscar Tajetti and Alberto

some of the most important rules and suggestions promulgated in ornamentation treatises.[8]

From early in the sixteenth century, performers were admonished to pick appropriate words to ornament and warned against embellishing more than one part at a time. Writers of this period advise that *passaggi* should begin and end with the same note so that there is no disruption in the original, unornamented melodic line. An exception to this rule may be made where the original melodic line contained a leap. In this case, the *passaggio* may fill out the leap and approach the next note of the melody by step. The rules of strict counterpoint need not always apply in embellishments, since their speed and the effectiveness of particular passages may override a few contrapuntal faults. Several writers say that embellishments must always be performed without slowing the underlying beat, but it is not clear that this was always followed in practice, especially with the flexible tempos advocated in the early seventeenth century. *Passaggi* should conclude with one or more slower notes, and very rapid *passaggi* should begin with a first note longer than the others. Good taste and discretion are the most important rules of thumb in determining where and how to ornament. [9]

Specifically vocal ornamentation required some additional considerations. Numerous theorists comment on the importance of singing softly and sweetly and of introducing variety into the performance. Zacconi, however, allows for repetition in *passaggi*: 'The art of the *gorgie* does not so much consist in variation or in the diversity of the *passaggi* as it does in a just and measured quantity of figures, the great speed of which does not permit one to perceive whether that which one hears has already been said and is being repeated. On the contrary, a small number of figures can be reused many times in the manner of a circle or a crown . . .'[10]

Colzani. See also Oliver Strunk, *Source Readings in Music History* (New York: W. W. Norton & Company, 1950), 377–92, 419–31. For full titles of relevant theoretical treatises, some available in facsimile and some translated into English, see in Appendix F: Agostino Agazzari, *Del sonare sopra'l basso*; Giovanni Bassano, *Ricercate, passaggi et cadentiae*; Giovanni Battista Bovicelli, *Regole, passaggi di musica*; Antonio Brunelli, *Varii esercitii*; Girolamo dalla Casa, *Il vero modo di diminuir*; Giovanni Luca Conforti, *Breve et facile maniera d'essercitarsi . . . a far passaggi*; Girolamo Diruta, *Il Transilvano* (i. 8–12; ii. 11–13; Eng. trans., i. 63–73; ii. 20–2); Hermann Finck, *Practica musica* (bk. v); Silvestro Ganassi, *Opera intitulata Fontegara*; Michael Praetorius, *Syntagmatis musici . . . tomus tertius* (pp. 229–40; Eng. trans., pp. 367–79); Francesco Rognoni, *Selva de varii passaggi*; Giovanni Battista Spadi, *Libro de passaggi ascendenti et descendenti*; Nicola Vicentino, *L'antica musica ridotta alla moderna prattica* (bk. iv, ch. 42); Aurelio Virgiliano, *Il Dolcimelo*; Lodovico Zacconi, *Prattica di musica* (vol. i, fos. 58–76); Gioseffo Zarlino, *Le istitutioni harmoniche* (pp. 203–4; Eng. trans. Guy A. Marco and Claude V. Palisca, pp. 109–11). Also relevant are the prefaces to Giulio Caccini, *Le nuove musiche*; id., *Nuove musiche e nuova maniera di scriverle*; and Ottavio Durante, *Arie devote*, listed in App. E.

[8] For convenient lists of rules regarding diminutions according to Virgiliano and Zacconi, see Bruce Dickey, 'Ornamentation in Early-Seventeenh-Century Italian Music', in Stewart Carter, ed., *A Performer's Guide to Seventeenth-Century Music* (New York: Schirmer Books, 1997), 247–54.

[9] Bovicelli, *Regole passaggi di musica*, 'Avertimenti intorno alle note', and Rognoni, *Selva de varii passaggi*, 'Avvertimenti alli benigni lettori' and 'Avertimenti à cantanti'.

[10] Quoted from Dickey, 'Ornamentation in Early-Seventeenth-Century Italian Music', 252 Original text in Zacconi, *Prattica di musica* (Venice: Girolamo Polo, 1592; fac. Bologna: Arnaldo Forni, 1967), 66.

Writers also warned against the singer showing affectation, ornamenting excessively, or ignoring the expression of the text. Ottavio Durante declares explicitly that singers should 'make the *passaggi* in places where they will not impede the understanding of the words.'[11] *Passaggi* should be made on the penultimate syllable of a word, so that the ornament concludes with the last syllable. The best vowel for vocal ornamentation is *o*, but *a* and *e* are also satisfactory; *u* and *i* are to be avoided. Since *passaggi* may require a redistribution of syllables of text, care must be taken not to make short syllables long or long syllables short. Syllables of text should not be repeated in the course of a *passaggio*. *Passaggi* or other ornaments that conclude with rapid notes should not proceed immediately to the next syllable; rather, a moderating note, taken from the rhythmic duration of the subsequent note, should be inserted. Quite naturally, such ornamentation can be applied only when one person is singing a part, not two or more.[12]

There is very little commentary in treatises of the period on the technique for producing *passaggi*. In Chapter 16 above, a passage from Zacconi's *Prattica di musica* of 1592 was quoted that bears on this question:

the *tremolo*, that is the trembling voice, is the true gate to enter the passages and to become proficient in the *gorgia* [ornaments]: because the boat moves with greater ease when it is first pushed . . . The *tremolo* should be short and beautiful, for if it is long and forceful, it tires and bores. And it is of such a nature that those who employ it must always use it, so that it becomes a habit. The continual movement of the voice aids and voluntarily pushes the movement of the *gorgia*, and admirably facilitates the beginnings of the passages. This movement I am speaking of should only be made with proper speed, and lively and vehemently.[13]

Zacconi is vague about what he means by a *tremolo*, and his use of the term has been the subject of considerable debate, though it is clear he sees it as a method for facilitating *passaggi* and *gorgie*. Sally A. Sanford and some others believe Zacconi is referring to an articulation in the throat, which greatly facilitates the singing of embellishments.[14] According to Sanford,

Both French and Italian singing in the seventeenth century differ significantly from modern singing with respect to the use of throat articulation, a technique for singing rapid passages and ornaments. Throat articulation . . . had reached a zenith in the 1580's with *garganta* singers such as the three ladies of Ferrara, who excelled in this *gorgia* technique. Bacilly called this technique, or

---

[11] Donald C. Sanders, 'Vocal Ornaments in Durante's *Arie devote* (1608)', *Performance Practice Review*, 6 (1993), 71. Durante's preface is published in its original Italian together with an English translation in Sanders, 'Vocal Ornaments', 70–6.

[12] Bovicelli, *Regole passaggi di musica*, 'Avertimenti intorno alle note'.

[13] Carol MacClintock, *Readings in the History of Music in Performance* (Bloomington, Ind.: Indiana University Press, 1979), 73, where the treatise is incorrectly dated 1596.

[14] See the discussion of this issue in Ch. 16.

the laryngeal set-up for using this technique, the *disposition de la gorge*.[15] The Italians called it the *dispositione*.[16]

According to Sanford, even the virtuoso *passaggi* notated by Monteverdi in *Possente spirto* from *L'Orfeo* are 'quite simple to sing' for someone who uses throat articulation and is familiar with characteristic seventeenth-century ornamental *affetti*.[17]

While commentaries on vocal *passaggi* also mention maintaining the underlying tempo in such embellishments, the affective style of singing, characterized by Caccini's concept of *nobile sprezzatura* (See Chapters 16 and 20), requires sufficient flexibility in *passaggi* that they may be sung with the grace that was so highly prized by all writers on singing of the period.

The proliferation of embellishments in the sixteenth century and early seventeenth century also led to objections by writers who complained of ornamental excesses as well as the ruin of good counterpoint.[18] According to several theorists, bass parts, in particular, should not be heavily embellished, since the foundation of the harmony could easily be disrupted.

From the last decade of the sixteenth century onwards, more and more emphasis was placed on the various graces as a means of enhancing individual notes and short phrases or of expressing the emotional import of individual words of the text. Caccini's preface and the notated embellishments in *Le nuove musiche* (1602) significantly de-emphasize *passaggi* in favour of such graces, which he says should be used to create a variety of affects in a composition.[19] The most common graces, both in the repertoire and in theoretical treatises, are *groppi*, *tremoli*, *trilli*, *intonazioni* (*clamazioni*), *accenti*, *escalmazioni*, the *ribattuta di gola*, and the *portar la voce*.[20] The *groppo* is an alternation between two adjacent notes followed by a turning figure. The word *tremolo* has various meanings, ranging from the vocal analogue of an organ *tremolo*, the latter produced mechanically by rhythmic impulses in the otherwise steady flow of air, to the measured reiteration of a single pitch.[21] The organ *tremolo*'s undulations in air supply produced

---

[15] Author's note, expanded: Bénigne de Bacilly, *Remarques curieuses sur l'art de bien chanter*, 2nd edn. (Paris: Guillaume de Luyne, 1679; repr. Geneva: Minkoff Reprints, 1971), 48 ff.

[16] 'A Comparison of French and Italian Singing in the Seventeenth Century', *Journal of Seventeeth-Century Music*, 1 (1995), ¶ 7.1 [http:// rism.harvard.edu/jscm/].

[17] Ibid., ¶ 8.1.

[18] See e.g. Rognoni, *Selva di varii passaggi*, 'Avertimenti à cantanti'. Caccini also complained of such excesses in the preface to *Le nuove musiche*. See *Giulio Caccini: Le nuove musiche*, ed. H. Wiley Hitchcock (Madison, Wis.: A-R Editions, 1970), 43.

[19] See Brown, *Embellishing Sixteenth-Century Music*, 1–16; and *Le nuove musiche*, ed. Hitchcock, 43–56.

[20] Among the authors listed in n. 7 above, particularly useful articles describing these ornaments are Stewart Carter, 'Francesco Rognoni's *Selva de varii passaggi* (1620): Fresh Details concerning Early-Baroque Vocal Ornamentation', *Performance Practice Review*, 2 (1989), 5–33; and Dickey, 'Ornamentation in Early-Seventeenth-Century Italian Music'.

[21] See Greta Moens-Haenen, *Das Vibrato in der Musik des Barock* (Graz: Akademische Druck und

undulations in pitch as well.[22] The vocal *tremolo*, on the other hand, is sometimes described as being similar to a measured breath vibrato, but slower than a vibrato (see below for a discussion of vibrato as an ornament).[23] The organ *tremolo* also frequently served as the reference in seventeenth-century sources for the string *tremolo*, consisting of measured repetitions of a note 'taken in a single stroke of the bow, articulated by a gentle pulsating motion of the bow arm without stopping the bow'.[24] But unlike the organ *tremolo*, the string *tremolo* does not result in an undulation in pitch. In addition to the mechanical *tremolo* of the organ, Girolamo Diruta prescribes a separate ornament on the manual, which he also calls a *tremolo*, consisting of the rapid alternation of adjacent notes, equivalent to a modern keyboard trill.[25] Some writers of the seventeenth century equate the *tremolo* with the *trillo*; the *trillo* is the rapid, unmeasured reiteration of a single pitch, a technique particularly suited to the voice and clearly described by Caccini.[26]

Agazzari seems to suggest in the passage quoted below that instruments could also perform the *trillo*. Bovicelli's description of the *tremolo* seemingly overlaps with Caccini's description of the *trillo*. The reason for the frequent confusion between these two terms may lie in the way in which the *trillo* was notated. Although it was intended to be sung freely, with increasing velocity, it could only be notated in a strictly measured fashion in pedagogical examples or in musical compositions. Consequently, the *trillo* appears on the page as a measured reiteration of a single note—the usual conception for a vocal *tremolo*, although the measure of the *tremolo* was normally considered slow in contrast to the rapid movement associated with the *trillo*.[27] Contributing further to the confusion is

---

Verlagsanstalt, 1988), 129. An extensive discussion of the *tremolo* in vocal and instrumental music is found on pp. 253–70. For further discussion of the organ *tremolo*, see Ch. 13 above.

[22] Stewart Carter, 'The String Tremolo in the 17th Century', *Early Music*, 19 (1991), 48.

[23] Moens-Haenen, *Das Vibrato*, 130–1.

[24] Carter, 'The String Tremolo', 44.

[25] Girolamo Diruta, *Il Transilvano, dialogo sopra il vero modo di sonar organi, et istromenti da penna* (Venice: Giacomo Vincenti, 1593); fac. ed. Luisa Cervelli (Bologna: Arnaldo Forni, 1969), i. 10–12; Eng. trans. Murray C. Bradshaw and Edward J. Soehnlen as *Girolamo Diruta: The Transylvanian* (Ottawa: Institute of Mediaeval Music, 1984), i. 67–72. Praetorius also illustrates a *tremolo* by means of the rapid alternation of adjacent notes (either above or below the notated pitch), which he defines as a 'trembling [*Zittern*] of the voice over a note, which organists call *Mordanten* or *Moderanten*'. See *Syntagmatis musici . . . tomus tertius*, 235; Eng. trans. in Hans Lampl, 'A Translation of *Syntagma musicum III* by Michael Praetorius' (DMA dissertation, University of Southern California, 1957), 374.

[26] *Le nuove musiche*, ed. Hitchcock, 50–1. The *trillo* is illustrated similarly by the Roman composer and virtuoso Giovanni Luca Conforti in his *Breve et facile maniera d'essercitarsi ad ogni scolari non solamente a far passaggi* (Rome, 1593; fac. New York: Broude Brothers Ltd., 1978).

[27] Carol MacClintock, 'Caccini's *Trillo*: A Re-examination', *NATS Bulletin*, 33/1 (1976), 38–44. In her discussion of Bovicelli, MacClintock refers to both the unmeasured and measured reiteration of a pitch as a *trillo*, articulating two kinds: (1) *formato*, consisting of a slower moving measured repetition, and (2) *non formato*, comprising a quick, unmeasured repetition in the midst of a rapid ornamental passage. Praetorius also gives examples of this second type in *Syntagmatis musici . . . tomus tertius*, 237–9; trans. Lampl, pp. 375–7. This latter type was often notated by composers of the Florentine circle with a *t* or *tr* written over a note; Praetorius says it is indicated by *t*, *tr*, or *tri*.

the notation of the *trillo* in Monteverdi's *Duo Seraphim*, where, because two, and later three, voices are performing this ornament at once, it must be not only notated in a strictly measured fashion but also sung measured.

Other typically vocal ornaments include the *accento*, the embellishment of a stepwise descending melodic line with upper *échapées* in dotted rhythms, or an ascending stepwise line with anticipations in dotted rhythms; and the *portar la voce*—the ornamentation of ascending or descending scale movement through repetition of each note in dotted rhythm.[28] Caccini also prints an example of the *ribattuta di gola*, consisting of the alternation of two adjacent pitches in long–short dotted rhythms, an ornament found frequently in the music of not only Caccini and Monteverdi, but also many of their contemporaries.

When used at cadences, the *groppo* may either ascend or descend to the final note, which is approached by a stepwise third or fourth. *Groppi* are described with the trill including either the note above or the note below the main pitch. Rhythmic values should be mixed, ranging from semiminims to *semicrome* (semiquavers) or even *biscrome* (demisemiquavers). One form of the *groppo* concludes with a note longer than the previous rhythmic values. The keyboard *tremolo* should always include the note above the main pitch, not the note below, and should last for half of the value of the main note. It should be rapid, light and flexible and may be introduced at the beginning of a composition as well as during its course and at its end. Another form of the *tremolo*, identified with the *trillo* by Durante and Praetorius, is found especially in Florentine vocal compositions of the early seventeenth century and consists of a rapid repeated note, usually in the midst of a descending ornamental figure.[29]

Both Praetorius and Caccini discuss the attack at the beginning of a song or phrase, called *intonatio* or *intonazione* by Praetorius and Caccini, but termed a *clamazione* by many writers. As usual, Praetorius is more comprehensive in his comments, although some of his remarks are obviously derived directly from Caccini: 'Intonatio is the way in which a song is started; and there are different opinions about this. Some want to start it on the proper note; others a second below the proper note, so that the voice climbs and rises gradually. Others say the third [below], others on the fourth [below]. Some begin with a graceful soft tone.'[30]

Caccini recognizes only the *intonazione* from the third below and

---

[28] See Brown, *Embellishing Sixteenth-Century Music*, 3–4. Rognoni's *Selva de varii passaggi* of 1620 begins with a useful table of these graces. Rognoni's valuable treatise is studied and the text translated in Carter, 'Francesco Rognoni's *Selva de varii passaggi* (1620)'.

[29] Durante, *Arie devote*, preface; trans. in Sanders, 'Vocal Ornaments', 74. Praetorius, *Syntagmatis musici . . . tomus tertius*, 237–8; trans. in MacClintock, *Readings*, 168–9. For examples of these ornaments, see Brown, *Embellishing Seventeenth-Century Music*. See also n. 20 above.

[30] *Syntagmatis musici . . . tomus tertius*, 231; trans. in MacClintock, *Readings*, 164.

recommends against it as a general rule because 'it is discordant with many harmonies, but even where it can be used it has become so commonplace (and also because some stay too long on the third below, whereas it should be scarcely suggested) that instead of having grace I should say it were rather unpleasant to the ear and ought to be used but seldom, especially by beginners.'[31] Rather than employ the ascending third, Caccini suggests that the singer execute a crescendo or a decrescendo on the first note. In the four motets of Monteverdi's 1610 Vespers there are several instances of the written-out *intonatio* or *clamazione*, where a phrase begins with a brief rising third to the principal note. The third is usually filled in with a passing-note in dotted rhythm. Ottavio Durante also commented in 1608 on how to begin a serious composition: 'At the beginning of any affective and weighty composition, one must commence with gravity and without *passaggi*, but not without graces [*affetti*].'[32]

Another solo vocal ornament described by Caccini, Praetorius, and Francesco Rognoni is the *esclamazione*. The descriptions are somewhat confusing, but seem to refer to a crescendo utilized in conjunction with the combination of a minim or dotted crotchet followed by a shorter, lower note, the latter often reached by leap. The shorter note should be hurried somewhat and, according to Rognoni, given spirit and vivacity by a slight *tremolo*, or quick repercussion. Caccini recommends a decrescendo on the longer note, with the crescendo falling on the shorter note. The crescendo itself should not be too forceful; Caccini describes it as 'nothing but a certain strengthening of the relaxed voice'.[33] Caccini's *esclamazione* has exactly the reverse dynamic progress of the *messa di voce*.[34] In fact, Caccini shows limited interest in the *messa di voce*, to which he refers as 'an increasing and decreasing of the voice', but considers the *esclamazione* 'the most basic means of moving the affect'.[35] Similarly, he declares the *esclamazione* to be a more affective beginning of a phrase than the simple crescendo described above. Longer notes, however, such as semibreves,

---

[31] *Le nuove musiche*, ed. Hitchcock, 48–9. Paul Anthony Luke Boncella, in 'From behind the Propaganda: A New Anatomy of Caccini's *esclamazioni*', paper delivered at Seventh Biennial Conference on Baroque Music, Birmingham, England, 4–7 July 1996, has interpreted Caccini's meaning in the phrase 'an increasing and decreasing of the voice' (*il crescere e scemare della voce*) as referring to two additional and distinct versions of the *intonazione*—one a crescendo, the other a decrescendo. Thus Caccini cites three types of *intonazione*, the first comprising an ascending third, the second comprising a crescendo, and the third comprising a decrescendo. The latter two do not add any antecedent notes to the affected pitch. I am grateful to Dr Boncella for sharing a copy of his paper with me.

[32] *Arie devote*, preface (my trans.).

[33] *Le nuove musiche*, ed. Hitchcock, 49.

[34] See Dickey, 'Ornamentation in Early-Seventeenth-Century Italian Music', 261.

[35] *Le nuove musiche*, ed. Hitchcock, 49. For Paul Boncella's interpretation of the phrase 'an increasing and decreasing of the voice', see n. 31 above. Boncella's analysis of Caccini's meaning makes the third form of the *intonazione* (the decrescendo) the initial element in an *esclamazione*.

should be sung with the *messa di voce* rather than the *esclamazione*.[36] Durante recommends a crescendo specifically on dotted notes.[37]

'Vibrato' is a word not found in Baroque sources, but some aspects of vocal style and a number of ornaments are described that may be subsumed under that term.[38] The types of vibrato and the manner in which they pertain to vocal style are discussed in Chapter 16. Here vibrato will be treated in its capacity as an ornament; indeed, Baroque sources usually describe the vibrato as an ornament to be used in specific places for particular affects.[39] Vibrato as a vocal ornament, whether a vibrato of intensity, pitch, or some combination of the two, must have been more pronounced and perceptible than the natural, imperceptible vibrato contributing to a good vocal quality advocated by Praetorius.[40] As with other ornaments, especially *passaggi*, over-frequent use of vibrato aroused criticism.[41] The vibrato was a soft affect, and according to Giambattista Doni, a vocal vibrato should be reserved for soft, feminine, or sorrowful subjects and not be used in music of masculine or heroic character.[42]

The ornamental vibrato was used most significantly for harmonic, rhythmic, or melodic emphasis, for example, at the beginning of a composition; at a change in rhythm; on a long note, especially before or after a leap; on a sustained note after the conclusion of a *passaggio*; at the end of a cadence formula; or on the final note of a piece. A particularly affective figure might be prepared or emphasized by means of a vibrato.

Vibrato was practised on instruments as well.[43] Sources from the sixteenth century testify to the use of vibrato on the recorder, produced by movement of the finger as well as by a 'tremulous quality in the breath'.[44] A measured breath vibrato was the means for producing a *tremolo*, that is, a measured repeated

[36] Caccini also includes undotted semibreves in his examples of *esclamazioni*. Further confirmation of the practice of singing a crescendo–diminuendo on a long note is found in the 1638 trumpet treatise of Girolamo Fantini: 'wherever notes of one, of two or of four beats' length are found, they should be held in a singing fashion, by starting softly, making a crescendo until the middle of the note, and making a diminuendo on the second half until the end of the beat, so that it may hardly be heard . . .' Quoted by Alan Lumsden in 'Woodwind and Brass', in Howard Mayer Brown and Stanley Sadie, eds., *Performance Practice: Music after 1600* (New York: W. W. Norton & Co., 1989), 83.

[37] Sanders, 'Vocal Ornaments', 62, 74.

[38] An exhaustive study of vibrato based on Baroque practical and theoretical sources is found in Moens-Haenen, *Das Vibrato*. My discussion here and in Ch. 16 above is based on her study as well as on Sanford, 'A comparison of French and Italian Singing'.

[39] Moens-Haenen, *Das Vibrato*, 24, 145.

[40] See Ch. 16 above.

[41] Moens-Haenen, *Das Vibrato*, 166, 273.

[42] Ibid. 164–5, 274.

[43] Moens-Haenen, ibid., devotes a number of chapters to instrumental vibrato. Frederick Neumann, in 'The Vibrato Controversy', *Performance Practice Review*, 4 (1991), 14–27, cites a number of 16th–18th cent. sources that discuss vibrato on various instruments.

[44] Herbert Myers, 'Recorder', in Jeffrey T. Kite-Powell, ed., *A Performer's Guide to Renaissance Music* (New York: Schirmer Books, 1994), 51.

pitch.[45] As with the voice, the role of vibrato was as an ornament, rather than for the continuous production of a particular tone quality. Sylvestro Ganassi describes a trill produced by 'trembling with the finger over a hole of the recorder'.[46] Such trills could be even smaller than a diesis and 'are barely perceptible to the ear with precision'.[47] Jerome Cardan, in his detailed discussion of recorders, notes that both partial covering of holes and restraint of the breath affect pitch. He is remarkably detailed in his explanation of how to create a 'trembling movement' in the sound: 'Then it is necessary to consider that a trill (*vox tremula*) is used very often with a higher or lower diesis or semitone. This is a twofold action, with a tremulous quality in the breath and with a trembling movement of the fingers. . . . when the trembling movement is made on a semitone or even on a whole tone by opening a hole very lightly, a sound running back and forth through dieses is created, a sound than which nothing finer, nothing sweeter, nothing more pleasant can be imagined. Thus trills (*voces*) are lively when a finger constantly opens and closes a hole, and tender when a finger trembles. But three conditions are necessary to create the sweetest trills: (1) lower and not higher tones should be trilled; (2) fingers should be raised from a hole lightly and very little; (3) the recoiling motion of the fingers should not stop but should tremble just as a sword strongly vibrated will repeatedly rebound. Moderate trills are formed variously in higher tones by a trembling motion of the fingers. A gentle breath produces a mild tone, an intense breath a rough tone.'[48]

String players likewise did not rely on vibrato for the continuous production of a good sound; the bow, rather than the left hand, was considered the source of expression.[49] But like singers and wind players, string players employed vibrato as an ornament. From the manner in which violins and violas were commonly held, it appears that an arm vibrato was not feasible, but it is often unclear from treatises whether the vibrato described was produced by oscillation of the finger or by wrist motion. Both these methods yield a pitch vibrato, while changes of finger pressure produce an intensity vibrato.[50] Ganassi describes a bow vibrato combined with a left-hand vibrato: 'For melancholy words and music, move the bow gracefully, and at times shake the bow arm and the finger of the hand on the neck, in order to make the effect conform to melancholy and tormented music.'[51] It is impossible to prove from theoretical sources the use of

[45] Moens-Haenen, *Das Vibrato*, 83, 137–8.
[46] *Opera intitulata Fontegara*, ch. 24. Eng. trans. in Dorothy Swainson, *Sylvestro Ganassi: Opera intitulata Fontegara* (Berlin and Lichterfelde: Robert Lienau, 1956), 87.
[47] Ibid.
[48] *Hieronymus Cardanus, Writings on Music*, trans. Miller, 63–4, 69–70.
[49] Moens-Haenen, *Das Vibrato*, 68; David Douglass, 'The Violin', in Kite-Powell, ed., *A Performer's Guide to Renaissance Music*, 135.
[50] Moens-Haenen, *Das Vibrato*, 68.
[51] Ganassi, in *Regola rubertina* (Venice, 1542; fac. edn. Bologna: Forni Editore, 1970); Eng. trans.

vibrato in members of the violin family in the early seventeenth century, since the subject is not discussed until an ambiguous reference by Mersenne in 1636.[52] However, it may be inferred from the documented use of vibrato as an ornament on the viola da gamba, in the voice, on plucked instruments, and on wind instruments that the *viole da braccio* of Monteverdi's Vespers also employed vibrato as an ornament in situations similar to those described above for the voice.

Another means for singing more expressively suggested by Caccini is rhythmic alteration. He offers several examples in which dotted rhythms, with either the long note or the short note first, are imposed on passages notated in even quavers.[53] He also introduces several forms of an ornament called a *cascata*, which replaces a moderately paced descending scale motion with elongation of the first note followed by a rapid descent.[54] The gracefulness of the uneven rhythms or the rapid descent improves upon the stodginess of the equal note values that had characterized typical *passaggi* ever since the early sixteenth century. Caccini's examples in the preface to *Le nuove musiche*, as well as the written-out ornamentation in the music itself, illustrate continually shifting rhythms, thus creating the 'variety [that] is most essential to this art'.[55]

Ottavio Durante described another vocal nuance in singing the interval of an ascending chromatic semitone resulting from the natural form of a note followed by its sharpened form: 'To raise the voice from the tone to the semitone, the sharp is assigned on the slurred note to make it understood that it is necessary to begin to rise little by little, keeping in mind that there are four commas, until one arrives at the perfect increase, which is very moving when it is done well.'[56] Durante seems to be calling for a gradual rise in pitch on the first note,

Daphne and Stephen Silvester (Berlin and Lichterfelde: Robert Lienau, 1972), ch. 2, p. vi. Quoted and translated in Stewart Carter, 'The String Tremolo', 44. According to Carter, Ganassi's 'shaking' (*tremar il braccio de l'archetto, e le dita de la mano del manico*) constitutes a 'gentle pulsating motion of the bow arm without stopping the bow', together with a left-hand vibrato.

[52] Moens-Haenen, *Das Vibrato*, 69–70.

[53] Brunelli also recommends dotted rhythms in quavers. See the quotation in Ch. 16 above.

[54] See *Le nuove musiche*, ed. Hitchcock, 51–2.

[55] Ibid. 49.

[56] *Arie devote*, preface. Sanders, 'Vocal Ornaments', 74, interprets this passage differently. The original text reads 'Per il crescimento della voce dal tuono al semituono si assegna il diesis nella nota ligata, per dar intendere, che bisogna cominciar à crescere a poco a poco, facendo conto che vi siano 4. come, sino che si arrivi al perfetto crescimento, il che quando è fatto bene, commove assai.' I have taken Durante's *come* as the plural of *comma*, usually spelled with two *m*s in 16th-century sources, while Sanders has omitted it from his translation and taken the words *crescimento* and *crescere* to refer to a crescendo in volume. He therefore interprets the entire passage in terms of a vocal crescendo accompanying a semitone rise in pitch. Much of the passage makes little sense, however, in terms of a crescendo, especially the phrase 'facendo conto che vi siano 4. come, sino che si arrivi al perfetto crescimento'. The number 4 and the concept of a 'perfect crescendo' seems especially problematic in Sanders's interpretation. Supporting my reading is an instruction from Domenico Mazzochi, in his *Dialoghi e sonetti* (Rome: Zannetti, 1638), calling in the enharmonic genus for an increase in the breath on a note while gradually raising the pitch. See Stewart Carter, 'Francesco Rognoni's *Selva de varii passaggi*', 14, n. 12.

passing through all four commas, until the full chromatic semitone is reached at the point where the second note is printed.[57]

The 1620 treatise by Francesco Rognoni offers comments on bowing for members of the violin family (*viole da braccio*), both when playing what is written and when playing ornaments:

The arm violas, particularly the violin, is [*sic*] an instrument in itself crude and harsh if it is not tempered and sweetened by gentle bowing. From here let those learn who have a certain raw sound by not stretching the bow over the viola, and lift it with so much vehemence that they make more noise with the bow than with the sound; and furthermore, they do not know how to draw four *cromae* or *semicromae* so that they are equal to one another, but go jumping with the bow over the viola so that it seems they are devouring the notes, not making them all heard with an equal bow, tightly pressed to the viola, as good players do. . . .

By *lireggiare* is meant making two, three, or more notes in only one bow. . . . If they are two, two downwards and two upwards; if they are three, the same; if four, four downwards and four upwards; if they are eight or twelve, the same, so that the bow stroke lasts until the line underneath arrives; this is also done for five and six notes. And wishing that they succeed well, it is necessary that they be done slowly, giving force to the wrist of the bow hand. . . . To *lireggiare* tenderly [*affettuoso*], that is, with affect, is the same as above as far as the bow is concerned, but requires that the wrist of the bow hand, almost hopping, strikes all the notes, one by one.[58]

Agostino Agazzari also comments on the way in which different instruments should play in adding their sonorities and ornaments to the ensemble:

But since each instrument has its own peculiar limitations, the player must take advantage of them and be guided by them to produce a good result. Bowed instruments, for example, have a different style than those plucked with a quill or with the finger . . . The violin requires beautiful passages, distinct and long, with playful figures and little echoes and imitations repeated in several places, passionate accents, mute strokes of the bow, groups, trills [*gruppi, trilli*], etc. The *violone*, as the lowest part, proceeds with gravity, supporting the harmony of the other parts with soft resonance, dwelling as much as possible on the heavier strings, frequently touching the lowest ones. The theorbo, with its full and gentle consonances, reinforces the melody greatly, restriking and lightly passing over the bass strings, its special excellence, with trills and mute accents [*trilli & accenti muti*] played with the left hand. The *arpa doppia*, which is everywhere useful, as much so in the soprano as in the bass, explores its entire range with gentle plucked notes, echoes of the two hands, trills [*trilli*], etc.; in short, it aims at good counterpoint . . . But all this must be done prudently; if the instruments are alone in the consort, they must lead it and do everything; if they play in company, each must regard the other, giving it room and not conflicting with it; if there are many, they must each await their turn and not, chirping all at once like sparrows, try to shout one another down.'[59]

---

[57] Durante probably intended the term *comma* to mean a quarter of a chromatic semitone rather than a mathematically precise syntonic comma of 22 cents, since the size of the chromatic semitone would depend on the tuning employed: in quarter-comma mean-tone tuning, four syntonic commas would be slightly larger than a chromatic semitone of 75.5 cents; in an approximately equal-tempered tuning the four commas would be less than the semitone of 100 cents. See Ch. 22 below for a discussion of tuning and temperaments.

[58] *Selva de varii passaggi*, pt. II, 3–4 (my trans.).

[59] *Del sonare sopra'l basso*, 9; Eng. trans. in Strunk, *Source Readings in Music History*, 42–9 (bracketed passages mine).

It is evident from the ornamentation manuals and from musical publications themselves that motets, psalms, and Magnificats were all suited to an embellished style—both written and improvised—in the early seventeenth century. Settings of *Domine ad adjuvandum*, on the other hand, were somewhat rare in the early part of the *Seicento* and usually in a simple style. Similarly, an embellished style is not found in hymn settings of this period. Thus, in principle, ornamentation may be applied to the motets, psalms, and Magnificats of Monteverdi's Vespers. On the other hand, Monteverdi himself supplied some of the most extensive written ornamentation to be found in printed musical sources of the early seventeenth century. Two performance issues arise from this circumstance. The first is the application of the performance criteria outlined in the paragraphs above to Monteverdi's notated ornamentation. The second is the question of what other ornamentation, if any, may be added, since the composer took such extraordinary pains in publishing his own embellishments. Has Monteverdi supplied all the ornamentation necessary for performing his music, and did he do so in order to prevent or inhibit the performer from taking liberties with it?[60] Certainly the simplest course of action would be to follow Monteverdi's composed ornamentation and leave matters at that. But the widespread practice of improvised embellishment in music of this time and the implication in Monteverdi's two versions of the aria *Possente spirto* from *L'Orfeo*, one highly embellished and one plain (the latter for the skilled performer to improvise his own ornamentation), suggest a less definitive conclusion.

Monteverdi's notated ornaments consist of both *passaggi* and graces. *Passaggi*, in both even and dotted rhythms, are found in the psalms, some of the motets, the *Sonata sopra Sancta Maria*, and the Magnificats. Although ornamentation manuals consistently comment that embellishments should be confined to one part at a time, Monteverdi's modern imitative duet style often produces *passaggi* in two parts simultaneously, or even three in the second part of *Duo Seraphim*. Most often imitative duets lead to *passaggi* in parallel thirds, or, more rarely, parallel sixths. Monteverdi's preference for duet textures over a single solo voice or instrument throughout his *œuvre* gives rise to similar notated embellishments in two parts simultaneously in many other works, both sacred and secular, aside from the 1610 Vespers.

Graces are especially prominent in the motets of the Vespers, but are also evident in the psalms, the Magnificats, and the *Sonata*. Monteverdi employs many of the standard early seventeenth-century graces, such as *accenti*, the *intonatio* or *clamatione*, the *esclamazione*, the *cascata*, the *groppo*, the *ribattuta di gola*, the

[60] Anna Maria Vacchelli argues the case against adding any further ornamentation to Monteverdi's music in 'Monteverdi as a Primary Source for the Performance of his own Music', in Raffaello Monterosso, ed., *Performing Practice in Monteverdi's Music: The Historic–Philological Background* (Cremona: Fondazione Claudio Monteverdi, 1995), 51.

tremolo, and the *trillo*; sometimes several such graces are strung together in a single passage. All of Monteverdi's notated graces as well as the *passaggi* are appropriately performed according to the methods described by the various theorists
quoted above.

Despite Monteverdi's extensive notated ornamentation, there are still passages where additional embellishments can be applied. Lengthy vocal *passaggi*
seem out of the question, since the composer has already pre-empted virtually
every place where a bass-line consisting of sustained notes or scale patterns can
support such extensive ornamentation. However, there are other places in the
psalms, the motets, and the hymn where short vocal *passaggi* could be employed.

The instrumental ritornellos in the hymn and the Magnificat *a 7*, however,
provide more fertile ground for improvised *passaggi*. Monteverdi has left
these ritornellos, unlike the vocal parts, unornamented, and the elaborate
embellishments suggested for instrumental music by late sixteenth-century
and early seventeenth-century writers leave the door open to considerable
ornamentation. In order to ensure the variety so often demanded by theorists,
the ornamentation should be different for each successive statement of a
ritornello.

Aside from brief *passaggi*, there is also room throughout the Vespers for the
addition of graces, especially in the motets. There are numerous places in these
compositions that invite brief, expressive ornaments of one kind or another.
Graces can occur not only in the course of a piece, but also at cadences, where
certain ones were particularly common (the *groppo*, *tremolo*, and *trillo*). In fact,
the theoretical sources make it apparent that while ornamentation during a
piece or section was optional, embellishment of cadences, especially final cadences, was virtually obligatory. Curiously, it is precisely the cadences that
Monteverdi has left unadorned throughout the Vespers. This is especially evident in the two Magnificats and *Duo Seraphim*, which have been highly embellished by the composer except at the cadences, where listeners were most likely
to expect ornamentation. This fact strongly suggests that whereas Monteverdi
preferred to specify most of the internal ornamentation he wanted performed
(apart from instrumental ritornellos), he left cadential ornaments to be improvised by the performers as a matter of course.

By far the most frequent cadential ornament in the treatises is some form of
the *groppo*, especially in cadences with a raised seventh degree. Numerous examples of *groppi* are illustrated in Dalla Casa, Bovicelli, Conforti, Caccini, and
Rognoni. The *trillo*, sometimes concluding with a turn extending to a third
below the cadence note, is also a common cadential ornament and can be
applied at numerous internal and final cadences throughout the Vespers. Since
groppi and *trilli* were by this time such standardized and frequently-used cadential embellishments, Monteverdi clearly expected performers to add them,

without concerning himself with details. Graces and *passaggi* within the course of a phrase or section, on the other hand, he notated with care.

Although discussion to this point has focused on embellishment of melodic lines, some recent editors of Monteverdi and some performers have also embellished the continuo part, in certain cases rather extensively. This practice does not accord, however, with what we can learn of the style of basso continuo playing in the early seventeenth century (see Chapter 14 above). Continuo playing in this period was simple in character, conceived almost exclusively as support for the other parts, and only rarely entered into any kind of counterpoint with those parts. Even where the right hand of the keyboard player doubled an ornamented vocal or instrumental line, the continuo player was instructed to play a simpler version.[61] The continuo realization, therefore, should not be subjected to elaborate embellishments. Ornamentation in the continuo should be limited mostly to simple cadential graces, especially *groppi*, but even these should be used only when the continuo ornaments will not interfere with embellishments in the other parts. Viadana is succinct in describing the role of the continuo: 'The organist is bound to play the organ part simply, and in particular with the left hand; if, however, he wants to execute some movement with the right hand, as by ornamenting the cadences, or by some appropriate embellishment, he must play in such a manner that the singer or singers are not covered or confused by too much movement.'[62] Viadana's admonition is particularly appropriate for the organ, with its sustained tone. Harpsichords, with their more quickly fading tone, might provide a greater degree of ornamentation without covering the singers, and plucked instruments, whose sound is softer and dies away even more quickly, may be still freer to interact ornamentally with the voices.[63]

To give the performer some idea of how ornamentation might be applied in the Vespers, a few examples are appended here. It should be noted that these examples attempt to illustrate a variety of ornaments and are in no way prescriptive. The version of *Nigra sum* given as Ex. 21.1, for instance, is not actually intended to be performed with such extensive ornamentation, which undoubtedly would have been considered excessive by Monteverdi, Caccini, and other composers in the new style of the early seventeenth century. Rather, the purpose of the example is to demonstrate the types of ornaments that might be applied throughout the composition, in the hope of stimulating the imagination of the performer to think about what ornaments he may wish to try. As in

---

[61] Monteverdi himself provides a simpler version of embellished instrumental or vocal lines in the *Sonata sopra Sancta Maria* and the *Quia fecit* of the Magnificat *a 7*. See also the preface to Giovanni Paolo Cima's *Concerti ecclesiastici* (1610), quoted in Luigi Ferdinando Tagliavini, 'Registrazioni organistiche nei Magnificat dei "Vespri" Monteverdiani', *Rivista italiana di musicologia*, 2 (1967), 366–7.

[62] *Cento concerti ecclesiastici*, preface; Eng. trans. in Strunk, *Source Readings in Music History*, 421.

[63] I am grateful to Sally Sanford for emphasizing this point.

Ex. 21.1. *Nigra sum*, typical ornaments

Ex. 21.1. *Continued*

Ex. 21.1. *Continued*

Ex. 21.2. *Ave maris stella*, ritornello ornaments: *a* cantus instrumental part; *b* sextus instrumental part, bar 74; *c* sextus instrumental part, faster ornamentation

Ex. 21.2. *Continued*

Ex. 21.3. Cadential ornaments: *a Dixit Dominus*, bars 256–8; *b Laudate pueri*, bars 128–32; *c Laudate pueri*, bars 224–5; *d Laetatus sum*, bars 229–31

the seventeenth century, good taste, the expression of the text, and one's own vocal capacities should be the principal guides to the performer in making decisions about ornamentation. Ex. 21.2 provides an embellished cantus part for the instrumental ritornello of *Ave maris stella* and an alternative, even more lavishly ornamented version for the sextus part. Ex. 21.3 illustrates typical cadential ornaments for three of the psalms. A convenient source manual for ornamentation of the sixteenth and early seventeenth centuries is Brown, *Embellishing Sixteenth-Century Music*.

22

Tuning and Temperament

⟨✢⟩

IF the performance practice issues discussed in the preceding chapters seem ambiguous and incapable of definitive resolution, matters of tuning and temperament are equally problematic. Tempered tuning, mean-tone tunings, just intonation, Pythagorean tuning, and Ptolemaic tuning were all discussed and argued by theorists in the Renaissance and early seventeenth century.[1] Pythagorean tuning, with its pure fifths, seems to have been preferred until about the middle of the fifteenth century.[2] However, with increasing emphasis on the sonority of thirds and full triads in the late fifteenth century and the sixteenth century, mean-tone tuning, with its richer-sounding major thirds, became more popular, especially for organs and other keyboard instruments.[3] In the late sixteenth century Vincenzo Galilei, in discussing the intonation of singers, expressed his belief that 'the major third is formed by an irrational pro-

---

[1] Brief overviews of tuning in this period can be found in Mark Lindley, 'Temperaments', in *The New Grove Dictionary of Music and Musicians*, ed. Stanley Sadie (London: Macmillan Publishers Ltd., 1980), xviii. 660–7; id., 'Tuning and Intonation', in Howard Mayer Brown and Stanley Sadie, eds., *Performance Practice: Music after 1600* (New York and London: W. W. Norton & Company, 1989), 169–75; and in Ross W. Duffin, 'Tuning and Temperament', in Jeffery T. Kite-Powell, ed., *A Performer's Guide to Renaissance Music* (New York: Schirmer Books, 1994), 238–47. A more detailed account of practical tuning instructions by Arnolt Schlick, Pietro Aaron, and Giovanni Maria Lanfranco is given in Mark Lindley, 'Early 16th-Century Keyboard Temperaments', *Musica disciplina*, 28 (1974), 129–51, and discussions of Pythagorean, equal, and mean-tone temperaments as well as just intonation are found in id., *Lutes, Viols and Temperaments* (Cambridge: Cambridge University Press, 1984). Easley Blackwood, *The Structure of Recognizable Diatonic Tunings* (Princeton: Princeton University Press, 1985) contains a comprehensive study of diatonic tuning systems, complete with the mathematical basis for each system.

[2] The particular Pythagorean tuning that yielded the greatest quantity of nearly pure thirds and pure fifths is outlined in Lindley, 'Tuning and Intonation', 170 and Duffin, 'Tuning and Temperament', 240.

[3] Ibid. 239–41. According to Lindley, already in 1482 Ramis de Pareia had 'indicated that mean-tone temperament was in common use on keyboard instruments of his day' in Tertia Pars, Tractatus Secundus, ch. 4 of his *Musica practica* (Bologna, 1482); ed. Johannes Wolf (Leipzig: Breitkopf & Härtel, 1901); Eng. trans. Clement A. Miller as *Bartolomeo Ramis de Pareia, Musica practica* (Neuhausen and Stuttgart: Hänssler Verlag, American Institute of Musicology, 1993). See Lindley, 'Temperaments', 661; id., *Lutes, Viols and Temperaments*, 43; id., 'Fifteenth-Century Evidence for Meantone Temperament', *Proceedings of the Royal Musical Association*, 102 (1975–6), 37–51. Herbert Myers notes that Renaissance recorders are much easier to play in tune in mean-tone tuning. See Myers, 'Recorder', in Kite-Powell, ed., *A Performer's Guide to Renaissance Music*, 48. Patrizio Barbieri asserts that 'violinists of all schools, at least until the middle of the 18th century, . . . used a tuning of the syntonic-mean-tone type'. See Barbieri, 'Violin Intonation: A Historical Survey', *Early Music*, 19 (1991), 69, 74.

portion very close to a *sesquiquarta* [$\frac{5}{4}$ = a pure third]'.[4] In 1619 Michael Praetorius was still recommending mean-tone tuning for all keyboard instruments.[5]

Mean-tone tuning (based on the pure tenth C–E), when superimposed on pure fifths, results in the syntonic comma below the larger C–E tenth that is generated by the succession of fifths C–G–D–A–E. One method of eliminating this comma was to divide it equally among the four intervals of a fifth above the original reference note, yielding the so-called quarter-comma mean-tone tuning somewhat ambiguously described by Pietro Aaron.[6]

Quarter-comma mean-tone tuning, producing a ' "pure" major third of 386 cents', requires fifths slightly smaller (696.5 cents) than a well-tempered fifth (700 cents), and even smaller than a perfect fifth (702 cents).[7] Pitches in this system are tuned in a series of fifths above and a series of fifths below the reference tone (normally c'). Consequently, the upward series of fifths becomes progressively flatter, while the lower series becomes progressively sharper. 'Thus, the two extremes, G♯, flat by 28 cents, and E♭, sharp by 10.5 cents, produce the "wolf-fifth", 36.5 cents larger than the equal tempered fifth; similarly, the discrepancy between G♯ and A♭ produces the true "wolf-tone" of 42 cents.'[8] For this reason, modulation in mean-tone tuning around the circle of fifths is limited, and split keys to accommodate the difference between D♯ and E♭ and between G♯ and A♭ were added to Italian organs as early as the fifteenth century and

---

[4] 'Tengo che la Terza maggiore sia contenuta da una proporzione irrazionale assai vicina La Sesquiquarta', *Dialogo della musica antica et della moderna* (Florence: Marescotti, 1581; fac. edn. New York: Broude Brothers, 1967), 31. In his *Discorso intorno all'opere di Gioseffo Zarlino* (Florence: Marescotti, 1589; fac. edn. Milan: Bollettino Bibliografico Musicale, 1933), 131, Galilei claimed that Aristoxenus, Didymus, and Ptolemy all prescribed 'consonant thirds and sixths'.

[5] *Syntagmatis musici . . . tomus secundus de organographia* (Wolfenbüttel: Elias Holwein, 1619); fac. ed. Wilibald Gurlitt (Kassel: Bärenreiter, 1958), 148–58. See Lindley, 'Temperaments', 666 and Vincent J. Panetta, Jr., *Treatise on Harpsichord Tuning by Jean Denis* (Cambridge: Cambridge University Press, 1987), 38–9.

[6] The quarter-comma mean-tone tuning results from Aaron's initial instructions for tuning, which use C as the reference point and begin with a pure third E. Each successive fifth above C is then narrowed from a pure fifth by an equal amount, thereby dividing the comma equally among the four fifths C–G–A–D–E. See Pietro Aaron, *Toscanello in musica* (Venice: Bernardino and Matheo de Vitali, 1523, rev. edn. 1529; fac. New York: Broude Brothers, 1965), ch. 51; Eng. trans. Peter Bergquist, as *Pietro Aaron: Toscanello in Music, Book II, Chapters XXXVII–XXXX, Supplement* (Colorado Springs, Colo.: Colorado College Music Press, 1970), 11. Lindley, in 'Early 16th-Century Keyboard Temperaments', illustrates that Aaron's further instructions tend to compromise the assumption that he is referring to a precise quarter-comma mean-tone. See the same observation in Mimi S. Waitzman, 'Meantone Temperament in Theory and Practice', *In Theory Only*, 5 (1979–81), 3–15. Zarlino was the first to publish a 'mathematically coherent' model of a mean-tone temperament in *Le istituzioni harmoniche* (Venice, 1558; fac. edn. New York: Broude Brothers, 1965), 125–42, and in 1571 he published a description of quarter-comma mean-tone tuning in *Dimostrationi harmoniche* (Venice: Francesco del Franceschi Senesi, 1571; fac. Ridgewood, NJ; Gregg Press), 267–9. See Lindley, 'Tuning and Intonation', 171–2. A clear exposition of the quarter-comma tuning system is given in Clare G. Rayner, 'The Enigmatic Cima: Meantone Tuning and Transpositions', *Galpin Society Journal*, 22 (1969), 23–34.

[7] Ibid. 24.

[8] Ibid.

became increasingly common on harpsichords in the late sixteenth and early seventeenth centuries.[9] The organ constructed by Graziado Antegnati for the ducal church of Santa Barbara in Mantua in 1565 had D♯ and A♭ split keys in all complete octaves except for *ab″*.[10]

The quarter-comma mean-tone system also produces two significantly different semitones (75.5 cents and 117.5 cents) and two substantially different whole tones (193 cents and 235 cents). However, in the scales normally encountered in the early seventeenth century (modal or minor: A, D, and G; and major: C, D, F, G, B♭, and more rarely, E♭ and A), there occur only semitones of 117.5 cents and whole tones of 193 cents.[11]

In Monteverdi's Vespers, the tonalities all fall within the normal limitations of early seventeenth-century music, and mean-tone tuning is feasible in the performance of all fourteen pieces. Indeed, many professional early music ensembles today use quarter-comma mean-tone tuning in performing works of this period.[12] The principal accidentals throughout Monteverdi's Vespers are B♭ and E♭ on the flat side and F♯, C♯, and G♯ on the sharp side. Only B♭ appears in a signature. The sharp accidentals are primarily, but not exclusively, used as *subsemitonium modi* at cadences, and in such cases are not essential to the definition of the mode or tonality of the piece. In quarter-comma mean-tone tuning, these *subsemitonium modi* and other chromatic alterations by sharp will be smaller, chromatic semitones (75.5 cents) above the natural forms of the notes they alter. Only *Domine ad adjuvandum* is written in a sharp tonality, with F♯ and C♯ as fundamental to the mode (whereas C♯ may be considered a *subsemitonium modi,* the uninflected c does not appear in this piece; hence the response is clearly in Glareanus's Ionian mode, transposed to D). Where Monteverdi uses flats, whether in a signature or as accidentals, the smaller chromatic semitone would occur between the notes B♭ or E♭ and their altered (natural) forms. Those pieces with both B♭ and E♭ (*Laetatus sum, Duo Seraphim, Nisi Dominus,* and the two Magnificats) avoid G♯, except for *Laetatus sum,* where G♯ occurs twice (bars 166 and the parallel passage in bar 220). Since in these passages both E♭ and *g♯* appear in the bottom part of the bassus generalis, the e♭ following the g♯ by three bars, the 'wolf' fifth would be present in mean-tone tuning, but mitigated by an intervening complete cadence.

---

[9] Christopher Stembridge, 'Music for the *cimbalo cromatico* and other Split-Keyed Instruments in Seventeenth-Century Italy', *Performance Practice Review*, 5 (1992), 6; Denzil Wraight and Christopher Stembridge, 'Italian Split-Keyed Instruments with Fewer than Nineteen Divisions to the Octave', *Performance Practice Review*, 7 (1994), 150–81. The manufacture of split-key harpsichords seems to have been particularly prominent in Florence in the period 1610–30 (ibid. 159). French harpsichords, on the other hand, did not have split keys. See Panetta, *Treatise*, 42–3.

[10] Wraight and Stembridge, 'Italian Split-Keyed Instruments', 164.

[11] Rayner, 'The Enigmatic Cima', 26.

[12] Paul O'Dette, for example, has indicated in private conversation that he and the Musicians of Swanne Alley regularly employ quarter-comma mean-tone tuning (Ex. (b) in Lindley's chart, Fig. 22.1) in performances of 17th-century music. Many other ensembles do so as well.

If *Lauda Jerusalem* and the two Magnificats are transposed down a fourth, as recommended in Chapter 17, then D♯ appears in *Lauda Jerusalem* in place of the originally notated G♯, and B♭ disappears in favour of F. The D♯ is a *subsemitonium modi*, a smaller semitone above D. The two Magnificats, when transposed, drop their E♭ and add G♯.

The only other D♯ is in *Nigra sum* (bars 39 and 61), where the chromatic alteration is part of a passage with other chromatic alterations related to the text (see the discussion in Chapter 9). The *d♯'* would also be a chromatic semitone above *d'* and a larger, diatonic semitone below the following *e'*, the two different intervals contributing to the expressive colouring and effectiveness of the chromatic passage. In this instance *d♯'* does not function as a *subsemitonium modi* to *e*, but rather as a momentary lower neighbour note, and in the larger melodic context of the passage as a chromatic passing-note between *d'* (even *c♯'*) and *e'*.

In contrast to the sharp accidentals, B♭ is found in the signature of several pieces in the Vespers: *Laetatus sum*, *Duo Seraphim*, *Nisi Dominus*, and the two Magnificats. In *Laetatus sum* and the Magnificats, the B♭ signature signals transposition of the psalm tone or Magnificat tone. Downward transposition of the Magnificats by a fourth removes the B♭ signature, but whether as a signature or as an accidental, B♭ would be a small semitone below B in mean-tone tuning. Similarly, E♭, which always occurs as a chromatic alteration, will be a smaller semitone below E.

Because the fifths in quarter-comma mean-tone tuning are substantially narrower than those in Pythagorean intonation and equal temperament, other mean-tone tunings, adjusting the thirds somewhat in order to improve the fifths, were also described or implied by sixteenth-century theorists ($\frac{1}{6}$-comma, $\frac{1}{5}$-comma, $\frac{2}{9}$-comma, $\frac{2}{7}$-comma, and $\frac{1}{3}$-comma), and all kinds of irregular adjustments were probably used in practice.[13] Fig. 22.1 shows four 'historically suitable' versions of mean-tone tuning, as given by Lindley, who recommends that 'one judge by ear (with appropriate music and on an appropriate instrument, of course) the relative strengths and weakness of the extreme types ... and then choose an intermediate shade by ear'.[14]

An approximately equal temperament was also in use in the sixteenth century

---

[13] Duffin, 'Tuning and Temperament', 240–2; Lindley, 'Early 16th-Century Keyboard Temperaments'; id., 'Temperaments', 662; and id., 'Tuning and Intonation', 171–5. A table comparing various mean-tone tunings is given in Panetta, *Treatise*, 18.

[14] 'Tuning and Intonation', 173. Lindley provides 'a general procedure for tuning any regular mean-tone temperament by ear' in 'Instructions for the Clavier Diversely Tempered', *Early Music*, 5 (1977), 18–23. He also provides instruction for quarter-comma, $\frac{1}{5}$ comma, and $\frac{1}{6}$ comma mean-tone tuning in 'Tuning Renaissance and Baroque Keyboard Instruments: Some Guidelines', *Performance Practice Review*, 7 (1994), 88–9. Other practical guides for tuning instruments in mean-tone temperament are Owen Jorgensen, *Tuning the Historical Temperaments by Ear* (Marquette, Mich.: The Northern Michigan University Press, 1977), 101–97; G. C. Klop, *Harpsichord Tuning, Course Outline* (Garderen, The Netherlands: Werkplaats voor Clavecimbelbouw, 1974), 12–17; Edward L. Kottick, *The Harpsichord Owner's Guide* (Chapel Hill, NC: The University of North Carolina Press, 1987), 159–62. See also the chapter 'Procedure for Tuning the Harpsichord Properly' in Panetta, *Treatise*, 71–4.

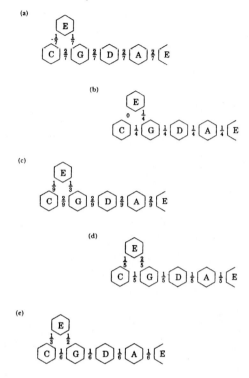

FIG. 22.1. Tempering of the triadic intervals in some representative shades of regular meantone temperament. The fifths are tempered by the following fractions of a syntonic comma: (a) $\frac{2}{7}$, (b) $\frac{1}{4}$, (c) $\frac{2}{9}$, (d) $\frac{1}{5}$, (e) $\frac{1}{6}$. In these diagrams a positive number means that the fourth, major third or major sixth in question is tempered larger than pure (and the fifth, minor third or minor sixth smaller). In the first of the schemes shown here, the major thirds are tempered smaller than pure.

Source: Lindley, 'Tuning and Intonation', 172 (reproduced with permission).

and early seventeenth century. Fretted instruments, with their strings tuned in fourths and a major third, were much more suited to an equal temperament than to a mean-tone tuning, and were therefore problematic to play with keyboard instruments, according to some theorists.[15] Nevertheless, there is evidence from

[15] Duffin, 'Tuning and Temperament', 242; Lindley, *Lutes, Viols and Temperaments*, 19; id., 'Temperaments', 664–5; and id., 'Tuning and Intonation', 173; Panetta, *Treatise*, 68–9; Patrizio Barbieri, 'Conflitti di intonazione tra cembalo, liuto e archi nel "Concerto" italiano del Seicento', in Pierluigi Petrobelli and Gloria Staffieri, eds., *Studi Corelliani IV: Atti del Quarto Congresso Internazionale*, Fusignano, 4–7 Sept. 1986 (1990), 123–52. For a detailed study of tuning systems on fretted instruments, see Lindley, *Lutes, Viols and Temperaments*. Lindley's opening observation is instructive regarding the imprecision of tuning: 'Any account of the history of tempered tuning on lutes and viols might well begin with an admission that even the best tuner cannot impose a theoretical scheme upon these instruments very exactly. For one thing players cannot help but alter, in greater or lesser degree, the tension and therefore the pitch of a stopped string when they press it down to the fret' (p. 5). And further: 'It may be informative to reduce a fretting formula to a set of intervals calculated in cents, but it would be very naïve to imagine that the frets will impose such an intonation of the scale upon the performance as definitively as the harpsichord or organ tuner's handiwork does' (p. 7).

the sixteenth century of adjustments of frets to achieve some shade of mean-tone tuning.[16] Jack Ashworth and Paul O'Dette also cite evidence of unequal tunings on Renaissance and early Baroque fretted instruments and note the large number of documented instances of ensembles combining keyboard and fretted instruments (see Ch. 12 above).[17] In the view of Ashworth and O'Dette, 'Despite the highly publicized and exaggerated paranoia of a few late Renaissance and early-Baroque theorists regarding unequal temperaments on fretted instruments, they were, in fact, widely used and are not at all difficult to achieve'.[18]

Violins and violas could also be adapted to mean-tone temperament by adjusting the tuning of the basic fifths. Adriano Banchieri describes in his *Conclusioni nel suono dell'organo . . . opera vigesima* of 1609 a large-scale performance in Verona in 1607 of a multi-choir mass of his own composition combining members of the violin family, violas da gamba, trombones, violoni, harpsichords, lutes, and theorbos.[19] Banchieri even gives tables for tuning each type of instrument to the keyboard. Patrizio Barbieri presents evidence of mean-tone tuning of lutes and viols in the first half of the seventeenth century, especially in Rome and Naples, and offers documentation that adjustments to mean-tone tuning were made on unfretted strings throughout the seventeenth and eighteenth centuries.[20] The combination of cornettos, trombones, and violins in numerous church ensembles of the late sixteenth and early seventeenth centuries (see Chapter 4) demonstrates that wind instruments as well could adjust their intonation to the mean-tone tuning of organs.

Monteverdi's antagonist, the theorist Giovanni Maria Artusi, claimed that Monteverdi had his own notions of tuning, which approximated equal temperament. Lindley cites a passage where Artusi complains that

---

[16] Ibid. 50–66; Panetta, *Treatise*, 69 n. 34. See n. 18 below for other literature dealing with this issue.

[17] Emilio de' Cavalieri's *Rappresentatione di anima, et di corpo* (Rome: Mutij, 1600; fac. ed. Farnborough, England: Gregg Press, 1967), whose preface calls for combining a *lira doppia*, a harpsichord, and a theorbo, or an organ and a theorbo, is only one of numerous examples. Eng. trans. in Tamar Clothylde Read, 'A Critical Study and Performance Edition of Emilio de' Cavalieri's *Rappresentatione di anima e di corpo'* (DMA dissertation, University of Southern California, 1969), 141–4.

[18] 'Proto-Continuo: Overview and Practical Applications', in Kite-Powell, ed., *A Performer's Guide to Renaissance Music*, 210, 213 n. 11. In *Lutes, Viols and Temperaments*, 65–6, Lindley offers two methods of achieving mean-tone tuning on fretted instruments. Eugen M. Dombois in 'Correct and Easy Fret Placement', *Journal of the Lute Society of America*, 6 (1973), 30–2, and 'Varieties of Meantone Temperament Realized on the Lute', *Journal of the Lute Society of America*, 7 (1974), 82–9 also presents practical recommendations for setting frets and responding to various situations where mean-tone tuning is desired on the lute.

[19] (Bologna: Rossi, 1609; fac. ed. Bologna: Forni Editore, 1968), 50–5; Eng. trans. Lee R. Garrett as *Adriano Banchieri: Conclusions for Playing the Organ (1609)* (Colorado Springs, Colo.: Colorado College Music Press, 1982), 45–8. Banchieri gives similar instructions for tuning violas da gamba, violins, lutes, and theorbos to the organ or harpsichord in the 2nd edn. of *L'organo suonarino opera ventesima quinta* (Venice: Amadino, 1611), 97–8; fac. ed. Giulio Cattin (Amsterdam: Frits Knuf, 1969), 44. Eng. trans. (from 1622 edn.) in Donald E. Marcase, 'Adriano Banchieri, *L'organo suonarino*: Translation, Transcription and Commentary' (Ph.D. dissertation, Indiana University, 1970), 288–9.

[20] 'Conflitti di intonazione', 125–38.

certain obstinate 'modern composers' (Monteverdi) entertained a theory of intonation according to which the C♯–B♭ is 'neither a sixth nor a seventh, but sounds very well' and F♯–B♭ 'is a third' and is divided into a Pythagorean whole-tone and two equal semitones' as follows:[21]

According to Lindley, 'this amounted to a theory of equal temperament', since the 'resulting semitones are less than a cent larger than $\frac{1}{12}$ of an octave'.[22] Such a temperament would have been especially suitable for the more chromatic madrigals of Monteverdi's Fourth and Fifth Books of 1603 and 1605, the objects of Artusi's attacks.

Not all of the pieces in the Vespers need necessarily be performed in the same temperament. While the cantus firmus compositions might be performed with an organ in quarter-comma mean-tone tuning, the motets, which could suitably utilize a fretted lute or chitarrone as the continuo instrument (see Chapter 12), might well be performed in an approximately equal temperament. Nevertheless, the motets could also be performed in some type of mean-tone tuning, even when accompanied by a lute or chitarrone, by adjusting the frets and pulling or pushing stopped strings.

In the last analysis, Lindley's own conclusions about the complications and vagaries of tuning and temperament in the sixteenth century and early seventeenth century highlight the difficulty of arriving at any definitive system: 'Given all these different views, modern singers of Renaissance music may as well forget about any particular system of intonation and be content to make a good ensemble with whatever instruments and other voices may be present.'[23]

---

[21] Lindley, 'Tuning and Intonation', 174–5. The matter is discussed in more detail in id., 'Chromatic Systems (or Non-Systems) from Vicentino to Monteverdi' (review of Karol Berger, *Theories of Chromatic and Enharmonic Music in Late 16th Century Italy*), *Early Music History*, 2 (1982), 393–404, and in id., *Lutes, Viols and Temperaments*, 84–92. Lindley gives an abbreviated version and translation of Artusi's extended commentary from the 'Nona consideratione' of *L'Artusi, della imperfettione della moderna musica, parte seconda* of 1603 in 'Chromatic Systems', 402–4, and in slightly altered form in *Lutes, Viols and Temperaments*, 90–2.

[22] 'Tuning and Intonation', 175.

[23] Ibid.

23
Historical Pronunciation

In recent years, increasing attention has been paid to the historical pronunciation of texts of vocal music as scholars and singers of early music have become more aware of the impact on performance of historical pronunciation. Andrea von Ramm succinctly highlighted the importance of pronunciation some twenty years ago, even though she was speaking about the differences of pronunciation between separate languages rather than between modern and historical pronunciation of the same language:

> The characteristic sound of a language can be imitated as a typical sequence of vowels and consonants, as a melody, as a phrasing. There is an established rhythmical impulse of a language and a specific area of resonance involved for this particular character of a language or a dialect. . . . This causes a different sound, a different resonance and a different singing voice, depending on the language sung. Each language thus possesses its own timbre. . . .
>
> It is an important duty of an early music singer to understand the projection of languages. The projection consists not only of understanding the words. The singing voice has to give way to the sound of a language, of its character, of its integration with music. In a spoken language errors in pronunciation are obvious. In music they can create a stylistic disaster. Language is important in a musical style, the sound character of a language has to be carefully trained.[1]

Von Ramm's remarks are equally applicable to the historical pronunciation of any language in which performers of early music sing.

Studies of historical pronunciation are very difficult, and are complicated by the fact that people in different geographical regions speaking the same language often used different pronunciations. Pronunciation also varied across social classes and between generations. The pronunciation of a composer (whose place of work might have been far away from his original home) did not necessarily agree with that of his audience. And how might the French pronunciation of north Italian courtiers singing French chansons have compared with the French of the Parisian court? As far as historical pronunciation is concerned, one can scarcely speak in terms of 'authenticity'.

One set of criteria for approaching this problem has been proposed by Alison Wray:

---

[1] 'Singing Early Music', *Early Music*, 4 (1976), 14.

The middle road is to hypothesize about what range of pronunciations the composer would have considered acceptable. Insofar as a composer had fairly average pronunciation for his age and place of residence, that range should comprise of a selection of sounds that co-existed at the given date and which, in certain combinations, would provide plausible pronunciations for ordinary, reasonably educated individuals. That is, pronunciations that *could* have existed at the time, and which, had they been heard, would have seemed quite unremarkable because they fell within the range of what people heard around them every day.

The key to reconstruction, then, if we are to be practical about it, is *plausibility*, and the key to plausibility is the correct *selection* of sound combinations from the range we know to have existed at any given time.[2]

According to Wray, the pronunciation of Latin is the most complicated problem of all: 'Latin had been around so long and was so central to the administration and religion of the European countries that it took on, in its pronunciation, the characteristics of the native language around it.'[3] Singing pronunciation, moreover, may have been somewhat different from spoken pronunciation 'both for reasons of vocal production and acoustics and because of fashions and traditions'.[4]

Andrew Parrott cites three benefits to be derived from a historical approach to singing Latin:

Firstly, a correctly underlaid text will tend to become easier to sing (given the correct voice-type, at the right pitch), by virtue of the fact that, at the extremities of the vocal range and on melismas, the appropriate vowel from the period is likely to be technically more helpful to the singer. (We know that Renaissance theorists were concerned that composers should set the words in this way.) Secondly, the rhythm of the music and language are more likely to match where sometimes they might fight. Thirdly, Latin is rescued from appearing to be a dead language, or the exclusive property of the modern Roman Church; and through its similarity to the vernacular in any country it acquires a paradoxically greater feeling of familiarity. (More specifically, the meaning of a word may become more apparent to singer and listener alike through a sound closer to that of the word's vernacular descendant.)[5]

A preliminary pronunciation guide to Latin in Italy in the Renaissance was published by Ross W. Duffin in the *Journal of Musicology*.[6] Duffin's guide is based on comments by humanistic writers of the period. I reproduce here his table of pronunciations for Italy:

All Vowels   Especially the Romans put a glottal stop between two vowels of the same word, as *egum* or *echum* for *eum*. (Erasmus)

C   Soft *c* = *s* with a closing of the teeth, perhaps *ts*, *sh* or even *tsch*. (Charles Estienne) In the late 16th century, soft *c* = *s*. (Lipsius) This may be a regionalism or it may be Lipsius' inability to hear

---

[2] 'Restored Pronunciation for the Performance of Vocal Music', in Tess Knighton and David Fallows, eds., *Companion to Medieval and Renaissance Music* (New York: Schirmer Books, 1992), 295.

[3] Ibid. 296.

[4] Ibid. 297.

[5] Quoted in Harold Copeman, *Singing in Latin or Pronunciation Explor'd* (Oxford, 1990), pp. vi–vii. I have omitted Parrott's footnotes from the quotation.

[6] 'National Pronunciations of Latin ca. 1490–1600', *Journal of Musicology*, 4 (1985–6), 217–26.

the actual consonant. George Abbot, in 1604, describes the speech of Giordano Bruno in 1583 by quoting him: '*chentrum & chirculus and circumferenchia* (after the pronunciation of his Country language).'

G   Soft *g* sometimes pronounced like *z* (Lipsius)

H   Slightly aspirated. Thus, *hominem* is distinguished from *omine*. (Erasmus) Intervocalic *h* = *k*.

I   Consonantal *i* and vocalic *i* are virtually the same. (Charles Estienne)

O   *o* = *au* to many Italians, as *aumnis* for *omnis*. (Charles Estienne)

S   Intervocalic *s* = *s*. (Erasmus)

U   Pronounced more toward the French than the German manner (Erasmus), yet also described as equivalent to the French *ou*. (Charles Estienne)

X   *x* = *s* (unvoiced). (Henri Estienne)

Z   *z* = *dz*.

AU   Sometimes pronounced *al*, as *laldo* for *laudo*, *aldio* for *audio*. (Erasmus)

CH   Highly aspirated, especially in Florence. (Erasmus)

GN   Neither *g* nor *n*, but halfway between the two. (Erasmus)

PH   *ph* = *f* (Erasmus)

At the time of this writing, the only detailed study of Latin pronunciation is Harold Copeman, *Singing in Latin or Pronunciation Explor'd* (Oxford, 1990). According to Copeman, 'This book explores how to bring about a marriage of words and music, in the style of the time and place.'[7]

The Latin of sixteenth-century Rome was the Latin adopted by the Catholic Church in 1903 as the official pronunciation of the liturgy and is described in the introduction to the *Liber usualis*.[8] In other areas of Italy, Copeman concludes, 'the speaker of Latin was free to follow the local dialect or the standard Italian, with or without local accent: and singers likewise, subject to their local traditions and to their directors'.[9] In considering the intonation of Monteverdi's response *Deus in adjutorium me intende*, Copeman declares that 'in western Vulgar Latin generally and in Italian and many of the Italian dialects the 'e' can be close, and would be in both *Deus* and *intende*. . .'.[10] He notes that 'by around 1500 final -*d*, -*t*, -*s*, -*m* had become mute, and *pt* had become [tt], *ct* [s], *ps* [ss], and that *cs/x* was [ss] or [s]. The [n] in -*ns* had ceased to be mute.'[11] Moreover,

in the (Celtic) Gallo-Italic north-west (extending in the Middle Ages as far east as Emilia) 'u', as in France, was 'ü', representing [y] or [Y]; and in the whole of the north beyond the Apennines *c*

---

[7] *Singing in Latin*, 2.
[8] Ibid. 171, 226. Sect. IX of the introduction to the *Liber usualis* treats the reading and pronunciation of liturgical Latin.
[9] *Singing in Latin*, 173.
[10] Ibid. 174.
[11] Ibid. The symbols in square brackets are from the alphabet of the International Phonetic Association. A chart of their sounds is given ibid., pp. viii–ix, but can also be found in any standard work on phonetics.

before *e*, *i* became sibilised to [ts] (and often further to [s]), instead of being palatalised to [tʃ] (and sometimes [ʃ]) as in Tuscany and central Italy. The *g* in the north similarly became [dz] and in some places [z], compared with [dʒ] and [ʒ] further south.[12]

Copeman describes regional variants in northern Italy as follows:

In the musically important north the Piedmontese, Ligurian, Lombard and Emilian dialects (and so their vernacular Latin) are Gallo-Italic, shading into Franco-Provençal. Venice is linguistically (not geographically) transitional between Tuscan and Gallo-Italic. The mountains had some influence on the spread of Tuscan, and in the cities between the Apennines and the River Po the linguistic frontier ebbed and flowed somewhat.[13]

I reproduce here Copeman's table of 'Regional Variants in Renaissance Italy':

A. In northern Italy this is (and perhaps then was) a fronted [a]; in parts of Tuscany and in central and southern Italy it is a more backward [ɑ], and in Piedmont a back vowel approximating to [ɔ]. In Emilia palatalised sounds like [æ] are heard, and even [ɛ] near the Tuscan–Umbrian border.

AU. In Rome, as [al] (*laudo*/laldo, *audio*/aldio).

C. In northern Italy *c* before *e*, *i*, after originally being [k], had passed through (or missed out) the palatal [tʃ] used in central and most of southern Italy; it was sibilised to [ts] or [s]; [s] is today the commonest in north Italy but [θ] is found in parts of the north-east. Erasmus says that *chorpus*, *chalidus*, *champus* were heard at Florence, but he didn't think the speaker came from there.

Deus, eum. Romans interpolate [g] or 'ch' ([k]?) as a glottal stop.

I/J in Upper Italy (the north) was [ʒ].

S. In Rome and in the north, softened to [z] between vowels; in Tuscany the *s*, including endings, is [s]. Florentine usage depends on the word.

SC. Erasmus seems to imply for the It. sound [sts] or [stʃ], not [ʃ].

U. This was 'ü' ([y] or [Y]) in north-west Italy (Piedmont, Liguria, Lombardy, Modena, Mantua, and the north of the Trentino) . . .

Z. The Romans often used 'SS duplex', a very strong [s], nearly [ts]. Standard speech uses both [ts] and [dz]/[z]; *zona* = [zona].[14]

Copeman notes that Monteverdi's Venetian sacred music would have been pronounced in a typically Venetian manner: 'On the important question of *c* before front vowels . . . one is reasonably safe with [tʃ] (the familiar "chees and chaws"), but [s] is quite possible. His *u* would be [u] in Venice, but local speech would suggest [y] in Mantua.'[15] Other features of Venetian pronunciation are as follows:

The 'r' is not trilled; endings may be omitted; *gn* is pronounced 'ñ', as in Italian, rather than other northern possibilities, [n] and [gn].

---

[12] *Singing in Latin.* Original footnotes omitted.
[13] Ibid. 272.
[14] Ibid. Original footnotes and references omitted. I am grateful to Harold Copeman for permission to reproduce this and the following table.
[15] Ibid. 275.

. . . consonants are not sounded double and are often written single.

Ce, ci may be written as *ze, zi* (cito/zito), pronounced as [ts] before the eighteenth century, then as [s] (cf. cinque/sinque). The intervocalic *c* in Venice is now [z], but before the eighteenth century it was [dz]. Venetian Latin *pacem* may earlier have been [patʃem]; in Florence it was [paʃem].

The *ch* may stand for [tʃ] or the [k] of standard Italian (and Venetian *ca, co, cu*), depending partly on spelling conventions. And *g* before *e, i* could be written in the sixteenth century in place of *ch* (chiesa/giesia), so it may here have stood for [tʃ] (rather than [k]); and *z* could (as in *zentildonna* . . .) be used in Venetian dialect in place of Italian (or Latin) *g*, so *ge* could also be [dz], not very far removed from [tʃ]. *Gi* can be [j] or [dʒ].

Sc (before *e, i*), *ss* and initial *s* are [s] (pesce/pesse, scimia/simia).

The Latin *x, xc* and *cc* may have sounded as [z].

Before any consonant *n* becomes [ŋ] (Venetian dialect *cento* = [seŋto], and in the Middle Ages and Renaissance the Latin *centum* may have been pronounced [tʃeŋtum].

Before a nasal consonant the *e* was probably pronounced [e] rather than the Tuscan [ɛ]. More generally, I have suggested . . . that close as well as open vowels may have been used in regional Latin (as distinct from Italian literary and academic Latin) when the local vernacular speech worked that way. In Venice, Latin *e* and *o* in an open syllable may well have sounded as [e] and [o].[16]

[16] Ibid. 274–5.

Appendix A
Psalm *Cursus* and their Feasts

ↂ

SOURCE: Antiphonarium Romanum Ad Ritum Breviarij, ex decreto Sacros. Concilij Tridentini restituti, Pij Quinti Pontificis Maximi iussi editi, Et Clementis viij. auctoritate recogniti, Ad usum omnium Ecclesiarum Cathedralium, et Collegiatarum nuper iuxta regulas Directorij Chori magno studio, ac labore redactum. Venetiis, Apud Iuntas. M DC XXIII.

Feasts of the second class, which have vespers only on the feast-day itself, are listed under second vespers. Feasts in editorial brackets have no rubric indicating psalm *cursus* for first vespers, but do have a Magnificat antiphon for first vespers. The bracketed feast is assigned to the psalm *cursus* according to modern liturgical books.

'MALE *CURSUS*'

Dixit Dominus
Confitebor tibi
Beatus vir
Laudate pueri
Laudate Dominum

First and second Vespers: Ascension of the Lord, St Andrew, Finding of the Holy Cross, Nativity of St John the Baptist, Transfiguration of the Lord Jesus Christ, Exaltation of the Holy Cross, Holy Custodian Angels, Common of Confessors not Pontiffs

First vespers only: Christmas, Epiphany, Octave of Epiphany, Pentecost, Holy Trinity, Chair of St Peter, [Saint Agnes], Conversion of St Paul, St Agatha, Apostles Philip and James, SS John and Paul Martyrs, Apostles Peter and Paul, St Peter in Chains, St Lawrence, Beheading of St John the Baptist, Dedication of St Michael the Archangel, All Saints, St Martin the Bishop, Common of Apostles and Evangelists, Common of One Martyr, Common of Two or More Martyrs, Common of Confessor Pontiffs

'FEMALE *CURSUS*'

Dixit Dominus
Laudate pueri
Laetatus sum
Nisi Dominus
Lauda Jerusalem

First and second vespers: Circumcision, Conception of the BVM, Saint Lucy, Purification of the BVM, Annunciation of the BVM, Visitation of the BVM, Mary Magdalene, Holy Mary of the Snow, Assumption of the BVM, Nativity of the BVM, Presentation of the BVM, St Cecilia, Common of Virgins, Common of Holy Women

'SUNDAY *CURSUS*'

Dixit Dominus
Confitebor tibi
Beatus vir
Laudate pueri
In exitu Israel (*Laudate Dominum* often served as an unofficial substitute.)[1]

Second vespers only: Sundays, Epiphany, Octave of Epiphany, Passion Sunday, Palm Sunday, Easter, Sundays after Easter, Pentecost, Sundays after Pentecost, Holy Trinity

'CHRISTMAS *CURSUS*'

Dixit Dominus
Confitebor tibi
Beatus vir
De profundis
Memento Domine David

Second vespers only: Christmas, St Stephen, St John Apostle and Evangelist, Holy Innocents

'CORPUS CHRISTI *CURSUS*'

Dixit Dominus
Confitebor
Credidi
Beati omnes
Lauda Jerusalem

First and second vespers: Corpus Christi

OTHER *CURSUS*

1. *Dixit Dominus*
   Confitebor tibi
   Beatus vir
   Laudate pueri
   Lauda Jerusalem

First and second vespers: Dedication of church
Second vespers only: St Agnes, St Agatha

2. *Dixit Dominus*
   Confitebor tibi
   Beatus vir
   Laudate pueri
   Credidi

Second vespers only: SS John and Paul Martyrs, St Lawrence, Beheading of St John the Baptist, All Saints, St Clement, Common of One Martyr, Common of Two or More Martyrs

3. *Dixit Dominus*
   Confitebor tibi
   Beatus vir

[1] I am grateful to Linda Maria Koldau for this observation.

Laudate pueri
Memento Domine David

Second vespers only: [Chair of St Peter], St Martin the Bishop, Common of Confessor Pontiffs

4. *Dixit Dominus*
   Confitebor tibi
   Beatus vir
   Laudate pueri
   Confitebor tibi . . . quoniam

Second vespers only: Dedication of St Michael the Archangel

5. *Dixit Dominus*
   Laudate pueri
   Credidi
   In convertendo
   Domine probasti me

Second Vespers only: Conversion of St Paul, Apostles Philip and James, Apostles Peter and Paul, St Peter in Chains, Common of Apostles and Evangelists

DIVERGENCE IN MODERN LITURGICAL BOOKS

Second vespers: Holy Custodian Angels
Dixit Dominus
Confitebor tibi
Beatus vir
Laudate pueri
Confitebor tibi . . . quoniam

Appendix B
Rubrics Regarding Vespers and Marian Antiphons

6❧9

SOURCE: *Breviarium Romanum Ex Decreto Sacrosancti Concilij Tridentini Restitutum. Pii V. Pont. Max. iussu editum . . . Venetiis. MDLXXXIII.* (Copy in London, British Library.)
Rubricae Generales

De vesperis[1]

Ad Vesperas Pater noster: Ave Maria: Deus in adiutorium, &c. Deinde dicuntur quinque psalmi, cum quinque antiphonis, ut in proprio, aut Commune sanctorum signatur. In dominicis aut, & ferijs: antiphonae & psalmi semper dicuntur ut in psalterio, ubi. Tempore paschali psalmi dicuntur sub una antiphona: nisi aliae propriae antiphonae, ut in dominicis Adventus, assignatur.

Post psalmos, & antiphonas dicitur capitulum hymnis, versus, antiphona ad Magnificat cum eodem cantico, & oratio, omnia de tempore, vel sancto pro qualitate officij.

Preces quando dicendae sunt, dicuntur ante orationem: commemorationes vero de Cruce, S. Maria, Apostolis, & pace post cani, ut infra in proprijs rubricis dicitur.

De Antiphonis[2]

. . . In duplicibus ad Vesp. & Matutin. & Laudes tantum, antiphonae dicuntur ante psalmos integrae, & post psalmos integrae repetuntur; & in alijs Horis, & in officio non duplici, in principio psalmi inchoatur tantum antiphona, deinde in fine integra dicitur. Et quando antiphona incipit sicut psalmus, post inceptam antiphonam dicitur quod sequitur in psalmo sine repetitione principij, ab eo loco, ub. desinit antiphona . . .

De Antiphonis Beatae Mariae in fine Officij[3]

Antiphonae beatae Mariae positae in fine Psalterij post Complet. singula dicunt pro temporis diversitate, ut ibi annotat, praeterquam in triduo maioris hebdomadae ante Pascha. Dicantur autem extra Chorum tantum in fine Completorij, & in fine matutini dictis Laudibus, si tunc terminandum sit officium; alioquin, si alia subsequatur Hora, in fine ultimae Horae. In Choro autem semper deantur, [sic] quandocunque terminata alia Hora discendum est a Choro.

Nunquam vero dicitur post aliquam Horam quando subsequitur cum officio diei officium Defunctorum, vel Litania, praeterquam post Completorium, in quo semper dicitur, etiam si praedicta subsequantur: neque etiam dicitur, quando post aliquam Horam subsequitur missa. Dicuntur autem semper flexis genibus, praeterquam tempore paschali, hebdomadario tamen ad orationem surgente.

---

[1] fo. with signature +++3^{v}.
[2] fo. with signature +++4^{v}.
[3] fo. without signature; final page of Rubricae Generales.

Appendix C
Texts and Structural Outlines of
Compositions Based on a Cantus Firmus

꧁✿꧂

Latin texts for the response, psalms, Magnificats, hymn, and *Sonata* given below are derived from the *Liber usualis*, following its spelling and division of verses. English translations are adapted from *The Revised English Bible* (Oxford: Oxford University Press, 1989) and *The Oxford Annotated Bible* (Oxford: Oxford University Press, 1962). Indications in structural outlines of transpositions of cantus firmus refer only to intervals other than an octave.

Domine ad adjuvandum   *Sex vocib. & sex Instrumentis, si placet* (For six voices and six instruments, if it pleases)
Deus in adjutorium/Domine ad adjuvandum (Psalm 69, verse 2)

℣ Deus in adjutorium meum intende.
℞ Domine ad adjuvandum me festina.

Gloria Patri et Filio et Spiritui Sancto.
Sicut erat in principio, et nunc et semper, et in saecula saeculorum, Amen. Alleluia.

℣ Make haste and save me, God.
℞ Lord, come quickly to my help.

Glory to the Father and Son and Holy Spirit.
As it was in the beginning and is now and shall be, for all ages, Amen. Alleluiah.

Verse 1: *Domine ad adjuvandum* (12 syllables)	8 bars
Ritornello (triple metre)	7 bars
Verse 2: *Gloria Patri* (16 syllables)	9 bars
Ritornello (triple metre)	7 bars
Verse 3: *Sicut erat* (25 syllables)	15 bars
Alleluia (Text plus partial ritornello; duple and triple metre)	13 bars (9 + 4)

Dixit Dominus   (Psalm 109) *Sex vocib. & sex Instrumentis. Li Ritornelli si ponno sonar, & anco tralasciar secondo il volere.* (For six voices and six instruments. The ritornellos may be played or omitted, according to your wish.) Tone 4e
1. Dixit Dominus Domino meo: Sede a dextris meis.
2. Donec ponam inimicos tuos, scabellum pedum tuorum.
3. Virgam virtutis tuae emittet Dominus ex Sion: dominare in medio inimicorum tuorum.
4. Tecum principium in die virtutis tuae in splendoribus sanctorum: ex utero ante luciferum genui te.
5. Juravit Dominus, et non paenitebit eum: Tu es sacerdos in aeternum secundum ordinem Melchisedech.
6. Dominus a dextris tuis, confregit in die irae suae reges.
7. Judicabit in nationibus, implebit ruinas; conquassabit capita in terra multorum.

8. De torrente in via bibet: propterea exaltabit caput.
9. Gloria Patri et Filio, et Spiritui Sancto.
10. Sicut erat in principio, et nunc, et semper, et in saecula saeculorum. Amen.

1. The Lord said to my lord: 'Sit at my right hand.
2. And I shall make your enemies your footstool.'
3. The Lord extends the sway of your powerful sceptre, saying, 'From Zion reign over your enemies.'
4. You gain the homage of your people on the day of your power, arrayed in holy garments, a child of the dawn, you have the dew of your youth.
5. The Lord has sworn an oath and will not change his mind: 'You are a priest for ever, a Melchizedek in my service.'
6. The Lord is at your right hand; he crushes kings on the day of his wrath.
7. He will judge the nations, he will fill them with destruction, he will shatter heads throughout the wide earth.
8. He will drink from the stream on his way; therefore he will hold his head high.
9. Glory to the Father and Son and Holy Spirit.
10. As it was in the beginning and is now and shall be, for all ages, Amen.

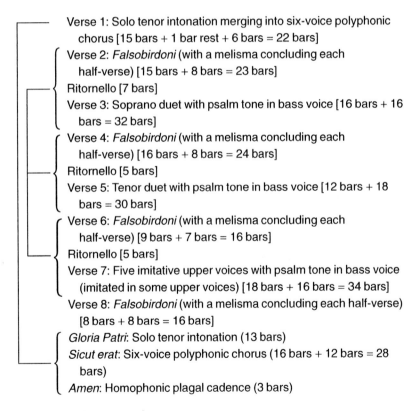

Fɪɢ. C.ɪ. *Dixit Dominus*, symmetries

Laudate pueri (Psalm 112) *à 8 voci sole nel Organo* (for eight solo voices with the organ). Tone 8g

1. Laudate, pueri, Dominum; laudate nomen Domini.
2. Sit nomen Domini benedictum, ex hoc nunc, et usque in saeculum.
3. A solis ortu usque ad occasum, laudabile nomen Domini.
4. Excelsus super omens gentes Dominus, et super caelos gloria ejus.
5. Quis sicut Dominus Deus noster, qui in altis habitat, et humilia respicit in caelo et in terra?
6. Suscitans a terra inopem, et de stercore erigens pauperem:
7. Ut collocet eum cum principibus, cum principibus populi sui.
8. Qui habitare facit sterilem in domo, matrem filiorum laetantem.
9. & 10. Gloria Patri et Filio etc.

1. Praise the Lord, you that are his servants, praise the name of the Lord.
2. Blessed be the name of the Lord now and evermore.
3. From the rising of the sun to its setting may the Lord's name be praised!
4. High is the Lord above all nations, high his glory above the heavens.
5. Who is like the Lord our God, who resides on high, but humbly cares for heaven and earth?
6. Who lifts the weak out of the dust and raises the poor from the rubbish heap,
7. Giving them a place among princes, among the princes of his people;
8. Who makes the woman in a childless house a happy mother of children.
9. & 10. Glory to the Father, etc.

Verse 1: Expanding polyphony based on psalm tone and countersubject. Reciting note: c' (15 bars + 12 bars = 27 bars).

Verse 2: Soprano duet with psalm tone in quintus. Reciting note: g ($9\frac{1}{2}$ bars + 5 bars = $14\frac{1}{2}$ bars).

Verse 3: Soprano duet with psalm tone in altus. Reciting note: g' ($7\frac{1}{2}$ bars + 4 bars = $11\frac{1}{2}$ bars).

Verse 4: Tenor duet with overlapped psalm tone from verse 3 in altus; subsequent psalm tone in cantus. Reciting note: d'' (5 bars (overlapped from verse 3) + 11 bars = 16 bars).

Verse 5: Bass duet with psalm tone in sextus. Entire verse completed in sextus during first half of verse in basses. Reciting note: c'' ($13\frac{1}{2}$ bars + $10\frac{1}{2}$ bars = 24 bars).

Verse 6: Triple-metre full-texture sequences interspersed with duple-metre psalm tone in altus. Reciting note: c' (8 bars + 9 bars = 17 bars).

Verse 7: Homophonic texture with psalm tone in quintus. Entire verse completed in quintus during first half of verse in other voices. Reciting note: c' ($15\frac{1}{2}$ bars + $10\frac{1}{2}$ bars = 26 bars).

Verse 8: Imitative texture expanding to all voices in triple metre with psalm tone in tenor. Almost entire verse completed in tenor during first half of verse in other voices. Reciting note: c' (12 bars + 12 bars = 24 bars).

Gloria Patri: Imitative and homophonic passages in duple and triple metre interspersed with solo recitation of psalm tone in quintus. Reciting note: c' (14 bars + 21 bars repetition of text = 35 bars).

Sicut erat: Repetition of material from verse 1 with psalm tone migrating from quintus to cantus, tenor, quintus, and bassus. Reciting note: c' (10 bars + 11 bars = 21 bars).

Amen: Imitative texture without psalm tone resolving to tenor and quintus duet, concluding with full cadence (15 bars).

Laetatus sum (Psalm 121) *A sei voci* (For six voices). Tone 2d transposed up a fourth, in *cantus mollis.*

1. Laetatus sum in his quae dicta sunt mihi: 'In domum Domini ibimus.'
2. Stantes erant pedes nostri, in atriis tuis Jerusalem.

3. Jerusalem, quae aedificatur ut civitas: cujus participatio ejus in idipsum.
4. Illuc enim ascenderunt tribus, tribus Domini: testimonium Israel, ad confitendum nomini Domini.
5. Quia illic sederunt sedes in judicio, sedes super domum David.
6. Rogate quae ad pacem sunt Jerusalem: et abundantia diligentibus te.
7. Fiat pax in virtute tua: et abundantia in turribus tuis.
8. Propter fratres meos et proximos meos, loquebar pacem de te.
9. Propter domum Domini Dei nostri, quaesivi bona tibi.
10. & 11. Gloria Patri et Filio etc.

1. I rejoiced when they said to me, 'Let us go to the house of the Lord.'
2. Our feet were standing within your gates, Jerusalem:
3. Jerusalem, a city built compactly and solidly.
4. There the tribes went up, the tribes of the Lord, the testimony of Israel, to acknowledge the name of the Lord.
5. For there the thrones of justice were set, the thrones of the house of David.
6. Pray for the peace of Jerusalem: 'May those who love you prosper.'
7. 'Peace be within your ramparts and prosperity in your palaces.'
8. For the sake of these my brothers and my friends, I shall say, 'Peace be within you.'
9. For the sake of the house of the Lord our God I shall pray for your well-being.
10. & 11. Glory to the Father, etc.

Verse 1: Solo cantus firmus over bass pattern a (see Ex. 6.12*a*) (10 bars + 1 bar rest + 6 bars = 17 bars).

Verse 2: Six-voice imitative polyphony over bass pattern b (see Ex. 6.12*b*). No cantus firmus (10 bars + 13 bars = 23 bars).

Verse 3: Tenor duet over bass pattern a. No cantus firmus (11 bars + 6 bars = 17 bars).

Verse 4: Soprano duet, then soprano and tenor duets with drone fifth in bassus and altus over pattern c (see Ex. 6.12*c*) (6 bars + 6 bars = 12 bars). Six-voice imitative and homophonic texture over bass pattern d (see Ex. 6.12*d*) with migrating cantus firmus (9 bars + $15\frac{1}{2}$ bars = $24\frac{1}{2}$ bars).

Verse 5: Trio texture with soprano duet and bass voice over bass pattern a. No cantus firmus (10 bars + 7 bars = 17 bars).

Verse 6: Four lower voices in imitative pairs over bass pattern b. Cantus firmus in cantus between first and second halves of verse as well as during second half. (14 bars + 7 bars = 21 bars).

Verse 7: Trio of lower voices with cantus firmus in sextus over pattern a (10 bars + 7 bars = 17 bars).

Verse 8: Tenor duet, then soprano and tenor duets with drone fifth in bassus and altus over pattern c (4 bars + 7 bars = 11 bars). Six-voice imitative texture over pattern d with migrating cantus firmus ($5\frac{1}{2}$ bars + $10\frac{1}{2}$ bars = 16 bars).

Verse 9: Six-voice imitative texture over pattern a. No cantus firmus ($9\frac{1}{2}$ bars + $7\frac{1}{2}$ bars = 17 bars).

Gloria Patri: Six-voice imitative and homophonic textures over varied version of bass pattern b. Cantus firmus transposed down a fourth in altus in second half of verse (10 bars + 1 bar rest + 12 bars = 23 bars).

Sicut erat: *Falsobordone* beginning leads to six-voice homophonic and imitative texture over pattern d, with migrating cantus firmus (5 bars + 11 bars = 16 bars).

Amen: Homophonic plagal cadence (3 bars).

Nisi Dominus   (Psalm 126) *A dieci voci* (For ten voices). Tone 6f

1. Nisi Dominus aedificaverit domum, in vanum laboraverunt qui aedificant eam.
2. Nisi Dominus custodierit civitatem, frustra vigilat qui custodit eam.
3. Vanum est vobis ante lucem surgere: surgite postquam sederitis, qui manducatis panem doloris.
4. Cum dederit dilectis suis somnum: ecce hereditas Domini, filii: merces, fructus ventris.
5. Sicut sagittae in manu potentis: ita filii excussorum.
6. Beatus vir qui implevit desiderium suum ex ipsis: non confundetur cum loquetur inimicis suis in porta.
7. & 8. Gloria Patri et Filio etc.

1. Unless the Lord builds the house, its builders labour in vain.
2. Unless the Lord keeps watch over the city, the watchman stands guard in vain.
3. It is vain for you to rise early and go late to rest, eating the bread of sorrow.
4. For he gives to his beloved sleep; behold, sons are a gift from the Lord, the fruit of the womb, a reward.
5. Like arrows in the hand of a warrior are the sons of one's youth.
6. Happy is the man who has fulfilled his desire with them; he shall not be confounded when he speaks with his enemies at the gate.
7. & 8. Glory to the Father, etc.

Verse 1: Double choirs in close imitative polyphony (19 bars + 16 bars = 35 bars).
Verse 2: *Cori spezzati* in homophonic style. Second choir echoes first choir ((first choir: 9 bars + 8 bars = 17 bars) + (second choir: 3-bar overlap with first choir + 14 bars = 17 bars) = 31 bars).
Verse 3: *Cori spezzati* in homophonic style. Second choir echoes first choir ((first choir: 9 bars + 8 bars = 17 bars) + (second choir: 3-bar overlap with first choir + 14 bars = 17 bars) = 31 bars).
Verse 4: *Cori spezzati* in homophonic style. Second choir echoes first choir ((first choir: 9 bars + 8 bars = 17 bars) + (second choir: 3-bar overlap with first choir + 14 bars = 17 bars) = 31 bars).
Verse 5: *Cori spezzati* in homophonic style in triple metre. Psalm tone transposed up a fourth. Second choir echoes first choir ((first choir: 9 bars + 8 bars = 17 bars) + (second choir: 3-bar overlap with first choir + 6 bars = 9 bars) = 23 bars).
Verse 6: *Cori spezzati* in homophonic style in triple metre. Psalm tone transposed up a fourth. Second choir overlaps first choir ((first choir: 8 bars + 14 bars = 22 bars) + (second choir: 16-bar overlap with first choir) = 22 bars).
Gloria Patri: Double-choir homophony with psalm tone transposed down a tone below original level ($6\frac{1}{2}$ bars + $6\frac{1}{2}$ bars = 13 bars).
Sicut erat: Repetition of verse 1. Psalm tone transposed back to original level (19 bars + 16 bars = 35 bars).
Amen: Homophonic plagal cadence (5 bars).

Lauda Jerusalem   (Psalm 147: 12–20) *A Sette voci* (For seven voices). Tone 3a

1. Lauda Jerusalem, Dominum: lauda Deum tuum, Sion.
2. Quoniam confortavit seras portarum tuarum: benedixit filiis tuis in te.
3. Qui posuit fines tuos pacem: et adipe frumenti satiat te.
4. Qui emittit eloquium suum terrae: velociter currit sermo ejus.
5. Qui dat nivem sicut lanam: nebulam sicut cinerem spargit.
6. Mittit crystallum suam sicut buccellas: ante faciem frigoris ejus quis sustinebit?
7. Emittet verbum suum, et liquefaciet ea: flabit spiritus ejus, et fluent aquae.
8. Qui annuntiat verbum suum Jacob: justitias et judicia sua Israel.

9. Non fecit taliter omni nationi: et judicia sua non manifestavit eis.

10. & 11. Gloria Patri et Filio etc.

1. Praise the Lord, Jerusalem, praise your God, O Zion,

2. For he has strengthened your barred gates; he has blessed your inhabitants.

3. He has brought peace to your realm and given you the best of wheat in plenty.

4. He sends his command over the earth, and his word runs swiftly.

5. He showers down snow, white as wool, and sprinkles hoar-frost like ashes;

6. He scatters crystals of ice like crumbs; who can stand before his cold?

7. He utters his word, and the ice is melted; he makes the wind blow, and the water flows again.

8. To Jacob he reveals his word, his statutes and decrees to Israel;

9. He has not done this for other nations, nor were his decrees made known to them.

10. & 11. Glory to the Father, etc.

Verse 1: Psalm tone in tenor interspersed with chordal homophony. Reciting note: c'. Psalm tone imitated in cantus part (9 bars + 10 bars = 19 bars).

Verse 2: Choirs, beginning with first choir, alternate at intervals of $2\frac{1}{2}$–$3\frac{1}{2}$ bars (8 bars + 8 bars (1 bar overlap) = 15 bars).

Verse 3: Choirs, beginning with first choir, alternate at intervals of 3 bars (4 bars + 5 bars (1 bar overlap) = 8 bars).

Verse 4: Choirs, beginning with first choir, alternate at intervals of 3 bars. Reciting note transposed up a fourth to f (4 bars + 4 bars = 8 bars).

Verse 5: Choirs, beginning with first choir, alternate at intervals of 1–$1\frac{1}{2}$ bars (4 bars + 5 bars (1 bar overlap) = 8 bars).

Verse 6: Choirs, beginning with second choir, alternate at intervals of $\frac{1}{2}$–$1\frac{1}{2}$ bars ($5\frac{1}{2}$ bars + $6\frac{1}{2}$ bars (1 bar overlap) = 11 bars).

Verse 7: Second choir imitates first choir at interval of semibreve (one bar). Reciting note transposed back to c' (7 bars + 7 bars (1 bar overlap) = 13 bars).

Verse 8: Second choir follows first choir (bass of second choir imitates first choir bass at fifth below) at interval of minim (half-bar) (4 bars + $7\frac{1}{2}$ bars = $11\frac{1}{2}$ bars).

Verse 9: Second choir imitates first choir at interval of semiminim ($6\frac{1}{2}$ bars + $11\frac{1}{2}$ bars = 18 bars).

Gloria Patri: Homophonic setting of first half of verse in both choirs. Reciting note shifted to cantus and transposed up a fourth to f''. First choir follows second choir at interval of five bars in second half of verse. Psalm tone at untransposed level in sextus of second choir, then repeated in septimus and imitated fourth higher in cantus of first choir (12 bars + 12 bars = 24 bars).

Sicut erat: Both choirs join in homophonic setting beginning with measured *falsobordone* and proceeding to imitations of reciting note at intervals of half-bar and full bar. Reciting note C in sextus (second choir soprano), bassus (second choir), and sextus (8 bars + 13 bars = 21 bars).

Amen: Six-voice imitative texture without psalm tone, concluding with full cadence (12 bars).

Sonata sopra Sancta Maria   (Litany of the Saints)

Sancta Maria, ora pro nobis.

Holy Mary, pray for us.

The number of bars shown includes the cadences overlapping the end of one section and the beginning of the next. The brackets illustrate the structural groupings and symmetries (see Ch. 8 above).

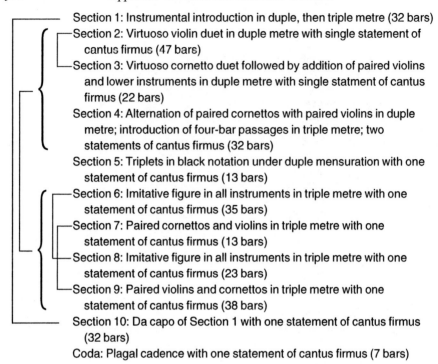

Section 1: Instrumental introduction in duple, then triple metre (32 bars)

Section 2: Virtuoso violin duet in duple metre with single statement of cantus firmus (47 bars)

Section 3: Virtuoso cornetto duet followed by addition of paired violins and lower instruments in duple metre with single statment of cantus firmus (22 bars)

Section 4: Alternation of paired cornettos with paired violins in duple metre; introduction of four-bar passages in triple metre; two statements of cantus firmus (32 bars)

Section 5: Triplets in black notation under duple mensuration with one statement of cantus firmus (13 bars)

Section 6: Imitative figure in all instruments in triple metre with one statement of cantus firmus (35 bars)

Section 7: Paired cornettos and violins in triple metre with one statement of cantus firmus (13 bars)

Section 8: Imitative figure in all instruments in triple metre with one statement of cantus firmus (23 bars)

Section 9: Paired violins and cornettos in triple metre with one statement of cantus firmus (38 bars)

Section 10: Da capo of Section 1 with one statement of cantus firmus (32 bars)

Coda: Plagal cadence with one statement of cantus firmus (7 bars)

Fig. C.2. *Sonata sopra Sancta Maria*, symmetries

Ave maris stella   *à 8* (Hymn for feasts of the BVM)

1. Ave, maris stella,   Hail, star of the sea,
Dei Mater alma,   The nourishing Mother of God,
Atque semper Virgo,   And always virgin,
Felix caeli porta.   The happy portal of heaven.

2. Sumens illud Ave   Taking that, 'Hail'
Gabrielis ore,   From the mouth of Gabriel,
Funda nos in pace,   Grant us peace,
Mutans Hevae nomen.   Changing the name of Eve [to Ave].

3. Solve vincla reis,   Release the bonds of sinners,
Profer lumen caecis,   Bring light to the blind,
Mala nostra pelle,   Drive away our evil,
Bona cuncta posce.   Pray for all our blessings.

4. Monstra te esse matrem: Show yourself a mother:
Sumat per te preces,   He will accept our prayers through you,
Qui pro nobis natus,   He who, born for us,
Tulit esse tuus.   Was carried by you.

5. Virgo singularis,   O peerless Virgin,
Inter omnes mitis,   Gentlest of all,
Nos culpis solutos,   Our sins dissolved,
Mites fac et castos.   Make us mild and pure.

6. Vitam praesta puram,   Grant a pure life,
Iter para tutum,   Prepare a safe journey,

Ut videntes Jesum,	That seeing Jesus,
Semper collaetemur.	We may rejoice for ever.

7. Sit laus Deo Patri, — Praise be to God the Father,
Summo Christo decus, — Glory to Christ on high,
Spiritui Sancto, — To the Holy Spirit,
Tribus honor unus. Amen. — Honour, one as three. Amen.

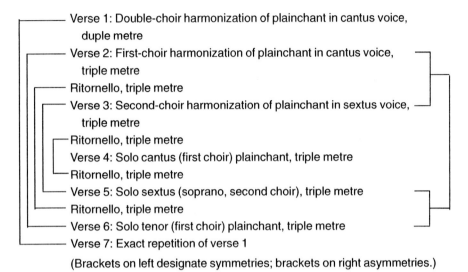

Verse 1: Double-choir harmonization of plainchant in cantus voice, duple metre

Verse 2: First-choir harmonization of plainchant in cantus voice, triple metre

Ritornello, triple metre

Verse 3: Second-choir harmonization of plainchant in sextus voice, triple metre

Ritornello, triple metre

Verse 4: Solo cantus (first choir) plainchant, triple metre

Ritornello, triple metre

Verse 5: Solo sextus (soprano, second choir), triple metre

Ritornello, triple metre

Verse 6: Solo tenor (first choir) plainchant, triple metre

Verse 7: Exact repetition of verse 1

(Brackets on left designate symmetries; brackets on right asymmetries.)

Fig. C.3. Ave maris stella, symmetries and asymmetries

Magnificats (Luke 1: 46–55) *A 6. voci* (for six voices) and *à Sette voci, & Sei instrumenti* (for seven voices and six instruments). Tone 1d, transposed up a fourth, in *cantus mollis*

1. Magnificat anima mea Dominum.
2. Et exsultavit spiritus meus in Deo salutari meo.
3. Quia respexit humilitatem ancillae suae: ecce enim ex hoc beatam me dicent omnes generationes.
4. Quia fecit mihi magna qui potens est: et sanctum nomen ejus.
5. Et misericordia ejus a progenie in progenies timentibus eum.
6. Fecit potentiam in brachio suo: dispersit superbos mente cordis sui.
7. Deposuit potentes de sede, et exaltavit humiles.
8. Esurientes implevit bonis: et divites dimisit inanes.
9. Suscepit Israel, puerum suum, recordatus misericordiae suae.
10. Sicut locutus est ad patres nostros, Abraham et semini ejus in saecula.
11. & 12. Gloria Patri et Filio etc.

1. My soul prizes the greatness of the Lord.
2. My spirit has rejoiced in God my Saviour;
3. For he has looked with favour on his lowly servant, and because of this all generations will call me blessed.
4. For the Mighty God has done great things for me; and his name is holy.
5. And his mercy [is] from generation to generation towards those who fear him.
6. He has shown the might of his arm; he has scattered the proud in the imagination of their hearts.

7. He has brought down the mighty from their thrones, and raised on high the lowly.

8. He has filled the hungry with good things, and sent the rich away empty.

9. He has supported Israel, his servant, in remembrance of his mercy,

10. As he spoke [promised] to our forefathers, Abraham and his seed, for ever.

11. & 12. Glory to the Father, etc.

Magnificat a 7

Verse 1: Increasing texture based on Magnificat tone intonation in overlapping four-bar units until full texture reached. Second half of verse harmonizes Magnificat tone with reciting note *d″* as cantus solo with walking bass (14 bars + 10 bars = 24 bars).

Verse 2: Tenor and quintus virtuoso duet in duple metre with cantus firmus in altus. Magnificat tone transposed down a fourth to reciting note *a′* (12 bars + 15 bars = 27 bars).

Verse 3: Instrumental ritornello in triple metre followed by Magnificat tone in quintus with reciting note *d′* in duple metre, accompanied by organ and obbligato *pifare*, trombones, and recorders in succession. At *omnes generationes*, tenor, after a long pause, joins an exact repetition of the ritornello in triple metre (16 bars ritornello + 17 bars + 4 bars obbligato instrumental interlude + 14 bars + 16 bars ritornello with tenor = 67 bars).

Verse 4: Bassus and septimus virtuoso duet in duple metre with two obbligato violins and cantus firmus in altus. Magnificat tone transposed down a fourth to reciting note *a* (17 bars + 15 bars (1 bar overlap) = 31 bars).

Verse 5: Alternating high and low trios each with cantus firmus in topmost voice of each trio. Magnificat tone alternates between tenor reciting note *a* and cantus reciting note *d″*. Trios combined at end. Conservative style (42 bars + 17 bars (1 bar overlap) = 58 bars).

Verse 6: Two violins and viola with cantus firmus in altus. Magnificat tone transposed down a fourth with reciting note *a′* (20 bars + 16 bars = 36 bars).

Verse 7: Virtuoso echo duet between two cornettos, then two violins. Magnificat tone in quintus with reciting note *d′* (16 bars + 15 bars = 31 bars).

Verse 8: Instrumental ritornello interspersed with unaccompanied chant in parallel thirds. Magnificat tone in cantus with reciting note *d″*. Ritornello joins voices at end (23 bars + 30 bars = 53 bars).

Verse 9: Virtuoso duet for cantus and sextus. Magnificat tone in tenor with reciting note *d′* (19 bars + 17 bars = 36 bars).

Verse 10: Dialogue between pair of violins and pair of cornettos. Magnificat tone in altus transposed down a fourth with reciting note *a′* (21 bars + 17 bars = 38 bars).

Gloria Patri: Virtuoso duet for tenor and quintus. Magnificat tone in cantus with reciting note *d″* (19 bars + 19 bars (1 bar overlap) = 37 bars).

Sicut erat: Seven-voice homophonic texture. Magnificat tone in cantus and sextus (canon), in cantus alone, in sextus with quintus (canon), and in cantus alone. Reciting note *d″* (20 bars + 33 bars = 53 bars).

Amen: Seven-voice imitative texture based on perpetually descending scale. No Magnificat tone (13 bars).

Magnificat a 6

Verse 1: Increasing texture based on Magnificat tone intonation at four-bar intervals until full texture reached. Second half of verse harmonizes Magnificat tone with reciting note *d″* as cantus solo with walking bass; repeat of tone in sextus accompanied by cantus in parallel thirds (16 bars + 16 bars = 32 bars).

Verse 2: Virtuoso duet in triple metre for tenor and quintus with cantus firmus in altus. Magnificat tone transposed down a fourth to reciting note *a′* (20 bars + 20 bars = 40 bars).

Verse 3: Organ ritornello in triple metre followed by Magnificat tone in tenor with reciting note *d'* in duple metre, harmonized by organ only. At *omnes generationes*, tenor is joined by an exact repetition of the ritornello in triple metre (13 bars ritornello + 15 bars + 23 bars (10 bars tenor alone + 13 bars tenor with ritornello) = 51 bars).

Verse 4: Alternating high and low trios each with cantus firmus in topmost voice of each trio. Magnificat tone alternates between cantus reciting note *d''* and tenor reciting note *a*. Trios combined at end. Conservative style (26 bars + 30 bars (1 bar overlap) = 55 bars).

Verse 5: Virtuoso duet in duple metre for cantus and sextus with cantus firmus in tenor. Magnificat tone untransposed with reciting note *d'* (16 bars + 20 bars = 36 bars).

Verse 6: Duet for cantus and sextus in modest style and duple metre with cantus firmus in a ltus. Magnificat tone transposed down a fourth with reciting note *a'* (23 bars + 14 bars = 37 bars).

Verse 7: Virtuoso echo duet between cantus and sextus. Magnificat tone in tenor with reciting note *d'* (15½ bars + 17½ bars = 33 bars).

Verse 8: Organ ritornello interspersed with unaccompanied chant in parallel thirds. Magnificat tone in altus transposed down a fourth with reciting note *a'*. Ritornello joins voices at end (25 bars + 28 bars = 53 bars).

Verse 9: Organ ritornello interspersed with unaccompanied chant in parallel thirds. Magnificat tone in sextus with reciting note *d''*. Ritornello joins voices at end (25 bars + 35 bars = 60 bars).

Verse 10: Dialogue between cantus-bassus pair and sextus-tenor pair. Magnificat tone in altus transposed down a fourth with reciting note *a'* (22 bars + 19 bars = 41 bars).

Gloria Patri: Six-voice imitative texture alternating with solo Magnificat tone in quintus with reciting note *d'* (20 bars + 39 bars = 59 bars).

Sicut erat and Amen: Six-voice homophonic texture. Magnificat tone in cantus with reciting note *d''*. Sextus in canon with cantus for first half of verse (17 bars + 29 bars = 46 bars).

Summary of Magnificat Tone Levels

Magnificat *a 6*

Verse 1: Untransposed; cantus reciting note *d''*
Verse 2: Transposed a fourth down; altus reciting note *a'*
Verse 3: Untransposed; tenor reciting note *d'*
Verse 4: Alternation between cantus reciting note *d''* and tenor reciting note *a*
Verse 5: Untransposed; tenor reciting note *d'*
Verse 6: Transposed a fourth down; altus reciting note *a'*
Verse 7: Untransposed; tenor reciting note *d'*
Verse 8: Transposed a fourth down; altus reciting note *a'*
Verse 9: Untransposed; sextus reciting note *d''*
Verse 10: Transposed a fourth down; altus reciting note *a'*
Gloria Patri: Untransposed; quintus reciting note *d'*
Sicut erat: Untransposed; cantus reciting note *d''*

Magnificat *a 7*

Verse 1: Untransposed; cantus reciting note *d''*
Verse 2: Transposed a fourth down; altus reciting note *a'*
Verse 3: Untransposed; quintus reciting note *d'*
Verse 4: Transposed a fourth down; altus reciting note *a'*
Verse 5: Alternation between tenor reciting note *a* and cantus reciting note *d''*

Verse 6: Transposed a fourth down; altus reciting note *a'*
Verse 7: Untransposed; quintus reciting note *d'*
Verse 8: Untransposed; cantus reciting note *d"*
Verse 9: Untransposed; tenor reciting note *d'*
Verse 10: Transposed a fourth down; altus reciting note *a'*
Gloria Patri: Untransposed; cantus reciting note *d"*
Sicut erat: Untransposed; cantus and sextus reciting note *d"*

The two Magnificats differ in their presentation of the Magnificat tone in verse 5, where the levels of the alternating versions are reversed, and in verse 8, where the reciting note is transposed to *a'* in the Magnificat *a 6* but remains at *d"* in the Magnificat *a 7*.

Appendix D
Discography

RECORDINGS listed here include only those which contain several items from the Vespers portion of Monteverdi's 1610 print and which pretend to some level of 'completeness'. By 'completeness' is meant the director's belief that the items recorded represent either the liturgical unity of Monteverdi's collection, or a large sampling of the vesper music contained in it. Recordings with one, two, or a few separate items from the print are not listed, nor are recordings of the *Missa in illo tempore*.

Recordings often appear in multiple formats: LP, CD, cassette tape, even video. Each separate performance is listed in the discography only once, regardless of the number of formats in which it may have appeared, unless the content of separate formats differs (as in items 31 and 32). The format is LP unless otherwise noted. In some instances, the number of a boxed set differs from the numbering of the individual discs, CDs, or tapes within it. My numberings represent, in so far as I have been able to ascertain them, the catalogue issue numbers. Recordings normally have different identification numbers in different formats; moreover, the same format sometimes has different numberings in different countries or in re-releases. Where I have been able to obtain these numberings they are listed; however, I have made no attempt to trace all such issues and reissues. Nor has it always been possible to verify numberings. For some items, I have had to rely exclusively on listings in other discographies.

Dates of issue are also often problematic. In most cases, the date of issue represents the copyright date, which is usually printed on LPs and CDs. Some items, however, display no copyright date for the recording, only for the liner notes, or not at all. In these cases, the dates of issue are drawn from other discographies or record reviews, but different sources often give somewhat different dates, rendering this information inexact. Where the date appears uncertain, I have appended a question mark. It has proved impossible to verify myself the accuracy of all details of information for these recordings. In the context of the present book, the descriptions of the recordings themselves, each representing the director's view of the Vespers at the time the recording was made, have seemed the most important consideration. Therefore, in addition to principal performers, notable aspects of the content, order of compositions, or instrumentation of each recording are listed. I have not attempted to 'review' these recordings.

The earliest discography of Monteverdi's music is Gunnar Westerlund and Eric Hughes, *Music of Claudio Monteverdi: A Discography* (London: British Institute of Recorded Sound, 1972). See the review by Jeffrey Kurtzman in *Music Library Association Notes*, 30 (1974), 532–3. The first discography specifically of the Vespers of 1610 was by Jerome F. Weber in *Fanfare*, 4/5 (1981), 108–9. A subsequent one is Denis Morrier, 'Pour une discographie critique des Vêpres de la Vierge', *Diapason-Harmonie*, 354 (1989), 54–5. These discographies have been especially useful in providing information on several early or rare recordings of the Vespers. The series of reviews of recordings of the Vespers by Weber in *Fanfare* has also been very helpful, and I am very grateful to him for assistance in providing many further details for the present discography. Additional information on specific recordings was kindly provided by Michael Beckerman, Roberto Giuliani, Edward Houghton, and Tom Moore.

1. UNIVERSITY OF ILLINOIS CRS 1; (MONOPHONIC) 1952/1953?

Leopold Stokowski, director. University of Illinois Symphony Orchestra and The Oratorio Society. Vocal soloists: Miriam Stewart, Dorothy Clark, William Miller, Bruce Foote. Paul Pettinga, organ. Modern instruments. Recorded 12 November 1952. Order of compositions random. Includes *Domine ad adjuvandum, Nigra sum, Lauda Jerusalem, Ave maris stella, Dixit Dominus, Sonata sopra Sancta Maria,* Magnificat *a 7,* and an unrelated setting of *O quam pulchra es.*

2. VOX PL 7902/1-2 (MONOPHONIC); VUX 2004/1-2 (MONOPHONIC); VOX STUX 52004 (ELECTRONIC STEREO RECHANNELLING) 1953

Hans Grischkat, director. Swabian Choral Singers and Stuttgart Bach Orchestra. Vocal soloists and instrumentalists: Margot Guilleaume, Friederike Sailer, Lotte Wolf-Matthäus, Heinz Marten, Werner Hohmann, Franz Kelch, H. Liedecke, H. Elsner. Modern instruments. Based on edition by Hans Redlich. *Nisi Dominus, Lauda Jerusalem,* Magnificat *a 6* not included. Order of compositions essentially random, following neither Monteverdi's print nor Redlich's edition. See discussion in Chapter 1.

3. LONDON OL 50021/22 (MONOPHONIC) 1953; OISEAU-LYRE OLS 107/8 (ELECTRONIC STEREO RECHANNELLING) 1953

Anthony Lewis, director. The London St Anthony Singers and L'Oiseau Lyre Orchestral Ensemble. Vocal and instrumental soloists: Margaret Ritchie, Elsie Morison, William Herbert, Richard Lewis, Bruce Boyce, Geraint Jones, Ruggero Gerlin. Modern instruments. Recorded in Paris, September 1953. Based on edition by Leo Schrade. Magnificat *a 6* not included. Order of compositions follows Monteverdi's print. See discussion in Chapter 1.

4. ERATO STU 70325-7; COLUMBIA SMC 95072-4; MUSICAL HERITAGE SOCIETY MHS 814-815-816; ZL 30548 EX. 1967; 2292-45446-2 (CD) 1990; MHS and TELDEC 0630-12981-2 (CD) 1996

Michel Corboz, director. Lausanne Vocal and Instrumental Ensemble. Vocal and instrumental soloists: Luciana Ticinelli-Fattori, Maria-Grazia Ferracini-Malacarne, Magali Schwartz, Eric Tappy, Hugues Cuénod, Philippe Huttenlocher, Enrico Fissore, François Loup. Period instruments. Based on edition by Walter Goehr. Recorded April 1966. All fourteen vesper items included in order of Monteverdi's print.

5. TELEFUNKEN AWT 9501/02 (MONOPHONIC); SAWT 9501/02-A (STEREO); 6.35045/A-B (STEREO) 1967; TELDEC 6.35045-1/2 (STEREO) 1980; TELDEC 4509-92175-2 (CD) 1994

Jürgen Jürgens, director. Soloists of Vienna Boys Choir, Capella Antiqua, Monteverdi Choir of Hamburg, Vienna Concentus Musicus. Vocal soloists: Rohtraud Hansmann, Irmgard Jacobeit, Nigel Rogers, Bert van t'Hoff, Max van Egmond, Jacques Villisech. Period instruments. Recorded in Vienna, 1–12 October 1966. Based on edition by Jürgen Jürgens. Magnificat *a 6* not included. Order of compositions as in Monteverdi's print except that *Sonata sopra Sancta Maria* is placed before Magnificat. Psalms and Magnificat immediately preceded and followed by plainchant antiphons with texts from the Song of Songs and the Magnificat antiphon *Sancta Maria, succurre miseris.* Plainchant chapter included after *Lauda Jerusalem;* plainchant versicle after hymn; plainchant *Benedicamus Domino* and *Deo gratias.* See discussion in Chapter 1.

6. COLUMBIA M2L 363 (MONOPHONIC); M2S 763 (STEREO); CBS BRG 72602/3 (MONOPHONIC); SBRG 72062/3 (STEREO); 77212 1967; SB2K 62656 (CD); SONY 62656 (CD) 1996

Robert Craft, director. Gregg Smith Singers, Texas Boys Choir of Fort Worth, Columbia Baroque Ensemble. Vocal soloists: Adrienne Albert, Melvin Brown, Archie Drake, Richard Levitt, Gloria Prosper. Modern instruments. Order of compositions random. Magnificat *a 6* not included.

7. CONCERT HALL SOCIETY SMS 2518, 1967; ADÈS 'OR' 13.270-2 (CD) 1988

Maurice Le Roux, director. Deller Consort, French National Radio Chorus, Choir School, and Orchestra. Vocal soloists: Mary Thomas, Sally Le Sage, Alfred Deller, Max Worthley, Philip Todd, Maurice Bevan. Order of compositions follows Monteverdi's print. Magnificat *a 6* not included. Modern instruments. Possibly recorded June 1962.

8. VANGUARD VCS 10001/2; (UK) VANGUARD VSL 11000/1; (FRANCE) VANGUARD 991026/7; (ITALY) RICORDI AOCL 216012 1967

Denis Stevens, director. The Ambrosian Singers, Orchestra of the Accademia Monteverdiana. Vocal Soloists: Ursula Connors, Shirley Sams, Shirley Minty, Nigel Rogers, Leslie Fyson, John Noble, Christopher Keyte. Modern instruments. Recorded June 1966. Based on edition by Denis Stevens. Omits *Nigra sum, Pulchra es, Duo Seraphim, Audi coelum, Sonata sopra Sancta Maria,* Magnificat *a 6.* Otherwise order of compositions follows Monteverdi's print. Plainchant antiphons from various feasts of the BVM, selected to match tones of psalms and canticle, immediately precede and follow each psalm and the Magnificat. See discussion in Chapter 1.

9. MUSICA ANTIQUA SACRA PAB 1306/7 1968

Giuseppe Biella, director. Polifonica Ambrosiana Chorus and Orchestra. Vocal Soloists: Luciana Ticinelli-Fattori, Cettina Cadelo, Nelly Crescimanno, Stefania Sina-Daris, Adriano Ferrario, Rodolfo Malacarne, Teodoro Rovetta, Giovanni Faverio. Based on edition by Giuseppe Biella. Omits *Nigra sum, Pulchra es, Duo Seraphim, Audi coelum, Sonata sopra Sancta Maria,* and Magnificat *a 6.*

10. ETERNA 8 26086/7; ARIOLA XF 80622 K; EURODISC 80 620/21 XFK 1970

Helmut Koch, director. Solo Ensemble of the Berlin Radio, Berlin Chamber Orchestra. Vocal soloists: Lilo Chroczinski, Gisela Beer, Günter Neumann, Manfred Peine, Günter Beyer, Siegfried Hausmann. Modern instruments. Based on edition by Walter Goehr. Order of compositions follows Monteverdi's print. Omits both Magnificats.

11. DECCA SET 593/4; 6.35 449 FA; 7346/7 1975; 414 573/4-2 (CD) 1986; LONDON DECCA 443-482-2 (CD) 1994

John Eliot Gardiner, director. Monteverdi Choir and Orchestra. Boys' choir of Salisbury Cathedral, Philip Jones Brass Ensemble, David Munrow Recorder Ensemble. Vocal soloists: Jill Gomez, Felicity Palmer, James Bowman, Robert Tear, Philip Langridge, John Shirley-Quirk, Michael Rippon. Period instruments. Recorded January 1974 at St Jude's on the Hill, Hampstead Garden, London. Based on edition by John Eliot Gardiner. Order of compositions follows

Monteverdi's print. Magnificat *a 6* not included. 1994 reissue includes several compositions by Giovanni Gabrieli, Giovanni Bassano, and Monteverdi appended at end.

12. ARCHIV 2710 017; 2723 043 1975; 447 719-2 (CD) 1996?

Hans-Martin Schneidt, director. Regensburg Cathedral Choir: male singers only. Vocal soloists: Paul Esswood, Kevin Smith, Ian Partridge, John Elwes, David Thomas, Christopher Keyte. Period instruments. Recorded 16–26 July 1974 and 10–16 May 1975 at St Emmeram, Regensburg. Based on Gottfried Wolters's edition of 1966. Order of compositions follows Monteverdi's print. All fourteen Vesper items plus *Missa in illo tempore* included.

13. MUSICA PACIFICA PCFM 1002 1975

Paul Vorwerk, director. Pacifica Singers, Musica Pacifica. Vocal soloists: Wesley Abbott, Lloyd Bunnell, Jonathan Mack, Myron Myers, Dennis Parnell, Maurita Thornburgh, Anne Turner, Paul Vorwerk. Period instruments except for oboes in place of cornettos. Recorded in live performance at Fritchman Auditorium, Los Angeles, 18 May 1974. *Duo Seraphim* recorded October 1974. Order of compositions follows Monteverdi's print except that *Sonata sopra Sancta Maria* is placed after *Ave maris stella*. Magnificat *a 6* not included.

14. EMI ASD 3256/7; SLS 5064; SB 3837; 1C 187-02759/60Q (QUADROPHONIC) 1976; EMI 7243 5 68632/3 (CD) 1995

Philip Ledger, director. Choir of King's College, Cambridge. Early Music Consort of London, David Munrow, director. Vocal soloists: Elly Ameling, Norma Burrowes, Charles Brett, Anthony Rolfe Johnson, Robert Tear, Martyn Hill, Peter Knapp, John Noble. Period instruments. Based on edition by Denis Arnold. Order of compositions follows Monteverdi's print. Magnificat *a 6* not included.

15. HARMONIA MUNDI 1C 165-99 681/82 Q; BASF JA 228 576 1976

Ireneu Segarra OSB, director. Boys' and Chapel Choirs of Musica Montserrat, Montserrat Collegium Aureum. Vocal soloists: 3 members of Boys' Choir, James Griffett, Stephen Roberts, David Thomas, Michael George. Period instruments. Order of compositions follows Monteverdi's print. Magnificat *a 6* not included.

16. INTERDISC ID 602 1980

Rudolf Pohl, director. Aachen Cathedral Choir and Orchestra. Recorded 20 August 1979.

17. INTERDISC ID 603; ARS MUSICI AM 1000-2 (CD) 1980

Heinz Hennig, director. Pro Cantione Antiqua, Hannover Boys Choir, Collegium Aureum, Musica Fiata. Vocal soloists: Barbara Schlick, Timothy Penrose, James Griffet, Ian Partridge, Stephen Roberts, Michael George. Period instruments. Extensive instrumental doubling in psalms and hymn. Recorded 6 July 1979 at the festival 'Music and Theatre in Herrenhausen'. Order of compositions follows Monteverdi's print. Magnificat *a 6* not included.

18. CBS MASTERWORKS D2 36943 1981

Jean-Claude Malgoire, director. La Grande Ecurie et La Chambre du Roy, Les Petits Chanteurs de Chaillot, boy soloists from the Vocal Ensemble Roger Thirot and the Choir School of Notre Dame, Les Sacqueboutiers de Toulouse. Vocal soloists: Nella Anfuso, Virginie Pattie, Veronique Diestchy, Paul Esswood, Henri Ledroit, Nigel Rogers, John Elwes, Bruce Fithian, Michel Verschaeve, Niklaus Tuller. Mostly one voice per part. Period instruments. Recorded in the church of Notre Dame de Liban, Paris, 24–9 May 1981. Order of compositions follows Monteverdi's print. Magnificat *a 6* not included.

19. ERATO NUM 75030/1; ECD 88 025/6 (CD); 2292-45183-2 (CD) 1983; 0630 12981-2.2 (CD) 1996

Michel Corboz, director. Vocal Ensemble of Lausanne, Schola des Petits Chanteurs de Notre-Dame de Sion, Ensemble of Ancient Instruments. Vocal soloists: Jennifer Smith, Audrey Michael, Wynford Evans, John Elwes, Philippe Huttenlocher, Michael Brodard. Period instruments. Recorded February 1982 at St Peter's Church, Geneva. Order of compositions follows Monteverdi's print. Magnificat *a 6* not included. Plainchant antiphons derived from Song of Songs immediately precede each psalm and the Magnificat.

20. TITANIC 120 AND 121 1983

Jameson Marvin, director. The Harvard-Radcliffe Collegium Musicum, Baroque Orchestra, The New York Cornet and Sacbut Ensemble. Vocal soloists: Judith Caldwell, Allegra Dunmoreland, Jon Humphrey, Jeffrey Gall, Arthur Burrows, James Maddalena. Period instruments. Recorded live 20 April 1980 in Sanders Theater at Harvard University. Order of compositions follows Monteverdi's print. Magnificat *a 6* not included.

21. EMI DSB 3963; EMI 27-0129-1/27-0130-1; (UK) EX 27 0129 3; EMI 2701295 (CASSETTE); CDC 7 47078/9 (CD) 1984; VIRGIN 7243 5 61347 20 (CD) 1996; AMADEUS DARP PARAGON AMS 040/41-2 PE (CD) 1997

Andrew Parrott, director. Taverner Consort, Taverner Players. Vocal soloists: Emma Kirkby, Tessa Bonner, Evelyn Tubb, Emily Van Evera, Margaret Philpot, Nigel Rogers, Joseph Cornwell, Rogers Covey-Crump, Charles Daniels, John Dudley, Andrew King, Peter Long, Stephen Charlesworth, Simon Grant, Richard Savage, David Thomas, Richard Wistreich. All pieces sung with one voice per part. Period instruments. Recorded 15–19 August 1983 and 30 March 1984 at All Saints, Tooting, London. Order of compositions follows Monteverdi's print except that *Duo Seraphim* is displaced to the end in lieu of the *Deo gratias* and the *Sonata sopra Sancta Maria* is displaced to follow the Magnificat. In the position vacated by *Duo Seraphim*, a *Sonata a 2* by Giovanni Paolo Cima from his *Concerti ecclesiastici* of 1610 follows *Laetatus sum*, and in the position vacated by the *Sonata sopra Sancta Maria*, a *Sonata a 3* from the same publication by Cima follows *Lauda Jerusalem*. Magnificat *a 6* not included. Monteverdi's *Salve O Regina* of 1624 follows *Duo Seraphim* as the seasonal Marian antiphon. Plainchant antiphons from the Feast of the Assumption of the BVM precede each psalm and the Magnificat. The plainchant chapter and response precede *Ave maris stella*, and the verse and response follow the hymn. The plainchant prayer, verse, and response follow the *Sonata sopra Sancta Maria*, and a plainchant verse and response, another prayer, and the concluding verse and response follow the Marian antiphon *Salve O Regina*. *Lauda*

Jerusalem and the Magnificat *a 7* are transposed down a fourth, following the convention of *chiavette*. See discussions in Chapters 1 and 17.

22. ETERNA 827780-91; (JAPAN) DEUTSCHE SCHALLPLATTEN ET 4037-8;
    BERLIN CLASSICS 0092042BC (CD)   1984, 1996

Martin Flämig, director. Dresdner Kreuzchor: male singers only. Capella Fidicinia of the Museum of Musical Instruments at the University of Leipzig. Vocal soloists: Matthias Trommler, Eckart Preu, Albrecht Kludzuweit, Christoph König, Andreas Jäpel, Werner Marschall, Ekkehard Wagner, Albrecht Lepetit, Reinhart Ginzel, Armin Ude, Gothart Stier, Günther Schmidt. Period instruments. Uses shawms as *fifare* in *Quia respexit* of Magnificat *a 7*. Employs *notes inégales* in violin parts of *Deposuit*. Normally uses multiple violins on a single part. Harpsichord added to continuo ensemble in full-textured passages. Bass-line doubled with viola da gamba in all few-voiced pieces. Recorded in St Luke's Church, Dresden, 12–13 March and 24–6 November 1981 and 29 January and 19–23 April 1982. Performing score by Hans Grüß. Order of compositions follows Monteverdi's print. Magnificat *a 6* not included. Plainchant antiphons selected from a variety of Marian feasts and feasts of virgins, whose tones do not necessarily match the psalms and canticles, precede each psalm and the Magnificat.

23. ETERNA 827780/81; TELDEC 8.35710 (CD); 2292-42671-2 (CD); 4509-
    92629-2 (CD); 0630-18955 (CD)   1987

Nikolaus Harnoncourt, director. Tölzer Boys' Choir, Choir School of the Vienna Court Chapel, Arnold Schoenberg Choir, Vienna Concentus Musicus. Vocal soloists: Margaret Marshall, Felicity Palmer, Philip Langridge, Kurt Equiluz, Thomas Hampson, Arthur Korn. Period instruments. Recorded at live performances in the cathedral in Graz, Austria, 8–9 July 1986. Instrumental doubling, with doubled strings, used for 'choruses'. Winds double cantus firmus in Magnificat. Order of compositions follows Monteverdi's print. Magnificat *a 6* not included. Plainchant antiphons selected from a variety of Marian feasts precede and follow each psalm and the Magnificat (see item 39 below). Plainchant chapter precedes *Sonata sopra Sancta Maria*, and plainchant versicle follows *Ave Maris stella*. The Magnificat is succeeded by the plainchant prayer *Dominus exaudi orationem meam* and the closing *Benedicamus Domino* and *Deo gratias*.

24. HARMONIA MUNDI FRANCE HMC 901247.48 (CD)   1987

Philippe Herreweghe, director. Choir and Orchestra of La Chapelle Royale, Collegium Vocale, Les Saqueboutiers de Toulouse. Vocal soloists: Agnès Mellon, Guillemette Laurens, Vincent Darras, Howard Crook, William Kendall, Gerard O'Beirne, Peter Kooy, David Thomas. Period instruments. Recorded July 1986. Order of compositions follows Monteverdi's print. Magnificat *a 6* not included. Plainchant antiphons, selected from a variety of Marian feasts and feasts of virgins, whose tones do not necessarily match the psalms and canticle, precede each psalm and the Magnificat. *Lauda Jerusalem* and Magnificat *a 7* transposed down a fourth.

25. MUSIC OF THE BAROQUE CONCERT SERIES MB105-2 (CD)   1987

Thomas Wikman, director. Music of the Baroque Chorus and Orchestra, St Luke's Choir of Men and Boys. Vocal soloists: Sarah Beatty, Karen Brunssen, Cynthia Anderson, Kurt R. Hansen, Jan Jarvis, Darrell Rowader, Willard Thomen, Richard Cohn, Jeffrey Horvath, William F. Walker.

Modern instruments with multiple players on a part. Recorded in live performance at Divine Word Chapel, Techny, Illinois, 4 May 1983. Order of compositions follows Monteverdi's print except that *Sonata sopra Sancta Maria* is displaced to follow *Ave maris stella*. Magnificat *a 6* not included. Plainchant antiphons from various feasts of the BVM, selected to match tones of psalms and canticle, immediately precede and follow each psalm and the Magnificat. Plainchant chapter *Ab initio* precedes hymn; versicle and response *Benedicamus Domino / Deo gratias* follow Magnificat antiphon at end.

26. HYPERION CDA 66311/2 (CD) 1988

Harry Christophers, director. The Sixteen Choir and Orchestra. Vocal soloists: Nicola Jenkin, Mary Seers, Christopher Royall, Andrew Murgatroyd, Neil MacKenzie, Mark Padmore, Simon Birchall, Jeremy White. Period instruments. Recorded in St Jude-on-the Hill, Hampstead, London, 28–30 March 1988. Recast as Vespers of Santa Barbara. Psalms and Magnificat in order of Monteverdi's print. *Sacri concentus* rearranged. *Ave maris stella* is placed at the end, apart from the liturgical order. Magnificat *a 6* not included. Plainchant antiphons from feast of Santa Barbara precede each psalm and Magnificat. Order of music: (1) organ improvisation; (2) *Deus in adjutorium / Domine ad adjuvandum*; (3) plainchant antiphon *Angelicam vitam*; (4) psalm *Dixit Dominus*; (5) *Pulchra es*; (6) plainchant antiphon *In Dei orto*; (7) psalm *Laudate pueri*; (8) *Sonata* presumed to be by Giovanni Amigoni; (9) plainchant antiphon *Paterni oblita*; (10) psalm *Laetatus sum*; (11) *Nigra sum*; (12) plainchant antiphon *In Sancte Trinitatis*; (13) psalm *Nisi Dominus*; (14) *Sonata* presumed to be by Giovanni Amigoni; (15) plainchant antiphon *Trinitatem venerata*; (16) psalm *Lauda Jerusalem*; (17) *Duo Seraphim*; (18) plainchant chapter *Confitebor tibi*; (19) plainchant hymn *Exultet celebres virginis*; (20) plainchant response *Ora pro nobis beata Barbara*; (21) plainchant antiphon *Hodie beata Barbara*; (22) Magnificat *a 7*; (23) plainchant *Dominus vobiscum*; (24) prayer *Deus cuius delectionem beata Barbara*; (25) *Benedicamus Domino / Deo gratias*; (26) Palestrina's motet *Gaude Barbara beata*; (27) plainchant blessing *Sit nomen Domini*; (28) *Audi coelum* as substitute for Advent Marian antiphon *Alma Redemptoris Mater*; (29) response/collect *Angelus Domini nunciavit*; (30) *Sonata sopra Sancta Maria* with text changed to *Sancta Barbara*; (31) hymn *Ave maris stella* as appendix. See discussion in Chapter 1.

27. DEUTSCHE HARMONIA MUNDI 77760-2-RC (CD); RK77760 (CASSETTE) 1989

Frieder Bernius, director. Musica Fiata Cologne, Stuttgart Chamber Choir, Chant Choir of Lower Alteich. Vocal soloists: Monique Zanetti, Gillian Fischer, David Cordier, John Elwes, William Kendall, Nico van der Meel, Peter Kooy, Philippe Cantor. Period instruments. Recorded 2–7 January 1989 in the Evangelical Church in Gönningen/Reutlingen. Order of compositions follows Monteverdi's print except that *Sonata sopra Sancta Maria* is displaced to the very end. Magnificat *a 6* not included. Plainchant antiphons derived from Song of Songs precede each psalm; antiphon *Sancta Maria succurre miseris* precedes Magnificat. Antiphon modes match tones of psalms but not canticle. Plainchant chapter *Ab initio* precedes hymn. Hymn followed by plainchant versicle and response. Magnificat followed by *Benedicamus Domino / Deo gratias*, then *Sonata sopra Sancta Maria*.

28. AUVIDIS ASTRÉE E 8719/20 (CD) 1989

Jordi Savall, director. La Capella Reial, Choir of the Centre for Early Music of Padua. Vocal soloists: Montserrat Figueras, Maria Cristina Kiehr, Livio Picotti, Paolo Costa, Guy de Mey, Gian

Paolo Fagotto, Gerd Turk, Pietro Spagnoli, Roberto Abbondanza, Daniele Carnovich. Period instruments. Recorded in basilica of Santa Barbara in Mantua, November 1988. Order of compositions follows Monteverdi's print. Magnificat *a 6* not included. *Lauda Jerusalem* transposed down an augmented fourth. Plainchant antiphons for feast of Santa Barbara precede each psalm and the Magnificat, turning set into a 'quasi'-vespers of Santa Barbara. See discussion in Chapter 1.

29. AMBITUS AMB 383826 (CD)   1989?

Jürgen Jürgens, director. Hamburg Monteverdi Choir and Camerata Accademica. Vocal soloists: Barbara Schlick, Ine Kollecker, John Elwes, Wilfried Jochens, Holger Hampel, Christfried Biebrach, Gustav Hehring. Period instruments. Recorded 12–13 November 1987 in the church of St Michael, Hamburg. Order of compositions follows Monteverdi's print. Magnificat *a 6* not included.

30. L'OISEAU-LYRE 425 823-2 (CD); 425 823-4 (CASSETTE)   1990

Philip Pickett, director. New London Consort. Vocal soloists: Catherine Bott, Tessa Bonner, Christopher Robson, Andrew King, John Mark Ainsley, Michael George, Simon Grant. Period instruments. Sung mostly one voice per part. Recorded in St Jude-on-the Hill, Hampstead, London, May 1989. Order of compositions follows Monteverdi's print except that *Sonata sopra Sancta Maria* is displaced to the end. Magnificat *a 6* not included. *Lauda Jerusalem* and Magnificat *a 7* transposed down a fourth. Plainchant antiphons from second vespers for the feast of the Nativity of the BVM, drawn from a 1571 breviary, immediately precede and follow each psalm and the Magnificat.

31. ARCHIV PRODUKTION 429 565-2 (CD)   1990

John Eliot Gardiner, director. Monteverdi Choir, London Oratory Junior Choir, His Majesties Sagbutts and Cornetts, English Baroque Soloists. Vocal soloists: Ann Monoyios, Marinella Pennicchi, Michael Chance, Mark Tucker, Nigel Robson, Sandro Naglia, Bryn Terfel, Alastair Miles. Period instruments. Recorded in live performances in St Mark's Basilica, Venice, 10–11 May 1989. Order of compositions follows Monteverdi's print. Magnificat *a 6* included. Uses shawms in *Quia respexit* of Magnificat *a 7* (see the discussion in Chapter 18).

32. ARCHIV PRODUKTION 072 248-3 (VIDEO)   1989, 1990

Video version of item 31, excluding Magnificat *a 6*. Includes an introduction by John Eliot Gardiner. See the discussion in Chapter 1.

33. EMI 7 54546 2; 567-754 546-2 (CD)   1993

Hermann Max, director. Rheinische Kantorei. Vocal soloists: Johanna Koslowsky, Martina Lins, Wilfried Jochens, Markus Brutscher, Reinhard Dingel-Schulten, Kai Wessel, Arno Tabertshofer, Hans-Georg Wimmer, Stephan Schreckenberger. Period continuo instruments. Other instruments are excluded, with the continuo ensemble substituting for the instrumental interludes in *Domine ad adjuvandum* and the ritornellos of *Ave maris stella*. The absence of obbligato instruments also leads to the omission of the optional ritornellos of *Dixit Dominus* as well as the use of the Magnificat *a 6* and the substitution of a Ricercar by Frescobaldi in place of the *Sonata sopra Sancta Maria*. Except for the Frescobaldi substitution and omission of the Magnificat *a 7*, the order of compositions follows Monteverdi's print. Recorded 1990.

34. MUSICAL HERITAGE SOCIETY MHS 523536W (CD) 1994

Frederick Renz, director. New York's Grande Bande. Vocal soloists: Tamara Crout, Karen Clark Young, Mark Bleeke, Robert Craig, Timothy Leight Evans, Grant Herreid, Kevin Deas, Joel Frederiksen, Paul Shipper, Curtis Streetman. Period instruments. Order of compositions follows Monteverdi's print. Magnificat *a 6* not included. *Lauda Jerusalem* and Magnificat *a 7* transposed down a fourth. Several other instrumental and secular vocal compositions by Monteverdi, Lappi, Viadana, Gussago, and Allegri appended at end.

35. CAPRICCIO 10516 (CD) 1995

Ralf Otto, director. Frankfurt Vocal Ensemble, Instrumental Ensemble 'Il Basso'. Vocal soloists: Mechthild Bach, Barbara Fleckenstein, Christoph Prégardien, Peter Schmitz, Klaus Mertens, Michael George. Period instruments. Recorded 18–23 October 1993 at Hessian Radio. Order of compositions follows Monteverdi's print. Magnificat *a 6* not included.

36. NAXOS 8.550662-3 (CD) 1995

The Scholars Baroque Ensemble, David van Asch, artistic coordinator. Vocal soloists: Kym Amps, Janet Coxwell, Angus Davidson, Frances Jellard, Robin Doveton, Julian Podger, John Bowen, David van Asch, Adrian Peacock. One singer per part throughout. Period instruments. Frequent use of doubling instruments. Extensive added ornamentation in solo motets. Based on edition by Clifford Bartlett. Recorded in St Augustine's Church, Ilburn, September 1993. Order of compositions follows Monteverdi's print. *Lauda Jerusalem* transposed down a whole tone. Magnificat *a 6* not included.

37. DEUTSCHE HARMONIA MUNDI 05472 77332 2 (CD) 1995

Konrad Junghänel, artistic director and lute. Cantus Cölln, Concerto Palatino. Vocal soloists: Johanna Koslowsky, Maria Cristina Kiehr, Pascal Bertin, Bernhard Landauer, Gerd Türk, Wilfried Jochens, Markus Brutscher, Stephan Schreckenberger, Stephan MacLeod, Matthias Gerchen. Recorded 8–12 September, 1994. One singer per part except for doubling of the cantus firmus in *Lauda Jerusalem*, the *Sonata sopra Sancta Maria* and the Magnificat *a 7*. *Lauda Jerusalem* transposed down a whole tone. Period instruments. Extensive ornamentation in ritornellos of *Ave maris stella*. Based on edition by Clifford Bartlett. Order of compositions follows Monteverdi's print. Magnificat *a 6* not included.

38. MEMORIES MEM 4598/99 1995

Lovro Matačič, director. Chorus of the Croation Radio Television, Zagreb Philharmonic. Vocal soloists: Eva Andor, Adrienne Csengery, Durdevka Čakarevič, Werner Krenn, Josip Novosel, Franjo Petrušanec, Ante Mijač. Modern instruments. Recorded from live performance in 'Vatroslav Lisinski' Concert Hall in Zagreb on 5 June 1974. Digitally remastered and published under sponsorship of Lovro & Lilly Matačič Foundation. Large orchestra of modern instruments. Extensive instrumental doubling of voices. Harpsichord sometimes added to organ, string basses and harp as a continuo instrument. Operatic-style singing with wide vibrato. Extensive vocal ornamentation and some instrumental ornamentation added. Considerable re-arrangement of Monteverdi's score, including newly composed contrapuntal lines in the continuo accompaniments of the motets and in the instrumental accompaniment of the choir in the psalms, use of a female soprano for *Nigra sum*, substitution of a mixed choir with instrumental counterpoint for the solo tenors in the *Pleni sunt caeli* sections of *Duo Seraphim*, use of sopranos, tenors, and the combination of sopranos and tenors in octaves for the cantus firmus in the *Sonata sopra Sancta Maria*, substitution of solo voices for the second and third choral verses of *Ave maris stella* (soprano and tenor in octaves in the third verse), and octave transposition of one ritornello in *Ave maris stella*. Order of compositions follows Monteverdi's print except for omission of *Lauda Jerusalem* and displacement of *Sonata sopra Sancta Maria* until after the hymn. Magnificat *a 6* not included.

39. HARMONIA MUNDI FRANCE 901566 67 (CD) 1996

René Jacobs, director. Netherlands Chamber Choir, Concerto Vocale. Vocal soloists: Maria Cristina Kiehr, Barbara Borden, Andreas Scholl, John Bowen, Andrew Murgatroyd, Victor Torres, Antonio Abete, Jelle Draijer. Period instruments. Recorded June 1995. One singer per part in all thinner textures and in *Laudate pueri*. Instruments double voices in full textures. Bass string instrument doubles bass-line in few-voiced passages. Order of compositions follows Monteverdi's print except that *Sonata sopra Sancta Maria* is displaced until before the Magnificat. Magnificat *a 6* not included. Plainchant antiphons selected from a variety of Marian feasts precede and follow each psalm and the Magnificat; these are same plainchant antiphons as in item 23 above.[1] Plainchant chapter precedes hymn. Plainchant *Benedicamus Domino* follows Magnificat antiphon.

40. BBC RECORDS 15656 9187-7 (CD) 1996

Louis Halsey, director. London Bach Orchestra, London Cornett & Sackbutt Ensemble, Louis Halsey Singers. Vocal soloists: April Cantelo, Angela Beale, Paul Esswood, Ian Partridge, John Elwes, David Thomas. Period Instruments. Recorded live 25 May 1970. Based on edition by Basil Lam. Order of compositions follows Monteverdi's print. Magnificat *a 6* not included.

41. RAUMKLANG 9605 (CD) 1996

Hans-Christoph Rademann, director. Dresden Chamber Choir, Early Music Ensemble of Dresden, Wind Collegium of Leipzig. Vocal soloists: Nele Gramß, Johanna Koslowski, Markus Brutscher, Wilfried Jochens, Martin Krumbiegel, Egbert Junghanns, Stephan Schreckenberger. Period Instruments. Recorded 9 July 1996 in live performance at Festival of Early Music in Erzgebirge. Order of compositions follows Monteverdi's print. Magnificat *a 6* not included. Each psalm and the Magnificat is preceded by a plainchant antiphon, all taken from the series of six antiphons provided in the appendix of Gottfried Wolters's edition (see Chapter 1 above). Lively tempos for psalms, hymn, many verses of the Magnificat, *Sonata sopra Sancta Maria*, and six-voice section of *Audi coelum*. Frequent instrumental doubling of voices.

42. TELARC 80453 (CD) 1997

Martin Pearlman, director. Boston Baroque. Vocal soloists: Janice Chandler, Karen Clift, Richard Croft, Lynton Atkinson, Brad Diamond, Christopheren Nomura, Jeff Mattsey. Period instruments. Extensive instrumental doubling in psalms and hymn. Violone and harpsichord frequently added to continuo. Lively tempos in psalms and *Sonata sopra Sancta Maria*. Substantial added ornamentation in motets and ritornellos of *Ave maris stella*. Recorded in the Campion Center, Weston Center, Massachusetts on 1–4 February 1997. Order of compositions follows Monteverdi's print. Magnificat *a 6* not included. Plainchant antiphons for feast of the Assumption of the BVM precede each psalm and the Magnificat.

---

[1] I am grateful to Jerome Weber for pointing this out to me.

Appendix E
Sixteenth- and Seventeenth-Century
Musical Sources

⁶€❀❧ↄ

SPELLING of names has been standardized according to RISM. All dates of publication are given in arabic numerals. RISM identification numbers appear at the end of entries, where applicable. In some instances the entries in RISM have incorrect dates of publication. The correct dates are given below. Publications by Monteverdi have been excluded from this list as unnecessary.

AGAZZARI, AGOSTINO. Agostino Agazzarii In Collegio Germanico musicae Praefecti, Sacrae Laudes de Jesu, B. Virgine, Angelis, Apostolis, Martyribus, Confessoribus, Virginibus. Quaternis, Quinis, Senis, Septenis, Octonisque vocibus. Cum Basso ad Organum & musica instrumenta. Liber Secundus. Romae, apud Aloysium Zannettum. 1603. A334

——. Augustini Agazzarii Armonici Intronati, Sacrae Cantiones, Binis Ternisque vocibus concinendae. Liber Quartus. Bassus ad Organum. Venetijs apud Ricciardum Amadinum. 1606. A340

——. Augustini Agazzarii Armonici Intronati, Sacrarum Cantionum, quae Binis, Ternis, Quaternisque vocibus concinuntur. Liber II. Opus V. Motectorum. Cum Basso ad Organum. Item del medsimo Del sonare sopra'l Basso con tutti li stromenti e dell'uso loro nel Conserto. Venetijs, Apud Ricciardum Amadinum, 1608. A353 (reprint of first edition, Milan, 1607, A352)

——. Psalmi Sex, qui in Vesperis ad Concentum varietatem interponuntur, Ternis vocibus. Eosdem sequitur Completorium Quaternis vocibus. Cum Basso ad Organum. Auctore Augustino Agazario Armonico Intronato. Opus Duodecimum. Venetijs, Apud Ricciardum Amadinum. 1609. A357

AGOSTINI, PAOLO. Salmi della Madonna Magnificat à 3. voci. Hinno Ave Maris Stella, Antifone A una 2. & 3. voci. Et Motetti Tutti Concertati. Di Paolo Agostino Maestro di Cappella in San Lorenzo in Damaso, Discepolo, & Genero di Gio. Bernardino Nanini. Con il Basso continuo per sonare. Divisa in due parti. Libro Primo. In Roma, Per Luca Antonio Soldi. 1619. A411

ANERIO, GIOVANNI FRANCESCO. Ioannis Francisci Anerii Sacerdotis Romani, Musicorum in Ecclesia Deiparae Virginis ad Montes concentuum Compositoris. Motecta singulis, binis, ternisque vocibus. Liber Primus. Cum Basso ad Organum. Romae, Apud Io. Baptistam Roblettum. 1609. A1096

——. Io. Francisci Anerii Sacerdotis Romani. In Ecclesia Santiss. Virginis ad Montes Capellae Magistri. Motectorum singulis, binis, ternis, quaternis, quinis, senisque vocibus, Una cum Litaniis Beatae Virginis quatuor vocibus, Cum Basso ad Organum. Liber Tertius. Romae, Apud. Io. Baptistam Roblettum. 1613. A1102

——. Antiphonae, seu Sacrae Cantiones, quae in totius anni Vesperarum ac Completorii solemnitatibus decantari solent; in tres partes distributae; Quarum prima Nativitatis Domini, Circumcisionis, Epiphaniae, & omnium Sanctorum. Secunda, Festa mobilia, & Communia

Sanctorum. Tertia, Praecipua Mendicantium Religionum festa complectitur. Binis, Ternis, & Quaternis vocibus concinendae. Una cum Basso ad Organum. Auctore, Io: Francisco Anerio Romano. In Ecclesia Sanctissimae Virginis ad Montes Capellae Magistro. Romae, Apud Io: Baptistam Roblectum. 1613. A1104

ANTIPHONARIUM ROMANUM AD RITUM BREVIARIJ, EX DECRETO SACROS. Concilij Tridentini restituti, Pii Quinti Pontificis Maximi iussu editi, et Clementis viij. auctoritate recogniti, Ad usum omnium Ecclesiarum Cathedralium, et Collegiatarum nuper iuxta regulas Directorijj Chori magno studio, ac labore redactum. Venetijs, Apud Iuntas. 1623. (Not listed in RISM.)

ARETINO, PAOLO. Musica cum Quatuor, Quinque, ac Sex Vocibus: Super Hymnos Totius Anni. Secundum ritum S. Romanae Ecclesiae, noviter in lucem aediti. Mediolani Apud Granciscum Moschenium. 1565. (Not listed in RISM. Copy at Cracow, Biblioteka Jagiellonska.)

ASOLA, GIOVANNI MATTEO. Vespertina Omnium Solemnitatum Psalmodia Canticum B. Virginis Duplici Modulatione Primi videlicet, & Octavi Toni. Salve Regina, Missa, et Quinque Divinae Laudes Omnia Duodenis Vocibus. Ternis variata Chorus, ac omni Instrumentorum genere modulanda. R.D.Io: Matthaeo Asula Veronensi Auctore Nunc primum in lucem prodita. Ad Perillustre Veronae Canonicorum Collegium. Cum Privilegio. Venetiis Apud Riciardum Amadinum. 1590. A2581.

——. Completorium Romanum. Beataeque Virginis Laudes, in terminatione officii decantandae. Videlicet Ave Regina Coelorum. Regina Coeli. Salve Regina. Omnes gentes. Omnia Duodenis Vocibus. Ternis variata Choris. Ac omni instrumentorum genere modulanda. R. D. Io: Matthaeo Asula Veron. Auctore. Venetijs apud Ricciardum Amadinum. 1599. (Not listed in RISM. Copy at Cracow, Biblioteka Jagiellonska.)

ASSANDRA, CATERINA. Motetti à dua, & tre voci, Per cantar nell'Organo con il Basso continuo, di Caterina Assandra Pavese, Nuovamente composti, & dati in luce. Opera Seconda. Aggiontovi una Canzon Francesca à 4. & le Letanie della B. V. à 6 del Rever. Don Benedetto Rè suo Maestro di contrapunto. In Milano, Per l'herede di Simon Tini, & Filippo Lomazzo. 1609. A2637, SD1609³

BACCUSI, IPPOLITO. Hippoliti Baccusii Ecclesiae Cathedr. Veronae Musices Praefecti. Psalmi Omnes qui a S. Romana Ecclesia in solemnitatibus ad Vesperas decantari solent, Cum Duobus Magnificat. Tum viva voce, tum omni instrumentorum genere, cantatu commodissimi. Cum Octo Vocibus. Nunc primum in lucem editi. Venetijs, Apud Ricciardum Amadinum. 1597 B34

BAGLIONI, GIROLAMO. Hieronymi Ballioni Mediolanensis In Ecclesia S. Mariae Scal. Reg. Duc. Mediolani Organici, ac Gulielmi Arnoni discipuli, Sacrarum Cantionum, quae una, binis, ternis, quatuor, quinque, & sex vocibus concinuntur, Liber primus, & Opus secundum. Mediolani, Apud haer. Simonis Tini & Philippum Lomatium. 1608 B644

BALBI, LUIGI. Ecclesiastici Concentus Canendi Una, Duabus, Tribus, & Quatuor Vocibus, aut Organo, aut alijs quibusuis [sic] Instrumentis eiusdem generis, & alij Quinq., Sex, Septem, & Octo, tum ad concertandum, tum ad vocibus canendum accommodati. Aloysii Balbi Veneti Ecclesiae Magnae Domus Venetiarum Musicae Moderatoris. Liber Primus. Venetiis, Apud Alexandrum Raverium. 1606. B748

BANCHIERI, ADRIANO. Concerti Ecclesiastici à otto voci, di D. Adriano da Bologna Monaco Olivetano, Discepolo del Sig. Gioseffo Guami, Aggiuntovi nel primo Choro la Spartitura per sonare nell'Organo commodissima, Nuovamente composti, & dati in luce. In Venetia Appresso Giacomo Vincenti. 1595. B799

——. Ecclesiastiche Sinfonie Dette Canzoni in aria Francese, à quatro voci, per sonare, & cantare, & sopra un Basso seguente concertare entro l'Organo. Opera Sedicesima di Adriano Banchieri

Bolognese, sotto moderno stile hor data in luce. Con Privilegio. In Venetia, Appresso Ricciardo Amadino. 1607. B802

——. Vezzo de perle Musicali Modernamente Conteste alla Regia Sposa effigiata nella Sacra Cantica: Opera Ventesima Terza. Del R.1P.D. Adriano Banchieri Bolognese Monaco Olivetano. Accomodata, che sopra il Basso seguente si può variare un'istesso Concerto in sei modi, con una & dui parti, cosi voci, come stromenti. Con privilegio. In Venetia, Appresso Ricciardo Amadino. 1610. B805

BARTEI, GIROLAMO. F. Hieronymi Barthaei Aretini Augustiniani Ecclesiae S. Augustini de urbe musices moderatoris. Liber Primus Sacrarum Modulationum quae Vulgo, Motecta Appellantur, duabus vocibus cum basso ad organum accomodato. Romae, Apud Ioannem Baptistam Roblettum. 1609. B1062

BIANCO, GIOVANNI BATTISTA. Musica A Due Voci Utilissima per instruir i figliuoli à cantar sicuramente in breve tempo, & commodi per sonar con ogni sorte di strumenti. Del R.P.F. Gio. Battista Bianco da Venetia Dell'Ordine Agostiniano Novamente data in luce. Con Privilegio. In Venetia, Appresso Giacomo Vincenti. 1610. B2607

BONA, VALERIO. Messa, e Vespro a Quattro Chori, Con il partito delli Bassi ridotti in un solo Basso generale, & doi continuati, per il primo, & secondo, terzo, & quarto Choro. Commodi per li Organisti, & Maestri di Capella, nelle occasioni delle loro Musiche. Di Valerio Bona Maestro della Musica in S. Francesco di Brescia. Opera Decimanona. Ad Reverendissimum P. Magistrum Gulielmum Hugo Avinion, Artium, et sacrae Theologiae Doctorem, universi ordinis Minorum Conventualium Ministrum Generalem. In Venetia, Appresso Giacomo Vincenti. 1611. B3433

BONINI, SEVERO. Il Secondo Libro de Madrigali, e Mottetti à una voce sola per cantare sopra gravicemboli chitarroni, et organi, Con Passaggi, e senza del Molto R. P. D. Severo Bonini Monaco di Vallambrosa. Dedicati al Molto Illustre Sig. Commendatore Angelo Minerbetti. In Firenze: Appresso Cristofano Marescotti. 1609. B3497

BORSARO, ARCHANGELO. Concerti Ecclesiastici, di Arcangelo Borsaro da Reggio, Nelli quali si contengo Mottetti a Una, Due, Tre, Quattro, Cinque, Sei, Sette, & Otto Voci. Domine ad adiuvandum. Dixit Dominus. Falsibordoni. Magnificat à Cinque Voci. Una Compieta à Otto voci. Messa à Otto Litanie che si cantano nella Santa Casa di Loreto à Otto Voci. Con il Basso Continuo per l'Organo. Novamente composti, & dati in luce. Opera Nona. In Venetia 1605. Appresso Ricciardo Amadino. B3779

——. Novo Giardino de Concerti a Quattro Voci, Per cantare à due Chori con due voci, e due Tromboni, ò altri Stromenti, ò voci, secondo la comodita de Cantori. Di Archangelo Borsaro da Reggio Nel quale si contengono alquante Antifone del Cantico della Beata Vergine, di alcune solennità principali dell'Anno, & altri Motetti. Con il Basso principale per l'organo. Opera Undecima. Dedicato All'Illustriss. & Reverendiss. mio Sig. & Patrone Colendissimo Il Sig. Conte Claudio Raugone, Vescovo di Reggio, e Prencipe, &c. In Venetia, Appresso Ricciardo Amadino. 1611. B3781

BOYLEAU, SIMON. Modulationes in Magnificat ad Omnes Tropos nuper aeditae à Simone Boyleau, In capella S. Mariae, apud D. Celsum, Phonasco: quatuor, quinque, ac sex vocibus distinctae. Addito Insuper Concentu, vulgò falso Bordon nominato, ad omnes tonos accommodato. Mediolani Apud Caesarem Puteum, 1566. B4186

BURLINI, ANTONIO. Fiori di Concerti Spirituali A Una, Due, Tre, e Quattro Voci, col Basso Continuo per l'Organo, & altro simile istrumento Commodi per li cantori che seguitano il moderno stile, e molto utile per quelli che desiderano impararlo di Don Antonio Burlini da Rovigo Organista di Monteoliveto Maggiore di Siena. Novamente composti, & dati in luce. Con Privilegio, In Venetia, Apresso Giacomo Vincenti. 1612. B5021

BURLINI, ANTONIO. Riviera Fiorita di Concerti Musicale à Una, Due, Tre, e Quattro Voci con
una Messa nel fine, Il tutto concertato col Basso continuo per l'Organo, Aggiuntevi ancora le
parti per uno, e due istrumenti per chi ne hà commodità, come nella Tavola si può avvertire, e
nelle parti per detti istrumenti è notato di D. Antonio Burlini da Rovigo Monaco Olivetano
Organista di Santa Elena di Venetia, Novamente date in luce. Con Privilegio. Opera Terza. In
Venetia, Apresso Giacomo Vincenti. 1612.   B5022

——. Salmi Intieri che si cantano al Vespro In alcune Solennità de l'Anno con due Magnificat. Il
tutto concertato à Quattro Voci co'l Basso continuo per l'Organo. Aggiuntevi ancora le parti
per due Istrumenti Gravi, & Acuto per chi hà commodità. Opera Quinta. Di D. Antonio
Burlini da Rovigo Monaco Olivetano Novamente composti & dati in luce. Con Privilegio. In
Venetia, Appresso Giacomo Vincenti. 1613.   B5023

——. Messa Salmi, et Motetti Concertati à Otto Voci in due Chori col Basso continuo per
l'Organo, & una parte per un Violino per chi n'hà commodità. Opera Ottava. Di D. Antonio
Burlini Monaco Olivetano. Nuovamente composta, & data in luce. Con Privilegio. In Venetia,
Appresso Giacomo Vincenti. 1615.   B5025

CACCINI, GIULIO. Le Nuove Musiche di Giulio Caccini detto Romano. In Firenze Appresso I
Marescotti, 1601 [recte 1602].   C6

——. Nuove Musiche e Nuova Maniera di Scriverle Con due Arie Particolari per Tenore, che
ricerchi le corde del Basso, di Giulio Caccini di Roma, detto Giulio Romano. Nelle quali si
dimostra, che da tal Maniera di scrivere con la pratica di essa, si poßano apprendere tutte le
squisitezze di quest'Arte, senza necessità del Canto dell'Autore, Adornate di Passaggi, Trilli,
Gruppi, e nuovi affetti per vero esercizio di qualunque voglia professare di cantar solo. In
Fiorenza, Appresso Zanobi Pignoni, e Compagni. 1614.   C11

CALESTANI, GIROLAMO. Sacrati Fiori Musicali a Otto Voci, Con il Te Deum à choro spezzato à
Quattro voci. Commodissimi per cantare in Capella, & Concertare nell'Organo, con ogni
sorte di Strumento Musico. Di Girolamo Calestani Luchese. Con il Basso continuato,
& Soprano, ove è stato necessario, per maggior commodità de'Sig. Organisti. Novamente
composta, & data in luce. Opera Seconda. In Parma, Nella Stamperia di Erasmo Viotti. 1603.
C68

CAMATERO, IPPOLITO. Salmi Corista a Otto Voci Per le feste di Natale di Pasqua & altre feste del
anno secondo l'ordine del Concilio di Trento Comodi alle voci, accompagnate anco con ogni
sorte di instrumenti Musicali, à misura breve, & anco alla ordinaria di Hippolito Chamatero di
Negro Romano Novamente posti in luce. Dixit dominus Confitebor Beatus vir Laudate pueri
Laudate dominum De profundis Memento In Exitu. In Vineggia, Appresso l'herede di
Girolamo Scotto, 1573.   C279

CAPECE, ALESSANDRO. Davidis Cithara Psalmorum quatuor vocum concentibus concors. Ab
Alexandro Capicio in primaria Reatina Ecclesia musices moderatore prolata. Cum Basso ad organum. Romae, Io. Baptistam Roblettum, 1615.   C890

CAPELLO, GIOVANNI FRANCESCO. Gio. Francisci Capello Veneti Fesulanae Congregationis Filij
Sacrorum Concentuum Unica, & Duabus Vocibus cum Litanijs B. Virginis Mariae. Opus
Primum. Venetijs, apud Ricciardum Amadinum, 1610.   C902

——. Lamentationi Benedictus, e Miserere da cantarsi il Mercordì, Giovedí, e Venerdí Santo di
sera à Matutino. Concertate à Cinque voci, et Istromenti à beneplacito. Dal R.P. Gio.
Francesco Capello da Venetia, della Congregat. Fiesolana. Opera Terza Novamente Stampata.
Dedicata al Molto Mag. & M. Rever. Sig. D. Antonio Bocco Honoratiss. Mansionario nel
Domo di Brescia. In Verona, Appresso Angelo Tamo. 1612.   C903

——. Cantici Spirituali A Una, Due, Tre, Quattro, Cinque et Sei Voci. Del R.P. Gio. Francesco
Capello da Venetia Organista nelle Gratie di Brescia. Opera Decima. Nuovamente composta,

& data in luce. Con Privilegio. Dedicata All'Illustrissimo Signore Fortunato Cesis Conte di
Gombola, & Castellano di Parma. In Venetia, Appresso Giacomo Vincenti. 1616.   (Not listed
in RISM. Copy at Cracow, Biblioteka Jagiellonska.)

CAVI, PIETRO PAOLO. F. Petri Pauli Cavensis Augustiniani Sacrae Cantiones Binis, Ternisque vocibus concinendae. Cum Basso ad Organum accommodato. Liber Tertius. Romae, Apud
Bartholomaeum Zannettum. 1609.   C1576b

CECCHINO, TOMASO. Salmi, et Motetti Concertati a Quattro Voci Piene Et mutate à beneplacito de Cantori con il Basso per l'Organo, Et un Echo nel fine à Otto voci di Tomaso Cecchino
Veronese. Maestro di Capella nella Catedrale di Lesina. Libro Primo. Opera Nona. In Venetia,
Apresso Giacomo Vincenti. 1616.   (Not listed in RISM. Viewed at the Musicology Faculty
of the University of Ljubljana.)

——. Psalmi, Missa, et alia Cantica Quinque Vocibus Unà cum gravi parte pro Organo, Auctore
Thoma Cechino Veronensi Opus Decimum Quartum. Nùnc primum in lucem aeditum. Cum
Privilegio. Venetiis, Apud Alexandrum Vincentium. 1619.   C1675

CIFRA, ANTONIO. Psalmi Septem, qui in Vesperis ad Concentus Varietatem Interponuntur.
Quaternis Vocibus cum Basso ad Organum. Auctore Antonio Cifra Romano, Opus Septimum.
Romae, Apud Io: Baptistam Roblettum. 1609.   C2184

——. Salmi Septem, qui in Vesperis ad Concentus Varietatem Interponuntur. Quaternis Vocibus,
cum Basso ad Organum. Auctore Antonio Cifra Romano, in Alma Aede Lauretana Musicae
praefecto. Opus Decimum. Romae, 1611. Apud Io. Baptistam Roblectum.   C2188

CIMA, GIOVANNI PAOLO. Concerti Ecclesiatici a' una, due, tre, quattro voci. Con doi a cinque,
et uno a otto. Messa, e doi Magnificat, & Falsi Bordoni à 4. & sei sonate, per Instrumenti à due,
tre, e quatro. Di Gio. Paolo Cima, Organista della Gloriosa Madonna presso S. Celso di Milano.
Novamente dati in luce. Con la Partitura per l'Organo. In Milano, Per gl'Heredi di Simon Tini,
& Filippo Lomazzo, 1610.   C2229, SD1610[1]

COLOMBANI, ORAZIO. Li Dilettevoli Magnificat Composti Sopra Li Otto Toni a Nove Voci:
Accomodati per cantar: & sonar in concerto: con uno a quatordeci voci: a tre Chori. Del R.P.F.
Oratio Colombano Da Verona Min. Con. Novamente composti & dati in luce. In Venetia
Appresso Giacomo Vincenci: [*sic*] & Ricciardo Amadino compagni: 1583.   C3423

CONFORTI, GIOVANNI LUCA. Salmi Passaggiati Sopra Tutti I Toni Che Ordinariamente Canta
Santa Chiesa, Ne I Vesperi Della Domenica, et ne i giorni festivi di tutto l'anno, Con Il Basso
sotto per sonare, et cantare con Organo, ò con altri stromenti. Ne i quali esercitando quei che
cantono, non solamente si assuefarano à cantar sicuri, & con gratia, ma anco in breve acquis-
teranno la dispositione per sapere ben passaggiare in ogni sorte di note. Li quali, anco possono
servire per quelli, che leggiadramente vogliono sonar di violino, viola, [tiorba], ò d'altri stromenti da fiato. Fatti da Gio. Luca Conforti della Città di Mileto, Cantore nella Capella di N.S.
Papa Clemente VIII. Libro Primo. In Roma, Per li Heredi di Nicolò Mutij. 1601 (Soprano),
1602 (Tenore), 1603 (Basso).   C3498

——. Passaggi sopra tutti li salmi che ordinariamente canta Santa chiesa. Ne i Vesperi della
Dominica, & ne i giorni Festivi di tutto l'anno. Con il Basso sotto per sonare, & cantare con
Organo, o con altri stromenti. Fatti da Gio. Luca Conforti della Città di Mileto, Cantore nella
Capella di sua santità. Libro Primo. Ne i quali esercitando quei che cantano, non solamente si
asuefaranno à cantar sicuri, & con gratia, ma anco in breve acquitteranno [*sic*] la dispositione
per sapere ben passaggiare in ogni sorte di note. Possono anco servire per quelli, che leggiadra-
mente vogliono sonare di viola, violino, o d'altri stromenti da fiato. In Venetia Appresso Angelo
Gardano & Fratelli. 1607.   C3499

CONTINO, GIOVANNI. Magnificat Ioannis Contini, nunc ab ipso authore in lucem editi. Liber
Primus. Ferrariae, Apud Franciscum Rubeum Ducale Typographum. 1571.   C3542

COSTA, FRANCESCO ANTONIO. Messa a Quattro con Sei Salmi, Et un Magnificat, A tre composti per interpositione ne i concerti, à i quali seguitano motetti à due, & tre voci. Novamente datti in luce. Da Francesco Antonio Costa Da Voghiera Maestro di Capella, & Organista, Di S. Francisco di Genova col Basso al Organo. Libro Primo. In Genova, Appresso Giuseppe Pavoni, 1615. C4215

CRISTIANELLI FILIPPO. F. Philippi Christianelli Perusini, In Ecclesia Cathedrali Beneventi Musicae Magistri. Psalmi cum primo, & secundo versu Tribus vocibus. Ac aliquae sacrae cantiones, Binis, Ternis, Octonisque vocibus concinendae. Liber Primus. Neapoli, Apud Io. Iacobum Carlinum, 1611. C4417

CROCE, GIOVANNI. Vespertina Omnium Solemnitatum Psalmodia octonis Vocibus decantanda, Auctore Ioanne A Cruce Clodiense In Ecclesia Divi Marci Musices Vice Magistri. Cum Privilegio. Venetiis, Apud Iacobum Vincentium. 1597. C4449

——. Magnificat Omnium Tonorum cum sex vocibus Auctore Ioanne A Cruce Clodiense Serenissimae Republicae Venetiarum in Ecclesia Divi Marci Musices Magistro. Nunc primum in lucem aeditum. Cum privilegio. Venetiis, Apud Iacobum Vincentium, 1605. C4461

——. Sacre Cantilene concertate à tre, à cinque, et sei voci, Con i suoi ripieni à Quattro voci, del R.D. Giovanni Croce Chiozzotto Maestro di Capella della Serenissima Signoria di Venetia in S. Marco, Nuovamente con ogni diligenza stampate, & date in luce. Con Privilegio. In Venetia, Appresso Giacomo Vincenti. 1610. C4463

CROTTI, ARCANGELO. Il Primo Libro de' Concerti Ecclesiastici à 1. à 2. à 3. à 4. & à 5. Parte con voci sole, & parte con voci, & Instrumenti di Fr. Archangelo Crotti da Ferrara Agostiniano Eremita Osservante. Nuovamente composti, & dati in luce. In Venetia, Appresso Giacomo Vincenti. 1608. C4552

DE' CAVALIERE, EMILIO. Rappresentatione di Anima, et di Corpo Nuovamente posta in Musica dal Sig. Emilio del Cavalliere, per recitar Cantando. Data in luce da Alessandro Guidotti Bolognese. Con Licenza de' Superiori. In Roma Appresso Nicolò Mutij l'Anno del Iubileo. 1600. D1291

DE VILLENA, GENESIUS DOMINICUS. Liber Secundus Magnificarum de Omnibus Tonis Noviter Conpositus [sic] Per Genesium Dominicum de Villena Clericum Ispanum. Stampatus in civitate Ml'i ad instantiam D. Mathiae Flamenghi, & Innocentii Cigognera, & sotiorum omni diligentia correctus & emendatus primo die Septembris Anno salutis 1548. D2115

DONATI, IGNAZIO. Ignatii Donati Ecclesiae Metropolitanae Urbini Musicae Praefecti. Sacri Concentus Unis, Binis, Ternis, Quaternis, & Quinis vocibus, Una cum parte Organica. Ad Illustrissimum Comitem D. Franciscum Mariam Saxatellum Ordinis S. Michaelis Equitem meritissimum. Venetiis, Apud Iacobum Vincentium. 1612. D3379

DULCINO, GIOVANNI BATTISTA. Sacrae Cantiones Octo Vocibus Unà cum Litanijs Beatae Mariae Virginis, & Magnificat cum Basso continuo pro Organo. Auctore Io. Baptista Dulcino Laudensi. Liber Primus Nunc primùm in lucem aeditus. Venetiis, Apud Iacobum Vincentium. 1609. D3679

DURANTE, OTTAVIO. Arie Devote Le quali contengono in se la Maniera di cantar con gratia l'imitation delle parole, et altri affetti. Novam.ti composti da Ottavio Durante Romano. In Roma appresso Simone Verovio. 1608. D3975

FAA, ORAZIO. Salmi di Davit [sic] Profeta con tre Magnificat, et altri Componimenti A Cinque, Sei, & Otto Voci. composti dal S. Horatio Faà Gentilhuomo di Casale di Monferrato, & dati in Luce per il Rever. M. Gio: Andrea Botta Canonico & Maestro di Capella della Catedrale di detta Citta Novamente stampati. In Venetia Apresso li Figliuoli di Antonio Gardano. 1573. F3

FALCONIERI, ANDREA. Sacrae Modulationes Quinque et Sex Vocibus Concinendae. Andrae Falconerii Neapolitani. Invinctissimo Ferdinando Austriaco Boemiae & Ungheriae Regi

Archiduci Austriae &c. Dicati Sub Signo Gardani. Venetiis, Apud Bartolomeum Magni. 1619. (Not listed in RISM. Copy at Cracow, Biblioteka Jagiellonska.)

FASOLO, GIOVANNI BATTISTA. Annuale Che contiene tutto quello, che deve far un Organista, per risponder al Choro tutto l'Anno. Cioè tutti gl'Hinni delli Vesperi, tutte le Messe, cioè doppia, che serve ad ambe le classi, della Domenica, & della Beatissima Vergine Madre di Dio. Sono regolate sotto l'ordine de Toni Ecclesiastici, otto Magnificat, li cui Versetti per pigliare tutti li toni possono servire à tutte l'occorenze di risposte, ciascuno ha sua risposta breve per l'Antifona, otto Ricercate, otto Canzoni francese; quattro fughe, la prima sopra la Bergamasca, la seconda sopra la Girometta, la terza sopra la Bassa fiamenga, la quarta sopra Ut, Re, Mi, Fa, Sol, La; la Salve Regina, & il Te Deum laudamus. Di Fra Giovanbattista Fasolo d'Asti, dell'Ordine de Minor Convent. di S. Francesco. Opera Ottava. Con privilegio. In Venetia, Appresso Allessandro [*sic*] Vincenti. 1645.   F123

FATTORINI, GABRIELE. Il Secondo Libro de Mottetti a Otto Voci di Gabrielle Fattorini da Faenza. Con un Basso generale per l'organo, & nel fine una Canzon Francese a quattro voci. Raccolti dal Reverendo Don Donato Beroaldi da Bologna, & da esso novamente dati in luce. In Venetia, Appresso Ricciardo Amadino, 1601.   F133

FERGUSIO, GIOVANNI BATTISTA. Motetti e Dialogi per Concertar A una sino à nove voci, con il suo Basso continuo per l'Organo Al Serenissimo Prencipe Vittorio Amedeo di Savoia Dedicati, E novamente stampati, e dati in luce. In Venetia, Appresso Giacomo Vincenti. 1612.   F249

FINETTI, GIACOMO. Psalmi ad Vesperas in Solemnitate Sanctissimi Corporis Christi Decantandi Octo Vocibus Varijs modis elaborati. Una cum Basso ad Organum. Per Iacobum Finetum Anconitanum In Anconitana Corporis Christi Aede Sacra, Vocum Moderatorem Quibus adduntur Duo Cantica Beatae Virginis. Venetijs, Apud Angelum Gardanum, & Fratres. 1611.   F813

FLACCOMIO, GIOVANNI PETRO. Liber Primus Concentus in Duos distincti Choros. In quibus Vespere Missa, sacraeque Cantiones in Nativitate, Beatae Mariae Virginis aliarumque Virginum Festivitatibus decantandi continentur. Authore, R. Don Io: Petro Flaccomio siculo, è Civitate Milatij. Venetiis, Apud Angelum Gardanum, & Fratres. 1611.   F1100

FRANZONI, AMANTE. Concerti Ecclesiastici a Una, Due, et a Tre Voci Col Basso Continuo per L'Organo. Di Fra Amante Franzoni Mantovano Servita Academico Olimpico. Maestro di Capella del Domo di Forli. Novamente stampati. Libro Primo. Al molto Illustre Sig. Antonio Torelli da Forli. In Venetia, Appresso Ricciardo Amadino. 1611.   F1812

——. Apparato Musicale di Messa, Sinfonie, Canzoni, Motetti, & Letanie della Beata Vergine. A otto voci. Con la partitura de Bassi, & un novo ordine, con che si mostra, come, & con Istromenti, & senza si possa nell'Organo rappresentare. Opera Quinta. D'Amante Franzoni Servita Academico Olimpico Maestro di Capella nella Chiesa Ducale di Santa Barbara di Mantova. Libro Primo. Novamente posto in luce. Serenisssimo, [*sic*] et Reverendiss. Signore Il Signor Cardinal Gonzaga. In Venetia, Appresso Ricciardo Amadino. 1613.   F1813

FREDDI, AMADIO. Messa Vespro et Compieta à cinque voci col suo basso continuo Aggiuntovi un Violino, & Corneto per le Sinfonie, & per li Ripieni. Di Amadio Freddi Maestro di Capella nel Duomo di Treviso. All'Illustriss. & Eccellentiss. Sign. Il Sig. Antonio Lando Procuratore di S. Marco. In Venetia, 1616. Appresso Ricciardo Amadino.   F1829

GABRIELI, ANDREA. Andree [*sic*] Gabrielis Organistae Sereniss. Reipub. Venetiarum Psalmi Davidici, qui Poenitentiales nuncupantur, tum omnis generis Instrumentorum, tum ad vocis modulationem accommodati. Sex Vocum. Venetijs Apud Angelum Gardanum. 1583. G56

GABRIELI, ANDREA and GIOVANNI. Concerti di Andrea, et di Gio: Gabrieli Organisti della Sereniss. Sig. di Venetia. Continenti Musica di Chiesa, Madrigali, & altro, per voci, &

stromenti Musicali: à 6.7.8.10.12. & 16. Novamente con ogni diligentia dati in luce. Libro Primo et Secondo. Con Privilegio. In Venetia. Appresso Angelo Gardano. 1587. G85, SD1587[16]

GABRIELI, GIOVANNI. Sacrae Symphoniae, Ioannis Gabrielii. Sereniss. Reip. Venetiar. Organistae in Ecclesia Divi Marci. Senis, 7, 8, 10, 12, 14, 15, & 16, Tam vocibus, Quam Instrumentis. Editio Nova. Cum Privilegio. Venetiis, Apud Angelum Gardanum. 1597. G86

——. Symphoniae Sacrae Ioanni Gabrielii Liber Secundus Senis, 7, 8, 10, 11, 13, 14, 15, 17, & 19. Tam vocibus; Quam instrumentis. Dedicate Reverendissimo et Amplissimo Domino D. Ioanni Imperialis Monasterii SS. Udalrici et Afrae Aug. Vind. Abbati. Editio Nova. Cum Privilegio. Venetiis 1615. Aere Bartholomei Magni. G87

GAGLIANO, MARCO DA. La Dafne di Marca da Gagliano nell'Accademia degl'Elevati l'Affannato rappresentata in Mantova. In Firenze, Appresso Cristofano Marescotti, 1608. G113

GALLERANO, LEANDRO. Messa e Salmi Concertati a Tre, Cinque, et Otto Voci Aggiontovi, il Terzo Choro ad libitum. Di Leandro Gallerano Accademico Occulto detto L'Involato Maestro di Capella della Venerand'Arca del Glorioso Sant'Antonio di Padova. Opera Decima Sesta. In Venetia, Appresso Alessandro Vincenti. 1629. G160

GALLO, VINCENZO. Salmi del Re David che ordinariamente canta Santa Chiesa ne i Vespèri. Posti in Musica dal P.M. Vincenzo Gallo Siciliano dell'Alcara. Maestro della Cappella Reale di Sicilia. Libro Primo a Otto Voci. Con il suo partimento per commodita degl'Organisti. In Palermo, Appresso Gio. Battista Maringo. 1607. G267

GASPARINI, FELICE. Concerti Ecclesiastici à dua, & tre voci, Per cantare nell'Organo, con il Basso continuo, di D. Felice Gasparini Monaco Olivetano, Nuovamente dati in luce. In Milano, Per l'herede di Simon Tini, & Filippo Lomazzo. 1608. G454

GASTOLDI, GIOVANNI GIACOMO. Del Reverendo M. D. Gio. Giacomo Gastoldi, Maestro di Capella nella Chiesa Ducale di Santa Barbara di Mantoa. Tutti li Salmi che nelle Solennità dell'anno al Vespro si cantano, à otto voci. Con duoi Cantici della B. Vergine, uno del Settimo tuono, & uno del Secondo tuono, che risponde in Eco. Novamente composti, & dati in luce. In Venetia appresso Ricciardo Amadino. 1601. G498

——. Vespertina Omnium Solemnitatum Psalmodia quinis vocibus decantanda. Io. Iacobi Gastoldi in Ecclesia Ducali Inclitae urbis Mantuae Musices Praefecti. Liber Secundus. Nunc primum in lucem aeditus. Venetijs Apud Ricciardum Amadinum. 1602. G501

——. Salmi Intieri che nelle Solennità dell'anno al Vespro si cantano, Con il Cantico della B. Vergine. A sei voci. Di Gio. Giacomo Gastoldi Maestro di Capella nella Chiesa Ducale di Santa Barbara di Mantoa. Con il Basso continuo per l'Organo. Libro Secondo. Novamente composti, & dati in luce. In Venetia, Appresso Ricciardo Amadino. 1607. G503

GHIZZOLO, GIOVANNI. Messa Salmi Lettanie B. V. Falsibordoni et Gloria Patri Concertati A Cinque, ò None Voci, servendosi del Secondo Choro à beneplacito, con il Basso per l'Organo di Giovanni Ghizzolo Maestro di Capella dell'Illustrissimo, & Reverendissimo Sig. Cardinale Aldobrandini, nella sua Metropoli di Ravenna. Opera Decimaquinta. In Venetia, Appresso Alessandro Vincenti. 1619. G1790

GIACCOBI, GIROLAMO. Prima parte dei Salmi Concertati a Due, e Piu Chori. Di Gieronimo Giacobbi, Maestro di Cappella in S: Petronio di Bologna. Commodi da Concertare in diverse maniere. In Venetia. Appresso Angelo Gardano, & Fratelli. 1609. G1821

GIOVANELLI, PIETRO. Novi Thesauri Musici Liber Primus Quo Selectissime Planeque novae, nec unquam in lucem aeditae cantiones sacrae (quas vulgo moteta vocant) continentur octo, septem, sex, quinque ac quatuor vocum, a prestantissimis ac huius aetatis, precipuis Symphoniacis compositae, quae in sacra Ecclesia catholica, summis solennibusque festivitatibus, canuntur, ad omnis generis instrumenta musica, accomodatae: Petri Ioannelli Bergomensis de Gandino, summo studio ac labore collectae, eiusque expensis impressae. Venetijs Apud Antonium Gardanum. 1568.   SD1568²

GRANDI, ALESSANDRO. Il Primo Libro de Motteti à due, tre, quatro, cinque, & otto voci, con una Messa à quatro. Accommodati per cantarsi nell'Organo, Clavicembalo, Chitarone, o altro simile Stromento. Con il Basso per sonare di Alessandro Grandi Maestro di Capella del Spirito Santo in Ferrara, Nuovamente dati in luce con privilegio. In Venetia, Appresso Giacomo Vincenti, 1610.   G3417

GRANDIS, VINCENZO DE. Psalmi ad Vesperas et Motecta Octonis Vocibus quorum aliqua Concertata cum Litaniis B.M.V. Autuore [sic] Vincentio de Grandis Cappellae Pontificae pro tempore Magistro Liber Primus Romae Apud Lucam Antonium Soldum 1604.   G3480

GUALTIERI, ANTONIO. Motecta Octonis Vocibus Antonii Gualterii in terra D. Danielis Musices Magistri, Liber Primus. Venetiis, Apud Iacobum Vincentium. 1604.   G4791, SD1604⁶

GUAMI, GIOSEFFE. Sacrarum Cantionum Variis, et Choris, et Instrumentorum generibus concinendarum Liber Alter Quem Iosephus Guamius Lucensis Organorum Modulator nuper elaboravit, edidit, ac Ser.mo Allogobrorum Duci Dicavit. Mediolani, Apud Haeredes Augustini Tradati. 1608.   G4803, SD1608³

KAPSBERGER, JOHANNES HIERONYMUS. Libro primo di Mottetti Passeggiati à una Voce del Sig.r Gio. Girolamo Kapsperger Nobile Alemano. Raccolte dal Sig.r Francesco de Nobili. In Roma, 1612.   K185

LAMBARDI, GIROLAMO. Antiphonarium Vespertinum Dierum Festorum Totius anni iuxta ritum Romani Breviarij iussu Pij V. reformati, nunc nuper pulcherrimis contrapuntis exornatum atque auctum. A Reverendo D. Hieronymo Lambardo Canonico Regulari sancti Spiritus prope Venetias. In Tres Partes Distributum, quarum una complectitur dies festos Domini altera Proprium sanctorum, tertia Commune. Impressum in Caenobio Sancti Spiritus prope Venetias. 1597.   L366

LANDI, STEFANO. Psalmi Integri Quattuor Vocibus. Auctore Stephano Lando Romano. Clerico Benefitiato in Basilica Principis Apostolorum, nec non in Ecclesia D. Mariae ad Montes Musicae Praefecto, Romae, Apud Io. Baptistam Roblettum. 1624.   L531

LASSO, ORLANDO DI. Orlandi Lassi Sacrae Cantiones (Vulgo Motecta Appellatae) Quinque, et Sex Vocum, Tum viva Voce tum omnis generis Instrumentis cantatu commodissimae. Liber Secundus. Venetijs Appud [sic] Antoniom [sic] Gardaunm [sic]. 1566.   L794

LEONI, LEO. Sacri Fiori. Mottetti a Due a Tre, et a Quatro Voci per Cantar nel Organo di Leon Leoni Maestro di Capella nel Duomo di Vicenza, Con la sua partitura corrente a comodo delli organisti. Libro Primo. Novamente composti, & dati in luce, & nella Tavola si vede l'ordine di cantarli. In Venetia, apresso Ricciardo Amadino. 1606.   L1997

LINDNERI, FEDERICI. Corollarium cantionum sacrarum quinque, sex, septem, octo, et plurium vocum, de festis praecipuis anni. Quarum quaedam anteà, à praestantissimis nostrae aetatis musicis, in Italia separatim editae sunt, quaedam vero nuperrimè concinnatae, nec uspiam typis excusae, at nunc in unum quasi corpus redactae studio & opera Friderici Lindneri &c. Nürnberg, C. Gerlach, 1590.   SD1590⁵

MARSOLO, PIETRO MARIA. Motecta Quinque Tantum Vocibus Decantanda in totius Anni solemnioribus diebus. Liber Secundus D. Petri Mariae Marsoli I.V.D. Siculi, NOB: Mess. In Cathedrali, nec non in Illustrissima Intrepidorum Academia Ferraria Musices Praefecti Opus Undecimum Recenter compositum; & impressum. Cum declaratione in calce cuiusque libri apprime necessaria. Catholico Regi Dicatum. Cum Privilegio. Venetijs Apud Iacobum Vincentium. 1614.   M750

MASSAINI, TIBURTIO. Musica per Cantare con L'Organo ad Una, Due, & Tre Voci, Di Tiburtio

Massaino. Opera Trentesima seconda. Novamente Composta, & data in luce. In Venetia, Appresso Alessandro Raverij. 1607.   M1286, SD1607[19]

MASSENZIO, DOMENICO. Sacrae cantiones singulis, binis, ternis, quaternis, quinisque vocibus cum Basso ad Organum decantandae auctore Dominico Massentio Collegiatae Ecclesiae Roncilionensis Canonico D. Io. Bernardini Nanini discipulo. Liber primus. Romae, apud Bartolomaeum Zannettum 1612.   M1309

——. Psalmi, qui in Vesperis, una, cum duplici Magnificat, & Hymno Confessoris, concinuntur Quaternis, Quinisque vocibus. Cum Basso ad Organum. Auctore Dominico Massentio Roncilionensi, Illustrissimorum Sodalium B.V. Assumptae In Aedibus Professorum Societatis Iesu Romae Musicae Praefecto. Liber Primus. Romae, Ex Typographia Bartholomaei Zannetti. 1618.   M1313

MAZZI, LUIGI. Li Salmi à cinque voci Che si cantano dalla Santa Chiesa Romana nelli Vesperi delle Solennità di tutto l'Anno, Con doi Magnificat et il Basso per l'Organo di Luigi Mazzi Organista & Maestro di Musica dell'Altezza Serenissima di Modena. Libro Primo Novamente composto & dato in luce. In Venetia Appresso Giacomo Vincenti. 1610.   M1527

MICHELI, ROMANO. Psalmi ad Officium Vesperarum Musicis Notis Expressi, Et Ternis Vocibus decantandi. Una cum parte Organica. Romano Michaele, Clerico Romano, Auctore. Liber Primus. Ad Illustriss.um et Reverendiss.um Federicum Bonromeum [sic] S.R.E. Card. Amplissimum. Romae, Apud Io: Baptistam Roblectum. 1610.   M2682

——. Compieta a Sei Voci Con tre Tenori. Concertata all'uso moderno, Con il Basso Continuo per l'Organo, & un altro Basso Particolare Autore D. Romano Micheli Romano. Maestro di Cappella nella Cathedrale di Concordia. Novamente composta, & data in luce. Opera Quarta. In Venetia, Appresso Giacomo Vincenti. 1616.   M2685

MISEROCA, BASTIANO. Messa, Vespro, Motetti, et Letanie della B. Vergine da cantarsi a Otto voci Con uno avertimento nella parte continuata per l'Organo di Bastiano Miseroca da Ravenna Mastro di Capella, & Organista della Collegiata di S. Paolo di Massa Lombardi. Libro Primo. In Venetia, Appresso Ricciardo Amadino. 1609.   M2876

MONTEVERDI, CLAUDIO. Sanctissimae Virgini Missa Senis Vocibus, ac Vesperae Pluribus Decantandae, Cum Nonnullis Sacris Concentibus, ad Sacella sive Principum Cubicula accommodata. Opera a Claudio Monteverde nuper effecta ac Beatiss. Paulo V. Pont. Max. Consecrata. Venetijs, Apud Ricciardum Amadinum. 1610.   M3445

——. Selva Morale et Spirituale di Claudio Monteverde Maestro di Capella della Serenissma Republica di Venetia Dedicata alla Sacra Cesarea Maestà della Imperatrice Eleonora Gonzaga Con Licenza de Superiori, & Privilegio. In Venetia 1641 Appresso Bartolomeo Magni. M3446

——. Messa a Quattro Voci et Salmi a Una, Due, Tre, Quattro, Cinque, Sei, Sette, & Otto Voci, Concertati, e Parte da Cappella, & con le Letanie della B.V. del Signor Claudio Monteverde gia Maestro di Cappella della Serenissima Republica di Venetia. Dedicata al R.mo P.D. Odoardo Baranardi Abbate di Santa Maria delle Carceri della Congregatione Camaldolense. In Venetia, Appresso Alessandro Vincenti. 1650.   M3447, SD1650[5]

MORALES, CRISTÓBAL DE. Magnificat Moralis Ispani aliorumque authorum. Liber Primus. Venetijs apud hieronymum Scotum. 1542.   M3592, SD1542[9]

——. Magnificat Moralis Ispani cum Quatuor Vocibus Liber Primus Venetijs Apud Antonium Gardane 1545.   M3594.

MORO, GIACOMO. Concerti Ecclesiastici di Giacomo Moro Viadana Nelliquali si contengono Mottetti, Magnificat, & Falsibordoni A una, Due, Tre, Quattro, Sei, & Otto voci, Alcuni de quali sono con passaggi che servono non solo alle voci, ma ad ogni sorte di stromenti. Una Compieta a Otto con le sue Antiphone della B. Vergine. Messa a otto. Litanie che si cantano nella santa Casa di Loretto a Otto. Canzoni a Quattro per suonare con diversi stromenti. Con il Basso continuo per l'Organo. Novamente posti in luce. Opera Ottava, Al M. Mag. & R. Mons: Ambrosio Magnanino Dottor de l'una e l'altra legge, Rettor della Chiesa di Fivizano, e per l'Illustrissimo, & Reverendissimo Vescovo di Sarzana Vicario meritissimo. In Venetia, Appresso Ricciardo Amadino. 1604. M3732

MORTARO, ANTONIO. Messa, Salmi, Motetti, et Magnificat, à Tre Chori, di Antonio Mortaro da Brescia, Organista nella Chiesa di S. Francesco di Milano. Alla Santa Casa di Loreto. In Milano, Appresso l'herede di Simon Tini, & Francesco Besozzi. 1599.   M3741

———. Secondo Libro Delle Messe, Salmi, Magnificat, Canzoni da suonare, & Falsa Bordoni, à XIII. Di Antonio Mortaro da Brescia, Nuovamente datto [*sic*] in luce. Al glorioso S. Antonio di Padova. In Milano, Appresso l'her. di Simon Tini, & Filippo Lomazzo. 1610.   M3749

NALDI, HORTENSIO. Hortensii Naldi Placentini Psalmi omnes, qui à S.R.E. in solemnitatibus decantari solent, Cum Duobus Magnificat, et Fal. Bord. Tum viva voce, tum omni instrumentorum genere cantatu commodissimi, Unà cum Sectione partium ad Organistarum usum, & commodum. Cum Quatuor Vocibus. Liber Primus. Venetijs, apud Ricciardum Amadinum. 1606. N10

NANINO, GIOVANNI BERNARDINO. Salmi Vespertini a Quatro per le Domeniche, Solennita della Madonna, & Apostoli, con doi Magnificat, uno à quatro, e l'altro à otto. Con il Basso per l'Organo se piace. Del Sig. Gio. Bernardino Nanini. Racolti dal Reverendo D. Giulio Subissati da Fossombrone. In Roma, Apresso Gio. Battista Robletti. 1620.   N20, SD1620[7]

NASCIMBENI, STEFANO. Concerti Ecclesiastici a Dodeci Voci divisi in Tre Chori di Stefano Nasimbeni Maestro di Capella della Chiesa Ducale di Santa Babara [*sic*] di Mantova. Nelli quali si contengono due Messe, & li Salmi per i Vesperi di S. Syro Primo Vescovo di Pavia, con il Cantico della Beata Vergine. & il partito per sonare. Novamente dati in luce. In Venetia, Appresso Ricciardo Amadino: 1610. N70

NEGRI, MARCO ANTONIO. Cantica Spiritualia in Missis, et Vesperis Solennibus Senis Vocibus et Organis Concinenda. Auctore Marco Ant. Nigro Veronense Abbate S. Michaelis Veglae ad Sereniss.mi Principis Illustrissimam Neptem Lauram Bembo Monialem in Monasterio Omnium Sanctorum Sub Signo Gardani Venetiis 1618. Apud Bartolomeum Magni.   N365

NODARI, GIOVANNI PAOLO. Io. Pauli Nodarii Brixiensis Mellifluus Concentus In Psalmis David, qui in praecipuis anni solemnitatibus ad Vesperas Quatuor Vocibus. Organo Aliisque Musicis Instrumentis decantandi erunt. Nec non in duo Beatissime Virginis Deipare Cantica Iisdem instrumentis concinenda. Venetijs, Apud Ricciardum Amadinum. 1605.   N732

ORTIZ, DIEGO. Musices Liber Primus Hymnos, Magnificat, Salves, Motecta, Psalmos, aliquae diversa cantica complectens. Venetiis, apud A. Gardanum, 1565. O135

PACE, PIETRO. Salmi a Otto Voci di Pietro Pace Organista della Santa Casa di Loreto; Parte di detti Salmi da Concertarsi senza sonarli (se piace,) e parte non potendo senza, quali saranno assignati; havertendo a ciaschedun' Cantore, che ad ogni Salmo si contino le Battute. Novamente dati in luce. Opera Vigesima. In Venetia, Appresso Alessandro Vincenti. 1619. P12

PACELLI, ASPRILIO. Asprilii Pacelli in Alma Urbe Collegii Germanici Musicae Magistri Motectorum et Psalmorum qui Octonis Vocibus concinuntur. Liber Primus. Romae, Apud Nicolaum Mutium 1597. P24

PASQUALE, BONIFACIO. Di Bonifacio Pasquale da Bologna Maestro di Capella del Santo da Padova I Salmi che si cantano tutto l'anno al Vespro à cinque voci, Et un Magnificat à otto. Novamente Posti in Luce. In Vineggia, Appresso l'herede di Girolamo Scotto 1576. P973, SD1576[7]

PATTA, SERAFINO. Missa Psalmi Motecta, Ac Litaniae in honorem Deiparae Virginis quinque vocibus D. Seraphini Pattae Mediolanensis in Ecclesia Sanctae Mariae Montis Cesennae Organistae. Adita etiam infima pars pro Organo continuata. Venetiis, Apud Iacobum Vincentium, 1606. P1036

——. Sacrorum Canticorum una, duabus, tribus, quatuor, et quinque vocibus, D. Seraphini Pattae Mediolanensis Monachi Cassinensis, & in Ecclesia Sancti Salvatoris Papiae Organistae Liber Secundus cui inseruntur Cantiones quaedam instrumentis tantum accommodatae, cum parte infima pro Organo. Nunc primum in lucem aeditum. Venetijs Apud Iacobum Vincentium. 1613. P1038

PERI, JACOPO. Le Musiche di Iacopo Peri Nobil Fiorentino Sopra L'Euridice del Sig. Ottavio Rinuccini Rappresentate Nello Sponsalizio della Cristianissima Maria Medici Regina di Francia e di Navarra. In Fiorenza Appresso Giorgio Marescotti. 1600. P1431

PHINOT, DOMINIQUE. Di Dominico Phinot, Il primo Libro, Di Salmi, A quatro voci, A uno Choro, con la gionta, di dui Magnificat, Novamente Stampato, et con somma Diligentia Corretto. Venetiis, Apud Hieronymum Scotum. 1555. P2022

——. Di Dominico Phinot Il Primo Libro di Salmi a Quatro Voci a uno Choro, Con la gionta di dui Magnificat Novamente ristampato & con somma diligentia corretto. In Venetia appresso di Antonio Gardano. 1563. P2023

PICCIOLI, GIACOMO ANTONIO. Ac. Anto. Piccioli a Corbario, Min. Conven. Musices Cathedralis Ecclesiae Vercellensis moderatoris, Missa, Cantica B.M.VIR. ac Sacrae Cantiones octo vocibus concinendae. Ab Illustriss. et Reveren. D.D. Constantiam, S.R.E. Presbyterum Cardinalem Sarnanum, Episcopum Vercellensem. Mediolani, Apud Franciscum, & haeredes Simonis Tini. 1587. P2218

PICCIONI, GIOVANNI. Concerti Ecclesiastici di Giovanni Piccioni à Una, à Due, à Tre, à Quattro, à Cinque, à Sei, à Sette, & à Otto voci, Con il suo Basso seguito per l'Organo. Novamente posti in luce. Opera Decimasettima. Con privilegio. In Venetia Appresso Giacomo Vincenti, 1610. P2221

——. Psalmi Sex Ternis vocibus, et Aliae Cantiones, Binis, & Ternis vocibus decantandae, Auctore Ioanne Picionio Organico in Templo Cathedrali Illustrissimae Urbis Veteris. Opus XVIII. Romae, Apud Bartholomaeum Zannettum. 1612. P2222

——. Salmi Intieri a Quattro Voci Concertati, con l'Organo. Di Giovan Piccioni Maestro di Capella, & Organista di Monte Fiascone Nuovamente composti, & dati in luce. Opera Decima Nona. In Venetia, Appresso Giacomo Vincenti. 1616. P2223

——. Concertus [sic] Ecclesiastici Ioannis Piccioni Binis, Ternis, Quaternisque vocibus. Sex cum Psalmis in fine. Cum Basso ad Organum. Noviter aediti, Opera Vigesima prima. Romae, 1619. Apud Io. Baptistam Roblettum. P2224

PORTA, ERCOLE. Giardino di Spirituali Concenti A Due, A Tre, e A Quattro Voci, Con il Basso per l'Organo. Di Hercole Porta Organista della Colleggiata di S. Giovanni Impersicetto. Novamente posto in luce. In Venetia, Appresso Alessandro Raverij. 1609. P5191

PORTINARO, FRANCESCO. Il Secondo Libro de Motetti a Sei Sette et Otto Voci All'Illustrissimo & Reverendissimo Signor il Signor D. Luigi d'Este Card. In Venetia Appresso di Antonio Gardano. 1568. P5222

QUINTIANI, LUCREZIO. D. Lucretti Quintiani Cremonensi Ordinis Cisterciensi, Cantica Deiparae Virginis Octo Vocibus concinenda: Quibus etiam in fine Canticum unum Quarti Toni Duodecim Vocibus decantandum adiunctum est, Tum omnis generis Instrumentorum, tum ad vocis modulationem accomodata. Nunc primum in lucem edita. Venetijs Apud Angelum Gardanum. 1591. Q115

RADINO, GIULIO PADOVANO. Concerti per Sonare et Cantare di Giulio Radino Padovano Cioè Canzone, & Ricercari à Quattro, & Otto, Mottetti, Messe, Salmi, & Magnificat, à Cinque, Sei,

Sette, Dieci, Dodeci, & Sedeci Voci. Novamente dati alle Stampe Da Gio. Maria Radino suo Padre. In Venetia, Appresso Angelo Gardano, & Fratelli. 1607.   R29, SD1607[8]

RAMELLA, FRANCESCO. Sacrae Cantiones Quinis, Senis, ac Octonis vocibus, unà cum Missa, & Cantico B.M. Virginis octo vocibus, Tùm vivae voci, tùm omnibus Musices Instrumentis aptissimae, Francisci Ramellae Novar. Liber Primus. Mediolani, Ex Typographia Michaelis Tini ad signum Famae. 1591.   R195

RIGHI, GIOVANNI. Ioannis Righi Civitatis Mirandulae Canonici, ac Musices prefecti: Missa, Motecta, Psalmi ad vesperas, cum duobus Canticis, ac Litanijs in omnibus B. Mariae Virginis Festivitatibus, Octo Vocibus decantanda. Nunc primum in lucem edita. Cum Basso ad usum, & commoditatem Organistarum. Venetiis, Apud Iacobum Vincentium. 1606.   R1540

RIPALTA, GIOVANNI DOMENICO. Missa, Psalmi ad Vesperas, Magnificat, Motecta, et Psalmorum modulationes qui Octonibus Vocibus concinuntur. Auctore Ioanne Dominico Ripalta Modoaetiensi In templo Sancti Ioannis Baptistae Modoaetiae Organista. Mediolani, Apud Augustinum Tradatum. 1604.   R1733

RODIO, ROCCO. Psalmi ad Vespera Dierum Festorum Solemnium per totum annum, quae vulgus Falso Bordone appellat. A Diversis Authoribus Conditi Necnon omnes Dierum Festorum Hymni, uni cum Communibus, atque quatuor Magnificat, & Haec dies, Regina caeli, & Salve Regina, quatuor vocibus. A Rocho Rodio Conciti Nuper et Impressi, in lucemque aediti. Cum Privilegio ad Decennium: Neapoli Mattias Cancer excudebat. 1573.   (Not listed in RISM. Copy at Pesaro, Duomo.)

ROINCI, LUIGI. Sacra Omnium Solemnitatum Vespertina. Duoq. B. Virginis Cantica Quinis vocibus, decantanda. Aloysii Royncii. A.R.D. Iulio Cesare de Colli eius Discipulo Nunc primum in lucem edita. Venetijs, Apud Ricciardum Amadinum. 1604.   R1957

RORE, CIPRIANO and JACHET OF MANTUA. Di Cipriano et di Iachet I Salmi a Quattro Voci a Uno Choro, con la Gionta de Tutti' I Toni a Falsibordoni, Figurati, et Fermi, a Voce Piena, et a Voce Pari, et con la gionta del Salmo In exitu, Nuovamente ristampati. Venetiis, Apud Claudium Correggiatem. 1570.   SD1570[2]

RUBICONI, GRISOSTOMO. Concerti Ecclesiastici alla moderna dove si contengono Messa, Salmi per il Vespero, e Compieta, & Magnificat à Tre, à Quattro, à Cinque, à Sei, à Sette, & à Otto di D. Grisostomo Rubiconi da Rimini Monaco Olivetano Organista di S. Benedetto Novello in Padua Con il Basso continuo per Sonare nell'Organo. Opera Seconda. Novamente composta, & data in luce. In Venetia, Appresso Giacomo Vincenti. 1611.   R3034

RUBINO, BONAVENTURA. Messa, e Salmi a otto Voci Cocertati nel Primo Choro di Fr. Bonaventura Rubino da Montecchio Di Lombardia. Maestro di Cappella del Duomo di Palermo. Dedicati all'Illustriss. Senato dell'istessa Felice Città Opera Seconda. Con licenza de' Superiori, e Privileggio [sic]. In Palermo, Appresso Francesco Terranova. 1651.   R3041

——. Salmi Varii Variamente Concertati con Sinfonie d'obligo, et a beneplacito di F. Bonaventura Rubino da Montecchio di Lombardia Min. Con. Maestro di Cappella del Duomo della Felice Città di Palermo Dedicati al Sig. D. Cesarela Grua Toch, Manriquez, e Talamanca Duca di Villa Reale, Barone dell'Oliviero, di Pancaldo, e Zaffarana, Signore di Baida, &c. Opera Quinta, con Privilegio. In Palermo, per Guseppe Bisagni 1655. Con Licenza de' Superiori. (Not listed in RISM. Copy at Mdina, Malta, Cathedral Museum.)

——. Salmi Concertati a Cinque Voci di F. Bonaventura Rubino da Montecchio di Lombardia, Maestro di Cappella del Duomo della Felice Città di Palermo Dedicati all'Illustriss. et Eccellentiss. Signore D. Pietro Martinez Rubio Arcivescovo di Palermo, Prelato Familiare, & Assistente Di Sua Santità, del Conseglio di S. M. Luogotenente, e Capitan Generale in questo Regno di Sicilia. Opera Sesta con Privilegio. In Palermo, Per Giuseppe Bisagni 1658. Con Licenza de' Superiori. (Not listed in RISM. Incomplete copy at Spello, Biblioteca Comunale.)

RUBINO, BONAVENTURA. Salmi Davidici Concertati a Tre, e Quattro Voci di Fra Bonaventura Rubbino [*sic*] da Montecchio di Lombardia Minore Convent. Maestro di Cappella del Duomo della Felicissima Città di Palermo Dedicati all'Illus. Signor Marchese Gio. Francesco Pallavicini Opera Settima. In Palermo, Per Giuseppe Bisagni 1658. (Not listed in RISM. Copy at Mdina, Malta, Cathedral Museum.)

SARTORIUS, PAUL. Sacrae Cantiones Sive Motecta Senis, Septenis, Octonis, Denis Et Duodenis Vocibus Canendae. Atque Instrumentis pro Ecclesiarum & Festorum quorundam commoditate, accommodande. Paulo Sartorio Normib. Sereniss. Archiducis Maximilliani Organista, Authore. Venetijs. Apud Angelum Gardanum. 1602.　S1084

SCALETTA, ORAZIO. Messa, et il Vespro della Beatissima Vergine Maria Nostra Signora. A Tre Voci. Per Concertar nell'Organo. Con alcuni Motetti nel fine, à una, & tre voci. Di Oratio Scaletta. Opera Dedicata al Molto Reverendo Padre Frate Amante Bonvicino. Priore Dignissimo in S. Alessandro di Bressa, Signor mio osservandissimo. In Milano, Appresso Filippo Lomazzo. 1615.　S1145

SCARPA, GIOVANNI MICHIEL. Messa, Salmi et Motetti A Una, Due, & Tre, Voci Con il suo Basso generale per sonar nell'Organo Di Gio. Michiel Scarpa Chiozzotto Libro Primo Novamente dato in luce. Dedicato Al Molto Illustre, & Eccellentissimo Sig. Baldissera Vianello Cavalliere. In Venetia, Appresso Giacomo Vincenti. 1613.　S1219

SEVERI, FRANCESCO. Salmi passaggiati per tutte le voci nella maniera che si cantano in Roma sopra i falsi bordoni di tutti i tuoni ecclesiastici da cantarsi ne i Vespri della Domenica e delli giorni festivi di tutto l'Anno con alcuni versi di Miserere sopra il Falso Bordone del Dentice composti da Francesco Severi Perugino cantore nella Capp. di N.S. Papa Paolo V. Libro Primo. In Roma da Nicolò Borboni l'Anno 1615. con licenza de Superiori & con Privil°. S2847

SIGNORUCCI, POMPEO. Salmi, Falsibordoni, e Motetti a Tre Voci Commodissimi per cantare, & concertare nel Organo, con ogni sorte di strumento: Con dui Magnificat: uno intiero l'altro à versi spezzati, Di Pompeo Signorucci Maestro di Capella, & Organista del Borgo San Sepolcro. Novamente composti, & dati in luce. E Con il Basso continuato per maggior commodità de gli Organisti. Opera Sesta. In Venetia, Appresso Giacomo Vincenti. 1603.　S3429

——. Il Secondo Libro de Concerti Ecclesiastici A Otto voci di Pompeo Signorucci I.C. Accademico Unisono di Perugia, Maestro di Capella nel Duomo di Pisa. Cioè Salmi, Magnificat, Motetti, & una Messa dell'Ottavo Tono, Novamente composti, & dati in luce. Et con il Basso continuato, potendosi cantare in Capella, e sonar nell'Organo con ogni sorte d'Instrumento. Opera Undecima In Venetia, Appresso Giacomo Vincenti. 1608. S3431

SIMONETTI, LEONARDO. Raccolta Terza di Leonardo Simonetti Musico nella Capella della Serenissima Repubblica. De Messa et Salmi del Sig. Alessandro Grandi et Gio † Chiozotto à 2. 3. 4. con Basso continuo. Aggiontovi li Ripieni à beneplacito. Con Licenza de Superiori, Et Privilegio. Stampa del Gardano. In Venetia. 1630. Appresso Bartholomeo Magni.　SD1630[1]

SITIBUNDUS, GUILELMUS. Antiphonae ad Magnificat Festorum Omnium per annum occurrentium secundum tonos ab Ecclesia Romana observatos, Authore Guyilelmo Sitibundo Ancon. Liber Primus. Cum Quinque Vocibus. Venetiis, Apud Ioannem Barillettum. 1574.　S3550

SORIANO, FRANCESCO. Psalmi et Mottecta Quae Octo Duodecim, & Sexdecim Vocibus concinuntur. Auctore Francisco Suriano Romano Sacro Sanctae Basilicae S. Petri in Vaticano Chori Musici Magistro. Liber Secundus. Venetiis, Apud Iacobum Vincentium. 1616.　S3984

STEFANINI, GIOVANNI BATTISTA. Motetti di Gio. Battista Steffanini da Modena Mastro [*sic*] di Capella nella Chiesa Ducale di S. Maria della Scala di Milano, Libro Primo, à due, e tre voci. All'Illustriss. & Eccellentiss. Sig. Don Amadeo di Savoia, Marchese di Peveragno, e di Boves,

Cavaliere dell'Ordine, Gran Comendatore di Savoia, & Luogo tenente generale di S.A.S.ma. In Milano, Per l'herede di Simon Tini, & Filippo Lomazzo. 1606. S4728

STIVORI, FRANCESCO. In Sanctissimae Virginis Mariae Canticum modulationes super omnes tonos. Et Ex Canticis Canticorum Quatuor Divinae Laudes. Quatuorque illae Beatae Virg. Antiphonae quae in fine officij pro tempore decantantur. Omnia Octonis Vocibus Modulanda, ac omni genere instrumentorum accommodata. Auctore Francisco Stivorio Magnificae Communitatis Montaneanae Organorum Moderatore. Liber Quintus. Nunc primum in lucem edita. Venetijs, Apud Ricciardum Amadinum. 1598. S6451

STRATA, GIOVANNI BATTISTA. Di Gio. Battista Strata Organista del Duomo della Serenissima Republica di Genova. Messa, Motteti, Magnificat, Falsi Bordoni a Cinque Voci, Con il Basso continuato per l'Organo, e Stromenti, Primo Libro Dedicato All'Illustrissimo Signor Bernardo Clavarezza Nuovamente composto, & dato in luce. In Venetia, Appresso Giacomo Vincenti, 1609. S6928

TARDITI, PAOLO. Psalmi Magnif. cum quatuor antiphonis ad Vesperas Octo Vocib. Una cum Basso ad Organum Decantandi Auctore Paulo Tardito Romano in Ecclesia SS. Iacobi, & Illefonsi Hispanicae Nationis, Musices Moderatore. Liber Secundus. Romae. Apud Luca Antonium Soldum 1620. T225

TERRIERA, FRANCESCO. Messa Salmi per i Vesperi, et Motetti, à otto voci Con il Basso per sonar nel'Organo, di Francesco Terriera da Conegliano. Libro Primo. Novamente composto, & dato in luce. In Venetia, Appresso Giacomo Vincenti. 1601. T537

TORTI, LODOVICO. Ludovico Torto Ticinensi Auctore, ac Metrop. Eccl. Teatinae Musicae Moderatore, Missa una, septem divinae laudes, aliquot, & Hymni, una cum Psalmis Vespertinis, ac B.V. Cantico Ternis vocibus decantanda. Opus Sextum. Infima Organi continuati parte adiecta. Venetijs, Apud Ricciardum Amadinum. 1607. T1013

USPER, FRANCESCO. Messa, e Salmi da Concertarsi nel'Organo et anco con diversi Stromenti, à Cinque Voci, & insieme Sinfonie, & Motetti à Una, Due, Tre, Quattro, Cinque, & Sei Voci di Francesco Usper Organista nella Chiesa di S. Salvatore di Venetia Novamente composti, & dati in luce. Con privilegio. In Venetia, Appresso Giacomo Vincenti. 1614. U116

——. Salmi Vespertini Per tutto l'Anno, Parte à Doi Chori, parte Concertati al'uso moderno, & parte alla Breve, come si Cantano nelle Capelle De Prencipi, A 4. 5. & Otto Voci. Con il Basso Continuo. Di D. Francesco Usper Capo della Gran Scola di S. Giovanni Evangelista Di Venetia. Opera Quinta. Con Privilegio. Stampa del Gardano. In Venetia 1627. Appresso Bartolomeo Magni. U117

VALENTE, ANTONIO. Versi Spirituali Sopra Tutte le Note, Con Diversi Canoni Spartiti per Sonar ne gli Organi, Messe, Vespere, et Altri Officii Divini. Di M. Antonio Valente Cieco, Libro secondo, Novamente da lui composto, & posto in luce. In Napoli. Appresso gli Eredi di Mattio Cancer. 1580. V34

VAROTTO, MICHELE. Reverendi D. Michaelis Varoti Cathedralis Ecclesiae Novariensis Canonici Lamentationes Hieremiae Prophetae, aliqaeque diviuae [*sic*] laudes in maiori hebdomada, tùm viva voce, tùm omnis generis instrumentis aptè concinendae, Cum quinque, & octo vocibus. Mediolani, Apud Franciscum, & haeredes Simonis Tini. 1587. V989

VECCHI, ORAZIO. Missae Senis et Octonis Vocibus ex Celeberrimis Auctoribus Horatio Vecchio Aliisque Collectae Nomina pagina versâ invenies. Antverpiae Apud Petrum Phalesium 1612. V1009, SD1612[1]

VECCHI, ORFEO. Missa, Psalmi ad Vesperas Dominicales, Magnificat et Psalmorum modulationes, quae passim in Ecclesiis usurpantur. Auctore Orpheo Vecchio Medio. Presb. apud S. Mariae a Scala Capellae Magistro. Octonis vocibus. Mediolani, apud Franciscum et haeredes Simonis Tini. 1590. V1057

VECCHI, ORFEO. Psalmi Integri in Totius Anni Solemnitatibus, Magnificat duo, Antiphonae quatuor ad B.V. post Completorium, & modulationes octo, quae vulgò Falsibordoni nuncupantur. Quinque vocibus. Orphei Vecchii Mediol. Ecclesiae Divae Mariae Scalensis Reg. Duc. Musicae, & Chori Magistri. Mediolani Apud haeredes Francisci, & Simonis Tini. 1596. V1058

——. Basso Principale da Sonare Delli Salmi Intieri a Cinque Voci di Orfeo Vecchi. In Milano, Appresso l'herede di Simon Tini, & Gio. Francesco Besozzo. 1598. V1059

VERNIZZI, OTTAVIO. Armonia Ecclesiasticorum Concertuum Octavii Vernitii Bonon: in Ecclesia Divi Petronij Organistae Qui Duabus, Tribus, & Quatuor concinuntur vocibus, cum parte generali pro Organo, seu quibuslibet alijs Musicalibus Instrumentis. Opus Authoris secundum. Venetiis, Apud Jacobum Vincentium. 1604. V1293

VIADANA, LODOVICO. Cento Concerti Ecclesiastici, A Una, a Due, a Tre, & a Quattro voci. Con il Basso continuo per Sonar nell'Organo. Nova inventione commoda per ogni sorte de Cantori, & per gli Organisti. Di Lodovico Viadana. Opera duodecima. In Venetia, Appresso Giacomo Vincenti. 1602. V1360

——. Ludovici Viadanae Psalmi omnes qui a S. Romana Ecclesia in solemnitatibus ad Vesperas decantari solent. Cum Duobus Magnificat Tum viva voce, tum omni Instrumentorum genere, cantatu commodissimi. Cum Quinque Vocibus Nunc primum in lucem editi. Liber Secundus. Opera XIII. Venetiis, Apud Iacobum Vincentium. 1604. V1368; second edition: 1607 V1369

——. Il Terzo Libro de' Concerti Ecclesiastici A Due, à Tre, & à Quattro voci. Di Lodovico Viadana Maestro di Capella nella Cathedrale di Concordia Novamente composti, e dati in luce. 1609. V1392

——. Salmi a Quattro Chori Per cantare, e concertare nelle gran Solennità di tutto l'Anno, con il Basso continuo per sonar nell'Organo Di Lodovico Viadana Maestro di Capella nel Domo di Fano. Opera XXVII. Novamente composta, & data in luce. Con Privilegio. In Venetia, Appresso Giacomo Vincenti. 1612. V1400

VICTORIA, TOMÁS LUIS. Motecta que Partim, Quaternis, Partim, Quinis, Alia, Senis, Alia Octonis, Alia Duodenis Vocibus, Concinuntur: quae quidem nunc vero melius excussa, & alia quam plurima adiuncta Noviter sunt impressa. Permissu Superiorum. Romae, Apud Alexandrum Gardanum. 1583. V1422

——. Liber Primus. Qui Missas, Psalmos, Magnificat, ad Virginem Dei Matrem Salutationes, Alia'que Complectitur. Venetijs apud Angelum Gardanum. Anno Domini 1576. V1427

VILLANI, GASPARE. Psalmi Omnes qui per annum ad Vesperas Decantari consueverunt. Gasparis Villani Placentini In Ecclesia Cathedrali Placentiae organista. Octo vocibus. Liber Quintus. Venetijs Apud Angelum Gardanum, 1611. V1552

VISCONTE, SISTO. Concenti Spirituali, ne' quali si contengono Messa, Salmi, Magnificat, Motetti, Letanie, & Falsibordoni, A Quattro Voci, Con il Basso continuo per l'Organo. Di F. Sisto Visconte Men. Con. Maestro di Musica in S. Francesco di Torino. Opera Seconda. In Milano, Per l'herede di Simon Tini, & Filippo Lomazzo. 1609. V2109

WILLAERT, ADRIAN. Hymnorum Musica Secundum Ordinem Romanae Ecclesiae, Excellentissimi Adriani Wilart ac aliorum authorum Noviter in lucem edita. Venetijs apud Hieronymum Scotum. 1542. W1113, SD1542[11]

——. I Sacri et Santi Salmi che si cantano a Vespro et Compieta Con li suoi Himni Responsorij et Benedicamus Composti da l'eccellentissimo Musico Adraino Vuillaert a uno Choro et a quattro voci Novamente per Antonio Gardano stampati et corretti. Con la gionta di dui Magnificat a Quattro Voci. In Venetia apresso di Antonio Gardano. 1555. W1123

——. I Sacri et Santi Salmi che si Cantano a Vespro et Compieta Con li suoi Hymni Responsorij

& Benedicamns. [*sic*] Composti da l'eccellentissimo Musico Adraino Willaert à uno Choro & a quatro voci Novamente per Antonio Gardano ristampati & corretti Con la gionta di dui Magnificat. In Venetia Appresso di Antonio Gardano. 1561. (Not in RISM. Copy at Bressanone, Seminario Maggiore.)

———. I Sacri et Santi Salmi che si Cantano a Vespro et Compieta con li suoi Hinni, Responsorij, et Benedicamus, Composti da l'eccellentissimo Musico Adraino Willaert a uno Choro, et a Quatro Voci Novamente Ristampato, Con la gionta di dui Magnificat. A Quatro Voci In Venetia, Appresso Francesco Rampazetto, 1565. W 1124

———. I Sacri et Santi Salmi che si Cantano a Vespro et Compieta Con li suoi Hymni, Responsorij, & Benedicamus. Composti da l'Eccellentiss: Musico Adraino Willaert à uno Choro, & a Quatro voci. Novamente con ogni dilligentia Ristampati, Con la gionta di dui Magnificat. In Venetia Apresso li Figliuoli di Antonio Gardano. 1571. W 1125

———, and JACHET DE MANTUA. Di Adriano et di Jachet i Salmi appertinenti alli Vesperi Per tutte le Feste Dell'anno, Parte a versi, & parte spezzadi Accomodati da Cantare a uno & a duoi Chori, Novamente Posti in Luce, & per Antonio Gardane con ogni Diligentia stampati & Correti. Con Privilegio In Venetia Apresso di Antonio Gardane. 1550. SD1550¹

———. Di Adriano et di Iachet I Salmi apertinenti alli Vesperi Per tutte le Feste Dell'anno, Parte a versi, & parte spezzadi Accomodati da Cantare a uno & a duoi Chori, Novamente per Antonio Gardano con ogni Diligentia ristampati & Corretti. Con Privilegio In Venetia Apresso di Antonio Gardane. 1557. SD1557⁶

ZINERONI, AGOSTINO. Augustini Zineroni Bergomensis, Ecclesiae Cathdr. Bergomi Musices Praefecti, Missa, Beatae Virginis Cantica, Sacraeque Cantiones vulgo Motecta appellatae, Tum viva voce, Tum omni instrumentorum genere Octonis vocibus concinendae. Venetijs apud Ricciardum Amadinum, 1599. Z240, SD1599⁵

ZUCCHINI, GREGORIO. Missa Quatuor Vocibus Decantanda Cum nonnullis Psalmis integris, divisis, Falsibordonibus Magnificat, & Letanijs Beatae Virginis. Cum Sectione Gravium partium pro Organistis Auctore D. Gregorio Zuchinio Brixiensi Monaco Casinensi, & Divi Georgij Maioris Venetiarum professo. Nunc primum in lucem aedita. Venetijs, Apud Iacobum Vincentium. 1615. Z363

Appendix F
Theoretical Treatises of the Sixteenth and Seventeenth Centuries

꒰✦꒱

AARON, PIETRO. *Thoscanello in musica* (Venice: Bernardino and Matheo de Vitali, 1523, rev. edn. 1529; fac. New York: Broude Brothers, 1970). Partial Eng. trans. Peter Bergquist as *Pietro Aaron: Toscanello in Music, Book II, Chapters XXXVII–XXXX, Supplement* (Colorado Springs, Colo.: Colorado College Music Press, 1970).

AGAZZARI, AGOSTINO. *Del sonare sopra'l basso con tutti li stromenti e dell'uso loro nel conserto* (Siena: Domenico Falcini, 1607; fac. Bologna: Forni Editore, 1985). Eng. trans. in Oliver Strunk, *Source Readings in Music History* (New York: W. W. Norton and Company, 1950), 424–31.

ANTEGNATI, COSTANZO. *L'arte organica di Costanzo Antegnati organista del duomo di Brescia* (Brescia: Francesco Tebaldino, 1608). Repr. and Ger. trans. by Renato Lunelli, ed., and Paolo Smets, trans. (Mainz: Rheingold-Verlag, 1958).

ARTUSI, GIOVANNI MARIA. *L'Artusi overo delle imperfettioni della moderna musica* (Venice: Vincenti, 1600); fac. ed. Giuseppe Vecchi (Bologna: Forni Editore, 1968).

——. *L'Artusi, della imperfettione della moderna musica, parte seconda* (Venice: Vincenti, 1603); fac. ed. Giuseppe Vecchi (Bologna: Forni Editore, 1968).

——. *Discorso secondo musicale di Antonio Braccino da Todi, per la dichiaratione della lettera posta ne' Scherzi Musicali del Sig. Claudio Monteverde* (Venice: Vincenti, 1608); fac. ed. Giuseppe Vecchi (Bologna: Forni Editore, 1968).

BANCHIERI, ADRIANO. *L'organo suonarino opera terza decima* (Venice: Amadino, 1605); 2nd edn. *opera ventesima quinta* (Venice: Amadino, 1611); *Appendice all'organo suonarino, opera xxxxiii* (Venice: Vincenti, 1638); fac. ed. Giulio Cattin (Amsterdam: Frits Knuf, 1969). Eng. trans. in Donald E. Marcase, 'Adriano Banchieri, "L'organo suonarino": Translation, Transcription and Commentary' (Ph.D. dissertation, Indiana University, 1970).

——. *Conclusioni nel suono dell'organo . . . opera vigesima* (Bologna: Giovanni Rossi, 1609; fac. ed. Bologna: Forni Editore, 1968). Eng. trans. Lee R. Garrett as *Adriano Banchieri: Conclusions for Playing the Organ (1609)* (Colorado Springs, Colo.: Colorado College Music Press, 1982).

——. *Cartella musicale nel canto figurato, fermo, & contrapunto . . . terza impressione* (Venice: Vincenti, 1614); fac. ed. Giuseppe Vecchi (Bologna: Forni Editore, 1968). Eng. trans. in Clifford Alan Cranna, Jr., 'Adriano Banchieri's *Cartella musicale* (1614): Translation and Commentary' (Ph.D. dissertation, Stanford University, 1981).

BARCOTTO, ANTONIO. *Regola, e breve raccordo Per far rendere agiustati, e regolati ogni sorta di istrumenti da vento, cioé Organi, Claviorgani, Regali e simili* (Padua, 1652). Ed. in Renato Lunelli, 'Un trattatello di Antonio Barcotto colma le lacune dell'"Arte Organica"', *Collectanea historiae musicae*, I (1953), 135–55.

BASSANO, GIOVANNI. *Ricercate, passaggi et cadentie* (Venice: Giacomo Vincenti and Ricciardo Amadino, 1585).

BERNHARD, CHRISTOPH. *Von der Singe-Kunst oder Manier* (1650), in Joseph Müller-Blattau, ed., *Die Kompositionslehre Heinrich Schützens in der Fassung seines Schülers Christoph Bernhard*, 2nd edn. (Kassel: Bärenreiter, 1963).

BIANCIARDI, FRANCESCO. *Breve regola per imparar'a sonare sopra il basso con ogni sorte d'istrumento* (Siena: Enrico Zucchifice, 1607).

BOVICELLI, GIOVANNI BATTISTA. *Regole, passaggi di musica* (Venice: Giacomo Vincenti, 1594); fac. ed. Nanie Bridgman (Kassel: Bärenreiter, 1957).

BRUNELLI, ANTONIO. *Regole utilissime per li scolari che desiderano imparare a cantare, sopra la pratica della musica* (Florence: Volemar Timan, 1606); partial trans. in Putnam Aldrich, *Rhythm in Seventeenth-Century Italian Monody* (New York: W.W. Norton & Co., 1966), 26–38.

——. *Varii esercitii . . . per i quali si potrà con facilità aquistare la dispositione per il cantare con passaggi* (Florence: Zanobi Pignoni e Comp., 1614), ed. Richard Erig (Zurich: Musikverlag zum Pelikan, 1977).

CARDANUS, HIERONYMUS. *Writings on Music*, trans. Clement A. Miller (American Institute of Musicology, 1973).

CERONE, PIETRO. *El melopeo y Maestro* (Naples: Iuan Bautista Gargano and Lucrecio Nucci, 1613); fac. ed. F. Alberto Gallo (Bologna: Editrice Forni, 1969).

CONFORTI, GIOVANNI LUCA. *Breve e facile maniera d'essercitarsi ad ogni scolaro non solamente a far passaggi . . .* (Rome, 1593; fac. New York: Broude Brothers, 1978), fac. with Ger. trans. by Johannes Wolf (Berlin: Martin Breslauer, 1922).

CRIVELLATI, CESARE. *Discorsi musicali, nelli quali si contengono non solo cose pertinenti alla teorica, ma eziandio alla pratica. Mediante le quali si potrà con facilità pervenire all'acquisto di così honorata scientia. Raccolti da diversi buoni autori da Cesare Crivellati medico Viterbese* (Viterbo: Agostino Discep., 1624).

DALLA CASA, GIROLAMO. *Il vero modo di diminuir con tutte le sorti di stromenti* (Venice: Angelo Gardano, 1584); fac. ed. Giuseppe Vecchi (Bologna: Arnaldo Forni, 1976).

DENIS, JEAN. *Traité de l'accord de l'espinette* (Paris: Robert Ballard, 1650); fac. ed. Alan Curtis (New York: Da Capo Press, 1969); Eng. trans. in Vincent J. Panetta, Jr., *Treatise on Harpsichord Tuning by Jean Denis* (Cambridge: Cambridge University Press, 1987).

DIRUTA, GIROLAMO. *Il Transilvano, dialogo sopra il vero modo di sonar organi, et istromenti da penna* (Venice: Giacomo Vincenti, 1593); fac. ed. Luisa Cervelli (Bologna: Forni Editore, 1969). Ed. with Eng. trans. in Murray C. Bradshaw and Edward J. Soehnlen, *Girolamo Diruta, 'The Transylvanian'*, 2 vols. (Ottawa: Institute of Mediaeval Music, 1984), i.

——. *Seconda parte del Transilvano, dialogo diviso in quattro libri* (Venice: Alessandro Vincenti, 1609; repr. 1622); fac. ed. Luisa Cervelli (Bologna: Forni Editore, 1969). Ed. with Eng. trans. in Murray C. Bradshaw and Edward J. Soehnlen, *Girolamo Diruta, 'The Transylvanian'*, 2 vols. (Ottawa: Institute of Mediaeval Music, 1984), ii.

DONI, GIOVANNI BATTISTA. *De' trattati di musica . . . tomo secondo* (Florence: La Stamperia Imperiale, 1763; fac. Bologna: Arnaldo Forni Editore, 1974).

FINCK, HERMANN. *Practica musica* (Wittenberg, Georg Rhaw, 1556; fac. Hildesheim: Georg Olms Verlag, 1971).

GAFFURIUS, FRANCHINUS. *Practica musice* (Milan, 1496; fac. edns. Westmead, UK: Gregg Press Ltd., 1967, and New York: Broude Brothers Ltd., 1979); Eng. trans. Clement A. Miller as *Franchinus Gaffurius, Practica musice* (American Institute of Musicology, 1968).

GALILEI, VINCENZO. *Dialogo della musica antica et della moderna* (Florence: Marescotti, 1581; fac. New York: Broude Brothers, 1967); Eng. trans. in Robert Henry Herman, '*Dialogo della musica antica et della moderna* of Vincenzo Galilei: Translation and Commentary', 2 vols. (Ph.D. dissertation, North Texas State University, 1973).

GALILEI, VINCENZO. *Discorso intorno all'opere di Gioseffo Zarlino* (Florence: Marescotti, 1589; fac. Milan: Bollettino Bibliografico Musicale, 1933).

GANASSI, SYLVESTRO. *Opera intitulata Fontegara* (Venice, 1535; fac. Milan: La Musica Moderna, 1934). Eng. trans. Dorothy Swainson as *Sylvestro Ganassi: Opera intitulata Fontegara* (Berlin and Lichterfelde: Robert Lienau, 1956).

———. *Regola rubertina* (Venice, 1542; fac. edn. Bologna: Forni Editore, 1970); Eng. trans. Daphne and Stephen Silvester (Berlin and Lichterfelde: Robert Lienau, 1972).

GIUSTINIANI, VINCENZO. *Discorso sopra la musica*; Eng. trans. Carol MacClintock (American Institute of Musicology, 1962).

HEYDEN, SEBALD. *De arte canendi* (Nuremberg: Joh. Petreium, 1540); trans. Clement A. Miller (American Institute of Musicology, 1972).

KIRCHER, ATHANASIUS. *Musurgia universalis*, 2 vols. (vol. i, Rome: Francisci Corbelletti, 1650; vol. ii, Rome: Grignani, 1650; fac. Hildesheim: Georg Olms Verlag, 1970).

LANFRANCO, GIOVANNI MARIA. *Scintille di musica* (Brescia: Lodovico Britannico, 1533); fac. ed. Giuseppe Massera (Bologna: Forni Editore, 1970); Eng. trans. in Barbara Lee, 'Giovanni Maria Lanfranco's *Scintille di musica* and its Relation to 16th-Century Music Theory' (Ph.D. dissertation, Cornell University, 1961).

MERSENNE, MARIN. *Harmonie universelle contenant la théorie et la pratique de la musique*, 2 vols. (Paris: Sebastien Cramoisy, 1636; fac. Paris: Centre National de la Recherche Scientifique, 1963).

NIVERS, GUILLAUME-GABRIEL. *Dissertation sur le chant grégorien* (Paris, 1683).

NORTH, ROGER. 'As to Musick', in *Notes of Me* (*c.*1695), ed. John Wilson in *Roger North on Music* (London: Novello and Company Ltd., 1959), 9–30.

OLIFANTE, GIOVANNI BATTISTA. *Trattato brevissimo intorno alle proportioni cantabili, composte dalli prattici musici, nelle loro messe, mottetti, madrigali, & altre opere* (Naples: Gio. Giacomo Carlino, 1611; fac. Bologna: Arnaldo Forni, 1981). Printed in Rocco Rodio, *Regole di musica* (see below).

PAREIA, BARTOLOMEO RAMIS DE. *Musica practica* (Bologna, 1482), ed. Johannes Wolf (Leipzig: Breitkopf und Härtel, 1901). Eng. trans. Clement A. Miller as *Bartolomeo Ramis de Pareia, Musica practica* (Neuhausen and Stuttgart: Hänssler Verlag, American Institute of Musicology, 1993).

PISA, AGOSTINO. *Battuta della musica dichiarata* (Rome: Bartolomeo Zannetti, 1611); fac. ed. Walther Dürr as *Breve dichiarazione della battuta musicale* (Bologna: Forni Editore, 1969).

PRAETORIUS, MICHAEL. *Syntagmatis musici . . . tomus secundus de organographia* (Wolfenbüttel: Elias Holwein, 1619); fac. ed. Wilibald Gurlitt (Kassel: Bärenreiter, 1958). Eng. trans. Harold Blumenfeld as *The Syntagma Musicum of Michael Praetorius: Volume Two De Organographia, First and Second Parts* (New York: Da Capo Press, 1980); Eng. trans. David Z. Crookes as *Praetorius, Syntagma Musicum II: De Organographia, Parts I and II tomus secundus* (Oxford: Clarendon Press, 1986).

———. *Syntagmatis musici . . . tomus tertius* (Wolfenbüttel: Elias Holwein, 1619); fac. ed. Wilibald Gurlitt (Kassel: Bärenreiter, 1958). Eng. trans. Hans A. Lampl as 'A Translation of *Syntagma musicum III* by Michael Praetorius' (DMA dissertation, University of Southern California, 1957).

RAVENSCROFT, THOMAS. *A Briefe Discourse of the True (but Neglected) Use of Charact'ring the Degrees . . .* (London: Edward Allde, 1614; fac. edn. New York: Broude Brothers Ltd., 1976).

RODIO, ROCCO. *Regole di musica . . . sotto brevissime risposte ad alcuni dubij propostigli da un Cavaliero, intorno alle varie opinioni de Contrapontisti con la dimostratione de tutti i canoni sopra il Canto Fermo, con li Contraponti doppij, e rivoltati, e loro Regole. Aggiontavi un'altra breve dimostratione de dodeci Tuoni Regolar, Finitie Trasportati. Et di nuovo da Don Gio. Battista Olifante aggiontovi un Trattato di Proportioni necessario à detto Libro, e ristampato* (Naples: Gio. Giacomo Carlino e Costantino Vitale, 1609; Olifante, *Trattato*, Naples: Carlino, 1611; fac. Bologna: Arnaldo Forni, 1981).

ROGNONI, FRANCESCO. *Selva de varii passaggi secondo l'uso moderno per cantare, & suonare con ogni sorte de stromenti* (Milan: Filippo Lomazzo, 1620); fac. ed. Guglielmo Barblan (Bologna: Arnaldo Forni, 1978).

SABBATINI, GALEAZZO. *Regola facile e breve per sonare sopra il basso continuo nell'organo, manacordo & altro simile istrumento* (Venice: Angelo Salvadori, 1628).

SPADI, GIOVANNI BATTISTA. *Libro de passaggi ascendenti et descendenti* (Venice: Alessandro Vincenti, 1624).

VICENTINO, NICOLA. *L'antica musica ridotta alla moderna prattica* (Rome: Antonio Barre, 1555); fac. ed. Edward E. Lowinsky (Kassel: Bärenreiter, 1959). Eng. trans. Maria Rika Maniates as *Nicola Vicentino, Ancient Music Adapted to Modern Practice* (New Haven: Yale University Press, 1996).

VIRGILIANO, AURELIO. *Il Dolcimelo*, fac. ed. Marcello Castellani, Archivum Musicum: Collana di testi rari, 11 (Florence: Studio per Edizioni Scelte, 1979).

ZACCONI, LODOVICO. *Prattica di musica* (Venice: Girolamo Polo, 1592; fac. Bologna: Forni Editore, 1976).

ZARLINO, GIOSEFFO. *Le istitutioni harmoniche* (Venice, 1558; fac. New York: Broude Brothers, 1965). Pt. III trans. Guy A. Marco and Claude V. Palisca as *Gioseffo Zarlino, The Art of Counterpoint: Part Three of 'Le istitutioni harmoniche,' 1558* (New Haven: Yale University Press, 1968); pt. IV trans. Vered Cohen as *On the Modes: Part Four of 'Le istitutioni harmoniche', 1558, Gioseffo Zarlino* (New Haven: Yale University Press, 1983).

——. *Dimostrationi harmoniche* (Venice: Francesco dei Francheschi Senese, 1571; fac. Ridgewood, NJ: Gregg Press, 1966).

Bibliography

⟨❦⟩

BOOKS, ARTICLES, AND REVIEWS

ADAMS, K. GARY, and KIEL, DYKE, *Claudio Monteverdi: A Guide to Research* (New York: Garland Publishing, Inc., 1989).

ADRIO, ADAM, *Die Anfänge des geistlichen Konzerts* (Berlin: Junker und Dünnhaupt Verlag, 1935).

ALDRICH, PUTNAM, *Rhythm in Seventeenth-Century Italian Monody* (New York: W. W. Norton & Co., 1966).

ALLSOP, PETER, 'The Role of the Stringed Bass as a Continuo Instrument in Italian Seventeenth Century Instrumental Music', *Chelys: The Journal of the Viola da Gamba Society*, 8 (1978–9), 31–7.

ALTENBURG, DETLEF, 'Die Toccata zu Monteverdis "Orfeo"', *Bericht über den internationalen musikwissenschaftlichen Kongress Berlin 1974* (Kassel: Bärenreiter, 1980), 271–4.

ANNIBALDI, CLAUDIO, 'L'archivio musicale Doria Pamphilj: Saggio sulla cultura aristocratica a Roma fra 16° e 19° secolo (II)', *Studi musicali*, 11 (1982), 277–344.

APEL, WILLI, *The History of Keyboard Music to 1700*, trans. Hans Tischler (Bloomington, Ind.: Indiana University Press, 1972).

APFEL, ERNST, 'Zur Frage des Rhythms in der italienischen Monodie des 17. Jahrhunderts', *Die Musikforschung*, 21 (1968), 473–81.

ARMSTRONG, JAMES FOSTER, 'The Vesper Psalms and Magnificats of Maurizio Cazzati' (Ph.D. dissertation, Harvard University, 1969).

——'The *Antiphonae, seu sacrae cantiones* (1613) of Giovanni Francesco Anerio: A Liturgical Study', *Analecta musicologica*, 14 (1974), 89–150.

——'How to Compose a Psalm: Ponzio and Cerone Compared', *Studi musicali*, 7 (1978), 103–39.

ARNOLD, DENIS, 'Giovanni Croce and the "Concertato" Style', *Musical Quarterly*, 39 (1953), 37–48.

——'Notes on Two Movements of the Monteverdi "Vespers"', *Monthly Musical Record*, 84 (Mar.–Apr. 1954), 59–66.

——'Instruments in Church: Some Facts and Figures', *Monthly Musical Record*, 85 (Feb. 1955), 32–8.

——'Alessandro Grandi, A Disciple of Monteverdi', *Musical Quarterly*, 43 (1957), 171–86.

——'Brass Instruments in Italian Church Music of the Sixteenth and Early Seventeenth Centuries', *Brass Quarterly*, 1 (1957), 81–92.

——'Monteverdi's Church Music: Some Venetian Traits', *Monthly Musical Record*, 88 (May–June 1958), 83–91.

——'The Influence of Ornamentation on the Structure of Early 17th Century Music', *Bericht über den siebenten internationalen musikwissenschaftlichen Kongress Köln 1958* (Kassel: Bärenreiter, 1959), 57–8.

——'Music at the Scuola di San Rocco', *Music & Letters*, 40 (1959), 229–41.

——'The Significance of "Cori spezzati"', *Music & Letters*, 40 (1959), 4–14.

——'The Monteverdian Succession at St Mark's', *Music & Letters*, 42 (1961), 205–11.

ARNOLD, DENIS, *Monteverdi* (London: J. M. Dent & Sons, Ltd., 1963).

—— 'Monteverdi and the Technique of "Concertato"', *Amor Artis Bulletin*, 6 (Apr. 1967), 7–10.

—— 'Formal Design in Monteverdi's Church Music', in Monterosso, ed., *Claudio Monteverdi e il suo tempo*, 187–216.

—— 'A Background Note on Monteverdi's Hymn Settings', in *Scritti in onore di Luigi Ronga* (Milan: Ricciardo Ricciardi, 1973), 33–44.

—— *Monteverdi*, rev. edn. (London: J. M. Dent & Sons Ltd., 1975).

—— Reviews of *L'Orfeo*, ed. Edward H. Tarr and *Vespro della Beata Vergine*, ed. Jürgen Jürgens, *Early Music*, 6 (1978), 459–64.

—— *Giovanni Gabrieli and the Music of the Venetian High Renaissance* (London: Oxford University Press, 1979).

—— 'Cori spezzati', in *The New Grove*, iv. 776.

—— *Monteverdi's Church Music* (BBC Music Guides; London: British Broadcasting Corporation, 1982).

—— *Monteverdi*, 3rd edn., rev. Tim Carter (London: J. M. Dent & Sons Ltd., 1990).

—— and FORTUNE, NIGEL, eds., *The Monteverdi Companion* (London: Faber and Faber, 1968).

—— —— eds., *The New Monteverdi Companion* (London: Faber and Faber, 1985).

ARNOLD, F. T., *The Art of Accompaniment from a Thorough-Bass as Practised in the XVIIth & XVIIIth Centuries* (Oxford: Oxford University Press, 1931; repr. edn. New York: Dover Publications, 1965).

ASHWORTH, JACK, 'Keyboard Instruments', in Kite-Powell, ed., *A Performer's Guide to Renaissance Music*, 175–88.

—— and O'DETTE, PAUL, 'Proto-Continuo: Overview and Practical Applications', in Kite-Powell, ed., *A Performer's Guide to Renaissance Music*, 203–13.

ATCHERSON, WALTER, 'Key and Mode in Seventeenth-Century Music Theory Books', *Journal of Music Theory*, 17 (1973), 204–32.

ATKINSON, CHARLES M., 'Micheli, Romano', *The New Grove*, xii. 267.

BAINES, FRANCIS, 'What Exactly is a Violone? A Note towards a Solution', *Early Music*, 5 (1977), 173–6.

BANK, J. A., *Tactus, Tempo and Notation in Mensural Music from the 13th to the 17th Century* (Amsterdam: Annie Bank, 1972).

BARBIERI, PATRIZIO, 'Conflitti di intonazione tra cembalo, liuto e archi nel "Concerto" italiano del Seicento', in Pierluigi Petrobelli and Gloria Staffieri, eds., *Studi Corelliani IV: Atti del Quarto Congresso Internazionale*, Fusignano, 4–7 Sept. 1986 (Florence: Leo S. Olschki Editore, 1990), 123–52.

—— 'Chiavette and Modal Transposition in Italian Practice (c.1500–1837), *Recercare*, 3 (1991), 5–79.

—— 'Violin Intonation: A Historical Survey', *Early Music*, 19 (1991), 69–88.

—— 'On a Continuo Organ Part Attributed to Palestrina', *Early Music*, 22 (1994), 587–605.

BARBLAN, GUGLIELMO, ed., *Musiche della Cappella di S. Barbara in Mantova* (Florence: Leo S. Olschki Editore, 1972).

—— GALLICO, CLAUDIO, and PANNAIN, GUIDO, *Claudio Monteverdi* (Turin: Edizioni RAI Radiotelevisione Italiana, 1967).

BARTLETT, CLIFFORD, *Monteverdi Vespers (1610): Guide to Liturgical Context* (Huntingdon, Cambs.: King's Music, 1989).

—— and HOLMAN, PETER, 'Giovanni Gabrieli: A Guide to the Performance of his Instrumental Music', *Early Music*, 3 (1975), 29–32.

BATES, ROBERT FREDERICK, 'From Mode to Key: A Study of Seventeenth-Century French Liturgical Organ Music and Music Theory' (Ph.D. dissertation, Stanford University, 1986).

BENADE, ARTHUR H., *Fundamentals of Musical Acoustics* (New York: Oxford University Press, 1976).

BERETTA, OTTAVIO, 'Documenti inediti su Giovanni Giacomo Gastoldi scoperti negli archivi mantovani', *Rivista internazionale di musica sacra*, 14 (1993), 270–7.

BERGER, ANNA MARIA BUSSE, 'The Relationship of Perfect and Imperfect Time in Italian Theory of the Renaissance', *Early Music History*, 5 (1985), 1–28.

—— 'The Myth of *diminutio per tertiam partem*', *Journal of Musicology*, 8 (1990), 398–426.

—— *Mensuration and Proportion Signs: Origins and Evolution* (Oxford: Clarendon Press, 1993).

BERGER, KAROL, *Musica ficta* (Cambridge: Cambridge University Press, 1987).

BESUTTI, PAOLA, 'Ceremoniale e repertorio liturgico della basilica palatina di Santa Barbara in Mantova' (Tesi di laurea, University of Parma, 1984–5).

—— 'Catalogo tematico delle monodie liturgiche della Basilica Palatina di S. Barbara in Mantova', *Le fonti musicali in Italia*, 2 (1988), 53–66.

—— 'Testi e molodie per la liturgia della Cappella di Santa Barbara in Mantova', in *Atti del XIV congresso della Società internazionale di musicologia* (Turin: E.D.T. Edizioni, 1990), 68–77.

—— 'Un tardivo repertorio di canto piano', in *Tradizione manoscritta e pratica musicale: I codici di Puglia* (Florence: Leo S. Olschki, 1990), 87–97.

—— 'Giovanni Pierluigi da Palestrina e la liturgia mantovana', in *Atti del II Convegno internazionale di studi palestriniani* (Palestrina: Fondazione G. Pierluigi da Palestrina, 1991), 157–64.

—— 'Ricorrenze motiviche, canti dati e "cantus firmus" nella produzione sacra di Claudio Monteverdi' (paper delivered at Convegno, Claudio Monteverdi: Studi e prospettive, Mantua, 21–4 Oct. 1993).

—— '"Ave Maris Stella": La tradizione mantovane nuovamente posta in musica da Monteverdi' in Paola Besutti, Teresa M. Gialdroni, and Rodolfo Baroncini, eds., *Claudio Monteverdi: Studi e prospettive, Atti del Convegno (Mantova, 21–24 ottobre 1993)* (Florence: Olschki, 1993), 57–77.

BIELLA, GIUSEPPE, 'La "Messa" il "Vespro" e i "Sacri Concenti" di Claudio Monteverdi', *Musica sacra*, 2nd ser., 9 (1964), 105–15.

BLACHLY, ALEXANDER, 'On Singing and the Vocal Ensemble I', in Kite-Powell, ed., *A Performer's Guide to Renaissance Music*, 13–25.

BLACKBURN, BONNIE J., 'On Compositional Process in the Fifteenth Century', *Journal of the American Musicological Society*, 40 (1987), 210–84.

BLACKWOOD, EASLEY, *The Structure of Recognizable Diatonic Tunings* (Princeton: Princeton University Press, 1985).

BLAZEY, DAVID A., 'A Liturgical Role for Montevedi's *Sonata sopra Sancta Maria*', *Early Music*, 18 (1989), 175–82.

—— 'The Litany in 17th-Century Italy', 2 vols. (Ph.D. dissertation, University of Durham, 1990).

BONCELLA, PAUL ANTHONY LUKE, 'From Behind the Propaganda: a New Anatomy of Caccini's *Esclamazioni*', paper delivered at Seventh Biennial Conference on Baroque Music, Birmingham, England, 4–7 July, 1996.

BONGE, DALE, 'Gaffurius on Pulse and Tempo: A Reinterpretation', *Musica disciplina*, 36 (1982), 167–74.

BONTA, STEPHEN, 'Liturgical Problems in Monteverdi's Marian Vespers', *Journal of the American Musicological Society*, 20 (1967), 87–106.

—— 'The Uses of the Sonata da Chiesa', *Journal of the American Musicological Society*, 22 (1969), 54–84.

BONTA, STEPHEN, 'A Formal Convention in 17th-Century Italien [*sic*] Instrumental Music', in *International Musicological Society: Report of the Eleventh Congress: Copenhagen 1972* (Copenhagen: Wilhelm Hansen, 1974), 288–93.

—— 'From Violone to Violoncello: A Question of Strings?', *Journal of the American Musical Instrument Society*, 3 (1977), 64–99.

—— 'Terminology for the Bass Violin in the 17th-Century', *Journal of the American Musical Instrument Society*, 4 (1978), 5–42.

—— 'Catline Strings Revisited', *Journal of the American Musical Instrument Society*, 14 (1988), 38–60.

—— 'Corelli's Heritage: The Early Bass Violin in Italy', in Pierluigi Petrobelli and Gloria Staffieri, eds., *Studi Corelliani IV: Atti del Quarto Congresso Internazionale*, Fusignano, 4–7 Sept. 1986 (Florence: Leo S. Olschki Editore, 1990), 217–31.

—— 'The Use of Instruments in Sacred Music in Italy, 1560–1700', *Early Music*, 18 (1990), 519–35.

—— 'The Use of Instruments in the Ensemble Canzona and Sonata in Italy, 1580–1650', *Recercare*, 4 (1992), 23–43.

—— 'Clef, Mode, and Instruments in Italy, 1540–1675' (unpublished paper).

BORGIR, THARALD, *The Performance of the Basso Continuo in Italian Baroque Music* (Ann Arbor: UMI Press, 1987).

BORROWDALE, ROBERT JAMES, 'The *Musices liber primus* of Diego Ortiz: Spanish Musician' (Ph.D. dissertation, University of Southern California, 1952).

BOUWSMA, WILLIAM J., *Venice and the Defense of Republican Liberty* (Berkeley: University of California Press, 1968).

BOWERS, JANE, 'New Light on the Development of the Transverse Flute between about 1650 and about 1770', *Galpin Society Journal*, 3 (1977), 5–56.

BOWERS, ROGER, 'Some Reflection upon Notation and Proportions in Monteverdi's Mass and Vespers of 1610', *Music & Letters*, 73 (1992), 347–98.

—— 'Correspondence', *Music & Letters*, 74 (1993), 487–95; and 75 (1994), 145–54.

—— 'Proportional Notations in Banchieri's Theory and Monteverdi's Music', in Monterosso, ed., *Performing Practice in Monteverdi's Music*, 53–92.

—— 'Proportional Notations in Montererdis "Orfeo"', *Music & Letters*, 76 (1995), 149–67.

BOYDEN, DAVID D., 'Monteverdi's *violini piccoli alla francese* and *viole da brazzo*', *Annales musicologiques*, 6 (1958–63), 387–401.

BRADSHAW, MURRAY C., *The Origin of the Toccata* (American Institute of Musicology, 1972).

—— 'Tonal Design in the Venetian Intonation and Toccata', *Music Review*, 35 (1974), 101–19.

—— *The Falsobordone, A Study in Renaissance and Baroque Music* (Musical Studies and Documents, 34; Stuttgart: American Institute of Musicology/Hänssler-Verlag, 1978).

—— 'The Craft of the Renaissance Organist', *American Organist*, 15/2 (Feb. 1981), 44–5.

—— 'Lodovico Viadana as a Composer of Falsobordoni', *Studi musicali*, 19 (1990), 91–131.

—— 'Giovanni Luca Conforti and Vocal Embellishment: From Formula to Artful Improvisation', *Performance Practice Review*, 8 (1995), 5–27.

BRAINARD, PAUL, 'Zur Deutung der Diminution in der Tactuslehre des Michael Praetorius', *Die Musikforschung*, 17 (1964), 169–74.

—— 'Proportional Notation in the Music of Schütz and his Contemporaries', *Current Musicology*, 50 (1992), 21–46.

BRATTON, LEE BRYANT, 'Amadio Freddi's "Messa, Vespro, et Compieta" of 1616' (DMA dissertation, University of Texas at Austin, 1986).

BRIDGMAN, NANIE, 'Giovanni Camillo Maffei et sa lettre sur le chant,' *Revue de musicologie*, 38 (1956), 3–34.

BROWN, HOWARD M., *Sixteenth-Century Instrumentation: The Music of the Florentine Intermedii* (American Institute of Musicology, 1973).

—— *Embellishing Sixteenth-Century Music* (London: Oxford University Press, 1976).

—— and SADIE, STANLEY, eds., *Performance Practice: Music before 1600* (New York and London: W. W. Norton & Company, 1989).

—— and —— eds., *Performance Practice: Music after 1600* (New York and London: W. W. Norton & Company, 1989).

BRYANT, DAVID DOUGLAS, 'Liturgy, Ceremonial and Sacred Music in Venice at the Time of the Counter-Reformation' (Ph.D. dissertation, King's College, London, 1981).

—— 'The *cori spezzati* of St Mark's: Myth and Reality', *Early Music History*, 1 (1981), 165–86.

—— 'Andrea Gabrieli e la "musica di Stato" Veneziana', in *XLII Festival internazionale di Musica Contemporanea: Andrea Gabrieli 1585–1985* (Venice, 1985), 29–45.

BUETENS, STANLEY, 'Theorbo Accompaniments of Early Seventeenth-Century Italian Monody', *Journal of the Lute Society of America*, 6 (1973), 37–45.

BUELOW, GEORGE, 'Symposium on Seventeenth-Century Music Theory: Germany', *Journal of Music Theory*, 16 (1972), 36–49.

BUKOFZER, MANFRED F., 'The Beginnings of Choral Polyphony', in *Studies in Medieval and Renaissance Music* (New York: W. W. Norton & Company, 1950), 181–6.

BURKE, JOHN, *Musicians of S. Maria Maggiore Rome, 1600–1700*, supplement to *Note d'archivio, nuova serie*, 2 (Venice: Fondazione Levi, 1984).

BUSSI, FRANCESCO, *Piacenza, Archivio del Duomo: Catalogo del fondo musicale* (Milan: Istituto Editoriale Italiano, 1967).

CALDWELL, JOHN, 'Historic Organs in Italy, Denmark and Switzerland', *Early Music*, 22 (1994), 341–2.

CARTER, STEWART, 'Francesco Rognoni's *Selva de varii passaggi* (1620): Fresh Details concerning Early-Baroque Vocal Ornamentation', *Performance Practice Review*, 2 (1989), 5–33.

—— 'The String Tremolo in the 17th Century', *Early Music*, 19 (1991), 43–59.

—— 'Sackbut', in Kite-Powell, ed., *A Performer's Guide to Renaissance Music*, 97–108.

—— ed., *A Performer's Guide to Seventeenth-Century Music* (New York: Schirmer Books, 1997).

CARTER, TIM, 'On the Composition and Performance of Caccini's *Le nuove musiche* (1602)', *Early Music*, 12 (1984), 208–17.

—— 'Artusi, Monteverdi, and the Poetics of Modern Music', in Nancy Kovaleff Baker and Barbara Russano Hanning, eds., *Musical Humanism and its Legacy: Essays in Honor of Claude V. Palisca* (Stuyvesant, NY: Pendragon Press, 1992), 171–94.

—— ' "An Air New and Grateful to the Ear": The Concept of *Aria* in Late Renaissance and Early Baroque Italy', *Music Analysis*, 12 (1993), 127–45.

CARVER, ANTHONY F., 'The Psalms of Willaert and his North Italian Contemporaries', *Acta musicologica*, 47 (1975), 270–83.

—— 'The Development of Sacred Polychoral Music to 1580' (Ph.D. dissertation, University of Birmingham, 1980).

—— 'Polychoral Music: A Venetian Phenomenon?', *Proceedings of the Royal Musical Association*, 107 (1981–2), 1–24.

CERVELLI, LUISA, ' "Del sonare sopra 'l basso con tutti li stromenti" ', *Rivista musicale italiana*, 57 (1955), 121–35.

CHAFE, ERIC T., *Monteverdi's Tonal Language* (New York: Schirmer Books, 1992).

CHARTERIS, RICHARD, 'The Performance of Giovanni Gabrieli's Vocal Works: Indications in the Early Sources', *Music & Letters*, 71 (1990), 336–51.

CHEW, GEOFFREY, 'The Perfections of Modern Music: Consecutive Fifths and Tonal Coherence in Monteverdi', *Music Analysis*, 8 (1989), 247–73.

——'The Platonic Agenda of Monteverdi's *Seconda pratica*: A Case Study from the Eighth Book of Madrigals', *Music Analysis*, 12 (1993), 147–68.

CHRYSANDER, FRIEDRICH, 'Ludovico Zacconi als Lehrer des Kunstgesangs', *Vierteljahrsschrift für Musikwissenschaft*, 7 (1891), 337–96; 9 (1893), 249–310; 10 (1894), 531–67.

CLARK, J. BUNKER, *Transposition in Seventeenth Century English Organ Accompaniments and the Transposing Organ* (Detroit Monographs in Musicology, 4; Detroit: Information Coordinators, Inc., 1974).

COHEN, ALBERT, 'Symposium on Seventeenth-Century Music Theory: France', *Journal of Music Theory*, 16 (1972), 17–35.

——'Pierre Maillart', *The New Grove*, xi. 536–7.

COLLINS, MICHAEL B., 'The Performance of Sesquialtera and Hemiolia in the 16th Century', *Journal of the American Musicological Society*, 17 (1964), 5–28.

COLUMBRO, MARY ELECTA, 'Ostinato Technique in the Franco-Flemish Motet: 1480–ca. 1562' (Ph.D. dissertation, Case Western Reserve University, 1974).

COPEMAN, HAROLD, *Singing in Latin or Pronunciation Explor'd* (Oxford, 1990).

CORYAT, THOMAS, *Coryat's Crudities* (London: William Stansby, 1611; repr. edn. Glasgow: James MacLehose and Sons, 1905).

COVEY-CRUMP, ROGERS, 'Pythagoras at the Forge: Tuning in Early Music', in Knighton and Fallows, eds., *Companion to Medieval and Renaissance Music*, 317–26.

CRAMER, EUGENE C., 'The Significance of Clef Combinations in the Music of Tomás Luis de Victoria', *American Choral Review*, 18 (1976), 3–11.

CRAWFORD, DAVID E., 'Vespers Polyphony at Modena's Cathedral in the First Half of the Sixteenth Century' (Ph.D. dissertation, University of Illinois, 1967).

CULLEY, THOMAS D., *Jesuits and Music*, i: *A Study of the Musicians Connected with the German College in Rome during the 17th Century and of their Activities in Northern Europe* (St Louis: St Louis University, 1970).

——'Musical Activity in some Sixteenth Century Jesuit Colleges, with Special Reference to the Venerable English College in Rome from 1579 to 1589', *Analecta musicologica*, 19 (1979), 1–29.

CUMMINGS, ANTHONY M., 'Toward an Interpretation of the Sixteenth-Century Motet', *Journal of the American Musicological Society*, 34 (1981), 43–59.

CUSICK, SUZANNE G., 'Gendering Modern Music: Thoughts on the Monteverdi–Artusi Controversy', *Journal of the American Musicological Society*, 46 (1993), 1–25.

CYR, MARY, *Performing Baroque Music* (Portland, Oreg.: Amadeus Press, 1992).

D'ACCONE, FRANK A., 'The Musical Chapels at the Florentine Cathedral and Baptistry during the First Half of the 16th Century', *Journal of the American Musicological Society*, 24 (1971), 1–50.

——'Music and Musicians at Santa Maria del Fiore in the Early Quattrocento', in *Scritti in onore di Luigi Ronga* (Milan: Ricciardo Ricciardi, 1973), 99–126.

DAHLHAUS, CARL, 'Über das Tempo in der Musik des späten 16. Jahrhunderts', *Musica*, 13 (1959), 767–9.

——'Zur Theorie des Tactus im 16. Jahrhundert', *Archiv für Musikwissenschaft*, 17 (1960), 22–39.

——'Zur Entstehung des modernen Taktsystems im 17. Jahrhundert', *Archiv für Musikwissenschaft*, 18 (1961), 223–40.

——'Zur Taktlehre des Michael Praetorius', *Die Musikforschung*, 17 (1964), 162–9.

——'Zur Geschichte des Taktschlagens im frühen 17. Jahrhundert', in Robert L. Marshall, ed.,

Studies in Renaissance and Baroque Music in Honor of Arthur Mendel (Kassel: Bärenreiter, 1974), 117–23.

—— 'Harmony', in *The New Grove*, viii. 175–88.

—— *Studies on the Origin of Harmonic Tonality*, trans. Robert O. Gjerdingen (Princeton: Princeton University Press, 1990).

D'ALESSI, GIOVANNI, 'Precursors of Adriano Willaert in the Practice of *coro spezzato*', *Journal of the American Musicological Society*, 5 (1952), 187–210.

DARBELLAY, ETIENNE, 'Tempo Relationships in Frescobaldi's *Primo libro di capricci*', in Alexander Silbiger, ed., *Frescobaldi Studies* (Durham, NC: Duke University Press, 1987), 301–26.

D'ARPA, NICOLETTA BILLIO, 'Amadio Freddi, musicista padovano', *Il Santo. Rivista Antoniana di storia dottrina arte*, 27 (1987), 241–63.

—— 'Musica sacra tra stile antico e moderno: La Messa, Vespro et Compieta (Venezia 1616) di Amadio Freddi', *Rivista internazionale di musica sacra*, 11 (1990), 287–322.

DAVARI, STEFANO, *Notizie biografiche del distinto Maestro di Musica Claudio Monteverdi* (Mantua: G. Mondovi, 1885).

DAVIDSON, JIM, *Lyrebird Rising* (Portland, Oreg.: Amadeus Press, 1994).

DEFORD, RUTH I., 'Tempo Relationships between Duple and Triple Time in the Sixteenth Century', *Early Music History*, 14 (1995), 1–51.

—— 'Zacconi's Theories of *Tactus* and Mensuration', *Journal of Musicology*, 14 (1996), 151–82.

DE' PAOLI, DOMENICO, *Claudio Monteverdi* (Milan: Editore Ulrico Hoepli, 1945).

—— *Claudio Monteverdi: Lettere, dediche e prefazioni* (Rome: Edizioni de Santis, 1973).

—— *Monteverdi* (Milan: Rusconi, 1979).

DEL'RIO, MARTIN ANTVERPIENSE, *In Canticum Canticorum Salomonis commentarius litteralis, et catena mystica* (Lyons: Cardon, 1611).

DICKEY, BRUCE, 'Cornett and Sackbut', in Stewart Carter, ed., *A Performer's Guide to Seventeenth-Century Music* (New York: Schirmer Books, 1997), 98–115.

—— 'Ornamentation in Early-Seventeenth-Century Italian Music', in Stewart Carter, ed., *A Performer's Guide to Seventeenth-Century Music*, 245–68.

DIXON, GRAHAM, 'The Origins of the Roman "Colossal Baroque"', *Proceedings of the Royal Musical Association*, 106 (1979–80), 115–28.

—— 'G. F. Anerio (1567–1630) and the Roman School', *Musical Times*, 121 (1980), 366–8.

—— 'Musical Activity in the Church of the Gesù in Rome during the Early Baroque', *Archivum historicum Societatis Iesu*, 49 (1980), 323–37.

—— 'The Cappella of S. Maria in Trastevere (1605–45): An Archival Study', *Music & Letters*, 62 (1981), 30–40.

—— 'Liturgical Music in Rome (1605–45)' (Ph.D. dissertation, University of Durham, 1981).

—— 'The Pantheon and Music in Minor Churches in Seventeenth-Century Rome', *Studi musicali*, 10 (1981), 265–77.

—— 'Progressive Tendencies in the Roman Motet during the Early Seventeenth Century', *Acta musicologica*, 53 (1981), 105–19.

—— 'Roman Church Music: The Place of Instruments after 1600', *Galpin Society Journal*, 34 (1981), 51–61.

—— 'Lenten Devotions: Some Memoriae of Baroque Rome', *Musical Times*, 124 (1983), 157–61.

—— 'Continuo Scoring in the Early Baroque: The Role of Bowed-Bass Instruments', *Chelys: The Journal of the Viola da Gamba Society*, 15 (1986), 38–53.

—— 'Agostino Agazzari (1578–after 1640): The Theoretical Writings', *Research Chronicle*, 20 (1986–7), 39–52.

DIXON, GRAHAM, 'Monteverdi's Vespers of 1610: "della Beata Vergine"?', *Early Music*, 15 (1987), 386–9.

—— 'Fine if Unauthentic Interpretations', *Classic CD* (Feb. 1991), 97.

—— 'Giovanni Amigone, un cantore lombardo del Seicento e il suo metodo didatico', in *Seicento inesplorato: Atti del II convegno internazionale sulla musica in area lombardo-padana del secolo XVII* (Como: AMIS, 1993), 318–38.

—— ' "Behold our Affliction": Celebration and Supplication in the Gonzaga Household', *Early Music*, 24 (1996), 250–61.

DOMBOIS, EUGEN M., 'Correct and Easy Fret Placement', *Journal of the Lute Society of America*, 6 (1973), 30–2.

—— Varieties of Meantone Temperament Realized on the Lute', *Journal of the Lute Society of America*, 7 (1974), 82–9.

DONATI, PIER PAOLO; GIORGETTI, RENZO; LIVI, CARLO ALBERTO; MISCHIATI, OSCAR, and TAGLIVAVINI, LUIGI GERDINANDO, *Arte nell'Aretino: La tutela e il restauro degli organi storici; organi restaurati dal XVI al XIX secolo* (Florence: Edam, 1980).

DONESMONDI, IPPOLITO, *Cronologia d'alcune cose più notabili di Mantova* (Mantua: Aurelio and Lodovico Osanna fratelli, 1615).

—— *Dell'istoria ecclesiastica di Mantova . . . parte seconda* (Mantua: Aurelio and Lodovico Osanna fratelli, 1616).

DONINGTON, ROBERT, *A Performer's Guide to Baroque Music* (New York: Charles Scribner's Sons, 1973).

—— *The Interpretation of Early Music* (New York: St Martin's Press, 1974).

—— *String Playing in Baroque Music* (New York: Charles Scribner's Sons, 1977).

—— Review of Greta Moens-Haenen, *Das Vibrato in der Musik des Barock*, *Early Music*, 16 (1988), 571–3.

DOUGLASS, DAVID, 'The Violin', in Kite-Powell, ed., *A Performer's Guide to Renaissance Music*, 125–38.

DUFFIN, ROSS W., 'National Pronunciations of Latin ca. 1490–1600', *Journal of Musicology*, 4 (1985–6), 217–26.

—— 'Tuning and Temperament', in Kite-Powell, ed., *A Performer's Guide to Renaissance Music*, 238–47.

—— 'Shawm and Curtal', in Kite-Powell, ed., *A Performer's Guide to Renaissance Music*, 69–75.

—— 'Pronunciation Guides', in Kite-Powell, ed., *A Performer's Guide to Renaissance Music*, 257–9.

DÜRR, WALTHER, 'Auftakt und Taktschlag in der Musik um 1600', in Georg von Dadelsen and Andreas Holschneider, eds., *Festschrift Walter Gerstenberg zum 60. Geburtstag* (Wolfenbüttel: Möseler Verlag, 1964), 26–36.

EBERLEIN, ROLAND, 'Die Taktwechsel in Monteverdis Marienvesper', *Music und Kirche*, 62 (1992), 184–9.

EDWARDS, JEAN, 'The Experience of Early Music Singing', *Continuo*, 8 (1984), 2–5.

EGGEBRECHT, HANS HEINRICH, 'Arten des Generalbasses im frühen und mittleren 17. Jahrhundert', *Archiv für Musikwissenschaft*, 14 (1957), 61–82.

EINSTEIN, ALFRED, *The Italian Madrigal*, 3 vols., 2nd edn. (Princeton: Princeton University Press, 1971).

EITNER, ROBERT, *Biographisch-bibliographisches Quellen-Lexikon* (Leipzig: Breitkopf und Härtel, 1898–1904).

ENGELBRECHT, CHRISTIANE, 'Eine Sonata con voce von Giovanni Gabrieli', in *Bericht über den internationalen musikwissenschaftlichen Kongress Hamburg 1956* (Kassel: Bärenreiter Verlag, 1957).

EPSTEIN, PETER, 'Zur Rhythmisierung eines Ritornells von Monteverdi', *Archiv für Musikwissenschaft*, 8 (1926), 416–19.

ERIG, RICHARD, *Italienische Diminutionen* (Zurich: Amadeus Verlag, 1979).

FABBRI, PAOLO, *Monteverdi* (Turin: E.D.T. Edizioni, 1985); Eng. trans. Tim Carter (Cambridge: Cambridge University Press, 1994).

FEDERHOFER, HELMUT, 'Zur Chiavetten-Frage', *Anzeiger der phil.-hist. Kl. der Österreichischen Akademie der Wissenschaft*, 10 (1952), 139–52.

—— 'Musica poetica und musikalische Figur in ihrer Bedeutung für die Kirchenmusik des 16. und 17. Jahrhunderts, *Acta musicologica*, 65 (1993), 119–33.

FELLER, MARILYN, 'The New Style of Giulio Caccini, Member of the Florentine Camerata', in *Bericht über den siebenten internationalen musikwissenschaftlichen Kongress Köln 1958* (Kassel: Bärenreiter, 1959), 102–4.

FELLERER, KARL GUSTAV, 'Monodie und Diminutionsmodelle', in *Sbornik Praci Filosoficke Fakulty Brnenske University*, 9 (1965), 79–85.

FENLON, IAIN, 'The Monteverdi Vespers: Suggested Answers to some Fundamental Questions', *Early Music*, 5 (1977), 380–7.

—— *Music and Patronage in Sixteenth-Century Mantua*, 2 vols. (Cambridge: Cambridge University Press, 1980).

FERAND, ERNEST T., 'Die Motetti, Madrigali, et Canzoni Francesi . . . Diminuiti . . . des Giovanni Bassano (1591)', in Lothar Hoffmann-Erbrecht and Helmut Hucke, eds., *Festschrift Helmuth Osthoff zum 65. Geburtstage* (Tutzing: Hans Schneider, 1961), 75–101.

—— *Improvisation in Nine Centuries of Western Music* (Anthology of Music, 12; Cologne: Arno Volk Verlag, 1961).

—— 'Didactic Embellishment Literature in the Late Renaissance: A Survey of Sources', in Jan La Rue, ed., *Aspects of Medieval and Renaissance Music: A Birthday Offering to Gustave Reese* (New York: W. W. Norton and Company, 1966), 154–72.

FINSCHER, LUDWIG, ed., *Claudio Monteverdi. Festschrift Reinhold Hammerstein zum 70. Geburtstag* (Laaber: Laaber Verlag, 1986).

FISCHER, HENRY GEORGE, *The Renaissance Sackbut and its Use Today* (New York: The Metropolitan Museum of Art, 1984).

FISCHER, KLAUS, *Die Psalmkompositionen in Rom um 1600 (ca. 1570–1630)* (Kölner Beiträge zur Musikforschung, 98; Regensburg: Gustav Bosse Verlag, 1979).

FOLLINO, FEDERICO, *Compendio delle sontuose feste fatte l'anno M.DC.VIII. nella città di Mantova, per le reali nozze del Serenissimo Prencipe D. Francesco Gonzaga, con la Serenissima Infante Margherita di Savoia* (Mantua: Aurelio et Lodovico Osanna, 1608).

FORTUNE, NIGEL, 'Continuo Instrumentation in Italian Monodies', *Galpin Society Journal*, 4 (1953), 10–13.

—— 'Italian 17th-Century Singing', *Music & Letters*, 35 (1954), 206–19.

FRANKLIN, HARRIET A., 'Musical Activity in Ferrara, 1578–1618', 2 vols. (Ph.D. dissertation, Brown University, 1976).

GABLE, FREDERICK K., 'Some Observations concerning Baroque and Modern Vibrato', *Performance Practice Review*, 5 (1992), 90–102.

—— 'Resource Materials', in Kite-Powell, ed., *A Performer's Guide to Renaissance Music*, 235–7.

GALLICO, CLAUDIO, 'Newly Discovered Documents Concerning Monteverdi', *Musical Quarterly*, 48 (1962), 68–72.

GALLIVER, DAVID, '"Cantare con la gorga": The Coloratura Technique of the Renaissance Singer', *Studies in Music*, 7 (1973), 10–18.

GALLO, F. ALBERTO; GROTH, RENATE; PALISCA, CLAUDE V.; and REMPP, FRIEDER, *Geschichte der Musiktheorie*, vii: *Italiensiche Musiktheorie im 16. und 17. Jahrhundert* (Darmstadt: Wissenschaftliche Buchgesellschaft, 1989).

GASPARI, GAETANO, *Catalogo della Biblioteca del Liceo Musicale di Bologna* (Bologna: Romagnoli dall'Acqua, 1893), ii, iii.

GÉNÉBRAND, GILBERT, *Canticum Canticorum Salomonis versibus et commentariis illustratum* (Paris: Gorbinum, 1585).

GHISLERI, MICHAELIS ROMANI, *Commentaria in Canticum Canticorum Salomonis* (Antwerp: Keerbergium, 1619).

GIANTURCO, CAROLYN, 'Caterina Assandra, suora compositrice', in Alberto Colzani, Andrea Luppi, and Maurizio Padoan, eds., *La musica sacra in Lombardia nella prima metà del Seicento* (Como: AMIS, 1988), 115–27.

GILLESPIE, WENDY, 'Bowed Instruments', in Kite-Powell, ed., *A Performer's Guide to Renaissance Music* (New York: Schirmer Books, 1994), 109–24.

GIUDETTO, IOANNE, *Directorium chori ad usum omnium ecclesiarum cathedralium, & collegiatarium* (Rome: Stephanum Paulinum, 1604).

GREENLEE, ROBERT, 'The Articulation Techniques of Florid Singing in the Renaissance: An Introduction', *Journal of Performance Practice*, 1 (1983), 1–18.

——'*Dispositione di voce*: Passage to Florid Singing', *Early Music*, 15 (1987), 47–55.

GROUT, DONALD J., *A Short History of Opera* (New York: Columbia University Press, 1947).

GRUBB, FRANCIS, 'Monteverdi's Vespers', Letters to the Editor, *Musical Times*, 102 (1961), 643.

HAAR, JAMES, 'The *note nere* Madrigal', *Journal of the American Musicological Society*, 18 (1965), 22–41.

HAMMOND, FREDERICK, *Girolamo Frescobaldi* (Cambridge, Mass.: Harvard University Press, 1983).

HARGIS, ELLEN, 'The Solo Voice', in Kite-Powell, ed., *A Performer's Guide to Renaissance Music*, 3–12.

HARNONCOURT, NIKOLAUS, *Baroque Music Today: Music as Speech*, trans. Mary O'Neill (Portland, Oreg.: Amadeus Press, 1988).

HARRIS, ELLEN T., 'Voices', in Brown and Sadie, eds., *Performance Practice: Music after 1600*, 97–116.

HAYNES, BRUCE, 'Johann Sebastian Bach's Pitch Standards: The Woodwind Perspective', *Journal of the American Musical Instrument Society*, 11 (1985), 87–8.

——'Cornetts and Historical Pitch Standards', *Historic Brass Society Journal*, 6 (1994), 84–109.

——'Pitch Standards in the Baroque and Classical Periods', 2 vols. (Ph.D. dissertation, University of Montreal, 1995).

HECKMANN, HARALD, 'Der Takt in der Musiklehre des siebzehnten Jahrhunderts', *Archiv für Musikwissenschaft*, 10 (1953), 116–39.

HELL, HELMUT, 'Zu Rhythmus und Notierung des "Vi ricorda" in Claudio Monteverdis *Orfeo*', *Analecta musicologica*, 15 (1975), 87–157.

HERMELINK, SIEGFRIED, 'Zur Chiavettenfrage', in *Bericht über den internationalen musikwissenschaftlichen Kongress Wien Mozartjahr 1956* (Graz and Cologne: Hermann Böhlaus Nachfolger, 1958), 264–71.

——'Über Zarlinos Kadenzbegriff', in *Scritti in onore di Luigi Ronga* (Milan: Ricciardo Ricciardi, 1973), 253–73.

——'Chiavette', in *The New Grove*, iv. 221–3.

HERRMANN-BENGEN, IRMGARD, *Tempobezeichnungen: Ursprung, Wandel im 17. und 18. Jahrhundert* (Tutzing: Hans Schneider, 1959).

HIEKEL, HANS OTTO, 'Der Madrigal- und Motettentypus in der Mensurallehre des Michael Praetorius', *Archiv für Musikwissenschaft*, 19–20 (1962–3), 40–55.

HILL, JOHN WALTER, 'Realized Continuo Accompaniments from Florence *c* 1600', *Early Music*, 11 (1983), 194–208.

HILLIER, PAUL, 'Framing the Life of the Words', in Knighton and Fallows, eds., *Companion to Medieval and Renaissance Music*, 307–10.

HILSE, WALTER, 'The Treatises of Christoph Bernhard', *Music Forum*, 3 (New York; Columbia University Press, 1973), 1–196.

HITCHCOCK, H. WILEY, 'Vocal Ornamentation in Caccini's "Nuove musiche"', *Musical Quarterly*, 56 (1970), 389–404.

—— 'Vittoria Archilei', in *The New Grove*, i. 551.

HOLMAN, PETER, '"Col nobilissimo esercitio della vivuola": Monteverdi's String Writing', *Early Music*, 21 (1993), 576–90.

—— *Four and Twenty Fiddlers: The Violin at the English Court 1540–1690* (Oxford: Clarendon Press, 1993).

HORNING, JOSEPH, 'The Italian Organ, Part I: From the Fifteenth to the Nineteenth Century', *American Organist*, 25/2 (Feb. 1991), 50–7; 'Part II: Registrations', 25/9 (Sept. 1991), 66–72.

HORSLEY, IMOGENE, 'Wind Techniques in the Sixteenth and Early Seventeenth Centuries', *Brass Quarterly*, 4 (1960–1), 49–63.

—— 'The Solo Ricercar in Diminution Manuals: New Light on Early Wind and String Techniques', *Acta musicologica*, 33 (1961), 29–40.

—— 'The Diminutions in Composition and Theory of Composition', *Acta musicologica*, 35 (1963), 124–53.

—— 'Symposium on Seventeenth-Century Music Theory: Italy', *Journal of Music Theory*, 16 (1972), 50–61.

—— 'Full and Short Scores in the Accompaniment of Italian Church Music in the Early Baroque', *Journal of the American Musicological Society*, 30 (1977), 466–99.

HOULE, GEORGE, *Meter in Music, 1600–1800: Performance, Perception, and Notation* (Bloomington, Ind.: Indiana University Press, 1987).

HOWELL, ALMONTE C., Jr., 'French Baroque Organ Music and the Eight Church Tones', *Journal of the American Musicological Society*, 11 (1958), 106–18.

—— 'Symposium on Seventeenth-Century Music Theory: Spain', *Journal of Music Theory*, 16 (1972), 62–71.

HOWELL, STANDLEY, 'Ramos de Pareja's "Brief Discussion of Various Instruments"', *Journal of the American Musical Instrument Society*, 11 (1985), 14–37.

HUCKE, HELMUT, 'Die Besetzung von Sopran und Alt in der Sixtinischen Kapelle', *Miscelánea en homenaje a Monseñor Higinio Anglés*, i (Barcelona: Consejo Superior de Investigaciones Científicas, 1958–61), 379–96.

—— 'Die fälschlich so genannte "Marien"-Vesper von Claudio Monteverdi', in *Bericht über den internationalen musikwissenschaftlichen Kongress Bayreuth 1981* (Kassel: Bärenreiter, 1984), 295–305.

HUST, GERHARD, 'Untersuchungen zu Claudio Monteverdis Messkompositionen' (Ph.D. dissertation, Ruprecht-Karl-Universität, Heidelberg, 1970).

ILLING, CARL-HEINZ, *Zur Technik der Magnificat-Komposition des 16. Jahrhunderts* (Kieler Beiträge zur Musikwissenschaft, 3; Wolfenbüttel and Berlin: Georg Kallmeyer Verlag, 1936).

JEPPESON, KNUD, 'Monteverdi, Kapellmeister an S.ta Barbara?', in Monterosso, ed., *Claudio Monteverdi e il suo tempo*, 313–19.

JONES, CHESLYN; WAINWRIGHT, GEOFFREY; and YARNOLD, EDWARD, S. J., eds., *The Study of Liturgy* (Oxford: Oxford University Press, 1978).

JORGENSEN, OWEN, *Tuning the Historical Temperaments by Ear* (Marquette, Mich.: The Northern Michigan University Press, 1977).

JUDD, CRISTLE COLLINS, 'Modal Types and *Ut, Re, Mi* Tonalities: Tonal Coherence in Sacred Vocal Polyphony from about 1500', *Journal of the American Musicological Society*, 45 (1992), 428–67.

JÜRGENS, JÜRGEN, 'Urtext und Affführungspraxis bei Monteverdis *Orfeo* und *Marien-Vesper*', in Monterosso, ed., *Claudio Monteverdi e il suo tempo*, 269–304.

KANAZAWA, MASAKATA, 'Polyphonic Music for Vespers during the Fifteenth Century' (Ph.D. dissertation, Harvard University, 1966).

—— 'Two Vesper Repertories from Verona, ca. 1500', *Rivista italiana di musicologia*, 10 (1975), 154–79.

KARP, CARY, 'Pitch', in Brown and Sadie, eds., *Performance Practice: Music after 1600*, 147–68.

KELLER, JINDRICH, 'Antique Trumpet Mutes', *Historic Brass Society Journal*, 2 (1990), 97–103.

KENDRICK, ROBERT L., 'Genres, Generations and Gender: Nuns' Music in Early Modern Milan, c. 1550–1706' (Ph.D. dissertation, New York University, 1993).

—— ' "Sonet vox tua in auribus meis": Song of Songs Exegesis and the Seventeenth-Century Motet', *Schütz-Jahrbuch*, 16 (1994), 99–118.

—— *Celestial Sirens: Nuns and their Music in Early Modern Milan* (Oxford: Clarendon Press, 1996).

KENTON, EGON F., 'The "Brass" Parts in Giovanni Gabrieli's Instrumental Ensemble Compositions', *Brass Quarterly*, 1 (1957), 73–80.

—— *Life and Works of Giovanni Gabrieli* (Musicological Studies and Documents, 16; American Institute of Musicology, 1967).

KENYON, NICHOLAS, ed., *Authenticity and Early Music: A Symposium* (Oxford: Oxford University Press, 1988).

KINKELDEY, OTTO, *Orgel und Klavier in der Musik des 16. Jahrhunderts* (Leipzig: Breitkopf und Härtel, 1910; repr. edn. Hildesheim: Georg Olms, 1968).

KIRK, DOUGLAS, 'Cornetti and Renaissance Pitch Standards in Italy and Germany', *Journal de musique ancienne*, 10 (1989), 16–22.

—— 'Cornetti and Renaissance Pitch Revisited', Correspondence, *Historic Brass Society Journal*, 2 (1990), 203–5.

—— 'Cornett', in Kite-Powell, ed., *A Performer's Guide to Renaissance Music*, 79–96.

KIRSCH, WINFRIED, *Die Quellen der mehrstimmigen Magnificat- und Te Deum-Vertonungen bis zur Mitte des 16. Jahrhunderts* (Tutzing: Hans Schneider, 1966).

KITE-POWELL, JEFFERY T., ed., *A Practical Guide to Historical Performance—The Renaissance* (New York: Early Music America, 1989).

—— ed., *A Performer's Guide to Renaissance Music* (New York: Schirmer Books, 1994).

—— 'Large Ensembles', in Kite-Powell, ed., *A Performer's Guide to Renaissance Music*, 228–32.

KLOP, G. C., *Harpsichord Tuning, Course Outline* (Garderen, The Netherlands: Werkplaats voor Clavecimbelbouw, 1974).

KNIGHTON, TESS, and FALLOWS, DAVID, eds., *Companion to Medieval and Renaissance Music* (New York: Schirmer Books, 1992).

KORY, AGNES, 'A Wider Role for the Tenor Violin?', *Galpin Society Journal*, 47 (1994), 123–53.

KOTTICK, EDWARD L., *The Harpsichord Owner's Guide* (Chapel Hill, NC: The University of North Carolina Press, 1987).

KREITNER, KENNETH, 'Renaissance Pitch', in Knighton and Fallows, eds., *Companion to Medieval and Renaissance Music*, 275–83.

KROYER, THEODOR, 'Dialog und Echo in der alten Chormusik', *Jahrbuch der Bibliothek Peters*, 16 (1909), 13–32.

KUHN, MAX, *Die Verzierungs-Kunst in der Gesangs-Musik des 16.–17. Jahrhunderts (1535–1650)* (Leipzig: Breitkopf & Härtel, 1902).

KUNZ, P. LUCAS, *Die Tonartenlehre des Römischen Theoretikers u. Komponisten Pier Francesco Valentini* (Münsterische Beiträge zur Musikwissenschaft, 8; Kassel: Bärenreiter-Verlag, 1937).

KURTZMAN, JEFFREY G., 'The Monteverdi Vespers of 1610 and their Relationship with Italian Sacred Music of the Early Seventeenth Century' (Ph.D. dissertation, University of Illinois at Urbana-Champaign, 1972).

——Review of Gunnar Westerlund and Eric Hughes, *Music of Claudio Monteverdi: A Discography*, *Music Library Association Notes*, 30 (1974), 532–3.

——'Some Historical Perspectives on the Monteverdi Vespers', *Analecta musicologica*, 15 (1974), 29–86.

——'Giovanni Francesco Capello, an Avant-Gardist of the Early Seventeenth Century', *Musica disciplina*, 31 (1977), 155–82.

——*Essays on the Monteverdi Mass and Vespers of 1610* (Houston: Rice University Studies, 1978).

——Review of *Claudio Monteverdi: Vespro della Beata Vergine*, ed. Jürgen Jürgens, *Music Library Association Notes*, 37 (1980), 981–3.

——Review of *Second Vespers for the Feast of Santa Barbara and Vespri di S. Giovanni Battista*, *Early Music*, 17 (1989), 429–35.

——'A Taxonomic and Affective Analysis of Monteverdi's "Hor che'l ciel e la terra"', *Music Analysis*, 12 (1993), 169–95.

——'Correspondence', *Music & Letters*, 74 (1993), 487–95; and 75 (1994), 145–54.

——'What Makes Claudio "Divine"? Criteria for Analysis of Monteverdi's Large-Scale *Concertato* Style', in *Seicento inesplorato, Atti del III convegno internazionale sulla musica in area lombardo-padana del secolo XVII* (Como: AMIS, 1993), 259–302.

——'Why would Monteverdi Publish a Vespers in 1610? Lifting the Shadows on the Development of a Repertoire', in Peter Cahn and Ann-Katrin Heiner, eds., *De musica et cantu: Studien zur Geschichte der Kirchenmusik und der Oper. Helmut Hucke zum 60. Geburtstag* (Hildesheim: Georg Olms Verlag, 1993), 419–45.

——'Monteverdi's Changing Aesthetics: A Semiotic Perspective', in Thomas J. Mathiesen and Benito Rivera, eds., *Festa musicologica: Essays in Honor of George Buelow* (Stuyvesant, NY: Pendragon Press, 1994), 233–55.

——'Tones, Modes, Clefs and Pitch in Roman Cyclic Magnificats of the 16th Century', *Early Music*, 22 (1994), 641–64.

——'Palestrina's Magnificats: A Brief Survey', in David Crawford and Grayson Wagstaff, eds., *Encomium musicae: Essays in Honor of Robert J. Snow* (Stuyvesant, NY: Pendragon Press, forthcoming).

LAMPL, HANS, and PLANK, S. E., 'Praetorius on Performance: Excerpts from *Syntagma musicum III*', *Historic Brass Society Journal*, 6 (1994), 244–68.

LA RUE, JAN, 'Bifocal Tonality: An Explanation for Ambiguous Baroque Cadences', *Essays on Music in Honor of Archibald Thompson Davison* (Cambridge, Mass.: Harvard University, 1957), 173–84.

LAX, EVA, *Claudio Monteverdi: Lettere* (Florence: Leo S. Olschki Editore, 1994).

LEE, BARBARA, 'Giovanni Maria Lanfranco's *Scintille di musica* and its Relation to 16th-Century Music Theory' (Ph.D. dissertation, Cornell University, 1961).

LEICHTENTRITT, HUGO, *Geschichte der Motette* (Leipzig: Breitkopf und Härtel, 1908; repr. edn. Hildesheim: Georg Olms, 1967).

LEONARDS, PETRA, 'Einige Gedanken zur Terminologie und Frühgeschichte des Zinken', *Basler Jahrbuch für historische Musikpraxis*, 5 (1981), 361–71.

LEONARDS, PETRA, 'Historische Quellen zur Spielweise des Zinken', *Basler Jahrbuch für historische Musikpraxis*, 5 (1981), 315–46.

LESURE, FRANÇOIS, and SARTORI, CLAUDIO, eds., *Bibliografia della musica italiana vocale profana publicata dal 1500 al 1700* (Pomezia: Staderini spa, 1977), ii.

LINDLEY, MARK, 'Early 16th-Century Keyboard Temperaments', *Musica disciplina*, 28 (1974), 129–51.

—— 'Fifteenth-Century Evidence for Meantone Temperament', *Proceedings of the Royal Musical Association*, 102 (1975–6), 37–51.

—— 'Instructions for the Clavier Diversely Tempered', *Early Music*, 5 (1977), 18–23.

—— 'Temperaments', in *The New Grove*, xviii. 660–74.

—— 'Chromatic Systems (or Non-Systems) from Vicentino to Monteverdi' (review of Karol Berger, *Theories of Chromatic and Enharmonic Music in Late 16th Century Italy*), *Early Music History*, 2 (1982), 393–404.

—— *Lutes, Viols and Temperaments* (Cambridge: Cambridge University Press, 1984).

—— 'Tuning and Intonation', in Brown and Sadie, eds., *Performance Practice: Music after 1600*, 169–75.

—— 'Renaissance Keyboard Fingering', in Kite-Powell, ed., *A Performer's Guide to Renaissance Music*, 189–99.

—— 'Tuning Renaissance and Baroque Keyboard Instruments: Some Guidelines', *Performance Practice Review*, 7 (1994), 85–92.

—— and BOXALL, MARIA, *Early Keyboard Fingerings: A Comprehensive Guide* (Mainz: Schott, 1992).

—— WACHSMANN, KLAUS; RHODES, J. J. K.; and THOMAS, W. R., 'Pitch', in *The New Grove*, xiv. 779–86.

LIONNET, JEAN, 'Performance Practice in the Papal Chapel during the 17th Century', *Early Music*, 15 (1987), 4–15.

LIPPMAN, EDWARD, 'Monteverdi: *Vespers of 1610*', *Musical Quarterly*, 41 (1955), 404–7.

LOCKWOOD, LEWIS, *The Counter-Reformation and the Masses of Vincenzo Ruffo* (Studi di musica veneta, 2; Venice: Fondazione Giorgio Cini, 1970).

—— 'Performance and "Authenticity"', *Early Music*, 19 (1991), 502–4.

—— 'Monteverdi and Gombert: The Missa *In illo tempore* of 1610', in Peter Cahn and Ann-Katrin Heiner, eds., *De musica et cantu: Studien zur Geschichte der Kirchenmusik und der Oper. Helmut Hucke zum 60. Geburtstag* (Hildesheim: Georg Olms Verlag, 1993), 457–69.

—— and OWENS, JESSIE ANN, 'Willaert, Adrian', in *The New Grove*, xx. 423–4.

LONG, JOAN, 'The Motets, Psalms and Hymns of Adrian Willaert—A Liturgico-Musical Study' (Ph.D. dissertation, Columbia University, 1971).

LOWINSKY, EDWARD E., *Secret Chromatic Art in the Netherlands Motet* (New York: Russell & Russell, 1946).

—— 'A Newly Discovered Sixteenth-Century Motet Manuscript at the Biblioteca Vallicelliana in Rome', *Journal of the American Musicological Society*, 3 (1950), 173–232.

—— *Tonality and Atonality in Sixteenth-Century Music* (Berkeley: University of California Press, 1962).

LUMSDEN, ALAN, 'Woodwind and Brass', in Brown and Sadie, eds., *Performance Practice: Music after 1600*, 80–96.

LUNELLI, RENATO, *Der Orgelbau in Italien in seinen Meisterwerken vom 14. Jahrhundert bis zur Gegenwart* (Mainz: Rheingold-Verlag, 1956).

McCLARY, SUSAN, 'The Transition from Modal to Tonal Organization in the Works of Monteverdi' (Ph.D. dissertation, Harvard University, 1976).

MacClintock, Carol, *Giaches de Wert: Life and Works* (Musicological Studies and Documents, 17; American Institute of Musicology, 1966).

—— Caccini's *Trillo*: A Re-examination', *NATS Bulletin*, 33/1 (1976), 38–44.

—— *Readings in the History of Music in Performance* (Bloomington, Ind.: Indiana University Press, 1979).

Macey, Patrick Paul, 'Josquin's "Miserere mei Deus": Context, Structure, and Influence', 2 vols. (Ph.D. dissertation, University of California at Berkeley, 1985).

Machatius, Franz Jochen, 'Über mensurale und spielmännische Reduktion', *Die Musikforschung*, 8 (1955), 139–51.

—— 'Die Tempo-Charactere', in *Bericht über den siebenten internationalen musikwissenschaftlichen Kongress Köln 1958* (Kassel: Bärenreiter, 1959), 185–7.

—— 'Dreiertakt und Zweiertakt als Eurhythmus und Ekrhythmus', in Georg von Dadelsen and Andreas Holschneider, eds., *Festschrift Walter Gerstenberg zum 60. Geburtstag* (Wolfenbüttel: Möseler Verlag, 1964), 88–97.

—— *Die Tempi in der Musik um 1600* (Laaber: Laaber Verlag, 1977).

McCreesh, Paul, 'Monteverdi Vespers: Three New Editions', *Early Music*, 23 (1995), 325–7.

McGee, Timothy J., *Medieval and Renaissance Music: A Performer's Guide* (Toronto: University of Toronto Press, 1985).

Malinowsky, Władysław, 'Zum Problem der Form in der mehrchörigen Musik', *Musiktheorie*, 6 (1991), 43–53.

Malipiero, Gian Francesco, *Claudio Monteverdi* (Milano: Fratelli Treves Editori, 1929).

Mangsen, Sandra, '*Ad libitum* Procedures in Instrumental Duos and Trios', *Early Music*, 19 (1991), 29–40.

Marcase, Donald E., 'Adriano Banchieri, "L'organo suonarino": Translation, Transcription and Commentary' (Ph.D. dissertation, Indiana University, 1970).

Martini, Giambattista, *Esemplare o sia Saggio fondamentale pratico di contrappunto fugato . . . parte seconda* (Bologna: Lelio della Volpe, 1776).

Marvin, Bob, 'Recorders & English Flutes in European Collections', *Galpin Society Journal*, 25 (1972), 30–57.

Mason, Kevin, *The Chitarrone and its Repertoire in Early Seventeenth-Century Italy* (Aberystwyth, Wales: Boethius Press, 1989).

Meier, Bernhard, 'Zur Tonart der Concertato-Motetten in Monteverdis *Marienvesper*', in Ludwig Finscher, ed., *Claudio Monteverdi. Festschrift Reinhold Hammerstein zum 70. Geburtstag* (Laaber: Laaber Verlag, 1986), 359–67.

—— *The Modes of Classical Vocal Polyphony*, trans. Ellen S. Beebe (New York: Broude Brothers Limited, 1988).

—— 'Rhetorical Aspects of the Renaissance Modes', *Journal of the Royal Musical Association*, 115 (1990), 182–90.

—— *Alte Tonarten dargestellt an der Instrumentalmusik des 16. und 17. Jahrhunderts* (Kassel: Bärenreiter, 1992).

—— 'Auf der Grenze von Modalem und Dur-Moll-Tonalem System', *Basler Jahrbuch für historische Musikpraxis*, 16 (1992), 53–69.

Mendel, Arthur, Pitch in the 16th and Early 17th Centuries', *Musical Quarterly*, 34 (1948), 28–45, 199–221, 336–57, 575–93.

—— 'Some Ambiguities of the Mensural System', in Harold Powers, ed., *Studies in Music History: Essays for Oliver Strunk* (Princeton: Princeton University Press, 1968), 137–60.

—— 'Pitch in Western Music since 1500, a Re-Examination', *Acta musicologica*, 50 (1978), 1–93.

MESSMER, FRANZPETER, Review of Claudio Monteverdi, *Vespro della Beata Vergine, Fono Forum*, 2 (1994), 58.

MILLER, CAROLINE ANNE, '*Chiavette*, A New Approach' (MA thesis, University of California at Berkeley, 1960).

MOENS-HAENEN, GRETA, *Das Vibrato in der Musik des Barock* (Graz: Akademische Druck- und Verlagsanstalt, 1988).

MOMPELLIO, FEDERICO, *Lodovico Viadana: Musicista fra due secoli* (Florence: Leo S. Olschki Editore, 1966).

—— ' "Un certo ordine di procedere che non si può scrivere" ', in *Scritti in onore di Luigi Ronga* (Milan: Ricciardo Ricciardi, 1973), 367–88.

—— ' "L'Apparato musicale" del Servita Amante Franzoni', *Rivista internazionale di musica sacra*, 14 (1993), 211–69.

MONK, CHRISTOPHER, 'First Steps towards Playing the Cornett', *Early Music*, 3 (1975), 132–3, 244–8.

MONTEROSSO, RAFFAELLO, ed., *Claudio Monteverdi e il suo tempo, Atti del Congresso internazionale di studi monteverdiani, May 3–May 7, 1968* (Verona: Stamperia Valdonega, 1969).

—— ed., *Performing Practice in Monteverdi's Music: The Historic-Philological Background* (Cremona: Fondazione Claudio Monteverdi, 1995).

—— 'Tempo and Dynamics in Monteverdi's Secular Polyphony' in Monterosso, ed., *Performing Practice in Monteverdi's Music*, 93–117.

MOORE, JAMES H., 'The *Vespero delli Cinque Laudate* and the Role of *salmi spezzati* at St Mark's', *Journal of the American Musicological Society*, 34 (1981), 249–78.

—— *Vespers at St Mark's: Music of Alessandro Grandi, Giovanni Rovetta and Francesco Cavalli* (Ann Arbor: UMI Research Press, 1981).

—— 'The Liturgical Use of the Organ in Seventeenth-Century Italy: New Documents, New Hypotheses', in Alexander Silbiger, ed., *Frescobaldi Studies* (Durham, NC: Duke University Press, 1987), 351–83.

MORELLI, ARNALDO, 'Basso Continuo on the Organ in Seventeenth-Century Italian Music', *Basler Jahrbuch für historische Musikpraxis*, 18 (1994), 31–45.

—— 'Monteverdi and Organ Practice', in Monterosso, ed., *Performing Practice in Monteverdi's Music*, 125–41.

MORRIER, DENIS, 'Pour une discographie critique des Vêpres de la Vierge', *Diapason-harmonie*, 354 (1989), 54–5.

MÜLLER-BLATTAU, JOSEPH MARIA, 'Zur vokalen Improvisation im 16. Jahrhundert', in *Bericht über den siebenten internationalen musikwissenschaftlichen Kongress Köln 1958* (Kassel: Bärenreiter, 1959), 195–6.

MURATA, MARGARET, 'Pier Francesco Valentini on Tactus and Proportion', in Alexander Silbiger, ed., *Frescobaldi Studies* (Durham, NC: Duke University Press, 1987), 327–50.

MYERS, HERBERT, 'Praetorius's Pitch', *Early Music*, 12 (1984), 369–71.

—— 'Pitch and Transposition', in Kite-Powell, ed., *A Practical Guide to Historical Performance—The Renaissance* (New York: Early Music America, 1989), 157–63.

—— 'Pitch and Transposition', in Kite-Powell, ed., *A Performer's Guide to Renaissance Music* (New York: Schirmer Books, 1994), 248–56.

—— 'Recorder', in Kite-Powell, ed., *A Performer's Guide to Renaissance Music*, 41–55.

—— 'Renaissance Flute', in Kite-Powell, ed., *A Performer's Guide to Renaissance Music*, 56–62.

—— 'Woodwinds', in Stewart Carter, ed., *A Performer's Guide to Baroque Music* (New York: Schirmer Books, 1997), 69–97.

NATHAN, HANS, 'Two Interpretations of Monteverdi's *Vespro della Beata Vergine*', *Music Review*, 15 (1954), 155–6.

NELSON, BERNADETTE, 'Alternatim Practice in 17th-century Spain: The Integration of Organ Versets and Plainchant in Psalms and Canticles', *Early Music*, 22 (1994), 239–56.

NEUMANN, FREDERICK, 'The Vibrato Controversy', *Performance Practice Review*, 4 (1991), 14–27.

—— *Performance Practices of the Seventeenth and Eighteenth Centuries* (New York: Schirmer Books, 1993).

The New Grove Dictionary of Music and Musicians, ed. Stanley Sadie (London: Macmillan Publishers Ltd., 1980).

NORTH, NIGEL, *Continuo Playing on the Lute, Archlute and Theorbo* (Bloomington, Ind.: Indiana University Press, 1987).

NURSE, RAY, 'Vibrato in Renaissance Music', *Musick*, 8 (1986), 2–9.

O'DETTE, PAUL, 'Plucked Instruments', in Kite-Powell, ed., *A Performer's Guide to Renaissance Music*, 139–53.

O'REGAN, THOMAS NOEL, 'Sacred Polychoral Music in Rome 1575–1621' (D. Phil. dissertation, University of Oxford, 1988), 2 vols.

—— 'Palestrina and the Oratory of Santissima Trinità dei Pellegrini', in *Atti del II convegno internazionale di studi palestriniani* (Palestrina: Fondazione G. Pierluigi da Palestrina, 1991), 95–121.

—— 'Processions and their Music in Post-Tridentine Rome', *Recercare*, 4 (1992), 45–80.

—— '"Blessed with the Holy Father's Entertainment": Roman Ceremonial Music as Experienced by the Irish Earls in Rome, 1608', *Irish Musical Studies*, 2 (1993), 41–61.

—— 'Music at the Roman Archconfraternity of San Rocco in the Late Sixteenth Century', in *Atti del Convegno 'La musica a Roma attraverso le fonti d'archivio', 4–7 Giugno 1992* (Lucca: Libreria musicale italiana, 1994), 521–52.

—— 'Musical Ambassadors in Rome and Loreto: Papal Singers at the Confraternities of Santissima Trinità dei Pellegrini and San Rocco in the Late 16th and Early 17th Centuries', in Adalbert Roth, ed., *Collectanea I* (Capellae Apostolicae Sixtinaeque Collectanea Acta Monumenta', 3; Vatican City: Biblioteca Apostolica Vaticana, 1994), 75–95.

—— 'Victoria, Soto and the Spanish Archconfraternity of the Resurrection in Rome', *Early Music*, 22 (1994), 279–95.

—— 'Palestrina, a Musician and Composer in the Market-Place', *Early Music*, 22 (1994), 551–72.

—— *Institutional Patronage in Post-Tridentine Rome: Music at Santissima Trinità dei Pellegrini 1550–1650* (Royal Musical Association Monographs, 7; London: Royal Musical Association, 1995).

—— 'The Performance of Roman Sacred Polychoral Music in the Late Sixteenth and Early Seventeenth Centuries: Evidence from Archival Sources', *Performance Practice Review*, 8 (fall 1995), 107–46.

OSTHOFF, WOLFGANG, 'Claudio Monteverdi: Vespro della Beata Vergine (1610)', *Die Musikforschung*, 11 (1958), 380–1.

—— 'Unità liturgica e artistica nei *Vespri* del 1610', *Rivista italiana di musicologia*, 2 (1967), 314–27.

OWEN, BARBARA, and WILLIAMS, PETER, *The New Grove: Organ* (The Grove Musical Instruments Series; New York: W. W. Norton & Co., 1980).

The Oxford Annotated Bible (Oxford: Oxford University Press, 1962).

PADOAN, MAURIZIO, *La musica in S. Maria Maggiore a Bergamo nel periodo di Giovanni Cavaccio (1598–1626)* (Como: AMIS, 1983).

PAINE, GORDON, 'Tactus, Tempo, and Praetorius', in Gordon Paine, ed., *Five Centuries of Choral Music: Essays in Honor of Howard Swan* (Stuyvesant, NY: Pendragon Press, 1988), 167–216.

PALISCA, CLAUDE V., 'The Artusi–Monteverdi Controversy', in Arnold and Fortune, eds., *The Monteverdi Companion*, 133–66.

PALISCA, CLAUDE V., 'Emilio de' Cavalieri', in *The New Grove*, iv. 20–3.

—— 'The Artusi–Monteverdi Controversy', in Arnold and Fortune, eds., *The New Monteverdi Companion*, 127–58.

PANETTA, VINCENT J., Jr., *Treatise on Harpsichord Tuning by Jean Denis* (Cambridge: Cambridge University Press, 1987).

PARISI, SUSAN, ' "Licenza alla Mantovana": Frescobaldi and the Recruitment of Musicians for Mantua, 1612–1615', in Alexander Silbiger, ed., *Frescobaldi Studies* (Durham, NC: Duke University Press, 1987), 55–91.

—— 'Ducal Patronage of Music in Mantua, 1587–1627: An Archival Study', 2 vols. (Ph.D. dissertation, University of Illinois at Urbana-Champaign, 1989).

—— 'Once Fired, Twice Almost Rehired: An Assessment of Monteverdi's Relations with the Gonzagas' (paper delivered at conference of the Society for Seventeenth-Century Music, St Louis, Missouri, Apr. 1993 and at the Convegno, Claudio Monteverdi: Studi e prospettive, Mantua, 21–4 Oct. 1993; published as 'New Documents Concerning Monteverdi's Relations with the Gonzagas' in Paola Besutti, Teresa M. Gialdroni, and Rodolfo Baroncini eds., *Claudio Monteverdi: Studi e prospettive, Atti del Convegno (Mantova, 21–24 ottobre 1993)* (Florence: Olschki, 1998), 477–511.

—— 'Musicians at the Court of Mantua during Monteverdi's Time: Evidence from the Payrolls', in Siegfried Gmeinwieser, David Hiley, and Jörg Riedlbauer, eds., *Musicologia Humana: Studies in Honor of Warren and Ursula Kirkendale* (Florence: Leo S. Olschki Editore, 1994), 183–208.

—— 'Acquiring Musicians and Instruments in the Early Baroque: Observations from Mantua', *Journal of Musicology*, 14 (1996), 117–50.

—— 'New Documents concerning Monteverdi's relations with the Gonzagas', in Paola Besutti, Jeresa M. Gialdroni, and Rodolfo Baroncini, eds., *Claudio Monteverdi: Studi e prospettive, Atti del Convegno (Mantova, 21–24 ottobre 1993)* (Florence: Olschki, 1998), 477–511.

PARROTT, ANDREW, 'Transposition in Monteverdi's Vespers of 1610: An Aberration Defended', *Early Music*, 12 (1984), 490–516.

—— 'Monteverdi's Vespers of 1610 Revisited', in Monterosso, ed., *Performing Practice in Monteverdi's Music*, 163–74.

PHILLIPS, ELIZABETH V., and JACKSON, JOHN-PAUL CHRISTOPHER, *Performing Medieval and Renaissance Music: An Introductory Guide* (New York: Schirmer Books, 1986).

PICENARDI, GUIDO SOMMI, 'Alcuni documenti concernenti Claudio Monteverde,' *Archivio storico lombardo*, 22 (1895), 154–62.

PICKER, MARTIN, *The Motet Books of Andrea Antico* (Chicago: University of Chicago Press, 1987).

PINESCHI, UMBERTO, 'Restoration of Historical Organs in Pistoia, Italy and its Area', *Diapason*, 66/6 (May 1975), 2–4.

PLANCHART, ALEJANDRO ENRIQUE, 'The Relative Speed of "Tempora" in the Period of Dufay', *Research Chronicle*, 17 (1981), 33–51.

—— 'On Singing and the Vocal Ensemble II', in Kite-Powell, ed., *A Performer's Guide to Renaissance Music*, 26–38.

PLANYAVSKY, ALEXANDER, *Geschichte des Kontrabasses* (Tutzing: Hans Schneider, 1970).

POTTER, JOHN, 'Reconstructing Lost Voices', in Knighton and Fallows, ed., *Companion to Medieval and Renaissance Music*, 311–16.

POWERS, HAROLD S., 'The Modality of "Vestiva i colli" ', in Robert Marshall, ed., *Studies in Renaissance and Baroque Music in Honor of Arthur Mendel* (Kassel: Bärenreiter, 1974), 31–46.

—— 'Mode', in *The New Grove*, xii. 376–418.

—— 'Tonal Types and Modal Categories in Renaissance Polyphony', *Journal of the American Musicological Society*, 34 (1981), 428–70.

—— 'Modal Representation in Polyphonic Offertories', *Early Music History*, 2 (1982), 43–86.

—— 'Monteverdi's Model for a Multimodal Madrigal', in Fabrizio della Seta and Franco Piperno, eds., *In cantu et in sermone: For Nino Pirrotta on his 8oth Birthday* (Florence: Leo S. Olschki Editore, University of Western Australia Press, 1989), 185–219.

—— 'Is Mode Real?', *Basler Jahrbuch für historische Musikpraxis*, 16 (1992), 9–52.

PUGLISI, FILADELFIO, A Survey of Renaissance Flutes', *Galpin Society Journal*, 41 (1988), 67–82.

RAMM, ANDREA VON, 'Singing Early Music', *Early Music*, 4 (1976), 12–15.

RANDEL, DON M., 'Emerging Triadic Tonality in the Fifteenth Century', *Musical Quarterly*, 57 (1971), 73–86.

RAVIZZA, VICTOR, 'Frühe Doppelchörigkeit in Bergamo', *Die Musikforschung*, 25 (1972), 127–42.

—— 'Formprobleme des frühen Coro spezzato', *International Musicological Society, Report of the Eleventh Congress, Copenhagen 1972* (Copenhagen: Wilhelm Hansen, 1974), 604–11.

RAYNER, CLARE G., 'The Enigmatic Cima: Meantone Tuning and Transpositions', *Galpin Society Journal*, 22 (1969), 23–34.

READ, TAMAR CLOTHYLDE, 'A Critical Study and Performance Edition of Emilio de' Cavalieri's *Rappresentatione di anima e di corpo*' (DMA dissertation, University of Southern California, 1969).

REARDON, COLLEEN, *Agostino Agazzari and Music at Siena Cathedral, 1597–1641* (Oxford: Clarendon Press, 1993).

REDLICH, HANS F., 'Claudio Monteverdi—zum Problem der praktischen Ausgabe seiner Werke (Vesper 1610)', *Schweizerische Musikzeitung*, 74 (1934), 609–17, 641–6.

—— 'Monteverdi's Religious Music', *Music & Letters*, 27 (1946), 208–15.

—— 'Monteverdi's "Vespers"', *Listener*, 943 (6 Feb. 1947), 260.

—— *Claudio Monteverdi: Leben und Werk* (Olten: Verlag Otto Walter, 1949).

—— 'Aufgaben und Ziele der Monteverdi-Forschung: Zu Leo Schrades Monteverdi-Buch', *Die Musikforschung*, 4 (1951), 318–32.

—— *Claudio Monteverdi: Life and Works*, trans. Kathleen Dale (London: Oxford University Press, 1952).

—— Review of Leo Schrade, *Monteverdi: Creator of Modern Music*, *Music Review*, 13 (1952), 316–18.

—— 'Editions of Monteverdi's Vespers of 1610', *Gramophone*, 31 (1954), 503.

—— 'Two Interpretations of Monteverdi's *Vespers*', Correspondence, *Music Review*, 15 (1954), 255–6.

—— 'Claudio Monteverdi: Some Problems of Textual Interpretation', *Musical Quarterly*, 41 (1955), 68.

—— 'Monteverdi and Schütz in New Editions', *Music Review*, 19 (1958), 72–6.

—— 'Monteverdi's Vespers', Letters to the Editor, *Musical Times*, 102 (1961), 564.

—— 'Monteverdi's Vespers Again', Letters to the Editor, *Musical Times*, 102 (1961), 713.

—— 'Early Baroque Church Music', in Gerald Abraham, ed., *The Age of Humanism, 1540–1630* (The New Oxford History of Music, 4; London: Oxford University Press, 1968), 520–46.

REESE, GUSTAVE, *Music in the Renaissance* (New York: W. W. Norton and Company, Inc., 1954).

REINER, STUART, 'La vag' Angioletta (and Others)', *Analecta musicologica*, 14 (1974), 26–88.

REISS, SCOTT, 'Articulation: The Key to Expressive Playing', *American Recorder*, 27/4 (Nov. 1986), 144–9.

Répertoire International des Sources Musicales (RISM), *Recueils imprimés XVIᵉ–XVIIᵉ siècles* (Munich and Duisburg: G. Henle Verlag, 1960).

Répertoire International des Sources Musicales (RISM), *Einzeldrucke vor 1800*, 9 vols. (Kassel: Bärenreiter, 1971–81).

The Revised English Bible (Oxford: Oxford University Press, 1989).

REYNOLDS, CHRISTOPHER A., 'Sacred Polyphony', in Brown and Sadie, eds., *Performance Practice: Music before 1600*, 185–200.

RISM: see Répertoire International des Sources Musicales.

ROCHE, JEROME, 'Music at S. Maria Maggiore, Bergamo, 1614–1643', *Music & Letters*, 47 (1966), 296–312.

—— 'The Duet in Early Seventeenth-Century Italian Church Music', *Proceedings of the Royal Musical Association*, 93 (1967), 33–50.

—— 'North Italian Liturgical Music in the Early 17th Century; its Evolution around 1600 and its Development until the Death of Monteverdi' (Ph.D. dissertation, Cambridge University, 1967).

—— 'Monteverdi and the *Prima Prattica*', in Arnold and Fortune, eds., *The Monteverdi Companion*, 167–91.

—— 'Musica diversa di Compietà: Compline and its Music in Seventeenth-Century Italy', *Proceedings of the Royal Musical Association*, 109 (1982–3), 60–79.

—— *North Italian Church Music in the Age of Monteverdi* (Oxford: Clarendon Press, 1984).

—— 'Monteverdi and the *Prima Prattica*', in Arnold and Fortune, eds., *The New Monteverdi Companion*, 159–82.

ROGERS, NIGEL, 'Voices', in Julie Anne Sadie, ed., *Companion to Baroque Music* (New York: Schirmer Books, 1991), 351–65.

RORKE, MARGARET ANN, 'Sacred Contrafacta of Monteverdi Madrigals and Cardinal Borromeo's Milan', *Music & Letters*, 65 (1984), 168–75.

ROSE, GLORIA, 'Agazzari and the Improvising Orchestra', *Journal of the American Musicological Society*, 18 (1965), 382–93.

ROSTIROLLA, GIANCARLO, 'Policoralità e impiego di strumenti musicali nella basilica di San Pietro in Vaticano durante gli anni 1597–1600', in Giuseppe Donato, ed., *La Policoralità in Italia nei secoli XVI e XVII* (Rome: Edizioni Torre d'Orfeo, 1987), 11–53.

ROWEN, RUTH HALLE, *Music through Sources and Documents* (Englewood Cliffs, NJ: Prentice-Hall, Inc., 1979).

ROWLAND-JONES, ANTHONY, 'Recorder Slurring I: Renaissance and Early Baroque', *American Recorder*, 34/2 (June 1993), 9–15.

RUHLAND, KONRAD, 'Der mehrstimmige Psalmvortrag im 15. und 16. Jahrhundert. Studien zur Psalmodie auf der Grundlage von Faburdon, Fauxbourdon und Falsbordone' (Ph.D. dissertation, University of Munich, 1978).

RUHNKE, MARTIN, *Joachim Burmeister* (Kassel: Bärenreiter-Verlag, 1955).

SANDERS, DONALD C., 'Vocal Ornaments in Durante's *Arie devote* (1608)', *Performance Practice Review*, 6 (1993), 60–76.

SANFORD, SALLY ALLIS, 'Seventeenth and Eighteenth Century Vocal Style and Technique' (DMA dissertation, Stanford University, 1979).

—— 'A Comparison of French and Italian Singing in the Seventeenth Century', *Journal of Seventeenth-Century Music*, 1 (1995) [http://rism.harvard.edu/jscm/].

—— 'Solo Singing 1', in Stewart Carter, ed., *A Performer's Guide to Seventeenth-Century Music*, 3–29.

SANTORO, ELIA, *La famiglia e la formazione di Claudio Monteverdi: Note biografiche con documenti inediti* (Cremona: Athenaeum Cremonese, 1967).

SARTORI, CLAUDIO, *Bibliografia della musica strumentale italiana* (Florence: Olschki, 1952).

—— 'Monteverdiana', *Musical Quarterly*, 38 (1952), 399–413.

SCHEMPF, WILLIAM H., 'Polychoral Magnificats from H. Praetorius to H. Schütz' (Ph.D. dissertation, University of Rochester, 1960).

SCHNOEBELEN, ANNE, 'The Concerted Mass at San Petronio in Bologna: ca. 1660–1730. A Documentary and Analytical Study' (Ph.D. dissertation, University of Illinois, 1966).

—— 'Cazzati vs. Bologna: 1657–1671', *Musical Quarterly*, 57 (1971), 26–39.

—— 'The Role of the Violin in the Resurgence of the Mass in the 17th Century', *Early Music*, 18 (1990), 537–42.

SCHRADE, LEO, *Monteverdi, Creator of Modern Music* (New York: W. W. Norton & Company, Inc., 1950).

—— 'Monteverdi', Correspondence, *Music Review*, 14 (1953), 336–40.

—— 'Monteverdi: *Vespro della Beata Vergine*', *Musical Quarterly*, 40 (1954), 138–45.

—— Review of 'Monteverdi, *Vespro della Beata Vergine*', ed. Hans Redlich, *Musical Quarterly*, 40 (1954), 139–45.

SCHROEDER, EUNICE, 'The Stroke Comes Full Circle: Φ and $\mathbb{C}$ in Writings on Music, ca. 1450–1540', *Musica disciplina*, 36 (1982), 119–66.

SCHROEDER, Revd. H. J., *Canons and Decrees of the Council of Trent* (St Louis: B. Herder Book Co., 1960).

SEGERMAN, EPHRAIM, 'Praetorius's Pitch?', *Early Music*, 13 (1985), 261–3.

—— 'Tempo and Tactus after 1500', in Knighton and Fallows, eds., *Companion to Medieval and Renaissance Music*, 337–44.

—— 'A Re-examination of the Evidence on Absolute Tempo before 1700: I', *Early Music*, 24 (1996), 227–49.

SELFRIDGE-FIELD, ELEANOR, *Venetian Instrumental Music from Gabrieli to Vivaldi* (New York: Praeger Publishers, 1975; rev. edn. New York: Dover Publications, Inc., 1994).

—— 'Bassano and the Orchestra of St Mark's', *Early Music*, 4 (1976), 153–8.

—— 'Instrumentation and Genre in Italian Music, 1600–1670', *Early Music*, 19 (1991), 61–7.

SHANN, R. T., 'Flemish Transposing Harpsichords—An Explanation', *Galpin Society Journal*, 37 (1984), 62–71.

SHERR, RICHARD, 'Performance Practice in the Papal Chapel during the 16th Century', *Early Music*, 15 (1987), 453–62.

SILBIGER, ALEXANDER, The Roman Frescobaldi Tradition, c.1640–1670', *Journal of the American Musicological Society*, 33 (1980), 42–87.

SMITHERS, DON L., 'Baroque Trumpet Mutes: A Retrospective Commentary', *Historic Brass Society Journal*, 2 (1990), 104–11.

SMITH, ANNE, 'Über Modus und Transposition um 1600', *Basler Jahrbuch für historische Musikpraxis*, 6 (1982), 9–43.

—— 'Belege zur Frage der Stimmtonhöhe bei Michael Praetorius', *Alte Musik: Praxis und Reflexion* (Winterthur: Amadeus, 1983), 340–5.

—— 'The Renaissance Flute', in John Solum, *The Early Flute* (Oxford: Clarendon Press, 1992), 11–33.

SOEHNLEN, EDWARD J., 'Diruta and his Contemporaries: Tradition and Innovation in the Art of Registration *c* 1610', *Organ Yearbook*, 10 (1979), 15–33.

SOLERTI, ANGELO, *Le origini del melodramma* (Turin, 1903; repr. edns. Hildesheim: Georg Olms, 1969, and Bologna: Arnaldo Forni Editore, 1983).

SOLUM, JOHN, *The Early Flute* (Oxford: Clarendon Press, 1992).

SPENCER, ROBERT, 'Chitarrone, Theorbo and Archlute', *Early Music*, 4 (1976), 407–23.

SPINELLI, GIANFRANCO, 'Confronto fra le registrazioni organistiche dei *Vespri* di Monteverdi e quelle de *L'arte organica* di Antegnati', in Monterosso, ed., *Claudio Monteverdi e il suo tempo*, 479–88.

STEFANI, GINO, *Musica e religione nell' Italia barocca* (Palermo: S. F. Flaccovio, Editore, 1975).

STEMBRIDGE, CHRISTOPHER, 'Music for the *cimbalo cromatico* and other Split-Keyed Instruments in Seventeenth-Century Italy', *Performance Practice Review*, 5 (1992), 5–43.

—— 'The *cimbalo cromatico* and other Italian Keyboard Instruments with Nineteen or More Divisions to the Octave', *Performance Practice Review*, 6 (1993), 33–59.

STEVENS, DENIS, 'Monteverdi's Vespers', *Musical Times*, 99 (1958), 673.

—— ' "Monteverdi's Vespers" Verified', *Musical Times*, 102 (1961), 422.

—— 'Monteverdi's Vespers', Letters to the Editor, *Musical Times*, 102 (1961), 564–5.

—— 'Monteverdi's Vespers Again', Letters to the Editor, *Musical Times*, 102 (1961), 713.

—— 'Where are the Vespers of Yesteryear?', *Musical Quarterly*, 47 (1961), 315–30.

—— *Monteverdi: Sacred, Secular, and Occasional Music* (Rutherford: Fairleigh Dickinson University Press, 1978).

—— 'Altri vespri di Monteverdi', *Nuova rivista musicale italiana*, 14 (1980), 167–77.

—— *The Letters of Claudio Monteverdi* (Cambridge: Cambridge University Press, 1980; rev. edn. Oxford: Clarendon Press, 1995).

—— *Musicology, A Practical Guide* (New York: Schirmer Books, 1980).

—— 'Monteverdiana', *Early Music*, 21 (1993), 565–74.

—— 'Claudio Monteverdi: Acoustics, Tempo, Interpretation', in Monterosso, ed., *Performing Practice in Monteverdi's Music*, 11–22.

STEVENSON, ROBERT, 'Morales, Cristóbal de', in *The New Grove*, xii. 553–8.

STOWALL, ROBIN, Review of Greta Moens-Haenen, *Das Vibrato in der Musick des Barock*, *Music & Letters*, 71 (1990), 241–2.

STRAINCHAMPS, EDMOND, 'The Life and Death of Caterina Martinelli: New Light on Monteverdi's "Arianna" ', *Early Music History*, 5 (1985), 155–86.

STRASSLER, PAUL GENE, 'Hymns for the Church Year, Magnificats and other Sacred Choral Works of Diego Ortiz' (Ph.D. dissertation, University of North Carolina, 1967).

STRUNK, OLIVER, *Source Readings in Music History* (New York: W. W. Norton & Company, Inc., 1950).

TAFT, ROBERT, SJ, *The Liturgy of the Hours in East and West* (Collegeville, Minn.: The Liturgical Press, 1986).

TAGLIAVINI, LUIGI FERDINANDO, 'The Old Italian Organ and its Music', *Diapason*, 57/2 (Feb. 1966), 14–16.

—— 'Registrazioni organistiche nei Magnificat dei "Vespri" monteverdiani', *Rivista italiana di musicologia*, 2 (1967), 365–71.

—— 'The Art of "not Leaving the Instrument Empty": Comments on Early Italian Harpsichord Playing', *Early Music*, 9 (1983), 299–308.

—— 'Considerazioni sugli ambiti delle tastiere degli organi italiani', in Friedemann Hellwig, ed., *Studia organologica: Festschrift für John Henry van der Meer zu seinem fünfundsechzigsten Geburtstag* (Tutzing: Hans Schneider, 1987), 453–60.

TAGMANN, PIERRE M., *Archivalische Studien zur Musikpflege am Dom von Mantua (1500–1627)* (Berne: Paul Haupt, 1967).

—— 'La cappella dei maestri cantori della basilica palatina di Santa Barbara a Mantova (1565–1630): Nuovo materiale scoperto negli archivi mantovani', *Civiltà mantovana*, 4 (1969–70), 376–99.

—— 'The Palace Church of Santa Barbara in Mantua, and Monteverdi's Relationship to its

Liturgy', in Burton L. Karson, ed., *Festival Essays for Pauline Alderman* (Provo, Ut.: Brigham Young University Press, 1976), 53–60.

TAJETTI, OSCAR, and COLZANI, ALBERTO, *Aspetti della vocalità secentesca* in *Studi sul primo Seicento* (Como: AMIS, 1983).

TARR, EDWARD, 'Monteverdi, Bach und die Trompetenmusik ihrer Zeit', in *Bericht über den internationalen musikwissenschaftlichen Kongress Bonn 1970* (Kassel: Bärenreiter, 1972), 592–6.

—— 'Ein Katalog erhaltener Zinken', *Basler Jahrbuch für historische Musikpraxis*, 5 (1981), 11–262.

THEIN, HEINRICH, 'Zur Geschichte der Renaissance-Posaune von Jörg Neuschel (1557) und zu ihrer Nachschöpfung', *Basler Jahrbuch für historische Musikpraxis*, 5 (1981), 377–404.

THOMAS, BERNARD, 'The Renaissance Flute', *Early Music*, 3 (1975), 2–10.

—— 'Divisions in Renaissance Music', in Knighton and Fallows, eds., *Companion to Medieval and Renaissance Music*, 345–53.

THOMAS, W. R., and RHODES, J. J. K., 'Schlick, Praetorius and the History of Organ-Pitch', *Organ Yearbook*, 2 (1971), 58–76.

TOFT, ROBERT, *Aural Images of Lost Traditions* (Toronto: University of Toronto Press, 1992).

TOWNE, GARY SPAULDING, 'Gaspar de Albertis and Music at Santa Maria Maggiore in Bergamo in the Sixteenth Century' (Ph.D. dissertation, University of California at Santa Barbara, 1985).

TYLER, JAMES, 'Mixed Ensembles', in Kite-Powell, ed., *A Performer's Guide to Renaissance Music*, 217–27.

UBERTI, MAURO, 'Vocal Techniques in Italy in the Second Half of the 16th Century', *Early Music*, 9 (1981), 486–95.

UBERTI, MAURO, and SCHINDLER, OSKAR, 'Contributo alla ricerca di una vocalità monteverdiana: il "colore"', in Monterosso, ed., *Monteverdi e il suo tempo*, 519–37.

ULRICH, BERNHARD, *Concerning the Principles of Voice Training during the A Cappella Period and until the Beginning of Opera (1474–1640)* (Ph.D. dissertation, Leipzig, 1910), trans. John W. Seale (Minneapolis: Pro Musica Press, 1973).

VACCHELLI, ANNA MARIA, 'Monteverdi as a Primary Source for the Performance of his own Music', in Monterosso, ed., *Performing Practice in Monteverdi's Music*, 23–52.

VANSCHEEUWIJCK, MARC, 'Musical Performance at San Petronio in Bologna: A Brief History', *Performance Practice Review*, 8 (1995), 73–82.

VOGEL, EMIL, 'Claudio Monteverdi', *Vierteljahrsschrift für Musikwissenschaft*, 3 (1887), 315–450.

VON RAMM, ANDREA, 'Singing Early Music', *Early Music*, 4 (1976), 12–15.

WAITZMAN, MIMI S., 'Meantone Temperament in Theory and Practice', *In Theory Only*, 5 (1979–81), 3–15.

WALDO, ANDREW, 'So you Want to Blow the Audience Away; Sixteenth-Century Ornamentation: A Perspective on Goals and Techniques', *American Recorder*, 27 (1986), 48–59.

WALLS, PETER, 'Strings', in Brown and Sadie, eds., *Performance Practice: Music after 1600*, 44–79.

WEBER, JEROME F., 'Monteverdi: *Vespro della Beata Vergine*, Discography', *Fanfare*, 4/5 (1981), 108–9.

WEGMAN, ROB C., 'What is "Acceleratio Mensurae"?', *Music & Letters*, 73 (1992), 515–24.

WEIL, MARK S., 'The Devotion of the Forty Hours and Roman Baroque Illusions', *Journal of the Warburg and Courtauld Institutes*, 37 (1974), 218–48.

WESTERLUND, GUNNAR, and HUGHES, ERIC, *Music of Claudio Monteverdi* (London: British Institute of Recorded Sound, 1972).

WHENHAM, JOHN, *Duet and Dialogue in the Age of Monteverdi*, 2 vols. (Ann Arbor: UMI Research Press, 1982).

—— *Monteverdi: Vespers (1610)* (Cambridge: Cambridge University Press, 1997).

WIERING, FRANS, 'The Language of the Modes: Studies in the History of Polyphonic Modality' (Ph.D. dissertation, University of Amsterdam, 1995).

WILLIAMS, PETER, *The European Organ, 1450–1850* (London: B. T. Batsford Ltd., 1966).

—— *A New History of the Organ* (Bloomington, Ind.: Indiana University Press, 1980).

—— 'Continuo', in *The New Grove*, iv. 685–99.

WILSON, JOHN, ed., *Roger North on Music* (London: Novello and Company Ltd, 1959).

WINTERFELD, CARL VON, *Johannes Gabrieli und sein Zeitalter*, 3 vols. (Berlin, 1834; fac. edn. Hildesheim: Georg Olms, 1965).

WISTREICH, RICHARD, ' "La voce è grata assai, ma . . .": Monteverdi on singing', *Early Music*, 22 (1994), 7–19.

WOLF, UWE, *Notation und Aufführungspraxis: Studien zum Wandel von Notenschrift und Notenbild in italienischen Musikdrucken der Jahre 1571–1630*, 2 vols. (Berlin and Kassel: Verlag Merseburger, 1992).

—— 'Monteverdi und die Proportionen: Eine Entgegnung auf Roland Eberleins Aufsatz "Die Taktwechsel in Monteverdis Marienvesper" ', *Musik und Kirche*, 63 (1993), 91–5.

WOLFF, HELMUTH CHRISTIAN, 'Orientalische Einflüsse in den Improvisationen des 16. und 17. Jahrhunderts', in *Bericht über den siebenten internationalen musikwissenschaftlichen Kongress Köln 1958* (Kassel: Bärenreiter, 1959), 308–15.

WRAIGHT, DENZIL, and STEMBRIDGE, CHRISTOPHER, 'Italian Split-Keyed Instruments with Fewer than Nineteen Divisions to the Octave', *Performance Practice Review*, 7 (1994), 150–81.

WRAY, ALISON, 'Restored Pronunciation for the Performance of Vocal Music', in Knighton and Fallows, eds., *Companion to Medieval and Renaissance Music*, 292–9.

WRIGHT, CRAIG, Dufay's *Nuper rosarum flores*, King Solomon's Temple, and the Veneration of the Virgin', *Journal of the American Musicological Society*, 47 (1994), 395–439.

ZENCK, HERMANN, 'Adrian Willaert's "Salmi spezzati" ', *Die Musikforschung*, 2 (1949), 97–107.

EDITIONS

CACCINI, GIULIO, *Le nuove musiche*, ed. H. Wiley Hitchcock (Madison, Wis.: A-R Editions, Inc., 1970).

—— *Le nuove musiche e nuova maniera di scriverle*, ed. H. Wiley Hitchcock (Madison, Wis.: A-R Editions, Inc., 1978).

—— *Le nuove musiche, Firenze, 1601*, fac. ed. Piero Mioli (Florence: Studio per Edizioni Scelte, 1983).

—— *Nuove musiche e nuova maniera di scriverle, Firenze, 1614*, fac. ed. Piero Mioli (Florence: Studio per Edizioni Scelte, 1983).

CONFORTI, GIOVANNI LUCA, *'Salmi passaggiati' (1601–1603)*, ed. Murray C. Bradshaw (Neuhausen and Stuttgart: American Institute of Musicology, Hänssler-Verlag, 1985).

DUFAY, GUILLELMI, *Opera omnia*, ed. Heinrich Besseler (Rome: American Institute of Musicology, 1966), v.

DUNSTABLE, JOHN, *Complete Works*, ed. Manfred F. Bukofzer (Musica Britannica, 8; London: Stainer and Bell, 1953).

FESTA, COSTANZO, *Opera omnia*, ed. Alexander Main (American Institute of Musicology, 1962–), ii.

FRESCOBALDI, GIROLAMO, *Opere complete, II: Il primo libro di Toccate d'intavolatura di cembalo e organo, 1615–1637*, ed. Étienne Darbellay (Milan: Edizioni Suvini Zerboni, 1977).

—— *Orgel- und Klavierwerke*, ed. Pierre Pidoux (Kassel: Bärenreiter, 1954), v.

GABRIELI, GIOVANNI, *Canzoni e sonate*, ed. Michel Sanvoisin (Le Pupitre, 27; Paris: Heugel & Cie., 1971).

—— *Opera omnia*, iii–v ed. Denis Arnold (Rome: American Institute of Musicology, 1956–74).

—— *Opera omnia*, vii ed. Richard Charteris (Neuhausen and Stuttgart: Hänssler-Verlag, 1991).

GAFURIUS, FRANCHINUS, *Collected Musical Works*, ed. Lutz Finscher (Rome: American Institute of Musicology, 1955).

JEPPESON, KNUD, ed., *Die mehrstimmige italienische Laude um 1500* (Leipzig: Breitkopf und Härtel, 1935).

KAPSBERGER, GEROLAMO, *Arie e mottetti passeggiati*, fac. ed. Piero Mioli (Florence: Studio per Edizioni Scelte, 1980).

KURTZMAN, JEFFREY, ed., *Vesper and Compline Music* (Seventeenth-Century Italian Sacred Music, 11–20; New York: Garland Publishing, Inc., 1995–).

The Liber Usualis with Introduction and Rubrics in English (New York: Desclée Co., 1963).

MACCLINTOCK, CAROL, ed., *The Solo Song: 1580–1730* (New York: W. W. Norton & Company, 1973).

MONTEVERDI, CLAUDIO, *Magnificat sechsstimmig*, ed. Karl Matthaei (Kassel: Bärenreiter-Verlag, 1941).

—— *Magnificat [a 7] from 'Vespers' of 1610*. ed. H.F. Redlich (Vienna: Universal Edition, 1949; rev. 1952).

—— *Magnificat a sei voci from the Vespers of 1610*, ed. Don Smithers (New York: Lawson-Gould Music Publishers, Inc., 1969).

—— *Missa in illo tempore*, ed. Jeffrey G. Kurtzman (Stuttgart: Carus-Verlag, 1994).

—— *Sanctissimae Virgini Missa senis vocibus ac Vesperae*, fac. ed. Greta Haenen (Peer, Belgium: Alamire, 1992).

—— *Sonata sopra 'Sancta Maria' di Claudio Monteverdi: Versione ritmica e strumentale*, ed. Bernardino Molinari (Milan: G. Ricordi, 1919).

—— *Sonata sopra Sancta Maria ora pro nobis from The Vespers of 1610*, ed. Robert King (Music for Brass, 71; North Easton, Mass.: Robert King Music Co., 1952).

—— *Tutte le opere*, ed. Gian Francesco Malipiero (Vienna: Universal Edition, 1932–42), xiv–xvi.

—— *Vespro della Beata Vergine*, ed. Clifford Bartlett (Huntingdon, Cambs.: King's Music, 1986).

—— *Vespro della Beata Vergine*, ed. Clifford Bartlett (Huntingdon, Cambs.: King's Music, 1990).

—— *Vespro della Beata Vergine (1610) da concerto, composta [sic] sopra canti fermi*, ed. Walter Goehr (Vienna: Universal Edition, 1957).

—— *Vespro della Beata Vergine*, ed. Jürgen Jürgens (Vienna: Universal Edition and Philharmonia miniature score, 1977).

—— *Vespro della Beata Vergine*, ed. Hans F. Redlich (Vienna: Universal Edition, 1949; rev. 1952).

—— *Vespro della Beata Vergine/Marienvesper*, ed. Hans F. Redlich (Vienna: Universal Edition, 1955).

—— *Vespro della Beata Vergine*, ed. Jerome Roche (London: Eulenburg, 1994).

—— *Vespers*, ed. Denis Stevens (London: Novello, 1961); rev. as *Claudio Monteverdi: Vespers 1610* (London: Novello, 1994).

—— *Vesperae Beatae Mariae Virginis (Marien-Vesper) 1610*, ed. Gottfried Wolters (Wolfenbüttel: Möseler Verlag, 1954).

—— *Vesperae Beatae Mariae Virginis*, ed. Gottfried Wolters (Wolfenbüttel: Möseler Verlag, 1966).

MORALES, CRISTÓBAL, *Opera omnia*, ii, ed. Higinio Anglés (Monumentos de la Musica Española, 13; Rome: Consejo Superior de Investigaciones Científicas, 1953).

—— *Opera omnia*, xvi, ed. Higinio Anglés (Monumentos de la Música Española, 17; Barcelona: Consejo Superior de Investigaciones Científicas, 1956).

PALESTRINA, GIOVANNI PIERLUIGI, *Le opere complete di Giovanni Pierluigi da Palestrina*, ed. Raffaele Casimiri (Rome: Edizione Fratelli Scalera, 1939–), xvi.

PERI, JACOPO, *Euridice*, ed. Howard M. Brown (Madison, Wis.; A-R Editions, Inc., 1981).

PETRUCCI, OTTAVIANO, ed., *Frottole, Buch I und IV*, ed. Rudolph Schwartz, in Theodor Kroyer, ed., *Publikationen älterer Music* (repr. Hildesheim: Georg Olms, 1967), viii.

PRAETORIUS, MICHAEL, *Polyhymnia caduceatrix*, in *Gesamtausgabe der musikalischen Werke von Michael Praetorius*, xvii, ed. Wilibald Gurlitt (Wolfenbüttel: Georg Kallmeyer Verlag, 1933).

—— *Terpsichore*, in *Gesamtausgabe der musikalischen Werke von Michael Praetorius*, xii, ed. Günther Oberst (Wolfenbüttel: Georg Kallmeyer Verlag, 1929).

ROCHE, JEROME and ELIZABETH, eds., *Motets, 1600–1650* (Seventeenth-Century Italian Sacred Music, 21–5; New York: Garland Publishing, Inc., forthcoming).

SCHÜTZ, HEINRICH, *Historia der Auferstehung Jesu Christi*, in *Neue Ausgabe sämtlicher Werke*, iii, ed. Walter Simon Huber (Kassel: Bärenreiter-Verlag, 1956).

SEVERI, FRANCESCO, *Francesco Severi: Salmi passaggiati (1615)*, ed. Murray C. Bradshaw (Madison, Wis.: A-R Editions, Inc., 1981).

TORCHI, LUIGI, ed., *L'arte musicale in Italia*, 8 vols. (Milan: G. Ricordi, 1897–1908?).

VIADANA, LODOVICO, *Cento concerti ecclesiastici opera duodecima 1602: Parte prima: Concerti a una voce con l'organo*, ed. Claudio Gallico (Kassel: Bärenreiter, 1964).

VICTORIA, TOMÁS, *Opera omnia*, ed. Higinio Anglés iv (Monumentos de la Musica Española, 31; Rome: Consejo Superior de Investigaciones Científicas, 1968).

—— *Opera omnia*, ed. Philippo Pedrell (Leipzig: Breitkopf & Härtel, 1902–13), v, vii, viii.

WILLAERT, ADRIANI, *Opera omnia*, ed. Hermann Zenck (American Institute of Musicology, 1972), viii.

Index of Text Incipits and
Composition Titles

⟨❦⟩

Note: Compositions by Monteverdi and compositions assignable to other composers are cross-listed in the INDEX OF NAMES.

Index of Names

Note: Under each composer are listed the relevant compositions (cross-listed alphabetically by text incipit or composition title in the INDEX OF INCIPITS AND COMPOSITION TITLES). In those cases where more than one publication by a single composer is the source of multiple compositions, the short title of the publication is listed under the composer and individual compositions are subsumed under the appropriate short title. Full titles of printed collections are listed by composer in App. E. In a similar manner, multiple theoretical treatises are listed under the name of the author, and references in the text drawn from these sources are subsumed under the appropriate theoretical source. Full titles of theoretical sources are listed by author in App. F. Names of performers, composers, authors, dedicatees, printers, and places listed in Apps. D–F are not indexed.

General Index

⟨❧⟩

Printed in the United Kingdom
by Lightning Source UK Ltd.
102117UKS00001B/5